The Money-Diggers

* This tale occurs within "Wolfert Webber."

EDITOR'S NOTE

The tales have been taken from the author's revised and collected works as published in the Autograph Edition, issued in forty volumes by G. P. Putnam's Sons in 1895. The tales are presented in the chronological sequence of the respective first editions and in their sequence within each particular work.

INTRODUCTION

Inasmuch as Washington Irving is relatively distant from us in time, I shall begin this introductory essay with a brief biographical summary but I shall not feel obliged to mention all of his various publications, many of which will be referred to later. He was born April 3, 1783 in New York City, the youngest of eleven children, three of whom died in infancy. His parents had emigrated from Great Britain, where his father at one time had been an officer in the merchant marine. Washington Irving was raised on William Street in Manhattan.

The year of his birth was of some note in the history of the new republic. On February 14 the King's Proclamation, announcing the end of hostilities between Great Britain and the United States, was read in New York. On September 3 the formal peace treaty between the two nations was signed in Paris. On November 25 the last British troops were evacuated from the city by way of the Battery. On December 4 General George Washington said farewell to his officers in Fraunces Tavern in Manhattan, a gesture which symbolically ended the Revolution. The young Irving had reason to be proud of his native city, which was the first capital of the nation and which, on April 30, 1789, witnessed the inauguration of George Washington as President at Federal Hall, the old city hall. According to Irving's official biographer, his nephew Pierre M. Irving, a young Scotch maid-servant of the family, on seeing George Washington enter a shop, followed him inside with her charge, the young Irving, and said, "Please, your honor, here's a bairn was named after you," upon which Washington, touching the boy's head, gave him his blessing.

Although Irving's father often displayed the puritanical strictness of a Scotch Covenanter, his household was more literary and intellectual than those of many of his neighbors, and young Irving's artistic tendencies benefited by the influence. Irving received a fragmentary education in male seminaries in the city. Pierre M. Irving wrote in his biography, "His education was completed before he had attained his sixteenth year; at least from this period he assumed the direction of his own studies. His brothers, Peter and John, had been sent to Columbia College, and why he did not receive the same advantage he could never satisfactorily explain except that he was more alive to the drudgery than the advantage of a course of academic training. He never failed, however,

to regret the omission in after life." Like many incipient writers before him, Irving was an addicted reader, and in the end his self-education adequately served his needs.

He was the first internationally prominent American author and was followed soon afterwards in the distinction of international fame by James Fenimore Cooper and somewhat later by William Cullen Bryant. All three had a negligible formal education and all came from comfortable, what we would now call middle-class, homes. Irving's father was a successful merchant, Cooper's a lawyer, Bryant's a physician. Although only Irving was a native New Yorker, the literary careers of all three were connected with New York, whose largely mercantile society was proud of its international, intellectual and literary pursuits.

Between the ages of sixteen and eighteen Irving studied law in a Manhattan law office. In 1800 he made a voyage up the Hudson to visit two of his sisters, and in 1803 he traveled to Montreal. He had never had a robust constitution. When, early in 1804, his health seemed to be declining, his family decided to send him to Europe for the sea air, a change of scene and a rounding out of his education. He sailed from New York in May at the age of twenty-one. He visited France, mainland Italy, Sicily, Switzerland and London. He returned to New York early in 1806. In the fall he was admitted to the bar but he was never seriously to practice law. In 1807 he attended the trial for treason of Aaron Burr in Richmond, Virginia. His father died October 25, 1807, when Washington Irving was twenty-four. In 1808 Irving began work on *Knickerbocker's History of New York.* Matilda Hoffman, whose death is supposed to have affected him for the rest of his life and to have contributed in some measure to his decision to remain a bachelor, died April 26, 1809 in her eighteenth and his twenty-seventh year. The *History of New York* was published in December.

In 1812, in a review of the recently issued works of Robert Treat Paine, a poet now long forgotten, Irving had some choice remarks to make about the condition of authorship in America.

"Unfitted for business, in a nation where every one is busy; devoted to literature, where literary leisure is confounded with idleness; the man of letters is almost an insulated being, with few to understand, less to value, and scarcely any to encourage his pursuits. It is not surprising, therefore, that our authors soon grow weary of a race which they have to run alone, and turn their attention to other callings of a more worldly and profitable nature. This is one of the reasons why the writers of this country so seldom attain to excellence. Before their genius is disciplined, and their taste refined, their talents are diverted into the ordinary channels of busy life, and occupied in what are con-

sidered its more useful purposes. In fact, the great demand for rough talent, as for common manual labor, in this country, prevents the appropriation of either mental or physical forces to elegant employments. The delicate mechanician may toil in penury, unless he devote himself to common manufactures, suitable to the ordinary consumption of the country; and the fine writer, if he depend upon his pen for a subsistence, will soon discover that he may starve on the very summit of Parnassus, while he sees herds of newspaper editors battening on the rank marshes of its borders."

One wonders if his visit to Europe helped give him the sharply focused perspective evident in the preceding statement, and if he didn't, while composing it, long for a return to the older continent, where, perhaps, he would not so soon grow weary of running the race alone. After him, Hawthorne and James would also complain eloquently of the burdens of authorship on native soil.

On May 25, 1815, by which time the war between Great Britain and France had ended, Irving embarked for England, where, in Liverpool, he worked in the declining family import-export business. It is doubtful that he had any intimation that he would stay in Europe so long and with such consequences for his career as a writer. During this visit he was to be absent from the United States for an unbroken seventeen years, a long stretch to be separated from family, friends, native roots and native idiom. As we shall see, he was to resist family pressure to come home. Perhaps he did so not only because of what he believed to be the necessities of his developing art but because, as the youngest sibling, he needed the opportunity to mature apart from his sometimes oversolicitous brothers and sisters.

His mother died April 9, 1817, just after he turned thirty-four. In August he visited Walter Scott, to whom he had a letter of introduction, at Abbotsford in Scotland. Scott, an enthusiastic admirer of the *History of New York,* excerpts of which he had read aloud to members of his family, was very cordial to him, and a few years later was to be instrumental in placing Irving's *Sketch Book* with John Murray, a prestigious London publisher. The romantic side of Irving revered Scott.

Early in 1818 the family business went bankrupt and Irving decided to try authorship as a means of earning his keep. During the summer he took up lodgings in London, where he worked on *The Sketch Book.* In October his brother William wrote him from Washington, saying he could get him a job in the Navy Department. Irving declined in favor of a possible literary career. On March 3, 1819, when he was

almost thirty-six, he wrote a revealing letter to his brother Ebenezer, in which he gave his reasons for turning the job down.

"I find my declining the situation at Washington has given you chagrin. The fact is, that situation would have given me barely a genteel subsistence. It would have led to no higher situations, for I am quite unfitted for political life. My talents are merely literary, and all my habits of thinking, reading, etc., have been in a different direction from that required for the active politician. It is a mistake also to suppose I would fill an office there, and devote myself at the same time to literature. I require much leisure and a mind entirely abstracted from other cares and occupations, if I would write much or write well. I should therefore at Washington be completely out of my element, and instead of adding to my reputation, stand a chance of impairing that which I already possess. If I ever get any solid credit with the public, it must be in the quiet and assiduous operations of my pen, under the mere guidance of fancy or feeling.

"I have been for some time past nursing my mind up for literary operations, and collecting materials for the purpose. I shall be able, I trust, now to produce articles from time to time that will be sufficient for my present support, and form a stock of copyright property, that may be a little capital for me hereafter. To carry this into better effect it is important for me to remain a little longer in Europe, where there is so much food for observation, and objects of taste on which to meditate and improve. I feel myself completely committed in literary reputation by what I have already written; and I feel by no means satisfied to rest my reputation on my preceding writings. I have suffered several precious years of youth and lively imagination to pass by unimproved, and it behooves me to make the most of what is left. If I indeed have the means within me of establishing a legitimate literary reputation, this is the very period of life most auspicious for it, and I am resolved to devote a few years exclusively to the attempt. Should I succeed, besides the literary property I shall amass in copyright, I trust it will not be difficult to obtain some official situation of a moderate, unpretentious kind, in which I may make my bread. But as to reputation I can only look for it through the exertions of my pen. . . .

"In fact, I consider myself at present as making a literary experiment, in the course of which I only care to be kept in bread and cheese. Should it not succeed—should my writings not acquire critical applause, I am content to throw up the pen and take to any commonplace employment. But if they should succeed it would repay me for a world of care and privation to be placed among the established authors of my country, and to win the affections of my countrymen.

". . . I have but one thing to add. I have now given you the leading motive of my actions—it may be a weak one, but it has full possession of me, and therefore the attainment of it is necessary to my comfort. I now wish to be left for a little while entirely to the bent of my own inclination, and not agitated by new plans for subsistence, or by entreaties to come home. My spirits are very unequal, and my mind depends upon them; and I am easily thrown into such a state of perplexity and such depression as to incapacitate me for any mental exertion. Do not, I beseech you, impute my lingering in Europe to any indifference to my own country or my friends. My greatest desire is to make myself worthy of the good-will of my country, and my greatest anticipation of happiness is the return to my friends. I am living here in a retired and solitary way, and partaking in little of the gayety of life, but I am determined not to return home until I have sent some writings before me that shall, if they have merit, make me return to the smiles, rather than skulk back to the pity of my friends."

Such a self-understanding statement is abundant proof that he was the first important American literary artist to come to grips with the allurements and traditions of Europe, the problems of European experiences and subjects, the pleasures and woes of expatriation, the need to obtain a long and cultured perspective on raw native materials, the artistic obligation to come to terms with the conflict between foreign interests and native debts. As such he was the first in a line that runs through Cooper, Hawthorne, Melville, James, Twain, T. S. Eliot, Ezra Pound, Hemingway and many others, and these have inevitably been influenced by the tradition he began. No discussion of the importance of expatriation in the production of works of American literature can be complete without beginning with his example. In order to help place him among the early prominent figures of American literature, we may note that in terms of the year of birth he was six years Cooper's senior, eleven Bryant's, twenty Emerson's, twenty-one Hawthorne's, twenty-four Longfellow's, twenty-six Poe's, thirty-four Thoreau's and thirty-six Melville's and Whitman's.

The same day Irving addressed a letter to his good friend Henry Brevoort in the United States.

"I feel great diffidence about this reappearance in literature. I am conscious of my imperfections, and my mind has been for a long time past so preyed upon and agitated by various cares and anxieties that I fear it has lost much of its cheerfulness and some of its activity.

"I have attempted no lofty theme, nor sought to look wise and learned, which appears to be very much the fashion among our American writers at present. I have preferred addressing myself to the feeling

and fancy of the reader more than to his judgment. My writings, therefore, may appear light and trifling in our country of philosophers and politicians; but if they possess merit in the class of literature to which they belong, it is all to which I aspire in the work. I seek only to blow a flute accompaniment in the national concert, and leave others to play the fiddle and French horn."

He wrote Brevoort again July 10.

"It is a long time since I have heard from my brother William, and I am apt to attribute his silence to dissatisfaction at my not accepting the situation at Washington; a circumstance which I apprehend has disappointed others of my friends. In these matters, however, just weight should be given to a man's tastes and inclinations. The value of a situation is only as it contributes to a man's happiness, and I should have been perfectly out of my element and uncomfortable in Washington. The place could merely have supported me, and instead of rising, as my friends appeared to anticipate, I should have sunk even in my own opinion. My mode of life has unfortunately been such as to render me unfit for almost any useful purpose. I have not the kind of knowledge or the habits that are necessary for business or regular official duty. My acquirements, tastes, and habits are just such as to adapt me for the kind of literary exertions I contemplate. It is only in this way I have any chance of acquiring real reputation, and I am desirous of giving it a fair trial."

With the publication of The Sketch Book (1819–20), a collection of essays, sketches and tales, written in England, Irving became an English and to some extent a European celebrity. He was a sensitive, handsome, shy, sloe-eyed man of middle height, with a sensuous mouth; a fashionable and expensive dresser in London and Paris in the days of the first flush of his success; a man of polished manners, humorous, benign; to some of his European acquaintances a surprisingly cultivated transplant from the rawness of the new republic. He enjoyed the good life; was no ascetic; yet later, at forty-nine, he would be rugged and plastic enough to undertake and to endure without undue complaint a hard trip into what was then the Far West in his country. From 1820 on he was to enjoy great popularity in his time and during four or five decades afterwards, when various uniform editions of his collected works were successfully marketed, some lavishly illustrated and bound. Like Dickens he was the darling of illustrators.

Very early the standard litany about him, which still has some currency, took hold: that he was the first writer of his native land to make his living by authorship; the first American man of letters to win European fame; the father of the American short story; the creator, in Knick-

erbocker's History of New York, of the first great work of American humor. At times it even included the large statement that he was the father of American literature, thus perhaps affording him a closer affinity with the so-called father of his country than the possession of part of George Washington's name.

Two years after the publication of *The Sketch Book,* in a preface to *Bracebridge Hall* (1822), another collection of sketches, essays and tales, Irving wrote:

"It has been a matter of marvel, to my European readers, that a man from the wilds of America should express himself in tolerable English. I was looked upon as something new and strange in literature; as a kind of demi-savage, with a feather in his hand instead of on his head; and there was a curiosity to hear what such a being had to say about civilized society. . . . Having been born and brought up in a new country, yet educated from infancy in the literature of an old one, my mind was early filled with historical and poetical associations, connected with places, and manners, and customs of Europe, but which could rarely be applied to those of my own country. To a mind thus peculiarly prepared, the most ordinary objects and scenes, on arriving in Europe, are full of strange matter in interest—in novelty. . . . My only aim is to paint characters and manners. I am no politician. The more I have considered the study of politics, the more I have found it full of perplexity; and I have contented myself, as I have in my religion, with the faith in which I was brought up, regulating my own conduct by its precepts, but leaving to abler heads the task of making converts." Irving, it has been said, had "a distaste for democratic Jeffersonian policies." He was baptized a Presbyterian.

In the years between 1820 and 1824 he traveled on the continent: Heidelberg, Munich, Salzburg, Vienna, Dresden, Prague, Paris. In Paris he was involved unsuccessfully in trying to write or doctor plays with John Howard Payne, author of "Home, Sweet Home." Irving's *Tales of a Traveller* appeared in the summer and fall of 1824. Its unexpected and distressingly poor, in places even savage, reception determined Irving, despite his belief in its artistic merits—he was dependent now on authorship for his bread—to move away from fiction to nonfiction. It may be said without fear of exaggeration that the reception of *Tales of a Traveller* brought about a turning point in his literary career. Whether a stronger talent or character would have refused to accept the largely mistaken verdict it is idle to speculate. Irving had a gentle, pliant nature and expensive tastes, and was only too familiar with the garish, pendulating, garret life of one of his literary heroes, Oliver Goldsmith, to wish to emulate it. His disappointment over the

fate of *Tales of a Traveller* spilled over into a letter he wrote in Paris on December 7, 1824 to his young nephew Pierre Paris Irving, who meant to embark on a career as a writer, in which he stated:

"I hope none of those whose interests and happiness are dear to me will be induced to follow my footsteps, and wander into the seductive but treacherous paths of literature. There is no life more precarious in its profits and fallacious in its enjoyments than that of an author. I speak from an experience which may be considered a favorable and prosperous one; and I would earnestly dissuade all those with whom my voice has any effect from trusting their fortunes to the pen. . . . Do not meddle much with works of the imagination. Your imagination needs no feeding; indeed it is a mental quality that always takes care of itself; and is too apt to interfere with the others. . . . If you think my path has been a flowery one, you are greatly mistaken; it has too often lain among thorns and brambles, and been darkened by care and despondency. Many and many a time have I regretted that at my early outset in life I had not been imperiously bound down to some regular and useful mode of life, and been thoroughly inured to habits of business; and I have a thousand times regretted with bitterness that ever I was led away by my imagination. Believe me, the man who earns his bread by the sweat of his brow, eats oftener a sweeter morsel, however coarse, than he who procures it by the labor of his brains."

In February 1826 Irving moved to Madrid to begin work on his life of Columbus. On April 4, 1827, at forty-four, he wrote from Madrid to his friend Brevoort:

"I am conscious that my long absence from home has subjected me to unfavorable representations, and has been used to my disadvantage. A man, however, must have firmness enough to pursue his plans when justified by his own conscience, without being diverted from them by the idle surmises and misconceptions of others. If my character and conduct are worth inquiring into, they will ultimately be understood and appreciated according to their merits; nor can anything I could say or do in contradiction place them an iota above or below their real standard. With the world, therefore, let these matters take their course; I shall not court it nor rail at it; but with cherished friends like yourself, my dear Brevoort, the present feeling is all-important to me. Do not let yourself be persuaded, therefore, that time or distance has estranged me in thought or feeling from my native country, my native place, or the friends of my youth. The fact is, that the longer I remain from home the greater charm it has in my eyes, and all the coloring that the imagination once gave to distant Europe now gathers about the scenes of my native country. I look forward to my return as to the only

event of any very desirable kind that may yet be in store for me. I do not know whether it is the case with other wanderers, but with me, the various shifting scenes through which I have passed in Europe have pushed each other out of place successively and alternately faded away from my mind, while the scenes and friends of my youth alone remain fixed in my memory and my affections with their original strength and freshness."

From 1826 to 1829, enthralled by his work on Spanish subjects and materials, he traveled in Spain. In July 1829, on being appointed Secretary of Legation to London, he left Granada for Paris and London after a stay of two or three months in the Alhambra in Granada. In December of that year he resolved to write a life of Washington. In June 1831, at the age of forty-eight, he was awarded an LL.D. by Oxford University. In September he retired from the Legation. In April 1832 he left Le Havre for New York, arriving on May 21 after an absence from the United States of seventeen years, as we have observed.

His native town, with its Dutch influence still palpable in architecture, speech, names and descendants, had contained some 23,000 inhabitants at the time of his birth and 33,000 when he was a boy of seven. It had grown to more than 60,000 by only a decade later, which was the turn of the politically fateful century, and had become the most populous city of the nation. When he had last embarked from it in the year of Waterloo the mother-country influence on it, although waning, was still strong; its population then had been 110,000. Since his departure the city had burgeoned for a variety of reasons, chief among them the opening of the Erie Canal in 1825, which linked it with the Great Lakes by means of the Hudson River and made it the country's greatest trade center, the chief port between the frontier, the eastern seaboard and the lands beyond the Atlantic. Now New York was an astonishing metropolis of 205,000 money-hungry, political-minded, ambitious, multilingual, freewheeling Americans with the usual and healthy proportion of recent immigrants. The degree of the city's change was an index of the extent the country at large had changed. Fortunately for Irving the change was not as severe as it would have been three years later, when the great fire of 1835 wiped out the business district and the last vestiges of old New Amsterdam.

A great public dinner was given in his honor by the city on May 30, shortly after which he went to Washington, Boston, the White Mountains, Tarrytown, N.Y., and Saratoga Springs. In August he began a visit to the Oklahoma Territory, which resulted in *A Tour on the Prairies*. A companion, Henry Leavitt Ellsworth, to whom we shall refer again later, described him in a letter as "rosy-faced and as plump as a

partridge. Mr. Irving has a complexion a little darker than mine, which you know is not very light. His height is less than mine, but he is every way thicker set, and weighs I should suppose 20 lbs. more than I do." In 1835, at fifty-two, Irving bought the property that would later be called "Sunnyside," his estate near Tarrytown. In the same year he was nominated by Tammany Hall as mayor of New York, an honor he declined, as he also turned down the post of Secretary of the Navy, offered him by his friend President Martin Van Buren. On June 27, 1838 his close brother, Peter, died. In 1840, at fifty-seven, he began work on his life of Washington.

In February 1842 he was appointed minister to Spain. In April he left New York for Liverpool, visited London and Paris, and reached Madrid late in July. In the next four years, which were devoid of literary works, he made occasional forays from Madrid, going to Bordeaux, Paris, Barcelona, London, Birmingham. Early in September of 1846 he departed from London for Boston, reaching the United States after an absence of four and a half years. He returned to Sunnyside and soon resumed work on his biography of Washington. In July 1848, when he was sixty-five, he agreed to issue a revised, uniform edition of his works. In that year John Jacob Astor, at Irving's suggestion, founded the Astor Library, which became the basis of the great New York Public Library.

Matthew Brady's photograph of Irving shows a thick-set, thoughtful, perhaps dyspeptic, perhaps absent-minded man who has possibly experienced too much solitude; a man who does not much resemble his sensitive, handsome, winning early self; who could be taken for a mere man of business, overfed, underexercised, overworked and in retreat from himself as well as the world; a man aloof from his time and whom Time has not handled gently in the physical sense; a person almost unattractive in his declining years and therefore so different in this respect from the elderly and photogenic Walt Whitman, who was also photographed by Brady.

Irving died November 28, 1859, shortly after the final volume of his five-volume life of Washington appeared. He was seventy-six, the same age as his father when the latter died.

Irving's first published tales appeared in *The Sketch Book,* whose two volumes contained only three stories, but at least two of them are masterpieces, and the third, "The Spectre Bridegroom," at the very least is superbly told. The masterpieces are "Rip Van Winkle" and "The Legend of Sleepy Hollow." The three tales stand out in their setting of sketches (or essays) on a variety of topics. We enjoy the

vividness of fiction, the play of the imagination, and especially the powerful effect of American-set tales in a work devoted chiefly to ruminations on such English subjects as "English Writers on America," "Rural Life in England" and "Westminster Abbey."

Irving was fascinated by the art of short fiction and without question he helped to perfect it. He understood its requirements of great economy and unity of effect. It seems to me no accident that "The Spectre Bridegroom," the sole tale of the three with a foreign setting (German), although its details are precise and vivid and its language never cold, and always beautifully handled, is the least authentic, appealing and moving of the trio. Irving seems to grant the tale's weakness when compared with its companions, for in the introductory remarks he states, "I fear, however, it derived its chief zest from the manner in which it was told, and the peculiar air and appearance of the narrator."

The other two stories have a wonderful tone of nostalgia that one must reckon as flowing from the fact the settings are personally so meaningful to Irving; and this tone permeates, affects and ultimately lends beauty to the style, warming our imagination as well as the author's. I first read them as a boy. Rereading them for perhaps the fifth or sixth time, I still find them masterly, bewitching, magical, with a great aptness of phrase and metaphor, and with the subtle, delicate, delicious irony that marks Irving's best work. The two stories became great favorites on both sides of the Atlantic. "Rip Van Winkle" was successfully staged, with Joseph Jefferson, a leading American actor of the nineteenth century, performing the role of Rip.

In a way the tale was personally prophetic, for, as we have noted, Irving was absent from the United States for seventeen years, and when he returned, in triumph as contrasted with Rip's social debasement, he must have strongly sensed Time's work on people and places he had known, and of its effect as something resembling a nightmare. The tale, which itself often feels like a nightmare, is particularly important because it reveals so early in his career his keen folkloristic interest and his intense and marvelous sense of place. It also has a larger than folkloristic meaning in that it emphasizes what a great revolution had occurred internally and externally in Rip's society during his twenty-year sleep. England had been successfully defied and rejected, and the Dutch influence in manners and architecture had been powerfully subordinated to the Anglo-American along the Hudson and especially in the city of New York.

"Rip Van Winkle" is a fairy tale of bewitchment and a story of the magical changes wrought by Time. It has been insufficiently stressed that Time is one of Irving's chief characters, both in his fiction

and in his non-fiction. Possibly because his native land, when he was
an impressionable, sensitive youth, was short on hoary monuments and
traditions as compared with the mother country, the country so recently
rejected but that nevertheless was *his* and that haunted him, he was
endlessly fascinated by the effects of Time. It was an artist's fascination.
This is perhaps an appropriate place to say what it seems to me has
been largely overlooked about Irving: that he is our first great literary
artist, with a degree of self-understanding as such that is in itself remarkable. Unless one comprehends him as an artist and accepts him on
his own terms rather than on those imposed upon him for one reason
or another, one may expect to reach strange conclusions, many of them
false.

In "The Legend of Sleepy Hollow" he senses the thinness of Time
in his country when he writes, "In this by-place of nature, there abode,
in a remote period of American history, that is to say, some thirty years
since. . . ." But "Sleepy Hollow," like "Rip Van Winkle," is far
from thin in its vivid and richly detailed description of Ichabod Crane,
of Brom Bones and of Crane's weird, spectral horse. Irving lays the
groundwork of what's to happen to Crane with such artistry and such
lovely stretches of irony and humor, and controls and develops his effects with such a masterful hand, that it's a great pleasure to linger in
this tale that embodies so well an older, forgotten way of life: rural,
Dutch in ancestry, and with the ever-present Hudson lore and magical
river life.

The whole story, which I first read many years ago, is still sharp and
vivid for me, its humor extremely viable. It is literary artistry at its finest. I believe I first encountered it in a junior high school in Richmond,
Virginia, where it was assigned reading in an English class. There was
a tall strong boy in that class, with long arms and legs and large feet,
who reminded me of Ichabod Crane, and one day, when he was absent,
we discussed the appropriateness of the word "pretty" as applied to girls
and the word "handsome" as applied to boys. This was southern culture
in its heartland, where no notions were entertained about feminism.
Boys were supposed to be manly, girls demure, and our teacher made
it amply clear that any true boy would be greatly insulted if he were
called pretty. Next day our tall athlete, whom we thought of as a Brom
Bones type, reappeared and our teacher, in a tone that indicated she
was positive he would give the correct answer, that is, with an assertion
of threat, asked him what he'd do if a boy called him pretty. He thought
awhile, smiling awkwardly, sensing a trap, then said softly, "Give him
a quarter," and meant it. The guffaws were deafening. A quarter, by

the way, was a significant sum to a schoolboy in those ancient days of half a century ago.

Bracebridge Hall (1822), which followed *The Sketch Book,* contained within its two volumes four tales, the first and the last of which are unquestionably masterpieces of literary art: "The Stout Gentleman" and "Dolph Heyliger." As in *The Sketch Book,* the fictions are strikingly vivid in their setting and easily outlive their more prosy neighbors, which have such titles as "Family Servants," "Ready-Money Jack," "Forest Trees," "Falconry," "May-Day Customs" and "A Village Politician." And yet the sketches are written extremely well. The chapter called "The Widow's Retinue" provides an example of Irving's ability to observe and describe brilliantly and with irony and humor.

"She has brought two dogs with her, also, out of a number of pets which she maintains at home. One is a fat spaniel called Zephyr—though heaven defend me from such a zephyr! He is fed out of all shape and comfort; his eyes are nearly strained out of his head; he wheezes with corpulency, and cannot walk without great difficulty. The other is a little, old, gray, muzzled curmudgeon, with an unhappy eye, that kindles like a coal if you only look at him; his nose turns up, his mouth is drawn into wrinkles, so as to show his teeth; in short, he has altogether the look of a dog far gone in misanthropy, and totally sick of the world. When he walks, he has his tail curled up so tight that it seems to lift his feet from the ground; and he seldom makes use of more than three legs at a time, keeping the other drawn up as a reserve. This last wretch is called Beauty."

"The Stout Gentleman," one of Irving's finest, most genial and graceful inspirations, prefigures the art of Chekhov in its allusiveness, gentle plasticity, mellow humor and above all in its large, lifelike quality, its ability to sound humane notes long after the tale is read. Both language and style perfectly suit its setting of an English country inn on a rainy day. It is a virtuoso performance in suspense, characterization and tempo. At times the details are presented quietly, slowly, at others rapidly and almost percussively. The lingering effect is that of literary magic mixed with great personal charm. Shortly after the tale's publication it was rumored in England that the model of the stout gentleman was Walter Scott, whom Irving had already met and whom he greatly admired both as an author and person. Certain readers and critics of the day professed to be offended by the tale's supposedly indelicate ending, the description of a posterior: "The skirts of a brown coat parted behind, and gave me a full view of the broad disk of a pair of drab breeches." This kind of constraint was not conducive to the full development of a talent as shy as Irving's.

Irving's shyness, his strong sense of a lack of old native literary roots, his desire to suggest resonance of space and time, and his feeling for the remoteness of old tales handed down with changes of voice in the retelling, led him to assume various literary personae. The author of *Knickerbocker's History of New York* was supposedly Diedrich Knickerbocker. The author of *The Sketch Book* and *Bracebridge Hall* was listed as Geoffrey Crayon. And so "The Stout Gentleman" is not told simply by Irving but by Geoffrey Crayon as the latter heard it told by the "thin, pale, weazen-faced man." Washington Irving: Geoffrey Crayon: the thin man: the story. Which leaves Irving apparently twice removed from the tale. In "The Student of Salamanca" he is even further removed from his story. Washington Irving: Geoffrey Crayon: the captain: the latter's friend, Charles Lightly: Lightly's manuscript: the tale. One of the effects of this sort of "distance" between author and subject is to suggest a sense of tradition as well as to counteract the greenness of immediacy. It is also part of the convention of a book like *Bracebridge Hall*, in which a number of people amuse each other by telling stories.

"The Student of Salamanca" is one of Irving's less fortunate productions. I'm at a loss to explain his errors of judgment and taste in the making or even the attempting of it. The setting is foreign and over-romantic even for the highly romantic and at times sentimental admirer of Byron and Scott: Spain, young love, danger, alchemy, student life, the glamour of Granada. The tale is too long for its thin subject and in it Irving has relinquished his usual tongue-in-cheek manner and has forsaken his own "voice," even, to a degree, his own style. Melodrama is the result. It's almost as if some untalented evil genius inhabiting Irving's skull wrote the tale while Irving was drugged. Mark Twain, a great humorist, could also fall into such errors leading to bathos.

"Annette Delarbre" at first glance may seem a superficial tale. In my opinion the story is handled extremely well. It is untypical of Irving, who is not usually good at portraying women in depth. He genuinely reaches out toward Annette and understands, empathizes with and projects her touching and deranged states of mind. The story, with its foreign setting (Honfleur in lower Normandy), might easily have been diffuse, its psychology maudlin. Instead it is tightly woven, its texture fine, its details vivid, excellent.

In "Dolph Heyliger" Irving is again at his very finest. Whenever he presents a tale in the guise of Diedrich Knickerbocker we can be sure it will have the richness and resonance of being based on native ground. "Dolph Heyliger," it seems to me, is a greater accomplishment than any fiction he had previously published. It is a good deal longer than any

of his earlier tales. "Rip Van Winkle" is about 7,000 words long,
"Sleepy Hollow" 11,500, whereas "Dolph Heyliger" is some 25,000, a
sizable work. It contains an excellent description of Dr. Knipperhausen
and his study or lab, and many times it approaches the sly and sometimes boisterous humor of the History of New York. The work is brilliantly written. Knipperhausen means, approximately, snipperhouse, or
perhaps by inference a house where you get snipped or clipped, which
is what happened to Dolph. Heyliger means the holy one. Dolph seems
like an early version of Huck Finn—he's "the abhorrence of all drowsy,
house-keeping old citizens, who hated noise, and had no relish for
waggery. . . . No one seemed to hold him in much regard except the
wild striplings of the place, who were captivated by his open-hearted,
daring manners,—and the negroes, who always looked upon every
idle, do-nothing youngster as a kind of gentleman."

Irving, who loved the Hudson, provides fine descriptions of the river
and its lore. How well he writes about natural scenes. "Some prepared
the mid-day meal, while others reposed under the shade of the trees, in
luxurious summer indolence, looking drowsily forth upon the beauty of
the scene. On the one side were the highlands, vast and cragged,
feathered to the top with forests, and throwing their shadows on the
glassy water that dimpled at their feet."

"Dolph Heyliger" is among other things a remarkable ghost story,
its details fully imagined and projected, its handiwork shipshape, its
suspense fine. There's even a tale within the tale: "The Storm-Ship,"
told by Antony Vander Heyden and based on a manuscript by Mynheer
Selyne. The structure of "Dolph Heyliger" is particularly complex. It's
as if Irving is suggesting the manner in which folk and fairy tales are
handed down, from mouth to mouth and with no single individual
being the author. Irving seems to need to shroud himself in veils
within veils. Many authors of the nineteenth century, the most famous
of them being Samuel Clemens, used pen names and personae, but
Irving carried literary disguises to an extreme. Did such a method, or
perhaps tendency, in the end play a substantial part in limiting his expression of fictional talent? Why does he seem so distrustful of his own
voice in his fictions? Is it because his fictional gifts, his ability to imagine, were slender, great though they were within their own scope?

At the end of the story are a couple of amusing surprises. The final
paragraph begins: "The foregoing tale rests on better authority than
most tales of the kind, as I have it at second-hand [my emphasis] from
the lips of Dolph Heyliger himself." With this ironic thrust Irving an-
nounces that there are two other voices in the chorus supposedly telling
the story. Now we have Washington Irving: Geoffrey Crayon: Die-

drich Knickerbocker: John Josse Vandermoere: Antony Vander Heyden: Mynheer Selyne: an unidentified friend of Dolph Heyliger:
Dolph Heyliger: the tale. The story ends: "It may not be amiss, before
concluding, to observe that, in addition to his other accomplishments,
Dolph Heyliger was noted by being the ablest drawer of the long-bow
in the whole province." Which suggests that Dolph didn't acquire his
wealth by supernatural means; in short that the whole story is a leg-
puller. Both of these amusing effects are typical of Irving's artistic
"resonance," what in our own time we like to call ambiguity.

After publishing three tales in *The Sketch Book* and four in *Bracebridge Hall,* Irving went all out and in 1824, only four years after the
appearance of *The Sketch Book,* brought out two volumes exclusively
devoted to stories. These, titled *Tales of a Traveller,* consisted of four
series containing, respectively, eight, ten, eight and four tales: a total of
thirty. As we have already noted, Irving received but little contemporary solace for his troubles. The work was attacked in Great Britain and
the United States for ribaldry, vulgarity and indecency, or what some
of the reviewers of the time construed to be such. He was also knuckle-
rapped for his conservatism in politics and for his alleged flattery of the
English and French nobility. As a consequence of all this, the work was
a financial failure. Such belittling of *Tales of a Traveller* continued
into our own time. Stanley T. Williams, an authority on Irving, in his
article on Irving in the *Dictionary of American Biography* (1932)
wrote, "Crossing to England in the spring, he rigged up and finished
. . . a pot-pourri of tales and sketches—a miserable travesty of his original purpose of a 'work on Germany.' " In the same article Williams
wrote, "*Bracebridge Hall . . .* seems today utterly insipid. . . ."

In my opinion Irving paid a large price for being bold. He had
moved too far in advance of his time or at least of his public, which
apparently expected him to repeat his winning formula of a collection
of pleasant, charming, sometimes sentimental essays and sketches and
including two or three tales. Instead, he had produced a work that
seemed extreme: four sets of "frame" stories, containing nothing *but*
stories; stories that often toyed with the reader; that at times had an unpleasant realistic bite despite a tacked-on happy ending; that included
rape, insanity, murder and, perhaps worse, lese majesty toward the London literary scene. Where were the comforting essays and sketches, the
easy changes of pace, the sense that reality was essentially gentle? And
he had gone too far in his preoccupation with the art of short fiction,
he had seemingly forgotten himself or had forgotten his obligation to
his public, and at a time when people wanted sentimental novels to
read, when Scott was still in vogue and Cooper beginning to be a

European sensation. To overlook the substantial artistic merits of *Tales of a Traveller* is to share the errors of his contemporaries and to deprive oneself of a great deal of literary pleasure. Despite its flaws the work is strong and full of treasures, not the least of them the stories with an American setting.

Poor Irving, too sensitive, shy and proud to attempt to defend himself in public and to set down publicly what he was really about, did so privately in a letter to Brevoort written in Paris on December 11, 1824.

"If my writings are worth anything, they will outlive temporary criticism; if not, they are not worth caring about. Some parts of my last work were written rather hastily; yet I am convinced that a great part of it was written in a freer and happier vein than almost any of my former writings. . . . I fancy much of what I value myself upon in writing, escapes the observation of the great mass of my readers, who are intent more upon a story than the way in which it is told. For my part, I consider a story merely as a frame on which to stretch my materials. It is the play of thought, and sentiment, and language; the weaving in of characters, lightly, yet expressively delineated; the familiar and faithful exhibition of scenes in common life; and the half-concealed vein of humor that is often playing through the whole,—these are among what I aim at, and upon which I felicitate myself in proportion as I think I succeed. I have preferred adopting the mode of sketches and short tales rather than long works, because I choose to take a line of writing peculiar to myself, rather than fall into the manner or school of any other writer; and there is a constant activity of thought and a nicety of execution required in writings of this kind, more than the world appears to imagine. It is comparatively easy to swell a story to any size when you have once the scheme and the characters in your mind; the mere interest of the story, too, carries the reader on through pages and pages of careless writing, and the author may often be dull for half a volume at a time, if he has some striking scene at the end of it; but in these shorter writings, every page must have its merit. The author must be continually piquant; woe to him if he makes an awkward sentence or writes a stupid page; the critics are sure to pounce upon it. Yet if he succeed, the very variety and piquancy of his writings—nay, their very brevity, make them frequently recurred to, and when the mere interest of the story is exhausted, he begins to get credit for his touches of pathos or humor; his points of wit or turns of language. I give these as some of the reasons that have induced me to keep on thus far in the way I had opened for myself; because I find by recent letters from E.I. [his brother, Ebenezer Irving] that you

are joining in the oft-repeated advice that I should write a novel. I believe the works that I have written will be oftener re-read than any novel of the size that I could have written. It is true other writers have crowded into the same branch of literature, and I now begin to find myself elbowed by men who have followed my footsteps; but at any rate I have had the merit of adopting a line for myself, instead of following others."

The tales of the first series in *Tales of a Traveller*, "Strange Stories by a Nervous Gentleman," are essentially virtuoso pieces, whose content is not considerable but whose display of mastery of the short form of fiction, a form Irving was still perfecting, is very impressive. He is interested in telling the tales for their own sake and so exquisitely that they will often be reread. His irony, which is a great part of his charm, is much in evidence, as in the following passage from "The Hunting-Dinner": "The choice spirits which flashed up at the beginning of the dinner, sparked for a time, then gradually went out one after another, or only emitted now and then a faint gleam from the socket. Some of the briskest talkers, who had given tongue so bravely at the first burst, fell fast asleep; and none kept on their way but certain of those long-winded prosers, who, like short-legged hounds, worry on unnoticed at the bottom of conversation, but are sure to be in at the death. Even these at length subsided into silence; and scarcely anything was heard but the nasal communications of two or three veteran masticators, who having been silent while awake, were indemnifying the company in their sleep."

Or consider this brilliant bit of rapid characterization: "'Do you believe in ghosts, then?' said a thin, hatchet-faced gentleman, with projecting eyes like a lobster.

"I had remarked this last personage during dinner-time for one of those incessant questioners, who have a craving, unhealthy appetite in conversation. He never seemed satisfied with the whole of a story; never laughed when others laughed; but always put the joke to the question. He never could enjoy the kernel of the nut, but pestered himself to get more out of the shell."

A number of "Strange Stories" are a kind of droll joke played on the reader, who has been promised, by hints, a budget of ghost stories but who is led by the nose and "taken"—that is, given only spoofs of such stories. Irving, enjoying his technical mastery, is deliberately playing with the narrative. Which reminds one of Mark Twain lecturing, leading his audience along, stalling, winding about, until they grasp the joke and break up with applause. It's a dangerous game, which can backfire; it takes virtuosity to pull it off. "Adventure of the German Stu-

dent" like its neighbors is a burlesque on ghost stories but it contains something real and pathetic: a portrait of a deranged young mind that strikes one sharply after the lighter themes of the previous tales in the sequence. Such an unexpected change of pace is found also in "Adventure of the Mysterious Stranger," in which the young Italian's agonized and mysterious state of mind is dramatically portrayed. And "The Story of the Young Italian," which emanates directly from the preceding tale and is actually a continuation of it, is nothing trivial, being a study of extreme emotional and psychological repression and their consequences. The tale has many unfortunate melodramatic touches, especially in those parts dealing with the excesses of love, but it's a suspenseful, moving one nevertheless.

In "Buckthorne and His Friends" we encounter an Irving who is less removed, less in hiding, than in many of his other fictions. This series is very rich in observed details concerning London literary life. Irving's "bite" in this portion of the work may well have caused retaliation among some critics. "The Poor-Devil Author" is painful, telling stuff. "I perceived that there were little knots of authors who lived with, and for, and by one another. They considered themselves the salt of the earth. They fostered and kept up a conventional vein of thinking and talking, and joking on all subjects; and they cried each other up to the skies. Each sect had its particular creed; and set up certain authors as divinities, and fell down and worshipped them; and considered every one who did not worship them, or who worshipped any other, as a heretic and an infidel."

"Buckthorne: or, the Young Man of Great Expectations" I believe to be the masterpiece of *Tales of a Traveller,* the most sustained work, the richest in human materials and the best observed and written, despite Irving's almost compulsive need to provide a happy ending, as he usually does. He deserves to be faulted for this excessive proneness to please. But here's an example of vivid, controlled writing which can come only from the hand of a master:

"Our meals were solitary and unsocial. My uncle rarely spoke; he pointed to whatever he wanted, and the servant perfectly understood him. Indeed, his man John, or Iron John, as he was called in the neighborhood, was a counterpart of his master. He was a tall, bony old fellow, with a dry wig, that seemed made of cow's tail, and a face as tough as though it had been made of cow's hide. He was generally clad in a long, patched livery coat, taken out of the wardrobe of the house, and which bagged loosely about him, having evidently belonged to some corpulent predecessor, in the more plenteous days of the mansion. From long habits of taciturnity the hinges of his jaws seemed to have

grown absolutely rusty, and it cost him as much effort to set them ajar, and to let out a tolerable sentence, as it would have done to set open the iron gates of the park, and let out the old family carriage, that was dropping to pieces in the coach-house."

Here's another example: "I was so bewildered by the scene, and so lost in the crowd of sensations that kept swarming upon me, that I was like one entranced. I lost my companion, Tom Dribble, in a tumult and scuffle that took place near one of the shows; but I was too much occupied in mind to think long about him. I strolled about until dark, when the fair was lighted up, and a new scene of magic opened upon me. The illumination of the tents and booths, the brilliant effect of the stages decorated with lamps, with dramatic groups flaunting about them in gaudy dresses, contrasted splendidly with the surrounding darkness; while the uproar of drums, trumpets, fiddles, hautboys, and cymbals, mingled with the harangues of the showmen, the squeaking of Punch, and the shouts and laughter of the crowd, all united to complete my giddy distraction."

"The Italian Banditti" series is written with extreme care and skill, with Irving's usual irony, brilliant observation, and excitement with foreign scenes, personages and events. And then, after the reader has been treated to twenty-six stories in *Tales of a Traveller*, he is presented with "The Money Diggers," four tales "found among the papers of the late Diedrich Knickerbocker." After traveling in England and Italy we return to the United States for two of Irving's strongest stories: "The Devil and Tom Walker" and "Wolfert Webber." How he can write! Here's a description from "Hell Gate":

"There was a wild story told to us of this being the wreck of a pirate, and some tale of bloody murder which I cannot now recollect, but which made us regard it with great awe, and keep far from it in our cruisings. Indeed, the desolate look of the forlorn hulk, and the fearful place where it lay rotting, were enough to awaken strange notions. A row of timber-heads, blackened by time, just peered above the surface at high water; but at low tide a considerable part of the hull was bare, and its great ribs or timbers, partly stripped of their planks, and dripping with sea-weeds, looked like the huge skeleton of some sea-monster. There was also the stump of a mast, with a few ropes and blocks swinging about and whistling in the wind, while the sea-gull wheeled and screamed around the melancholy carcass. I have a faint recollection of some hobgoblin tale of sailors' ghosts being seen about this wreck at night, with bare skulls, and blue lights in their sockets instead of eyes, but I have forgotten all the particulars."

As we have seen in the biographical summary, Irving understandably

recoiled from the unfriendly reception accorded *Tales of a Traveller*. He depended on writing for his livelihood, and he was forced to believe that the products of his imagination and art would fail to provide him with bread. Perhaps he simply did not have it in him to be a fertile and voluminous fabulist; possibly he had mined his fictional vein pretty deeply. In any event for the next eight years he retreated from the writing of short fiction and sketches to what apparently gave him a greater sense both of financial and literary security: the production of non-fictional works based on Spanish and Moorish materials. Between the publication of *Tales of a Traveller* and *The Alhambra* (1832) he issued *Life and Voyages of Christopher Columbus* (1828), *Conquest of Granada* (1829) and *Voyages and Discoveries of the Companions of Columbus* (1831).

We have already noted that it was in February 1826, after travels in Europe, that he moved to Madrid to work on the life of Columbus. In March 1828, when he was almost forty-four, he set off for Cordova and Granada, and at Granada he visited for the first time the Moorish palace of the Alhambra before proceeding to Malaga, Gibraltar, Cadiz and Seville. He remained in Seville for more than a year and left it in May 1829 for a second and this time historic visit to the Alhambra, for now he was fortunate enough, through the good offices of the Governor of Granada, to whom he had a letter of recommendation, to be able to take up residence in the palace itself, a sprawling building mostly in a state of neglect and decay at the time. The result of his visit of some two or three months was *The Alhambra*, a work in two volumes which enjoyed great popularity.

His eleven Alhambra tales are probably best appreciated in their original setting, the book. They are more akin to fairy than to folk tales. Like a good deal of the rest of the work in which they appear, they permit Irving to hide his voice behind the walls of Moorish and Spanish lore, legend, romance and history. They are not much to my liking, for in them too often I miss his irony, humor, his subtle charm—qualities, by the way, not lacking in the rest of the work. They contain the expected technical mastery but absent are the vitality of native inspiration and idiom. However, many readers may enjoy precisely this superromantic side of him. Also, the Alhambra tales vary in subject as well as style, and some, notably "Legend of the Moor's Legacy," contain many ironic touches.

Almost a quarter of a century elapsed between the appearance of *The Alhambra* and Irving's next publication of tales in volume form, *Wolfert's Roost* (1855), a collection of tales and sketches. There are twelve tales in *Wolfert's Roost*, four of them, the latter in my opinion

the best of the dozen, being American in setting. During that long stretch of time Irving produced three important works on the American West; a life of Oliver Goldsmith; a life of Mahomet; and began the issuance of his monumental and panoramic life of Washington. His works on the American West have been underestimated, in my opinion. For example, Stanley T. Williams of Yale, whom I have already mentioned, said of them in his article in the *Dictionary of American Biography*, ". . . all Irving's compositions on Western themes were commonplace, defining him still more sharply, indirectly, as an urban writer and as a born dweller in cities. *Astoria* . . . and *The Adventures of Captain Bonneville* are frank hackwork." Williams was not very consistent. In 1935, three years after labeling Irving as "an urban writer and as a born dweller in cities," he wrote in his biography of Irving, "As a traveler he was always at his worst in great cities; an Andalusian peasant evoked more of his true self than all Madrid; the enchanted stream of the Saal outweighed Vienna."

To admire Irving's Spanish writings while denigrating his American ones is to fail utterly to comprehend Irving's true passion for his native materials and his great devotion and artistry in handling them. In the very year in which he published *The Alhambra* he was making his excursion into the Oklahoma Territory, which resulted in *A Tour on the Prairies*, published as part of *The Crayon Miscellany* three years later. How different these two works are! In *A Tour on the Prairies* Irving writes with great vividness. He has a wonderful ability to capture landscape with words. His language here, under the influence of the trip, his companions, his return to native soil, is strong, simple, direct as compared with that of *The Alhambra*. And some of his humor, for example in the way he describes Tonish's propensity to lying, is as freewheeling as Mark Twain's. He makes the details of frontier life, including Indian dress and manners, fascinating. He is an inveterate journal keeper, which is vital for the work at hand inasmuch as the literary success of such a journey depends on the quality of the journal entries and therefore on one's discipline in observing, and in writing down one's impressions promptly. He was sensitive about the charge of having stayed away from his country too long. As if in a moment of penitence as well as belated understanding, in *A Tour on the Prairies* he says, "We send our youth abroad to grow luxurious and effeminate in Europe; it appears to me that a previous tour on the prairies would be more likely to produce that manliness, simplicity, and self-dependence most in unison with our political institutions."

It's true, as he notes in a preface to the work, that he doesn't have any stirring adventures to relate here but the book is the greater triumph

for it: he gives us the feel of the frontier in ordinary nights and days. Almost anyone could have written about great adventures; only an artist could succeed in fascinating us with the routines of life on such a trip. He's a very hard worker, a true professional. When considering a master like Irving what's important is not so much what happens to *him* as what he happens *upon*. One wonders where Williams's eyes and ears were when, after reading such a work as *A Tour on the Prairies*, he could write, ". . . all Irving's compositions on Western themes were commonplace. . . ." The following from *A Tour on the Prairies* shows the precision with which Irving often observes and takes notes.

"It was a splendid autumnal evening. The horizon, after sunset, was of a clear apple-green, rising into a delicate lake which gradually lost itself in a deep purple blue. One narrow streak of cloud, of a mahogany color, edged with amber and gold, floated in the west, and just beneath it was the evening star, shining with the pure brilliancy of a diamond. In unison with this scene there was an evening concert of insects of various kinds, all blended and harmonized into one sober and somewhat melancholy note, which I have always found to have a soothing effect upon the mind, disposing it to quiet musings.

"The night that succeeded was calm and beautiful. There was a faint light from the moon, now in its second quarter, and after it had set, a fine starlight, with shooting meteors. The wearied rangers, after a little murmuring conversation round their fires, sank to rest at an early hour, and I seemed to have the whole scene to myself. It is delightful, in thus bivouacking on the prairies, to lie awake and gaze at the stars; it is like watching them from the deck of a ship at sea, when at one view we have the whole scope of heaven. . . . I do not know why it was, but I felt this night unusually affected by the solemn magnificence of the firmament; and seemed, as I lay thus under the open vault of heaven, to inhale with the pure untainted air an exhilarating buoyancy of spirit, and, as it were, an ecstasy of mind. I slept and walked alternately; and when I slept, my dreams partook of the happy tone of my waking reveries."

Or take the following as an example of his vivid descriptive writing. It too is taken from *A Tour on the Prairies*.

"It was a bright sunny morning, with a pure transparent atmosphere that seemed to bathe the very heart with gladness. Our march continued parallel to the Arkansas, through a rich and varied country;— sometimes we had to break our way through alluvial bottoms matted with redundant vegetation, where the gigantic trees were entangled with grapevines, hanging like cordage from their branches; sometimes we coasted along sluggish brooks, whose feebly trickling current just

served to link together a succession of glassy pools, imbedded like mirrors in the quiet bosom of the forest, reflecting its autumnal foliage and patches of the clear blue sky. Sometimes we scrambled up broken and rocky hills, from the summits of which we had wide views stretching on one side over distant prairies diversified by groves and forests, and on the other ranging along a line of blue and shadowy hills beyond the waters of the Arkansas. . . . At one time we passed through a luxuriant bottom of meadow bordered by thickets, where the tall grass was pressed down into numerous 'deer beds,' where those animals had couched the preceding night. Some oak-trees also bore signs of having been clambered by bears, in quest of acorns, the marks of their claws being visible in the bark."

An illuminating description of Irving as he appeared and revealed himself during the trip on the prairies is contained in a long letter the leader of the expedition, Henry Leavitt Ellsworth, a Connecticut man, mentioned earlier, sent home to his wife.

"In his person Mr. Irving is very neat—he carries a great change of dresses, and says he never feels well unless he is clean. Before he sits down to write his sketches or other works, he always washes himself up nice, and with everything clean on him and around him, he says his ideas flow properly—but when he is dirty, the power of association dries up every literary pore. He longs to get into a neat little room, where he can be by himself, and complete some of the numerous things now half finished. . . . He desires most to ramble among the natural actions of men. . . . His mode of recording events, is not to confide much to the memory, but to sketch in a little book every occurence worthy of remembrance and especially *dates & facts*. These he says are his foundations. He makes additional rooms when he builds his fabric and adds the rest, which he terms 'filligree work' . . . In private conversation he seldom takes up a 'set subject.' He dislikes political or polemic discussions. He dislikes to confine the mind long to any one point. . . . On religious subjects his sentiments are termed liberal. He seldom speaks on this subject, unless to condemn the strictness of puritanical folks. In all his readings, he has not perused the bible as much, as I should suppose he would have done, from its sublimity and pathos, if nothing more. That you may not think me incorrect in this particular I only noticed the fact, of his joy at finding Pourteles had with him on our tour to the West, a French bible. He commenced it and read many pages but made a great merriment about the curious things that took place in those ancient days, and made many strange remarks about courtships & marriages & & during those old times. . . . He is very particular to shave every day—and in this respect

Carson City

Library

Date: 8/31/2020

Time: 2:14:57 PM

Fines/Fees Owed: $0.00

Total Checked Out: 1

Checked Out

Title: The complete tales of Washington Irving
Barcode: 31472701586202
Due Date: 09/28/2020 23:59:59

neither of us failed, while travelling together—but we were forced to perform the operation *without a glass,* which none took with them. It is difficult to shave without a glass at first, and experience is gained through *blood,* till at length a mirror becomes unnecessary. . . . His age is 49. In looking back upon his past life he could not tell how he had got along. He had staggered *through the world like a drunken man.* . . . He was a poor scholar—fond of roguery, with no disposition to bone down to study. He had a great thirst for reading voyages and travelled all over the world and became acquainted with all nations. He applauded acts of daring interprise, and felt a longing to visit every place of interest described by travellers. . . . A taste for novels, plays, and light reading succeeded or grew up with the relish for voyages & travels."

Nor does Irving's artistry fail him in *Astoria* and *Adventures of Captain Bonneville,* works not based on first-hand observation but in which he writes so vividly, not only about landscape but about the life of outdoor action, that one tends to forget he had not witnessed the scenes himself. He's as much a master at exploiting other people's journals and letters as his own. *Astoria* is a history of John Jacob Astor's unsuccessful attempt to set up a trading post at the mouth of the Columbia River despite British opposition by way of Canada. *Adventures of Captain Bonneville* relates the adventures of an army officer who had been granted leave to explore the West and whom Irving met at Astor's house. The difference between these works and those that other writers might have produced from the documents and stories made available resides quite simply in Irving's literary and artistic genius together with the fact that he could bring personal experience of the West to bear on the composition of the works. Far from being hackwork, these books, together with *A Tour on the Prairies,* are a significant contribution to the history of the American West as well as to American literature. *The Alhambra* is European in subject and Latinate in language, whereas the books on the American West are written with native verve and fresh idiom, almost as though Irving had spent a professional lifetime in preparing to deal with such materials.

An appreciation of his western works is necessary for a proper recognition of his accomplishment in certain sketches and stories of *Wolfert's Roost,* such as "The Creole Village" and above all "The Early Experiences of Ralph Ringwood." The latter is one of the most remarkable tales Irving ever wrote. He not only delights in its western materials but has great control of them. Its frontier humor is evidenced in such displays as, "I was a stout boy for my years, while my uncle was a little wiffet of a man; one that in Kentucky we would not call even an 'in-

dividual'; nothing more than a 'remote circumstance.' I soon, therefore, brought him to a parley, and learned the whole extent of the charge against me." How authentic and beautiful are many of the story's details. "At Wheeling I embarked in a flat-bottomed family boat, technically called a broad-horn, a prime river conveyance in those days. In this ark for two weeks I floated down the Ohio. The river was as yet in all its wild beauty. Its loftiest trees had not been thinned out. The forest overhung the water's edge, and was occasionally skirted by immense canebrakes. Wild animals of all kinds abounded. We heard them rushing through the thickets and plashing in the water. Deer and bears would frequently swim across the river; others would come down to the bank, and gaze at the boat as it passed."

And the dialogue is free and easy, and economical and authentic, and not inane, windy and unbelievable as it is in Cooper's Leatherstocking Tales. And there is beauty in the rough-spun tale. "The more I knew of a hunter's life, the more I relished it. The country, too, which had been the promised land of my boyhood, did not, like most promised lands, disappoint me. No wilderness could be more beautiful than this part of Kentucky in those times. The forests were open and spacious, with noble trees, some of which looked as if they had stood for centuries. There were beautiful prairies, too, diversified with groves and clumps of trees, which looked like vast parks, and in which you could see the deer running, at a great distance. In the proper season, these prairies would be covered in many places with wild strawberries, where your horse's hoofs would be dyed to the fetlock. I thought there could not be another place in the world equal to Kentucky;—and I think so still." What a lovely detail: dyed to the fetlock.

I have quoted liberally from Irving for the purpose of showing the reader his excellences at large, that is, beyond the scope of his tales, and of encouraging him to explore Irving's world for himself. It is the world of an extraordinarily gifted, romantic, sometimes sentimental, strikingly humane, shy and often solitary writer who looked outside himself for inspiration and materials, who declined, in his later years, several suggestions that he write his autobiography but who, realizing the extent of his popularity in his own time—he was not merely popular, he was a "loved" writer, like Dickens—and his unique position in the origins of our literature, delegated to his devoted nephew Pierre M. Irving the responsible task of composing his posthumous biography. Such an exploration would be an enriching adventure at any time. It is especially relevant and rewarding in a year which is only one short of our bicentennial.

In any event I hope the present essay serves at least as a partial corrective of the prejudices against Irving that arose most virulently in the 1930s, when, like Henry James, he was judged deficient for a lack of virility; when he was too often taken to be little more than a charming, genteel literary professional over-eager to please and to mint coin; too bent on aping English literary manners or steeping himself in unpatriotically foreign themes; when he was blamed for his overlengthy expatriation and for his opinions in religion and politics, a trinity quite beside the point in an unbiased discussion of his artistic flaws or merits; when it was wondered if he was the worthy competitor of Cooper for early American literary glory, as had been thought in his time. By the way, Cooper's supposed greatness as an authentic portraitist of our early frontier was brilliantly demolished by Mark Twain in an essay called "Fenimore Cooper's Literary Offenses," published in 1895. Clemens had a remarkable ear; frontier knowledge gained the hard way; linguistic as well as literary genius; a devastating gift of invective; and a trait Cooper lacked: self-humor. He was well positioned for the attack on Cooper's reputation. His essay is hilariously convincing but even more convincing and hilarious is a rereading of any of the novels in the Leatherstocking Tales series.

It was in the same '30s that the proletarian novel, with its notable deficiency of aesthetic taste and gifts, seemed to some critics to be American literature's best hope. The prejudices against Irving stemming from or renewed in that time have seemingly continued, although with waning strength, to the present day; or, where they have disappeared, have been replaced by a kind of studied indifference to the work of an early American author worthy of our serious admiration, not our lip service.

Irving, who lived his life between the margins of two great civil wars, the keen and professional observer standing aside from the mainstream, the lifelong bachelor, the inveterate traveler attracted by exotic scenes, is an author much of whose work still lives, and contains a great deal of beauty, and for whom one can still feel genuine affection and respect. Basically the reason is to be found in his artistry. He is an artistic fountainhead who influenced such different writers as Hawthorne, James and Twain, and who can offer much pleasure today.

Princeton, New Jersey
July 1974

RIP VAN WINKLE

A Posthumous Writing of Diedrich Knickerbocker*

By Woden, God of Saxons,
From whence comes Wensday, that is Wodensday,
Truth is a thing that ever I will keep
Unto thylke day in which I creep into
My sepulchre——

CARTWRIGHT.

. [The following Tale was found among the papers of the late Diedrich Knickerbocker, an old gentleman of New York, who was very curious in the Dutch history of the province, and the manners of the descendants from its primitive settlers. His historical researches, however, did not lie so much among books as among men; for the former are lamentably scanty on his favorite topics; whereas he found the old burghers, and still more their wives, rich in that legendary lore so invaluable to true history. Whenever, therefore, he happened upon a genuine Dutch family, snugly shut up in its low-roofed farmhouse, under a spreading sycamore, he looked upon it as a little clasped volume of black-letter, and studied it with the zeal of a book-worm.

The result of all these researches was a history of the province during the reign of the Dutch governors, which he published some years since. There have been various opinions as to the literary character of his work, and, to tell the truth, it is not a whit better than it should be. Its chief merit is its scrupulous accuracy, which indeed was a little questioned on its first appearance, but has since been completely established; and it is now admitted into all historical collections as a book of unquestionable authority.

The old gentleman died shortly after the publication of his work; and now that he is dead and gone, it cannot do much harm to his memory to say that his time might have been much better employed in weightier labors. He, however, was apt to ride his hobby his own way; and though it did now and then kick up the dust a little in the eyes of his neighbors, and grieve the spirit of some friends, for whom he felt the truest deference and

---

* Diedrich Knickerbocker was the imaginary character who was supposed to have written Irving's *History of New York*, published in 1809.—C.N.

affection, yet his errors and follies are remembered "more in sorrow than in anger," and it begins to be suspected that he never intended to offend. But however his memory may be appreciated by critics, it is still held dear by many folk whose good opinion is well worth having; particularly by certain biscuit-makers, who have gone so far as to imprint his likeness on their New-Year cakes; and have thus given him a chance for immortality, almost equal to being stamped on a Waterloo Medal, or a Queen Anne's Farthing.]

WHOEVER has made a voyage up the Hudson must remember the Kaatskill mountains. They are a dismembered branch of the great Appalachian family, and are seen away to the west of the river, swelling up to a noble height, and lording it over the surrounding country. Every change of season, every change of weather, indeed, every hour of the day, produces some change in the magical hues and shapes of these mountains, and they are regarded by all the good wives, far and near, as perfect barometers. When the weather is fair and settled, they are clothed in blue and purple, and print their bold outlines on the clear evening sky; but sometimes, when the rest of the landscape is cloudless, they will gather a hood of gray vapors about their summits, which, in the last rays of the setting sun, will glow and light up like a crown of glory.

At the foot of these fairy mountains, the voyager may have descried the light smoke curling up from a village, whose shingle-roofs gleam among the trees, just where the blue tints of the upland melt away into the fresh green of the nearer landscape. It is a little village, of great antiquity, having been founded by some of the Dutch colonists in the early times of the province, just about the beginning of the government of the good Peter Stuyvesant, (may he rest in peace!) and there were some of the houses of the original settlers standing within a few years, built of small yellow bricks brought from Holland, having latticed windows and gable fronts, surmounted with weathercocks.

In that same village, and in one of these very houses (which, to tell the precise truth, was sadly time-worn and weather-beaten), there lived, many years since, while the country was yet a province of Great Britain, a simple, good-natured fellow, of the name of Rip Van Winkle. He was a descendant of the Van Winkles who figured so gallantly in the chivalrous days of Peter Stuyvesant, and accompanied him to the siege of Fort Christina. He inherited, however, but little of the martial character of his ancestors. I have observed that he was a simple, good-natured man; he was, moreover, a kind neighbor, and an obedient, hen-

pecked husband. Indeed, to the latter circumstance might be owing that meekness of spirit which gained him such universal popularity; for those men are most apt to be obsequious and conciliating abroad, who are under the discipline of shrews at home. Their tempers, doubtless, are rendered pliant and malleable in the fiery furnace of domestic tribulation; and a curtain-lecture is worth all the sermons in the world for teaching the virtues of patience and long-suffering. A termagant wife may, therefore, in some respects, be considered a tolerable blessing; and if so, Rip Van Winkle was thrice blessed.

Certain it is, that he was a great favorite among all the good wives of the village, who, as usual with the amiable sex, took his part in all family squabbles; and never failed, whenever they talked those matters over in their evening gossipings, to lay all the blame on Dame Van Winkle. The children of the village, too, would shout with joy whenever he approached. He assisted at their sports, made their playthings, taught them to fly kites and shoot marbles, and told them long stories of ghosts, witches, and Indians. Whenever he went dodging about the village, he was surrounded by a troop of them, hanging on his skirts, clambering on his back, and playing a thousand tricks on him with impunity; and not a dog would bark at him throughout the neighborhood.

The great error in Rip's composition was an insuperable aversion to all kinds of profitable labor. It could not be from the want of assiduity or perseverance; for he would sit on a wet rock, with a rod as long and heavy as a Tartar's lance, and fish all day without a murmur, even though he should not be encouraged by a single nibble. He would carry a fowling-piece on his shoulder for hours together, trudging through woods and swamps, and up hill and down dale, to shoot a few squirrels or wild pigeons. He would never refuse to assist a neighbor even in the roughest toil, and was a foremost man at all country frolics for husking Indian corn, or building stone fences; the women of the village, too, used to employ him to run their errands, and to do such little odd jobs as their less obliging husbands would not do for them. In a word, Rip was ready to attend to anybody's business but his own; but as to doing family duty, and keeping his farm in order, he found it impossible.

In fact, he declared it was of no use to work on his farm; it was the most pestilent little piece of ground in the whole country; everything about it went wrong, and would go wrong, in spite of him. His fences were continually falling to pieces; his cow would either go astray, or get among the cabbages; weeds were sure to grow quicker in his fields than anywhere else; the rain always made a point of setting in just as

he had some out-door work to do; so that though his patrimonial estate had dwindled away under his management, acre by acre, until there was little more left than a mere patch of Indian corn and potatoes, yet it was the worst conditioned farm in the neighborhood.

His children, too, were as ragged and wild as if they belonged to nobody. His son Rip, an urchin begotten in his own likeness, promised to inherit the habits, with the old clothes, of his father. He was generally seen trooping like a colt at his mother's heels, equipped in a pair of his father's cast-off galligaskins, which he had much ado to hold up with one hand, as a fine lady does her train in bad weather.

Rip Van Winkle, however, was one of those happy mortals, of foolish, well-oiled dispositions, who take the world easy, eat white bread or brown, whichever can be got with least thought or trouble, and would rather starve on a penny than work for a pound. If left to himself, he would have whistled life away in perfect contentment; but his wife kept continually dinning in his ears about his idleness, his carelessness, and the ruin he was bringing on his family. Morning, noon, and night, her tongue was incessantly going, and everything he said or did was sure to produce a torrent of household eloquence. Rip had but one way of replying to all lectures of the kind, and that, by frequent use, had grown into a habit. He shrugged his shoulders, shook his head, cast up his eyes, but said nothing. This, however, always provoked a fresh volley from his wife; so that he was fain to draw off his forces, and take to the outside of the house—the only side which, in truth, belongs to a hen-pecked husband.

Rip's sole domestic adherent was his dog Wolf, who was as much hen-pecked as his master; for Dame Van Winkle regarded them as companions in idleness, and even looked upon Wolf with an evil eye, as the cause of his master's going so often astray. True it is, in all points of spirit befitting an honorable dog, he was as courageous an animal as ever scoured the woods; but what courage can withstand the ever-enduring and all-besetting terrors of a woman's tongue? The moment Wolf entered the house his crest fell, his tail drooped to the ground, or curled between his legs, he sneaked about with a gallows air, casting many a sidelong glance at Dame Van Winkle, and at the least flourish of a broomstick or ladle he would fly to the door with yelping precipitation.

Times grew worse and worse with Rip Van Winkle as years of matrimony rolled on; a tart temper never mellows with age, and a sharp tongue is the only edged tool that grows keener with constant use. For a long while he used to console himself, when driven from home, by frequenting a kind of perpetual club of the sages, philosophers, and other idle personages of the village, which held its sessions on a bench

before a small inn, designated by a rubicund portrait of His Majesty George the Third. Here they used to sit in the shade through a long, lazy summer's day, talking listlessly over village gossip, or telling endless sleepy stories about nothing. But it would have been worth any statesman's money to have heard the profound discussions that sometimes took place, when by chance an old newspaper fell into their hands from some passing traveller. How solemnly they would listen to the contents, as drawled out by Derrick Van Bummel, the schoolmaster, a dapper learned little man, who was not to be daunted by the most gigantic word in the dictionary; and how sagely they would deliberate upon public events some months after they had taken place.

The opinions of this junto were completely controlled by Nicholas Vedder, patriarch of the village, and landlord of the inn, at the door of which he took his seat from morning till night, just moving sufficiently to avoid the sun and keep in the shade of a large tree; so that the neighbors could tell the hour by his movements as accurately as by a sun-dial. It is true he was rarely heard to speak, but smoked his pipe incessantly. His adherents, however (for every great man has his adherents), perfectly understood him, and knew how to gather his opinions. When anything that was read or related displeased him, he was observed to smoke his pipe vehemently, and to send forth short, frequent, and angry puffs; but when pleased, he would inhale the smoke slowly and tranquilly, and emit it in light and placid clouds; and sometimes, taking the pipe from his mouth, and letting the fragrant vapor curl about his nose, would gravely nod his head in token of perfect approbation.

From even this stronghold the unlucky Rip was at length routed by his termagant wife, who would suddenly break in upon the tranquillity of the assemblage and call the members all to naught; nor was that august personage, Nicholas Vedder himself, sacred from the daring tongue of this terrible virago, who charged him outright with encouraging her husband in habits of idleness.

Poor Rip was at last reduced almost to despair; and his only alternative, to escape from the labor of the farm and clamor of his wife, was to take gun in hand and stroll away into the woods. Here he would sometimes seat himself at the foot of a tree, and share the contents of his wallet with Wolf, with whom he sympathized as a fellow-sufferer in persecution. "Poor Wolf," he would say, "thy mistress leads thee a dog's life of it, but never mind, my lad, whilst I live thou shalt never want a friend to stand by thee!" Wolf would wag his tail, look wistfully in his master's face, and if dogs can feel pity, I verily believe he reciprocated the sentiment with all his heart.

In a long ramble of the kind on a fine autumnal day, Rip had un-

consciously scrambled to one of the highest parts of the Kaatskill mountains. He was after his favorite sport of squirrel-shooting, and the still
solitudes had echoed and re-echoed with the reports of his gun. Panting
and fatigued, he threw himself, late in the afternoon, on a green
knoll, covered with mountain herbage, that crowned the brow of a
precipice. From an opening between the trees he could overlook all the
lower country for many a mile of rich woodland. He saw at a distance
the lordly Hudson, far, far below him, moving on its silent but majestic
course, with the reflection of a purple cloud, or the sail of a lagging
bark, here and there sleeping on its glassy bosom, and at last losing
itself in the blue highlands.

On the other side he looked down into a deep mountain glen, wild,
lonely, and shagged, the bottom filled with fragments from the impending cliffs, and scarcely lighted by the reflected rays of the setting sun.
For some time Rip lay musing on this scene; evening was gradually advancing; the mountains began to throw their long blue shadows over
the valleys; he saw that it would be dark long before he could reach the
village, and he heaved a heavy sigh when he thought of encountering
the terrors of Dame Van Winkle.

As he was about to descend, he heard a voice from a distance, hal-
looing, "Rip Van Winkle, Rip Van Winkle!" He looked around, but
could see nothing but a crow winging its solitary flight across the mountain. He thought his fancy must have deceived him, and turned again
to descend, when he heard the same cry ring through the still evening
air: "Rip Van Winkle! Rip Van Winkle!"—at the same time Wolf
bristled up his back, and giving a low growl, skulked to his master's
side, looking fearfully down into the glen. Rip now felt a vague apprehension stealing over him; he looked anxiously in the same direction,
and perceived a strange figure slowly toiling up the rocks, and bending
under the weight of something he carried on his back. He was surprised
to see any human being in this lonely and unfrequented place; but supposing it to be some one of the neighborhood in need of his assistance,
he hastened down to yield it.

On nearer approach he was still more surprised at the singularity of
the stranger's appearance. He was a short, square-built old fellow, with
thick bushy hair, and a grizzled beard. His dress was of the antique
Dutch fashion,—a cloth jerkin strapped around the waist—several pair
of breeches, the outer one of ample volume, decorated with rows of
buttons down the sides, and bunches at the knees. He bore on his
shoulders a stout keg, that seemed full of liquor, and made signs for
Rip to approach and assist him with the load. Though rather shy and
distrustful of this new acquaintance, Rip complied with his usual alac-

rity; and mutually relieving one another, they clambered up a narrow gully, apparently the dry bed of a mountain torrent. As they ascended, Rip every now and then heard long, rolling peals, like distant thunder, that seemed to issue out of a deep ravine, or rather cleft, between lofty rocks, toward which their rugged path conducted. He paused for an instant, but supposing it to be the muttering of one of those transient thunder-showers which often take place in mountain heights, he proceeded. Passing through the ravine, they came to a hollow, like a small amphitheatre, surrounded by perpendicular precipices, over the brinks of which impending trees shot their branches, so that you only caught glimpses of the azure sky and the bright evening cloud. During the whole time Rip and his companion had labored on in silence; for though the former marvelled greatly what could be the object of carrying a keg of liquor up this wild mountain, yet there was something strange and incomprehensible about the unknown, that inspired awe and checked familiarity.

On entering the amphitheatre, new objects of wonder presented themselves. On a level spot in the centre was a company of odd-looking personages playing at ninepins. They were dressed in a quaint, outlandish fashion; some wore short doublets, others jerkins, with long knives in their belts, and most of them had enormous breeches, of similar style with that of the guide's. Their visages, too, were peculiar: one had a large beard, broad face, and small piggish eyes; the face of another seemed to consist entirely of nose, and was surmounted by a white sugar-loaf hat, set off with a little red cock's tail. They all had beards, of various shapes and colors. There was one who seemed to be the commander. He was a stout old gentleman, with a weather-beaten countenance; he wore a laced doublet, broad belt and hanger, high crowned hat and feather, red stockings, and high-heeled shoes, with roses in them. The whole group reminded Rip of the figures in an old Flemish painting, in the parlor of Dominie Van Shaick, the village parson, and which had been brought over from Holland at the time of the settlement.

What seemed particularly odd to Rip was, that, though these folks were evidently amusing themselves, yet they maintained the gravest faces, the most mysterious silence, and were, withal, the most melancholy party of pleasure he had ever witnessed. Nothing interrupted the stillness of the scene but the noise of the balls, which, whenever they rolled, echoed along the mountains like rumbling peals of thunder.

As Rip and his companion approached them, they suddenly desisted from their play, and stared at him with such fixed, statue-like gaze, and such strange, uncouth, lack-lustre countenances, that his heart turned

within him, and his knees smote together. His companion now emptied the contents of the keg into large flagons, and made signs to him to wait upon the company. He obeyed with fear and trembling; they quaffed the liquor in profound silence, and then returned to their game.

By degrees Rip's awe and apprehension subsided. He even ventured, when no eye was fixed upon him, to taste the beverage, which he found had much of the flavor of excellent Hollands. He was naturally a thirsty soul, and was soon tempted to repeat the draught. One taste provoked another; and he reiterated his visits to the flagon so often that at length his senses were overpowered, his eyes swam in his head, his head gradually declined, and he fell into a deep sleep.

On waking, he found himself on the green knoll whence he had first seen the old man of the glen. He rubbed his eyes—it was a bright sunny morning. The birds were hopping and twittering among the bushes, and the eagle was wheeling aloft, and breasting the pure mountain breeze. "Surely," thought Rip, "I have not slept here all night." He recalled the occurrences before he fell asleep. The strange man with a keg of liquor—the mountain ravine—the wild retreat among the rocks—the woe-begone party at ninepins—the flagon—"Oh! that flagon! that wicked flagon!" thought Rip, "what excuse shall I make to Dame Van Winkle?"

He looked round for his gun, but in place of the clean, well-oiled fowling-piece, he found an old firelock lying by him, the barrel encrusted with rust, the lock falling off, and the stock worm-eaten. He now suspected that the grave roisters of the mountains had put a trick upon him, and, having dosed him with liquor, had robbed him of his gun. Wolf, too, had disappeared, but he might have strayed away after a squirrel or partridge. He whistled after him, and shouted his name, but all in vain; the echoes repeated his whistle and shout, but no dog was to be seen.

He determined to revisit the scene of the last evening's gambol, and if he met with any of the party, to demand his dog and gun. As he rose to walk, he found himself stiff in the joints, and wanting in his usual activity. "These mountain beds do not agree with me," thought Rip, "and if this frolic should lay me up with a fit of the rheumatism, I shall have a blessed time with Dame Van Winkle." With some difficulty he got down into the glen: he found the gully up which he and his companion had ascended the preceding evening; but to his astonishment a mountain stream was now foaming down it, leaping from rock to rock, and filling the glen with babbling murmurs. He, however, made shift to scramble up its sides, working his toilsome way through thickets of birch, sassafras, and witch-hazel, and sometimes tripped up

or entangled by the wild grape-vines that twisted their coils or tendrils from tree to tree, and spread a kind of network in his path.

At length he reached to where the ravine had opened through the cliffs to the amphitheatre; but no traces of such opening remained. The rocks presented a high, impenetrable wall, over which the torrent came tumbling in a sheet of feathery foam, and fell into a broad deep basin, black from the shadows of the surrounding forest. Here, then, poor Rip was brought to a stand. He again called and whistled after his dog; he was only answered by the cawing of a flock of idle crows, sporting high in air about a dry tree that overhung a sunny precipice; and who, secure in their elevation, seemed to look down and scoff at the poor man's perplexities. What was to be done? the morning was passing away, and Rip felt famished for want of his breakfast. He grieved to give up his dog and gun; he dreaded to meet his wife; but it would not do to starve among the mountains. He shook his head, shouldered the rusty firelock, and, with a heart full of trouble and anxiety, turned his footsteps homeward.

As he approached the village he met a number of people, but none whom he knew, which somewhat surprised him, for he had thought himself acquainted with every one in the country round. Their dress, too, was of a different fashion from that to which he was accustomed. They all stared at him with equal marks of surprise, and whenever they cast their eyes upon him, invariably stroked their chins. The constant recurrence of this gesture induced Rip, involuntarily, to do the same, when, to his astonishment, he found his beard had grown a foot long!

He had now entered the skirts of the village. A troop of strange children ran at his heels, hooting after him, and pointing at his gray beard. The dogs, too, not one of which he recognized for an old acquaintance, barked at him as he passed. The very village was altered; it was larger and more populous. There were rows of houses which he had never seen before, and those which had been his familiar haunts had disappeared. Strange names were over the doors—strange faces at the windows—everything was strange. His mind now misgave him; he began to doubt whether both he and the world around him were not bewitched. Surely this was his native village, which he had left but the day before. There stood the Kaatskill mountains—there ran the silver Hudson at a distance—there was every hill and dale precisely as it had always been. Rip was sorely perplexed. "That flagon last night," thought he, "has addled my poor head sadly!"

It was with some difficulty that he found the way to his own house, which he approached with silent awe, expecting every moment to hear the shrill voice of Dame Van Winkle. He found the house gone to de-

cay—the roof fallen in, the windows shattered, and the doors off the hinges. A half-starved dog that looked like Wolf was skulking about it. Rip called him by name, but the cur snarled, showed his teeth, and passed on. This was an unkind cut indeed. "My very dog," sighed poor Rip, "has forgotten me!"

He entered the house, which to tell the truth, Dame Van Winkle had always kept in neat order. It was empty, forlorn, and apparently abandoned. This desolateness overcame all his connubial fears—he called loudly for his wife and children—the lonely chambers rang for a moment with his voice, and then all again was silence.

He now hurried forth, and hastened to his old resort, the village inn, but it too was gone. A large rickety wooden building stood in its place, with great gaping windows, some of them broken and mended with old hats and petticoats, and over the door was painted, "The Union Hotel, by Jonathan Doolittle." Instead of the great tree that used to shelter the quiet little Dutch inn of yore, there now was reared a tall naked pole, with something on top that looked like a red night-cap, and from it was fluttering a flag, on which was a singular assemblage of stars and stripes;—all this was strange and incomprehensible. He recognized on the sign, however, the ruby face of King George, under which he had smoked so many a peaceful pipe; but even this was singularly metamorphosed. The red coat was changed for one of blue and buff, a sword was held in the hand instead of a sceptre, the head was decorated with a cocked hat, and underneath was painted in large characters, GENERAL WASHINGTON.

There was, as usual, a crowd of folk about the door, but none that Rip recollected. The very character of the people seemed changed. There was a busy, bustling, disputatious tone about it, instead of the accustomed phlegm and drowsy tranquillity. He looked in vain for the sage Nicholas Vedder, with his broad face, double chin, and fair long pipe, uttering clouds of tobacco-smoke instead of idle speeches; or Van Bummel, the schoolmaster, doling forth the contents of an ancient newspaper. In place of these, a lean, bilious-looking fellow, with his pockets full of handbills, was haranguing vehemently about rights of citizens—elections—members of congress—liberty—Bunker's Hill—heroes of seventy-six—and other words, which were a perfect Babylonish jargon to the bewildered Van Winkle.

The appearance of Rip, with his long, grizzled beard, his rusty fowling-piece, his uncouth dress, and an army of women and children at his heels, soon attracted the attention of the tavern-politicians. They crowded round him, eying him from head to foot with great curiosity. The orator bustled up to him, and, drawing him partly aside, inquired

"On which side he voted?" Rip stared in vacant stupidity. Another short but busy little fellow pulled him by the arm, and, rising on tiptoe, inquired in his ear, "Whether he was Federal or Democrat?" Rip was equally at a loss to comprehend the question; when a knowing, self-important old gentleman, in a sharp cocked hat, made his way through the crowd, putting them to the right and left with his elbows as he passed, and planting himself before Van Winkle, with one arm akimbo, the other resting on his cane, his keen eyes and sharp hat penetrating, as it were, into his very soul, demanded in an austere tone, "What brought him to the election with a gun on his shoulder, and a mob at his heels; and whether he meant to breed a riot in the village?"—"Alas! gentlemen," cried Rip, somewhat dismayed, "I am a poor quiet man, a native of the place, and a loyal subject of the King, God bless him!"

Here a general shout burst from the by-standers—"A tory! a tory! a spy! a refugee! hustle him! away with him!" It was with great difficulty that the self-important man in the cocked hat restored order; and, having assumed a tenfold austerity of brow, demanded again of the unknown culprit, what he came there for, and whom he was seeking? The poor man humbly assured him that he meant no harm, but merely came there in search of some of his neighbors, who used to keep about the tavern.

"Well—who are they?—name them."

Rip bethought himself a moment, and inquired, "Where's Nicholas Vedder?"

There was a silence for a little while, when an old man replied, in a thin piping voice, "Nicholas Vedder! why, he is dead and gone these eighteen years! There was a wooden tombstone in that churchyard that used to tell all about him, but that's rotten and gone too."

"Where's Brom Dutcher?"

"Oh, he went off to the army in the beginning of the war; some say he was killed at the storming of Stony Point—others say he was drowned in a squall at the foot of Antony's Nose. I don't know—he never came back again."

"Where's Van Bummel, the schoolmaster?"

"He went off to the wars too, was a great militia general, and is now in congress."

Rip's heart died away at hearing of these sad changes in his home and friends, and finding himself thus alone in the world. Every answer puzzled him too, by treating of such enormous lapses of time, and of matters which he could not understand: war—congress—Stony Point— he had no courage to ask after any more friends, but cried out in despair, "Does nobody here know Rip Van Winkle?"

"Oh, Rip Van Winkle!" exclaimed two or three, "oh, to be sure! that's Rip Van Winkle yonder, leaning against the tree."

Rip looked, and he beheld a precise counterpart of himself, as he went up the mountain; apparently as lazy, and certainly as ragged. The poor fellow was now completely confounded. He doubted his own identity, and whether he was himself or another man. In the midst of his bewilderment, the man in the cocked hat demanded who he was, and what was his name.

"God knows," exclaimed he, at his wit's end; "I'm not myself—I'm somebody else—that's me yonder—no—that's somebody else got into my shoes—I was myself last night, but I fell asleep on the mountain, and they've changed my gun, and everything's changed, and I'm changed, and I can't tell what's my name, or who I am!"

The by-standers began now to look at each other, nod, wink significantly, and tap their fingers against their foreheads. There was a whisper, also, about securing the gun, and keeping the old fellow from doing mischief, at the very suggestion of which the self-important man in the cocked hat retired with some precipitation. At this critical moment a fresh, comely woman pressed through the throng to get a peep at the gray-bearded man. She had a chubby child in her arms, which, frightened at his looks, began to cry. "Hush, Rip," cried she, "hush, you little fool; the old man won't hurt you." The name of the child, the air of the mother, the tone of her voice, all awakened a train of recollections in his mind. "What is your name, my good woman?" asked he.

"Judith Gardenier."

"And your father's name?"

"Ah, poor man, Rip Van Winkle was his name, but it's twenty years since he went away from home with his gun, and never has been heard of since,—his dog came home without him; but whether he shot himself, or was carried away by the Indians, nobody can tell. I was then but a little girl."

Rip had but one question more to ask; but he put it with a faltering voice:

"Where's your mother?"

"Oh, she too had died but a short time since; she broke a bloodvessel in a fit of passion at a New England pedler."

There was a drop of comfort, at least, in this intelligence. The honest man could contain himself no longer. He caught his daughter and her child in his arms. "I am your father!" cried he—"Young Rip Van Winkle once—old Rip Van Winkle now!—Does nobody know poor Rip Van Winkle?"

All stood amazed, until an old woman, tottering out from among the

crowd, put her hand to her brow, and peering under it in his face for a moment, exclaimed, "Sure enough! it is Rip Van Winkle—it is himself! Welcome home again, old neighbor. Why, where have you been these twenty long years?"

Rip's story was soon told, for the whole twenty years had been to him but as one night. The neighbors stared when they heard it; some were seen to wink at each other, and put their tongues in their cheeks: and the self-important man in the cocked hat, who, when the alarm was over, had returned to the field, screwed down the corners of his mouth, and shook his head—upon which there was a general shaking of the head throughout the assemblage.

It was determined, however, to take the opinion of old Peter Vander-donk, who was seen slowly advancing up the road. He was a descend-ant of the historian of that name, who wrote one of the earliest ac-counts of the province. Peter was the most ancient inhabitant of the village, and well versed in all the wonderful events and traditions of the neighborhood. He recollected Rip at once, and corroborated his story in the most satisfactory manner. He assured the company that it was a fact, handed down from his ancestor the historian, that the Kaatskill mountains had always been haunted by strange beings. That it was af-firmed that the great Hendrick Hudson, the first discoverer of the river and country, kept a kind of vigil there every twenty years, with his crew of the *Half-moon;* being permitted in this way to revisit the scenes of his enterprise, and keep a guardian eye upon the river and the great city called by his name. That his father had once seen them in their old Dutch dresses playing at ninepins in a hollow of the mountain; and that he himself had heard, one summer afternoon, the sound of their balls, like distant peals of thunder.

To make a long story short, the company broke up and returned to the more important concerns of the election. Rip's daughter took him home to live with her; she had a snug, well-furnished house, and a stout, cheery farmer for a husband, whom Rip recollected for one of the urchins that used to climb upon his back. As to Rip's son and heir, who was the ditto of himself, seen leaning against the tree, he was employed to work on the farm; but evinced an hereditary disposition to attend to anything else but his business.

Rip now resumed his old walks and habits; he soon found many of his former cronies, though all rather the worse for the wear and tear of time; and preferred making friends among the rising generation, with whom he soon grew into great favor.

Having nothing to do at home, and being arrived at that happy age when a man can be idle with impunity, he took his place once more on

the bench at the inn-door, and was reverenced as one of the patriarchs of the village, and a chronicle of the old times "before the war." It was some time before he could get into the regular track of gossip, or could be made to comprehend the strange events that had taken place during his torpor. How that there had been a revolutionary war,—that the country had thrown off the yoke of old England,—and that, instead of being a subject of his Majesty George the Third, he was now a free citizen of the United States. Rip, in fact, was no politician; the changes of states and empires made but little impression on him; but there was one species of despotism under which he long groaned, and that was— petticoat government. Happily that was at an end; he had got his neck out of the yoke of matrimony, and could go in and out whenever he pleased, without dreading the tyranny of Dame Van Winkle. Whenever her name was mentioned, however, he shook his head, shrugged his shoulders, and cast up his eyes; which might pass either for an expression of resignation to his fate, or joy at his deliverance.

He used to tell his story to every stranger that arrived at Mr. Doolittle's hotel. He was observed, at first, to vary on some points every time he told it, which was, doubtless, owing to his having so recently awaked. It at last settled down precisely to the tale I have related, and not a man, woman, or child in the neighborhood but knew it by heart. Some always pretended to doubt the reality of it, and insisted that Rip had been out of his head, and that this was one point on which he always remained flighty. The old Dutch inhabitants, however, almost universally gave it full credit. Even to this day they never hear a thunderstorm of a summer afternoon about the Kaatskill, but they say Hendrick Hudson and his crew are at their game of ninepins; and it is a common wish of all hen-pecked husbands in the neighborhood, when life hangs heavy on their hands, that they might have a quieting draught out of Rip Van Winkle's flagon.

NOTE.

The foregoing Tale, one would suspect, had been suggested to Mr. Knickerbocker by a little German superstition about the Emperor Frederick der Rothbart, and the Kypphäuser mountain: the subjoined note, however, which he had appended to the tale, shows that it is an absolute fact, narrated with his usual fidelity.

"The story of Rip Van Winkle may seem incredible to many, but nevertheless I give it my full belief, for I know the vicinity of our old Dutch settlements to have been very subject to marvellous events and appearances. Indeed, I have heard many stranger stories than this, in the villages along the Hudson; all of which were too well authenticated to admit of a doubt.

I have even talked with Rip Van Winkle myself, who, when last I saw him, was a very venerable old man, and so perfectly rational and consistent on every other point, that I think no conscientious person could refuse to take this into the bargain; nay, I have seen a certificate on the subject taken before a country justice and signed with a cross, in the justice's own handwriting. The story, therefore, is beyond the possibility of doubt.

"D.K."

POSTSCRIPT.

The following are travelling notes from a memorandum-book of Mr. Knickerbocker.

The Kaatsberg, or Catskill Mountains, have always been a region full of fable. The Indians considered them the abode of spirits, who influenced the weather, spreading sunshine or clouds over the landscape, and sending good or bad hunting-seasons. They were ruled by an old squaw spirit, said to be their mother. She dwelt on the highest peak of the Catskills, and had charge of the doors of day and night to open and shut them at the proper hour. She hung up the new moons in the skies, and cut up the old ones into stars. In times of drought, if properly propitiated, she would spin light summer clouds out of cobwebs and morning dew, and send them off from the crest of the mountain, flake after flake, like flakes of carded cotton, to float in the air; until, dissolved by the heat of the sun, they would fall in gentle showers, causing the grass to spring, the fruits to ripen, and the corn to grow an inch an hour. If displeased, however, she would brew up clouds black as ink, sitting in the midst of them like a bottle-bellied spider in the midst of its web; and when these clouds broke, woe betide the valleys!

In old times, say the Indian traditions, there was a kind of Manitou or Spirit, who kept about the wildest recesses of the Catskill Mountains, and took a mischievous pleasure in wreaking all kinds of evils and vexations upon the red men. Sometimes he would assume the form of a bear, a panther, or a deer, lead the bewildered hunter a weary chase through tangled forests and among ragged rocks; and then spring off with a loud ho! ho! leaving him aghast on the brink of a beetling precipice or raging torrent.

The favorite abode of this Manitou is still shown. It is a great rock or cliff on the loneliest part of the mountains, and, from the flowering vines which clamber about it, and the wild flowers which abound in its neighborhood, is known by the name of the Garden Rock. Near the foot of it is a small lake, the haunt of the solitary bittern, with water-snakes basking in the sun on the leaves of the pond-lilies which lie on the surface. This place was held in great awe by the Indians, insomuch that the boldest hunter would not pursue his game within its precincts. Once upon a time, however, a hunter who had lost his way, penetrated to the Garden Rock,

where he beheld a number of gourds placed in the crotches of trees. One of these he seized and made off with it, but in the hurry of his retreat he let it fall among the rocks, when a great stream gushed forth, which washed him away and swept him down precipices, where he was dashed to pieces, and the stream made its way to the Hudson, and continues to flow to the present day; being the identical stream known by the name of the Kaaterskill.

From *The Sketch Book*

THE SPECTRE BRIDEGROOM

A Traveller's Tale*

> Shall I not take mine ease in mine inn!
> FALSTAFF.

DURING a journey that I once made through the Netherlands, I had arrived one evening at the *Pomme d' Or*, the principal inn of a small Flemish village. It was after the hour of the *table d' hôte*, so that I was obliged to make a solitary supper from the relics of its ampler board. The weather was chilly; I was seated alone in one end of a great gloomy dining-room, and, my repast being over, I had the prospect before me of a long dull evening, without any visible means of enlivening it. I summoned mine host, and requested something to read; he brought me the whole literary stock of his household, a Dutch family Bible, an almanac in the same language, and a number of old Paris newspapers. As I sat dozing over one of the latter, reading old and stale criticisms, my ear was now and then struck with bursts of laughter which seemed to proceed from the kitchen. Every one that has travelled on the continent must know how favorite a resort the kitchen of a country inn is to the middle and inferior order of travellers; particularly in that equivocal kind of weather, when a fire becomes agreeable toward evening. I threw aside the newspaper, and explored my way to the kitchen, to take a peep at the group that appeared to be so merry. It was composed partly of travellers who had arrived some hours before in a diligence, and partly of the usual attendants and hangers-on of inns. They were seated round a great burnished stove, that might have been mistaken for an altar, at which they were worshipping. It was covered with various kitchen vessels of resplendent brightness; among which steamed and hissed a huge copper tea-kettle. A large lamp threw a strong mass of light

---

* The erudite reader, well versed in good-for-nothing lore, will perceive that the above Tale must have been suggested to the old Swiss by a little French anecdote, a circumstance said to have taken place at Paris.

This tale consists of two chapters of *The Sketch Book*, the first an introductory one titled "The Inn Kitchen."—C.N.

upon the group, bringing out many odd features in strong relief. Its yellow rays partially illumined the spacious kitchen, dying duskily away into remote corners, except where they settled, in mellow radiance on the broad side of a flitch of bacon, or were reflected back from well-scoured utensils, that gleamed from the midst of obscurity. A strapping Flemish lass, with long golden pendants in her ears, and a necklace with a golden heart suspended to it, was the presiding priestess of the temple.

Many of the company were furnished with pipes, and most of them with some kind of evening potation. I found their mirth was occasioned by anecdotes, which a little swarthy Frenchman, with a dry weazen face and large whiskers, was giving of his love adventures; at the end of each of which there was one of those bursts of honest unceremonious laughter, in which a man indulges in that temple of true liberty, an inn.

As I had no better mode of getting through a tedious blustering evening, I took my coat near the stove, and listened to a variety of traveller's tales, some very extravagant, and most very dull. All of them, however, have faded from my treacherous memory except one, which I will endeavor to relate. I fear, however, it derived its chief zest from the manner in which it was told, and the peculiar air and appearance of the narrator. He was a corpulent old Swiss, who had the look of a veteran traveller. He was dressed in a tarnished green travelling-jacket, with a broad belt round his waist, and a pair of overalls, with buttons from the hips to the ankles. He was of a full, rubicund countenance, with a double chin, aquiline nose and a pleasant, twinkling eye. His hair was light, and curled from under an old green velvet travelling-cap stuck on one side of his head. He was interrupted more than once by the arrival of guests, or the remarks of his auditors; and paused now and then to replenish his pipe; at which times he had generally a roguish leer, and a sly joke for the buxom kitchen-maid.

I wish my readers could imagine the old fellow lolling in a huge arm-chair, one arm akimbo, the other holding a curiously twisted tobacco-pipe, formed of genuine *écume de mer*, decorated with silver chain and silken tassel,—his head cocked on one side, and a whimsical cut of the eye occasionally, as he related the following story.

He that supper for is dight,
He lyes full cold, I trow, this night!
Yestreen to chamber I him led,
This night Gray-Steel has made his bed.
SIR EGER, SIR GRAHAME, AND SIR GRAY-STEEL.

ON the summit of one of the heights of the Odenwald, a wild and romantic tract of Upper Germany, that lies not far from the confluence of the Main and the Rhine, there stood, many, many years since, the Castle of the Baron Von Landshort. It is now quite fallen to decay, and almost buried among beechtrees and dark firs; above which, however, its old watch-tower may still be seen struggling, like the former possessor I have mentioned, to carry a high head, and look down upon the neighboring country.

The baron was a dry branch of the great family of Katzenellen-bogen,* and inherited the relics of the property, and all the pride of his ancestors. Though the warlike disposition of his predecessors had much impaired the family possessions, yet the baron still endeavored to keep up some show of former state. The times were peaceable, and the German nobles, in general, had abandoned their inconvenient old castles, perched like eagles' nests among the mountains, and had built more convenient residences in the valleys: still the baron remained proudly drawn up in his little fortress, cherishing, with hereditary inveteracy, all the old family feuds; so that he was on ill terms with some of his nearest neighbors, on account of disputes that had happened between their great-great-grandfathers.

The baron had but one child, a daughter; but nature, when she grants but one child, always compensates by making it a prodigy; and so it was with the daughter of the baron. All the nurses, gossips, and country-cousins assured her father that she had not her equal for beauty in all Germany; and who should know better than they? She had, moreover, been brought up with great care under the superintendence of two maiden aunts, who had spent some years of their early life at one of the little German courts, and were skilled in all the branches of knowledge necessary to the education of a fine lady. Under their instructions she became a miracle of accomplishments. By the time she was eighteen, she could embroider to admiration, and had worked whole histories of the saints in tapestry, with such strength of expression in their countenance, that they looked like so many souls in purgatory. She could read without great difficulty, and had spelled her way through several church legends, and almost all the chivalric wonders of the Heldenbuch. She had even made considerable proficiency in writing; could sign her own name without missing a letter, and so legibly that her aunts could read it without spectacles. She excelled in making

---

* I.e., CAT's-ELBOW. The name of a family of those parts, very powerful in former times. The appellation, we are told, was given in compliment to a peerless dame of the family, celebrated for her fine arm.

little elegant good-for-nothing lady-like knickknacks of all kinds; was versed in the most abstruse dancing of the day; played a number of airs on the harp and guitar; and knew all the tender ballads of the Minnelieders by heart.

Her aunts, too, having been great flirts and coquettes in their younger days, were admirably calculated to be vigilant guardians and strict censors of the conduct of their niece; for there is no duenna so rigidly prudent, and inexorably decorous, as a superannuated coquette. She was rarely suffered out of their sight; never went beyond the domains of the castle, unless well attended, or rather well watched; had continual lectures read to her about strict decorum and implicit obedience; and as to the men—pah!—she was taught to hold them at such a distance, and in such absolute distrust, that, unless properly authorized, she would not have cast a glance upon the handsomest cavalier in the world—no, not if he were even dying at her feet.

The good effects of this system were wonderfully apparent. The young lady was a pattern of docility and correctness. While others were wasting their sweetness in the glare of the world, and liable to be plucked and thrown aside by every hand, she was coyly blooming into fresh and lovely womanhood under the protection of those immaculate spinsters like a rose-bud blushing forth among guardian thorns. Her aunts looked upon her with pride and exultation, and vaunted that though all the other young ladies in the world might go astray, yet, thank Heaven, nothing of the kind could happen to the heiress of Katzenellenbogen.

But, however scantily the Baron Von Landshort might be provided with children, his household was by no means a small one; for Providence had enriched him with abundance of poor relations. They, one and all, possessed the affectionate disposition common to humble relatives; were wonderfully attached to the baron, and took every possible occasion to come in swarms and enliven the castle. All family festivals were commemorated by these good people at the baron's expense; and when they were filled with good cheer, they would declare that there was nothing on earth so delightful as these family meetings, these jubilees of the heart.

The baron, though a small man, had a large soul, and it swelled with satisfaction at the consciousness of being the greatest man in the little world about him. He loved to tell long stories about the dark old warriors whose portraits looked grimly down from the walls around, and he found no listeners equal to those who fed at his expense. He was much given to the marvellous, and a firm believer in all those supernatural tales with which every mountain and valley in Germany abounds. The

faith of his guests exceeded even his own; they listened to every tale of wonder with open eyes and mouth, and never failed to be astonished, even though repeated for the hundredth time. Thus lived the Baron Von Landshort, the oracle of his table, the absolute monarch of his little territory, and happy, above all things, in the persuasion that he was the wisest man of the age.

At the time of which my story treats, there was a great family-gathering at the castle, on an affair of the utmost importance: it was to receive the destined bridegroom of the baron's daughter. A negotiation had been carried on between the father and an old nobleman of Bavaria, to unite the dignity of their houses by the marriage of their children. The preliminaries had been conducted with proper punctilio. The young people were betrothed without seeing each other; and the time was appointed for the marriage ceremony. The young Count Von Altenburg had been recalled from the army for the purpose, and was actually on his way to the baron's to receive his bride. Missives had even been received from him, from Würtzburg, where he was accidentally detained, mentioning the day and hour when he might be expected to arrive.

· The castle was in a tumult of preparation to give him a suitable welcome. The fair bride had been decked out with uncommon care. The two aunts had superintended her toilet, and quarrelled the whole morning about every article of her dress. The young lady had taken advantage of their contest to follow the bent of her own taste; and fortunately it was a good one. She looked as lovely as youthful bridegroom could desire; and the flutter of expectation heightened the lustre of her charms.

The suffusions that mantled her face and neck, the gentle heaving of the bosom, the eye now and then lost in reverie, all betrayed the soft tumult that was going on in her little heart. The aunts were continually hovering around her; for maiden aunts are apt to take great interest in affairs of this nature. They were giving her a world of staid counsel how to deport herself, what to say, and in what manner to receive the expected lover.

The baron was no less busied in preparations. He had, in truth, nothing exactly to do; but he was naturally a fuming, bustling little man, and could not remain passive when all the world was in a hurry. He worried from top to bottom of the castle with an air of infinite anxiety; he continually called the servants from their work to exhort them to be diligent; and buzzed about every hall and chamber, as idly restless and importunate as a blué-bottle fly on a warm summer's day.

In the meantime the fatted calf had been killed; the forests had rung with the clamor of the huntsmen; the kitchen was crowded with good

cheer; the cellars had yielded up whole oceans of *Rhein-wein* and *Ferne-wein;* and even the great Heidelberg tun had been laid under contribution. Everything was ready to receive the distinguished guest with *Saus* and *Braus* in the true spirit of German hospitality;—but the guest delayed to make his appearance. Hour rolled after hour. The sun, that had poured his downward rays upon the rich forest of the Odenwald, now just gleamed along the summits of the mountains. The baron mounted the highest tower, and strained his eyes in the hope of catching a distant sight of the count and his attendants. Once he thought he beheld them; the sound of horns came floating from the valley, prolonged by the mountain echoes. A number of horsemen were seen far below, slowly advancing along the road; but when they had nearly reached the foot of the mountain, they suddenly struck off in a different direction. The last ray of sunshine departed,—the bats began to flit by in the twilight,—the road grew dimmer and dimmer to the view, and nothing appeared stirring in it but now and then a peasant lagging homeward from his labor.

While the old castle of Landshort was in this state of perplexity, a very interesting scene was transacting in a different part of the Odenwald.

The young Count Von Altenburg was tranquilly pursuing his route in that sober jogtrot way, in which a man travels toward matrimony when his friends have taken all the trouble and uncertainty of courtship off his hands, and a bride is waiting for him, as certainly as a dinner at the end of his journey. He had encountered at Würtzburg a youthful companion in arms, with whom he had seen some service on the frontiers,—Herman Von Starkenfaust, one of the stoutest hands and worthiest hearts of German chivalry, who was now returning from the army. His father's castle was not far distant from the old fortress of Landshort, although an hereditary feud rendered the families hostile, and strangers to each other.

In the warm-hearted moment of recognition, the young friends related all their past adventures and fortunes, and the count gave the whole history of his intended nuptials with a young lady whom he had never seen, but of whose charms he had received the most enrapturing descriptions.

As the route of the friends lay in the same direction, they agreed to perform the rest of their journey together; and, that they might do it the more leisurely, set off from Würtzburg at an early hour, the count having given directions for his retinue to follow and overtake him.

They beguiled their wayfaring with recollections of their military scenes and adventures; but the count was apt to be a little tedious, now

and then, about the reputed charms of his bride, and the felicity that awaited him.

In this way they had entered among the mountains of the Odenwald, and were traversing one of its most lonely and thickly-wooded passes. It is well known that the forests of Germany have always been as much infested by robbers, as its castles by spectres; and, at this time, the former were particularly numerous, from the hordes of disbanded soldiers wandering about the country. It will not appear extraordinary, therefore, that the cavaliers were attacked by a gang of these stragglers, in the midst of the forest. They defended themselves with bravery, but were nearly overpowered, when the count's retinue arrived to their assistance. At sight of them the robbers fled, but not until the count had received a mortal wound. He was slowly and carefully conveyed back to the city of Würtzburg, and a friar summoned from a neighboring convent, who was famous for his skill in administering to both soul and body; but half of his skill was superfluous; the moments of the unfortunate count were numbered.

With his dying breath he entreated his friend to repair instantly to the castle of Landshort, and explain the fatal cause of his not keeping his appointment with his bride. Though not the most ardent of lovers, he was one of the most punctilious of men, and appeared earnestly solicitous that his mission should be speedily and courteously executed. "Unless this is done," said he, "I shall not sleep quietly in my grave!" He repeated these last words with peculiar solemnity. A request, at a moment so impressive, admitted no hesitation. Starkenfaust endeavored to soothe him to calmness; promised faithfully to execute his wish, and gave him his hand in solemn pledge. The dying man pressed it in acknowledgment, but soon lapsed into delirium—raved about his bride—his engagements—his plighted word; ordered his horse, that he might ride to the castle of Landshort; and expired in the fancied act of vaulting into the saddle.

Starkenfaust bestowed a sigh and a soldier's tear on the untimely fate of his comrade; and then pondered on the awkward mission he had undertaken. His heart was heavy, and his head perplexed; for he was to present himself an unbidden guest among hostile people, and to damp their festivity with tidings fatal to their hopes. Still there were certain whisperings of curiosity in his bosom to see this far-famed beauty of Katzenellenbogen, so cautiously shut up from the world; for he was a passionate admirer of the sex, and there was a dash of eccentricity and enterprise in his character that made him fond of all singular adventure.

Previous to his departure he made all due arrangements with the holy fraternity of the convent for the funeral solemnities of his friend, who

was to be buried in the cathedral of Würtzburg, near some of his illustrious relatives; and the mourning retinue of the count took charge of his remains.

It is now high time that we should return to the ancient family of Katzenellenbogen, who were impatient for their guest, and still more for their dinner; and to the worthy little baron, whom we left airing himself on the watch-tower.

Night closed in, but still no guest arrived. The baron descended from the tower in despair. The banquet, which had been delayed from hour to hour, could no longer be postponed. The meats were already overdone; the cook in an agony; and the whole household had the look of a garrison that had been reduced by famine. The baron was obliged reluctantly to give orders for the feast without the presence of the guest. All were seated at table, and just on the point of commencing, when the sound of a horn from without the gate gave notice of the approach of a stranger. Another long blast filled the old courts of the castle with its echoes, and was answered by the warder from the walls. The baron hastened to receive his future son-in-law.

The drawbridge had been let down, and the stranger was before the gate. He was a tall, gallant cavalier, mounted on a black steed. His countenance was pale, but he had a beaming, romantic eye, and an air of stately melancholy. The baron was a little mortified that he should have come in this simple, solitary style. His dignity for a moment was ruffled, and he felt disposed to consider it a want of proper respect for the important occasion, and the important family with which he was to be connected. He pacified himself, however, with the conclusion, that it must have been youthful impatience which had induced him thus to spur on sooner than his attendants.

"I am sorry," said the stranger, "to break in upon you thus unseasonably——"

Here the baron interrupted him with a world of compliments and greetings; for, to tell the truth, he prided himself upon his courtesy and eloquence. The stranger attempted, once or twice, to stem the torrent of words, but in vain, so he bowed his head and suffered it to flow on. By the time the baron had come to a pause, they had reached the inner court of the castle; and the stranger was again about to speak, when he was once more interrupted by the appearance of the female part of the family, leading forth the shrinking and blushing bride. He gazed on her for a moment as one entranced; it seemed as if his whole soul beamed forth in the gaze, and rested upon that lovely form. One of the maiden aunts whispered something in her ear; she made an effort to speak; her moist blue eye was timidly raised; gave a shy glance of

inquiry on the stranger; and was cast again to the ground. The words died away; but there was a sweet smile playing about her lips, and a soft dimpling of the cheek that showed her glance had not been unsatisfactory. It was impossible for a girl of the fond age of eighteen, highly predisposed for love and matrimony, not to be pleased with so gallant a cavalier.

The late hour at which the guest had arrived left no time for parley. The baron was peremptory, and deferred all particular conversation until the morning, and led the way to the untasted banquet.

It was served up in the great hall of the castle. Around the walls hung the hard-favored portraits of the heroes of the house of Katzenellenbogen, and the trophies which they had gained in the field and in the chase. Hacked corselets, splintered jousting spears, and tattered banners, were mingled with the spoils of sylvan warfare; the jaws of the wolf, and the tusks of the boar, grinned horribly among cross-bows and battle-axes, and a huge pair of antlers branched immediately over the head of the youthful bridegroom.

The cavalier took but little notice of the company or the entertainment. He scarcely tasted the banquet, but seemed absorbed in admiration of his bride. He conversed in a low tone that could not be overheard—for the language of love is never loud; but where is the female ear so dull that it cannot catch the softest whisper of the lover? There was a mingled tenderness and gravity in his manner, that appeared to have a powerful effect upon the young lady. Her color came and went as she listened with deep attention. Now and then she made some blushing reply, and when his eye was turned away, she would steal a sidelong glance at his romantic countenance, and heave a gentle sigh of tender happiness. It was evident that the young couple were completely enamored. The aunts, who were deeply versed in the mysteries of the heart, declared that they had fallen in love with each other at first sight.

The feast went on merrily, or at least noisily, for the guests were all blessed with those keen appetites that attend upon light purses and mountain-air. The baron told his best and longest stories, and never had he told them so well, or with such great effect. If there was anything marvellous, his auditors were lost in astonishment; and if anything facetious, they were sure to laugh exactly in the right place. The baron, it is true, like most great men, was too dignified to utter any joke but a dull one; it was always enforced, however, by a bumper of excellent Hockheimer; and even a dull joke, at one's own table, served up with jolly old wine, is irresistible. Many good things were said by poorer and keener wits, that would not bear repeating, except on similar occasions; many sly speeches whispered in ladies' ears, that almost con-

vulsed them with suppressed laughter; and a song or two roared out by a poor, but merry and broad-faced cousin of the baron, that absolutely made the maiden aunts hold up their fans.

Amidst all this revelry, the stranger guest maintained a most singular and unseasonable gravity. His countenance assumed a deeper caste of dejection as the evening advanced; and, strange as it may appear, even the baron's jokes seemed only to render him the more melancholy. At times he was lost in thought, and at times there was a perturbed and restless wandering of the eye that bespoke a mind but ill at ease. His conversations with the bride became more and more earnest and mysterious. Lowering clouds began to steal over the fair serenity of her brow, and tremors to run through her tender frame.

All this could not escape the notice of the company. Their gayety was chilled by the unaccountable gloom of the bridegroom; their spirits were infected; whispers and glances were interchanged, accompanied by shrugs and dubious shakes of the head. The song and the laugh grew less and less frequent; there were dreary pauses in the conversation, which were at length succeeded by wild tales and supernatural legends. One dismal story produced another still more dismal, and the baron nearly frightened some of the ladies into hysterics with the history of the goblin horseman that carried away the fair Leonora: a dreadful story, which has since been put into excellent verse, and is read and believed by all the world.

The bridegroom listened to this tale with profound attention. He kept his eyes steadily fixed on the baron and, as the story drew to a close, began gradually to rise from his seat, growing taller and taller, until, in the baron's entranced eye, he seemed almost to tower into a giant. The moment the tale was finished, he heaved a deep sigh, and took a solemn farewell of the company. They were all amazement. The baron was perfectly thunderstruck.

"What! going to leave the castle at midnight? why, everything was prepared for his reception; a chamber was ready for him if he wished to retire."

The stranger shook his head mournfully and mysteriously; "I must lay my head in a different chamber to-night!"

There was something in this reply, and the tone in which it was uttered, that made the baron's heart misgive him; but he rallied his forces, and repeated his hospitable entreaties.

The stranger shook his head silently, but positively, at every offer; and, waving his farewell to the company, stalked slowly out of the hall. The maiden aunts were absolutely petrified; the bride hung her head, and a tear stole to her eye.

The baron followed the stranger to the great court of the castle, where the black charger stood pawing the earth, and snorting with impatience. When they had reached the portal, whose deep archway was dimly lighted by a cresset, the stranger paused, and addressed the baron in a hollow tone of voice, which the vaulted roof rendered still more sepulchral.

"Now that we are alone," said he, "I will impart to you the reason of my going. I have a solemn, an indispensable engagement——"

"Why," said the baron, "cannot you send some one in your place?"

"It admits of no substitute—I must attend it in person—I must away to Würtzburg cathedral——"

"Ay," said the baron, plucking up spirit, "but not until to-morrow—to-morrow you shall take your bride there."

"No! no!" replied the stranger, with tenfold solemnity, "my engagement is with no bride—the worms! the worms expect me! I am a dead man—I have been slain by robbers—my body lies at Würtzburg—at midnight I am to be buried—the grave is waiting for me—I must keep my appointment!"

He sprang on his black charger, dashed over the drawbridge, and the clattering of his horse's hoofs was lost in the whistling of the night-blast.

The baron returned to the hall in the utmost consternation, and related what had passed. Two ladies fainted outright, others sickened at the idea of having banqueted with a spectre. It was the opinion of some, that this might be the wild huntsman, famous in German legend. Some talked of mountain sprites, of wood-demons, and of other supernatural beings, with which the good people of Germany have been so grievously harassed since time immemorial. One of the poor relations ventured to suggest that it might be some sportive evasion of the young cavalier, and that the very gloominess of the caprice seemed to accord with so melancholy a personage. This, however, drew on him the indignation of the whole company, and especially of the baron, who looked upon him as little better than an infidel; so that he was fain to abjure his heresy as speedily as possible, and come into the faith of the true believers.

But whatever may have been the doubts entertained, they were completely put to an end by the arrival, next day, of regular missives, confirming the intelligence of the young count's murder, and his interment in Würtzburg cathedral.

The dismay at the castle may well be imagined. The baron shut himself up in his chamber. The guests, who had come to rejoice with him, could not think of abandoning him in his distress. They wandered

about the courts, or collected in groups in the hall, shaking their heads
and shrugging their shoulders, at the troubles of so good a man; and sat
longer than ever at table, and ate and drank more stoutly than ever, by
way of keeping up their spirits. But the situation of the widowed bride
was the most pitiable. To have lost a husband before she had even embraced him—and such a husband! if the very spectre could be so gracious and noble, what must have been the living man. She filled the
house with lamentations.

On the night of the second day of her widowhood, she had retired to
her chamber, accompanied by one of her aunts, who insisted on sleeping with her. The aunt, who was one of the best tellers of ghost-stories
in all Germany, had just been recounting one of her longest, and had
fallen asleep in the very midst of it. The chamber was remote, and
overlooked a small garden. The niece lay pensively gazing at the beams
of the rising moon, as they trembled on the leaves of an aspen tree before the lattice. The castle clock had just tolled midnight, when a soft
strain of music stole up from the garden. She rose hastily from her bed,
and stepped lightly to the window. A tall figure stood among the shadows of the trees. As it raised its head, a beam of moonlight fell upon the
countenance. Heaven and earth! she beheld the Spectre Bridegroom!
A loud shriek at that moment burst upon her ear, and her aunt, who
had been awakened by the music, and had followed her silently to the
window, fell into her arms. When she looked again, the spectre had disappeared.

Of the two females, the aunt now required the most soothing, for she
was perfectly beside herself with terror. As to the young lady, there was
something, even in the spectre of her lover, that seemed endearing.
There was still the semblance of manly beauty; and though the shadow
of a man is but little calculated to satisfy the affections of a lovesick girl,
yet, where the substance is not to be had, even that is consoling. The
aunt declared she would never sleep in that chamber again; the niece,
for once, was refractory, and declared as strongly that she would sleep
in no other in the castle: the consequence was, that she had to sleep in
it alone; but she drew a promise from her aunt not to relate the story of
the spectre, lest she should be denied the only melancholy pleasure left
her on earth—that of inhabiting the chamber over which the guardian
shade of her lover kept its nightly vigils.

How long the good old lady would have observed this promise is uncertain, for she dearly loved to talk of the marvellous, and there is a
triumph in being the first to tell a frightful story; it is, however, still
quoted in the neighborhood, as a memorable instance of female secrecy, that she kept it to herself for a whole week; when she was sud-

denly absolved from all further restraint, by intelligence brought to the breakfast-table one morning that the young lady was not to be found. Her room was empty—the bed had not been slept in—the window was open, and the bird had flown!

The astonishment and concern with which the intelligence was received can only be imagined by those who have witnessed the agitation which the mishaps of a great man cause among his friends. Even the poor relations paused for a moment from the indefatigable labors of the trencher; when the aunt, who had at first been struck speechless, wrung her hands, and shrieked out, "The goblin! the goblin! she's carried away by the goblin!"

In a few words she related the fearful scene in the garden, and concluded that the spectre must have carried off his bride. Two of the domestics corroborated the opinion, for they had heard the clattering of a horse's hoofs down the mountain about midnight, and had no doubt that it was the spectre on his black charger, bearing her away to the tomb. All present were struck with the direful probability; for events of the kind are extremely common in Germany, as many well-authenticated histories bear witness.

What a lamentable situation was that of the poor baron! What a heart-rending dilemma for a fond father, and a member of the great family of Katzenellenbogen! His only daughter had either been rapt away to the grave, or he was to have some wood-demon for a son-in-law, and, perchance, a troop of goblin grandchildren. As usual, he was completely bewildered, and all the castle in an uproar. The men were ordered to take horse, and scour every road and path and glen of the Odenwald. The baron himself had just drawn on his jack-boots, girded on his sword, and was about to mount his steed and sally forth on a doubtful quest, when he was brought to a pause by a new apparition. A lady was seen approaching the castle, mounted on a palfrey, attended by a cavalier on horseback. She galloped up to the gate, sprang from her horse, and falling at the baron's feet, embraced his knees. It was his lost daughter, and her companion—the Spectre Bridegroom! The baron was astounded. He looked at his daughter, then at the spectre, and almost doubted the evidence of his senses. The latter, too, was wonderfully improved in his appearance since his visit to the world of spirits. His dress was splendid, and set off a noble figure of manly symmetry. He was no longer pale and melancholy. His fine countenance was flushed with the glow of youth, and joy rioted in his large dark eye.

The mystery was soon cleared up. The cavalier (for, in truth, as you must have known all the while, he was no goblin) announced himself as Sir Herman Von Starkenfaust. He related his adventure with the

young count. He told how he had hastened to the castle to deliver the unwelcome tidings, but that the eloquence of the baron had interrupted him in every attempt to tell his tale. How the sight of the bride had completely captivated him, and that to pass a few hours near her, he had tacitly suffered the mistake to continue. How he had been sorely perplexed in what way to make a decent retreat, until the baron's goblin stories had suggested his eccentric exit. How, fearing the feudal hostility of the family, he had repeated his visits by stealth—had haunted the garden beneath the young lady's window—had wooed—had won— had borne away in triumph—and, in a word, had wedded the fair.

Under any other circumstances the baron would have been inflexible, for he was tenacious of paternal authority, and devoutly obstinate in all family feuds; but he loved his daughter; he had lamented her as lost; he rejoiced to find her still alive; and, though her husband was of a hostile house, yet, thank heaven, he was not a goblin. There was something, it must be acknowledged, that did not exactly accord with his notions of strict veracity, in the joke the knight has passed upon him of his being a dead man; but several old friends present, who had served in the wars, assured him that every stratagem was excusable in love, and that the cavalier was entitled to especial privilege, having lately served as a trooper.

Matters, therefore, were happily arranged. The baron pardoned the young couple on the spot. The revels at the castle were resumed. The poor relations overwhelmed this new member of the family with loving-kindness; he was so gallant, so generous—and so rich. The aunts, it is true, were somewhat scandalized that their system of strict seclusion and passive obedience should be so badly exemplified, but attributed it all to their negligence in not having the windows grated. One of them was particularly mortified at having her marvellous story marred, and that the only spectre she had ever seen should turn out a counterfeit; but the niece seemed perfectly happy at having found him substantial flesh and blood—and so the story ends.

From *The Sketch Book*

THE LEGEND OF SLEEPY HOLLOW

Found Among the Papers of the Late Diedrich Knickerbocker

A pleasing land of drowsy head it was,
Of dreams that wave before the half-shut eye,
And of gay castles in the clouds that pass,
For ever flushing round a summer sky.
Castle of Indolence.

IN the bosom of one of those spacious coves which indent the eastern shore of the Hudson, at that broad expansion of the river denominated by the ancient Dutch navigators the Tappan Zee, and where they always prudently shortened sail, and implored the protection of St. Nicholas when they crossed, there lies a small market-town or rural port, which by some is called Greensburgh, but which is more generally and properly known by the name of Tarry Town. This name was given, we are told, in former days, by the good housewives of the adjacent country, from the inveterate propensity of their husbands to linger about the village tavern on market-days. Be that as it may, I do not vouch for the fact, but merely advert to it for the sake of being precise and authentic. Not far from this village, perhaps about two miles, there is a little valley, or rather lap of land, among high hills, which is one of the quietest places in the whole world. A small brook glides through it, with just murmur enough to lull one to repose; and the occasional whistle of a quail, or tapping of a woodpecker, is almost the only sound that ever breaks in upon the uniform tranquillity.

I recollect that, when a stripling, my first exploit in squirrel-shooting was in a grove of tall walnut-trees that shades one side of the valley. I had wandered into it at noon-time, when all nature is particularly quiet, and was startled by the roar of my own gun, as it broke the Sabbath stillness around, and was prolonged and reverberated by the angry echoes. If ever I should wish for a retreat, whither I might steal from

the world and its distractions, and dream quietly away the remnant of a troubled life, I know of none more promising than this little valley.

From the listless repose of the place, and the peculiar character of its inhabitants, who are descendants from the original Dutch settlers, this sequestered glen has long been known by the name of SLEEPY HOLLOW, and its rustic lads are called the Sleepy Hollow Boys throughout all the neighboring country. A drowsy, dreamy influence seems to hang over the land, and to pervade the very atmosphere. Some say that the place was bewitched by a high German doctor, during the early days of the settlement; others, that an old Indian chief, the prophet or wizard of his tribe, held his pow-wows there before the country was discovered by Master Hendrick Hudson. Certain it is, the place still continues under the sway of some bewitching power, that holds a spell over the minds of the good people, causing them to walk in a continual reverie. They are given to all kinds of marvellous beliefs; are subject to trances and visions; and frequently see strange sights, and hear music and voices in the air. The whole neighborhood abounds with local tales, haunted spots, and twilight superstitions; stars shoot and meteors glare oftener across the valley than in any other part of the country, and the nightmare, with her whole ninefold, seems to make it the favorite scene of her gambols.

The dominant spirit, however, that haunts this enchanted region, and seems to be commander-in-chief of all the powers of the air, is the apparition of a figure on horseback without a head. It is said by some to be the ghost of a Hessian trooper, whose head had been carried away by a cannon-ball, in some nameless battle during the Revolutionary War, and who is ever and anon seen by the country folk, hurrying along in the gloom of night, as if on the wings of the wind. His haunts are not confined to the valley, but extend at times to the adjacent roads, and especially to the vicinity of a church at no great distance. Indeed, certain of the most authentic historians of those parts, who have been careful in collecting and collating the floating facts concerning this spectre, allege that the body of the trooper, having been buried in the churchyard, the ghost rides forth to the scene of battle in nightly quest of his head; and that the rushing speed with which he sometimes passes along the Hollow, like a midnight blast, is owing to his being belated, and in a hurry to get back to the churchyard before daybreak.

Such is the general purport of this legendary superstition, which has furnished materials for many a wild story in that region of shadows; and the spectre is known, at all the country firesides, by the name of the Headless Horseman of Sleepy Hollow.

It is remarkable that the visionary propensity I have mentioned is not confined to the native inhabitants of the valley, but is unconsciously imbibed by every one who resides there for a time. However wide awake they may have been before they entered that sleepy region, they are sure, in a little time, to inhale the witching influence of the air, and begin to grow imaginative, to dream dreams, and see apparitions.

I mention this peaceful spot with all possible laud; for it is in such little retired Dutch valleys, found here and there embosomed in the great State of New York, that population, manners, and customs remain fixed; while the great torrent of migration and improvement, which is making such incessant changes in other parts of this restless country, sweeps by them unobserved. They are like those little nooks of still water which border a rapid stream; where we may see the straw and bubble riding quietly at anchor, or slowly revolving in their mimic harbor, undisturbed by the rush of the passing current. Though many years have elapsed since I trod the drowsy shades of Sleepy Hollow, yet I question whether I should not still find the same trees and the same families vegetating in its sheltered bosom.

In this by-place of nature, there abode, in a remote period of American history, that is to say, some thirty years since, a worthy wight of the name of Ichabod Crane; who sojourned, or, as he expressed it, "tarried," in Sleepy Hollow, for the purpose of instructing the children of the vicinity. He was a native of Connecticut, a State which supplies the Union with pioneers for the mind as well as for the forest, and sends forth yearly its legions of frontier woodsmen and country schoolmasters. The cognomen of Crane was not inapplicable to his person. He was tall, but exceedingly lank, with narrow shoulders, long arms and legs, hands that dangled a mile out of his sleeves, feet that might have served for shovels, and his whole frame most loosely hung together. His head was small, and flat at top, with huge ears, large green glassy eyes, and a long snipe nose, so that it looked like a weathercock perched upon his spindle neck, to tell which way the wind blew. To see him striding along the profile of a hill on a windy day, with his clothes bagging and fluttering about him, one might have mistaken him for the genius of famine descending upon the earth, or some scarecrow eloped from a corn-field.

His school-house was a low building of one large room, rudely constructed of logs; the windows partly glazed, and partly patched with leaves of old copy-books. It was most ingeniously secured at vacant hours by a withe twisted in the handle of the door, and stakes set against the window-shutters; so that, though a thief might get in with

perfect ease, he would find some embarrassment in getting out: an idea most probably borrowed by the architect, Yost Van Houten, from the mystery of an eel-pot. The school-house stood in a rather lonely but pleasant situation, just at the foot of a woody hill, with a brook running close by, and a formidable birch-tree growing at one end of it. From hence the low murmur of his pupils' voices, conning over their lessons, might be heard on a drowsy summer's day, like the hum of a bee-hive; interrupted now and then by the authoritative voice of the master, in the tone of menace or command; or, peradventure, by the appalling sound of the birch, as he urged some tardy loiterer along the flowery path of knowledge. Truth to say, he was a conscientious man, and ever bore in mind the golden maxim, "Spare the rod and spoil the child."—Ichabod Crane's scholars certainly were not spoiled.

I would not have it imagined, however, that he was one of those cruel potentates of the school, who joy in the smart of their subjects; on the contrary, he administered justice with discrimination rather than severity, taking the burden off the backs of the weak, and laying it on those of the strong. Your mere puny stripling, that winced at the least flourish of the rod, was passed by with indulgence; but the claims of justice were satisfied by inflicting a double portion on some little, tough, wrong-headed, broad-skirted Dutch urchin, who sulked and swelled and grew dogged and sullen beneath the birch. All this he called "doing his duty" by their parents; and he never inflicted a chastisement without following it by the assurance, so consolatory to the smarting urchin, that "he would remember it, and thank him for it the longest day he had to live."

When school-hours were over, he was even the companion and playmate of the larger boys; and on holiday afternoons would convoy some of the smaller ones home, who happened to have pretty sisters, or good housewives for mothers, noted for the comforts of the cupboard. Indeed it behooved him to keep on good terms with his pupils. The revenue arising from his school was small, and would have been scarcely sufficient to furnish him with daily bread, for he was a huge feeder, and, though lank, had the dilating powers of an anaconda; but to help out his maintenance, he was, according to country custom in those parts, boarded and lodged at the houses of the farmers, whose children he instructed. With these he lived successively a week at a time; thus going the rounds of the neighborhood, with all his worldly effects tied up in a cotton handkerchief.

That all this might not be too onerous on the purses of his rustic patrons, who are apt to consider the costs of schooling a grievious burden, and schoolmasters as mere drones, he had various ways of render-

ing himself both useful and agreeable. He assisted the farmers occasionally in the lighter labors of their farms; helped to make hay;
mended the fences; took the horses to water; drove the cows from pasture; and cut wood for the winter fire. He laid aside, too, all the dominant dignity and absolute sway with which he lorded it in his little empire, the school, and became wonderfully gentle and ingratiating. He
found favor in the eyes of the mothers, by petting the children, particularly the youngest; and like the lion bold, which whilom so magnani-
mously the lamb did hold, he would sit with a child on one knee, and
rock a cradle with his foot for whole hours together.

In addition to his other vocations, he was the singing-master of
the neighborhood, and picked up many bright shillings by instructing
the young folks in psalmody. It was a matter of no little vanity to him,
on Sundays, to take his station in front of the church-gallery, with a
band of chosen singers; where, in his own mind, he completely carried
away the palm from the parson. Certain it is, his voice resounded far
above all the rest of the congregation; and there are peculiar quavers
still to be heard in that church, and which may even be heard half a
mile off, quite to the opposite side of the mill-pond, on a still Sunday
morning, which are said to be legitimately descended from the nose of
Ichabod Crane. Thus, by divers little makeshifts in that ingenious way
which is commonly denominated "by hook and by crook," the worthy
pedagogue got on tolerably enough, and was thought, by all who understood nothing of the labor of headwork, to have a wonderfully easy life
of it.

The schoolmaster is generally a man of some importance in the female circle of a rural neighborhood; being considered a kind of idle,
gentleman-like personage, of vastly superior taste and accomplishments
to the rough country swains, and, indeed, inferior in learning only to
the parson. His appearance, therefore, is apt to occasion some little stir
at the tea-table of a farm-house, and the addition of a supernumerary
dish of cakes or sweet-meats, or, peradventure, the parade of a silver
tea-pot. Our man of letters, therefore, was peculiarly happy in the smiles
of all the country damsels. How he would figure among them in the
churchyard, between services on Sundays! gathering grapes for them
from the wild vines that overrun the surrounding trees; reciting for
their amusement all the epitaphs on the tombstones; or sauntering, with
a whole bevy of them, along the banks of the adjacent mill-pond; while
the more bashful country bumpkins hung sheepishly back, envying his
superior elegance and address.

From his half itinerant life, also, he was a kind of travelling gazette,
carrying the whole budget of local gossip from house to house: so that

his appearance was always greeted with satisfaction. He was, moreover, esteemed by the women as a man of great erudition, for he had read several books quite through, and was a perfect master of Cotton Mather's *History of New England Witchcraft*, in which, by the way, he most firmly and potently believed.

He was, in fact, an odd mixture of small shrewdness and simple credulity. His appetite for the marvellous, and his powers of digesting it, were equally extraordinary; and both had been increased by his residence in this spellbound region. No tale was too gross or monstrous for his capacious swallow. It was often his delight, after his school was dismissed in the afternoon, to stretch himself on the rich bed of clover bordering the little brook that whimpered by his school-house, and there con over old Mather's direful tales, until the gathering dusk of the evening made the printed page a mere mist before his eyes. Then, as he wended his way, by swamp and stream, and awful woodland, to the farm-house where he happened to be quartered, every sound of nature, at that witching hour, fluttered his excited imagination; the moan of the whippoorwill* from the hill-side, the boding cry of the tree-toad, that harbinger of storm; the dreary hooting of the screech-owl, or the sudden rustling in the thicket of birds frightened from their roost. The fire-flies, too, which sparkled most vividly in the darkest places, now and then startled him, as one of uncommon brightness would stream across his path; and if, by chance, a huge blockhead of a beetle came winging his blundering flight against him, the poor varlet was ready to give up the ghost, with the idea that he was struck with a witch's token. His only resource on such occasions, either to drown thought or drive away evil spirits, was to sing psalm-tunes; and the good people of Sleepy Hollow, as they sat by their doors of an evening, were often filled with awe, at hearing his nasal melody, "in linkèd sweetness long drawn out," floating from the distant hill, or along the dusky road.

Another of his sources of fearful pleasure was, to pass long winter evenings with the old Dutch wives, as they sat spinning by the fire, with a row of apples roasting and spluttering along the hearth, and listen to their marvellous tales of ghosts and goblins, and haunted fields, and haunted brooks, and haunted bridges, and haunted houses, and particularly of the headless horseman, or Galloping Hessian of the Hollow, as they sometimes called him. He would delight them equally by his anecdotes of witchcraft, and the direful omens and portentous

---

* The whippoorwill is a bird which is only heard at night. It receives its name from its note, which is thought to resemble those words.

sights and sounds in the air, which prevailed in the earlier times of Connecticut; and would frighten them wofully with speculations upon comets and shooting-stars, and with the alarming fact that the world did absolutely turn round, and that they were half the time topsy-turvy!

But if there was a pleasure in all this, while snugly cuddling in the chimney-corner of a chamber that was all of a ruddy glow from the crackling wood-fire, and where, of course, no spectre dared to show his face, it was dearly purchased by the terrors of his subsequent walk homewards. What fearful shapes and shadows beset his path amidst the dim and ghastly glare of a snowy night!—With what wistful look did he eye every trembling ray of light streaming across the waste fields from some distant window!—How often was he appalled by some shrub covered with snow, which, like a sheeted spectre, beset his very path!—How often did he shrink with curdling awe at the sound of his own steps on a frosty crust beneath his feet; and dread to look over his shoulder, lest he should behold some uncouth being tramping close behind him!—and how often was he thrown into complete dismay by some rushing blast, howling among the trees, in the idea that it was the Galloping Hessian on one of his nightly scourings!

All these, however, were mere terrors of the night, phantoms of the mind that walk in darkness; and though he had seen many spectres in his time, and been more than once beset by Satan in divers shapes, in his lonely perambulations, yet daylight put an end to all these evils; and he would have passed a pleasant life of it, in despite of the devil and all his works, if his path had not been crossed by a being that causes more perplexity to mortal man than ghosts, goblins, and the whole race of witches put together, and that was—a woman.

Among the musical disciples who assembled, one evening in each week, to receive his instructions in psalmody, was Katrina Van Tassel, the daughter and only child of a substantial Dutch farmer. She was a blooming lass of fresh eighteen; plump as a partridge; ripe and melting and rosy-cheeked as one of her father's peaches, and universally famed, not merely for her beauty, but her vast expectations. She was withal a little of a coquette, as might be perceived even in her dress, which was a mixture of ancient and modern fashions, as most suited to set off her charms. She wore the ornaments of pure yellow gold, which her great-great-grandmother had brought over from Saardam; the tempting stomacher of the olden·time; and withal a provokingly short petticoat, to display the prettiest foot and ankle in the country round.

Ichabod Crane had a soft and foolish heart towards the sex; and it is not to be wondered at that so tempting a morsel soon found favor in his eyes; more especially after he had visited her in her paternal mansion.

Old Baltus Van Tassel was a perfect picture of a thriving, contented, liberal-hearted farmer. He seldom, it is true, sent either his eyes or his thoughts beyond the boundaries of his own farm; but within those everything was snug, happy, and well-conditioned. He was satisfied with his wealth, but not proud of it; and piqued himself upon the hearty abundance rather than the style in which he lived. His stronghold was situated on the banks of the Hudson, in one of those green, sheltered, fertile nooks in which the Dutch farmers are so fond of nestling. A great elm-tree spread its broad branches over it; at the foot of which bubbled up a spring of the softest and sweetest water, in a little well, formed of a barrel; and then stole sparkling away through the grass, to a neighboring brook, that bubbled along among alders and dwarf willows. Hard by the farm-house was a vast barn, that might have served for a church; every window and crevice of which seemed bursting forth with the treasures of the farm; the flail was busily resounding within it from morning till night; swallows and martins skimmed twittering about the eaves; and rows of pigeons, some with one eye turned up, as if watching the weather, some with their heads under their wings, or buried in their bosoms, and others swelling, and cooing, and bowing about their dames, were enjoying the sunshine on the roof. Sleek unwieldly porkers were grunting in the repose and abundance of their pens; whence sallied forth, now and then, troops of sucking pigs, as if to snuff the air. A stately squadron of snowy geese were riding in an adjoining pond, convoying whole fleets of ducks; regiments of turkeys were gobbling through the farm-yard, and guinea fowls fretting about it, like ill-tempered housewives, with their peevish discontented cry. Before the barn-door strutted the gallant cock, that pattern of a husband, a warrior, and a fine gentleman, clapping his burnished wings, and crowing in the pride and gladness of his heart—sometimes tearing up the earth with his feet, and then generously calling his ever-hungry family of wives and children to enjoy the rich morsel which he had discovered.

The pedagogue's mouth watered, as he looked upon this sumptuous promise of luxurious winter fare. In his devouring mind's eye he pictured to himself every roasting-pig running about with a pudding in his belly, and an apple in his mouth; the pigeons were snugly put to bed in a comfortable pie, and tucked in with a coverlet of crust; the geese were swimming in their own gravy; and the ducks pairing cosily in dishes, like snug married couples, with a decent competency of onion-sauce. In the porkers he saw carved out the future sleek side of bacon, and juicy relishing ham; not a turkey but he beheld daintily trussed up, with its gizzard under its wing, and, peradventure, a neck-

lace of savory sausages; and even bright chanticleer himself lay sprawling on his back, in a side-dish, with uplifted claws, as if craving that quarter which his chivalrous spirit disdained to ask while living.

As the enraptured Ichabod fancied all this, and as he rolled his great green eyes over the fat meadow-lands, the rich fields of wheat, of rye, of buckwheat, and Indian corn, and the orchard burdened with ruddy fruit, which surrounded the warm tenement of Van Tassel, his heart yearned after the damsel who was to inherit these domains, and his imagination expanded with the idea how they might be readily turned into cash, and the money invested in immense tracts of wild land, and shingle palaces in the wilderness. Nay, his busy fancy already realized his hopes, and presented to him the blooming Katrina, with a whole family of children, mounted on the top of a wagon loaded with household trumpery, with pots and kettles dangling beneath; and he beheld himself bestriding a pacing mare, with a colt at her heels, setting out for Kentucky, Tennessee, or the Lord knows where.

When he entered the house, the conquest of his heart was complete. It was one of those spacious farm-houses, with high-ridged, but lowly-sloping roofs, built in the style handed down from the first Dutch settlers; the low projecting eaves forming a piazza along the front, capable of being closed up in bad weather. Under this were hung flails, harness, various utensils of husbandry, and nets for fishing in the neighboring river. Benches were built along the sides for summer use; and a great spinning-wheel at one end, and a churn at the other, showed the various uses to which this important porch might be devoted. From this piazza the wandering Ichabod entered the hall, which formed the centre of the mansion and the place of usual residence. Here, rows of resplendent pewter, ranged on a long dresser, dazzled his eyes. In one corner stood a huge bag of wool ready to be spun; in another a quantity of linsey-woolsey just from the loom; ears of Indian corn, and strings of dried apples and peaches, hung in gay festoons along the walls, mingled with the gaud of red peppers; and a door left ajar gave him a peep into the best parlor, where the claw-footed chairs and dark mahogany tables shone like mirrors; and irons, with their accompanying shovel and tongs, glistened from their covert of asparagus tops; mock-oranges and conch-shells decorated the mantel-piece; strings of various colored birds' eggs were suspended above it, a great ostrich egg was hung from the centre of the room, and a corner-cupboard, knowingly left open, displayed immense treasures of old silver and well-mended china.

From the moment Ichabod laid his eyes upon these regions of delight, the peace of his mind was at an end, and his only study was how

to gain the affections of the peerless daughter of Van Tassel. In this enterprise, however, he had more real difficulties than generally fell to the lot of a knight-errant of yore, who seldom had anything but giants, enchanters, fiery dragons, and such like easily conquered adversaries, to contend with; and had to make his way merely through gates of iron and brass, and walls of adamant, to the castle-keep, where the lady of his heart was confined; all which he achieved as easily as a man would carve his way to the centre of a Christmas pie; and then the lady gave him her hand as a matter of course. Ichabod, on the contrary, had to win his way to the heart of a country coquette, beset with a labyrinth of whims and caprices, which were forever presenting new difficulties and impediments; and he had to encounter a host of fearful adversaries of real flesh and blood, the numerous rustic admirers, who beset every portal to her heart; keeping a watchful and angry eye upon each other, but ready to fly out in the common cause against any new competitor.

Among those the most formidable was a burly, roaring, roistering blade, of the name of Abraham, or, according to the Dutch abbreviation, Brom Van Brunt, the hero of the country round, which rang with his feats of strength and hardihood. He was broad-shouldered and double-jointed, with short, curly black hair, and a bluff but not unpleasant countenance, having a mingled air of fun and arrogance. From his Herculean frame and great powers of limb, he had received the nickname of BROM BONES, by which he was universally known. He was famed for great knowledge and skill in horsemanship, being as dexterous on horseback as a Tartar. He was foremost at all races and cockfights; and, with the ascendency which bodily strength acquires in rustic life, was the umpire in all disputes, setting his hat on one side, and giving his decisions with an air and tone admitting of no gainsay or appeal. He was always ready for either a fight or a frolic; but had more mischief than ill-will in his composition; and, with all his overbearing roughness, there was a strong dash of waggish good-humor at the bottom. He had three or four boon companions, who regarded him as their model, and at the head of whom he scoured the country, attending every scene of feud or merriment for miles round. In cold weather he was distinguished by a fur cap, surmounted with a flaunting fox's tail; and when the folks at a country gathering descried this well-known crest at a distance, whisking about among a squad of hard riders, they always stood by for a squall. Sometimes his crew would be heard dashing along past the farm-houses at midnight, with whoop and halloo, like a troop of Don Cossacks; and the old dames, startled out of their sleep, would listen for a moment till the hurry-scurry had clattered by, and then exclaim, "Ay, there goes Brom Bones and his gang!" The

neighbors looked upon him with a mixture of awe, admiration, and good-will; and when any madcap prank, or rustic brawl, occurred in the vicinity, always shook their heads, and warranted Brom Bones was at the bottom of it.

This rantipole hero had for some time singled out the blooming Katrina for the object of his uncouth gallantries; and though his amorous toyings were something like the gentle caresses and endearments of a bear, yet it was whispered that she did not altogether discourage his hopes. Certain it is, his advances were signals for rival candidates to retire, who felt no inclination to cross a line in his amours; insomuch, that, when his horse was seen tied to Van Tassel's paling on a Sunday night, a sure sign that his master was courting, or, as it is termed, "sparking," within, all other suitors passed by in despair, and carried the war into other quarters.

Such was the formidable rival with whom Ichabod Crane had to contend, and, considering all things, a stouter man than he would have shrunk from the competition, and a wiser man would have despaired. He had, however, a happy mixture of pliability and perseverance in his nature; he was in form and spirit like a supple-jack—yielding, but tough; though he bent, he never broke; and though he bowed beneath the slightest pressure yet, the moment it was away—jerk! he was as erect, and carried his head as high as ever.

To have taken the field openly against his rival would have been madness; for he was not a man to be thwarted in his amours, any more than that stormy lover, Achilles. Ichabod, therefore, made his advances in a quiet and gently insinuating manner. Under cover of his character of singing-master, he had made frequent visits at the farmhouse; not that he had anything to apprehend from the meddlesome interference of parents, which is so often a stumbling-block in the path of lovers. Balt Van Tassel was an easy, indulgent soul; he loved his daughter better even than his pipe, and, like a reasonable man and an excellent father, let her have her way in everything. His notable little wife, too, had enough to do to attend to her housekeeping and manage her poultry; for, as she sagely observed, ducks and geese are foolish things, and must be looked after, but girls can take care of themselves. Thus while the busy dame bustled about the house, or plied her spinning-wheel at one end of the piazza, honest Balt would sit smoking his evening pipe at the other, watching the achievements of a little wooden warrior, who, armed with a sword in each hand, was most valiantly fighting the wind on the pinnacle of the barn. In the meantime, Ichabod would carry on his suit with the daughter by the side of

the spring under the great elm, or sauntering along in the twilight,—that hour so favorable to the lover's eloquence.

I profess not to know how women's hearts are wooed and won. To me they have always been matters of riddle and admiration. Some seem to have but one vulnerable point or door of access, while others have a thousand avenues, and may be captured in a thousand different ways. It is a great triumph of skill to gain the former, but a still greater proof of generalship to maintain possession of the latter, for the man must battle for his fortress at every door and window. He who wins a thousand common hearts is therefore entitled to some renown; but he who keeps undisputed sway over the heart of a coquette, is indeed a hero. Certain it is, this was not the case with the redoubtable Brom Bones; and from the moment Ichabod Crane made his advances, the interests of the former evidently declined; his horse was no longer seen tied at the palings on Sunday nights, and a deadly feud gradually arose between him and the preceptor of Sleepy Hollow.

Brom, who had a degree of rough chivalry in his nature, would fain have carried matters to open warfare, and have settled their pretensions to the lady according to the mode of those most concise and simple reasoners, the knights-errant of yore—by single combat; but Ichabod was too conscious of the superior might of his adversary to enter the lists against him: he had overheard a boast of Bones, that he would "double the schoolmaster up, and lay him on a shelf of his own schoolhouse;" and he was too wary to give him an opportunity. There was something extremely provoking in this obstinately pacific system; it left Brom no alternative but to draw upon the funds of rustic waggery in his disposition, and to play off boorish practical jokes upon his rival. Ichabod became the object of whimsical persecution to Bones and his gang of rough riders. They harried his hitherto peaceful domains; smoked out his singing-school, by stopping up the chimney; broke into the school-house at night, in spite of its formidable fastenings of withe and window-stakes, and turned everything topsy-turvy: so that the poor schoolmaster began to think all the witches in the country held their meetings there. But what was still more annoying, Brom took opportunities of turning him into ridicule in presence of his mistress, and had a scoundrel dog whom he taught to whine in the most ludicrous manner, and introduced as a rival of Ichabod's to instruct her in psalmody.

In this way matters went on for some time, without producing any material effect on the relative situation of the contending powers. On a fine autumnal afternoon, Ichabod, in pensive mood, sat enthroned on the lofty stool whence he usually watched all the concerns of his little literary realm. In his hand he swayed a ferule, that sceptre of despotic

power; the birch of justice reposed on three nails, behind the throne, a constant terror to evil-doers; while on the desk before him might be seen sundry contraband articles and prohibited weapons, detected upon the persons of idle urchins; such as half-munched apples, pop-guns, whirligigs, fly-cages, and whole legions of rampant little paper game-cocks. Apparently there had been some appalling act of justice recently inflicted, for his scholars were all busily intent upon their books, or slyly whispering behind them with one eye kept upon the master; and a kind of buzzing stillness reigned throughout the school-room. It was suddenly interrupted by the appearance of a negro, in tow-cloth jacket and trousers, a round-crowned fragment of a hat, like the cap of Mercury, and mounted on the back of a ragged, wild, half-broken colt, which he managed with a rope by way of halter. He came clattering up to the school-door with an invitation to Ichabod to attend a merry-making or "quilting frolic," to be held that evening at Mynheer Van Tassel's; and having delivered his message with that air of importance, and effort at fine language, which a negro is apt to display on petty embassies of the kind, he dashed over the brook, and was seen scampering away up the Hollow, full of the importance and hurry of his mission.

All was now bustle and hubbub in the late quiet school-room. The scholars were hurried through their lessons, without stopping at trifles; those who were nimble skipped over half with impunity, and those who were tardy had a smart application now and then in the rear, to quicken their speed, or help them over a tall word. Books were flung aside without being put away on the shelves, inkstands were overturned, benches thrown down, and the whole school was turned loose an hour before the usual time, bursting forth like a legion of young imps, yelping and racketing about the green, in joy at their early emancipation.

The gallant Ichabod now spent at least an extra half-hour at his toilet, brushing and furbishing up his best and indeed only suit of rusty black, and arranging his locks by a bit of broken looking-glass, that hung up in the school-house. That he might make his appearance before his mistress in the true style of a cavalier, he borrowed a horse from the farmer with whom he was domiciliated, a choleric old Dutchman, of the name of Hans Van Ripper, and, thus gallantly mounted, issued forth, like a knight-errant in quest of adventures. But it is meet I should, in the true spirit of romantic story, give some account of the looks and equipments of my hero and his steed. The animal he bestrode was a broken-down plough-horse, that had outlived almost everything but his viciousness. He was gaunt and shagged, with a ewe neck and a head like a hammer; his rusty mane and tail were tangled and knotted with burrs; one eye had lost its pupil, and was glaring and spectral; but the

other had the gleam of a genuine devil in it. Still he must have had fire and mettle in his day, if we may judge from the name he bore of Gunpowder. He had, in fact, been a favorite steed of his master's, the choleric Van Ripper, who was a furious rider, and had infused, very probably, some of his own spirit into the animal; for, old and broken-down as he looked, there was more of the lurking devil in him than in any young filly in the country.

Ichabod was a suitable figure for such a steed. He rode with short stirrups, which brought his knees nearly up to the pommel of the saddle; his sharp elbows stuck out like grasshoppers'; he carried his whip perpendicularly in his hand, like a sceptre, and, as his horse jogged on, the motion of his arms was not unlike the flapping of a pair of wings. A small wool hat rested on the top of his nose, for so his scanty strip of forehead might be called; and the skirts of his black coat fluttered out almost to the horse's tail. Such was the appearance of Ichabod and his steed, as they shambled out of the gate of Hans Van Ripper, and it was altogether such an apparition as is seldom to be met with in broad daylight.

It was, as I have said, a fine autumnal day, the sky was clear and nature wore that rich and golden livery which we always associate with the idea of abundance. The forests had put on their sober brown and yellow, while some trees of the tenderer kind had been nipped by the frosts into brilliant dyes of orange, purple, and scarlet. Streaming files of wild ducks began to make their appearance high in the air; the bark of the squirrel might be heard from the groves of beech and hickory nuts, and the pensive whistle of the quail at intervals from the neighboring stubble-field.

The small birds were taking their farewell banquets. In the fulness of their revelry, they fluttered, chirping and frolicking, from bush to bush, and tree to tree, capricious from the very profusion and variety around them. There was the honest cockrobin, the favorite game of stripling sportsmen, with its loud querulous notes; and the twittering blackbirds flying in sable clouds; and the golden-winged woodpecker, with his crimson crest, his broad black gorget, and splendid plumage; and the cedar-bird, with its red-tipt wings and yellow-tipt tail, and its little monteiro cap of feathers; and the blue jay, that noisy coxcomb, in his gay light-blue coat and white under-clothes, screaming and chattering, nodding and bobbing and bowing, and pretending to be on good terms with every songster of the grove.

As Ichabod jogged slowly on his way, his eye, ever open to every symptom of culinary abundance, ranged with delight over the treasures of jolly autumn. On all sides he beheld vast store of apples; some hang-

ing in oppressive opulence on the trees; some gathered into baskets and barrels for the market; others heaped up in rich piles for the cider-press. Farther on he beheld great fields of Indian corn, with its golden ears peeping from their leafy coverts, and holding out the promise of cakes and hasty-pudding; and the yellow pumpkins lying beneath them, turning up their fair round bellies to the sun, and giving ample prospects of the most luxurious of pies; and anon he passed the fragrant buckwheat fields, breathing the odor of the bee-hive, and as he beheld them, soft anticipations stole over his mind of dainty slapjacks, well buttered, and garnished with honey or treacle, by the delicate little dimpled hand of Katrina Van Tassel.

Thus feeding his mind with many sweet thoughts and "sugared suppositions," he journeyed along the sides of a range of hills which look out upon some of the goodliest scenes of the mighty Hudson. The sun gradually wheeled his broad disk down into the west. The wide bosom of the Tappan Zee lay motionless and glossy, excepting that here and there a gentle undulation waved and prolonged the blue shadow of the distant mountain. A few amber clouds floated in the sky, without a breath of air to move them. The horizon was of a fine golden tint, changing gradually into a pure apple-green, and from that into the deep blue of the mid-heaven. A slanting ray lingered on the woody crests of the precipices that overhung some parts of the river, giving greater depth to the dark-gray and purple of their rocky sides. A sloop was loitering in the distance, dropping slowly down with the tide, her sail hanging uselessly against the mast; and as the reflection of the sky gleamed along the still water, it seemed as if the vessel was suspended in the air.

It was toward evening that Ichabod arrived at the castle of the Heer Van Tassel, which he found thronged with the pride and flower of the adjacent country. Old farmers, a spare leathern-faced race, in homespun coats and breeches, blue stockings, huge shoes, and magnificent pewter buckles. Their brisk withered little dames, in close crimped caps, long-waisted shortgowns, homespun petticoats, with scissors and pincushions, and gay calico pockets hanging on the outside. Buxom lasses, almost as antiquated as their mothers, excepting where a straw hat, a fine ribbon, or perhaps a white frock, gave symptoms of city innovation. The sons, in short square-skirted coats with rows of stupendous brass buttons, and their hair generally queued in the fashion of the times, especially if they could procure an eel-skin for the purpose, it being esteemed, throughout the country, as a potent nourisher and strengthener of the hair.

Brom Bones, however, was the hero of the scene, having come to the

gathering on his favorite steed, Daredevil, a creature, like himself, full of mettle and mischief, and which no one but himself could manage. He was, in fact, noted for preferring vicious animals, given to all kinds of tricks, which kept the rider in constant risk of his neck, for he held a tractable well-broken horse as unworthy of a lad of spirit.

Fain would I pause to dwell upon the world of charms that burst upon the enraptured gaze of my hero, as he entered the state parlor of Van Tassel's mansion. Not those of the bevy of buxom lasses, with their luxurious display of red and white; but the ample charms of a genuine Dutch country tea-table, in the sumptuous time of autumn. Such heaped-up platters of cakes of various and almost indescribable kinds, known only to experienced Dutch housewives! There was the doughty doughnut, the tenderer oly koek, and the crisp and crumbling cruller; sweet cakes and short cakes, ginger-cakes and honey-cakes, and the whole family of cakes. And then there were apple-pies and peach-pies and pumpkin-pies; besides slices of ham and smoked beef; and more-over delectable dishes of preserved plums, and peaches, and pears, and quinces; not to mention broiled shad and roasted chickens; together with bowls of milk and cream, all mingled higgledy-piggledy, pretty much as I have enumerated them, with the motherly tea-pot sending up its clouds of vapor from the midst—Heaven bless the mark! I want breath and time to discuss this banquet as it deserves, and am too eager to get on with my story. Happily, Ichabod Crane was not in so great a hurry as his historian, but did ample justice to every dainty.

He was a kind and thankful creature, whose heart dilated in proportion as his skin was filled with good cheer; and whose spirits rose with eating as some men's do with drink. He could not help, too, rolling his large eyes round him as he ate, and chuckling with the possibility that he might one day be lord of all this scene of almost unimaginable luxury and splendor. Then, he thought, how soon he'd turn his back upon the old school-house; snap his fingers in the face of Hans Van Ripper, and every other niggardly patron, and kick any itinerant pedagogue out-of-doors that should dare to call him comrade!

Old Baltus Van Tassel moved about among his guests with a face dilated with content and good-humor, round and jolly as the harvest-moon. His hospitable attentions were brief, but expressive, being confined to a shake of the hand, a slap on the shoulder, a loud laugh, and a pressing invitation to "fall to, and help themselves."

And now the sound of the music from the common room, or hall, summoned to the dance. The musician was an old gray-headed negro, who had been the itinerant orchestra of the neighborhood for more than half a century. His instrument was as old and battered as himself.

The greater part of the time he scraped on two or three strings, accompanying every movement of the bow with a motion of the head; bowing almost to the ground, and stamping with his foot whenever a fresh couple were to start.

Ichabod prided himself upon his dancing as much as upon his vocal powers. Not a limb, not a fibre about him was idle; and to have seen his loosely hung frame in full motion, and clattering about the room, you would have thought Saint Vitus himself, that blessed patron of the dance, was figuring before you in person. He was the admiration of all the negroes; who, having gathered, of all ages and sizes, from the farm and the neighborhood, stood forming a pyramid of shining black faces at every door and window, gazing with delight at the scene, rolling their white eyeballs, and showing grinning rows of ivory from ear to ear. How could the flogger of urchins be otherwise than animated and joyous? the lady of his heart was his partner in the dance, and smiling graciously in reply to all his amorous oglings; while Brom Bones, sorely smitten with love and jealousy, sat brooding by himself in one corner.

When the dance was at an end, Ichabod was attracted to a knot of the sager folks, who, with old Van Tassel, sat smoking at one end of the piazza, gossiping over former times, and drawing out long stories about the war.

This neighborhood, at the time of which I am speaking, was one of those highly favored places which abound with chronicle and great men. The British and American line had run near it during the war; it had, therefore, been the scene of marauding, and infested with refugees, cow-boys, and all kinds of border chivalry. Just sufficient time has elapsed to enable each story-teller to dress up his tale with a little becoming fiction, and, in the indistinctness of his recollection, to make himself the hero of every exploit.

There was the story of Doffue Martling, a large blue-bearded Dutchman, who had nearly taken a British frigate with an old iron nine-pounder from a mud breastwork, only that his gun burst at the sixth discharge. And there was an old gentleman who shall be nameless, being too rich a mynheer to be lightly mentioned, who, in the battle of White Plains, being an excellent master of defence, parried a musket-ball with a small sword, insomuch that he absolutely felt it whiz round the blade, and glance off at the hilt; in proof of which he was ready at any time to show the sword, with the hilt a little bent. There were several more that had been equally great in the field, not one of whom but was persuaded that he had a considerable hand in bringing the war to a happy termination.

But all these were nothing to the tales of ghosts and apparitions that

succeeded. The neighborhood is rich in legendary treasures of the kind. Local tales and superstitions thrive best in these sheltered long-settled retreats; but are trampled underfoot by the shifting throng that forms the population of most of our country places. Besides, there is no encouragement for ghosts in most of our villages, for they have scarcely had time to finish their first nap, and turn themselves in their graves before their surviving friends have travelled away from the neighborhood; so that when they turn out at night to walk their rounds, they have no acquaintance left to call upon. This is perhaps the reason why we so seldom hear of ghosts, except in our long-established Dutch communities.

The immediate cause, however, of the prevalence of supernatural stories in these parts was doubtless owing to the vicinity of Sleepy Hollow. There was a contagion in the very air that blew from the haunted region; it breathed forth an atmosphere of dreams and fancies infecting all the land. Several of the Sleepy Hollow people were present at Van Tassel's and, as usual, were doling out their wild and wonderful legends. Many dismal tales were told about funeral trains, and mourning cries and wailings heard and seen about the great tree where the unfortunate Major André was taken, and which stood in the neighborhood. Some mention was made also of the woman in white, that haunted the dark glen at Raven Rock, and was often heard to shriek on winter nights before a storm, having perished there in the snow. The chief part of the stories, however, turned upon the favorite spectre of Sleepy Hollow, the headless horseman, who had been heard several times of late, patrolling the country; and, it was said, tethered his horse nightly among the graves in the churchyard.

The sequestered situation of this church seems always to have made it a favorite haunt of troubled spirits. It stands on a knoll, surrounded by locust-trees and lofty elms, from among which its decent whitewashed walls shine modestly forth, like Christian purity beaming through the shades of retirement. A gentle slope descends from it to a silver sheet of water, bordered by high trees, between which, peeps may be caught at the blue hills of the Hudson. To look upon its grassgrown yard, where the sunbeams seem to sleep so quietly, one would think that there at least the dead might rest in peace. On one side of the church extends a wide woody dell, along which raves a large brook among broken rocks and trunks of fallen trees. Over a deep black part of the stream, not far from the church, was formerly thrown a wooden bridge; the road that led to it, and the bridge itself, were thickly shaded by overhanging trees, which cast a gloom about it, even in the daytime, but occasioned a fearful darkness at night. This was one of the favorite

haunts of the headless horseman; and the place where he was most frequently encountered. The tale was told of old Brouwer, a most heretical disbeliever in ghosts, how he met the horseman returning from his foray into Sleepy Hollow, and was obliged to get up behind him; how they galloped over bush and brake, over hill and swamp, until they reached the bridge; when the horseman suddenly turned into a skeleton, threw old Brouwer into the brook, and sprang away over the tree-tops with a clap of thunder.

This story was immediately matched by a thrice marvellous adventure of Brom Bones, who made light of the galloping Hessian as an arrant jockey. He affirmed that, on returning one night from the neighboring village of Sing Sing, he had been overtaken by this midnight trooper; that he had offered to race with him for a bowl of punch, and should have won it too, for Daredevil beat the goblin horse all hollow, but, just as they came to the church bridge, the Hessian bolted, and vanished in a flash of fire.

All these tales, told in that drowsy undertone with which men talk in the dark, the countenances of the listeners only now and then receiving a casual gleam from the glare of a pipe, sank deep in the mind of Ichabod. He repaid them in kind with large extracts from his invaluable author, Cotton Mather, and added many marvellous events that had taken place in his native State of Connecticut, and fearful sights which he had seen in his nightly walks about the Sleepy Hollow.

The revel now gradually broke up. The old farmers gathered together their families in their wagons, and were heard for some time rattling along the hollow roads, and over the distant hills. Some of the damsels mounted on pillions behind their favorite swains, and their light-hearted laughter, mingling with the clatter of hoofs, echoed along the silent woodlands, sounding fainter and fainter until they gradually died away —and the late scene of noise and frolic was all silent and deserted. Ichabod only lingered behind, according to the custom of country lovers, to have a tête-à-tête with the heiress, fully convinced that he was now on the high road to success. What passed at this interview I will not pretend to say, for in fact I do not know. Something, however, I fear me, must have gone wrong, for he certainly sallied forth, after no very great interval, with an air quite desolate and chop-fallen.—Oh, these women! these women! Could that girl have been playing off any of her coquettish tricks?—Was her encouragement of the poor pedagogue all a mere sham to secure her conquest of his rival?—Heaven only knows, not I!— Let it suffice to say, Ichabod stole forth with the air of one who had been sacking a hen-roost, rather than a fair lady's heart. Without looking to the right or left to notice the scene of rural wealth on which he

had so often gloated, he went straight to the stable, and with several hearty cuffs and kicks, roused his steed most uncourteously from the comfortable quarters in which he was soundly sleeping, dreaming of mountains of corn and oats, and whole valleys of timothy and clover.

It was the very witching time of night that Ichabod, heavy-hearted and crestfallen, pursued his travel homewards, along the sides of the lofty hills which rise above Tarry Town, and which he had traversed so cheerily in the afternoon. The hour was as dismal as himself. Far below him, the Tappan Zee spread its dusky and indistinct waste of waters, with here and there the tall mast of a sloop riding quietly at anchor under the land. In the dead hush of midnight he could even hear the barking of the watch-dog from the opposite shore of the Hudson; but it was so vague and faint as only to give an idea of his distance from this faithful companion of man. Now and then, too, the long-drawn crowing of a cock, accidentally awakened, would sound far, far off, from some farm-house away among the hills—but it was like a dreaming sound in his ear. No signs of life occurred near him, but occasionally the melancholy chirp of a cricket, or perhaps the guttural twang of a bull-frog, from a neighboring marsh, as if sleeping uncomfortably, and turning suddenly in his bed.

All the stories of ghosts and goblins that he had heard in the afternoon, now came crowding upon his recollection. The night grew darker and darker; the stars seemed to sink deeper in the sky, and driving clouds occasionally hid them from his sight. He had never felt so lonely and dismal. He was, moreover, approaching the very place where many of the scenes of the ghost-stories had been laid. In the centre of the road stood an enormous tulip-tree, which towered like a giant above all the other trees of the neighborhood, and formed a kind of landmark. Its limbs were gnarled, and fantastic, large enough to form trunks for ordinary trees, twisting down almost to the earth, and rising again into the air. It was connected with the tragical story of the unfortunate André, who had been taken prisoner hard by; and was universally known by the name of Major André's tree. The common people regarded it with a mixture of respect and superstition, partly out of sympathy for the fate of its ill-starred namesake, and partly from the tales of strange sights and doleful lamentations told concerning it.

As Ichabod approached this fearful tree, he began to whistle: he thought his whistle was answered,—it was but a blast sweeping sharply through the dry branches. As he approached a little nearer, he thought he saw something white, hanging in the midst of the tree,—he paused and ceased whistling; but on looking more narrowly, perceived that it was a place where the tree had been scathed by lightning, and the white

wood laid bare. Suddenly he heard a groan,—his teeth chattered and his knees smote against the saddle: it was but the rubbing of one huge bough upon another, as they were swayed about by the breeze. He passed the tree in safety; but new perils lay before him.

About two hundred yards from the tree a small brook crossed the road, and ran into a marshy and thickly wooded glen, known by the name of Wiley's swamp. A few rough logs, laid side by side, served for a bridge over this stream. On that side of the road where the brook entered the wood, a group of oaks and chestnuts, matted thick with wild grape-vines, threw a cavernous gloom over it. To pass this bridge was the severest trial. It was at this identical spot that the unfortunate André was captured, and under the covert of those chestnuts and vines were the sturdy yeomen concealed who surprised him. This has ever since been considered a haunted stream, and fearful are the feelings of the school boy who has to pass it alone after dark.

As he approached the stream, his heart began to thump; he summoned up, however, all his resolution, gave his horse half a score of kicks in the ribs, and attempted to dash briskly across the bridge; but instead of starting forward, the perverse old animal made a lateral movement, and ran broadside against the fence. Ichabod, whose fears increased with the delay, jerked the reins on the other side, and kicked lustily with the contrary foot: it was all in vain; his steed started, it is true, but it was only to plunge to the opposite side of the road into a thicket of brambles and alder bushes. The schoolmaster now bestowed both whip and heel upon the starveling ribs of old Gunpowder, who dashed forward, snuffling and snorting, but came to a stand just by the bridge, with a suddenness that had nearly sent his rider sprawling over his head. Just at this moment a plashy tramp by the side of the bridge caught the sensitive ear of Ichabod. In the dark shadow of the grove, on the margin of the brook, he beheld something huge, misshapen, black, and towering. It stirred not, but seemed gathered up in the gloom, like some gigantic monster ready to spring upon the traveller.

The hair of the affrighted pedagogue rose upon his head with terror. What was to be done? To turn and fly was now too late; and besides, what chance was there of escaping ghost or goblin, if such it was, which could ride upon the wings of the wind? Summoning up, therefore, a show of courage, he demanded in stammering accents—"Who are you?" He received no reply. He repeated his demand in a still more agitated voice. Still there was no answer. Once more he cudgelled the sides of the inflexible Gunpowder, and, shutting his eyes, broke forth with involuntary fervor into a psalm-tune. Just then the shadowy object of alarm put itself in motion, and, with a scramble and a bound, stood

at once in the middle of the road. Though the night was dark and dismal, yet the form of the unknown might now in some degree be ascertained. He appeared to be a horseman of large dimensions, and mounted on a black horse of powerful frame. He made no offer of molestation or sociability, but kept aloof on one side of the road, jogging along on the blind side of old Gunpowder, who had now got over his fright and waywardness.

Ichabod, who had no relish for this strange midnight companion, and bethought himself of the adventure of Brom Bones with the Galloping Hessian, now quickened his steed, in hopes of leaving him behind. The stranger, however, quickened his horse to an equal pace. Ichabod pulled up, and fell into a walk, thinking to lag behind,—the other did the same. His heart began to sink within him; he endeavored to resume his psalm-tune, but his parched tongue clove to the roof of his mouth, and he could not utter a stave. There was something in the moody and dogged silence of this pertinacious companion, that was mysterious and appalling. It was soon fearfully accounted for. On mounting a rising ground, which brought the figure of his fellow-traveller in relief against the sky, gigantic in height, and muffled in a cloak, Ichabod was horror-struck, on perceiving that he was headless!—but his horror was still more increased, on observing that the head, which should have rested on his shoulders, was carried before him on the pommel of the saddle: his terror rose to desperation; he rained a shower of kicks and blows upon Gunpowder, hoping, by a sudden movement, to give his companion the slip,—but the spectre started full jump with him. Away then they dashed, through thick and thin; stones flying, and sparks flashing at every bound. Ichabod's flimsy garments fluttered in the air, as he stretched his long lank body away over his horse's head, in the eagerness of his flight.

They had now reached the road which turns off to Sleepy Hollow; but Gunpowder, who seemed possessed with a demon, instead of keeping up it, made an opposite turn, and plunged headlong downhill to the left. This road leads through a sandy hollow, shaded by trees for about a quarter of a mile, where it crosses the bridge famous in goblin story, and just beyond swells the green knoll on which stands the whitewashed church.

As yet the panic of the steed had given his unskilful rider an apparent advantage in the chase; but just as he had got half-way through the hollow, the girths of the saddle gave way, and he felt it slipping from under him. He seized it by the pommel, and endeavored to hold it firm, but in vain; and had just time to save himself by clasping old Gunpowder round the neck, when the saddle fell to the earth, and he heard

it trampled underfoot by his pursuer. For a moment, the terror of Hans Van Ripper's wrath passed across his mind—for it was his Sunday saddle; but this was no time for petty fears; the goblin was hard on his haunches; and (unskilful rider that he was!) he had much ado to maintain his seat; sometimes slipping on one side, sometimes on another, and sometimes jolted on the high ridge of his horse's backbone, with a violence that he verily feared would cleave him asunder.

An opening in the trees now cheered him with the hopes that the church-bridge was at hand. The wavering reflection of a silver star in the bosom of the brook told him that he was not mistaken. He saw the walls of the church dimly glaring under the trees beyond. He recollected the place where Brom Bones' ghostly competitor had disappeared. "If I can but reach that bridge," thought Ichabod, "I am safe." Just then he heard the black steed panting and blowing close behind him; he even fancied that he felt his hot breath. Another convulsive kick in the ribs, and old Gunpowder sprang upon the bridge; he thundered over the resounding planks; he gained the opposite side; and now Ichabod cast a look behind to see if his pursuer should vanish, according to rule, in a flash of fire and brimstone. Just then he saw the goblin rising in his stirrups, and in the very act of hurling his head at him. Ichabod endeavored to dodge the horrible missile, but too late. It encountered his cranium with a tremendous crash,—he was tumbled headlong into the dust, and Gunpowder, the black steed, and the goblin rider, passed by like a whirlwind.

The next morning the old horse was found without his saddle, and with the bridle under his feet, soberly cropping the grass at his master's gate. Ichabod did not make his appearance at breakfast;—dinner-hour came, but no Ichabod. The boys assembled at the school-house, and strolled idly about the banks of the brook; but no schoolmaster. Hans Van Ripper now began to feel some uneasiness about the fate of poor Ichabod, and his saddle. An inquiry was set on foot, and after diligent investigation they came upon his traces. In one part of the road leading to the church was found the saddle trampled in the dirt; the tracks of horses' hoofs deeply dented in the road, and evidently at furious speed, were traced to the bridge, beyond which, on the bank of a broad part of the brook, where the water ran deep and black, was found the hat of the unfortunate Ichabod, and close beside it a shattered pumpkin.

The brook was searched, but the body of the schoolmaster was not to be discovered. Hans Van Ripper, as executor of his estate, examined the bundle which contained all his worldly effects. They consisted of two shirts and a half; two stocks for the neck; a pair or two of worsted stockings, an old pair of corduroy small-clothes; a rusty razor; a book

of psalm-tunes, full of dogs' ears; and a broken pitch-pipe. As to the books and furniture of the school-house, they belonged to the community, excepting Cotton Mather's *History of Witchcraft*, a *New England Almanac*, and a book of dreams and fortune-telling; in which last was a sheet of foolscap much scribbled and blotted in several fruitless attempts to make a copy of verses in honor of the heiress of Van Tassel. These magic books and the poetic scrawl were forthwith consigned to the flames by Hans Van Ripper; who from that time forward determined to send his children no more to school; observing, that he never knew any good come of this same reading and writing. Whatever money the schoolmaster possessed, and he had received his quarter's pay but a day or two before, he must have had about his person at the time of his disappearance.

The mysterious event caused much speculation at the church on the following Sunday. Knots of gazers and gossips were collected in the churchyard, at the bridge, and at the spot where the hat and pumpkin had been found. The stories of Brouwer, of Bones, and a whole budget of others, were called to mind; and when they had diligently considered them all, and compared them with the symptoms of the present case, they shook their heads, and came to the conclusion that Ichabod had been carried off by the Galloping Hessian. As he was a bachelor, and in nobody's debt, nobody troubled his head any more about him. The school was removed to a different quarter of the Hollow, and another pedagogue reigned in his stead.

It is true, an old farmer, who had been down to New York on a visit several years after, and from whom this account of the ghastly adventure was received, brought home the intelligence that Ichabod Crane was still alive; that he had left the neighborhood, partly through fear of the goblin and Hans Van Ripper, and partly in mortification at having been suddenly dismissed by the heiress; that he had changed his quarters to a distant part of the country; had kept school and studied law at the same time, had been admitted to the bar, turned politician, electioneered, written for the newspapers, and finally had been made a justice of the Ten Pound Court. Brom Bones too, who shortly after his rival's disappearance conducted the blooming Katrina in triumph to the altar, was observed to look exceedingly knowing whenever the story of Ichabod was related, and always burst into a hearty laugh at the mention of the pumpkin; which led some to suspect that he knew more about the matter than he chose to tell.

The old country wives, however, who are the best judges of these matters, maintain to this day that Ichabod was spirited away by supernatural means; and it is a favorite story often told about the neighbor-

hood round the winter evening fire. The bridge became more than ever an object of superstitious awe, and that may be the reason why the road has been altered of late years, so as to approach the church by the border of the millpond. The school-house, being deserted, soon fell to decay, and was reported to be haunted by the ghost of the unfortunate pedagogue; and the plough-boy, loitering homeward of a still summer evening, has often fancied his voice at a distance, chanting a melancholy psalm-tune, among the tranquil solitudes of Sleepy Hollow.

POSTSCRIPT,

Found in the Handwriting of Mr. Knickerbocker.

The preceding Tale is given, almost in the precise words in which I heard it related at a Corporation meeting of the ancient city of Manhattoes, at which were present many of its sagest and most illustrious burghers. The narrator was a pleasant, shabby, gentlemanly old fellow, in pepper-and-salt clothes, with a sadly humorous face; and one whom I strongly suspected of being poor,—he made such efforts to be entertaining. When his story was concluded, there was much laughter and approbation, particularly from two or three deputy aldermen, who had been asleep the greater part of the time. There was, however, one tall, dry-looking old gentleman, with beetling eyebrows, who maintained a grave and rather severe face throughout; now and then folding his arms, inclining his head, and looking down upon the floor, as if turning a doubt over in his mind. He was one of your wary men, who never laugh, but on good grounds— when they have reason and the law on their side. When the mirth of the rest of the company had subsided and silence was restored, he leaned one arm on the elbow of his chair, and sticking the other akimbo, demanded, with a slight but exceedingly sage motion of the head, and contraction of the brow, what was the moral of the story, and what it went to prove?

The story-teller, who was just putting a glass of wine to his lips, as a refreshment after his toils, paused for a moment, looked at his inquirer with an air of infinite deference, and, lowering the glass slowly to the table, observed, that the story was intended most logically to prove:

"There is no situation in life but has its advantages and pleasures—provided we will but take a joke as we find it;

"That, therefore, he that runs races with goblin troopers is likely to have rough riding of it.

"*Ergo,* for a country schoolmaster to be refused the hand of a Dutch heiress, is a certain step to high preferment in the state."

The cautious old gentleman knit his brows tenfold closer after this explanation, being sorely puzzled by ratiocination of the syllogism; while,

methought, the one in pepper-and-salt eyed him with something of a triumphant leer. At length he observed, that all this was very well, but still he thought the story a little on the extravagant—there were one or two points on which he had his doubts.

"Faith, sir," replied the story-teller, "as to that matter, I don't believe one half of it myself."

D.K.

From *The Sketch Book*

THE STOUT GENTLEMAN

A Stage-coach Romance

I'll cross it though it blast me!—*Hamlet.*

A FAVORITE evening pastime at the Hall, and one which the worthy Squire is fond of promoting, is story-telling, a "good old-fashioned fireside amusement," as he terms it. Indeed, I believe he promotes it chiefly because it was one of the choice recreations in those days of yore when ladies and gentlemen were not much in the habit of reading. Be this as it may, he will often, at supper-table, when conversation flags, call on some one or other of the company for a story, as it was formerly the custom to call for a song; and it is edifying to see the exemplary patience, and even satisfaction, with which the good old gentleman will sit and listen to some hackneyed tale that he has heard for at least a hundred times.

In this way one evening the current of anecdotes and stories ran upon mysterious personages that have figured at different times, and filled the world with doubts and conjecture; such as the Wandering Jew, the Man with the Iron Mask, who tormented the curiosity of all Europe; the Invisible Girl, and last, though not least, the Pig-faced Lady.

At length one of the company was called upon who had the most unpromising physiognomy for a story-teller that ever I had seen. He was a thin, pale, weazen-faced man, extremely nervous, who had sat at one corner of the table, shrunk up, as it were, into himself, and almost swallowed up in the cape of his coat, as a turtle in its shell.

The very demand seemed to throw him into a nervous agitation, yet he did not refuse. He emerged his head out of his shell, made a few odd grimaces and gesticulations, before he could get his muscles into order, or his voice under command, and then offered to give some account of a mysterious personage whom he had recently encountered in

---

"The Stout Gentleman" fills two chapters in Irving's *Bracebridge Hall*, published in 1822, the first a brief introductory one called "Story-Telling."—C.N.

the course of his travels, and one whom he thought fully entitled of being classed with the Man with the Iron Mask.

I was so much struck with his extraordinary narrative, that I have written it out to the best of my recollection, for the amusement of the reader. I think it has in it all the elements of that mysterious and romantic narrative so greedily sought after at the present day.

IT was a rainy Sunday in the gloomy month of November. I had been detained, in the course of a journey, by a slight indisposition, from which I was recovering; but was still feverish, and obliged to keep within doors all day, in an inn of the small town of Derby. A wet Sunday in a country inn!—whoever has had the luck to experience one can alone judge of my situation. The rain pattered against the casements; the bells tolled for church with a melancholy sound. I went to the windows in quest of something to amuse the eye; but it seemed as if I had been placed completely out of the reach of all amusement. The windows of my bedroom looked out among tiled roofs and stacks of chimneys, while those of my sitting-room commanded a full view of the stable-yard. I know of nothing more calculated to make a man sick of this world than a stable-yard on a rainy day. The place was littered with wet straw that had been kicked about by travellers and stable-boys. In one corner was a stagnant pool of water, surrounding an island of muck; there were several half-drowned fowls crowded together under a cart, among which was a miserable, crestfallen cock, drenched out of all life and spirit; his drooping tail matted, as it were, into a single feather, along which the water trickled from his back; near the cart was a half-dozing cow, chewing the cud, and standing patiently to be rained on, with wreaths of vapor rising from her reeking hide; a wall-eyed horse, tired of the loneliness of the stable, was poking his spectral head out of a window, with the rain dripping on it from the eaves; an unhappy cur, chained to a dog-house hard by, uttered something, every now and then, between a bark and a yelp; a drab of a kitchen-wench tramped backwards and forwards through the yard in patterns, looking as sulky as the weather itself; everything, in short, was comfortless and forlorn, excepting a crew of hardened ducks, assembled like boon companions round a puddle, and making a riotous noise over their liquor.

I was lonely and listless, and wanted amusement. My room soon became insupportable. I abandoned it, and sought what is technically called the travellers' room. This is a public room set apart at most inns for the accommodation of a class of wayfarers called travellers, or rid-

ers; a kind of commercial knights-errant, who are incessantly scouring the kingdom in gigs, on horseback, or by coach. They are the only successors that I know of at the present day to the knights-errant of yore. They lead the same kind of roving, adventurous life, only changing the lance for a driving-whip, the buckler for a pattern-card, and the coat of mail for an upper Benjamin. Instead of vindicating the charms of peerless beauty, they rove about, spreading the fame and standing of some substantial tradesman, or manufacturer, and are ready at any time to bargain in his name; it being the fashion nowadays to trade, instead of fight, with one another. As the room of the hostel, in the good old fighting times, would be hung round at night with the armor of way-worn warriors, such as coats of mail, falchions, and yawning helmets, so the travellers' room is garnished with box-coats, whips of all kinds, spurs, gaiters, and oil-cloth covered hats.

I was in hopes of finding some of these worthies to talk with, but was disappointed. There were, indeed, two or three in the room; but I could make nothing of them. One was just finishing his breakfast, quarrelling with his bread and butter, and huffing the waiter; another buttoned on a pair of gaiters, with many execrations at Boots for not having cleaned his shoes well; a third sat drumming on the table with his fingers and looking at the rain as it streamed down the window-glass; they all appeared infected by the weather, and disappeared, one after the other, without exchanging a word.

I sauntered to the window, and stood gazing at the people, picking their way to church, with petticoats hoisted midleg high, and dripping umbrellas. The bell ceased to toll, and the streets became silent. I then amused myself with watching the daughters of a tradesman opposite; who, being confined to the house for fear of wetting their Sunday finery, played off their charms at the front windows, to fascinate the chance tenants of the inn. They at length were summoned away by a vigilant, vinegar-faced mother, and I had nothing further from without to amuse me.

What was I to do to pass away the long-lived day? I was sadly nervous and lonely; and everything about an inn seems calculated to make a dull day ten times duller. Old newspapers, smelling of beer and to-bacco-smoke, and which I had already read half a dozen times. Good-for-nothing books, that were worse than rainy weather. I bored myself to death with an old volume of the *Lady's Magazine*. I read all the commonplace names of ambitious travellers scrawled on the panes of glass; the eternal families of the Smiths, and the Browns, and the Jacksons, and the Johnsons, and all the other sons; and I deciphered several

scraps of fatiguing inn-window poetry which I have met with in all parts of the world.

The day continued lowering and gloomy; the slovenly, ragged, spongy cloud drifted heavily along; there was no variety even in the rain: it was one dull, continued, monotonous patter—patter—patter, excepting that now and then I was enlivened by the idea of a brisk shower, from the rattling of the drops upon a passing umbrella.

It was quite *refreshing* (if I may be allowed a hackneyed phrase of the day) when, in the course of the morning, a horn blew, and a stage-coach whirled through the street, with outside passengers stuck all over it, cowering under cotton umbrellas, and seethed together, and reeking with the steams of wet box-coats and upper Benjamins.

The sound brought out from their lurking-places a crew of vagabond boys, and vagabond dogs, and the carroty-headed hostler, and that non-descript animal ycleped Boots, and all the other vagabond race that infest the purlieus of an inn. But the bustle was transient; the coach again whirled on its way; and boy and dog, and hostler and Boots, all slunk back again to their holes; the street again became silent, and the rain continued to rain on. In fact, there was no hope of its clearing up; the barometer pointed to rainy weather; mine hostess's tortoise-shell cat sat by the fire washing her face, and rubbing her paws over her ears; and, on referring to the Almanac, I found a direful prediction stretching from the top of the page to the bottom through the whole month, "expect—much—rain—about—this—time!"

I was dreadfully hipped. The hours seemed as if they would never creep by. The very ticking of the clock became irksome. At length the stillness of the house was interrupted by the ringing of a bell. Shortly after I heard the voice of a waiter at the bar: "The stout gentleman in No. 13 wants his breakfast. Tea and bread and butter, with ham and eggs; the eggs not to be too much done."

In such a situation as mine, every incident is of importance. Here was a subject of speculation presented to my mind, and ample exercise for my imagination. I am prone to paint pictures to myself, and on this occasion I had some materials to work upon. Had the guest upstairs been mentioned as Mr. Smith, or Mr. Brown, or Mr. Jackson, or Mr. Johnson, or merely as "the gentleman in No. 13," it would have been a perfect blank to me. I should have thought nothing of it; but "The stout gentleman"!—the very name had something in it of the picturesque. It at once gave the size; it embodied the personage to my mind's eye, and my fancy did the rest.

He was stout, or, as some term it, lusty; in all probability, therefore, he was advanced in life, some people expanding as they grow old. By

his breakfasting rather late, and in his own room, he must be a man accustomed to live at his ease, and above the necessity of early rising; no doubt a round, rosy, lusty old gentleman.

There was another violent ringing. The stout gentleman was impatient for his breakfast. He was evidently a man of importance; "well to do in the world"; accustomed to be promptly waited upon; of a keen appetite, and a little cross when hungry; "perhaps," thought I, "he may be some London Alderman; or who knows but he may be a Member of Parliament?"

The breakfast was sent up, and there was a short interval of silence; he was, doubtless, making the tea. Presently there was a violent ringing; and before it could be answered, another ringing still more violent. "Bless me! what a choleric old gentleman!" The waiter came down in a huff. The butter was rancid, the eggs were overdone, the ham was too salt;—the stout gentleman was evidently nice in his eating; one of those who eat and growl, and keep the waiter on the trot, and live in a state militant with the household.

The hostess got into a fume. I should observe that she was a brisk, coquettish woman; a little of a shrew, and something of a slammerkin, but very pretty withal; with a nincompoop for a husband, as shrews are apt to have. She rated the servants roundly for their negligence in sending up so bad a breakfast, but said not a word against the stout gentleman; by which I clearly perceived that he must be a man of consequence, entitled to make a noise and to give trouble at a country inn. Other eggs, and ham, and bread and butter were sent up. They appeared to be more graciously received; at least there was no further complaint.

I had not made many turns about the travellers' room, when there was another ringing. Shortly afterwards there was a stir and an inquest about the house. The stout gentleman wanted the *Times* or the *Chronicle* newspaper. I set him down, therefore, for a Whig; or rather, from his being so absolute and lordly where he had a chance, I suspected him of being a Radical. Hunt, I had heard, was a large man; "who knows," thought I, "but it is Hunt himself!"

My curiosity began to be awakened. I inquired of the waiter who was this stout gentleman that was making all this stir; but I could get no information. Nobody seemed to know his name. The landlords of bustling inns seldom trouble their heads about the names or occupations of their transient guest. The color of a coat, the shape or size of a person, is enough to suggest a travelling name. It is either the tall gentleman, or the short gentleman, or the gentleman in black, or the gentleman in snuff-color; or, as in the present instance, the stout gentleman.

A designation of the kind once hit on, answers every purpose, and saves all further inquiry.

Rain—rain—rain! pitiless, ceaseless rain! No such thing as putting a foot out of doors, and no occupation or amusement within. By and by I heard some one walking overhead. It was in the stout gentleman's room. He evidently was a large man by the heaviness of his tread; and an old man from his wearing such creaking soles. "He is doubtless," thought I, "some rich old square-toes of regular habits, and is now taking exercise after breakfast."

I now read all the advertisements of coaches and hotels that were stuck about the mantelpiece. The *Lady's Magazine* had become an abomination to me; it was as tedious as the day itself. I wandered out, not knowing what to do, and ascended again to my room. I had not been there long, when there was a squall from a neighboring bedroom. A door opened and slammed violently; a chamber-maid, that I had re-marked for having a ruddy, good-humored face, went down stairs in a violent flurry. The stout gentleman had been rude to her!

This sent a whole host of my deductions to the deuce in a moment. The unknown personage could not be an old gentleman; for old gentlemen are not apt to be so obstreperous to chamber-maids. He could not be a young gentleman; for young gentlemen are not apt to inspire such indignation. He must be a middle-aged man, and confounded ugly into the bargain, or the girl would not have taken the matter in such terrible dudgeon. I confess I was sorely puzzled.

In a few minutes I heard the voice of my landlady. I caught a glance of her as she came tramping up stairs,—her face glowing, her cap flaring, her tongue wagging the whole way. "She'd have no such doings in her house, she'd warrant. If gentlemen did spend money freely, it was no rule. She'd have no servant-maids of hers treated in that way, when they were about their work, that's what she wouldn't."

As I hate squabbles, particularly with women, and above all with pretty women, I slunk back into my room, and partly closed the door; but my curiosity was too much excited not to listen. The landlady marched intrepidly to the enemy's citadel, and entered it with a storm. The door closed after her. I heard her voice in high windy clamor for a moment or two. Then it gradually subsided, like a gust of wind in a garret; then there was a laugh; then I heard nothing more.

After a little while my landlady came out with an odd smile on her face, adjusting her cap, which was a little on one side. As she went down stairs, I heard the landlord ask her what was the matter. She said, "Nothing at all, only the girl's a fool."—I was more than ever perplexed what to make of this unaccountable personage, who could put a good-

natured chamber-maid in a passion, and send away a termagant landlady in smiles. He could not be so old, nor cross, nor ugly either. I had to go to work at his picture again, and to paint him entirely different. I now set him down for one of those stout gentlemen that are frequently met with swaggering about the doors of country inns. Moist, merry fellows, in Belcher handkerchiefs, whose bulk is a little assisted by malt liquors. Men who have seen the world, and been sworn at Highgate; who are used to tavern-life, up to all the tricks of tapsters, and knowing in the ways of sinful publicans. Free-livers on a small scale; who are prodigal within the compass of a guinea, who call all the waiters by name, tousle the maids, gossip with the landlady at the bar, and prose over a pint of port, or a glass of negus, after dinner.

The morning wore away in forming these and similar surmises. As fast as I wove one system of belief, some movement of the unknown would completely overturn it, and throw all my thoughts again into confusion. Such are the solitary operations of a feverish mind. I was, as I have said, extremely nervous; and the continual meditation on the concerns of this invisible personage began to have its effect. I was getting a fit of the fidgets.

Dinner-time came. I hoped the stout gentleman might dine in the travellers' room, and that I might at length get a view of his person; but no—he had dinner served in his own room. What could be the meaning of this solitude and mystery? He could not be a radical; there was something too aristocratical in thus keeping himself apart from the rest of the world, and condemning himself to his own dull company throughout a rainy day. And then, too, he lived too well for a discontented politician. He seemed to expatiate on a variety of dishes, and to sit over his wine like a jolly friend of good living. Indeed, my doubts on this head were soon at an end; for he could not have finished his first bottle before I could faintly hear him humming a tune; and on listening I found it to be "God save the King." 'Twas plain, then, he was no radical, but a faithful subject; one who grew loyal over his bottle and was ready to stand by king and constitution, when he could stand by nothing else. But who could he be? My conjectures began to run wild. Was he not some personage of distinction travelling incog.? "God knows!" said I, at my wit's end; "it may be one of the royal family for aught I know, for they are all stout gentlemen!"

The weather continued rainy. The mysterious unknown kept his room, and, as far as I could judge, his chair, for I did not hear him move. In the meantime, as the day advanced, the travellers' room began to be frequented. Some, who had just arrived, came in buttoned up in box-coats; others came home who had been dispersed about the town;

64 THE COMPLETE TALES OF WASHINGTON IRVING

some took their dinners, and some their tea. Had I been in a different mood, I should have found entertainment in studying this peculiar class of men. There were two especially, who were regular wags of the road, and up to all the standing jokes of travellers. They had a thousand sly things to say to the waiting-maid, whom they called Louisa, and Ethelinda, and a dozen other fine names, changing the name every time, and chuckling amazingly at their own waggery. My mind, however, had been completely engrossed by the stout gentleman. He had kept my fancy in chase during a long day, and it was not now to be diverted from the scent.

The evening gradually wore away. The travellers read the papers two or three times over. Some drew round the fire and told long stories about their horses, about their adventures, their overturns, and breakings-down. They discussed the credit of different merchants and different inns; and the two wags told several choice anecdotes of pretty chamber maids and kind landladies. All this passed as they were quietly taking what they called their night-caps, that is to say, strong glasses of brandy and water and sugar, or some other mixture of the kind; after which they one after another rang for "Boots" and the chamber-maid, and walked off to bed in old shoes cut down into marvellously uncomfortable slippers.

There was now only one man left: a short-legged, long-bodied, plethoric fellow, with a very large, sandy head. He sat by himself, with a glass of port-wine negus, and a spoon; sipping and stirring, and meditating and sipping, until nothing was left but the spoon. He gradually fell asleep bolt upright in his chair, with the empty glass standing before him; and the candle seemed to fall asleep too, for the wick grew long, and black, and cabbaged at the end, and dimmed the little light that remained in the chamber. The gloom that now prevailed was contagious. Around hung the shapeless, and almost spectral box-coats of departed travellers, long since buried in deep sleep. I only heard the ticking of the clock, with the deep-drawn breathings of the sleeping topers, and the drippings of the rain, drop—drop—drop, from the eaves of the house. The church-bells chimed midnight. All at once the stout gentleman began to walk overhead, pacing slowly backwards and forwards. There was something extremely awful in all this especially to one in my state of nerves. These ghastly great-coats, these guttural breathings, and the creaking footsteps of this mysterious being. His steps grew fainter and fainter, and at length died away. I could bear it no longer. I was wound up to the desperation of a hero of romance. "Be he who or what he may," said I to myself, "I'll have a sight of him!" I seized a chamber-candle, and hurried up to No. 13. The door stood

ajar. I hesitated—I entered; the room was deserted. There stood a large, broad-bottomed elbow-chair at a table, on which was an empty tumbler, and a *Times*, newspaper, and the room smelt powerfully of Stilton cheese.

The mysterious stranger had evidently but just retired. I turned off, sorely disappointed, to my room, which had been changed to the front of the house. As I went along the corridor, I saw a large pair of boots, with dirty, waxed tops, standing at the door of a bed-chamber. They doubtless belonged to the unknown; but it would not do to disturb so redoubtable a personage in his den: he might discharge a pistol, or something worse, at my head. I went to bed, therefore, and lay awake half the night in a terribly nervous state; and even when I fell asleep, I was still haunted in my dreams by the idea of the stout gentleman and his wax-topped boots.

I slept rather late the next morning, and was awakened by some stir and bustle in the house, which I could not at first comprehend; until getting more awake, I found there was a mail-coach starting from the door. Suddenly there was a cry from below: "The gentleman has forgot his umbrella! Look for the gentleman's umbrella in No. 13!" I heard an immediate scampering of a chamber-maid along the passage, and a shrill reply as she ran. "Here it is! here's the gentleman's um-brella!"

The mysterious stranger then was on the point of setting off. This was the only chance I should ever have of knowing him. I sprang out of bed, scrambled to the window, snatched aside the curtains, and just caught a glimpse of the rear of a person getting in at the coach-door. The skirts of a brown coat parted behind, and gave me a full view of the broad disk of a pair of drab breeches. The door closed—"All right!" was the word—the coach whirled off;—and that was all I ever saw of the stout gentleman!

From *Bracebridge Hall*

THE STUDENT OF SALAMANCA

What a life doe I lead with my master; nothing but blowing of bellowes, beating of spirits, and scraping of croslets! It is a very secret science, for none almost can understand the language of it; sublimation, almigation, calcination, rubification, albification, and fermentation; with as many termes unpossible to be uttered as the arte to be compassed.—Lilly's *Gallathea.*

YESTERDAY the fair Julia made her first appearance down-stairs since her accident; and the sight of her spread a universal cheerfulness through the household. She was extremely pale, however, and could not walk without pain and difficulty. She was assisted, therefore, to a sofa in the library, which is pleasant and retired, looking out among trees, and so quiet that the little birds come hopping upon the windows, and peering curiously into the apartment. Here several of the family gathered round, and devised means to amuse her, and make the day pass pleasantly. Lady Lillycraft lamented the want of some new novel to while away the time; and was almost in a pet, because the author of *Waverley* had not produced a work for the last three months.

There was a motion made to call on the parson for some of his old legends or ghost-stories; but to this Lady Lillycraft objected, as they were apt to give her the vapors. General Harbottle gave a minute account, for the sixth time, of the disaster of a friend in India, who had his leg bitten off by a tiger whilst he was hunting,—and was proceeding to menace the company with a chapter or two about Tippoo Saib.

At length the captain bethought himself, and said he believed he had a manuscript tale lying in one corner of his campaigning trunk, which, if he could find, and the company were desirous, he would read to them. The offer was eagerly accepted. He retired, and soon returned with a roll of blotted manuscript, in a very gentlemanlike, but nearly illegible hand, and a great part written on cartridge paper.

"It is one of the scribblings," said he, "of my poor friend, Charles Lightly, of the dragoons. He was a curious, romantic, studious, fanciful fellow; the favorite, and often the unconscious butt of his fellow-

---

This tale is drawn from two chapters of *Bracebridge Hall,* the first a brief introductory one titled "The Library."—C.N.

officers, who entertained themselves with his eccentricities. He was in
some of the hardest service in the peninsula, and distinguished himself
by his gallantry. When the intervals of duty permitted, he was fond of
roving about the country, visiting noted places, and was extremely fond
of Moorish ruins. When at his quarters, he was a great scribbler, and
passed much of his leisure with his pen in his hand.

"As I was a much younger officer, and a very young man, he took
me, in a manner, under his care, and we became close friends. He used
often to read his writings to me, having a great confidence in my taste,
for I always praised them. Poor fellow! he was shot down close by me at
Waterloo. We lay wounded together for some time during a hard contest that took place near at hand. As I was least hurt, I tried to relieve
him, and to stanch the blood which flowed from a wound in his breast.
He lay with his head in my lap, and looked up thankfully in my face,
but shook his head faintly, and made a sign that it was all over with
him; and, indeed, he died a few minutes afterwards, just as our men
had repulsed the enemy, and came to our relief. I have his favorite dog
and his pistols to this day, and several of his manuscripts, which he gave
to me at different times. The one I am now going to read is a tale which
he said he wrote in Spain, during the time that he lay ill of a wound
received at Salamanca."

We now arranged ourselves to hear the story. The captain seated
himself on the sofa, beside the fair Julia, who I had noticed to be somewhat affected by the picture he had carelessly drawn of wounds and
dangers in a field of battle. She now leaned her arm fondly on his
shoulder, and her eye glistened as it rested on the manuscript of the
poor literary dragoon. Lady Lillycraft buried herself in a deep, well-
cushioned elbow-chair. Her dogs were nestled on soft mats at her feet,
and the gallant general took his station in an armchair at her side, and
toyed with her elegantly ornamented work-bag. The rest of the circle
being all equally well accommodated, the captain began his story, a
copy of which I have procured for the benefit of the reader.

ONCE upon a time, in the ancient city of Grenada, there sojourned a
young man of the name of Antonio de Castros. He wore the garb of a
student of Salamanca, and was pursuing a course of reading in the library of the university; and, at intervals of leisure, indulging his curiosity by examining those remains of Moorish magnificence for which
Grenada is renowned.

Whilst occupied in his studies, he frequently noticed an old man of
singular appearance, who was likewise a visitor to the library. He was

lean and withered, though apparently more from study than from age. His eyes, though bright and visionary, were sunk in his head, and thrown into shade by overhanging eyebrows. His dress was always the same,—a black doublet, a short black coat, very rusty and threadbare, a small ruff, and a large overshadowing hat.

His appetite for knowledge seemed insatiable. He would pass whole days in the library, absorbed in study, consulting a multiplicity of authors, as though he were pursuing some interesting subject through all its ramifications; so that, when evening came, he was almost buried among books and manuscripts.

The curiosity of Antonio was excited, and he inquired of the attendants concerning the stranger. No one could give him any information, excepting that he had been for some time past a casual frequenter of the library; that his reading lay chiefly among works treating of the occult sciences, and that he was particularly curious in his inquiries after Arabian manuscripts. They added, that he never held communication with any one, excepting to ask for particular works; that, after a fit of studious application, he would disappear for several days, and even weeks, and when he revisited the library, he would look more withered and haggard than ever. The student felt interested by this account; he was leading rather a desultory life, and had all that capricious curiosity which springs up in idleness. He determined to make himself acquainted with this bookworm, and find out who and what he was.

The next time that he saw the old man at the library, he commenced his approaches by requesting permission to look into one of the volumes with which the unknown appeared to have done. The latter merely bowed his head in token of assent. After pretending to look through the volume with great attention, he returned it with many acknowledgments. The stranger made no reply.

"May I ask, señor," said Antonio, with some hesitation, "may I ask what you are searching after in all these books?"

The old man raised his head, with an expression of surprise at having his studies interrupted for the first time, and by so intrusive a question. He surveyed the student with a side-glance from head to foot: "Wisdom, my son," said he, calmly, "and the search requires every moment of my attention." He then cast his eyes upon his book and resumed his studies.

"But, father," said Antonio, "cannot you spare a moment to point out the road to others? It is to experienced travellers, like you, that we strangers in the path of knowledge must look for directions on our journey."

The stranger looked disturbed. "I have not time enough, my son, to

learn," said he, "much less to teach. I am ignorant myself of the path of true knowledge; how then can I show it to others?"

"Well, but father——"

"Señor," said the old man, mildly, but earnestly, "you must see that I have but a few more steps to the grave. In that short space have I to accomplish the whole business of my existence. I have no time for words; every word is as one grain of sand of my glass wasted. Suffer me to be alone."

There was no replying to so complete a closing of the door of intimacy. The student found himself calmly but totally repulsed. Though curious and inquisitive, he was naturally modest, and on after-thoughts blushed at his own intrusion. His mind soon became occupied by other objects. He passed several days wandering among the mouldering piles of Moorish architecture, those melancholy monuments of an elegant and voluptuous people. He paced the deserted halls of the Alhambra, the paradise of the Moorish kings. He visited the great court of the lions, famous for the perfidious massacre of the gallant Abencerrages. He gazed with admiration at its Mosaic cupolas, gorgeously painted in gold and azure; its basins of marble, its alabaster vase, supported by lions, and storied with inscriptions.

His imagination kindled as he wandered among these scenes. They were calculated to awaken all the enthusiasm of a youthful mind. Most of the halls have anciently been beautified by fountains. The fine taste of the Arabs delighted in the sparkling purity and reviving freshness of water, and they erected, as it were, altars on every side, to that delicate element. Poetry mingles with architecture in the Alhambra. It breathes along the very walls. Wherever Antonio turned his eye, he beheld inscriptions in Arabic, wherein the perpetuity of Moorish power and splendor within these walls was confidently predicted. Alas! how has the prophecy been falsified! Many of the basins, where the fountains had once thrown up their sparkling showers, were dry and dusty. Some of the palaces were turned into gloomy convents, and the barefoot monk paced through those courts which had once glittered with the array and echoed to the music of Moorish chivalry.

In the course of his rambles, the student more than once encountered the old man of the library. He was always alone, and so full of thought as not to notice any one about him. He appeared to be intent upon studying those half-buried inscriptions, which are found, here and there, among the Moorish ruins, and seem to murmur from the earth the tale of former greatness. The greater part of these have since been translated; but they were supposed by many, at the time, to contain symbolical revelations, and golden maxims of the Arabian sages and as-

trologers. As Antonio saw the stranger apparently deciphering these inscriptions, he felt an eager longing to make his acquaintance, and to participate in his curious researches; but the repulse he had met with at the library deterred him from making any further advances.

He had directed his steps one evening to the sacred mount which overlooks the beautiful valley watered by the Darro, the fertile plains of the Vega, and all that rich diversity of vale and mountain which surrounds Grenada with an earthly paradise. It was twilight when he found himself at the place where, at the present day, are situated the chapels known by the name of the Sacred Furnaces. They are so called from grottos, in which some of the primitive saints are said to have been burnt. At the time of Antonio's visit the place was an object of much curiosity. In an excavation of these grottos, several manuscripts had recently been discovered, engraved on plates of lead. They were written in the Arabian language, excepting one, which was in unknown characters. The Pope had issued a bull forbidding any one, under pain of excommunication, to speak of these manuscripts. The prohibition had only excited the greater curiosity; and many reports were whispered about, that these manuscripts contained treasures of dark and forbidden knowledge.

As Antonio was examining the place whence these mysterious manuscripts had been drawn, he again observed the old man of the library wandering among the ruins. His curiosity was now fully awakened; the time and place served to stimulate it. He resolved to watch this groper after secret and forgotten lore, and to trace him to his habitation. There was something like adventure in the thing, which charmed his romantic disposition. He followed the stranger, therefore, at a little distance; at first cautiously, but he soon observed him to be so wrapped in his own thoughts, as to take little heed of external objects.

They passed along the skirts of the mountain, and then by the shady banks of the Darro. They pursued their way, for some distance from Grenada, along a lonely road leading among the hills. The gloom of evening was gathering, and it was quite dark when the stranger stopped at the portal of a solitary mansion.

It appeared to be a mere wing, or ruined fragment, of what had once been a pile of some consequence. The walls were of great thickness, the windows narrow, and generally secured by iron bars. The door was of planks, studded with iron spikes, and had been of great strength, though at present much decayed. At one end of the mansion was a ruinous tower, in the Moorish style of architecture. The edifice had probably been a country retreat, or castle of pleasure, during the occupation

of Grenada by the Moors, and rendered sufficiently strong to withstand any casual assault in those warlike times.

The old man knocked at the portal. A light appeared at a small window just above it, and a female head looked out: it might have served as a model for one of Raphael's saints. The hair was beautifully braided, and gathered in a silken net; and the complexion, as well as could be judged from the light, was that soft, rich brunette so becoming in southern beauty.

"It is I, my child," said the old man. The face instantly disappeared, and soon after a wicket-door in the large portal opened. Antonio, who had ventured near to the building, caught a transient sight of a delicate female form. A pair of fine black eyes darted a look of surprise at seeing a stranger hovering near, and the door was precipitately closed.

There was something in this sudden gleam of beauty that wonderfully struck the imagination of the student. It was like a brilliant flashing from its dark casket. He sauntered about, regarding the gloomy pile with increasing interest. A few simple, wild notes, from among some rocks and trees at a little distance, attracted his attention. He found there a group of Gitanas, a vagabond gypsy race, which at that time abounded in Spain, and lived in hovels and caves of the hills about the neighborhood of Grenada. Some were busy about a fire, and others were listening to the uncouth music which one of their companions, seated on a ledge of the rock, was making with a split reed.

Antonio endeavored to obtain some information of them concerning the old building and its inhabitants. The one who appeared to be their spokesman was a gaunt fellow, with a subtle gait, a whispering voice, and a sinister roll of the eye. He shrugged his shoulders on the student's inquiries, and said: "All was not right in that building. An old man inhabited it, whom nobody knew, and whose family appeared to be only a daughter and a female servant. I and my companions," he added, "live up among the neighboring hills; and as we have been about at night, we have often seen strange lights and heard strange sounds from the tower. Some of the country people, who work in the vineyards among the hills, believe the old man deals in the black art, and they are not over-fond of passing rear the tower at night. But for our parts, we Gitanas are not a people to trouble ourselves with fears of that kind."

The student endeavored to gain more precise information, but they had none to furnish him. They began to be solicitous for a compensation for what they had already imparted; and recollecting the loneliness of the place, and the vagabond character of his companions, he was glad to give them a gratuity and hasten homewards.

He sat down to his studies, but his brain was too full of what he had seen and heard; his eye was upon the page, but his fancy still returned to the tower, and he was continually picturing the little window, with the beautiful head peeping out; or the door half open, and the nymph-like form within. He retired to bed, but the same objects haunted his dreams. He was young and susceptible; and the excited state of his feelings, from wandering among the abodes of departed grace and gallantry, had predisposed him for a sudden impression from female beauty.

The next morning he strolled again in the direction of the tower. It was still more forlorn by the broad glare of day than in the gloom of evening. The walls were crumbling, and weeds and moss were growing in every crevice. It had the look of a prison rather than a dwelling-house. In one angle, however, he remarked a window which seemed an exception to the surrounding squalidness. There was a curtain drawn within it, and flowers standing on the window-stone. Whilst he was looking at it, the curtain was partially withdrawn, and a delicate white arm, of the most beautiful roundness, was put forth to water the flowers.

The student made a noise to attract the attention of the fair florist. He succeeded. The curtain was further drawn, and he had a glance of the same lovely face he had seen the evening before. It was but a mere glance; the curtain again fell, and the casement closed. All this was calculated to excite the feelings of a romantic youth. Had he seen the unknown under other circumstances, it is probable he would not have been struck with her beauty; but this appearance of being shut up and kept apart gave her the value of a treasured gem. He passed and re-passed before the house several times in the course of the day, but saw nothing more. He was there again in the evening. The whole aspect of the house was dreary. The narrow windows emitted no rays of cheerful light, to indicate social life within. Antonio listened at the portal, but no sound of voices reached his ear. Just then he heard the clapping to of a distant door, and fearing to be detected in the unworthy act of eavesdropping, he precipitately drew off to the opposite side of the road, and stood in the shadow of a ruined archway.

He now remarked a light from a window in the tower. It was fitful and changeable; commonly feeble and yellowish, as if from a lamp; with an occasional glare of some vivid metallic color, followed by a dusky glow. A column of dense smoke would now and then rise in the air, and hang like a canopy over the tower. There was altogether such a loneliness and seeming mystery about the building and its inhabitants, that Antonio was half inclined to indulge the country people's notions,

and to fancy it the den of some powerful sorcerer, and the fair damsel he had seen to be some spellbound beauty.

After some time had elapsed, a light appeared in the window where he had seen the beautiful arm. The curtain was down, but it was so thin that he could perceive the shadow of some one passing and repassing between it and the light. He fancied he could distinguish that the form was delicate; and from the alacrity of its movements, it was evidently youthful. He had not a doubt but this was the bedchamber of his beautiful unknown.

Presently he heard the sound of a guitar, and a female voice singing. He drew near cautiously, and listened. It was a plaintive Moorish ballad, and he recognized in it the lamentations of one of the Abencerrages on leaving the walls of lovely Grenada. It was full of passion and tenderness. It spoke of the delights of early life; the hours of love it had enjoyed on the banks of the Darro, and among the blissful abodes of the Alhambra. It bewailed the fallen honors of the Abencerrages, and imprecated vengeance on their oppressors. Antonio was affected by the music. It singularly coincided with the place. It was like the voice of past times echoed in the present, and breathing among the monuments of its departed glories.

The voice ceased; after a time the light disappeared, and all was still. "She sleeps!" said Antonio, fondly. He lingered about the building with the devotion with which a lover lingers about the bower of sleeping beauty. The rising moon threw its silver beams on the gray walls, and glittered on the casement. The late gloomy landscape gradually became flooded with its radiance. Finding, therefore, that he could no longer move about in obscurity, and fearful that his loiterings might be observed, he reluctantly retired.

The curiosity which had at first drawn the young man to the tower was now seconded by feelings of a more romantic kind. His studies were almost entirely abandoned. He maintained a kind of blockade of the old mansion; he would take a book with him, and pass a great part of the day under the trees in its vicinity; keeping a vigilant eye upon it, and endeavoring to ascertain what were the walks of his mysterious charmer. She never went out, however, except to mass, when she was accompanied by her father. He waited at the door of the church, and offered her the holy water, in the hopes of touching her hand—a little office of gallantry common in Catholic countries. She modestly declined, without raising her eyes to see who made the offer, and always took it herself from the font. She was attentive in her devotion; her eyes were never taken from the altar or the priest; and on returning home, her countenance was almost entirely concealed by her mantilla.

Antonio had now carried on the pursuit for several days, and was hourly getting more and more interested in the chase, but never a step nearer to the game. His lurkings about the house had probably been noticed, for he no longer saw the fair face at the widow, nor the white arm put forth to water the flowers. His only consolation was to repair nightly to his post of observation and listen to her warbling; and if by chance he could catch a sight of her shadow, passing and repassing before the window, he thought himself most fortunate.

As he was indulging in one of these evening vigils, which were complete revels of the imagination, the sound of approaching footsteps made him withdraw into the deep shadow of the ruined archway, opposite to the tower. A cavalier approached, wrapped in a large Spanish cloak. He paused under the window of the tower, and after a little while began a serenade, accompanied by his guitar, in the usual style of Spanish gallantry. His voice was rich and manly; he touched the instrument with skill, and sang with amorous and impassioned eloquence. The plume of his hat was buckled by jewels that sparkled in the moonbeams; and, as he played on the guitar, his cloak falling off from one shoulder showed him to be richly dressed. He was evidently a person of rank.

The idea now flashed across Antonio's mind, that the affections of his unknown beauty might be engaged. She was young, and doubtless susceptible; and it was not in the nature of Spanish females to be deaf and insensible to music and admiration. The surmise brought with it a feeling of dreariness. There was a pleasant dream of several days suddenly dispelled. He had never before experienced anything of the tender passion; and, as its morning dreams are always delightful, he would fain have continued in the delusion.

"But what have I to do with her attachments?" thought he; "I have no claim on her heart, nor even on her acquaintance. How do I know that she is worthy of affection? Or if she is, must not so gallant a lover as this, with his jewels, his rank, and his detestible music, have completely captivated her? What idle humor is this that I have fallen into? I must again to my books. Study, study will soon chase away all these idle fancies!"

The more he thought, however, the more he became entangled in the spell which his lively imagination had woven round him; and now that a rival had appeared, in addition to the other obstacles that environed this enchanted beauty, she appeared ten times more lovely and desirable. It was some slight consolation to him to perceive that the gallantry of the unknown met with no apparent return from the tower. The light at the window was extinguished. The curtain remained un-

drawn, and none of the customary signals were given to intimate that the serenade was accepted.

The cavalier lingered for some time about the place and sang several other tender airs with a taste and feeling that made Antonio's heart ache; at length he slowly retired. The student remained with folded arms, leaning against the ruined arch, endeavoring to summon up resolution to depart; but a romantic fascination still enchained him to the place. "It is the last time," said he, willing to compromise between his feelings and his judgment, "it is the last time; then let me enjoy the dream a few moments longer."

As his eye ranged about the old building to take a farewell look, he observed the strange light in the tower, which he had noticed on a former occasion. It kept beaming up, and declining, as before. A pillar of smoke rose in the air, and hung in sable volumes. It was evident the old man was busied in some of those operations which had gained him the reputation of a sorcerer throughout the neighborhood.

Suddenly an intense and brilliant glare shone through the casement, followed by a loud report, and then a fierce and ruddy glow. A figure appeared at the window, uttering cries of agony or alarm, but immediately disappeared, and a body of smoke and flame whirled out of the narrow aperture. Antonio rushed to the portal, and knocked at it with vehemence. He was only answered by loud shrieks, and found that the females were already in helpless consternation. With an exertion of desperate strength, he forced the wicket from its hinges, and rushed into the house.

He found himself in a small vaulted hall, and by the light of the moon which entered at the door, he saw a staircase to the left. He hurried up it to a narrow corridor, through which was rolling a volume of smoke. He found here the two females in a frantic state of alarm; one of them clasped her hands, and implored him to save her father.

The corridor terminated in a spiral flight of steps, leading up to the tower. He sprang up it to a small door, through the chinks of which came a glow of light, and smoke was spuming out. He burst it open, and found himself in an antique vaulted chamber, furnished with furnace, and various chemical apparatus. A shattered retort lay on the stone floor; a quantity of combustibles, nearly consumed, with various half-burnt books and papers, were sending up an expiring flame, and filling the chamber with stifling smoke. Just within the threshold lay the reputed conjurer. He was bleeding, his clothes were scorched, and he appeared lifeless. Antonio caught him up, and bore him down the stairs to a chamber in which there was a light, and laid him on a bed. The female domestic was dispatched for such appliances as the house

afforded; but the daughter threw herself frantically beside her parent, and could not be reasoned out of her alarm. Her dress was all in disorder; her dishevelled hair hung in rich confusion about her neck and bosom, and never was there beheld a lovelier picture of terror and affliction.

The skilful assiduities of the scholar soon produced signs of returning animation in his patient. The old man's wounds, though severe, were not dangerous. They had evidently been produced by the bursting of the retort; in his bewilderment he had been enveloped in the stifling metallic vapors which had overpowered his feeble frame, and had not Antonio arrived to his assistance, it is possible he might never have recovered.

By slow degrees he came to his senses. He looked about with a bewildered air at the chamber, the agitated group around, and the student who was leaning over him.

"Where am I?" said he, wildly.

At the sound of his voice his daughter uttered a faint exclamation of delight. "My poor Inez!" said he, embracing her; then putting his hand to his head, and taking it away stained with blood, he seemed suddenly to recollect himself, and to be overcome with emotion.

"Ah!" cried he, "all is over with me! all gone! all vanished! gone in a moment! the labor of a lifetime lost!"

His daughter attempted to soothe him, but he became slightly delirious, and raved incoherently about malignant demons, and about the habitation of the green lion being destroyed. His wounds being dressed, and such other remedies administered as his situation required, he sank into a state of quiet. Antonio now turned his attention to the daughter, whose sufferings had been little inferior to those of her father. Having with great difficulty succeeded in tranquillizing her fears, he endeavored to prevail upon her to retire, and seek the repose so necessary to her frame, proffering to remain by her father until morning. "I am a stranger," said he, "it is true, and my offer may appear intrusive; but I see you are lonely and helpless, and I cannot help venturing over the limits of mere ceremony. Should you feel any scruple or doubt, however, say but a word, and I will instantly retire."

There was a frankness, a kindness, and a modesty mingled in Antonio's deportment, which inspired instant confidence; and his simple scholar's garb was a recommendation in the house of poverty. The females consented to resign the sufferer to his care, as they would be the better able to attend to him on the morrow. On retiring, the old domestic was profuse in her benedictions; the daughter only looked her

thanks; but as they shone through the tears that filled her fine black eyes, the student thought them a thousand times the most eloquent.

Here, then, he was, by a singular turn of chance, completely housed within this mysterious mansion. When left to himself, and the bustle of the scene was over, his heart throbbed as he looked round the chamber in which he was sitting. It was the daughter's room, the promised land toward which he had cast so many a longing gaze. The furniture was old, and had probably belonged to the building in its prosperous days; but everything was arranged with propriety. The flowers which he had seen her attend stood in the window; a guitar leaned against a table, on which stood a crucifix, and before it lay a missal and a rosary. There reigned an air of purity and serenity about this little nestling-place of innocence; it was the emblem of a chaste and quiet mind. Some few articles of female dress lay on the chairs; and there was the very bed on which she had slept; the pillow on which her soft cheek had reclined! The poor scholar was threading enchanted ground; for what fairy land has more magic in it than the bedchamber of innocence and beauty?

From various expressions of the old man in his ravings, and from what he had noticed on a subsequent visit to the tower, to see that the fire was extinguished, Antonio had gathered that his patient was an alchemist. The philosopher's stone was an object eagerly sought after by visionaries in those days; but in consequence of the superstitious prejudices of the times, and the frequent persecutions of its votaries, they were apt to pursue their experiments in secret, in lonely houses, in caverns and ruins, or in the privacy of cloistered cells.

In the course of the night the old man had several fits of restlessness and delirium; he would call out upon Theophrastus, and Geber, and Albertus Magnus, and other sages of his art; and anon would murmur about fermentation and projection, until, toward daylight, he once more sunk into a salutary sleep. When the morning sun darted his rays into the casement, the fair Inez, attended by the female domestic, came blushing into the chamber. The student now took his leave, having himself need of repose, but obtained ready permission to return and inquire after the sufferer.

When he called again, he found the alchemist languid and in pain, but apparently suffering more in mind than in body. His delirium had left him, and he had been informed of the particulars of his deliverance and of the subsequent attentions of the scholar. He could do little more than look his thanks, but Antonio did not require them; his own heart repaid him for all that he had done, and he almost rejoiced in the disaster that had gained him an entrance into this mysterious habita-

tion. The alchemist was so helpless as to need much assistance; Antonio remained with him, therefore, the greater part of the day. He repeated his visit the next day, and the next. Every day his company seemed more pleasing to the invalid; and every day he felt his interest in the latter increasing. Perhaps the presence of the daughter might have been at the bottom of this solicitude.

He had frequent and long conversations with the alchemist. He found him, as men of his pursuits were apt to be, a mixture of enthusiasm and simplicity; of curious and extensive reading on points of little utility, with great inattention to the every-day occurrences of life, and profound ignorance of the world. He was deeply versed in singular and obscure branches of knowledge, and much given to visionary speculations. Antonio, whose mind was of a romantic cast, had himself given some attention to the occult sciences, and he entered upon these themes with an ardor that delighted the philosopher. Their conversations frequently turned upon astrology, divination, and the great secret. The old man would forget his aches and wounds, rise up like a spectre in his bed, and kindle into eloquence on his favorite topics. When gently admonished of his situation, it would but prompt him to another sally of thought.

"Alas, my son!" he would say, "is not this very decrepitude and suffering another proof of the importance of those secrets with which we are surrounded? Why are we trammelled by disease, withered by old age, and our spirits quenched, as it were, within us, but because we have lost those secrets of life and youth which were known to our parents before their fall? To regain these have philosophers been ever since aspiring; but just as they are on the point of securing the precious secrets forever, their brief period of life is at an end. They die, and with them all their wisdom and experience. 'Nothing,' as De Nuysment observes,—'nothing is wanting for man's perfection but a longer life, less crossed with sorrows and maladies, to the attaining of the full and perfect knowledge of things.'"

At length Antonio so far gained on the heart of his patient as to draw from him the outlines of his story.

Felix de Vasques, the alchemist, was a native of Castile, and of an ancient and honorable line. Early in life he had married a beautiful female, a descendant from one of the Moorish families. The marriage displeased his father, who considered the pure Spanish blood contaminated by this foreign mixture. It is true, the lady traced her descent from one of the Abencerrages, the most gallant of Moorish cavaliers, who had embraced the Christian faith on being exiled from the walls of Grenada. The injured pride of the father, however, was not to be ap-

peased. He never saw his son afterwards, and on dying left him but a scanty portion of his estate; bequeathing the residue, in the piety and bitterness of his heart, to the erection of convents, and the performance of masses for souls in purgatory. Don Felix resided for a long time in the neighborhood of Valladolid, in a state of embarrassment and obscurity. He devoted himself to intense study, having, while at the university of Salamanca, imbibed a taste for the secret sciences. He was enthusiastic and speculative; he went on from one branch of knowledge to another, until he became zealous in the search after the grand Arcanum.

He had at first engaged in the pursuit with the hopes of raising himself from his present obscurity, and resuming the rank and dignity to which his birth entitled him; but, as usual, it ended in absorbing every thought, and becoming the business of his existence. He was at length aroused from this mental abstraction by the calamities of his household. A malignant fever swept off his wife and all his children, excepting an infant daughter. These losses for a time overwhelmed and stupefied him. His home had in a manner died away from around him, and he felt lonely and forlorn. When his spirit revived within him, he determined to abandon the scene of his humiliation and disaster; to bear away the child that was still left him, beyond the scene of contagion, and never to return to Castile until he should be enabled to reclaim the honors of his line.

He had ever since been wandering and unsettled in his abode. Sometimes the resident of populous cities, at other times of absolute solitudes. He had searched libraries, meditated on inscriptions, visited adepts of different countries, and sought to gather and concentrate the rays which had been thrown by various minds upon the secrets of alchemy. He had at one time travelled quite to Padua to search for the manuscripts of Pietro d'Abano, and to inspect an urn which had been dug up near Este, supposed to have been buried by Maximus Olybius, and to have contained the grand elixir.*

---

* This urn was found in 1533. It contained a lesser one, in which was a burning lamp between two small vials, the one of gold, the other of silver, both of them full of a very clear liquor. On the largest was an inscription stating that Maximus Olybius shut up in this small vessel elements which he had prepared with great toil. There were many disquisitions among the learned on the subject. It was the most received opinion that this Maximus Olybius was an inhabitant of Padua; that he had discovered the great secret, and that these vessels contained liquor, one to transmute metals to gold, the other to silver. The peasants who found the urns, imagining this precious liquor to be common water, spilt every drop, so that the art of transmuting metals remains as much a secret as ever.

While at Padua he met with an adept versed in Arabian lore, who talked of the invaluable manuscripts that must remain in the Spanish libraries, preserved from the spoils of the Moorish academies and universities; of the probability of meeting with precious unpublished writings of Geber, and Alfarabius, and Avicenna the great physicians of the Arabian schools, who, it was well known, had treated much of alchemy; but, above all, he spoke of the Arabian tablets of lead, which had recently been dug up in the neighborhood of Grenada, and which, it was confidently believed among adepts, contained the lost secrets of the art.

The indefatigable alchemist once more bent his steps for Spain, full of renovated hope. He had made his way to Grenada; he had wearied himself in the study of Arabic, in deciphering inscriptions, in rummaging libraries, and exploring every possible trace left by the Arabian sages.

In all his wanderings he had been accompanied by Inez; through the rough and the smooth, the pleasant and the adverse; never complaining, but rather seeking to soothe his cares by her innocent and playful caresses. Her instruction had been the employment and the delight of his hours of relaxation. She had grown up while they were wandering, and had scarcely ever known any home but by his side. He was family, friends, home, everything to her. He had carried her in his arms when they first began their wayfaring; had nestled her, as an eagle does its young, among the rocky heights of the Sierra Morena; she had sported about him in childhood in the solitudes of the Bateucas; had followed him, as the lamb does the shepherd, over the rugged Pyrenees, and into the fair plains of Languedoc; and now she was grown up to support his feeble footsteps among the ruined abodes of her maternal ancestors.

His property had gradually wasted away in the course of his travels and his experiments. Still hope, the constant attendant of the alchemist, had led him on; ever on the point of reaping the reward of his labors, and ever disappointed. With the credulity that often attended his art, he attributed many of his disappointments to the machinations of the malignant spirits which beset the path of the alchemist, and torment him in his solitary labors. "It is their constant endeavor," he observed, "to close up every avenue to those sublime truths which would enable man to rise above the abject state into which he has fallen, and to return to his original perfection." To the evil offices of these demons he attributed his late disaster. He had been on the very verge of the glorious discovery; never were the indications more completely auspicious; all was going on prosperously, when, at the critical moment

which should have crowned his labors with success, and have placed him at the very summit of human power and felicity, the bursting of a retort had reduced his laboratory and himself to ruins.

"I must now," said he, "give up at the very threshold of success. My books and papers are burnt; my apparatus is broken. I am too old to bear up against these evils. The ardor that once inspired me is gone; my poor frame is exhausted by study and watchfulness, and this last misfortune has hurried me towards the grave." He concluded in a tone of deep dejection. Antonio endeavored to comfort and reassure him; but the poor alchemist had for once awakened to a consciousness of the worldly ills gathering around him, and had sunk into dispondency. After a pause, and some thoughtfulness and perplexity of brow, Antonio ventured to make a proposal.

"I have long," said he, "been filled with a love for the secret sciences, but have felt too ignorant and diffident to give myself up to them. You have acquired experience; you have amassed the knowledge of a lifetime; it were a pity it should be thrown away. You say you are too old to renew the toils of the laboratory; suffer me to undertake them. Add your knowledge to my youth and activity, and what shall we not accomplish? As a probationary fee, and a fund on which to proceed, I will bring into the common stock a sum of gold, the residue of a legacy, which has enabled me to complete my education. A poor scholar cannot boast much; but I trust we shall soon put ourselves beyond the reach of want; and if we should fail, why, I must depend, like other scholars, upon my brains to carry me through the world."

The philosopher's spirits, however, were more depressed than the student had imagined. This last shock, following in the rear of so many disappointments, had almost destroyed the reaction of his mind. The fire of an enthusiast, however, is never so low, but that it may be blown again into a flame. By degrees the old man was cheered and reanimated by the buoyancy and ardor of his sanguine companion. He at length agreed to accept of the services of the student, and once more to renew his experiments. He objected, however, to using the student's gold, notwithstanding his own was nearly exhausted; but this objection was soon overcome; the student insisted on making it a common stock and common cause;—and then how absurd was any delicacy about such a trifle, with men who looked forward to discovering the philosopher's stone?

While, therefore, the alchemist was slowly recovering, the student busied himself in getting the laboratory once more in order. It was strewed with the wrecks of retorts and alembics, with old crucibles,

boxes and phials of powders and tinctures, and half-burnt books and manuscripts.

As soon as the old man was sufficiently recovered, the studies and experiments were renewed. The student became a privileged and frequent visitor, and was indefatigable in his toils in the laboratory. The philosopher daily derived new zeal and spirits from the animation of his disciple. He was now enabled to prosecute the enterprise with continued exertion, having so active a coadjutor to divide the toil. While he was pouring over the writings of Sandivogius, and Philalethes, and Dominus de Nuysment, and endeavoring to comprehend the symbolical language in which they have locked up their mysteries, Antonio would occupy himself among the retorts and crucibles, and keep the furnace in a perpetual glow.

With all his zeal, however, for the discovery of the golden art, the feelings of the student had not cooled as to the object that first drew him to this ruinous mansion. During the old man's illness, he had frequent opportunities of being near the daughter; and every day made him more sensible to her charms. There was a pure simplicity, and an almost passive gentleness in her manners; yet with all this was mingled something, whether mere maiden shyness, or a consciousness of high descent, or a dash of Castilian pride, or perhaps all united, that prevented undue familiarity, and made her difficult of approach. The danger of her father, and the measures to be taken for his relief, had at first overcome this coyness and reserve; but as he recovered and her alarm subsided, she seemed to shrink from the familiarity she had indulged with the youthful stranger, and to become every day more shy and silent.

Antonio had read many books, but this was the first volume of womankind that he had ever studied. He had been captivated with the very title-page; but the further he read the more he was delighted. She seemed formed to love; her soft black eye rolled languidly under its long silken lashes, and wherever it turned, it would linger and repose; there was tenderness in every beam. To him alone she was reserved and distant. Now that the common cares of the sick-room were at an end, he saw little more of her than before his admission to the house. Sometimes he met her on his way to and from the laboratory and at such times there was ever a smile and a blush; but, after a simple salutation, she glided on and disappeared.

" 'Tis plain," thought Antonio, "my presence is indifferent, if not irksome to her. She has noticed my admiration, and is determined to discourage it; nothing but a feeling of gratitude prevents her treating me with marked distaste;—and then has she not another lover, rich, gallant,

splendid, musical? how can I suppose she would turn her eyes from so brilliant a cavalier to a poor obscure student, raking among the cinders of her father's laboratory?"

Indeed, the idea of the amorous serenader continually haunted his mind. He felt convinced that he was a favored lover; yet, if so, why did he not frequent the tower? Why did he not make his approaches by noonday? There was mystery in this eavesdropping and musical court-ship. Surely Inez could not be encouraging a secret intrigue! Oh, no! she was too artless, too pure, too ingenuous! But then the Spanish fe-males were so prone to love and intrigue; and music and moonlight were so seductive, and Inez had such a tender soul languishing in every look. "Oh!" would the poor scholar exclaim, clasping his hands,—"oh, that I could but once behold those loving eyes beaming on me with af-fection!"

It is incredible to those who have not experienced it, on what scanty aliment human life and human love may be supported. A dry crust, thrown now and then to a starving man, will give him a new lease of existence; and a faint smile, or a kind look, bestowed at casual intervals, will keep a lover loving on, when a man in his sober senses would de-spair.

When Antonio found himself alone in the laboratory, his mind would be haunted by one of these looks, or smiles, which he had re-ceived in passing. He would set it in every possible light, and argue on it with all the self-pleasing, self-teasing logic of a lover.

The country around was enough to awaken that voluptuousness of feeling so favorable to the growth of passion. The windows of the tower rose above the trees of the romantic valley of the Darro, and looked down upon some of the loveliest scenery of the Vega, where groves of citron and orange were refreshed by cool springs and brooks of the purest water. The Xenel and the Darro wound their shining streams along the plain, and gleamed from among its bowers. The sur-rounding hills were covered with vineyards, and the mountains, crowned with snow, seemed to melt into the blue sky. The delicate airs that played about the tower were perfumed by the fragrance of myrtle and orange blossoms, and the ear was charmed with the fond warbling of the nightingale, which, in these happy regions, sings the whole day long. Sometimes, too, there was the idle song of the muleteer, saunter-ing along the solitary road, or the notes of the guitar from some group of peasants dancing in the shade. All these were enough to fill the head of a young lover with poetic fancies; and Antonio would picture to him-self how he could loiter among those happy groves, and wander by those gentle rivers, and love away his life with Inez.

He felt at times impatient at his own weakness, and would endeavor to brush away these cobwebs of the mind. He would turn his thought, with sudden effort, to his occult studies, or occupy himself in some perplexing process; but often, when he had partially succeeded in fixing his attention, the sound of Inez's lute, or the soft notes of her voice, would come stealing upon the stillness of the chamber, and, as it were, floating round the tower. There was no great art in her performance; but Antonio thought he had never heard music comparable to this. It was perfect witchcraft to hear her warble forth some of her national melodies; those little Spanish romances and Moorish ballads which transport the hearer, in idea, to the banks of the Guadalquiver, or the walls of the Alhambra, and make him dream of beauties, and balconies, and moonlight serenades.

Never was poor student more sadly beset than Antonio. Love is a troublesome companion in a study at the best of times; but in the laboratory of an alchemist his intrusion is terribly disastrous. Instead of attending to the retorts and crucibles, and watching the process of some experiment intrusted to his charge, the student would get entranced in one of these love-dreams, from which he would often be aroused by some fatal catastrophe. The philosopher, on returning from his researches in the libraries, would find everything gone wrong, and Antonio in despair over the ruins of the whole day's work. The old man, however, took all quietly, for his had been a life of experiment and failure.

"We must have patience, my son," would he say, "as all the great masters that have gone before us have had. Errors, and accidents, and delays, are what we have to contend with. Did not Pontanus err two hundred times before he could obtain even the matter on which to found his experiments? The great Flamel, too, did he not labor four-and-twenty years, before he ascertained the first agent? What difficulties and hardships did not Cartilaceus encounter, at the very threshold of his discoveries? And Bernard de Treves, even after he had attained a knowledge of all the requisites, was he not delayed full three years? What you consider accidents, my son, are the machinations of our invisible enemies. The treasures and golden secrets of nature are surrounded by spirits hostile to man. The air about us teems with them. They lurk in the fire of the furnace, in the bottom of the crucible and the alembic, and are ever on the alert to take advantage of those moments when our minds are wandering from intense meditation on the great truth that we are seeking. We must only strive the more to purify ourselves from those gross and earthly feelings which becloud the soul, and prevent her from piercing into nature's arcana."

"Alas!" thought Antonio, "if to be purified from all earthly feeling requires that I should cease to love Inez, I fear I shall never discover the philosopher's stone!"

In this way matters went on for some time at the alchemist's. Day after day was sending the student's gold in vapor up the chimney; every blast of the furnace made him a ducat the poorer, without apparently helping him a jot nearer to the golden secret. Still the young man stood by, and saw piece after piece disappearing without a murmur; he had daily an opportunity of seeing Inez, and felt as if her favor would be better than silver or gold, and that every smile was worth a ducat.

Sometimes, in the cool of the evening, when the toils of the laboratory happened to be suspended, he would walk with the alchemist in what had once been a garden belonging to the mansion. There were still the remains of terraces and balustrades, and here and there a marble urn, or mutilated statue overturned, and buried among weeds and flowers run wild.

It was the favorite resort of the alchemist in his hours of relaxation, where he would give full scope to his visionary flights. His mind was tinctured with the Rosicrucian doctrines. He believed in elementary beings; some favorable, others adverse to his pursuits; and in the exaltation of his fancy, had often imagined that he held communion with them in his solitary walks about the whispering groves and echoing walls of this old garden.

When accompanied by Antonio, he would prolong these evening recreations. Indeed, he sometimes did it out of consideration for his disciple, for he feared lest his too close application, and his incessant seclusion in the tower, should be injurious to his health. He was delighted and surprised by this extraordinary zeal and perseverance in so young a tyro, and looked upon him as destined to be one of the great luminaries of the art. Lest the student should repine at the time lost in these relaxations, the good alchemist would fill them up with wholesome knowledge, in matters connected with their pursuits; and would walk up and down the alleys with his disciple, imparting oral instruction like an ancient philosopher. In all his visionary schemes there breathed a spirit of lofty, though chimerical philanthropy, that won the admiration of the scholar. Nothing sordid nor sensual, nothing petty nor selfish seemed to enter into his views, in respect to the grand discoveries he was anticipating. On the contrary, his imagination kindled with conceptions of widely dispensated happiness. He looked forward to the time when he should be able to go about the earth relieving the indigent, comforting the distressed; and, by his unlimited means, devising and executing plans for the complete extirpation of poverty, and all its

attendant sufferings and crimes. Never were grander schemes for general good, for the distribution of boundless wealth and universal competence, devised, than by this poor, indigent alchemist in his ruined tower.

Antonio would attend these peripatetic lectures with all the ardor of a devotee; but there was another circumstance which may have given a secret charm to them. The garden was the resort also of Inez, where she took her walks of recreation, the only exercise her secluded life permitted. As Antonio was duteously pacing by the side of his instructor, he would often catch a glimpse of the daughter, walking pensively about the alleys in the soft twilight. Sometimes they would meet her unexpectedly, and the heart of the student would throb with agitation. A blush, too, would crimson the cheek of Inez, but still she passed on, and never joined them.

He had remained one evening, until rather a late hour, with the alchemist in this favorite resort. It was a delightful night after a sultry day, and the balmy air of the garden was peculiarly reviving. The old man was seated on a fragment of a pedestal, looking like a part of the ruin on which he sat. He was edifying his pupil by long lessons of wisdom from the stars, as they shone out with brilliant lustre in the dark-blue vault of a southern sky; for he was deeply versed in Behmen, and other of the Rosicrucians, and talked much of the signature of earthly things, and passing events, which may be discerned in the heavens; of the power of the stars over corporeal beings, and their influence on the fortunes of the sons of men.

By degrees the moon rose and shed her gleaming light among the groves. Antonio apparently listened with fixed attention to the sage, but his ear was drinking in the melody of Inez's voice, who was singing to her lute in one of the moonlight glades of the garden. The old man having exhausted his theme, sat gazing in silent reverie at the heavens. Antonio could not resist an inclination to steal a look at this coy beauty, who was thus playing the part of the nightingale, so sequestered and musical. Leaving the alchemist in his celestial reverie, he stole gently along one of the alleys. The music had ceased, and he thought he heard the sound of voices. He came to an angle of a copse that had screened a kind of green recess, ornamented by a marble fountain. The moon shone full upon the place, and by its light he beheld his unknown serenading rival at the feet of Inez. He was detaining her by the hand, which he covered with kisses; but at sight of Antonio he started up and half drew his sword, while Inez, disengaged, fled back to the house.

All the jealous doubts and fears of Antonio were now confirmed. He

did not remain to encounter the resentment of his happy rival at being thus interrupted, but turned from the place in sudden wretchedness of heart. That Inez should love another would have been misery enough; but that she should be capable of a dishonorable amour, shocked him to the soul. The idea of deception in so young and apparently artless a being, brought with it that sudden distrust in human nature, so sickening to a youthful and ingenuous mind; but when he thought of the kind, simple parent she was deceiving, whose affections all centred in her, he felt for a moment a sentiment of indignation, and almost of aversion.

He found the alchemist still seated in his visionary contemplation of the moon. "Come hither, my son," said he, with his usual enthusiasm, "come, read with me in this vast volume of wisdom, thus nightly unfolded for our perusal. Wisely did the Chaldean sages affirm, that the heaven is as a mystic page, uttering speech to those who can rightly understand; warning them of good and evil, and instructing them in the secret decrees of fate."

The student's heart ached for his venerable master; and, for a moment, he felt the futility of all his occult wisdom. "Alas! poor old man!" thought he, "of what avails all thy study? Little dost thou dream, while busied in airy speculations among the stars, what a treason against thy happiness is going on under thine eyes,—as it were, in thy very bosom! —Oh, Inez! Inez! where shall we look for truth and innocence; where shall we repose confidence in woman, if even you can deceive?"

It was a trite apostrophe, such as every lover makes when he finds his mistress not quite such a goddess as he had painted her. With the student, however, it sprang from honest anguish of heart. He returned to his lodgings in pitiable confusion of mind. He now deplored the infatuation which had led him on until his feelings were so thoroughly engaged. He resolved to abandon his pursuits at the tower, and trust to absence to dispel the fascination by which he had been spellbound. He no longer thirsted after the discovery of the grand elixir: the dream of alchemy was over; for without Inez, what was the value of the philosopher's stone?

He rose, after a sleepless night, with the determination of taking his leave of the alchemist, and tearing himself from Grenada. For several days did he rise with the same resolution, and every night saw him come back to his pillow to repine at his want of resolution, and to make fresh determinations for the morrow. In the meanwhile he saw less of Inez than ever. She no longer walked in the garden, but remained almost entirely in her apartment. When she met him, she blushed more than usual; and once hesitated, as if she would have spoken; but after a

temporary embarrassment, and still deeper blushes, she made some casual observation, and retired. Antonio read, in this confusion, a consciousness of fault, and of that fault's being discovered. "What could she have wished to communicate? Perhaps to account for the scene in the garden;—but how can she account for it, or why should she account for it to me? What am I to her?—or rather, what is she to me?" exclaimed he, impatiently; with a new resolution to break through these entanglements of the heart, and fly from this enchanted spot forever.

He was returning that very night to his lodgings, full of this excellent determination, when, in a shadowy part of the road, he passed a person whom he recognized, by his height and form, for his rival; he was going in the direction of the tower. If any lingering doubts remained, here was an opportunity of settling them completely. He determined to follow this unknown cavalier, and, under favor of the darkness, observe his movements. If he obtained access to the tower, or in any way a favorable reception, Antonio felt as if it would be a relief to his mind, and would enable him to fix his wavering resolution.

The unknown, as he came near the tower, was more cautious and stealthy in his approaches. He was joined under a clump of trees by another person, and they had much whispering together. A light was burning in the chamber of Inez, the curtain was down, but the casement was left open, as the night was warm. After some time the light was extinguished. A considerable interval elapsed. The cavalier and his companion remained under covert of the trees, as if keeping watch. At length they approached the tower with silent and cautious steps. The cavalier received a dark lantern from his companion, and threw off his cloak. The other then softly brought something from the clump of trees, which Antonio perceived to be a light ladder. They placed it against the wall, and the serenader gently ascended. A sickening sensation came over Antonio. Here was indeed a confirmation of every fear. He was about to leave the place, never to return, when he heard a stifled shriek from Inez's chamber.

In an instant the fellow that stood at the foot of the ladder lay prostrate on the ground. Antonio wrested a stiletto from his nerveless hand, and hurried up the ladder. He sprang in at the window, and found Inez struggling in the grasp of his fancied rival. The latter, disturbed from his prey, caught up his lantern, turned its full light upon Antonio, and drawing his sword, made a furious assault; luckily the student saw the light gleam along the blade, and parried the thrust with the stiletto. A fierce, but unequal combat ensued. Antonio fought exposed to the full glare of the light, while his antagonist was in a shadow. His stiletto, too, was but a poor defence against a rapier. He saw that noth-

ing would save him but closing with his adversary and getting within his weapon. He rushed furiously upon him, and gave him a severe blow with the stiletto; but received a wound in return from the shortened sword. At the same moment a blow was inflicted from behind, by the confederate, who had ascended the ladder; it felled him to the floor, and his antagonists made their escape.

By this time the cries of Inez had brought her father and the domestic to the room. Antonio was found weltering in his blood, and senseless. He was conveyed to the chamber of the alchemist, who now repaid in kind the attentions which the student had once bestowed upon him. Among his varied knowledge he possessed some skill in surgery, which at this moment was of more value than even his chemical lore. He stanched and dressed the wounds of his disciple, which on examination proved less desperate than he had at first apprehended. For a few days, however, his case was anxious, and attended with danger. The old man watched over him with the affection of a parent. He felt a double debt of gratitude towards him on account of his daughter and himself; he loved him too as a faithful and zealous disciple; and he dreaded lest the world should be deprived of the promising talents of so aspiring an alchemist.

An excellent constitution soon medicined his wounds; and there was a balsam in the looks and words of Inez, that had a healing effect on the still severer wounds which he carried in his heart. She displayed the strongest interest in his safety; she called him her deliverer, her preserver. It seemed as if her grateful disposition sought, in the warmth of its acknowledgments, to repay him for past coldness. But what most contributed to Antonio's recovery, was her explanation concerning his supposed rival. It was some time since he had first beheld her at church, and he had ever since persecuted her with his attentions. He had beset her in her walks, until she had been obliged to confine herself to the house, except when accompanied by her father. He had besieged her with letters, serenades, and every art by which he could urge a vehement, but clandestine and dishonorable suit. The scene in the garden was as much of a surprise to her as to Antonio. Her persecutor had been attracted by her voice, and had found his way over a ruined part of the wall. He had come upon her unawares, and was detaining her by force, and pleading his insulting passion, when the appearance of the student interrupted him, and enabled her to make her escape. She had forborne to mention to her father the persecution which she suffered; she wished to spare him unavailing anxiety and distress, and had determined to confine herself more rigorously to the house; though

it appeared that even here she had not been safe from his daring enterprise.

Antonio inquired whether she knew the name of this impetuous admirer? She replied that he had made his advances under a fictitious name; but that she had heard him once called by the name of Don Ambrosio de Loxa.

Antonio knew him, by report, for one of the most determined and dangerous libertines in all Grenada. Artful, accomplished, and if he chose to be so, insinuating; but daring and headlong in the pursuit of his pleasures; violent and implacable in his resentments. He rejoiced to find that Inez had been proof against his seductions, and had been inspired with aversion by his splendid profligacy; but he trembled to think of the dangers she had run, and he felt solicitude about the dangers that must yet environ her.

At present, however, it was probable the enemy had a temporary quietus. The traces of blood had been found for some distance from the ladder, until they were lost among thickets; and as nothing had been heard or seen of him since, it was concluded that he had been seriously wounded.

As the student recovered from his wounds, he was enabled to join Inez and her father in their domestic intercourse. The chamber in which they usually met had probably been a saloon of state in former times. The floor was of marble; the walls were partially covered with remains of tapestry; the chairs, richly carved and gilt, were crazed with age, and covered with tarnished and tattered brocade. Against the wall hung a long, rusty rapier, the only relic that the old man retained of the chivalry of his ancestors. There might have been something to provoke a smile in the contrast between the mansion and its inhabitants, between present poverty and the traces of departed grandeur; but the fancy of the student had thrown so much romance about the edifice and its inmates, that everything was clothed with charms. The philosopher, with his broken-down pride, and his strange pursuits, seemed to comport with the melancholy ruin he inhabited; and there was a native elegance of spirit about the daughter, that showed she would have graced the mansion in its happier days.

What delicious moments were these to the student! Inez was no longer coy and reserved. She was naturally artless and confiding; though the kind of persecution she had experienced from one admirer had rendered her, for a time, suspicious and circumspect towards the other, she now felt an entire confidence in the sincerity and worth of Antonio, mingled with an overflowing gratitude. When her eyes met his, they

beamed with sympathy and kindness; and Antonio, no longer haunted by the idea of a favored rival, once more aspired to success.

At these domestic meetings, however, he had little opportunity of paying his court, except by looks. The alchemist, supposing him, like himself, absorbed in the study of alchemy, endeavored to cheer the tediousness of his recovery by long conversations on the art. He even brought several of his half-burnt volumes, which the student had once rescued from the flames, and rewarded him for their preservation by reading copious passages. He would entertain him with the great and good acts of Flamel, which he effected through means of the philosopher's stone, relieving widows and orphans, founding hospitals, building churches, and what not; or with the interrogatories of King Kalid, and the answers of Morienus, the Roman hermit of Hierusalem; or the profound questions which Elardus, a necromancer of the province of Catalonia, put to the devil, touching the secrets of alchemy, and the devil's replies.

All these were couched in occult language, almost unintelligible to the unpractised ear of the disciple. Indeed, the old man delighted in the mystic phrases and symbolical jargon in which the writers that have treated of alchemy have wrapped their communications; rendering them incomprehensible except to the initiated. With what rapture would he elevate his voice at a triumphant passage, announcing the grand discovery! "Thou shalt see," would he exclaim, in the words of Henry Kuhnrade,* "the stone of the philosophers (our king) go forth of the bed-chamber of his glassy sepulchre into the theatre of this world; that is to say, regenerated and made perfect, a shining carbuncle, a most temperate splendor, whose most subtle and dephurated parts are inseparable, united into one with a concordial mixture, exceeding equal, transparent as crystal, shining red like a ruby, permanently coloring or ringing, fixt in all temptations or trials; yea, in the examination of the burning sulphur itself, and the devouring waters, and in the most vehement persecution of the fire, always incombustible and permanent as a salamander!"

The student had a high veneration for the fathers of alchemy, and a profound respect for his instructor; but what was Henry Kuhnrade, Geber, Lully, or even Albertus Magnus himself, compared to the countenance of Inez, which presented such a page of beauty to his perusal? While, therefore, the good alchemist was doling out knowledge by the hour, his disciple would forget books, alchemy, everything but the lovely object before him. Inez, too, unpractised in the science of the

---

* *Amphitheatre of the Eternal Wisdom.*

heart, was gradually becoming fascinated by the silent attentions of her lover. Day by day she seemed more and more perplexed by the kindling and strangely pleasing emotions of her bosom. Her eye was often cast down in thought. Blushes stole to her cheek without any apparent cause, and light, half-suppressed sighs would follow these short fits of musing. Her little ballads, though the same that she had always sung, yet breathed a more tender spirit. Either the tones of her voice were more soft and touching, or some passages were delivered with a feeling which she had never before given them. Antonio, beside his love for the abstruse sciences, had a pretty turn for music; and never did philosopher touch the guitar more tastefully. As, by degrees, he conquered the mutual embarrassment that kept them asunder, he ventured to accompany Inez in some of her songs. He had a voice full of fire and tenderness; as he sang, one would have thought, from the kindling blushes of his companion, that he had been pleading his own passion in her ear. Let those who would keep two youthful hearts asunder beware of music. Oh! this leaning over chairs, and conning the same music-book, and entwining of voices and melting away in harmonies!— the German waltz is nothing to it.

The worthy alchemist saw nothing of all this. His mind could admit of no idea that was not connected with the discovery of the grand arcanum, and he supposed his youthful coadjutor equally devoted. He was a mere child as to human nature, and, as to the passion of love, whatever he might once have felt of it, he had long since forgotten that there was such an idle passion in existence. But, while he dreamed, the silent amour went on. The very quiet and seclusion of the place were favorable to the growth of romantic passion. The opening bud of love was able to put forth leaf by leaf, without an adverse wind to check its growth. There was neither officious friendship to chill by its advice, nor insidious envy to wither by its sneers, nor an observing world to look on and stare it out of countenance. There was neither declaration, nor vow, nor any other form of Cupid's canting school. Their hearts mingled together, and understood each other without the aid of language. They lapsed into the full current of affection, unconscious of its depth, and thoughtless of the rocks that might lurk beneath its surface. Happy lovers! who wanted nothing to make their felicity complete but the discovery of the philosopher's stone.

At length Antonio's health was sufficiently restored to enable him to return to his lodgings in Grenada. He felt uneasy, however, at leaving the tower, while lurking danger might surround its almost defenceless inmates. He dreaded lest Don Ambrosio, recovered from his wounds, might plot some new attempt, by secret art or open violence. From all

that he had heard, he knew him to be too implacable to suffer his defeat to pass unavenged, and too rash and fearless, when his arts were unavailing, to stop at any daring deed in the accomplishment of his purposes. He urged his apprehensions to the alchemist and his daughter, and proposed that they should abandon the dangerous vicinity of Grenada.

"I have relations," said he, "in Valencia, poor indeed, but worthy and affectionate. Among them you will find friendship and quiet, and we may there pursue our labors unmolested." He went on to paint the beauties and delights of Valencia with all the fondness of a native, and all the eloquence with which a lover paints the fields and groves which he is picturing as the future scenes of his happiness. His eloquence, backed by the apprehensions of Inez, was successful with the alchemist, who, indeed, had led too unsettled a life to be particular about the place of his residence; and it was determined that, as soon as Antonio's health was perfectly restored, they should abandon the tower, and seek the delicious neighborhood of Valencia.*

To recruit his strength, the student suspended his toils in the laboratory, and spent the few remaining days, before departure, in taking a farewell look at the enchanting environs of Grenada. He felt returning health and vigor as he inhaled the pure temperate breezes that play about its hills; and the happy state of his mind contributed to his rapid recovery. Inez was often the companion of his walks. Her descent, by the mother's side, from one of the ancient Moorish families, gave her an interest in this once favorite seat of Arabian power. She gazed with enthusiasm upon its magnificent monuments, and her memory was filled with the traditional tales and ballads of Moorish chivalry. Indeed, the solitary life she had led, and the visionary turn of her father's mind, had produced an effect upon her character, and given it a tinge of what, in modern days, would be termed romance. All this was called into full force by this new passion; for, when a woman first begins to love, life is all romance to her.

In one of their evening strolls, they had ascended to the mountain

* Here are the strongest silks, the sweetest wines, the excellent'st almonds, the best oyls and beautifull'st females of all Spain. The very bruit animals make themselves beds of rosemary, and other fragrant flowers hereabouts; and when one is at sea, if the winde blow from the shore, he may smell this soyl before he come in sight of it many leagues off, by the stong odoriferous scent it casts. As it is the most pleasant, so it is also the temperat'st clime of all Spain, and they commonly call it the second Italy, which made the Moors, whereof many thousands were disterr'd and banish'd hence to Barbary to think that Paradise was in that part of the heavens which hung over this citie.—Howell's *Letters*.

of the Sun, where is situated the Generaliffe, the palace of pleasure, in the days of Moorish dominion, but now a gloomy convent of capuchins. They had wandered about its garden, among groves of orange, citron, and cypress, where the waters, leaping in torrents, or gushing in fountains, or tossed aloft in sparkling jets, fill the air with music and freshness. There is a melancholy mingled with all the beauties of this garden, that gradually stole over the feelings of the lovers. The place is full of the sad story of past times. It was the favorite abode of the lovely queen of Grenada, where she was surrounded by the delights of a gay and voluptuous court. It was here, too, amidst her own bowers of roses, that her slanderers laid the base story of her dishonor, and struck a fatal blow to the line of the gallant Abencerrages.

The whole garden has a look of ruin and neglect. Many of the fountains are dry and broken; the streams have wandered from their marble channels, and are choked by weeds and yellow leaves. The reed whistles to the wind where it had once sported among roses, and shaken perfume from the orange-blossom. The convent bell flings its sullen sound, or the drowsy vesper hymn floats along these solitudes, which once resounded with the song, and the dance, and the lover's serenade. Well may the Moors lament over the loss of this earthly paradise; well may they remember it in their prayers, and beseech Heaven to restore it to the faithful; well may their ambassadors smite their breasts when they behold these monuments of their race, and sit down and weep among the fading glories of Grenada!

It is impossible to wander about these scenes of departed love and gayety, and not feel the tenderness of the heart awakened. It was then that Antonio first ventured to breathe his passion, and to express by words what his eyes had long since so eloquently revealed. He made his avowal with fervor, but with frankness. He had no gay prospects to hold out; he was a poor scholar, dependent on his "good spirits to feed and clothe him." But a woman in love is no interested calculator. Inez listened to him with downcast eyes, but in them was a humid gleam that showed her heart was with him. She had no prudery in her nature; and she had not been sufficiently in society to acquire it. She loved him with all the absence of worldliness of a genuine woman; and, amidst timid smiles and blushes, he drew from her a modest acknowledgment of her affection.

They wandered about the garden with that sweet intoxication of the soul which none but happy lovers know. The world about them was all fairyland; and, indeed, it spread forth one of its fairest scenes before their eyes, as if to fulfil their dream of earthly happiness. They looked out from between groves of orange upon the towers of Grenada below

them; the magnificent plain of the Vega beyond, streaked with evening sunshine, and the distant hills tinted with rosy and purple hues; it seemed an emblem of the happy future that love and hope was decking out for them.

As if to make the scene complete, a group of Andalusians struck up a dance, in one of the vistas of the garden, to the guitars of two wandering musicians. The Spanish music is wild and plaintive, yet the people dance to it with spirit and enthusiasm. The picturesque figures of the dance, the girls with their hair in silken nets that hung in knots and tassels down their backs, their mantillas floating round their graceful forms, their slender feet peeping from under their basquinas, their arms tossed up in the air to play the castanets, had a beautiful effect on this airy height, with the rich evening landscape spreading out below them.

When the dance was ended, two of the parties approached Antonio and Inez; one of them began a soft and tender Moorish ballad, accompanied by the other on the lute. It alluded to the story of the garden, the wrongs of the fair queen of Grenada, and the misfortunes of the Abencerrages. It was one of those old ballads that abound in this part of Spain, and live, like echoes, about the ruins of Moorish greatness. The heart of Inez was at that moment open to every tender impression; the tears rose into her eyes as she listened to the tale. The singer approached nearer to her; she was striking in her appearance; young, beautiful, with a mixture of wildness and melancholy in her fine black eyes. She fixed them mournfully and expressively on Inez, and suddenly varying her manner, sang another ballad, which treated of impending danger and treachery. All this might have passed for a mere accidental caprice of the singer, had there not been something in her look, manner, and gesticulation, that made it pointed and startling.

Inez was about to ask the meaning of this evidently personal application of the song, when she was interrupted by Antonio, who gently drew her from the place. Whilst she had been lost in attention to the music, he had remarked a group of men, in the shadows of the trees, whispering together. They were enveloped in the broad hats and great cloaks so much worn by the Spanish, and while they were regarding himself and Inez attentively, seemed anxious to avoid observation. Not knowing what might be their character or intention, he hastened to quit a place where the gathering shadows of evening might expose them to intrusion and insult. On their way down the hill, as they passed through the wood of elms, mingled with poplars and oleanders, that skirts the road leading from the Alhambra, he again saw these men, apparently following at a distance; and he afterwards caught sight of

them among the trees on the banks of the Darro. He said nothing on the subject to Inez, nor her father, for he would not awaken unnecessary alarm; but he felt at a loss how to ascertain or to avert any machinations that might be devising against the helpless inhabitants of the tower.

He took his leave of them late at night, full of this perplexity. As he left the dreary old pile, he saw someone lurking in the shadow of the wall, apparently watching his movements. He hastened after the figure, but it glided away, and disappeared among some ruins. Shortly after he heard a low whistle, which was answered from a little distance. He had no longer a doubt but that some mischief was on foot, and turned to hasten back to the tower, and put its inmates on their guard. He had scarcely turned, however, before he found himself suddenly seized from behind by someone of Herculean strength. His struggles were in vain; he was surrounded by armed men. One threw a mantle over him that stifled his cries, and enveloped him in its folds; and he was hurried off with irresistible rapidity.

The next day passed without the appearance of Antonio at the alchemist's. Another, and another day succeeded, and yet he did not come; nor had anything been heard of him at his lodgings. His absence caused, at first, surprise and conjecture, and at length alarm. Inez recollected the singular intimations of the ballad singer upon the mountain, which seemed to warn her of impending danger, and her mind was full of vague forebodings. She sat listening to every sound at the gate, or footstep on the stairs. She would take up her guitar and strike a few notes, but it would not do; her heart was sickening with suspense and anxiety. She had never before felt what it was to be really lonely. She now was conscious of the force of that attachment which had taken possession of her breast; for never do we know how much we love, never do we know how necessary the object of our love is to our happiness, until we experience the weary void of separation.

The philosopher, too, felt the absence of his disciple almost as sensibly as did his daughter. The animating buoyancy of the youth had inspired him with new ardor, and had given to his labors the charm of full companionship. However, he had resources and consolations of which his daughter was destitute. His pursuits were of a nature to occupy every thought, and keep the spirits in a state of continual excitement. Certain indications, too, had lately manifested themselves, of the most favorable nature. Forty days and forty nights had the process gone on successfully; the old man's hopes were constantly rising, and he now considered the glorious moment once more at hand, when he should obtain not merely the major lunaria, but likewise the tinctura solaris,

the means of multiplying gold, and of prolonging existence. He remained, therefore, continually shut up in his laboratory, watching his furnace; for a moment's inadvertency might once more defeat all his expectations.

He was sitting one evening at one of his solitary vigils, wrapped up in meditation; the hour was late, and his neighbor, the owl, was hooting from the battlement of the tower, when he heard the door open behind him. Supposing it to be his daughter coming to take leave of him for the night, as was her frequent practice, he called her by name, but a harsh voice met his ear in reply. He was grasped by the arms, and looking up, perceived three strange men in the chamber. He attempted to shake them off, but in vain. He called for help, but they scoffed at his cries.

"Peace, dotard!" cried one, "think'st thou the servants of the most holy inquisition are to be daunted by thy clamors? Comrades, away with him!"

Without heeding his remonstrances and entreaties, they seized upon his books and papers, took some note of the apartment, and the utensils, and then bore him off a prisoner.

Inez, left to herself, had passed a sad and lonely evening; seated by a casement which looked into the garden, she had pensively watched star after star sparkle out of the blue depths of the sky, and was indulging a crowd of anxious thoughts about her lover, until the rising tears began to flow. She was suddenly alarmed by the sound of voices that seemed to come from a distant part of the mansion. There was not long after a noise of several persons descending the stairs. Surprised at these unusual sounds in their lonely habitation, she remained for a few moments in a state of trembling yet indistinct apprehension, when the servant rushed into the room, with terror in her countenance, and informed her that her father was carried off by armed men.

Inez did not stop to hear further, but flew down-stairs to overtake them. She had scarcely passed the threshold when she found herself in the grasp of strangers.

"Away! away!" cried she, wildly; "do not stop me—let me follow my father."

"We come to conduct you to him, señora," said one of the men, respectfully.

"Where is he then?"

"He is gone to Grenada," replied the man. "An unexpected circumstance requires his presence there immediately; but he is among friends."

"We have no friends in Grenada," said Inez, drawing back. But then the idea of Antonio rushed into her mind; something relating to him

might have called her father thither. "Is Señor Antonio de Castros with him?" demanded she, with agitation.

"I know not, señora," replied the man. "It is very possible. I only know that your father is among friends, and is anxious for you to follow him."

"Let us go, then," cried she, eagerly. The men led her a little distance to where a mule was waiting, and, assisting her to mount, they conducted her slowly towards the city.

Grenada was on that evening a scene of fanciful revel. It was one of the festivals of the Maestranza, an association of the nobility to keep up some of the gallant customs of ancient chivalry. There had been a representation of a tournament in one of the squares; the streets would still occasionally resound with the beat of a solitary drum, or the bray of a trumpet, from some straggling party of revellers. Sometimes they were met by cavaliers, richly dressed in ancient costumes, attended by their squires; and at one time they passed in sight of a palace brilliantly illuminated, whence came the mingled sounds of music and the dance. Shortly after they came to the square, where the mock tournament had been held. It was thronged by the populace, recreating themselves among booths and stalls where refreshments were sold, and the glare of torches showed the temporary galleries, and gay-colored awnings, and armorial trophies, and other paraphernalia of the show. The conductors of Inez endeavored to keep out of observation, and to traverse a gloomy part of the square, but they were detained at one place by the pressure of a crowd surrounding a party of wandering musicians, singing one of those ballads of which the Spanish populace are so passionately fond. The torches which were held by some of the crowd, threw a strong mass of light upon Inez, and the sight of so beautiful a being, without mantilla or veil, looking so bewildered, and conducted by men who seemed to take no gratification in the surrounding gayety, occasioned expressions of curiosity. One of the ballad-singers approached, and striking her guitar with peculiar earnestness, began to sing a doleful air, full of sinister forebodings. Inez started with surprise. It was the same ballad-singer that had addressed her in the garden of Generaliffe. It was the same air that she had then sung. It spoke of impending dangers; they seemed, indeed, to be thickening around her. She was anxious to speak with the girl, and to ascertain whether she really had a knowledge of any definite evil that was threatening her; but as she attempted to address her, the mule on which she rode was suddenly seized and led forcibly through the throng by one of her conductors, while she saw another addressing menacing words to the ballad-singer. The latter raised her hand with a warning gesture as Inez lost sight of her.

While she was yet lost in perplexity, caused by this singular occurrence, they stopped at the gate of a large mansion. One of her attendants knocked, the door was opened, and they entered a paved court. "Where are we?" demanded Inez, with anxiety. "At the house of a friend, señora," replied the man. "Ascend this staircase with me, and in a moment you will meet your father.

They ascended a staircase that led to a suite of splendid apartments. They passed through several until they came to an inner chamber. The door opened; some one approached; but what was her terror on perceiving, not her father, but Don Ambrosio!

The men who had seized upon the alchemist had, at least, been more honest in their professions. They were, indeed, familiars of the inquisition. He was conducted in silence to the gloomy prison of that horrible tribunal. It was a mansion whose very aspect withered joy, and almost shut out hope. It was one of those hideous abodes which the bad passions of men conjure up in this fair world, to rival the fancied dens of demons and the accursed.

Day after day went heavily by, without anything to mark the lapse of time but the decline and reappearance of the light that feebly glimmered through the narrow window of the dungeon in which the unfortunate alchemist was buried rather than confined. His mind was harassed with uncertainties and fears about his daughter, so helpless and inexperienced. He endeavored to gather tidings of her from the man who brought his daily portion of food. The fellow stared, as if astonished at being asked a question in that mansion of silence and mystery, but departed without saying a word. Every succeeding attempt was equally fruitless.

The poor alchemist was oppressed with many griefs; and it was not the least that he had been again interrupted in his labors on the very point of success. Never was alchemist so near attaining the golden secret;—a little longer, and all his hopes would have been realized. The thoughts of these disappointments afflicted him more than even the fear of all that he might suffer from the merciless inquisition. His waking thoughts would follow him into his dreams. He would be transported in fancy to his laboratory, busied again among retorts and alembics, and surrounded by Lully, by D'Abano, by Olybius, and the other masters of the sublime art. The moment of projection would arrive; a seraphic form would arise out of the furnace, holding forth a vessel containing the precious elixir; but, before he could grasp the prize, he would awake, and find himself in a dungeon.

All the devices of inquisitorial ingenuity were employed to ensnare the old man, and to draw from him evidence that might be brought

against himself, and might corroborate certain secret information given against him. He had been accused of practising necromancy and judicial astrology, and a cloud of evidence had been secretly brought forward to substantiate the charge. It would be tedious to enumerate all the circumstances, apparently corroborative, which had been industriously cited by the secret accuser. The silence which prevailed about the tower, its desolateness, the very quiet of its inhabitants, had been adduced as proofs that something sinister was perpetrated within. The alchemist's conversations and soliloquies in the garden had been overheard and misrepresented. The lights and strange appearances at night, in the tower, were given with violent exaggerations. Shrieks and yells were said to have been heard thence at midnight, when, it was confidently asserted, the old man raised familiar spirits by his incantations, and even compelled the dead to rise from their graves, and answer to his questions.

The alchemist, according to the custom of the inquisition, was kept in complete ignorance of his accuser; of the witnesses produced against him; even of the crimes of which he was accused. He was examined generally, whether he knew why he was arrested, and was conscious of any guilt that might deserve the notice of the holy office? He was examined as to his country, his life, his habits, his pursuits, his actions, and opinions. The old man was frank and simple in his replies; he was conscious of no guilt, capable of no art, practised in no dissimulation. After receiving a general admonition to bethink himself whether he had not committed any act deserving of punishment, and to prepare, by confession, to secure the well-known mercy of the tribunal, he was remanded to his cell.

He was now visited in his dungeon by crafty familiars of the inquisition; who, under pretence of sympathy and kindness, came to beguile the tediousness of his imprisonment with friendly conversation. They casually introduced the subject of alchemy, on which they touched with great caution and pretended indifference. There was no need of such craftiness. The honest enthusiast had no suspicion in his nature; the moment they touched upon his favorite theme, he forgot his misfortunes and imprisonment, and broke forth into rhapsodies about the divine science.

The conversation was artfully turned to the discussion of elementary beings. The alchemist readily allowed his belief in them; and that there had been instances of their attending upon philosophers, and administering to their wishes. He related many miracles said to have been performed by Apollonius Thyaneus, through the aid of spirits or demons; insomuch that he was set up by the heathens in opposition to the Mes-

siah; and was even regarded with reverence by many Christians. The familiars eagerly demanded whether he believed Apollonius to be a true and worthy philosopher. The unaffected piety of the alchemist protected him even in the midst of his simplicity; for he condemned Apollonius as a sorcerer and an imposter. No art could draw from him an admission that he had ever employed or invoked spiritual agencies in the prosecution of his pursuits, though he believed himself to have been frequently impeded by their invisible interference.

The inquisitors were sorely vexed at not being able to inveigle him into a confession of a criminal nature; they attributed their failure to craft, to obstinacy, to every cause but the right one, namely, that the harmless visionary had nothing guilty to confess. They had abundant proof of a secret nature against him; but it was the practice of the inquisition to endeavor to procure confession from the prisoners. An *auto da fé* was at hand; the worthy fathers were eager for his conviction, for they were always anxious to have a good number of culprits condemned to the stake, to grace these solemn triumphs. He was at length brought to a final examination.

The chamber of trial was spacious and gloomy. At one end was a huge crucifix, the standard of the inquisition. A long table extended through the centre of the room, at which sat the inquisitors and their secretary. At the other end a stool was placed for the prisoner.

He was brought in, according to custom, bare-headed and bare-legged. He was enfeebled by confinement and affliction; by constantly brooding over the unknown fate of his child, and the disastrous interruption of his experiments. He sat bowed down and listless, his head sunk upon his breast; his whole appearance that of one "past hope, abandoned, and by himself given over."

The accusation alleged against him was now brought forward in a specific form; he was called upon by name, Felix de Vasquez, formerly of Castile, to answer to the charges of necromancy and demonology. He was told that the charges were amply substantiated; and was asked whether he was ready, by full confession, to throw himself upon the well-known mercy of the holy inquisition.

The philosopher testified some little surprise at the nature of the accusation, but simply replied: "I am innocent."

"What proof have you to give of your innocence?"

"It rather remains for you to prove your charges," said the old man. "I am a stranger and a sojourner in the land, and know no one out of the doors of my dwelling. I can give nothing in my vindication but the word of a nobleman and a Castilian."

The inquisitor shook his head, and went on to repeat the various in-

quiries that had before been made as to his mode of life and pursuits. The poor alchemist was too feeble and too weary at heart to make any but brief replies. He requested that some man of science might examine his laboratory, and all his books and papers, by which it would be made abundantly evident that he was merely engaged in the study of alchemy.

To this the inquisitor observed, that alchemy had become a mere covert for secret and deadly sins. That the practisers of it were apt to scruple at no means to satisfy their inordinate greediness of gold. Some had been known to use spells and impious ceremonies; to conjure the aid of evil spirits; nay, even to sell their souls to the enemy of mankind, so that they might riot in boundless wealth while living.

The poor alchemist had heard all patiently, or, at least, passively. He had disdained to vindicate his name otherwise than by his word; he had smiled at the accusations of sorcery, when applied merely to himself; but when the sublime art, which had been the study and passion of his life, was assailed, he could no longer listen in silence. His head gradually rose from his bosom, a hectic color came in faint streaks to his cheeks, played about there, disappeared, returned, and at length kindled into a burning glow. The clammy dampness dried from his forehead; his eyes, which had been nearly extinguished, lighted up again, and burned with their wonted and visionary fires. He entered into a vindication of his favorite art. His voice at first was feeble and broken; but it gathered strength as he proceeded, until it rolled in a deep and sonorous volume. He gradually rose from his seat as he rose with his subject; he threw back the scanty black mantle which had hitherto wrapped his limbs; the very uncouthness of his form and looks gave an impressive effect to what he uttered; it was as though a corpse had become suddenly animated.

He repelled with scorn the aspersions cast upon alchemy by the ignorant and vulgar. He affirmed it to be the mother of all art and science, citing the opinions of Paracelsus, Sandivogius, Raymond Lully, and others, in support of his assertions. He maintained that it was pure and innocent, and honorable both in its purposes and means. What were its objects? The perpetuation of life and youth, and the production of gold. "The elixir vitæ," says he, "is no charmed potion, but merely a concentration of those elements of vitality which nature has scattered through her works. The philosopher's stone, or tincture, or powder, as it is variously called, is no necromantic talisman, but consists simply of those particles which gold contains within itself for its reproduction; for gold, like other things, has its seed within itself, though bound up with inconceivable firmness, from the vigor of innate fixed salts and

sulphurs. In seeking to discover the elixir of life, then," continued he, "we seek only to apply some of nature's own specifics against the disease and decay to which our bodies are subjected; and what else does the physician, when he tasks his art, and uses subtle compounds and cunning distillations to revive our languishing powers, and avert the stroke of death for a season?

"In seeking to multiply the precious metals, also, we seek but to germinate and multiply, by natural means, a particular species of nature's productions; and what else does the husbandman, who consults times and seasons, and, by what might be deemed a natural magic, from the mere scattering of his hand, covers a whole plain with golden vegetation? The mysteries of our art, it is true, are deeply and darkly hidden; but it requires so much the more innocence and purity of thought to penetrate unto them. No, father, the true alchemist must be pure in mind, and body; he must be temperate, patient, chaste, watchful, meek, humble, devout. 'My son,' says Hermes Trismegestes, the great master of our art, 'my son, I recommend you above all things to fear God.' And indeed it is only by devout castigation of the senses and purification of the soul, that the alchemist is enabled to enter into the sacred chambers of truth. 'Labor, pray, and read,' is the motto of our science. As De Nuysement well observes, 'these high and singular favors are granted unto none save only unto the sons of God (that is to say, the virtuous and devout), who, under his paternal benediction, have obtained the opening of the same, by the helping hand of the queen of arts, divine philosophy.' Indeed, so sacred has the nature of this knowledge been considered, that we are told it has four times been expressly communicated by God to man, having made a part of that cabalistical wisdom which was revealed to Adam to console him for the loss of Paradise, to Moses in the bush, to Solomon in a dream, and to Esdras by the angel.

"So far from demons and malign spirits being the friends and abettors of the alchemist, they are the continual foes with which he has to contend. It is their constant endeavor to shut up the avenues to those truths which would enable him to rise above the abject state into which he has fallen, and return to that excellence which was his original birthright. For what would be the effect of this length of days, and this abundant wealth, but to enable the possessor to go on from art to art, from science to science, with energies unimpaired by sickness, uninterrupted by death? For this have sages and philosophers shut themselves up in cells and solitudes; buried themselves in caves and dens of the earth; turning from the joys of life, and the pleasance of the world; enduring scorn, poverty, persecution. For this was Raymond Lully stoned to death in Mauritania. For this did the immortal Pietro d'Abano

suffer persecution at Padua, and when he escaped from his oppressors by death, was despitefully burnt in effigy. For this have illustrious men of all nations intrepidly suffered martyrdom. For this, if unmolested, have they assiduously employed the latest hour of life, the expiring throb of existence, hoping to the last that they might yet seize upon the prize for which they had struggled, and pluck themselves back even from the very jaws of the grave.

"For, when once the alchemist shall have attained the object of his toils, when the sublime secret shall be revealed to his gaze, how glorious will be the change in his condition! How will he emerge from his solitary retreat, like the sun breaking forth from the darksome chamber of the night, and darting his beams throughout the earth! Gifted with perpetual youth and boundless riches, to what heights of wisdom may he attain! How may he carry on, uninterrupted, the thread of knowledge, which has hitherto been snapped at the death of each philosopher! And, as the increase of wisdom is the increase of virtue, how may he become the benefactor of his fellow-men; dispensing with liberal, but cautious and discriminating hand, that inexhaustible wealth which is at his disposal; banishing poverty, which is the cause of so much sorrow and wickedness; encouraging the arts; promoting discoveries, and enlarging all the means of virtuous enjoyment! His life will be the connecting band of generations. History will live in his recollection; distant ages will speak with his tongue. The nations of the earth will look to him as their preceptor, and kings will sit at his feet and learn wisdom. Oh glorious! oh celestial alchemy!"

Here he was interrupted by the inquisitor, who had suffered him to go on thus far, in hopes of gathering something from his unguarded enthusiasm. "Señor," said he, "this is all rambling, visionary talk. You are charged with sorcery, and in defence you give us a rhapsody about alchemy. Have you nothing better than this to offer in your defence?"

The old man slowly resumed his seat, but did deign no reply. The fire that had beamed in his eye gradually expired. His cheek resumed its wonted paleness; but he did not relapse into inanity. He sat with a steady, serene, patient look, like one prepared not to contend but to suffer.

His trial continued for a long time with cruel mockery of justice, for no witnesses were ever, in this court, confronted with the accused, and the latter had continually to defend himself in the dark. Some unknown and powerful enemy had alleged charges against the unfortunate alchemist, but who he could not imagine. Stranger and sojourner as he was in the land, solitary and harmless in his pursuits, how could he have provoked such hostility? The tide of secret testimony, however,

was too strong against him. He was convicted of the crime of magic, and condemned to expiate his sins at the stake, at the approaching *auto da fé*.

While the unhappy alchemist was undergoing his trial at the inquisition, his daughter was exposed to trials no less severe. Don Ambrosio, into whose hands she had fallen, was, as has before been intimated, one of the most daring and lawless profligates in all Grenada. He was a man of hot blood and fiery passions, who stopped at nothing in the gratification of his desires; yet with all this he possessed manners, address, and accomplishments, that had made him eminently successful among the sex. From the palace to the cottage he had extended his amorous enterprises; his serenades harassed the slumbers of half the husbands in Grenada; no balcony was too high for his adventurous attempts; nor any cottage too lowly for his perfidious seductions. Yet he was as fickle as he was ardent; success had made him vain and capricious; he had no sentiment to attach him to the victim of his arts; and many a pale cheek and fading eye, languishing amidst the sparkling of jewels, and many a breaking heart, throbbing under the rustic bodice, bore testimony to his triumphs and his faithlessness.

He was sated, however, by easy conquests, and wearied of a life of continual and prompt gratification. There had been a degree of difficulty and enterprise in the pursuit of Inez, that he had never before experienced. It had aroused him from the monotony of mere sensual life, and stimulated him with the charm of adventure. He had become an epicure in pleasure; and now that he had this coy beauty in his power, he was determined to protract his enjoyment, by the gradual conquest of her scruples, and downfall of her virtue. He was vain of his person and address, which he thought no woman could long withstand; and it was a kind of trial of skill to endeavor to gain by art and fascination what he was secure of obtaining at any time by violence.

When Inez, therefore, was brought to his presence by his emissaries, he affected not to notice her terror and surprise, but received her with formal and stately courtesy. He was too wary a fowler to flutter the bird when just entangled in the net. To her eager and wild inquiries about her father, he begged her not to be alarmed; that he was safe, and had been there, but was engaged elsewhere in an affair of moment, from which he would soon return; in the meantime he had left word that she should await his return in patience. After some stately expressions of general civility, Don Ambrosio made a ceremonious bow, and retired.

The mind of Inez was full of trouble and perplexity. The stately formality of Don Ambrosio was so unexpected as to check the accusations and reproaches that were springing to her lips. Had he had evil

designs, would he have treated her with such frigid ceremony when he had her in his power? But why, then, was she brought to his house? Was not the mysterious disappearance of Antonio connected with this? A thought suddenly darted into her mind. Antonio had again met with Don Ambrosio—they had fought—Antonio was wounded—perhaps dying!—It was him to whom her father had gone. It was at his request that Don Ambrosio had sent for them to soothe his dying moments! These, and a thousand such horrible suggestions harassed her mind; but she tried in vain to get information from the domestics; they knew nothing but that her father had been there, had gone, and would soon return.

Thus passed a night of tumultuous thought and vague yet cruel apprehensions. She knew not what to do, or what to believe; whether she ought to fly, or to remain. But if to fly, how was she to extricate herself? and where was she to seek her father? As the day dawned without any intelligence of him, her alarm increased. At length a message was brought from him, saying that circumstances prevented his return to her, but begging her to hasten to him without delay.

With an eager and throbbing heart did she set forth with the men that were to conduct her. She little thought, however, that she was merely changing her prison-house. Don Ambrosio had feared lest she should be traced to his residence in Grenada; or that he might be interrupted there before he could accomplish his plan of seduction. He had her now conveyed, therefore, to a mansion which he possessed in one of the mountain solitudes in the neighborhood of Grenada; a lonely, but beautiful retreat. In vain, on her arrival, did she look around for her father, or Antonio; none but strange faces met her eye; menials profoundly respectful, but who knew nor saw anything but what their master pleased.

She had scarcely arrived before Don Ambrosio made his appearance, less stately in his manner, but still treating her with the utmost delicacy and deference. Inez was too much agitated and alarmed to be baffled by his courtesy, and became vehement in her demand to be conducted to her father.

Don Ambrosio now put on an appearance of the greatest embarrassment and emotion. After some delay, and much pretended confusion, he at length confessed that the seizure of her father was all a stratagem; a mere false alarm to procure him the present opportunity of having access to her, and endeavoring to mitigate that obduracy, and conquer that repugnance, which he declared had almost driven him to distraction.

He assured her that her father was again at home in safety, and oc-

cupied in his usual pursuits; having been fully satisfied that his daughter was in honorable hands, and would soon be restored to him. In vain she threw herself at his feet, and implored to be set at liberty; he only replied by gentle entreaties, that she would pardon the seeming violence he had to use; and that she would trust a little while to his honor. "You are here," said he, "absolute mistress of everything. Nothing shall be said or done to offend you; I will not even intrude upon your ear the unhappy passion that is devouring my heart. Should you require it, I will even absent myself from your presence; but to part with you entirely at present, with your mind full of doubts and resentments, would be worse than death to me. No, beautiful Inez, you must first know me a little better, and know my conduct, that my passion for you is as delicate and respectful as it is vehement."

The assurance of her father's safety had relieved Inez from one cause of torturing anxiety, only to render her fears more violent on her own account. Don Ambrosio, however, continued to treat her with artful deference, that insensibly lulled her apprehensions. It is true she found herself a captive, but no advantage appeared to be taken of her helplessness. She soothed herself with the idea that a little while would suffice to convince Don Ambrosio of the fallacy of his hopes, and that he would be induced to restore her to her home. Her transports of terror and affliction, therefore, subsided, in a few days, into a passive yet anxious melancholy, with which she awaited the hoped-for event.

In the meanwhile all those artifices were employed that are calculated to charm the senses, ensnare the feelings, and dissolve the heart into tenderness. Don Ambrosio was a master of the subtle arts of seduction. His very mansion breathed an enervating atmosphere of languor and delight. It was here, amidst twilight saloons and dreamy chambers, buried among groves of orange and myrtle, that he shut himself up at times from the prying world, and gave free scope to the gratification of his pleasures.

The apartments were furnished in the most sumptuous and voluptuous manner; the silken couches swelled to the touch, and sank in downy softness beneath the slightest pressure. The paintings and statues all told some classic tale of love, managed, however, with an insidious delicacy; which, while it banished the grossness that might disgust, was the more calculated to excite the imagination. There the blooming Adonis was seen, not breaking away to pursue the boisterous chase, but crowned with flowers, and languishing in the embraces of celestial beauty. There Acis wooed his Galatea in the shade, with the Sicilian sea spreading in halcyon serenity before them. There were depicted groups of fauns and dryads, fondly reclining in summer bowers, and

listening to the liquid piping of the reed; or the wanton satyrs surprising some wood-nymph during her noontide slumber. There, too, on the storied tapestry, might be seen the chaste Diana, stealing, in the mystery of moonlight, to kiss the sleeping Endymion; while Cupid and Psyche, entwined in immortal marble, breathed on each other's lips the early kiss of love.

The ardent rays of the sun were excluded from these balmy halls. Soft and tender music from unseen musicians floated around, seeming to mingle with the perfumes exhaled from a thousand flowers. At night, when the moon shed a fairy light over the scene, the tender serenade would rise from among the bowers of the garden, in which the fine voice of Don Ambrosio might often be distinguished; or the amorous flute would be heard along the mountain breathing in its pensive cadences the very soul of a lover's melancholy.

Various entertainments were also devised to dispel her loneliness and to charm away the idea of confinement. Groups of Andalusian dancers performed, in the splendid saloons, the various picturesque dances of their country; or represented little amorous ballets, which turned upon some pleasing scene of pastoral coquetry and courtship. Sometimes there were bands of singers, who, to the romantic guitar, warbled forth ditties full of passion and tenderness.

Thus all about her enticed to pleasure and voluptuousness; but the heart of Inez turned with distaste from this idle mockery. The tears would rush into her eyes as her thoughts reverted from this scene of profligate splendor to the humble but virtuous home whence she had been betrayed; or if the witching power of music ever soothed her into a tender reverie, it was to dwell with fondness on the image of Antonio. But if Don Ambrosio, deceived by this transient calm, should attempt at such time to whisper his passion, she would start as from a dream, and recoil from him with involuntary shuddering.

She had passed one long day of more than ordinary sadness, and in the evening a band of these hired performers were exerting all the animating powers of song and dance to amuse her. But while the lofty saloon resounded with their warblings, and the light sound of feet upon its marble pavement kept time to the cadence of the song, poor Inez, with her face buried in the silken couch on which she reclined, was only rendered more wretched by the sound of gayety.

At length her attention was caught by the voice of one of the singers, that brought with it some indefinite recollections. She raised her head, and cast an anxious look at the performers, who, as usual, were at the lower end of the saloon. One of them advanced a little before the others. It was a female, dressed in a fanciful pastoral garb, suited to the

character she was sustaining; but her countenance was not to be mistaken. It was the same ballad-singer that had twice crossed her path, and given her mysterious intimations of the lurking mischief that surrounded her. When the rest of the performances were concluded, she seized a tambourine, and tossing it aloft, danced alone to the melody of her own voice. In the course of her dancing she approached to where Inez reclined; and as she struck the tambourine, contrived, dexterously, to throw a folded paper on the couch. Inez seized it with avidity, and concealed it in her bosom. The singing and dancing were at an end; the motley crew retired; and Inez, left alone, hastened with anxiety to unfold the paper thus mysteriously conveyed. It was written in an agitated, and almost illegible, handwriting: "Be on your guard! you are surrounded by treachery. Trust not to the forbearance of Don Ambrosio; you are marked out for his prey. An humble victim to his perfidy gives you this warning; she is encompassed by too many dangers to be more explicit. Your father is in the dungeons of the inquisition!"

The brain of Inez reeled as she read this dreadful scroll. She was less filled with alarm at her own danger, than horror at her father's situation. The moment Don Ambrosio appeared, she rushed and threw herself at his feet, imploring him to save her father. Don Ambrosio started with astonishment; but immediately regaining his self-possession, endeavored to soothe her by his blandishments, and by assurances that her father was in safety. She was not to be pacified; her fears were too much aroused to be trifled with. She declared her knowledge of her father's being a prisoner of the inquisition, and reiterated her frantic supplications that he would save him.

Don Ambrosio paused for a moment in perplexity, but was too adroit to be easily confounded. "That your father is a prisoner," replied he, "I have long known. I have concealed it from you, to save you from fruitless anxiety. You now know the real reason of the restraint I have put upon your liberty. I have been protecting instead of detaining you. Every exertion has been made in your father's favor; but I regret to say, the proofs of the offences of which he stands charged have been too strong to be controverted. Still," added he, "I have it in my power to save him; I have influence, I have means at my beck; it may involve me, it is true, in difficulties, perhaps in disgrace; but what would I not do in the hopes of being rewarded by your favor? Speak, beautiful Inez," said he, his eyes kindling with sudden eagerness; "it is with you to say the word that seals your father's fate. One kind word—say but you will be mine, and you will behold me at your feet, your father at liberty and in affluence, and we shall all be happy!"

Inez drew back from him with scorn and disbelief. "My father," ex-

claimed she, "is too innocent and blameless to be convicted of crime; this is some base, some cruel artifice!" Don Ambrosio repeated his asseverations, and with them also his dishonorable proposals; but his eagerness overshot its mark. Her indignation and her incredulity were alike awakened by his base suggestions; and he retired from her presence checked and awed by the sudden pride and dignity of her demeanor.

The unfortunate Inez now became a prey to the most harrowing anxieties. Don Ambrosio saw that the mask had fallen from his face, and that the nature of his machinations was revealed. He had gone too far to retrace his steps, and assume the affectation of tenderness and respect; indeed, he was mortified and incensed at her insensibility to his attractions, and now only sought to subdue her through her fears. He daily represented to her the dangers that threatened her father, and that it was in his power alone to avert them. Inez was still incredulous. She was too ignorant of the nature of the inquisition to know that even innocence was not always a protection from its cruelties; and she confided too surely in the virtue of her father to believe that any accusation could prevail against him.

At length Don Ambrosio, to give an effectual blow to her confidence, brought her the proclamation of the approaching *auto da fé* in which the prisoners were enumerated. She glanced her eye over it, and beheld her father's name, condemned to the stake for sorcery.

For a moment she stood transfixed with horror. Don Ambrosio seized upon the transient calm. "Think now, beautiful Inez," said he, with a tone of affected tenderness, "his life is still in your hands; one word from you, one kind word, and I can yet save him."

"Monster! wretch!" cried she, coming to herself, and recoiling from him with insuperable abhorrence: "'tis you that are the cause of this—'tis you that are his murderer!" Then, wringing her hands, she broke forth into exclamations of the most frantic agony.

The perfidious Ambrosio saw the torture of her soul, and anticipated from it a triumph. He saw that she was in no mood, during her present paroxysm, to listen to his words; but he trusted that the horrors of lonely rumination would break down her spirit, and subdue her to his will. In this, however, he was disappointed. Many were the vicissitudes of mind of the wretched Inez. One time she would embrace his knees with piercing supplications; at another she would shrink with nervous horror at his very approach; but any intimation of his passion only excited the same emotion of loathing and detestation.

At length the fatal day drew nigh. "To-morrow," said Don Ambrosio, as he left her one evening,—"to-morrow is the *auto da fé*. To-morrow

you will hear the sound of the bell that tolls your father to his death. You will almost see the smoke that rises from his funeral-pile. I leave you to yourself. It is yet in my power to save him. Think whether you can stand to-morrow's horror without shrinking. Think whether you can endure the after-reflection, that you were the cause of his death, and that merely through a perversity in refusing proffered happiness."

What a night it was to Inez! Her heart, already harassed and almost broken by repeated and protracted anxieties; her strength wasted and enfeebled. On every side horrors awaited her; her father's death, her own dishonor. There seemed no escape from misery or perdition. "Is there no relief from man—no pity in heaven?" exclaimed she. "What have we done that we should be thus wretched?"

As the dawn approached, the fever of her mind arose to agony. A thousand times did she try the doors and windows of her apartment, in the desperate hope of escaping. Alas! with all the splendor of her prison, it was too faithfully secured for weak hands to work deliverance. Like a poor bird, that beats its wings against its gilded cage, until it sinks panting in despair, so she threw herself on the floor in hopeless anguish. Her blood grew hot in her veins, her tongue was parched, her temples throbbed with violence, she gasped rather than breathed; it seemed as if her brain was on fire. "Blessed Virgin!" exclaimed she, clasping her hands, and turning up her strained eyes, "look down with pity, and support me in this dreadful hour!"

Just as the day began to dawn, she heard a key turn softly in the door of her apartment. She dreaded lest it should be Don Ambrosio, and the very thought of him gave her a sickening pang. It was a female, clad in a rustic dress, with her face concealed by her mantilla. She stepped silently into the room, looked cautiously round, and then, uncovering her face, revealed the well-known features of the ballad-singer. Inez uttered an exclamation of surprise, almost of joy. The unknown started back, pressed her finger on her lips enjoining silence, and beckoned her to follow. She hastily wrapped herself in her veil, and obeyed. They passed with quick but noiseless steps through an antechamber, across a spacious hall, and along a corridor. All was silent; the household was yet locked in sleep. They came to the door, to which the unknown applied a key. Inez's heart misgave her; she knew not but some new treachery was menacing her. She laid her cold hand on the stranger's arm: "Whither are you leading me?" said she. "To liberty," replied the other in a whisper.

"Do you know the passages about this mansion?"

"But too well!" replied the girl, with a melancholy shake of the head. There was an expression of sad veracity in her countenance that was

not to be distrusted. The door opened on a small terrace which was overlooked by several windows of the mansion.

"We must move across this quickly," said the girl, "or we may be observed."

They glided over it as if scarce touching the ground. A flight of steps led down into the garden; a wicket at the bottom was readily unbolted. They passed with breathless velocity along one of the alleys, still in sight of the mansion, in which, however, no person appeared to be stirring. At length they came to a low private door in the wall, partly hidden by a fig-tree. It was secured by rusty bolts, that refused to yield to their feeble efforts.

"Holy Virgin!" exclaimed the stranger,—"what is to be done? one moment more, and we may be discovered."

She seized a stone that lay near by. A few blows, and the bolts flew back. The door grated harshly as they opened it, and the next moment they found themselves in a narrow road.

"Now," said the stranger, "for Grenada as quickly as possible! The nearer we approach it, the safer we shall be; for the road will be more frequented."

The imminent risk they ran of being pursued and taken gave supernatural strength to their limbs; they flew rather than ran. The day had dawned; the crimson streaks on the edge of the horizon gave tokens of approaching sunrise; already the light clouds that floated in the western sky were tinged with gold and purple, though the broad plain of the Vega, which now began to open upon their view, was covered with the dark haze of the morning. As yet they only passed a few straggling peasants on the road, who could have yielded them no assistance in case of their being overtaken. They continued to hurry forward, and had gained a considerable distance, when the strength of Inez, which had only been sustained by the fever of her mind, began to yield to fatigue. She slackened her pace, and faltered.

"Alas!" said she, "my limbs fail me! I can go no farther!"

"Bear up, bear up," replied her companion cheeringly; "a little farther, and we shall be safe. Look! Yonder is Grenada, just showing itself in the valley below us. A little farther, and we shall come to the main road, and then we shall find plenty of passengers to protect us."

Inez, encouraged, made fresh efforts to get forward, but her weary limbs were unequal to the eagerness of her mind. Her mouth and throat were parched by agony and terror; she gasped for breath, and leaned for support against a rock. "It is all in vain!" exclaimed she; "I feel as though I should faint."

"Lean on me," said the other; "let us get into the shelter of yon

thicket, that will conceal us from view. I hear the sound of water, which will refresh you."

With much difficulty they reached the thicket which overhung a small mountain-stream, just where its sparkling waters leaped over the rock and fell into a natural basin. Here Inez sank upon the ground exhausted. Her companion brought water in the palms of her hands, and bathed her pallid temples. The cooling drops revived her; she was enabled to get to the margin of the stream, and drink of its crystal current; then, reclining her head on the bosom of her deliverer, she was first enabled to murmur forth her heartfelt gratitude.

"Alas!" said the other, "I deserve no thanks; I deserve not the good opinion you express. In me you behold a victim of Don Ambrosio's arts. In early years he seduced me from the cottage of my parents. Look! at the foot of yonder blue mountain in the distance lies my native village; but it is no longer a home for me. He lured me thence when I was too young for reflection; he educated me, taught me various accomplishments, made me sensible to love, to splendor, to refinement; then, having grown weary of me, he neglected me, and cast me upon the world. Happily, the accomplishments he taught me have kept me from utter want; and the love with which he inspired me has kept me from further degradation. Yes! I confess my weakness; all his perfidy and wrongs cannot efface him from my heart. I have been brought up to love him; I have no other idol. I know him to be base, yet I cannot help adoring him. I am content to mingle among the hireling throng that administer to his amusements, that I may still hover about him, and linger in those halls where I once reigned mistress. What merit, then, have I in assisting your escape? I scarce know whether I am acting from sympathy and a desire to rescue another victim from his power, or jealousy and an eagerness to remove too powerful a rival!"

While she was yet speaking, the sun rose in all its splendor; first lighting up the mountain summits, then stealing down height by height, until its rays gilded the domes and towers of Grenada, which they could partially see from between the trees, below them. Just then the heavy tones of a bell came sounding from a distance, echoing, in sullen clang, along the mountain. Inez turned pale at the sound. She knew it to be the great bell of the cathedral, rung at sunrise on the day of the *auto da fé*, to give note of funeral preparation. Every stroke beat upon her heart, and inflicted an absolute, corporeal pang. She started up wildly. "Let us be gone!" cried she; "there is not a moment for delay!"

"Stop!" exclaimed the other, "yonder are horsemen coming over the brow of that distant height; If I mistake not, Don Ambrosio is at their head. Alas! 'tis he. We are lost. Hold!" continued she; "give me your

scarf and veil; wrap yourself in this mantilla. I will fly up yon footpath that leads to the heights. I will let the veil flutter as I ascend; perhaps they may mistake me for you, and they must dismount to follow me. Do you hasten forward. You will soon reach the main road. You have jewels on your fingers; bribe the first muleteer you meet to assist you on your way."

All this was said with hurried and breathless rapidity. The exchange of garments was made in an instant. The girl darted up the mountain-path, her white veil fluttering among the dark shrubbery; while Inez, inspired with new strength, or rather new terror, flew to the road, and trusted to Providence to guide her tottering steps to Grenada.

All Grenada was in agitation on the morning of this dismal day. The heavy bell of the cathedral continued to utter its clanging tones, that pervaded every part of the city, summoning all persons to the tremendous spectacle about to be exhibited. The streets through which the procession was to pass were crowded with the populace. The windows, the roofs, every place that could admit a face or a foothold, was alive with spectators. In the great square a spacious scaffolding, like an amphitheatre, was erected, where the sentences of the prisoners were to be read, and the sermon of faith to be preached; and close by were the stakes prepared, where the condemned were to be burnt to death. Seats were arranged for the great, the gay, the beautiful; for such is the horrible curiosity of human nature, that this cruel sacrifice was attended with more eagerness than a theatre, or even a bull-feast.

As the day advanced, the scaffolds and balconies were filled with expecting multitudes; the sun shone brightly upon fair faces and gallant dresses; one would have thought it some scene of elegant festivity, instead of an exhibition of human agony and death. But what a different spectacle and ceremony was this from those which Grenada exhibited in the days of her Moorish splendor. "Her galas, her tournaments, her sports of the ring, her fêtes of St. John, her music, her Zambras, and admirable tilts of canes! Her serenades, her concerts, her songs in Generaliffe! The costly liveries of the Abencerrages, their exquisite inventions, the skill and valor of the Alabaces, the superb dresses of the Zegries, Mazas, and Gomeles!"*—all these were at an end. The days of chivalry were over. Instead of the prancing cavalcade, with neighing steed and lively trumpet; with burnished lance, and helm, and buckler; with rich confusion of plume, and scarf, and banner, where purple, and scarlet, and green, and orange, and every gay color were mingled

---

* Rodd's *Civil Wars of Grenada*.

with cloth of gold and fair embroidery;—instead of this crept on the gloomy pageant of superstition, in cowl and sackcloth; with cross and coffin and frightful symbols of human suffering. In place of the frank, hardy knight, open and brave, with his lady's favor in his casque, and amorous motto on his shield, looking, by gallant deeds, to win the smile of beauty, came the shaven, unmanly monk, with downcast eyes, and head and heart bleached in the cold cloister, secretly exulting in this bigot triumph.

The sound of the bells gave notice that the dismal procession was advancing. It passed slowly through the principal streets of the city, bearing in advance the awful banner of the holy office. The prisoners walked singly attended by confessors, and guarded by familiars of the inquisition. They were clad in different garments, according to the nature of their punishments;—those who were to suffer death wore the hideous Samarra, painted with flames and demons. The procession was swelled by choirs of boys, different religious orders, and public dignitaries; and, above all, by the fathers of the faith, moving "with slow pace, and profound gravity, truly triumphing as becomes the principal generals of that great victory."*

As the sacred banner of the inquisition advanced, the countless throng sank on their knees before it. They bowed their faces to the very earth as it passed, and then slowly rose again, like a great undulating billow. A murmur of tongues prevailed as the prisoners approached, and eager eyes were strained, and fingers pointed, to distinguish the different orders of penitents, whose habits denoted the degree of punishment they were to undergo. But as those drew near whose frightful garb marked them as destined to the flames, the noise of the rabble subsided; they seemed almost to hold in their breaths; filled with that strange and dismal interest with which we contemplate a human being on the verge of suffering and death.

It is an awful thing—a voiceless, noiseless multitude! The hushed and gazing stillness of the surrounding thousands, heaped on walls, and gates, and roofs, and hanging, as it were, in clusters, heightened the effect of the pageant that moved drearily on. The low murmuring of the priests could now be heard in prayer and exhortation, with the faint responses of the prisoners, and now and then the voices of the choir at a distance, chanting the litanies of the saints.

The faces of the prisoners were ghastly and disconsolate. Even those who had been pardoned, and wore the Sanbenito, or penitential garment, bore traces of the horrors they had undergone. Some were feeble

* Gonsalvius, p. 135.

and tottering from long confinement; some crippled and distorted by various tortures; every countenance was a dismal page on which might be read the secrets of their prison-house. But in the looks of those condemned to death there was something fierce and eager. They seemed men harrowed up by the past, and desperate as to the future. They were anticipating, with spirits fevered by despair, and fixed and clenched determination, the vehement struggle with agony and death they were shortly to undergo. Some cast now and then a wild and anguished look about them upon the shining day; the "sun-bright palaces," the gay, the beautiful world, which they were soon to quit forever; or a glance of sudden indignation at the thronging thousands, happy in liberty and life, who seemed, in contemplating their frightful situation, to exult in their own comparative security.

One among the condemned, however, was an exception to these remarks. It was an aged man, somewhat bowed down, with a serene, though dejected countenance, and a beaming, melancholy eye. It was the alchemist. The populace looked upon him with a degree of compassion, which they were not prone to feel towards criminals condemned by the inquisition; but when they were told that he was convicted of the crime of magic, they drew back with awe and abhorrence.

The procession had reached the grand square. The first part had already mounted the scaffolding, and the condemned were approaching. The press of the populace became excessive, and was repelled, as it were, in billows by the guards. Just as the condemned were entering the square, a shrieking was heard among the crowd. A female, pale, frantic, dishevelled, was seen struggling through the multitude. "My father! my father!" was all the cry she uttered, but it thrilled through every heart. The crowd instinctively drew back, and made way for her as she advanced.

The poor alchemist had made his peace with Heaven, and, by hard struggle, had closed his heart upon the world, when the voice of his child called him once more back to worldly thought and agony. He turned towards the well-known voice; his knees smote together; he endeavored to reach forth his pinioned arms, and felt himself clasped in the embraces of his child. The emotions of both were too agonizing for utterance. Convulsive sobs, and broken exclamations, and embraces more of anguish than tenderness, were all that passed between them. The procession was interrupted for a moment. The astonished monks and familiars were filled with involuntary respect at this agony of natural affection. Ejaculations of pity broke from the crowd, touched by the filial piety, the extraordinary and hopeless anguish of so young and beautiful a being.

Every attempt to soothe her, and prevail on her to retire, was unheeded. At length they endeavored to separate her from her father by force. The movement roused her from her temporary abandonment. With a sudden paroxysm of fury, she snatched a sword from one of the familiars. Her pale countenance was flushed with rage, and fire flashed from her once soft and languishing eyes. The guard shrunk back with awe. There was something in this filial frenzy, this feminine tenderness wrought up to desperation, that touched even their hardened hearts. They endeavored to pacify her, but in vain. Her eye was eager and quick as the she-wolf's guarding her young. With one arm she pressed her father to her bosom, with the other she menaced every one that approached.

The patience of the guards was soon exhausted. They had held back in awe, but not in fear. With all her desperation the weapon was soon wrested from her feeble hand, and she was borne shrieking and struggling among the crowd. The rabble murmured compassion; but such was the dread inspired by the inquisition, that no one attempted to interfere.

The procession again resumed its march. Inez was ineffectually struggling to release herself from the hands of the familiars that detained her, when suddenly she saw Don Ambrosio before her. "Wretched girl!" exclaimed he with fury, "why have you fled from your friends? Deliver her," said he to the familiars, "to my domestics; she is under my protection."

His creatures advanced to seize her. "Oh no! oh no!" cried she, with new terrors, and clinging to the familiars, "I have fled from no friends. He is not my protector! He is the murderer of my father!"

The familiars were perplexed; the crowd pressed on with eager curiosity. "Stand off!" cried the fiery Ambrosio, dashing the throng from around him. Then turning to the familiars, with sudden moderation, "My friends," said he, "deliver this poor girl to me. Her distress has turned her brain; she has escaped from her friends and protectors this morning; but a little quiet and kind treatment will restore her to tranquillity."

"I am not mad! I am not mad!" cried she, vehemently. "Oh, save me! —save me from these men! I have no protector on earth but my father, and him they are murdering!"

The familiars shook their heads; her wildness corroborated the assertions of Don Ambrosio, and his apparent rank commanded respect and belief. They relinquished their charge to him, and he was consigning the struggling Inez to his creatures——

"Let go your hold, villain!" cried a voice from among the crowd, and Antonio was seen eagerly tearing his way through the press of people.

"Seize him! seize him!" cried Don Ambrosio to the familiars; "'tis an accomplice of the sorcerer's."

"Liar!" retorted Antonio, as he thrust the mob to the right and left, and forced himself to the spot.

The sword of Don Ambrosio flashed in an instant from the scabbard; the student was armed and equally alert. There was a fierce clash of weapons; the crowd made way for them as they fought, and closed again, so as to hide them from the view of Inez. All was tumult and confusion for a moment; when there was a kind of shout from the spectators, and the mob again opening, she beheld, as she thought, Antonio weltering in his blood.

This new shock was too great for her already over-strained intellects. A giddiness seized upon her; everything seemed to whirl before her eyes; she gasped some incoherent words, and sank senseless upon the ground.

Days, weeks, elapsed before Inez returned to consciousness. At length she opened her eyes, as if out of a troubled sleep. She was lying upon a magnificent bed, in a chamber richly furnished with pier-glasses and massive tables inlaid with silver, of exquisite workmanship. The walls were covered with tapestry; the cornices richly gilded. Through the door which stood open, she perceived a superb saloon, with statues and crystal lustres, and a magnificent suit of apartments beyond. The casements of the room were open to admit the soft breath of summer, which stole in, laden with perfumes from a neighboring garden; whence, also, the refreshing sound of fountains and the sweet notes of birds came in mingled music to her ear.

Female attendants were moving, with noiseless step, about the chamber; but she feared to address them. She doubted whether this were not all delusion, or whether she was not still in the palace of Don Ambrosio, and that her escape, and all its circumstances, had not been but a feverish dream. She closed her eyes again, endeavoring to recall the past, and to separate the real from the imaginary. The last scenes of consciousness, however, rushed too forcibly, with all their horrors, to her mind to be doubted, and she turned shuddering from the recollection, to gaze once more on the quiet and serene magnificence around her. As she again opened her eyes, they rested on an object that at once dispelled every alarm. At the head of her bed sat a venerable form watching over her with a look of fond anxiety,—it was her father!

I will not attempt to describe the scene that ensued; nor the moments of rapture which more than repaid all the sufferings her affectionate

heart had undergone. As soon as their feelings had become more calm, the alchemist stepped out of the room to introduce a stranger, to whom he was indebted for his life and liberty. He returned, leading in Antonio, no longer in his poor scholar's garb, but in the rich dress of a nobleman.

The feelings of Inez were almost overpowered by these sudden reverses, and it was some time before she was sufficiently composed to comprehend the explanation of this seeming romance.

It appeared that the lover, who had sought her affections in the lowly guise of a student, was only son and heir of a powerful grandee of Valencia. He had been placed at the university at Salamanca; but a lively curiosity, and an eagerness for adventure, had induced him to abandon the university, without his father's consent, and to visit various parts of Spain. His rambling inclination satisfied, he had remained incognito for a time at Grenada, until, by further study and self-regulation, he could prepare himself to return home with credit, and atone for his trangressions against paternal authority.

How hard he had studied does not remain on record. All that we know is his romantic adventure of the tower. It was at first a mere youthful caprice, excited by a glimpse of a beautiful face. In becoming a disciple of the alchemist, he probably thought of nothing more than pursuing a light love-affair. Further acquaintance, however, had completely fixed his affections; and he had determined to conduct Inez and her father to Valencia, and trust to her merits to secure his father's consent to their union.

In the meantime he had been traced to his concealment. His father had received intelligence of his being entangled in the snares of a mysterious adventurer and his daughter, and likely to become the dupe of the fascinations of the latter. Trusty emissaries had been dispatched to seize upon him by main force, and convey him without delay to the paternal home.

What eloquence he had used with his father to convince him of the innocence, the honor, and the high descent of the alchemist, and of the exalted worth of his daughter, does not appear. All that we know is, that the father, though a very passionate, was a very reasonable man, as appears by his consenting that his son should return to Grenada, and conduct Inez, as his affianced bride, to Valencia.

Away, then, Don Antonio hurried back, full of joyous anticipations. He still forbore to throw off his disguise, fondly picturing to himself what would be the surprise of Inez, when, having won her heart and hand as a poor wandering scholar, he should raise her and her father at once to opulence and splendor.

On his arrival he had been shocked at finding the tower deserted of its inhabitants. In vain he sought for intelligence concerning them; a mystery hung over their disappearance which he could not penetrate, until he was thunderstruck, on accidently reading a list of the prisoners at the impending *auto da fé,* to find the name of his venerable master among the condemned.

It was the very morning of the execution. The procession was already on its way to the grand square. Not a moment was to be lost. The grand inquisitor was a relation of Don Antonio, though they had never met. His first impulse was to make himself known; to exert all his family influence, the weight of his name, and the power of his eloquence, in vindication of the alchemist. But the grand inquisitor was already proceeding, in all his pomp, to the place where the fatal ceremony was to be performed. How was he to be approached? Antonio threw himself into the crowd, in a fever of anxiety, and was forcing his way to the scene of horror, where he arrived just in time to rescue Inez, as has been mentioned.

It was Don Ambrosio that fell in the contest. Being desperately wounded and thinking his end approaching, he had confessed, to an attending father of the inquisition, that he was the sole cause of the alchemist's condemnation, and that the evidence on which it was grounded was altogether false. The testimony of Don Antonio came in corroboration of this avowal; and his relationship to the grand inquisitor had, in all probability, its proper weight. Thus was the poor alchemist snatched, in a manner, from the very flames; and so great had been the sympathy awakened in his case, that for once a populace rejoiced at being disappointed of an execution.

The residue of the story may readily be imagined by every one versed in this valuable kind of history. Don Antonio espoused with the lovely Inez, and took her and her father with him to Valencia. As she had been a loving and dutiful daughter, so she proved a true and tender wife. It was not long before Don Antonio succeeded to his father's titles and estates, and he and his fair spouse were renowned for being the handsomest and happiest couple in all Valencia.

As to Don Ambrosio, he partially recovered to the enjoyment of a broken constitution and a blasted name, and hid his remorse and disgraces in a convent; while the poor victim of his arts, who had assisted Inez in her escape, unable to conquer the early passion that he had awakened in her bosom, though convinced of the baseness of the object, retired from the world, and became an humble sister in a nunnery.

The worthy alchemist took up his abode with his children. A pavilion, in the garden of their palace, was assigned to him as a laboratory,

where he resumed his researches, with renovated ardor, after the grand secret. He was now and then assisted by his son-in-law; but the latter slackened grievously in his zeal and diligence after marriage. Still he would listen with profound gravity and attention to the old man's rhapsodies, and his quotations from Paracelsus, Sandivogius, and Pietro d'Abano, which daily grew longer and longer. In this way the good alchemist lived on quietly and comfortably, to what is called a good old age, that is to say, an age that is good for nothing, and, unfortunately for mankind, was hurried out of life in his ninetieth year, just as he was on the point of discovering the philosopher's stone.

Such was the story of the captain's friend, with which we whiled away the morning. The captain was, every now and then, interrupted by questions and remarks, which I have not mentioned, lest I should break the continuity of the tale. He was a little disturbed, also, once or twice, by the general, who fell asleep, and breathed rather hard, to the great horror and annoyance of Lady Lillycraft. In a long and tender love-scene, also, which was particularly to her ladyship's taste, the unlucky general, having his head a little sunk upon his breast kept making a sound at regular intervals, very much like the word *pish*, long drawn out. At length he made an odd, abrupt, guttural sound, that suddenly awoke him; he hemmed, looked about with a slight degree of consternation, and then began to play with her ladyship's work-bag, which, however, she rather pettishly withdrew. The steady sound of the captain's voice was still too potent a soporific for the poor general; he kept gleaming up and sinking in the socket, until the cessation of the tale again roused him, when he started awake, put his foot down upon Lady Lillycraft's cur, the sleeping Beauty, which yelped, seized him by the leg, and in a moment the whole library resounded with yelpings and exclamations. Never did a man more completely mar his fortunes while he was asleep. Silence being at length restored, the company expressed their thanks to the captain, and gave various opinions of the story. The parson's mind, I found, had been continually running upon the leaden manuscripts, mentioned in the beginning, as dug up at Grenada, and he put several eager questions to the captain on the subject. The general could not well make out the drift of the story, but thought it a little confused. "I am glad, however," said he, "that they burnt the old chap in the tower; I have no doubt he was a notorious impostor."

From *Bracebridge Hall*

ANNETTE DELARBRE

The soldier frae the war returns,
And the merchant from the main,
But I hae parted wi' my love,
And ne'er to meet again,
                My dear,
And ne'er to meet again.
When day is gone, and night is come,
And a' are boun to sleep,
I think on them that's far awa
The lee-lang night and weep,
                My dear,
The lee-lang night and weep.
                        Old Scotch Ballad

YESTERDAY was a day of quiet and repose after the bustle of May-day. During the morning I joined the ladies in a small sitting-room, the windows of which came down to the floor, and opened upon a terrace of the garden, which was set out with delicate shrubs and flowers. The soft sunshine falling into the room through the branches of trees that overhung the windows, the sweet smell of flowers, and the singing of birds, produced a pleasing yet calming effect on the whole party. Some time elapsed without any one speaking. Lady Lillycraft and Miss Templeton were sitting by an elegant work-table, near one of the windows, occupied with some pretty lady-like work. The captain was on a stool at his mistress's feet, looking over some music; and poor Phœbe Wilkins, who has always been a kind of pet among the ladies, but who has risen vastly in favor with Lady Lillycraft in consequence of some tender confessions, sat in one corner of the room, with swollen eyes, working pensively at some of the fair Julia's wedding ornaments.

The silence was interrupted by her ladyship, who suddenly proposed a task to the captain. "I am in your debt," said she, "for that tale you read to us the other day; I will now furnish one in return, if you'll

---

I have drawn this tale from two chapters of *Bracebridge Hall.* The first is called "The Manuscript."—C.N.

read it; and it is just suited to this sweet May morning, for it is all about love!"

The proposition seemed to delight every one present. The captain smiled assent. Her ladyship rang for her page, and despatched him to her room for the manuscript. "As the captain," said she, "gave us an account of the author of his story, it is but right I should give one of mine. It was written by the parson of the parish where I reside. He is a thin, elderly man, of a delicate constitution, but positively one of the most charming men that ever lived. He lost his wife a few years since; one of the sweetest women you ever saw. He has two sons, whom he educates himself; both of whom already write delightful poetry. His parsonage is a lovely place, close by the church, all overrun with ivy and honeysuckles, with the sweetest flower-garden about it; for, you know, our country clergymen are almost always fond of flowers, and make their parsonages perfect pictures.

"His living is a very good one, and he is very much beloved, and does a great deal of good in the neighborhood, and among the poor. And then such sermons as he preaches! Oh, if you could only hear one taken from a text in Solomon's Song, all about love and matrimony, one of the sweetest things you ever heard! He preaches it at least once a year, in springtime, for he knows I am fond of it. He always dines with me on Sundays, and often brings me some of the sweetest pieces of poetry, all about the pleasures of melancholy, and such subjects, that make me cry so, you can't think. I wish he would publish. I think he has some things as sweet as anything of Moore or Lord Byron.

"He fell into very ill health, some time ago, and was advised to go to the Continent; and I gave him no peace until he went, and promised to take care of his two boys until he returned.

"He was gone for above a year, and was quite restored. When he came back, he sent me the tale I'm going to show you—Oh, here it is!" said she, as the page put in her hands a beautiful box of satin-wood. She unlocked it, and among several parcels of notes on embossed paper, cards of charades, and copies of verses, she drew out a crimson velvet case, that smelt very much of perfumes. From this she took a manuscript, daintily written on gilt-edged vellum paper, and stitched with a light-blue ribbon. This she handed to the captain, who read the following tale, which I have procured for the entertainment of the reader.

IN the course of a tour in Lower Normandy I remained for a day or two in the old town of Honfleur, which stands near the mouth of the Seine. It was the time of a fête, and all the world was thronging in the

evening to dance at the fair, held before the chapel of Our Lady of Grace. As I like all kinds of innocent merry-making, I joined the throng.

The chapel is situated at the top of a high hill, or promontory, whence its bell may be heard at a distance by a mariner at night. It is said to have given the name to the port of Havre de Grace, which lies directly opposite, on the other side of the Seine. The road up to the chapel went in a zigzag course along the brow of the steep coast; it was shaded by trees, from between which I had beautiful peeps at the ancient towers of Honfleur below, the varied scenery of the opposite shore, the white buildings of Havre in the distance, and the wide sea beyond. The road was enlivened by groups of peasant girls, in bright crimson dresses, and tall caps, and I found all the flower of the neighborhood assembled on the green that crowds the summit of the hill.

The chapel of Notre Dame de Grace is a favorite resort of the inhabitants of Honfleur and its vicinity, both for pleasure and devotion. At this little chapel prayers are put up by the mariners of the port previous to their voyages, and by their friends during their absence; and votive offerings are hung about its walls, in fulfilment of vows made during times of shipwreck and disaster. The chapel is surrounded by trees. Over the portal is an image of the Virgin and Child, with an inscription which struck me as being quite poetical:

"Etoile de la mer, priez pour nous!"
(Star of the sea, pray for us.)

On a level spot near the chapel, under a grove of noble trees, the populace dance on fine summer evenings; and here are held frequent fairs and fêtes, which assemble all the rustic beauty of the loveliest parts of Lower Normandy. The present was an occasion of the kind. Booths and tents were erected among the trees; there were the usual displays of finery to tempt the rural coquette, and of wonderful shows to entice the curious; mountebanks were exerting their eloquence; jugglers and fortune-tellers astonishing the credulous; while whole rows of grotesque saints, in wood and wax-work, were offered for the purchase of the pious.

The fête had assembled in one view all the picturesque costumes of the Pays d'Auge and the Coté de Caux. I beheld tall, stately caps, and trim bodices, according to fashions which have been handed down from mother to daughter for centuries; the exact counterparts of those worn in the time of the Conqueror; and which surprised me by their faithful resemblance to those in the old pictures of Froissart's Chronicles, and in the paintings of illuminated manuscripts. Any one, also, who has

been in Lower Normandy, must have remarked the beauty of the peasantry, and that air of native elegance which prevails among them. It is to this country, undoubtedly, that the English owe their good looks. It was hence that the bright carnation, the fine blue eye, the light auburn hair, passed over to England in the train of the Conqueror, and filled the land with beauty.

The scene before me was perfectly enchanting: the assemblage of so many fresh and blooming faces; the gay groups in fanciful dresses; some dancing on the green, others strolling about, or seated on the grass; the fine clumps of trees in the foreground, bordering the brow of this airy height, and the broad green sea, sleeping in summer tranquillity, in the distance.

Whilst I was regarding this animated picture, I was struck with the appearance of a beautiful girl, who passed through the crowd without seeming to take any interest in their amusements. She was slender and delicate, without the bloom upon her cheek usual among the peasantry of Normandy, and her blue eyes had a singular and melancholy expression. She was accompanied by a venerable-looking man, whom I presumed to be her father. There was a whisper among the by-standers, and a wistful look after her as she passed; the young men touched their hats, and some of the children followed her at a little distance, watching her movements. She approached the edge of the hill, where there is a little platform, whence the people of Honfleur look out for the approach of vessels. Here she stood for some time waving her handkerchief, though there was nothing to be seen but two or three fishing-boats, like mere specks on the bosom of the distant ocean.

These circumstances excited my curiosity, and I made some inquiries about her, which were answered with readiness and intelligence by a priest of the neighboring chapel. Our conversation drew together several of the by-standers, each of whom had something to communicate, and from them all I gathered the following particulars.

Annette Delarbre was the only daughter of one of the higher order of farmers, or small proprietors, as they are called, of Pont l'Eveque, a pleasant village not far from Honfleur, in that rich pastoral part of Lower Normandy called the Pays d'Auge. Annette was the pride and delight of her parents, who brought her up with the fondest indulgence. She was gay, tender, petulant, and susceptible. All her feelings were quick and ardent; and having never experienced contradiction nor restraint she was little practised in self-control; nothing but the native goodness of her heart kept her from running continually into error.

Even while a child, her susceptibility was evinced in an attachment formed to a playmate, Eugene la Forgue, the only son of a widow of the

neighborhood. Their childish love was an epitome of maturer passion; it had its caprices, and jealousies, and quarrels, and reconciliations. It was assuming something of a graver character as Annette entered her fifteenth and Eugene his nineteenth year, when he was suddenly carried off to the army by the conscription.

It was a heavy blow to his widowed mother, for he was her only pride and comfort; but it was one of those sudden bereavements which mothers were perpetually doomed to feel in France, during the time that continual and bloody wars were incessantly draining her youth. It was a temporary affliction also to Annette, to lose her lover. With tender embraces, half childish, half womanish she parted from him. The tears streamed from her blue eyes as she bound a braid of her fair hair round his wrist; but the smiles still broke through; for she was yet too young to feel how serious a thing is separation, and how many chances there are, when parting in this wide world, against our ever meeting again.

Weeks, months, years flew by. Annette increased in beauty as she increased in years, and was the reigning belle of the neighborhood. Her time passed innocently and happily. Her father was a man of some consequence in the rural community, and his house was the resort of the gayest of the village. Annette held a kind of rural court; she was always surrounded by companions of her own age, among whom she shone unrivalled. Much of their time was passed in making lace, the prevalent manufacture of the neighborhood. As they sat at this delicate and feminine labor, the merry tale and sprightly song went round. None laughed with a lighter heart than Annette; and if she sang, her voice was perfect melody. Their evenings were enlivened by the dance, or by those pleasant social games so prevalent among the French; and when she appeared at the village ball on Sunday evenings, she was the theme of universal admiration.

As she was a rural heiress, she did not want for suitors. Many advantageous offers were made her, but she refused them all. She laughed at the pretended pangs of her admirers, and triumphed over them with the caprice of buoyant youth and conscious beauty. With all her apparent levity, however, could any one have read the story of her heart, they might have traced in it some fond remembrance of her early playmate, not so deeply graven as to be painful, but too deep to be easily obliterated; and they might have noticed, amidst all her gayety, the tenderness that marked her manner towards the mother of Eugene. She would often steal away from her youthful companions and their amusements, to pass whole days with the good widow; listening to her fond talk about her boy, and blushing with secret pleasure, when his letters were read, at finding herself a constant theme of recollection and inquiry.

At length the sudden return of peace, which sent many a warrior to his native cottage, brought back Eugene, a young sunburnt soldier, to the village. I need not say how rapturously his return was greeted by his mother, who saw in him the pride and staff of her old age. He had risen in the service by his merit; but brought away but little from the wars excepting a soldierlike air, a gallant name, and, a scar across the forehead. He brought back however, a nature unspoiled by the camp. He was frank, open, generous, and ardent. His heart was quick and kind in its impulses, and was perhaps a little softer from having suffered. It was full of tenderness for Annette. He had received frequent accounts of her from his mother; and the mention of her kindness to his lonely parent had rendered her doubly dear to him. He had been wounded. He had been a prisoner; he had been in various troubles but had always preserved the braid of hair which she had bound round his arm. It had been a kind of talisman to him; he had many a time looked upon it as he lay on the hard ground, and the thought that he might one day see Annette again, and the fair fields about his native village, had cheered his heart, and enabled him to bear up against every hardship.

He had left Annette almost a child; he found her a blooming woman. If he had loved her before, he now adored her. Annette was equally struck with the improvement time had made in her lover. She noticed, with secret admiration, his superiority to the young men of the village; the frank, lofty, military air, that distinguished him from all the rest at their rural gatherings. The more she saw him, the more her light, playful fondness of former years deepened into ardent and powerful affection. But Annette was a rural belle. She had tasted the sweets of dominion, and had been rendered wilful and capricious by constant indulgence at home, and admiration abroad. She was conscious of her power over Eugene, and delighted in exercising it. She sometimes treated him with petulant caprice, enjoying the pain which she inflicted by her frowns, from the idea how soon she would chase it away again by her smiles. She took a pleasure in alarming his fears, by affecting a temporary preference for some one or other of his rivals; and then would delight in allaying them by an ample measure of returning kindness. Perhaps there was some degree of vanity gratified by all this; it might be a matter of triumph to show her absolute power over the young soldier, who was a universal object of female admiration. Eugene, however, was of too serious and ardent a nature to be trifled with. He loved too fervently not to be filled with doubt. He saw Annette surrounded by admirers, and full of animation, the gayest among the gay at all their rural festivities, and apparently most gay when he was most

dejected. Every one saw through this caprice but himself; every one saw that in reality she doted on him; but Eugene alone suspected the sincerity of her affection. For some time he bore the coquetry with secret impatience and distrust; but his feelings grew sore and irritable, and overcame his self-command. A slight misunderstanding took place; a quarrel ensued. Annette, unaccustomed to be thwarted and contradicted, and full of the insolence of youthful beauty, assumed an air of disdain. She refused all explanations to her lover, and they parted in anger. That very evening Eugene saw her, full of gayety, dancing with one of his rivals; and as her eye caught his, fixed on her with unfeigned distress, it sparkled with more than usual vivacity. It was a finishing blow to his hopes, already so much impaired by secret distrust. Pride and resentment both struggled in his breast, and seemed to rouse his spirit to all his wonted energy. He retired from her presence with the hasty determination never to see her again.

A woman is more considerate in affairs of love than a man; because love is more the study and business of her life. Annette soon repented of her indiscretion; she felt that she had used her lover unkindly; she felt that she had trifled with his sincere and generous nature—and then he looked so handsome when he parted after their quarrel—his fine features lighted up by indignation. She had intended making up with him at the evening dance; but his sudden departure prevented her. She now promised herself that when next they met she would amply repay him by the sweets of a perfect reconciliation, and that, thenceforward, she would never—never tease him more! That promise was not to be fulfilled. Day after day passed; but Eugene did not make his appearance. Sunday evening came, the usual time when all the gayety of the village asssembled; but Eugene was not there. She inquired after him; he had left the village. She now became alarmed, and, forgetting all coyness and affected indifference, called on Eugene's mother for an explanation. She found her full of affliction, and learnt with surprise and consternation that Eugene had gone to sea.

While his feelings were yet smarting with her affected disdain, and his heart a prey to alternate indignation and despair, he had suddenly embraced an invitation which had repeatedly been made him by a relative, who was fitting out a ship from the port of Honfleur, and who wished him to be the companion of his voyage. Absence appeared to him the only cure for his unlucky passion; and in the temporary transports of his feelings there was something gratifying in the idea of having half the world intervene between them. The hurry necessary for his departure left no time for cool reflection; it rendered him deaf to the remonstrances of his afflicted mother. He hastened to Honfleur just in

time to make the needful preparations for the voyage; and the first news that Annette received of this sudden determination was a letter delivered by his mother, returning her pledges of affection, particularly the long-treasured braid of her hair, and bidding her a last farewell, in terms more full of sorrow and tenderness than upbraiding.

This was the first stroke of real anguish that Annette had ever received, and it overcame her. The vivacity of her spirits were apt to hurry her to extremes; she for a time gave way to ungovernable transports of affliction and remorse, and manifested, in the violence of her grief, the real ardor of her affection. The thought occurred to her that the ship might not yet have sailed; she seized on the hope with eagerness, and hastened with her father to Honfleur. The ship had sailed that very morning. From the heights above the town she saw it lessening to a speck on the broad bosom of the ocean, and before evening the white sail had faded from her sight. She turned, full of anguish, to the neighboring chapel of Our Lady of Grace, and throwing herself on the pavement, poured out prayers and tears for the safe return of her lover.

When she returned home, the cheerfulness of her spirits was at an end. She looked back with remorse and self-upbraiding on her past caprices; she turned with distaste from the adulation of her admirers, and had no longer any relish for the amusements of the village. With humiliation and diffidence she sought the widowed mother of Eugene; but was received by her with an overflowing heart, for she only beheld in Annette one who could sympathize in her doting fondness for her son. It seemed some alleviation of her remorse to sit by the mother all day, to study her wants, to beguile her heavy hours, to hang about her with the caressing endearments of a daughter, and to seek by every means, if possible, to supply the place of the son, whom she reproached herself with having driven away.

In the meantime the ship made a prosperous voyage to her destined port. Eugene's mother received a letter from him, in which he lamented the precipitancy of his departure. The voyage had given him time for sober reflection. If Annette had been unkind to him, he ought not to have forgotten what was due to his mother, who was now advanced in years. He accused himself of selfishness in only listening to the suggestions of his own inconsiderate passions. He promised to return with the ship, to make his mind up to his disappointment, and to think of nothing but making his mother happy——"And when he does return," said Annette, clasping her hands with transport, "it shall not be my fault if he ever leaves us again."

The time approached for the ship's return. She was daily expected, when the weather became dreadfully tempestuous. Day after day

brought news of vessels foundered, or driven on shore, and the coast was strewed with wrecks. Intelligence was received of the looked-for ship having been seen dismasted in a violent storm, and the greatest fears were entertained for her safety.

Annette never left the side of Eugene's mother. She watched every change of her countenance with painful solicitude, and endeavored to cheer her with hopes, while her own mind was racked by anxiety. She tasked her efforts to be gay; but it was a forced and unnatural gayety. A sigh from the mother would completely check it; and when she could no longer restrain the rising tears, she would hurry away and pour out her agony in secret. Every anxious look, every anxious inquiry of the mother, whenever a door opened, or a strange face appeared, was an arrow to her soul. She considered every disappointment as a pang of her own infliction, and her heart sickened under the care-worn expression of the maternal eye. At length this suspense became insupportable. She left the village and hastened to Honfleur, hoping every hour, every moment, to receive some tidings of her lover. She paced the pier, and wearied the seamen of the port with her inquiries. She made a daily pilgrimage to the chapel of Our Lady of Grace, hung votive garlands on the wall, and passed hours either kneeling before the altar, or looking out from the brow of the hill upon the angry sea.

At length word was brought that the long-wished-for vessel was in sight. She was seen standing into the mouth of the Seine, shattered and crippled, bearing marks of having been sadly tempest-tossed. A general joy was diffused by her return; and there was not a brighter eye, nor a lighter heart, than Annette's in the little port of Honfleur. The ship came to anchor in the river; and a boat put off for the shore. The populace crowded down to the pier head to welcome it. Annette stood blushing, and smiling, and trembling, and weeping; for a thousand painfully pleasing emotions agitated her breast at the thoughts of the meeting and reconciliation about to take place.

Her heart throbbed to pour itself out, and atone to her gallant lover for all its errors. At one moment she would place herself in a conspicuous situation, where she might catch his view at once, and surprise him by her welcome; but the next moment a doubt would come across her mind, and she would shrink among the throng, trembling and faint, and gasping with her emotions. Her agitation increased as the boat drew near, until it became distressing; and it was almost a relief to her when she perceived that her lover was not there. She presumed that some accident had detained him on board of the ship, and felt that the delay would enable her to gather more self-possession for the meeting. As the boat neared the shore, many inquiries were made, and laconic

answers returned. At length Annette heard some inquiries after her lover. Her heart palpitated; there was a moment's pause; the reply was brief, but awful. He had been washed from the deck, with two of the crew, in the midst of a stormy night, when it was impossible to render any assistance. A piercing shriek broke from among the crowd, and Annette had nearly fallen into the waves.

The sudden revulsion of feelings after such a transient gleam of happiness was too much for her harassed frame. She was carried home senseless. Her life was for some time despaired of, and it was months before she recovered her health; but she never had perfectly recovered her mind. It still remained unsettled with respect to her lover's fate.

"The subject," continued my informer, "is never mentioned in her hearing; but she sometimes speaks of it herself, and it seems as though there were some vague train of impressions in her mind, in which hope and fear are strangely mingled; some imperfect idea of her lover's shipwreck, and yet some expectation of his return.

"Her parents have tried every means to cheer her, and to banish these gloomy images from her thoughts. They assemble round her the young companions in whose society she used to delight; and they will work and chat, and sing, and laugh, as formerly; but she will sit silently among them, and will sometimes weep in the midst of their gayety; and if spoken to, will make no reply, but look up with streaming eyes, and sing a dismal little song, which she has learned somewhere, about a shipwreck. It makes everyone's very heart ache to see her in this way, for she used to be the happiest creature in the village.

"She passes the greater part of the time with Eugene's mother; whose only consolation is her society, and who dotes on her with a mother's tenderness. She is the only one that has perfect influence over Annette in every mood. The poor girl seems, as formerly, to make an effort to be cheerful in her company; but will sometimes gaze upon her with the most piteous look, and then kiss her gray hairs, and fall on her neck and weep.

"She is not always melancholy, however; there are occasional intervals when she will be bright and animated for days together; but a degree of wildness attends these fits of gayety, that prevents their yielding any satisfaction to her friends. At such times she will arrange her room, which is all covered with pictures of ships and legends of saints; and will wreathe a white chaplet, as for a wedding, and prepare wedding ornaments. She will listen anxiously at the door, and look frequently out at the window, as if expecting some one's arrival. It is supposed that at such times she is looking for her lover's return; but, as no one touches upon the theme, or mentions his name in her presence, the current of

her thoughts is mere matter of conjecture. Now and then she will make a pilgrimage to the chapel of Notre Dame de Grace; where she will pray for hours at the altar, and decorate the images with wreathes that she has woven; or will wave her handkerchief from the terrace, as you have seen if there is any vessel in the distance."

Upwards of a year, he informed me, had now elapsed without effacing from her mind this singular taint of insanity, still her friends hoped it might gradually wear away. They had at one time removed her to a distant part of the country, in hopes that absence from the scenes connected with her story might have a salutary effect; but, when her periodical melancholy returned, she became more restless and wretched than usual, and, secretly escaping from her friends, set out on foot, without knowing the road, on one of her pilgrimages to the chapel.

This little story entirely drew my attention from the gay scene of the fête, and fixed it upon the beautiful Annette. While she was yet standing on the terrace, the vesper-bell rang from the neighboring chapel. She listened for a moment, and then drawing a small rosary from her bosom, walked in that direction. Several of the peasantry followed her in silence; and I felt too much interested not to do the same.

The chapel, as I said before, is in the midst of a grove, on the high promontory. The inside is hung round with little models of ships, and rude paintings of wrecks and perils at sea, and providential deliverances, the votive offerings of captains and crews that have been saved. On entering, Annette paused for a moment before a picture of the Virgin, which, I observed, had recently been decorated with a wreath of artificial flowers. When she reached the middle of the chapel she knelt down, and those who followed her involuntarily did the same at a little distance. The evening sun shone softly through the checkered grove into one window of the chapel. A perfect stillness reigned within; and this stillness was the more impressive, contrasted with the distant sound of music and merriment from the fair. I could not take my eyes off from the poor suppliant; her lips moved as she told her beads, but her prayers were breathed in silence. It might have been mere fancy excited by the scene, that, as she raised her eyes to heaven, I thought they had an expression truly seraphic. But I am easily affected by female beauty, and there was something in this mixture of love, devotion, and partial insanity, inexpressibly touching.

As the poor girl left the chapel, there was a sweet serenity in her looks; and I was told she would return home, and in all probability be calm and cheerful for days, and even weeks; in which time it was supposed that hope predominated in her mental malady; and when the dark side of her mind, as her friends call it, was about to turn up, it

would be known by her neglecting her distaff or her lace, singing plaintive songs, and weeping in silence.

She passed on from the chapel without noticing the fête, but smiling and speaking to many as she passed. I followed her with my eyes as she descended the winding road towards Honfleur, leaning on her father's arm. "Heaven," thought I, "has ever its store of balms for the hurt mind and wounded spirit, and may in time rear up this broken flower to be once more the pride and joy of the valley. The very delusion in which the poor girl walks may be one of those mists kindly diffused by Providence over the regions of thought, when they become too fruitful of misery. The veil may gradually be raised which obscures the horizon of her mind, as she is enabled steadily and calmly to contemplate the sorrows at present hidden in mercy from her view."

On my return from Paris, about a year afterwards, I turned off from the beaten route at Rouen, to revisit some of the most striking scenes of Lower Normandy. Having passed through the lovely country of the Pays d'Auge, I reached Honfleur on a fine afternoon, intending to cross to Havre the next morning, and embark for England. As I had no better way of passing the evening, I strolled up the hill to enjoy the fine prospect from the chapel of Notre Dame de Grace; and while there, I thought of inquiring after the fate of poor Annette Delarbre. The priest who had told me her story was officiating at vespers, after which I accosted him, and learnt from him the remaining circumstances. He told me that from the time I had seen her at the chapel, her disorder took a sudden turn for the worse, and her health rapidly declined. Her cheerful intervals became shorter and less frequent, and attended with more incoherency. She grew languid, silent, and moody in her melancholy; her form was wasted, her looks were pale and disconsolate, and it was feared she would never recover. She became impatient of all sounds of gayety, and was never so contented as when Eugene's mother was near her. The good woman watched over her with patient, yearning solicitude; and in seeking to beguile her sorrows, would half forget her own. Sometimes, as she sat looking upon her pallid face, the tears would fill her eyes, which when Annette perceived, she would anxiously wipe them away, and tell her not to grieve, for that Eugene would soon return; and then she would effect a forced gayety, as in former times, and sing a lively air; but a sudden recollection would come over her, and she would burst into tears, hang on the poor mother's neck, and entreat her not to curse her for having destroyed her son.

Just at this time, to the astonishment of every one, news was received of Eugene; who, it appears, was still living. When almost drowned, he

had fortunately seized upon a spar, washed from the ship's deck. Finding himself nearly exhausted, he fastened himself to it, and floated for a day and night, until all sense left him. On recovering, he found himself on board a vessel bound to India, but so ill as not to move without assistance. His health continued precarious throughout the voyage. On arriving in India, he experienced many vicissitudes, and was transferred from ship to ship, and hospital to hospital. His constitution enabled him to struggle through every hardship; and he was now in a distant port, waiting only for the sailing of a ship to return home.

Great caution was necessary in imparting these tidings to the mother, and even then she was nearly overcome by the transports of her joy. But how to impart them to Annette was a matter of still greater perplexity. Her state of mind had been so morbid, she had been subject to such violent changes, and the cause of her derangement had been of such an inconsolable and hopeless kind, that her friends had always forborne to tamper with her feelings. They had never even hinted at the subject of her griefs, nor encouraged the theme when she adverted to it, but had passed it over in silence, hoping that time would gradually wear the traces of it from her recollection, or, at least, would render them less painful. They now felt at a loss how to undeceive her even in her misery, lest the sudden recurrence of happiness might confirm the estrangement of her reason, or might overpower her feeble frame. They ventured, however, to probe those wounds which they formerly did not dare to touch, for they now had the balm to pour into them. They led the conversation to those topics which they had hitherto shunned, and endeavored to ascertain the current of her thoughts in those varying moods which had formerly perplexed them. They found her mind even more affected than they had imagined. All her ideas were confused and wandering. Her bright and cheerful moods, which now grew seldomer than ever, were all the effects of mental delusion. At such times she had no recollection of her lover's having been in danger, but was only anticipating his arrival. "When the winter has passed away," said she, "and the trees put on their blossoms, and the swallow comes back over the sea, he will return." When she was drooping and desponding, it was in vain to remind her of what she had said in her gayer moments, and to assure her that Eugene would indeed return shortly. She wept on in silence, and appeared insensible to their words. But at times her agitation became violent, when she would upbraid herself with having driven Eugene from his mother, and brought sorrow on her gray hairs. Her mind admitted but one leading idea at a time, which nothing could avert or efface; or if they ever succeeded in interrupting the current of her fancy, it only became the more incoherent, and increased

the feverishness that preyed upon both mind and body. Her friends felt more alarm for her than ever, for they feared her senses were irrevocably gone, and her constitution completely undermined.

In the meantime Eugene returned to the village. He was violently affected when the story of Annette was told him. With bitterness of heart he upbraided his own rashness and infatuation that had hurried him away from her, and accused himself as the author of all her woes. His mother would describe to him all the anguish and remorse of poor Annette; the tenderness with which she clung to her, and endeavored, even in the midst of her insanity, to console her for the loss of her son; and the touching expressions of affection mingled with her most incoherent wanderings of thought, until his feelings would be wound up to agony, and he would entreat her to desist from the recital. They did not dare as yet to bring him into Annette's sight; but he was permitted to see her when she was sleeping. The tears streamed down his sunburnt cheeks as he contemplated the ravages which grief and malady had made; and his heart swelled almost to breaking as he beheld round her neck the very braid of hair which she once gave him in token of girlish affection, and which he had returned to her in anger.

At length the physician that attended her determined to adventure upon an experiment; to take advantage of one of those cheerful moods when her mind was visited by hope, and to engraft, as it were, the reality upon the delusions of her fancy. These moods had now become very rare, for nature was sinking under the continual pressure of her mental malady, and the principle of reaction was daily growing weaker. Every effort was tried to bring on a cheerful interval of the kind. Several of her most favorite companions were kept continually about her; they chatted gayly, they laughed, and sang, and danced; but Annette reclined with languid frame and hollow eye, and took no part in their gayety. At length the winter was gone; the trees put forth their leaves; the swallows began to build in the eaves of the house, and the robin and wren piped all day beneath the window. Annette's spirits gradually revived. She began to deck her person with unusual care; and bringing forth a basket of artificial flowers, went to work to wreathe a bridal chaplet of white roses. Her companions asked her why she prepared the chaplet. "What!" said she with a smile, "have you not noticed the trees putting on their wedding-dresses of blossoms? Has not the swallow flown back over the sea? Do you not know that the time is come for Eugene to return? that he will be home tomorrow, and that on Sunday we are to be married?"

Her words were repeated to the physician, and he seized on them at once. He directed that her idea should be encouraged and acted upon.

Her words were echoed through the house. Every one talked of the return of Eugene as a matter of course; they congratulated her upon her approaching happiness, and assisted her in her preparations. The next morning the same theme was resumed. She was dressed out to receive her lover. Every bosom fluttered with anxiety. A cabriolet drove into the village. "Eugene is coming!" was the cry. She saw him alight at the door, and rushed with a shriek into his arms.

Her friends trembled for the result of this critical experiment; but she did not sink under it, for her fancy had prepared her for his return. She was as one in a dream, to whom a tide of unlooked-for prosperity, that would have overwhelmed his waking reason, seems but the natural current of circumstances. Her conversation, however, showed that her senses were wandering. There was an absolute forgetfulness of all past sorrow; a wild and feverish gayety that at times was incoherent.

The next morning she awoke languid and exhausted. All the occurrences of the preceding day had passed away from her mind as though they had been the mere illusions of her fancy. She rose melancholy and abstracted, and as she dressed herself, was heard to sing one of her plaintive ballads. When she entered the parlor, her eyes were swollen with weeping. She heard Eugene's voice without, and started; passed her hand across her forehead, and stood musing, like one endeavoring to recall a dream. Eugene entered the room, and advanced towards her. She looked at him with an eager, searching look, murmured some indistinct words, and, before he could reach her, sank upon the floor.

She relapsed into a wild and unsettled state of mind; but now that the first shock was over, the physician ordered that Eugene should keep continually in her sight. Sometimes she did not know him; at other times she would talk to him as if he were going to sea, and would implore him not to part from her in anger; and when he was not present, she would speak of him as if buried in the ocean, and would sit, with clasped hands, looking upon the ground, the picture of despair.

As the agitation of her feelings subsided, and her frame recovered from the shock it had received, she became more placid and coherent. Eugene kept almost continually near her. He formed the real object round which her scattered ideas once more gathered, and which linked them once more with the realities of life. But her changeful disorder now appeared to take a new turn. She became languid and inert, and would sit for hours silent, and almost in a state of lethargy. If roused from this stupor, it seemed as if her mind would make some attempt to follow up a train of thought, but would soon become confused. She would regard every one that approached her with an anxious and inquiring eye, that seemed continually to disappoint itself. Sometimes, as

her lover sat holding her hand, she would look pensively in his face without saying a word, until his heart was overcome; and after these transient fits of intellectual exertion, she would sink again into lethargy.

By degrees this stupor increased; her mind appeared to have subsided into a stagnant and almost deathlike calm. For the greater part of the time her eyes were closed; her face was almost as fixed and passionless as that of a corpse. She no longer took any notice of surrounding objects. There was an awfulness in this tranquillity that filled her friends with apprehensions. The physician ordered that she should be kept perfectly quiet; or that, if she evinced any agitation, she should be gently lulled, like a child, by some favorite tune.

She remained in this state for hours, hardly seeming to breathe, and apparently sinking into the sleep of death. Her chamber was profoundly still. The attendants moved about it with noiseless tread; everything was communicated by signs and whispers. Her lover sat by her side watching her with painful anxiety, and fearing every breath which stole from her pale lips would be the last.

At length she heaved a deep sigh; and from some convulsive motions, appeared to be troubled in her sleep. Her agitation increased, accompanied by an indistinct moaning. One of her companions, remembering the physician's instructions, endeavored to lull her by singing, in a low voice, a tender little air, which was a particular favorite of Annette's. Probably it had some connection in her mind with her own story; for every fond girl has some ditty of the kind, linked in her thoughts with sweet and sad remembrances.

As she sang, the agitation of Annette subsided. A streak of faint color came into her cheeks; her eyelids became swollen with rising tears, which trembled there for a moment, and then, stealing forth, coursed down her pallid cheek. When the song was ended, she opened her eyes, and looked about her, as one awaking in a strange place.

"Oh, Eugene! Eugene!" said she, "it seems as if I have had a long and dismal dream; what has happened, and what has been the matter with me?"

The questions were embarrassing; and before they could be answered, the physician, who was in the next room, entered. She took him by the hand, looked up in his face, and made the same inquiry. He endeavored to put her off with some evasive answer. "No, no!" cried she, "I know I have been ill, and I have been dreaming strangely. I thought Eugene had left us—and that he had gone to sea—and that— and that he was drowned!—but he *has* been to sea!" added she earnestly, as recollection kept flashing upon her, "and he has been wrecked—and we were all so wretched—and he came home again one bright morning

—and—oh!" said she, pressing her hand against her forehead with a sickly smile, "I see how it is; all has not been right here. I begin to recollect—but it is all past now—Eugene is here! and his mother is happy —and we will never—never part again—shall we, Eugene?"

She sunk back in her chair exhausted; the tears streamed down her cheeks. Her companions hovered round her, not knowing what to make of this sudden dawn of reason. Her lover sobbed aloud. She opened her eyes again, and looked upon them with an air of the sweetest acknowledgment. "You are all so good to me!" said she, faintly.

The physician drew the father aside. "Your daughter's mind is restored," said he; "she is sensible that she has been deranged; she is growing conscious of the past, and conscious of the present. All that now remains is to keep her calm and quiet until her health is re-established, and then let her be married, in God's name!"

"The wedding took place," continued the good priest, "but a short time since; they were here at the last fête during their honeymoon, and a handsomer and happier couple was not to be seen as they danced under yonder trees. The young man, his wife, and mother, now live on a fine farm at Pont l'Eveque; and the model of a ship which you see yonder, with white flowers wreathed round it, is Annette's offering of thanks to our Lady of Grace, for having listened to her prayers, and protected her lover in the hour of peril."

The captain having finished, there was a momentary silence. The tender-hearted Lady Lillycraft, who knew the story by heart, had led the way in weeping, and indeed often began to shed tears before they came to the right place.

The fair Julia was a little flurried at the passage where wedding preparations were mentioned; but the auditor most affected was the simple Phœbe Wilkins. She had gradually dropped her work in her lap, and sat sobbing through the latter part of the story, until towards the end, when the happy reverse had nearly produced another scene of hysterics. "Go, take this case to my room again, child," said Lady Lillycraft kindly, "and don't cry so much."

"I won't, an't please your ladyship, if I can help it;—but I'm glad they made all up again, and were married!"

From *Bracebridge Hall*

DOLPH HEYLIGER

The Historian

Hermione. Pray you sit by us, And tell's a tale.
Mamilius. Merry or sad shall 't be?
Hermione. As merry as you will.
Mamilius. A sad tale's best for winter.
I have one of sprites and goblins.
Hermione. Let's have that, sir.

Winter's Tale.

A S this is a story-telling age, I have been tempted occasionally to
give the reader one of the many tales served up with supper at the
Hall. I might, indeed, have furnished a series almost equal in number
to the *Arabian Nights;* but some were rather hackneyed and tedious;
others I did not feel warranted in betraying into print; and many more
were of the old general's relating, and turned principally upon tiger
hunting, elephant riding, and Seringapatam, enlivened by the wonderful deeds of Tippoo Saib, and the excellent jokes of Major Pendergast.

I had all along maintained a quiet post at a corner of the table, where
I had been able to indulge my humor undisturbed; listening attentively
when the story was very good, and dozing a little when it was rather
dull, which I consider the perfection of auditorship.

I was roused the other evening from a slight trance, into which I had
fallen during one of the general's histories, by a sudden call from the
Squire to furnish some entertainment of the kind in my turn. Having
been so profound a listener to others, I could not in conscience refuse;
but neither my memory nor invention being ready to answer so unexpected a demand, I begged leave to read a manuscript tale from the
pen of my fellow-countryman, the late Mr. Diedrich Knickerbocker, the
historian of New York. As this ancient chronicler may not be better
known to my readers than he was to the company at the Hall, a word or

---

This tale has two introductory chapters in *Bracebridge Hall*, both of which I
have included.—C.N.

two concerning him may not be amiss, before proceeding to his manuscript.

Diedrich Knickerbocker was a native of New York, a descendant from one of the ancient Dutch families which originally settled that province, and remained there after it was taken possession of by the English in 1664. The descendants of these Dutch families still remain in villages and neighborhoods in various parts of the country, retaining, with singular obstinacy, the dresses, manners, and even language of their ancestors, and forming a very distinct and curious feature in the motley population of the State. In a hamlet whose spire may be seen from New York, rising from above the brow of a hill on the opposite side of the Hudson, many of the old folks, even at the present day, speak English with an accent, and the Dominie preaches in Dutch; and so completely is the hereditary love of quiet and silence maintained, that in one of these drowsy villages, in the middle of a warm summer's day, the buzzing of a stout bluebottle fly will resound from one end of the place to the other.

With the laudable hereditary feeling thus kept up among these worthy people, did Mr. Knickerbocker undertake to write a history of his native city, comprising the reign of its three Dutch governors during the time that it was yet under the domination of the Hogenmogens of Holland. In the execution of this design the little Dutchman has displayed great historical research, and a wonderful consciousness of the dignity of his subject. His work, however, has been so little understood as to be pronounced a mere work of humor, satirizing the follies of the times, both in politics and morals, and giving whimsical views of human nature.

Be this as it may,—among the papers left behind him were several tales of a lighter nature, apparently thrown together from materials gathered during his profound researches for his history, and which he seems to have cast by with neglect, as unworthy of publication. Some of these have fallen into my hands by an accident which it is needless at present to mention; and one of these very stories, with its prelude in the words of Mr. Knickerbocker, I undertook to read, by way of acquitting myself of the debt which I owed to the other story-tellers at the Hall. I subjoin it for such of my readers as are fond of stories.

The Haunted House

FROM THE MSS. OF THE LATE DIEDRICH KNICKER-
BOCKER

Formerly almost every place had a house of this kind. If a house was
seated on some melancholy place, or built in some old romantic manner,
or if any particular accident had happened in it, such as murder, sudden
death, or the like, to be sure that house had a mark set on it, and was afterwards esteemed the habitation of a ghost.—Bourne's *Antiquities*.

IN the neighborhood of the ancient city of the Manhattoes there
stood, not very many years since, an old mansion, which, when I was a
boy, went by the name of the Haunted House. It was one of the very
few remains of the architecture of the early Dutch settlers, and must
have been a house of some consequence at the time when it was built.
It consisted of a centre and two wings, the gable ends of which were
shaped like stairs. It was built partly of wood and partly of small Dutch
bricks, such as the worthy colonists brought with them from Holland,
before they discovered that bricks could be manufactured elsewhere.
The house stood remote from the road, in the centre of a large field,
with an avenue of old locust* trees leading up to it, several of which
had been shivered by lightning, and two or three blown down. A few
apple trees grew straggling about the field; there were traces also of
what had been a kitchen garden; but the fences were broken down, the
vegetables had disappeared, or had grown wild, and turned to little
better than weeds, with here and there a ragged rosebush, or a tall sun-
flower shooting up from among the brambles, and hanging its head
sorrowfully, as if contemplating the surrounding desolation. Part of the
roof of the old house had fallen in, the windows were shattered, the
panels of the doors broken, and mended with rough boards, and two
rusty weather-cocks at the ends of the house made a great jingling and
whistling as they whirled about, but always pointed wrong. The appearance of the whole place was forlorn and desolate at the best of
times; but, in unruly weather, the howling of the wind about the crazy
old mansion, the screeching of the weather-cocks, and the slamming
and banging of a few loose window shutters, had altogether so wild
and dreary an effect, that the neighborhood stood perfectly in awe of

* Acacias.

the place, and pronounced it the rendezvous of hobgoblins. I recollect the old building well; for many times, when an idle, unlucky urchin, I have prowled round its precinct, with some of my graceless companions, on holiday afternoons when out on a free-booting cruise among the orchards. There was a tree standing near the house that bore the most beautiful and tempting fruit; but then it was on enchanted ground, for the place was so charmed by frightful stories that we dreaded to approach it. Sometimes we would venture in a body, and get near the Hesperian tree, keeping an eye upon the old mansion, and darting fearful glances into its shattered windows, when, just as we were about to seize upon our prize, an exclamation from some one of the gang, or an accidental noise, would throw us all into a panic, and we would scamper headlong from the place, nor stop until we had got quite into the road. Then there was sure to be a host of fearful anecdotes told of strange cries and groans, or of some hideous face suddenly seen staring out of one of the windows. By degrees we ceased to venture into these lonely grounds, but would stand at a distance, and throw stones at the building; and there was something fearfully pleasing in the sound as they rattled along the roof, or sometimes struck some jingling fragments of glass out of the windows.

The origin of this house was lost in the obscurity that covers the early period of the province, while under the government of their high mightinesses the states-general. Some reported it to have been a country residence of Wilhelmus Kieft, commonly called the Testy, one of the Dutch governors of New Amsterdam; others said it had been built by a naval commander who served under Van Tromp, and who, on being disappointed of preferment, retired from the service in disgust, became a philosopher through sheer spite, and brought over all his wealth to the province, that he might live according to his humor, and despise the world. The reason of its having fallen to decay was likewise a matter of dispute. Some said it was in chancery, and had already cost more than its worth in legal expense; but the most current, and, of course, the most probable account, was that it was haunted, and that nobody could live quietly in it. There can, in fact, be very little doubt that this last was the case, there were so many corroborating stories to prove it,— not an old woman in the neighborhood but could furnish at least a score. A gray-headed curmudgeon of a negro who lived hard by had a whole budget of them to tell, many of which had happened to himself. I recollect many a time stopping with my schoolmates, and getting him to relate some. The old crone lived in a hovel, in the midst of a small patch of potatoes and Indian corn, which his master had given him on setting him free. He would come to us, with his hoe in his hand, and

as we sat perched, like a row of swallows, on the rail of a fence, in the mellow twilight of a summer evening, would tell us such fearful stories, accompanied by such awful rollings of his white eyes, that we were almost afraid of our own footsteps as we returned home afterwards in the dark.

Poor old Pompey! many years are past since he died, and went to keep company with the ghosts he was so fond of talking about. He was buried in a corner of his own little potato patch; the plough soon passed over his grave, and levelled it with the rest of the field, and nobody thought any more of the gray-headed negro. By singular chance I was strolling in that neighborhood, several years afterwards, when I had grown up to be a young man, and I found a knot of gossips speculating on a skull which had just been turned up by a plough-share. They of course determined it to be the remains of some one who had been murdered and they had raked up with it some of the traditionary tales of the haunted house. I knew it at once to be the relic of poor Pompey, but I held my tongue; for I am too considerate of other people's enjoyment even to mar a story of a ghost or a murder. I took care, however, to see the bones of my old friend once more buried in a place where they were not likely to be disturbed. As I sat on the turf and watched the interment, I fell into a long conversation with an old gentleman of the neighborhood, John Josse Vandermoere, a pleasant gossiping man, whose whole life was spent in hearing and telling the news of the province. He recollected old Pompey, and his stories about the Haunted House; but he assured me he could give me one still more strange than any that Pompey had related, and on my expressing a great curiosity to hear it, he sat down beside me on the turf, and told the following tale. I have endeavored to give it as nearly as possible in his words; but it is now many years since, and I am grown old, and my memory is not over good. I cannot therefore vouch for the language, but I am always scrupulous as to facts.

D.K.

I take the town of concord, where I dwell,
All Kilborn be my witness, if I were not
Begot in bashfulness, brought up in shamefacedness.
Let 'un bring a dog but to my vace that can
Zay I have beat 'un, and without a vault;
Or but a cat will swear upon a book,
I have as much as zet a vire her tail,
And I'll give him or her a crown for 'mends.
Tale of a Tub

IN the early time of the province of New York, while it groaned under the tyranny of the English governor, Lord Cornbury, who carried
his cruelties towards the Dutch inhabitants so far as to allow no dominie
or schoolmaster to officiate in their language without his special license;
about this time there lived in the jolly little old city of the Manhattoes
a kind motherly dame, known by the name of Dame Heyliger. She was
the widow of a Dutch sea-captain, who died suddenly of a fever, in
consequence of working too hard and eating too heartily, at a time
when all the inhabitants turned out in a panic, to fortify the place
against the invasion of a small French privateer.* He left her with
very little money and one infant son, the only survivor of several children. The good woman had need of much management to make both
ends meet, and keep up a decent appearance. However, as her husband
had fallen a victim to his zeal for the public safety, it was universally
agreed that "something ought to be done for the widow"; and on the
hopes of this "something" she lived tolerably for some years; in the
meantime everybody pitied and spoke well of her, and that helped
along.

She lived in a small house, in a small street, called Garden Street,
very probably from a garden which may have flourished there some
time or other. As her necessities every year grew greater, and the talk
of the public about doing "something for her" grew less, she had to
cast about for some mode of doing something for herself, by way of
helping out her slender means, and maintaining her independence, of
which she was somewhat tenacious.

Living in a mercantile town, she had caught something of the spirit,
and determined to venture a little in the great lottery of commerce. On
a sudden, therefore, to the great surprise of the street, there appeared
at her window a grand array of gingerbread kings and queens, with
their arms stuck akimbo, after the invariable royal manner. There were
also several broken tumblers, some filled with sugar-plums, some with
marbles; there were, moreover, cakes of various kinds, and barley-sugar,
and Holland dolls, and wooden horses, with here and there gilt-covered
picture-books, and now and then a skein of thread, or a dangling pound
of candles. At the door of the house sat the good old dame's cat, a decent demure-looking personage, who seemed to scan everybody that
passed, to criticise their dress, and now and then to stretch her neck,
and to look out with sudden curiosity, to see what was going on at the
other end of the street; but if by chance any idle vagabond dog came
by, and offered to be uncivil—hoity-toity!—how she would bristle up,

---

* 1705.

and growl, and spit, and strike out her paws! she was as indignant as ever was an ancient and ugly spinster on the approach of some graceless profligate.

But though the good woman had to come down to those humble means of subsistence, yet she still kept up a feeling of family pride, being descended from the Vanderspiegels, of Amsterdam; and she had the family arms painted and framed, and hung over her mantel-piece. She was, in truth, much respected by all the poorer people of the place; her house was quite a resort of the old wives of the neighborhood; they would drop in there of a winter's afternoon, as she sat knitting on one side of her fireplace, her cat purring on the other, and the tea-kettle singing before it; and they would gossip with her until late in the evening. There was always an arm-chair for Peter de Groodt, sometimes called Long Peter, and sometimes Peter Longlegs, the clerk and sexton of the little Lutheran church, who was her great crony, and indeed the oracle of her fireside. Nay, the Dominie himself did not disdain, now and then, to step in, converse about the state of her mind, and take a glass of her special good cherry-brandy. Indeed, he never failed to call on New-Year's day, and wish her a happy New Year; and the good dame, who was a little vain on some points, always piqued herself on giving him as large a cake as any one in town.

I have said that she had one son. He was the child of her old age; but could hardly be called the comfort, for, of all unlucky urchins, Dolph Heyliger was the most mischievous. Not that the whipster was really vicious; he was only full of fun and frolic, and had that daring, gamesome spirit which is extolled in a rich man's child, but execrated in a poor man's. He was continually getting into scrapes; his mother was incessantly harassed with complaints of some waggish pranks which he had played off; bills were sent in for windows that he had broken; in a word, he had not reached his fourteenth year before he was pronounced, by all the neighborhood, to be a "wicked dog, the wickedest dog in the street!" Nay, one old gentleman, in a claret-colored coat with a thin red face, and ferret eyes, went so far as to assure Dame Heyliger, that her son would, one day or other, come to the gallows!

Yet, notwithstanding all this, the poor old soul loved her boy. It seemed as though she loved him the better the worse he behaved, and that he grew more in her favor the more he grew out of favor with the world. Mothers are foolish, fond-hearted beings; there's no reasoning them out of their dotage; and, indeed, this poor woman's child was all that was left to love her in this world;—so we must not think it hard that she turned a deaf ear to her good friends, who sought to prove to her that Dolph would come to a halter.

To do the varlet justice, too, he was strongly attached to his parent. He would not willingly have given her pain on any account; and when he had been doing wrong, it was but for him to catch his poor mother's eye fixed wistfully and sorrowfully upon him, to fill his heart with bitterness and contrition. But he was a heedless youngster, and could not, for the life of him, resist any new temptation to fun and mischief. Though quick at his learning, whenever he could be brought to apply himself, he was always prone to be led away by idle company, and would play truant to hunt after birds' nests, to rob orchards, or to swim in the Hudson.

In this way he grew up, a tall, lubberly boy; and his mother began to be greatly perplexed what to do with him, or how to put him in a way to do for himself; for he had acquired such an unlucky reputation, that no one seemed willing to employ him.

Many were the consultations that she held with Peter de Groodt, the clerk and sexton, who was her prime counsellor. Peter was as much perplexed as herself, for he had no great opinion of the boy, and thought he would never come to good. He at once advised her to send him to sea; a piece of advice only given in the most desperate cases; but Dame Heyliger would not listen to such an idea; she could not think of letting Dolph go out of her sight. She was sitting one day knitting by her fireside, in great perplexity, when the sexton entered with an air of unusual vivacity and briskness. He had just come from a funeral. It had been that of a boy of Dolph's years, who had been apprentice to a famous German doctor, and had died of a consumption. It is true, there had been a whisper that the deceased had been brought to his end by being made the subject of the doctor's experiments, on which he was apt to try the effects of a new compound, or a quieting draught. This, however, it is likely, was a mere scandal; at any rate, Peter de Groodt did not think it worth mentioning; though, had we time to philosophize, it would be a curious matter for speculation, why a doctor's family is apt to be so lean and cadaverous, and a butcher's so jolly and rubicund.

Peter de Groodt, as I said before, entered the house of Dame Heyliger with unusual alacrity. A bright idea had popped into his head at the funeral, over which he had chuckled as he shovelled the earth into the grave of the doctor's disciple. It had occurred to him, that, as the situation of the deceased was vacant at the doctor's, it would be the very place for Dolph. The boy had parts, and could pound a pestle, and run an errand with any boy in the town; and what more was wanted in a student?

The suggestion of the sage Peter was a vision of glory to the mother.

She already saw Dolph, in her mind's eye, with a cane at his nose, a knocker at his door, and an M.D. at the end of his name,—one of the established dignitaries of the town.

The matter, once undertaken, was soon effected; the sexton had some influence with the doctor, they having had much dealing together in the way of their separate professions; and the very next morning he called and conducted the urchin, clad in his Sunday clothes, to undergo the inspection of Dr. Karl Lodovick Knipperhausen.

They found the doctor seated in an elbow-chair, in one corner of his study, or laboratory, with a large volume, in German print, before him. He was a short fat man, with a dark square face, rendered more dark by a black velvet cap. He had a little nobbed nose, not unlike the ace of spades, with a pair of spectacles gleaming on each side of his dusky countenance, like a couple of bow-windows.

Dolph felt struck with awe on entering into the presence of this learned man; and gazed about him with boyish wonder at the furniture of this chamber of knowledge; which appeared to him almost as the den of a magician. In the centre stood a claw-footed table, with pestle and mortar, phials and gallipots, and a pair of small burnished scales. At one end was a heavy clothes-press, turned into a receptacle for drugs and compounds; against which hung the doctor's hat and cloak, and gold-headed cane, and on the top grinned a human skull. Along the mantelpiece were glass vessels, in which were snakes and lizards, and a human fœtus preserved in spirits. A closet, the doors of which were taken off, contained three whole shelves of books, and some, too, of mighty folio dimensions,—a collection the like of which Dolph had never before beheld. As, however, the library did not take up the whole of the closet, the doctor's thrifty housekeeper had occupied the rest with pots of pickles and preserves; and had hung about the room, among awful implements of the healing art, strings of red pepper and corpulent cucumbers, carefully preserved for seed.

Peter de Groodt and his protégé were received with great gravity and stateliness by the doctor, who was a very wise, dignified little man, and never smiled. He surveyed Dolph from head to foot, above, and under, and through his spectacles, and the poor lad's heart quailed as these great glasses glared on him like two full moons. The doctor heard all that Peter de Groodt had to say in favor of the youthful candidate; and then wetting his thumb with the end of his tongue, he began deliberately to turn over page after page of the great black volume before him. At length, after many hums and haws, and strokings of the chin, and all that hesitation and deliberation with which a wise man proceeds to do what he intended to do from the very first, the doctor agreed to take

the lad as a disciple; to give him bed, board, and clothing, and to instruct him in the healing art, in return for which he was to have his services until his twenty-first year.

Behold, then, our hero, all at once transformed from an unlucky urchin running wild about the streets, to a student of medicine, diligently pounding a pestle, under the auspices of the learned Doctor Karl Lodovick Knipperhausen. It was a happy transition for his fond old mother. She was delighted with the idea of her boy's being brought up worthy of his ancestors; and anticipated the day when he would be able to hold up his head with the lawyer, that lived in the large house opposite; or, peradventure, with the Dominie himself.

Doctor Knipperhausen was a native of the Palatinate in Germany; whence, in company with many of his countrymen, he had taken refuge in England, on account of religious persecution. He was one of nearly three thousand Palatines, who came over from England in 1710, under the protection of Governor Hunter. Where the doctor had studied, how he had acquired his medical knowledge, and where he had received his diploma, it is hard at present to say, for nobody knew at the time; yet it is certain that his profound skill and abstruse knowledge were the talk and wonder of the common people, far and near.

His practice was totally different from that of any other physician,—consisting in mysterious compounds, known only to himself, in the preparing and administering of which, it was said, he always consulted the stars. So high an opinion was entertained of his skill, particularly by the German and Dutch inhabitants, that they always resorted to him in desperate cases. He was one of those infallible doctors that are always effecting sudden and surprising cures, when the patient has been given up by all the regular physicians; unless, as is shrewdly observed, the case has been left too long before it was put into their hands. The doctor's library was the talk and marvel of the neighborhood, I might almost say of the entire burgh. The good people looked with reverence at a man who had read three whole shelves full of books, and some of them, too, as large as a family Bible. There were many disputes among the members of the little Lutheran church, as to which was the wisest man, the doctor or the Dominie. Some of his admirers even went so far as to say, that he knew more than the governor himself. In a word, it was thought that there was no end to his knowledge!

No sooner was Dolph received into the doctor's family, than he was put in possession of the lodging of his predecessor. It was a garret room of a steep-roofed Dutch house, where the rain had pattered on the shingles, and the lightning gleamed, and the wind piped through the cran-

nies in stormy weather; and where whole troops of hungry rats, like
Don Cossacks, galloped about, in defiance of traps and ratsbane.

He was soon up to his ears in medical studies, being employed, morning, noon and night, in rolling pills, filtering tinctures, or pounding the
pestle and mortar in one corner of the laboratory; while the doctor
would take his seat in another corner, when he had nothing else to do,
or expected visitors, and arrayed in his morning gown and velvet cap,
would pore over the contents of some folio volume. It is true, that the
regular thumping of Dolph's pestle, or perhaps the drowsy buzzing of
the summer flies, would now and then lull the little man into a slumber; but then his spectacles were always wide awake, and studiously regarding the book.

There was another personage in the house, however, to whom Dolph
was obliged to pay allegiance. Though a bachelor, and a man of such
great dignity and importance, the doctor was, like many other wise men,
subject to petticoat government. He was completely under the sway of
his housekeeper,—a spare, busy, fretting housewife, in a little, round,
quilted German cap, with a huge bunch of keys jingling at the girdle
of an exceedingly long waist. Frau Ilsé (or Frow Ilsy, as it was pronounced) had accompanied him in his various migrations from Germany to England, and from England to the province; managing his establishment and himself too; ruling him, it is true, with a gentle hand,
but carrying a high hand with all the world beside. How she had acquired such ascendency I do not pretend to say. People, it is true, did
talk—but have not people been prone to talk ever since the world began? Who can tell how women generally continue to get the upper-
hand? A husband, it is true, may now and then be master in his own
house; but who ever knew a bachelor that was not managed by his
housekeeper?

Indeed, Frau Ilsy's power was not confined to the doctor's household.
She was one of those prying gossips who know every one's business
better than they do themselves; and whose all-seeing eyes, and all-telling
tongues, are terrors throughout a neighborhood.

Nothing of any moment transpired in the world of scandal of this little burgh, but it was known to Frau Ilsy. She had her crew of cronies, that were perpetually hurrying to her little parlor with some
precious bit of news; nay, she would sometimes discuss a whole volume
of secret history, as she held the street-door ajar, and gossiped with one
of these garrulous cronies in the very teeth of a December blast.

Between the doctor and the housekeeper it may easily be supposed
that Dolph had a busy life of it. As Frau Ilsy kept the keys, and literally
ruled the roast, it was starvation to offend her, though he found the

study of her temper more perplexing even than that of medicine. When not busy in the laboratory, she kept him running hither and thither on her errands; and on Sundays he was obliged to accompany her to and from church, and carry her Bible. Many a time has the poor varlet stood shivering and blowing his fingers, or holding his frost-bitten nose, in the churchyard, while Ilsy and her cronies were huddled together, wagging their heads, and tearing some unlucky character to pieces.

With all his advantages, however, Dolph made very slow progress in his art. This was no fault of the doctor's, certainly, for he took unwearied pains with the lad, keeping him close to the pestle and mortar, or on the trot about town with phials and pill-boxes; and if he ever flagged in his industry, which he was rather apt to do, the doctor would fly into a passion, and ask him if he ever expected to learn his profession, unless he applied himself closer to the study. The fact is, he still retained the fondness for sport and mischief that had marked his childhood; the habit, indeed, had strengthened with his years, and gained force from being thwarted and constrained. He daily grew more and more untractable, and lost favor in the eyes, both of the doctor and the housekeeper.

In the meantime the doctor went on, waxing wealthy and renowned. He was famous for his skill in managing cases not laid down in the books. He had cured several old women and young girls of witchcraft, —a terrible complaint, and nearly as prevalent in the province in those days as hydrophobia is at present. He had even restored one strapping country girl to perfect health, who had gone so far as to vomit crooked pins and needles; which is considered a desperate stage of the malady. It was whispered, also, that he was possessed of the art of preparing love-powders; and many applications had he in consequence from love-sick patients of both sexes. But all these cases formed the mysterious part of his practice, in which, according to the cant phrase, "secrecy and honor might be depended on." Dolph, therefore, was obliged to turn out of the study whenever such consultations occurred, though it is said he learnt more of the secrets of the art at the keyhole than by all the rest of his studies put together.

As the doctor increased in wealth, he began to extend his possessions, and to look forward, like other great men, to the time when he should retire to the repose of a country-seat. For this purpose he had purchased a farm, or as the Dutch settlers called it, a *bowerie*, a few miles from town. It had been the residence of a wealthy family, that had returned some time since to Holland. A large mansion-house stood in the centre of it, very much out of repair, and which, in consequence of certain reports, had received the appellation of the Haunted House. Either

from these reports, or from its actual dreariness, the doctor found it impossible to get a tenant; and that the place might not fall to ruin before he could reside in it himself, he placed a country boor, with his family, in one wing, with the privilege of cultivating the farm on shares.

The doctor now felt all the dignity of a landholder rising within him. He had a little of the German pride of territory in his composition, and almost looked upon himself as owner of a principality. He began to complain of the fatigue of business; and was fond of riding out "to look at his estate." His little expeditions to his lands were attended with a bustle and parade that created a sensation throughout the neighborhood. His wall-eyed horse stood, stamping and whisking off the flies, for a full hour before the house. Then the doctor's saddle-bags would be brought out and adjusted; then, after a little while, his cloak would be rolled up and strapped to the saddle; then his umbrella would be buttoned to the cloak; while, in the meantime, a group of ragged boys, that observant class of beings, would gather before the door. At length the doctor would issue forth, in a pair of jackboots that reached above his knees, and a cocked hat flapped down in front. As he was a short, fat man, he took some time to mount into the saddle; and when there, he took some time to have the saddle and stirrups properly adjusted, enjoying the wonder and admiration of the urchin crowd. Even after he had set off, he would pause in the middle of the street, or trot back two or three times to give some parting orders; which were answered by the housekeeper from the door, or Dolph from the study, or the black cook from the cellar, or the chambermaid from the garret window; and there were generally some last words bawled after him, just as he was turning the corner.

The whole neighborhood would be aroused by this pomp and circumstance. The cobbler would leave his last; the barber would thrust out his frizzled head, with a comb sticking in it; a knot would collect at the grocer's door, and the word would be buzzed from one end of the street to the other, "The doctor's riding out to his country-seat!"

These were golden moments for Dolph. No sooner was the doctor out of sight, than pestle and mortar were abandoned; the laboratory was left to take care of itself, and the student was off on some mad-cap frolic.

Indeed, it must be confessed, the youngster, as he grew up, seemed in a fair way to fulfil the prediction of the old claret-colored gentleman. He was the ringleader of all holiday sports and midnight gambols; ready for all kinds of mischievous pranks and hare-brained adventures.

There is nothing so troublesome as a hero on a small scale, or, rather a hero in a small town. Dolph soon became the abhorrence of all drowsy, housekeeping old citizens, who hated noise, and had no relish

for waggery. The good dames, too, considered him as little better than a reprobate, gathered their daughters under their wings whenever he approached, and pointed him out as a warning to their sons. No one seemed to hold him in much regard except the wild striplings of the place, who were captivated by his open-hearted, daring manners,—and the negroes, who always looked upon every idle, do-nothing youngster as a kind of gentleman. Even the good Peter de Groodt, who had considered himself a kind of patron of the lad, began to despair of him; and would shake his head dubiously, as he listened to a long complaint from the housekeeper, and sipped a glass of her raspberry brandy.

Still his mother was not be be wearied out of her affection by all the waywardness of her boy; nor disheartened by the stories of his misdeeds, with which her good friends were continually regaling her. She had, it is true, very little of the pleasure which rich people enjoy, in always hearing their children praised; but she considered all this ill-will as a kind of persecution which he suffered, and she liked him the better on that account. She saw him growing up a fine, tall, good-looking youngster, and she looked at him with the secret pride of a mother's heart. It was her great desire that Dolph should appear like a gentleman, and all the money she could save went towards helping out his pocket and his wardrobe. She would look out of the window after him, as he sallied forth in his best array, and her heart would yearn with delight; and once, when Peter de Groodt, struck with the youngster's gallant appearance on a bright Sunday morning, observed, "Well, after all, Dolph does grow a comely fellow!" the tear of pride started into the mother's eye. "Ah, neighbor! neighbor!" exclaimed she, "they may say what they please; poor Dolph will yet hold up his head with the best of them!"

Dolph Heyliger had now nearly attained his one-and-twentieth year, and the term of his medical studies was just expiring; yet it must be confessed that he knew little more of the profession than when he first entered the doctor's doors. This, however, could not be from any want of quickness of parts, for he showed amazing aptness in mastering other branches of knowledge, which he could only have studied at intervals. He was, for instance, a sure marksman, and won all the geese and turkeys at Christmas holidays. He was a bold rider; he was famous for leaping and wrestling; he played tolerably on the fiddle; could swim like a fish; and was the best hand in the whole place at fives and ninepins.

All these accomplishments, however, procured him no favor in the eyes of the doctor, who grew more and more crabbed and intolerant the nearer the term of apprenticeship approached. Frau Ilsy, too, was forever finding some occasion to raise a windy tempest about his ears, and seldom encountered him about the house without a clatter of the

tongue; so that at length the jingling of her keys, as she approached, was to Dolph like the ringing of the prompter's bell, that gives notice of a theatrical thunder-storm. Nothing but the infinite good-humor of the heedless youngster enabled him to bear all this domestic tyranny without open rebellion. It was evident that the doctor and his housekeeper were preparing to beat the poor youth out of the nest, the moment his term should have expired—a short-hand mode which the doctor had of providing for useless disciples.

Indeed, the little man had been rendered more than usually irritable lately in consequence of various cares and vexations which his country estate had brought upon him. The doctor had been repeatedly annoyed by the rumors and tales which prevailed concerning the old mansion, and found it difficult to prevail even upon the country-man and his family to remain there rent-free. Every time he rode out to the farm he was teased by some fresh complaint of strange noises and fearful sights, with which the tenants were disturbed at night; and the doctor would come home fretting and fuming, and vent his spleen upon the whole household. It was indeed a sore grievance that affected him both in pride and purse. He was threatened with an absolute loss of the profits of his property; and then, what a blow to his territorial consequence, to be the landlord of a haunted house!

It was observed, however, that with all his vexation, the doctor never proposed to sleep in the house himself; nay, he could never be prevailed upon to remain on the premises after dark, but made the best of his way for town as soon as the bats began to flit about in the twilight. The fact was, the doctor had a secret belief in ghosts, having passed the early part of his life in a country where they particularly abound; and indeed the story went, that, when a boy, he had once seen the devil upon the Hartz Mountains in Germany.

At length the doctor's vexations on this head were brought to a crisis. One morning as he sat dozing over a volume in his study, he was suddenly startled from his slumbers by the bustling in of the housekeeper.

"Here's a fine to do!" cried she, as she entered the room. "Here's Claus Hopper come in, bag and baggage, from the farm, and swears he'll have nothing more to do with it. The whole family have been frightened out of their wits; for there's such racketing and rummaging about the old house, that they can't sleep quiet in their beds!"

"Donner and blitzen!" cried the doctor, impatiently; "will they never have done chattering about that house? What a pack of fools, to let a few rats and mice frighten them out of good quarters!"

"Nay, nay," said the housekeeper, wagging her head knowingly, and piqued at having a good ghost-story doubted, "there's more in it than

rats and mice. All the neighborhood, talks about the house; and then such sights as have been seen in it! Peter de Groodt tells me, that the family that sold you the house, and went to Holland, dropped several strange hints about it, and said, 'they wished you joy of your bargain'; and you know yourself there's no getting any family to live in it."

"Peter de Groodt's a ninny—an old woman," said the doctor, peevishly; "I'll warrant he's been filling these people's heads full of stories. It's just like his nonsense about the ghost that haunted the church belfry, as an excuse for not ringing the bell that cold night when Harmanus Brinkerhoff's house was on fire. Send Claus to me."

Claus Hopper now made his appearance: a simple country lout, full of awe at finding himself in the very study of Dr. Knipperhausen, and too much embarrassed to enter in much detail of the matters that had caused his alarm. He stood twirling his hat in one hand, resting sometimes on one leg, sometimes on the other, looking occasionally at the doctor, and now and then stealing a fearful glance at the death's-head that seemed ogling him from the top of the clothes-press.

The doctor tried every means to persuade him to return to the farm, but all in vain; he maintained a dogged determination on the subject; and at the close of every argument or solicitation would make the same brief, inflexible reply: "Ich kan nicht, mynheer." The doctor was a "little pot, and soon hot"; his patience was exhausted by these continual vexations about his estate. The stubborn refusal of Claus Hopper seemed to him like flat rebellion; his temper suddenly boiled over, and Claus was glad to make a rapid retreat to escape scalding.

When the bumpkin got to the housekeeper's room, he found Peter de Groodt, and several other true believers, ready to receive him. Here he indemnified himself for the restraint he had suffered in the study, and opened a budget of stories about the haunted house that astonished all his hearers. The housekeeper believed them all, if it was only to spite the doctor for having received her intelligence so uncourteously. Peter de Groodt matched them with many a wonderful legend of the times of the Dutch dynasty, and of the Devil's Stepping-stones; and of the pirate hanged at Gibbet Island, that continued to swing there at night long after the gallows was taken down; and of the ghost of the unfortunate Governor Leisler, hanged for treason, which haunted the old fort and the government house. The gossiping knot dispersed, each charged with direful intelligence. The sexton disburdened himself at a vestry meeting that was held that very day, and the black cook forsook her kitchen, and spent half the day at the street pump, that gossiping-place of servants, dealing forth the news to all that came for water. In a little time the whole town was in a buzz with tales about the

haunted house. Some said that Claus Hopper had seen the devil, while others hinted that the house was haunted by the ghosts of some of the patients whom the doctor had physicked out of the world, and that was the reason why he did not venture to live in it himself.

All this put the little doctor in a terrible fume. He threatened vengeance on any one who should affect the value of his property by exciting popular prejudices. He complained loudly of thus being in a manner dispossessed of his territories by mere bugbears; but he secretly determined to have the house exorcised by the Dominie. Great was his relief, therefore, when in the midst of his perplexities, Dolph stepped forward and undertook to garrison the haunted house. The youngster had been listening to all the stories of Claus Hopper and Peter de Groodt: he was fond of adventure, he loved the marvellous, and his imagination had become quite excited by these tales of wonder. Besides, he had led such an uncomfortable life at the doctor's, being subjected to the intolerable thraldom of early hours, that he was delighted at the prospect of having a house to himself, even though it should be a haunted one. His offer was eagerly accepted, and it was determined he should mount guard that very night. His only stipulation was, that the enterprise should be kept secret from his mother; for he knew the poor soul would not sleep a wink if she knew her son was waging war with the powers of darkness.

When night came on he set out on this perilous expedition. The old black cook, his only friend in the household, had provided him with a little mess for supper, and a rushlight; and she tied round his neck an amulet, given her by an African conjurer, as a charm against evil spirits. Dolph was escorted on his way by the doctor and Peter de Groodt, who had agreed to accompany him to the house, and to see him safe lodged. The night was overcast, and it was very dark when they arrived at the grounds which surrounded the mansion. The sexton led the way with the lantern. As they walked along the avenue of acacias, the fitful light, catching from bush to bush, and tree to tree, often startled the doughty Peter, and made him fall back upon his followers; and the doctor grappled still closer hold of Dolph's arm, observing that the ground was very slippery and uneven. At one time they were nearly put to total rout by a bat, which came flitting about the lantern; and the notes of the insects from the trees and the frogs from a neighboring pond, formed a most drowsy and doleful concert. The front door of the mansion opened with a grating sound, that made the doctor turn pale. They entered a tolerably large hall, such as is common in American country houses, and which serves for a sitting-room in warm weather. From this they went up a wide staircase, that groaned and creaked as they trod, every step

making its particular note, like the key of a harpsichord. This led to another hall on the second story, whence they entered the room where Dolph was to sleep. It was large, and scantily furnished; the shutters were closed; but as they were much broken, there was no want of a circulation of air. It appeared to have been that sacred chamber, known among Dutch housewives by the name of "the best bedroom"; which is the best furnished room in the house, but in which scarce anybody is ever permitted to sleep. Its splendor, however, was all at an end. There were a few broken articles of furniture about the room, and in the centre stood a heavy deal table and a large arm-chair, both of which had the look of being coeval with the mansion. The fireplace was wide, and had been faced with Dutch tiles, representing Scripture stories; but some of them had fallen out of their places, and lay scattered about the hearth. The sexton lit the rushlight; and the doctor, looking fearfully about the room, was just exhorting Dolph to be of good cheer, and to pluck up a stout heart, when a noise in the chimney, like voices and struggling, struck a sudden panic into the sexton. He took to his heels with the lantern; the doctor followed hard after him; the stairs groaned and creaked as they hurried down, increasing their agitation and speed by its noise. The front door slammed after them; and Dolph heard them scrabbling down the avenue, till the sound of their feet was lost in the distance. That he did not join in this precipitate retreat might have been owing to his possessing a little more courage than his companions, or perhaps that he had caught a glimpse of the cause of their dismay, in a nest of chimney-swallows, that came tumbling down into the fireplace.

Being now left to himself, he secured the front door by a strong bolt and bar; and having seen that the other entrances were fastened, returned to his desolate chamber. Having made his supper from the basket which the good old cook had provided, he locked the chamber door, and retired to rest on a mattress in one corner. The night was calm and still; and nothing broke upon the profound quiet but the lonely chirping of a cricket from the chimney of a distant chamber. The rushlight, which stood in the centre of the deal table, shed a feeble yellow ray, dimly illumining the chamber, and making uncouth shapes and shadows on the walls, from the clothes which Dolph had thrown over a chair.

With all his boldness of heart, there was something subduing in this desolate scene; and he felt his spirits flag within him, as he lay on his hard bed and gazed about the room. He was turning over in his mind his idle habits, his doubtful prospects, and now and then heaving a heavy sigh as he thought on his poor old mother; for there is nothing

like the silence and loneliness of night to bring dark shadows over the brightest mind. By and by he thought he heard a sound as of some one walking below stairs. He listened, and distinctly heard a step on the great staircase. It approached solemnly and slowly, tramp—tramp—tramp! It was evidently the tread of some heavy personage; and yet how could he have got into the house without making a noise? He had examined all the fastenings, and was certain that every entrance was secure. Still the steps advanced, tramp—tramp—tramp! It was evident that the person approaching could not be a robber, the step was too loud and deliberate; a robber would either be stealthy or precipitate. And now the footsteps had ascended the staircase; they were slowly advancing along the passage, resounding through the silent and empty apartments. The very cricket had ceased its melancholy note, and nothing interrupted their awful distinctness. The door, which had been locked on the inside, slowly swung open, as if self-moved. The footsteps entered the room; but no one was to be seen. They passed slowly and audibly across it, tramp—tramp—tramp! but whatever made the sound was invisible. Dolph rubbed his eyes, and stared about him; he could see to every part of the dimly lighted chamber; all was vacant; yet still he heard those mysterious footsteps, solemnly walking about the chamber. They ceased, and all was dead silence. There was something more appalling in this invisible visitation than there would have been in anything that addressed itself to the eyesight. It was awfully vague and indefinite. He felt his heart beat against his ribs; a cold sweat broke out upon his forehead; he lay for some time in a state of violent agitation: nothing, however, occurred to increase his alarm. His light gradually burnt down into the socket, and he fell asleep. When he awoke it was broad daylight; the sun was peering through the cracks of the window-shutters, and the birds were merrily singing about the house. The bright cheery day soon put to flight all the terrors of the preceding night. Dolph laughed, or rather tried to laugh, at all that had passed, and endeavored to persuade himself that it was a mere freak of the imagination, conjured up by the stories he had heard; but he was a little puzzled to find the door of his room locked on the inside, notwithstanding that he had positively seen it swing open as the footsteps had entered. He returned to town in a state of considerable perplexity; but he determined to say nothing on the subject, until his doubts were either confirmed or removed by another night's watching. His silence was a grievous disappointment to the gossips who had gathered at the doctor's mansion. They had prepared their minds to hear direful tales, and were almost in a rage of being assured he had nothing to relate.

The next night, then, Dolph repeated his vigil. He now entered the

house with some trepidation. He was particular in examining the fastenings of all the doors, and securing them well. He locked the door of his chamber, and placed a chair against it; then having despatched his supper, he threw himself on his mattress and endeavored to sleep. It was all in vain; a thousand crowding fancies kept him waking. The time slowly dragged on, as if minutes were spinning themselves out into hours. As the night advanced, he grew more and more nervous; and he almost started from his couch when he heard the mysterious footstep again on the staircase. Up it came, as before, solemnly and slowly, tramp—tramp—tramp! It approached along the passage; the door again swung open, as if there had been neither lock nor impediment, and a strange looking figure stalked into the room. It was an elderly man, large and robust, clothed in the old Flemish fashion. He had on a kind of short cloak, with a garment under it, belted round the waist; trunk-hose, with great bunches or bows at the knees; and a pair of russet boots, very large at top, and standing widely from his legs. His hat was broad and slouched, with a feather trailing over one side. His iron-gray hair hung in thick masses on his neck; and he had a short grizzled beard. He walked slowly round the room, as if examining that all was safe; then, hanging his hat on a peg beside the door, he sat down in the elbow-chair, and, leaning his elbow on the table, fixed his eyes on Dolph with an unmoving and deadening stare.

Dolph was not naturally a coward; but he had been brought up in an implicit belief in ghosts and goblins. A thousand stories came swarming to his mind that he had heard about this building; and as he looked at this strange personage, with his uncouth garb, his pale visage, his grizzly beard, and his fixed, staring, fishlike eye, his teeth began to chatter, his hair to rise on his head, and a cold sweat to break out all over his body. How long he remained in this situation he could not tell, for he was like one fascinated. He could not take his gaze off from the spectre; but lay staring at him, with his whole intellect absorbed in the contemplation. The old man remained seated behind the table, without stirring, or turning an eye, always keeping a dead steady glare upon Dolph. At length the household cock, from a neighboring farm, clapped his wings, and gave a loud cheerful crow that rung over the fields. At the sound the old man slowly rose, and took down his hat from the peg; the door opened, and closed after him; he was heard to go slowly down the staircase, tramp—tramp—tramp!—and when he had got to the bottom, all was again silent. Dolph lay and listened earnestly; counted every footfall; listened, and listened, if the steps should return, until, exhausted by watching and agitation, he fell into a troubled sleep.

Daylight again brought fresh courage and assurance. He would fain have considered all that had passed as a mere dream; yet there stood the chair in which the unknown had seated himself; there was the table on which he had leaned; there was the peg on which he had hung his hat; and there was the door, locked precisely as he himself had locked it, with the chair placed against it. He hastened down-stairs, and examined the doors and windows; all were exactly in the same state in which he had left them, and there was no apparent way by which any being could have entered and left the house, without leaving some trace behind. "Pooh!" said Dolph to himself, "it was all a dream;"—but it would not do. The more he endeavored to shake the scene off from his mind, the more it haunted him.

Though he persisted in a strict silence as to all that he had seen or heard, yet his looks betrayed the uncomfortable night that he had passed. It was evident that there was something wonderful hidden under this mysterious reserve. The doctor took him into the study, locked the door, and sought to have a full and confidential communication; but he could get nothing out of him. Frau Ilsy took him aside into the pantry, but to as little purpose; and Peter de Groodt held him by the button for a full hour, in the churchyard, the very place to get at the bottom of a ghost story, but came off not a whit wiser than the rest. It is always the case, however, that one truth concealed makes a dozen current lies. It is like a guinea locked up in a bank, that has a dozen paper representatives. Before the day was over, the neighborhood was full of reports. Some said that Dolph Heyliger watched in the haunted house, with pistols loaded with silver bullets; others, that he had a long talk with a spectre without a head; others, that Doctor Knipperhausen and the sexton had been hunted down the Bowery lane, and quite into town, by a legion of ghosts of their customers. Some shook their heads, and thought it a shame the doctor should put Dolph to pass the night alone in that dismal house, where he might be spirited away no one knew whither; while others observed, with a shrug, that if the devil did carry off the youngster, it would be but taking his own.

These rumors at length reached the ears of the good Dame Heyliger, and, as may be supposed, threw her into a terrible alarm. For her son to have opposed himself to danger from living foes would have been nothing so dreadful in her eyes, as to dare alone the terrors of the haunted house. She hastened to the doctor's, and passed a great part of the day in attempting to dissuade Dolph from repeating his vigil; she told him a score of tales, which her gossiping friends had just related to her, of persons who had been carried off when watching alone in old ruinous houses. It was all to no effect. Dolph's pride, as well as curios-

ity, was piqued. He endeavored to calm the apprehensions of his mother, and to assure her that there was no truth in all the rumors she had heard; she looked at him dubiously and shook her head; but finding his determination was not to be shaken, she brought him a little thick Dutch Bible, with brass clasps, to take with him, as a sword wherewith to fight the powers of darkness; and, lest that might not be sufficient, the housekeeper gave him the Heidelberg catechism by way of dagger.

The next night, therefore, Dolph took up his quarters for the third time in the old mansion. Whether dream or not, the same thing was repeated. Towards midnight, when everything was still, the same sound echoed through the empty halls, tramp—tramp—tramp! The stairs were again ascended; the door again swung open; the old man entered; walked round the room; hung up his hat, and seated himself by the table. The same fear and trembling came over poor Dolph, though not in so violent a degree. He lay in the same way, motionless and fascinated, staring at the figure, which regarded him as before, with a dead, fixed, chilling gaze. In this way they remained for a long time, till, by degrees, Dolph's courage began gradually to revive. Whether alive or dead, this being had certainly some object in his visitation; and he recollected to have heard it said, spirits have no power to speak until spoken to. Summoning up resolution, therefore, and making two or three attempts, before he could get his parched tongue in motion, he addressed the unknown in the most solemn form of adjuration, and demanded to know what was the motive of his visit.

No sooner had he finished, than the old man rose, took down his hat, the door opened, and he went out, looking back upon Dolph just as he crossed the threshold, as if expecting him to follow. The youngster did not hesitate an instant. He took the candle in his hand and the Bible under his arm, and obeyed the tacit invitation. The candle emitted a feeble, uncertain ray, but still he could see the figure before him slowly descend the stairs. He followed trembling. When it had reached the bottom of the stairs, it turned through the hall towards the back door of the mansion. Dolph held the light over the balustrades; but, in his eagerness to catch a sight of the unknown, he flared his feeble taper so suddenly, that it went out. Still there was sufficient light from the pale moonbeams, that fell through a narrow window, to give him an indistinct view of the figure near the door. He followed, therefore, down-stairs, and turned towards the place; but when he arrived there the unknown had disappeared. The door remained fast barred and bolted; there was no other mode of exit, yet the being, whatever he might be, was gone. He unfastened the door, and looked out into the

fields. It was a hazy, moonlight night, so that the eye could distinguish objects at some distance. He thought he saw the unknown in a foot-path which led from the door. He was not mistaken; but how had he got out of the house? He did not pause to think, but followed on. The old man proceeded at a measured pace, without looking about him, his footsteps sounding on the hard ground. He passed through the orchard of apple-trees, always keeping the footpath. It led to a well, situated in a little hollow, which had supplied the farm with water. Just at this well Dolph lost sight of him. He rubbed his eyes and looked again; but nothing was to be seen of the unknown. He reached the well, but no-body was there. All the surrounding ground was open and clear; there was no bush nor hiding-place. He looked down the well, and saw, at a great depth, the reflection of the sky in the still water. After remaining here for some time, without seeing or hearing anything more of his mysterious conductor, he returned to the house, full of awe and won-der. He bolted the door, groped his way back to bed, and it was long before he could compose himself to sleep.

His dreams were strange and troubled. He thought he was following the old man along the side of a great river, until they came to a vessel on the point of sailing, and that his conductor led him on board and vanished. He remembered the commander of the vessel, a short, swarthy man, with crisped black hair, blind of one eye, and lame of one leg; but the rest of his dream was very confused. Sometimes he was sailing, sometimes on shore; now amidst storms and tempests, and now wan-dering quietly in unknown streets. The figure of the old man was strangely mingled up with the incidents of the dream, and the whole distinctly wound up by his finding himself on board of the vessel again, returning home, with a great bag of money!

When he woke, the gray, cool light of dawn was streaking the hori-zon, and the cocks passing the reveille from farm to farm throughout the country. He rose more harassed and perplexed than ever. He was singularly confounded by all that he had seen and dreamt, and began to doubt whether his mind was not affected, and whether all that passing in his thoughts might not be mere feverish fantasy. In his present state of mind, he did not feel disposed to return immediately to the doctor's, and undergo the cross-questioning of the household. He made a scanty breakfast, therefore, on the remains of the last night's provisions, and then wandered out into the fields to meditate on all that had befallen him. Lost in thought, he rambled about, gradually approaching the town, until the morning was far advanced, when he was aroused by a hurry and bustle around him. He found himself near the water's edge, in a throng of people, hurrying to a pier, where was a

vessel ready to make sail. He was unconsciously carried along by the impulse of the crowd, and found that it was a sloop, on the point of sailing up the Hudson to Albany. There was much leave-taking, and kissing of old women and children, and great activity in carrying on board baskets of bread and cakes, and provisions of all kinds, notwithstanding the mighty joints of meat that dangled over the stern; for a voyage to Albany was an expedition of great moment in those days. The commander of the sloop was hurrying about, and giving a world of orders, which were not very strictly attended to; one man being busy in lighting his pipe, and another in sharpening his snicker-snee.

The appearance of the commander suddenly caught Dolph's attention. He was short and swarthy, with crisped black hair; blind of one eye, and lame of one leg—the very commander that he had seen in his dream! Surprised and aroused, he considered the scene more attentively, and recalled still further traces of his dream: the appearance of the vessel, of the river, and of images, a variety of other objects accorded with the imperfect images vaguely rising to recollection.

As he stood musing on these circumstances, the captain suddenly called out to him in Dutch: "Step on board, young man, or you'll be left behind!" He was startled by the summons; he saw that the sloop was cast loose, and was actually moving from the pier. It seemed as if he was actuated by some irresistible impulse; he sprang upon the deck, and the next moment the sloop was hurried off by the wind and tide. Dolph's thoughts and feelings were all in tumult and confusion. He had been strongly worked upon by the events which had recently befallen him, and could not but think there was some connection between his present situation and his last night's dream. He felt as if under supernatural influence, and tried to assure himself with an old and favorite maxim of his, that "one way or other all would turn out for the best." For a moment, the indignation of the doctor at his departure, without leave, passed across his mind; but that was matter of little moment. Then he thought of the distress of his mother at his strange disappearance, and the idea gave him a sudden pang. He would have entreated to be put on shore; but he knew with such wind and tide the entreaty would have been in vain. Then the inspiring love of novelty and adventure came rushing in full tide through his bosom. He felt himself launched strangely and suddenly on the world, and under full way to explore the regions of wonder that lay up this mighty river, and beyond those blue mountains which had bounded his horizon since childhood. While he was lost in this whirl of thought, the sails strained to the breeze; the shores seemed to hurry away behind him; and before he perfectly recovered his self-possession, the sloop was

ploughing her way past Spiking-Devil and Yonkers, and the tallest chimney of the Manhattoes had faded from his sight.

I have said that a voyage up the Hudson in those days was an undertaking of some moment; indeed, it was as much thought of as a voyage to Europe is at present. The sloops were often many days on the way, the cautious navigators taking in sail when it blew fresh, and coming to anchor at night; and stopping to send the boat ashore for milk for tea, without which it was impossible for the worthy old lady passengers to subsist. And there were the much-talked-of perils of the Tappaan Zee and the highlands. In short, a prudent Dutch burgher would talk of such a voyage for months, and even years, beforehand; and never undertook it without putting his affairs in order, making his will, and having prayers said for him in the Low Dutch churches.

In the course of such a voyage, therefore, Dolph was satisfied he would have time enough to reflect, and to make up his mind as to what he should do when he arrived at Albany. The captain, with his blind eye, and lame leg, would, it is true, bring his strange dream to mind, and perplex him sadly for a few moments; but of late his life had been made up so much of dreams and realities, his nights and days had been so jumbled together, that he seemed to be moving continually in a delusion. There is always, however, a kind of vagabond consolation in a man's having nothing in this world to lose; with this Dolph comforted his heart, and determined to make the most of the present enjoyment.

In the second day of the voyage they came to the highlands. It was the latter part of a calm, sultry day, that they floated gently with the tide between these stern mountains. There was that perfect quiet which prevails over nature in the languor of summer heat; the turning of a plank, or the accidental falling of an oar on deck, was echoed from the mountain-side, and reverberated along the shores; and if by chance the captain gave a shout of command, there were airy tongues which mocked it from every cliff.

Dolph gazed about him in mute delight and wonder at these scenes of nature's magnificence. To the left the Dunderberg reared its woody precipices, height over height, forest over forest, away into the deep summer sky. To the right, strutted forth the bold promontory of Anthony's Nose, with a solitary eagle wheeling about it; while beyond, mountain succeeded to mountain, until they seemed to lock their arms together, and confine this mighty river in their embraces. There was a feeling of quiet luxury in gazing at the broad, green bosoms here and there scooped out among the precipices; or at woodlands high in air, nodding over the edge of some beetling bluff, and their foliage all transparent in the yellow sunshine.

In the midst of his admiration, Dolph remarked a pile of bright, snowy clouds, peering above the western heights. It was succeeded by another, and another, each seemingly pushing onwards its predecessor, and towering, with dazzling brilliancy, in the deep blue atmosphere. And now muttering peals of thunder were faintly heard rolling behind the mountains. The river, hitherto still and glassy, reflecting pictures of the sky and land, now showed a dark ripple at a distance, as the breeze came creeping up it. The fish-hawks wheeled and screamed, and sought their nests on the high dry trees. The crows flew clamorously to the crevices of the rocks, and all nature seemed conscious of the approaching thundergust.

The clouds now rolled in volumes over the mountain-tops; their summits still bright and snowy, but the lower parts of an inky blackness. The rain began to patter down in broad and scattered drops; the wind freshened, and curled up the waves. At length it seemed as if the bellying clouds were torn open by the mountain-tops, and complete torrents of rain came rattling down. The lightning leaped from cloud to cloud, and streamed quivering against the rocks, splitting and rending the stoutest forest trees. The thunder burst in tremendous explosions; the peals were echoed from mountain to mountain; they crashed upon Dunderberg, and rolled up the long defile of the highlands, each headland making a new echo, until old Bull Hill seemed to bellow back the storm.

For a time the scudding rack and mist, and the sheeted rain, almost hid the landscape from the sight. There was a fearful gloom, illumined still more fearfully by the streams of lightning which glittered among the raindrops. Never had Dolph beheld such an absolute warring of the elements; it seemed as if the storm was tearing and rending its way through this mountain defile, and had brought all the artillery of heaven into action.

The vessel was hurried on by the increasing wind, until she came to where the river makes a sudden bend, the only one in the whole course of its majestic career.* Just as they turned the point, a violent flaw of wind came sweeping down a mountain gully, bending the forest before it, and, in a moment, lashing up the river into white froth and foam. The captain saw the danger, and cried out to lower the sail. Before the order could be obeyed, the flaw struck the sloop, and threw her on her beam ends. Everything now was fright and confusion: the flapping of the sails, the whistling and rushing of the wind, the bawling of the captain and crew, the shrieking of the passengers, all

---

* This must have been the bend at West Point.

mingled with the rolling and bellowing of the thunder. In the midst of the uproar the sloop righted; at the same time the mainsail shifted, the boom came sweeping the quarter-deck, and Dolph, who was gazing unguardedly at the clouds, found himself, in a moment, floundering in the river.

For once in his life one of his idle accomplishments was of use to him. The many truant hours he had devoted to sporting in the Hudson had made him an expert swimmer. Yet with all his strength and skill he found great difficulty in reaching the shore. His disappearance from the deck had not been noticed by the crew, who were all occupied by their own danger. The sloop was driven along with inconceivable rapidity. She had hard work to weather a long promontory on the eastern shore, round which the river turned, and which completely shut her from Dolph's view.

It was on a point of the western shore that he landed, and, scrambling up the rocks, threw himself, faint and exhausted, at the foot of a tree. By degrees the thunder-gust passed over. The clouds rolled away to the east, where they lay piled in feathery masses, tinted with the last rosy rays of the sun. The distant play of the lightning might be seen about the dark bases, and now and then might be heard the faint muttering of the thunder. Dolph rose, and sought about to see if any path led from the shore, but all was savage and trackless. The rocks were piled upon each other; great trunks of trees lay shattered about, as they had been blown down by the strong winds which draw through these mountains, or had fallen through age. The rocks, too, were overhung with wild vines and briers, which completely matted themselves together, and opposed a barrier to all ingress; every movement that he made shook down a shower from the dripping foliage. He attempted to scale one of these almost perpendicular heights; but, though strong and agile, he found it a Herculean undertaking. Often he was supported merely by crumbling projections of the rock, and sometimes he clung to roots and branches of trees, and hung almost suspended in the air. The wood-pigeon came cleaving his whistling flight by him, and the eagle screamed from the brow of the impending cliff. As he was thus clambering, he was on the point of seizing hold of a shrub to aid his ascent, when something rustled among the leaves, and he saw a snake quivering along like lightning, almost from under his hand. It coiled itself up immediately, in an attitude of defiance, with flattened head, distended jaws, and quickly vibrating tongue, that played like a little flame about its mouth. Dolph's heart turned faint within him, and he had well-nigh let go his hold and tumbled down the precipice. The serpent stood on the defensive but for an instant; and finding there was no at-

tack, glided away into a cleft of the rock. Dolph's eye followed it with fearful intensity, and saw a nest of adders, knotted, and writhing, and hissing in the chasm. He hastened with all speed from so frightful a neighborhood. His imagination, full of this new horror, saw an adder in every curling vine, and heard the tail of a rattlesnake in every dry leaf that rustled.

At length he succeeded in scrambling to the summit of a precipice; but it was covered by a dense forest. Wherever he could gain a lookout between trees, he beheld heights and cliffs, one rising beyond another, until huge mountains overtopped the whole. There were no signs of cultivation; no smoke curling among the trees to indicate a human residence. Everything was wild and solitary. As he was standing on the edge of a precipice overlooking a deep ravine fringed with trees, his feet detached a great fragment of rock; it fell, crashing its way through the tree-tops, down into the chasm. A loud whoop, or rather yell, issued from the bottom of the glen; the moment after there was a report of a gun; and a ball came whistling over his head, cutting the twigs and leaves, and burying itself deep in the bark of a chesnut tree.

· Dolph did not wait for a second shot, but made a precipitate retreat; fearing every moment to hear the enemy in pursuit. He succeeded, however, in returning unmolested to the shore, and determined to penetrate no farther into a country so beset with savage perils.

He sat himself down, dripping, disconsolately, on a stone. What was to be done? where was he to shelter himself? The hour of repose was approaching; the birds were seeking their nests, the bat began to flit about in the twilight, and the night-hawk, soaring high in the heaven, seemed to be calling out the stars. Night gradually closed in, and wrapped everything in gloom; and though it was the latter part of summer, the breeze stealing along the river, and among these dripping forests, was chilly and penetrating, especially to a half-drowned man.

As he sat drooping and despondent in this comfortless condition, he perceived a light gleaming through the trees near the shore, where the winding of the river made a deep bay. It cheered him with the hope of a human habitation, where he might get something to appease the clamorous cravings of his stomach, and what was equally necessary in his shipwrecked condition, a comfortable shelter for the night. With extreme difficulty he made his way toward the light, along ledges of rocks, down which he was in danger of sliding into the river, and over great trunks of fallen trees; some of which had been blown down in the late storm, and lay so thickly together that he had to struggle through their branches. At length he came to the brow of a rock overhanging a small dell, whence the light proceeded. It was from a fire at the foot of a

great tree in the midst of a grassy interval or plat among the rocks. The fire cast up a red glare among the gray crags, and impending trees; leaving chasms of deep gloom, that resembled entrances to caverns. A small brook rippled close by, betrayed by the quivering reflection of the flame. There were two figures moving about the fire, and others squatted before it. As they were between him and the light, they were in complete shadow; but one of them happening to move round to the opposite side, Dolph was startled at perceiving, by the glare falling on painted features, and glittering on silver ornaments, that he was an Indian. He now looked more narrowly, and saw guns leaning against a tree, and a dead body lying on the ground. Here was the very foe that had fired at him from the glen. He endeavored to retreat quietly, not caring to intrust himself to these half-human beings in so savage and lonely a place. It was too late; the Indian, with that eagle quickness of eye so remarkable in his race, perceived something stirring among the bushes on the rock; he seized one of the guns that leaned against the tree; one moment more, and Dolph might have had his passion for adventure cured by a bullet. He halloed loudly, with the Indian salutation of friendship; the whole party sprang upon their feet; the salutation was returned, and the straggler was invited to join them at the fire.

On approaching, he found, to his consolation, the party was composed of white men as well as Indians. One, evidently the principal personage, or commander, was seated on a trunk of a tree before the fire. He was a large, stout man, somewhat advanced in life, but hale and hearty. His face was bronzed almost to the color of an Indian's; he had strong but rather jovial features, an aquiline nose, and a mouth shaped like a mastiff's. His face was half thrown in shade by a broad hat, with a buck's tail in it. His gray hair hung short on his neck. He wore a hunting-frock, with Indian leggins, and moccasins, and a tomahawk in the broad wampum-belt round his waist. As Dolph caught a distinct view of his person and features, something reminded him of the old man of the haunted house. The man before him, however, was different in dress and age; he was more cheery too in aspect, and it was hard to find where the vague resemblance lay; but a resemblance there certainly was. Dolph felt some degree of awe in approaching him; but was assured by a frank, hearty welcome. He was still further encouraged by perceiving that the dead body, which had caused him some alarm, was that of a deer; and his satisfaction was complete in discerning by savory steams from a kettle, suspended by a hooked stick over the fire, that there was a part cooking for the evening's repast.

He had, in fact, fallen in with a rambling hunting-party, such as often took place in those days among the settlers along the river. The

hunter is always hospitable; and nothing makes men more social and unceremonious than meeting in the wilderness. The commander of the party poured out a dram of cheering liquor, which he gave him with a merry leer, to warm his heart; and ordered one of his followers to fetch some garments from a pinnace, moored in a cove close by, while those in which our hero was dripping might be dried before the fire.

Dolph found, as he had suspected, that the shot from the glen, which had come so near giving him his quietus when on the precipice, was from the party before him. He had nearly crushed one of them by the fragments of rock which he had detached; and the jovial old hunter, in the broad hat and buck-tail, had fired at the place where he saw the bushes move, supposing it to be the sound of some wild animal. He laughed heartily at the blunder, it being what is considered an exceeding good joke among hunters: "But faith, my lad," said he, "if I had but caught a glimpse of you to take sight at, you would have followed the rock. Antony Vander Heyden is seldom known to miss his aim." These last words were at once a clue to Dolph's curiosity; and a few questions let him completely into the character of the man before him, and of his band of woodland rangers. The commander in the broad hat and hunting-frock was no less a personage than the Heer Antony Vander Heyden, of Albany, of whom Dolph had many a time heard. He was, in fact, the hero of many a story, his singular humors and whimsical habits being matters of wonder to his quiet Dutch neighbors. As he was a man of property, having had a father before him from whom he inherited large tracts of wild land, and whole barrels full of wampum, he could indulge his humors without control. Instead of staying quietly at home, eating and drinking at regular mealtimes, amusing himself by smoking his pipe on the bench before the door, and then turning into a comfortable bed at night, he delighted in all kinds of rough, wild expeditions; never so happy as when on a hunting-party in the wilderness, sleeping under trees or bark sheds, or cruising down the river, or on some woodland lake, fishing and fowling, and living the Lord knows how.

He was a great friend to Indians, and to an Indian mode of life; which he considered true natural liberty and manly enjoyment. When at home he had always several Indian hangers-on who loitered about his house, sleeping like hounds in the sunshine; or preparing hunting and fishing tackle for some new expedition; or shooting at marks with bows and arrows.

Over these vagrant beings Heer Antony had as perfect command as a huntsman over his pack; though they were great nuisances to the regular people of his neighborhood. As he was a rich man, no one ventured

to thwart his humors; indeed, his hearty, joyous manner made him universally popular. He would troll a Dutch song as he tramped along the street; hail everyone a mile off, and when he entered a house, would slap the good man familiarly on the back, shake him by the hand till he roared, and kiss his wife and daughter before his face,—in short, there was no pride nor ill humor about Heer Antony.

Besides his Indian hangers-on, he had three or four humble friends among the white men, who looked up to him as a patron, and had the run of his kitchen, and the favor of being taken with him occasionally on his expeditions. With a medley of such retainers he was at present on a cruise along the shores of the Hudson, in a pinnace kept for his own recreation. There were two white men with him, dressed partly in the Indian style, with moccasins and hunting-shirts; the rest of his crew consisted of four favorite Indians. They had been prowling about the river, without any definite object, until they found themselves in the highlands; where they had passed two or three days, hunting the deer which still lingered among these mountains.

"It is lucky for you, young man," said Antony Vander Heyden, "that you happened to be knocked overboard to-day, as to-morrow morning we start early on our return homewards; and you might then have looked in vain for a meal among the mountains—but come, lads, stir about! stir about! Let's see what prog we have for supper; the kettle has boiled long enough; my stomach cries cupboard; and I'll warrant our guest is in no mood to dally with his trencher."

There was a bustle now in the little encampment; one took off the kettle and turned a part of the contents into a huge wooden bowl. Another prepared a flat rock for a table; while a third brought various utensils from the pinnace; Heer Antony himself brought a flask or two of precious liquor from his own private locker; knowing his boon companions too well to trust any of them with the key.

A rude but hearty repast was soon spread; consisting of venison smoking from the kettle, with cold bacon, boiled Indian corn, and mighty loaves of good brown household bread. Never had Dolph made a more delicious repast; and when he had washed it down with two or three draughts from the Heer Antony's flask, and felt the jolly liquor sending its warmth through his veins, and glowing round his very heart, he would not have changed his situation, no, not with the governor of the province.

The Heer Antony, too, grew chirping and joyous; told half a dozen fat stories, at which his white followers laughed immoderately, though the Indians, as usual, maintained an invincible gravity.

"This is your true life, my boy!" said he, slapping Dolph on the

shoulder; "a man is never a man till he can defy wind and weather, range woods and wilds, sleep under a tree, and live on basswood leaves!"

And then would he sing a stave or two of a Dutch drinking-song, swaying a short swab Dutch bottle in his hand, while his myrmidons would join in the chorus, until the woods echoed again;—as the good old song has it,

> "They all with a shout made the elements ring
>   So soon as the office was o'er,
> To feasting they went, with true merriment,
>   And tippled strong liquor gillore."

In the midst of his joviality, however, Heer Antony did not lose sight of discretion. Though he pushed the bottle without reserve to Dolph, he always took care to help his followers himself, knowing the beings he had to deal with; and was particular in granting but a moderate allowance to the Indians. The repast being ended, the Indians having drunk their liquor, and smoked their pipes, now wrapped themselves in their blankets, stretched themselves on the ground, with their feet to the fire, and soon fell asleep, like so many tired hounds. The rest of the party remained chatting before the fire, which the gloom of the forest, and the dampness of the air from the late storm, rendered extremely grateful and comforting. The conversation gradually moderated from the hilarity of supper-time, and turned upon hunting-adventures, and exploits and perils in the wilderness, many of which were so strange and improbable, that I will not venture to repeat them, lest the veracity of Antony Vander Heyden and his comrades should be brought into question. There were many legendary tales told, also, about the river, and the settlements on its borders; in which valuable kind of lore the Heer Antony seemed deeply versed. As the sturdy bush-beater sat in a twisted root of a tree, that served him for an arm-chair, dealing forth these wild stories, with the fire gleaming on his strongly marked visage, Dolph was again repeatedly perplexed by something that reminded him of the phantom of the haunted house; some vague resemblance not to be fixed upon any precise feature or lineament, but pervading the general air of his countenance and figure.

The circumstance of Dolph's falling overboard led to the relation of divers disasters and singular mishaps that had befallen voyagers on this great river, particularly in the earlier periods of colonial history; most of which the Heer deliberately attributed to supernatural causes. Dolph stared at this suggestion; but the old gentleman assured him it was very

currently believed by the settlers along the river, that these highlands were under the dominion of supernatural and mischievous beings, which seemed to have taken some pique against the Dutch colonists in the early time of the settlement. In consequence of this, they have ever taken particular delight in venting their spleen, and indulging their humors upon the Dutch skippers; bothering them with flaws, head-winds, counter-currents, and all kinds of impediments, insomuch, that a Dutch navigator was always obliged to be exceedingly wary and deliberate in his proceedings; to come to anchor at dusk; to drop his peak, or take in sail, whenever he saw a swag-bellied cloud rolling over the mountains; in short, to take so many precautions, that he was often apt to be an incredible time in toiling up the river.

Some, he said, believed these mischievous powers of the air to be the evil spirits conjured up by the Indian wizards, in the early times of the province, to revenge themselves on the strangers who had dispossessed them of their country. They even attributed to their incantations the misadventure which befell the renowned Hendrick Hudson, when he sailed so gallantly up this river in quest of a northwest passage, and, as he thought, ran his ship aground; which they affirm was nothing more nor less than a spell of these same wizards, to prevent his getting to China in this direction.

The greater part, however, Heer Antony observed, accounted for all the extraordinary circumstances attending this river, and the perplexities of the skippers who navigated it, by the old legend of the Storm-ship which haunted Point-no-point. On finding Dolph to be utterly ignorant of this tradition, the Heer stared at him for a moment with surprise, and wondered where he had passed his life, to be uninformed on so important a point of history. To pass away the remainder of the evening, therefore, he undertook the tale, as far as his memory would serve, in the very words in which it had been written out by Mynheer Selyne, an early poet of the New Netherlands. Giving, then, a stir to the fire, that sent up its sparks among the trees like a little volcano, he adjusted himself comfortably in his root of a tree, and throwing back his head, and closing his eyes for a few moments, to summon up his recollection, he related the following legend.

The Storm-ship

IN the golden age of the province of the New Netherlands, when under the sway of Wouter Van Twiller, otherwise called the Doubter, the people of the Manhattoes were alarmed one sultry afternoon, just

about the time of the summer solstice, by a tremendous storm of thunder and lightning. The rain fell in such torrents as absolutely to spatter up and smoke along the ground. It seemed as if the thunder rattled and rolled over the very roofs of the houses; the lightning was seen to play about the church of St. Nicholas, and to strive three times, in vain, to strike its weather-cock. Garret Van Horne's new chimney was split almost from top to bottom; Doffue Mildeberger was struck speechless from his baldfaced mare, just as he was riding into town. In a word, it was one of those unparalleled storms which only happen once within the memory of that venerable personage known in all towns by the appellation of "the oldest inhabitant."

Great was the terror of the good old women of the Manhattoes. They gathered their children together, and took refuge in the cellars; after having hung a shoe on the iron point of every bedpost, lest it should attract the lightning. At length the storm abated; the thunder sank ino a growl, and the setting sun, breaking from under the fringed borders of the clouds, made the broad bosom of the bay to gleam like a sea of molten gold.

. The word was given from the fort that a ship was standing up the bay. It passed from mouth to mouth, and street to street, and soon put the little capital in a bustle. The arrival of a ship, in those early times of the settlement, was an event of vast importance to the inhabitants. It brought them news from the old world, from the land of their birth, from which they were so completely severed; to the yearly ship, too, they looked for their supply of luxuries, of finery, of comforts, and almost of necessaries. The good vrouw could not have her new cap nor new gown until the arrival of the ship; the artist waited for it for his tools, the burgomaster for his pipe and his supply of Hollands, the schoolboy for his top and marbles, and the lordly landholder for the bricks with which he was to build his new mansion. Thus every one, rich and poor, great and small, looked out for the arrival of the ship. It was the great yearly event of the town of New Amsterdam; and from one end of the year to the other, the ship—the ship—the ship—was the continual topic of conversation.

The news from the fort, therefore, brought all the populace down to the Battery, to behold the wished-for sight. It was not exactly the time when she had been expected to arrive, and the circumstance was a matter of some speculation. Many were the groups collected about the Battery. Here and there might be seen a burgomaster, of slow and pompous gravity, giving his opinion with great confidence to a crowd of old women and idle boys. At another place was a knot of old weatherbeaten fellows, who had been seamen or fishermen in their times, and

were great authorities on such occasions. These gave different opinions, and caused great disputes among their several adherents; but the man most looked up to, and followed and watched by the crowd, was Hans Van Pelt, an old Dutch sea-captain retired from service, the nautical oracle of the place. He reconnoitred the ship through an ancient tele-scope, covered with tarry canvas, hummed a Dutch tune to himself, and said nothing. A hum, however, from Hans Van Pelt, had always more weight with the public than a speech from another man.

In the meantime the ship became more distinct to the naked eye: she was a stout, round, Dutch-built vessel, with high bow and poop, and bearing Dutch colors. The evening sun gilded her bellying canvas, as she came riding over the long waving billows. The sentinel who had given notice of her approach, declared, that he first got sight of her when she was in the centre of the bay; and that she broke suddenly on his sight, just as if she had come out of the bosom of the black thunder-cloud. The bystanders looked at Hans Van Pelt, to see what he would say to this report; Hans Van Pelt screwed his mouth closer together, and said nothing; upon which some shook their heads, and others shrugged their shoulders.

The ship was now repeatedly hailed, but made no reply, and passing by the fort, stood on up the Hudson. A gun was brought to bear on her, and, with some difficulty, loaded and fired by Hans Van Pelt, the gar-rison not being expert in artillery. The shot seemed absolutely to pass through the ship, and to skip along the water on the other side, but no notice was taken of it! What was strange, she had all her sails set, and sailed right against wind and tide, which were both down the river. Upon this Hans Van Pelt, who was likewise harbor-master, ordered his boat, and set off to board her; but after rowing two or three hours, he re-turned without success. Sometimes he would get within one or two hundred yards of her, and then, in a twinkling, she would be half a mile off. Some said it was because his oarsmen, who were rather pursy and short-winded, stopped every now and then to take breath, and spit on their hands; but this it is probable was a mere scandal. He got near enough, however, to see the crew; who were all dressed in the Dutch style, the officers in doublets and high hats and feathers. Not a word was spoken by any one on board; they stood as motionless as so many statues, and the ship seemed as if left to her own government. Thus she kept on, away up the river, lessening and lessening in the evening sun-shine, until she faded from sight, like a little white cloud melting away in the summer sky.

The appearance of this ship threw the governor into one of the deep-est doubts that ever beset him in the whole course of his administration.

Fears were entertained for the security of the infant settlements on the river, lest this might be an enemy's ship in disguise, sent to take possession. The governor called together his council repeatedly to assist him with their conjectures. He sat in his chair of state, built of timber from the sacred forest of the Hague, smoking his long jasmin pipe, and listening to all that his counsellors had to say on a subject about which they knew nothing; but in spite of all the conjecturing of the sagest and oldest heads, the governor still continued to doubt.

Messengers were despatched to different places on the river; but they returned without any tidings—the ship had made no port. Day after day, and week after week, elapsed, but she never returned down the Hudson. As, however, the council seemed solicitous for intelligence, they had it in abundance. The captains of the sloops seldom arrived without bringing some report of having seen the strange ship at different parts of the river; sometimes near the Pallisadoes, sometimes off Croton Point, and sometimes in the highlands; but she never was reported as having been seen above the highlands. The crews of the sloops, it is sure, generally differed among themselves in their accounts of these apparitions; but that may have arisen from the uncertain situations in which they saw her. Sometimes it was by the flashes of the thunder-storm lighting up a pitchy night, and giving glimpses of her careering across Tappaan Zee, or the wide waste of Haverstraw Bay. At one moment she would appear close upon them, as if likely to run them down, and would throw them into great bustle and alarm; but the next flash would show her far off, always sailing against the wind. Sometimes, in quiet moonlight nights, she would be seen under some high bluff of the highlands, all in deep shadow, excepting her top-sails glittering in the moonbeams; by the time, however, that the voyagers reached the place, no ship was to be seen; and when they had passed on for some distance, and looked back, behold! there she was again, with her topsails in the moonshine! Her appearance was always just after, or just before, or just in the midst of unruly weather; and she was known among the skippers and voyagers of the Hudson by the name of the *Storm-Ship*.

These reports perplexed the governor and his council more than ever; and it would be endless to repeat the conjectures and opinions uttered on the subject. Some quoted cases in point, of ships seen off the coast of New England, navigated by witches and goblins. Old Hans Van Pelt, who had been more than once to the Dutch colony at the Cape of Good Hope, insisted that this must be the flying Dutchman, which had so long haunted Table Bay; but being unable to make port, had now sought another harbor. Others suggested, that, if it really was

a supernatural apparition, as there was every natural reason to believe, it might be Hendrick Hudson, and his crew of the *Half-Moon;* who, it was well known, had once run aground in the upper part of the river in seeking a northwest passage to China. This opinion had very little weight with the governor, but it passed current out of doors; for indeed it had already been reported, that Hendrick Hudson and his crew haunted the Kaatskill Mountains; and it appeared very reasonable to suppose, that his ship might infest the river where the enterprise was baffled, or that it might bear the shadowy crew to their periodical revels in the mountain.

Other events occurred to occupy the thoughts and doubts of the sage Wouter and his council, and the *Storm-Ship* ceased to be a subject of deliberation at the board. It continued, however, a matter of popular belief and marvellous anecdote through the whole time of the Dutch government, and particularly just before the capture of New Amsterdam, and the subjugation of the province by the English squadron. About that time the *Storm-Ship* was repeatedly seen in the Tappaan Zee; and about Weehawk, and even down as far as Hoboken; and her approaching squall in public affairs, and the downfall of Dutch domination.

Since that time we have no authentic accounts of her; though it is said she still haunts the highlands, and cruises about Point-no-point. People who live along the river insist that they sometimes see her in summer moonlight; and that in a deep still midnight they have heard the chant of her crew, as if heaving the lead; but sights and sounds are so deceptive along the mountainous shores, and about the wide bays and long reaches of this great river, that I confess I have very strong doubts upon the subject.

It is certain, nevertheless, that strange things have been seen in these highlands in storms, which are considered as connected with the old story of the ship. The captains of the river craft talk of a little bulbous-bottomed Dutch goblin, in trunk-hose and sugar-loafed hat, with a speaking-trumpet in his hand, which they say keeps about the Dunderberg.* They declare that they have heard him, in stormy weather, in the midst of the turmoil, giving orders in Low Dutch for the piping up of a fresh gust of wind, or the rattling off of another thunder-clap. That sometimes he has been seen surrounded by a crew of little imps in broad breeches and short doublets; tumbling head-over-heels in the rack and mist, and playing a thousand gambols in the air; or buzzing like a swarm of flies about Antony's Nose; and that, at such times, the hurry-scurry of the storm was always greatest. One time a sloop, in passing by

---

* *i.e.*, The "Thunder-Mountain," so called from its echoes.

the Dunderberg, was overtaken by a thunder-gust, that came scouring round the mountain, and seemed to burst just over the vessel. Though tight and well ballasted, she labored dreadfully, and the water came over the gunwale. All the crew were amazed when it was discovered that there was a little white sugar-loaf hat on the mast-head, known at once to be the hat of the Heer of the Dunderberg. Nobody, however, dared to climb to the mast-head, and get rid of this terrible hat. The sloop continued laboring and rocking, as if she would have rolled her mast overboard, and seemed in continual danger either of upsetting or of running on shore. In this way she drove quite through the highlands, until she had passed Pollopol's Island, where, it is said, the jurisdiction of the Dunderberg potentate ceases. No sooner had she passed this bourn, than the little hat spun up into the air like a top, whirled up all the clouds into a vortex, and hurried them back to the summit of the Dunderberg; while the sloop righted herself, and sailed on as quietly as if in a mill-pond. Nothing saved her from utter wreck but the fortunate circumstances of having a horse-shoe nailed against the mast, —a wise precaution against evil spirits, since adopted by all the Dutch captains that navigate this haunted river.

There is another story told of this foul-weather urchin, by Skipper Daniel Ouselsticker, of Fishkill, who was never known to tell a lie. He declared, that, in a severe squall, he saw him seated astride of his bowsprit, riding the sloop ashore, full butt against Antony's Nose, and that he was exorcised by Dominie Van Gieson, of Esopus, who happened to be on board, and who sang the hymn of St. Nicholas; whereupon the goblin threw himself up in the air like a ball, and went off in a whirlwind, carrying away with him the nightcap of the Dominie's wife; which was discovered the next Sunday morning hanging on the weather-cock of Esopus church-steeple, at least forty miles off! Several events of this kind having taken place, the regular skippers of the river, for a long time, did not venture to pass the Dunderberg without lowering their peaks, out of homage to the Heer of the mountain; and it was observed that all such as paid this tribute of respect were suffered to pass unmolested.*

---

* Among the superstitions which prevailed in the colonies, during the early times of the settlements, there seems to have been a singular one about phantom ships. The superstitious fancies of men are always apt to turn upon those objects which concern their daily occupations. The solitary ship, which, from year to year, came like a raven in the wilderness, bringing to the inhabitants of a settlement the comforts of life from the world from which they were cut off, was apt to be present to their dreams, whether sleeping or waking. The accidental sight from shore of a sail gliding along the horizon in those as yet lonely seas, was apt to be a mat-

"Such," said Antony Vander Heyden, "are, a few of the stories written down by Selyne, the poet, concerning the *Storm-Ship*,—which he affirms to have brought a crew of mischievous imps into the province, from some old ghost-ridden country of Europe. I could give a host more, if necessary; for all the accidents that so often befall the river craft in the highlands are said to be tricks played off by these imps of the Dunderberg; but I see that you are nodding, so let us turn in for the night."

The moon had just raised her silver horns above the round back of Old Bull Hill, and lit up the gray rocks and shagged forests, and glittered on the waving bosom of the river. The night dew was falling, and the late gloomy mountains began to soften and put on a gray aërial tint in the dewy light. The hunters stirred the fire, and threw on fresh fuel to qualify the damp of the night air. They then prepared a bed of branches and dry leaves under a ledge of rocks for Dolph; while Antony Vander Heyden, wrapping himself in a huge coat of skins, stretched himself before the fire. It was some time, however, before Dolph could close his eyes. He lay contemplating the strange scene before him: the wild woods and rocks around; the fire throwing fitful gleams on the faces of the sleeping savages; and the Heer Antony, too, who so singularly, yet vaguely, reminded him of the nightly visitant to the haunted house. Now and then he heard the cry of some wild animal from the forest; or the hooting of the owl; or the notes of the whippoorwill, which seemed to abound among these solitudes; or the splash of a sturgeon, leaping out of the river and falling back full-length on its placid surface. He contrasted all this with his accustomed nest in the garret room of the doctor's mansion;—where the only sounds at night were the church clock telling the hour; the drowsy voice of the watchman, drawling out all was well; the deep snoring of the doctor's clubbed nose from below stairs; or the cautious labors of some carpenter rat gnawing in the wainscot. His thoughts then wandered to his poor old

---

ter of much talk and speculation. There is mention made in one of the early New England writers of a ship navigated by witches, with a great horse that stood by the mainmast. I have met with another story, somewhere, of a ship that drove on shore, in fair, sunny, tranquil weather, with sails all set, and a table spread in the cabin, as if to regale a number of guests, yet not a living being on board. These phantom ships always sailed in the eye of the wind; or ploughed their way with great velocity, making the smooth sea foam before their bows, when not a breath of air was stirring.

Moore has finely wrought up one of these legends of the sea into a little tale, which, within a small compass, contains the very essence of this species of supernatural fiction. I allude to his *Spectre-Ship*, bound to Deadman's Isle.

mother: what would she think of his mysterious disappearance—what anxiety and distress would she not suffer? This thought would continually intrude itself to mar his present enjoyment. It brought with it a feeling of pain and compunction, and he fell asleep with the tears yet standing in his eyes.

Were this a mere tale of fancy, here would be a fine opportunity for weaving in strange adventures among these wild mountains, and roving hunters; and, after involving my hero in a variety of perils and difficulties, rescuing him from them all by some miraculous contrivance. But as this is absolutely a true story, I must content myself with simple facts, and keep to probabilities.

At an early hour of the next day, therefore, after a hearty morning's meal, the encampment broke up, and our adventurers embarked in the pinnace of Antony Vander Heyden. There being no wind for the sails, the Indians rowed her gently along, keeping time to a kind of chant of one of the white men. The day was serene and beautiful; the river without a wave; and as the vessel cleft the glassy water, it left a long, undulating track behind. The crows, who had scented the hunters' banquet, were already gathering and hovering in the air, just where a column of thin, blue smoke, rising from among the trees showed the place of their last night's quarters. As they coasted along the bases of the mountains, the Heer Antony pointed out to Dolph a bald eagle, the sovereign of these regions, who sat perched on a dry tree that projected over the river, and, with eye turned upwards, seemed to be drinking in the splendor of the morning sun. Their approach disturbed the monarch's meditations. He first spread one wing, and then the other; balanced himself for a moment, and then, quitting his perch with dignified composure, wheeled slowly over their heads. Dolph snatched up a gun, and sent a whistling ball after him, that cut some of the feathers from his wing. The report of the gun leaped sharply from rock to rock, and awakened a thousand echoes. But the monarch of the air sailed calmly on, ascending higher and higher, and wheeling widely as he ascended, soaring up the green bosom of the woody mountain, until he disappeared over the brow of a beetling precipice. Dolph felt in a manner rebuked by this proud tranquillity, and almost reproached himself for having so wantonly insulted this majestic bird. Heer Antony told him, laughing, to remember that he was not yet out of the territories of the lord of the Dunderberg; and an old Indian shook his head, and observed, that there was bad luck in killing an eagle. The hunter, on the contrary, should always leave him a portion of his spoils.

Nothing, however, occurred to molest them on their voyage. They passed pleasantly through magnificent and lonely scenes, until they

came to where Pollopol's Island lay, like a floating bower at the extremity of the highlands. Here they landed, until the heat of the day should abate, or a breeze spring up that might supersede the labor of the oar. Some prepared the mid-day meal, while others reposed under the shade of the trees, in luxurious summer indolence, looking drowsily forth upon the beauty of the scene. On the one side were the highlands, vast and cragged, feathered to the top with forests, and throwing their shadows on the glassy water that dimpled at their feet. On the other side was a wide expanse of the river, like a broad lake, with long sunny reaches, and green headlands; and the distant line of Shawangunk mountains waving along a clear horizon, or checkered by a fleecy cloud.

But I forbear to dwell on the particulars of their cruise along the river. This vagrant, amphibious life, careering across silver sheets of water, coasting wild woodland shores, banqueting on shady promontories, with the spreading tree overhead, the river curling its light foam to one's feet, and distant mountain, and rock, and tree, and snowy cloud, and deep-blue sky, all mingling in summer beauty before one,—all this, though never cloying in the enjoyment, would be but tedious in narration.

When encamped by the water-side, some of the party would go into the woods and hunt; others would fish. Sometimes they would amuse themselves by shooting at a mark, by leaping, by running, by wrestling; and Dolph gained great favor in the eyes of Antony Vander Heyden, by his skill and adroitness in all these exercises, which the Heer considered as the highest of manly accomplishments.

Thus did they coast jollily on, choosing only the pleasant hours for voyaging; sometimes in the cool morning dawn, sometimes in the sober evening twilight, and sometimes when the moonshine spangled the crisp curling waves that whispered along the sides of their little bark. Never had Dolph felt so completely in his element; never had he met with anything so completely to his taste as this wild haphazard life. He was the very man to second Antony Vander Heyden in his rambling humors, and gained continually on his affections. The heart of the old bushwhacker yearned toward the young man, who seemed thus growing up in his own likeness; and as they approached to the end of their voyage, he could not help inquiring a little into his history. Dolph frankly told him his course of life, his severe medical studies, his little proficiency, and his very dubious prospects. The Heer was shocked to find that such amazing talents and accomplishments were to be cramped and buried under a doctor's wig. He had a sovereign contempt for the healing art, having never had any other physician than the butcher. He bore a mortal grudge to all kinds of study also, ever since he had been

flogged about an unintelligible book when he was a boy. But to think that a young fellow like Dolph, of such wonderful abilities, who could shoot, fish, run, jump, ride, and wrestle, should be obliged to roll pills, and administer juleps for a living—'t was monstrous! He told Dolph never to despair, but to "throw physic to the dogs"; for a young fellow of his prodigious talents could never fail to make his way. "As you seem to have no acquaintance in Albany," said Heer Antony, "you shall go home with me, and remain under my roof until you can look about you; and in the meantime we can take an occasional bout at shooting and fishing, for it is a pity that such talents should lie idle."

Dolph, who was at the mercy of chance, was not hard to be persuaded. Indeed, on turning over matters in his mind, which he did very sagely and deliberately, he could not but think that Antony Vander Heyden was, "somehow or other," connected with the story of the haunted house; that the misadventure in the highlands, which had thrown them so strangely together, was, "somehow or other," to work out something good: in short, there is nothing so convenient as this "somehow-or-other" way of accommodating one's self to circumstances; it is the mainstay of a heedless actor, and tardy reasoner, like Dolph Heyliger; and he who can, in this loose, easy way, link foregone evil to anticipated good, possesses a secret of happiness almost equal to the philosopher's stone.

On their arrival at Albany, the sight of Dolph's companion seemed to cause universal satisfaction. Many were the greetings at the river-side, and the salutations in the streets; the dogs bounded before him; the boys whooped as he passed; everybody seemed to know Antony Vander Heyden. Dolph followed on in silence, admiring the neatness of this worthy burgh; for in those days Albany was in all its glory, and inhabited almost exclusively by the descendants of the original Dutch settlers, not having as yet been discovered and colonized by the restless people of New England. Everything was quiet and orderly; everything was conducted calmly and leisurely; no hurry, no bustle, no struggling and scrambling for existence. The grass grew about the unpaved streets, and relieved the eye by its refreshing verdure. Tall sycamores or pendent willows shaded the houses, with caterpillars swinging in long silken strings from their branches; or moths, fluttering about like coxcombs, in joy at their gay transformation. The houses were built in the old Dutch style, with the gable-ends toward the street. The thrifty housewife was seated on a bench before her door, in close-crimped cap, bright-flowered gown, and white apron, busily employed in knitting. The husband smoked his pipe on the opposite bench; and the little pet negro girl, seated on the step at her mistress's feet, was industriously

plying her needle. The swallows sported about the eaves, or skimmed along the streets, and brought back some rich booty for their clamorous young; and the little housekeeping wren flew in and out of a Liliputian house, or an old hat nailed against the wall. The cows were coming home, lowing through the streets, to be milked at their owner's door; and if, perchance, there were any loiterers, some negro urchin, with a long goad, was gently urging them homewards.

As Dolph's companion passed on, he received a tranquil nod from the burghers, and a friendly word from their wives; all calling him familiarly by the name of Antony; for it was the custom in this stronghold of the patriarchs, where they had all grown up together from childhood, to call each other by the Christian name. The Heer did not pause to have his usual jokes with them, for he was impatient to reach his home. At length they arrived at his mansion. It was of some magnitude, in the Dutch style, with large iron figures on the gables, that gave the date of its erection, and showed that it had been built in the earliest times of the settlement.

The news of Heer Antony's arrival had preceded him, and the whole household was on the look-out. A crew of negroes, large and small, had collected in front of the house to receive him. The old, white-headed ones, who had grown gray in his service, grinned for joy, and made many awkward bows and grimaces, and the little ones capered about his knees. But the most happy being in the household was a little, plump, blooming lass, his only child, and the darling of his heart. She came bounding out of the house; but the sight of a strange young man with her father called up, for a moment, all the bashfulness of a home-bred damsel. Dolph gazed at her with wonder and delight; never had he seen, as he thought, anything so comely in the shape of a woman. She was dressed in the good old Dutch taste, with long stays, and full, short petticoats, so admirably adapted to show and set off the female form. Her hair, turned up under a small round cap, displayed the fairness of her forehead; she had fine blue, laughing eyes, a trim, slender waist, and soft swell—but, in a word, she was a little Dutch divinity; and Dolph, who never stopped half-way in a new impulse, fell desperately in love with her.

Dolph was now ushered into the house with a hearty welcome. In the interior was a mingled display of Heer Antony's taste and habits, and of the opulence of his predecessors. The chambers were furnished with good old mahogany; the beaufets and cupboards glittered with embossed silver and painted china. Over the parlor fireplace was, as usual, the family coat-of-arms, painted and framed; above which was a long duck fowling-piece, flanked by an Indian pouch and a powder-horn.

The room was decorated with many Indian articles, such as pipes of peace, tomahawks, scalping-knives, hunting-pouches, and belts of wampum; and there were various kinds of fishing-tackle, and two or three fowling-pieces in the corners. The household affairs seemed to be conducted, in some measure, after the master's humors; corrected, perhaps, by a little quiet management of the daughter's. There was a great degree of patriarchal simplicity, and good-humored indulgence. The negroes came into the room without being called, merely to look at their master, and hear of his adventures; they would stand listening at the door until he had finished a story, and then go off on a broad grin, to repeat it in the kitchen. A couple of pet negro children were playing about the floor with the dogs, and sharing with them their bread and butter. All the domestics looked hearty and happy; and when the table was set for the evening repast, the variety and abundance of good household luxuries bore testimony to the open-handed liberality of the Heer, and the notable housewifery of his daughter.

In the evening there dropped in several of the worthies of the place, the Van Renssellaers, and the Gansevoorts, and the Rosebooms, and others of Antony Vander Heyden's intimates, to hear an account of his expedition; for he was the Sinbad of Albany, and his exploits and adventures were favorite topics of conversation among the inhabitants. While these sat gossiping together about the door of the hall, and telling long twilight stories, Dolph was cosily seated, entertaining the daughter, on a window-bench. He had already got on intimate terms; for those were not times of false reserve and idle ceremony; and, besides, there is something wonderfully propitious to a lover's suit in the delightful dusk of a long summer evening; it gives courage to the most timid tongue, and hides the blushes of the bashful. The stars alone twinkled brightly, and now and then a fire-fly streamed his transient light before the window, or, wandering into the room, flew gleaming about the ceiling.

What Dolph whispered in her ear that long summer evening, it is impossible to say; his words were so low and indistinct, that they never reached the ear of the historian. It is probable, however, that they were to the purpose; for he had a natural talent at pleasing the sex, and was never long in company with a petticoat without paying proper court to it. In the meantime the visitors, one by one, departed; Antony Vander Heyden, who had fairly talked himself silent, sat nodding alone in his chair by the door, when he was suddenly aroused by a hearty salute with which Dolph Heyliger had unguardedly rounded off one of his periods, and which echoed through the still chamber like the report of a pistol. The Heer started up, rubbed his eyes, called for lights, and ob-

served that it was high time to go to bed; though, on parting for the night, he squeezed Dolph heartily by the hand, looked kindly in his face, and shook his head knowingly; for the Heer well remembered what he himself had been at the youngster's age.

The chamber in which our hero was lodged was spacious, and panelled with oak. It was furnished with clothes-presses, and mighty chests of drawers, well waxed, and glittering with brass ornaments. These contained ample stock of family linen; for the Dutch housewives had always a laudable pride in showing off their household treasures to strangers.

Dolph's mind, however, was too full to take particular note of the objects around him; yet he could not help continually comparing the free, open-hearted cheeriness of this establishment with the starveling, sordid, joyless housekeeping at Doctor Knipperhausen's. Still, something marred the enjoyment: the idea that he must take leave of his hearty host and pretty hostess, and cast himself once more adrift upon the world. To linger here would be folly. He should only get deeper in love; and for a poor varlet, like himself, to aspire to the daughter of the great Heer Vander Heyden—it was madness to think of such a thing! The very kindness that the girl had shown towards him prompted him, on reflection, to hasten his departure; it would be a poor return for the frank hospitality of his host to entangle his daughter's heart in an injudicious attachment. In a word, Dolph was like many other young reasoners of exceeding good hearts and giddy heads,—who think after they act, and act differently from what they think,—who make excellent determinations overnight, and forget to keep them the next morning.

"This is a fine conclusion, truly, of my voyage," said he, as he almost buried himself in a sumptuous feather bed, and drew the fresh white sheets up to his chin. "Here am I, instead of finding a bag of money to carry home, launched in a strange place, with scarcely a stiver in my pocket; and, what is worse, have jumped ashore up to my very ears in love into the bargain. However," added he, after some pause, stretching himself, and turning himself in bed, "I'm in good quarters for the present, at least; so I'll e'en enjoy the present moment, and let the next take care of itself; I dare say all will work out, 'somehow or other,' for the best."

As he said these words, he reached out his hand to extinguish the candle, when he was suddenly struck with astonishment and dismay, for he thought he beheld the phantom of the haunted house, staring on him from a dusky part of the chamber. A second look reassured him, as he perceived that what he had taken for the spectre was, in fact, nothing but a Flemish portrait, hanging in a shadowy corner, just behind a

clothes-press. It was, however, the precise representation of his nightly visitor. The same cloak and belted jerkin, the same grizzled beard and fixed eye, the same broad slouched hat, with a feather hanging over one side. Dolph now called to mind the resemblance he had frequently remarked between his host and the old man of the haunted house; and was fully convinced they were in some way connected, and that some especial destiny had governed his voyage. He lay gazing on the portrait with almost as much awe as he had gazed on the ghostly original, until the shrill house-clock warned him of the lateness of the hour. He put out the light, but remained for a long time turning over these curious circumstances and coincidences in his mind, until he fell asleep. His dreams partook of the nature of his waking thoughts. He fancied that he still lay gazing on the picture, until, by degrees, it became animated; that the figure descended from the wall, and walked out of the room; that he followed it, and found himself by the well to which the old man pointed, smiled on him, and disappeared.

In the morning, when he waked, he found his host standing by his bedside, who gave him a hearty morning's salutation, and asked him how he had slept. Dolph answered cheerily; but took occasion to inquire about the portrait that hung against the wall. "Ah," said Heer Antony, "that's a portrait of old Killian Vander Spiegel, once a burgomaster of Amsterdam, who, on some popular troubles, abandoned Holland, and came over to the province during the government of Peter Stuyvesant. He was my ancestor by the mother's side, and an old miserly curmudgeon he was. When the English took possession of New Amsterdam, in 1664, he retired into the country. He fell into a melancholy, apprehending that his wealth would be taken from him and he come to beggary. He turned all his property into cash, and used to hide it away. He was for a year or two concealed in various places, fancying himself sought after by the English, to strip him of his wealth; and finally he was found dead in his bed one morning, without any one being able to discover where he had concealed the greater part of his money."

When his host had left the room, Dolph remained for some time lost in thought. His whole mind was occupied by what he had heard. Vander Spiegel was his mother's family name; and he recollected to have heard her speak of this very Killian Vander Spiegel as one of her ancestors. He had heard her say, too, that her father was Killian's rightful heir, only that the old man died without leaving anything to be inherited. It now appeared that Heer Antony was likewise a descendant, and perhaps an heir also, of this poor rich man; and that thus the Heyligers and the Vander Heydens were remotely connected. "What," thought he, "if, after all, this is the interpretation of my dream, that

this is the way I am to make my fortune by this voyage to Albany, and that I am to find the old man's hidden wealth in the bottom of that well? But what an odd roundabout mode of communicating the matter! Why the plague could not the old goblin have told me about the well at once, without sending me all the way to Albany, to hear a story that was to send me all the way back again?"

These thoughts passed through his mind while he was dressing. He descended the stairs, full of perplexity, when the bright face of Marie Vander Heyden suddenly beamed in smiles upon him, and seemed to give him a clue to the whole mystery. "After all," thought he, "the old goblin is in the right. If I am to get his wealth, he means that I shall marry his pretty descendant; thus both branches of the family will again be united, and the property go on in the proper channel."

No sooner did this idea enter his head, than it carried conviction with it. He was now all impatience to hurry back and secure the treasure, which, he did not doubt, lay at the bottom of the well, and which he feared every moment might be discovered by some other person. "Who knows," thought he, "but this night-walking old fellow of the haunted house may be in the habit of haunting every visitor, and may give a hint to some shrewder fellow than myself, who will take a shorter cut to the well than by the way of Albany?" He wished a thousand times that the babbling old ghost was laid in the Red Sea, and his rambling portrait with him. He was in a perfect fever to depart. Two or three days elapsed before any opportunity presented for returning down the river. They were ages to Dolph, notwithstanding that he was basking in the smiles of the pretty Marie, and daily getting more and more enamoured.

At length the very sloop from which he had been knocked overboard prepared to make sail. Dolph made an awkward apology to his host for his sudden departure. Antony Vander Heyden was sorely astonished. He had concerted half a dozen excursions into the wilderness; and his Indians were actually preparing for a grand expedition to one of the lakes. He took Dolph aside, and exerted his eloquence to get him to abandon all thoughts of business and to remain with him, but in vain; and he at length gave up the attempt, observing, "that it was a thousand pities so fine a young man should throw himself away." Heer Antony, however, gave him a hearty shake by the hand at parting, with a favorite fowling-piece, and an invitation to come to his house whenever he revisited Albany. The pretty little Marie said nothing; but as he gave her a farewell kiss, her dimpled cheek turned pale, and a tear stood in her eye.

Dolph sprang lightly on board of the vessel. They hoisted sail; the wind was fair; they soon lost sight of Albany, its green hills and em-

bowered islands. They were wafted gayly past the Kaatskill Mountains, whose fairy heights were bright and cloudless. They passed prosperously through the highlands, without any molestation from the Dunderberg goblin and his crew; they swept on across Haverstraw Bay, and by Croton Point, and through the Tappaan Zee, and under the Palisadoes, until, in the afternoon of the third day, they saw the promontory of Hoboken hanging like a cloud in the air; and, shortly after, the roofs of the Manhattoes rising out of the water.

Dolph's first care was to repair to his mother's house; for he was continually goaded by the idea of the uneasiness she must experience on his account. He was puzzling his brains, as he went along, to think how he should account for his absence without betraying the secrets of the haunted house. In the midst of these cogitations he entered the street in which his mother's house was situated, when he was thunderstruck at beholding it a heap of ruins.

There had evidently been a great fire, which had destroyed several large houses, and the humble dwelling of poor Dame Heyliger had been involved in the conflagration. The walls were not so completely destroyed, but that Dolph could distinguish some traces of the scene of his childhood. The fireplace, about which he had often played, still remained, ornamented with Dutch tiles, illustrating passages in Bible history, on which he had many a time gazed with admiration. Among the rubbish lay the wreck of the good dame's elbow-chair, from which she had given him so many a wholesome precept; and hard by it was the family Bible, with brass clasps,—now, alas! reduced almost to a cinder.

For a moment Dolph was overcome by this dismal sight, for he was seized with the fear that his mother had perished in the flames. He was relieved, however, from his horrible apprehension by one of the neighbors, who happened to come by and informed him that his mother was yet alive.

The good woman had, indeed, lost everything by this unlooked-for calamity; for the populace had been so intent upon saving the fine furniture of her rich neighbors, that the little tenement, and the little all of poor Dame Heyliger, had been suffered to consume without interruption; nay, had it not been for the gallant assistance of her old crony, Peter de Groodt, the worthy dame and her cat might have shared the fate of their habitation.

As it was, she had been overcome with fright and affliction, and lay ill in body and sick at heart. The public, however, had showed her its wonted kindness. The furniture of her rich neighbors being, as far as possible, rescued from the flames; themselves duly and ceremoniously visited and condoled with on the injury of their property, and their

ladies commiserated on the agitation of their nerves; the public, at length, began to recollect something about poor Dame Heyliger. She forthwith became again a subject of universal sympathy; everybody pitied her more than ever; and if pity could but have been coined into cash—good Lord! how rich she would have been!

It was now determined, in good earnest, that something ought to be done for her without delay. The Dominie, therefore, put up prayers for her on Sunday, in which all the congregation joined most heartily. Even Cobus Groesbeek, the alderman, and Mynheer Milledollar, the great Dutch merchant, stood up in their pews, and did not spare their voices on the occasion; and it was thought the prayers of such great men could not but have their due weight. Doctor Knipperhausen, too, visited her professionally, and gave her abundance of advice gratis, and was universally lauded for his charity. As to her old friend, Peter de Groodt, he was a poor man, whose pity and prayers and advice could be of but little avail, so he gave her all that was in his power— he gave her shelter.

To the humble dwelling of Peter de Groodt, then, did Dolph turn his steps. On his way thither he recalled all the tenderness and kindness of his simple-hearted parent, her indulgence of his errors, her blindness to his faults; and then he bethought himself of his own idle, harum-scarum life. "I've been a sad scapegrace," said Dolph, shaking his head sorrowfully. "I've been a complete sink-pocket, that's the truth of it. But," added he briskly, and clasping his hands, "only let her live —only let her live—and I will show myself indeed a son!"

As Dolph approached the house he met Peter de Groodt coming out of it. The old man started back aghast, doubting whether it was not a ghost that stood before him. It being bright daylight, however, Peter soon plucked up heart, satisfied that no ghost dare show his face in such clear sunshine. Dolph now learned from the worthy sexton the consternation and rumor to which his mysterious disappearance had given rise. It had been universally believed that he had been spirited away by those hobgoblin gentry that infested the haunted house; and old Abraham Vandozer, who lived by the great buttonwood trees, near the three-mile stone, affirmed that he had heard a terrible noise in the air, as he was going home late at night, which seemed just as if a flock of wild geese were overhead, passing off towards the northward. The haunted house was, in consequence, looked upon with ten times more awe than ever; nobody would venture to pass a night in it for the world, and even the doctor had ceased to make his expeditions to it in the day-time.

It required some preparation before Dolph's return could be made

known to his mother, the poor soul having bewailed him as lost; and her spirits having been sorely broken down by a number of comforters, who daily cheered her with stories of ghosts, and of people carried away by the devil. He found her confined to her bed, with the other member of the Heyliger family, the good dame's cat, purring beside her, but sadly singed, and utterly despoiled of those whiskers which were the glory of her physiognomy. The poor woman threw her arms about Dolph's neck. "My boy! my boy! art thou still alive?" For a time she seemed to have forgotten all her losses and troubles in her joy at his return. Even the sage grimalkin showed indubitable signs of joy at the return of the youngster. She saw, perhaps, that they were a forlorn and undone family, and felt a touch of that kindliness which fellow-sufferers only know. But, in truth, cats are a slandered people; they have more affection in them than the world commonly gives them credit for.

The good dame's eyes glistened as she saw one being at least, besides herself, rejoiced at her son's return. "Tib knows thee! poor dumb beast!" said she, smoothing down the mottled coat of her favorite; then recollecting herself, with a melancholy shake of the head, "Ah, my poor Dolph!" exclaimed she, "thy mother can help thee no longer! She can no longer help herself! What will become of thee, my poor boy!"

"Mother," said Dolph, "don't talk in that strain; I've been too long a charge upon you; it's now my part to take care of you in your old days. Come, be of good cheer! you and I and Tib will all see better days. I'm here, you see, young and sound and hearty; then don't let us despair; I dare say things will all, somehow or other, turn out for the best."

While this scene was going on with the Heyliger family, the news was carried to Doctor Knipperhausen of the safe return of his disciple. The little doctor scarce knew whether to rejoice or be sorry at the tidings. He was happy at having the foul reports which had prevailed concerning his country mansion thus disproved; but he grieved at having his disciple, of whom he had supposed himself fairly disencumbered, thus drifting back a heavy charge upon his hands. While balancing between these two feelings, he was determined by the councils of Frau Ilsy, who advised him to take advantage of the truant absence of the youngster, and shut the door upon him forever.

At the hour of bedtime, therefore, when it was supposed the recreant disciple would seek his old quarters, everything was prepared for his reception. Dolph, having talked his mother into a state of tranquillity, sought the mansion of his quondam master, and raised the knocker with a faltering hand. Scarcely, however, had it give a dubious rap, when the doctor's head, in a red nightcap, popped out of one window, and

the housekeeper's, in a white nightcap, out of another. He was now greeted with a tremendous volley of hard names and hard language, mingled with invaluable pieces of advice, such as are seldom ventured to be given excepting to a friend in distress, or a culprit at the bar. In a few moments, not a window in the street but had its particular nightcap, listening to the shrill treble of Frau Ilsy, and the gutteral croaking of Dr. Knipperhausen; and the word went from window to window, "Ah! here's Dolph Heyliger come back, and at his old pranks again." In short, poor Dolph found he was likely to get nothing from the doctor but good advice; a commodity so abundant as even to be thrown out of the window; so he was fain to beat a retreat, and take up his quarters for the night under the lowly roof of honest Peter de Groodt.

The next morning, bright and early, Dolph was out at the haunted house. Everything looked just as he had left it. The fields were grass-grown and matted, and appeared as if nobody had traversed them since his departure. With palpitating heart he hastened to the well. He looked down into it, and saw that it was of great depth, with water at the bottom. He had provided himself with a strong line, such as the fishermen use on the banks of Newfoundland. At the end was a heavy plummet and a large fish-hook. With this he began to sound the bottom of the well, and to angle about in the water. The water was of some depth; there was also much rubbish, stones from the top having fallen in. Several times his hook got entangled, and he came near breaking his line. Now and then, too, he hauled up mere trash, such as the skull of a horse, an iron hoop, and a shattered iron-bound bucket. He had now been several hours employed without finding anything to repay his trouble, or to encourage him to proceed. He began to think himself a great fool, to be thus decoyed into a wild-goose chase by mere dreams, and was on the point of throwing line and all into the well, and giving up all further angling.

"One more cast of the line," said he, "and that shall be the last." As he sounded, he felt the plummet slip, as it were, through the interstices of loose stones; and as he drew back the line, he felt that the hook had taken hold of something heavy. He had to manage his line with great caution, lest it should be broken by the strain upon it. By degrees the rubbish which lay upon the article he had hooked gave way; he drew it to the surface of the water, and what was his rapture at seeing something like silver glittering at the end of his line! Almost breathless with anxiety, he drew it up to the mouth of the well, surprised at its great weight, and fearing every instant that his hook would slip from its hold, and his prize tumble again to the bottom. At length he

landed it safe beside the well. It was a great silver porringer, of an ancient form, richly embossed, and with armorial bearings engraved on its side, similar to those over his mother's mantelpiece. The lid was fastened on by several twists of wire; Dolph loosened them with a trembling hand, and, on lifting the lid, behold! the vessel was filled with broad golden pieces, of a coinage which he had never seen before! It was evident he had lit on the place where Killian Vander Spiegel had concealed his treasure.

Fearful of being seen by some straggler, he cautiously retired, and buried his pot of money in a secret place. He now spread terrible stories about the haunted house, and deterred every one from approaching it, while he made frequent visits to it in stormy days, when no one was stirring in the neighboring fields; though, to tell the truth, he did not care to venture there in the dark. For once in his life he was diligent and industrious, and followed up his new trade of angling with such perseverance and success, that in a little while he had hooked up wealth enough to make him, in those modern days, a rich burgher for life.

· It would be tedious to detail minutely the rest of this story. To tell how he gradually managed to bring his property into use without exciting surprise and inquiry,—how he satisfied all scruples with regard to retaining the property, and at the same time gratified his own feelings by marrying the pretty Marie Vander Heyden,—and how he and Heer Antony had many a merry and roving expedition together.

I must not omit to say, however, that Dolph took his mother home to live with him, and cherished her in her old days. The good dame, too, had the satisfaction of no longer hearing her son made the theme of censure; on the contrary, he grew daily in public esteem; everybody spoke well of him and his wines; and the lordliest burgomaster was never known to decline his invitation to dinner. Dolph often related, at his own table, the wicked pranks which had once been the abhorrence of the town; but they were now considered excellent jokes, and the gravest dignitary was fain to hold his sides when listening to them. No one was more struck with Dolph's increasing merit than his old master the doctor; and so forgiving was Dolph, that he absolutely employed the doctor as his family physician, only taking care that his prescriptions should be always thrown out of the window. His mother had often her junto of old cronies to take a snug cup of tea with her in her comfortable little parlor; and Peter de Groodt, as he sat by the fireside, with one of her grandchildren on his knee, would many a time congratulate her upon her son turning out so great a man; upon which the good old soul would wag her head with exultation, and exclaim: "Ah, neigh-

bor, neighbor! did I not say that Dolph would one day or other hold up his head with the best of them?"

Thus did Dolph Heyliger go on, cheerily and prosperously, growing merrier as he grew older and wiser, and completely falsifying the old proverb about money got over the devil's back; for he made good use of his wealth, and became a distinguished citizen, and a valuable member of the community. He was a great promoter of public institutions, such as beefsteak societies and catch-clubs. He presided at all public dinners, and was the first that introduced turtle from the West Indies. He improved the breed of race-horses and game cocks, and was so great a patron of modest merit, that any one who could sing a good song, or tell a good story, was sure to find a place at his table.

He was a member, too, of the corporation, made several laws for the protection of game and oysters, and bequeathed to the board a large silver punch-bowl, made out of the identical porringer before mentioned, and which is in the possession of the corporation to this very day.

Finally, he died, in a florid old age, of an apoplexy at a corporation feast, and was buried with great honors in the yard of the little Dutch church in Garden Street, where his tombstone may still be seen with a modest epitaph in Dutch, by his friend Mynheer Justus Benson, an ancient and excellent poet of the province.

The foregoing tale rests on better authority than most tales of the kind, as I have it at second-hand from the lips of Dolph Heyliger himself. He never related it till towards the latter part of his life, and then in great confidence (for he was very discreet), to a few of his particular cronies at his own table, over a supernumerary bowl of punch; and, strange as the hobgoblin parts of the story may seem, there never was a single doubt expressed on the subject by any of his guests. It may not be amiss, before concluding, to observe that, in addition to his other accomplishments, Dolph Heyliger was noted for being the ablest drawer of the long-bow in the whole province.

From *Bracebridge Hall*

Strange Stories by a
Nervous Gentleman

I'll tell you more, there was a fish taken,
A monstrous fish, with a sword by 's side, a long sword,
A pike in 's neck, and a gun in 's nose, a huge gun,
And letters of mart in 's mouth from the Duke of
    Florence.
    Cleanthes.—This is a monstrous lie.
    Tony.—   I do confess it.
Do you think I'd tell you truths?
                FLETCHER's *Wife for a month*

The following prefatory chapter and eight tales, which form a single narrative,
are taken in a body from *Tales of a Traveller.*—C.N.

THE GREAT UNKNOWN [*a preface*]

THE following adventures were related to me by the same nervous gentleman who told me the romantic tale of the Stout Gentleman, published in *Bracebridge Hall*. It is very singular, that, although I expressly stated that story to have been told to me, and described the very person who told it, still it has been received as an adventure that happened to myself. Now I protest I never met with any adventure of the kind. I should not have grieved at this, had it not been intimated by the author of *Waverley* in an introduction to his novel of *Peveril of the Peak*, that he was himself the stout gentleman alluded to. I have ever since been importuned by questions and letters from gentlemen, and particularly from ladies without number, touching what I had seen of the Great Unknown.

Now all this is extremely tantalizing. It is like being congratulated on the high prize when one has drawn a blank; for I have just as great a desire as any one of the public to penetrate the mystery of that very singular personage, whose voice fills every corner of the world, without any one being able to tell whence it comes.

My friend, the nervous gentleman, also, who is a man of very shy, retired habits, complains that he has been excessively annoyed in consequence of its getting about in his neighborhood that he is the fortunate personage. Insomuch, that he has become a character of considerable notoriety in two or three country-towns, and has been repeatedly teased to exhibit himself at blue-stocking parties, for no other reason than that of being "the gentleman who has had a glimpse of the author of *Waverley*."

Indeed the poor man has grown ten times as nervous as ever since he has discovered, on such good authority, who the stout gentleman was; and will never forgive himself for not having made a more resolute effort to get a full sight of him. He has anxiously endeavored to call up a recollection of what he saw of that portly personage; and has ever since kept a curious eye on all gentlemen of more than ordinary dimensions, whom he has seen getting into stage-coaches. All in vain! The features he had caught a glimpse of seem common to the whole race of stout

gentlemen, and the Great Unknown remains as great an unknown as ever.

Having premised these circumstances, I will now let the nervous gentleman proceed with his stories.

THE HUNTING-DINNER

I WAS once at a hunting-dinner, given by a worthy fox-hunting old Baronet, who kept bachelor's hall in jovial style in an ancient rook-haunted family-mansion, in one of the middle counties. He had been a devoted admirer of the fair sex in his younger days; but, having travelled much, studied the sex in various countries with distinguished success, and returned home profoundly instructed, as he supposed, in the ways of woman, and a perfect master of the art of pleasing, had the mortification of being jilted by a little boarding-school girl, who was scarcely versed in the accidence of love.

The Baronet was completely overcome by such an incredible defeat; retired from the world in disgust; put himself under the government of his housekeeper; and took to fox-hunting like a perfect Nimrod. Whatever poets may say to the contrary, a man will grow out of love as he grows old; and a pack of fox-hounds may chase out of his heart even the memory of a boarding-school goddess. The Baronet was, when I saw him, as merry and mellow an old bachelor as ever followed a hound; and the love he had once felt for one woman had spread itself over the whole sex, so that there was not a pretty face in the whole country round but came in for a share.

The dinner was prolonged till a late hour; for our host having no ladies in his household to summon us to the drawing-room, the bottle maintained its true bachelor sway, unrivalled by its potent enemy, the tea-kettle. The old hall in which we dined echoed to bursts of robustious fox-hunting merriment, that made the ancient antlers shake on the walls. By degrees, however, the wine and the wassail of mine host began to operate upon bodies already a little jaded by the chase. The choice spirits which flashed up at the beginning of the dinner, sparkled for a time, then gradually went out one after another, or only emitted now and then a faint gleam from the socket. Some of the briskest talkers, who had given tongue so bravely at the first burst, fell fast asleep; and none kept on their way but certain of those long-winded prosers, who, like short-legged hounds, worry on unnoticed at the bottom of conversation, but are sure to be in at the death. Even these at length subsided into silence; and scarcely anything was heard but the nasal

communications of two or three veteran masticators, who having been silent while awake, were indemnifying the company in their sleep.

At length the announcement of tea and coffee in the cedar-parlor roused all hands from this temporary torpor. Every one awoke marvellously renovated, and while sipping the refreshing beverage out of the Baronet's old-fashioned hereditary china, began to think of departing for their several homes. But here a sudden difficulty arose. While we had been prolonging our repast, a heavy winter storm had set in, with snow, rain, and sleet, driven by such bitter blasts of wind, that they threatened to penetrate to the very bone.

"It's all in vain," said our hospitable host, "to think of putting one's head out of doors in such weather. So, gentlemen, I hold you my guests for this night at least, and will have your quarters prepared accordingly."

The unruly weather, which became more and more tempestuous, rendered the hospitable suggestion unanswerable. The only question was, whether such an unexpected accession of company to an already crowded house would not put the housekeeper to her trumps to accommodate them.

"Pshaw," cried mine host; "did you ever know a bachelor's hall that was not elastic, and able to accommodate twice as many as it could hold?" So, out of a good-humored pique, the housekeeper was summoned to a consultation before us all. The old lady appeared in her gala suit of faded brocade, which rustled with flurry and agitation; for, in spite of our host's bravado, she was a little perplexed. But in a bachelor's house, and with bachelor guests, these matters are readily managed. There is no lady of the house to stand upon squeamish points about lodging gentlemen in odd holes and corners, and exposing the shabby parts of the establishment. A bachelor's housekeeper is used to shifts and emergencies; so, after much worrying to and fro, and divers consultations about the red-room, and the blue-room, and the chintz-room, and the damask-room, and the little room with the bow-window, the matter was finally arranged.

When all this was done, we were once more summoned to the standing rural amusement of eating. The time that had been consumed in dozing after dinner, and in the refreshment and consultation of the cedar-parlor, was sufficient, in the opinion of the rosy-faced butler, to engender a reasonable appetite for supper. A slight repast had, therefore, been tricked up from the residue of dinner, consisting of a cold sirloin of beef, hashed venison, a devilled leg of a turkey or so, and a few other of those light articles taken by country gentlemen to ensure sound sleep and heavy snoring.

The nap after dinner had brightened up every one's wit; and a great

deal of excellent humor was expended upon the perplexities of mine host and his housekeeper, by certain married gentlemen of the company, who considered themselves privileged in joking with a bachelor's establishment. From this the banter turned as to what quarters each would find, on being thus suddenly billeted in so antiquated a mansion.

"By my soul," said an Irish captain of dragoons, one of the most merry and boisterous of the party, "by my soul, but I should not be surprised if some of those good-looking gentlefolks that hang along the walls should walk about the rooms of this stormy night; or if I should find the ghosts of one of those longwaisted ladies turning into my bed in mistake for her grave in the churchyard."

"Do you believe in ghosts, then?" said a thin, hatchet-faced gentleman, with projecting eyes like a lobster.

I had remarked this last personage during dinner-time for one of those incessant questioners, who have a craving, unhealthy appetite in conversation. He never seemed satisfied with the whole of a story; never laughed when others laughed; but always put the joke to the question. He never could enjoy the kernel of the nut, but pestered himself to get more out of the shell. "Do you believe in ghosts, then?" said the inquisitive gentleman.

"Faith, but I do," replied the jovial Irishman. "I was brought up in the fear and belief of them. We had a Benshee in our own family, honey."

"A Benshee, and what's that?" cried the questioner.

"Why, an old lady ghost that tends upon your real Milesian families, and waits at their window to let them know when some of them are to die."

"A mighty pleasant piece of information!" cried an elderly gentleman with a knowing look, and with a flexible nose, to which he could give a whimsical twist when he wished to be waggish.

"By my soul, but I'd have you to know it's a piece of distinction to be waited on by a Benshee. It's a proof that one has pure blood in one's veins. But i' faith, now we are talking of ghosts, there never was a house or a night better fitted than the present for a ghost adventure. Pray, Sir John, haven't you such a thing as a haunted chamber to put a guest in?"

"Perhaps," said the Baronet, smiling, "I might accommodate you even on that point."

"Oh, I should like it of all things, my jewel. Some dark oaken room, with ugly woe-begone portraits, that stare dismally at one; and about which the housekeeper has a power of delightful stories of love and murder. And then a dim lamp, a table with a rusty sword across it, and a spectre all in white, to draw aside one's curtains at midnight——"

"In truth," said an old gentleman at one end of the table, "you put me in mind of an anecdote——"

"Oh, a ghost-story! a ghost-story!" was vociferated round the board, every one edging his chair a little nearer.

The attention of the whole company was now turned upon the speaker. He was an old gentleman, one side of whose face was no match for the other. The eyelid drooped and hung down like an unhinged window-shutter. Indeed, the whole side of his head was dilapidated, and seemed like the wing of a house shut up and haunted. I'll warrant that side was well stuffed with ghost-stories.

There was a universal demand for the tale.

"Nay," said the old gentleman, "it's a mere anecdote, and a very commonplace one; but such as it is you shall have it. It is a story that I once heard my uncle tell as having happened to himself. He was a man very apt to meet with strange adventures. I have heard him tell of others much more singular."

"What kind of a man was your uncle?" said the questioning gentleman.

"Why, he was rather a dry, shrewd kind of body; a great traveller, and fond of telling his adventures."

"Pray, how old might he have been when that happened?"

"When what happened?" cried the gentleman with the flexible nose, impatiently. "Egad, you have not given anything a chance to happen. Come, never mind our uncle's age; let us have his adventures."

The inquisitive gentleman being for the moment silenced, the old gentleman with the haunted head proceeded.

THE ADVENTURE OF MY UNCLE

MANY years since, some time before the French Revolution, my uncle passed several months at Paris. The English and French were on better terms in those days than at present, and mingled cordially in society. The English went abroad to spend money then, and the French were always ready to help them: they go abroad to save money at present, and that they can do without French assistance. Perhaps the travelling English were fewer and choicer than at present, when the whole nation has broke loose and inundated the continent. At any rate, they circulated more readily and currently in foreign society, and my uncle, during his residence in Paris, made many very intimate acquaintances among the French noblesse.

· Some time afterwards, he was making a journey in the winter-time in that part of Normandy called the Pays de Caux, when, as evening was closing in, he perceived the turrets of an ancient chateau rising out of the trees of its walled park; each turret with its high conical roof of gray slate, like a candle with an extinguisher on it.

"To whom does the chateau belong, friend?" cried my uncle to a meagre but fiery postilion, who, with tremendous jack-boots and cocked hat, was floundering on before him.

"To Monseigneur the Marquis de ——," said the postilion, touching his hat, partly out of respect to my uncle, and partly out of reverence to the noble name pronounced.

My uncle recollected the Marquis for a particular friend in Paris, who had often expressed a wish to see him at his paternal chateau. My uncle was an old traveller, one who knew well how to turn things to account. He revolved for a few moments in his mind, how agreeable it would be to his friend the Marquis to be surprised in this sociable way by a pop visit; and how much more agreeable to himself to get into snug quarters in a chateau, and have a relish of the Marquis's well-known kitchen, and a smack of his superior Champagne and Burgundy, rather than put up with the miserable lodgment and miserable fare of a provincial inn. In a few minutes, therefore, the meagre postilion was cracking his whip like a very devil, or like a true Frenchman, up the long, straight avenue that led to the chateau.

You have no doubt all seen French chateaus, as everybody travels in

France nowadays. This was one of the oldest; standing naked and alone in the midst of a desert of gravel walks and cold stone terraces; with a cold-looking, formal garden, cut into angles and rhomboids; and a cold, leafless park, divided geometrically by straight alleys; and two or three cold-looking noseless statues; and fountains spouting cold water enough to make one's teeth chatter. At least such was the feeling they imparted on the wintry day of my uncle's visit; though, in hot summer weather, I'll warrant there was glare enough to scorch one's eyes out.

The smacking of the postilion's whip, which grew more and more intense the nearer they approached, frightened a flight of pigeons out of a dove-cot, and rooks out of the roofs, and finally a crew of servants out of the chateau, with the Marquis at their head. He was enchanted to see my uncle, for his chateau, like the house of our worthy host, had not many more guests at the time than it could accommodate. So he kissed my uncle on each cheek, after the French fashion, and ushered him into the castle.

The Marquis did the honors of the house with the urbanity of his country. In fact, he was proud of his old family chateau, for part of it was extremely old. There was a tower and chapel which had been built almost before the memory of man; but the rest was more modern, the castle having been nearly demolished during the wars of the league. The Marquis dwelt upon this event with great satisfaction, and seemed really to entertain a grateful feeling towards Henry the Fourth, for having thought his paternal mansion worth battering down. He had many stories to tell of the prowess of his ancestors; and several skull-caps, helmets, and cross-bows, and divers huge boots and buff jerkins, to show, which had been worn by the leaguers. Above all, there was a two-handed sword, which he could hardly wield, but which he displayed, as a proof that there had been giants in his family.

In truth, he was but a small descendant from such great warriors. When you looked at their bluff visages and brawny limbs, as depicted in their portraits, and then at the little Marquis, with his spindle shanks, and his sallow lantern visage, flanked with a pair of powdered earlocks, or *aîles de pigeon*, that seemed ready to fly away with it, you could hardly believe him to be of the same race. But when you looked at the eyes that sparkled out like a beetle's from each side of his hooked nose, you saw at once that he inherited all the fiery spirit of his forefathers. In fact, a Frenchman's spirit never exhales, however his body may dwindle. It rather rarefies, and grows more inflammable, as the earthly particles diminish; and I have seen valor enough in a little fiery-hearted French dwarf to have furnished out a tolerable giant.

When once the Marquis, as was his wont, put on one of the old helmets stuck up in his hall, though his head no more filled it than a dry pea its peascod, yet his eyes flashed from the bottom of the iron cavern with the brilliancy of carbuncles; and when he poised the ponderous two-handed sword of his ancestors, you would have thought you saw the doughty little David wielding the sword of Goliath, which was unto him like a weaver's beam.

However, gentlemen, I am dwelling too long on this description of the Marquis and his chateau, but you must excuse me; he was an old friend of my uncle; and whenever my uncle told the story, he was always fond of talking a great deal about his host.—Poor little Marquis! He was one of that handful of gallant courtiers who made such a devoted but hopeless stand in the cause of their sovereign, in the chateau of the Tuileries, against the irruption of the mob on the sad tenth of August. He displayed the valor of a *preux* French chevalier to the last; flourishing feebly his little court-sword with a *ça-ça!* in face of a whole legion of *sans-culottes;* but was pinned to the wall like a butterfly, by the pike of a *poissarde,* and his heroic soul was borne up to heaven on his *aîles de pigeon.*

But all this has nothing to do with my story. To the point, then. When the hour arrived for retiring for the night, my uncle was shown to his room in a venerable old tower. It was the oldest part of the chateau, and had in ancient times been the donjon or stronghold; of course the chamber was none of the best. The Marquis had put him there, however, because he knew him to be a traveller of taste, and fond of antiquities; and also because the better apartments were already occupied. Indeed, he perfectly reconciled my uncle to his quarters by mentioning the great personages who had once inhabited them, all of whom were, in some way or other, connected with the family. If you would take his word for it, John Baliol, or as he called him, Jean de Bailleul, had died of chagrin in this very chamber, on hearing of the success of his rival, Robert de Bruce, at the battle of Bannockburn. And when he added that the Duke de Guise had slept in it, my uncle was fain to felicitate himself on being honored with such distinguished quarters.

The night was shrewd and windy, and the chamber none of the warmest. An old long-faced, long-bodied servant, in quaint livery, who attended upon my uncle, threw down an armful of wood beside the fireplace, gave a queer look about the room, and then wished him *bon repos* with a grimace and a shrug that would have been suspicious from any other than an old French servant.

The chamber had indeed a wild, crazy look, enough to strike any one who had read romances with apprehension and foreboding. The windows were high and narrow, and had once been loop-holes, but had been rudely enlarged, as well as the extreme thickness of the walls would permit; and the ill-fitted casements rattled to every breeze. You would have thought, on a windy night, some of the old leaguers were tramping and clanking about the apartment in their huge boots and rattling spurs. A door which stood ajar, and, like a true French door, would stand ajar in spite of every reason and effort to the contrary, opened upon a long dark corridor, that led the Lord knows whither, and seemed just made for ghosts to air themselves in, when they turned out of their graves at midnight. The wind would spring up into a hoarse murmur through this passage, and creak the door to and fro, as if some dubious ghost were balancing in its mind whether to come in or not. In a word, it was precisely the kind of comfortless apartment that a ghost, if ghost there were in the chateau, would single out for its favorite lounge.

My uncle, however, though a man accustomed to meet with strange adventures, apprehended none at the time. He made several attempts to shut the door, but in vain. Not that he apprehended anything, for he was too old a traveller to be daunted by a wild-looking apartment; but the night, as I have said, was cold and gusty, and the wind howled about the old turret pretty much as it does round this old mansion at this moment, and the breeze from the long dark corridor came in as damp and as chilly as if from a dungeon. My uncle, therefore, since he could not close the door, threw a quantity of wood on the fire, which soon sent up a flame in the great wide-mouthed chimney that illumined the whole chamber; and made the shadow of the tongs on the opposite wall look like a long-legged giant. My uncle now clambered on the top of the half-score of mattresses which form a French bed, and which stood in a deep recess; then tucking himself snugly in, and burying himself up to the chin in the bedclothes, he lay looking at the fire, and listening to the wind, and thinking how knowingly he had come over his friend the Marquis for a night's lodging—and so he fell asleep.

He had not taken above half of his first nap when he was awakened by the clock of the chateau, in the turret over his chamber, which struck midnight. It was just such an old clock as ghosts are fond of. It had a deep, dismal tone, and struck so slowly and tediously that my uncle thought it would never have done. He counted and counted till he was confident he counted thirteen, and then it stopped.

The fire had burnt low, and the blaze of the last fagot was almost

expiring, burning in small blue flames, which now and then lengthened up into little white gleams. My uncle lay with his eyes half closed, and his nightcap drawn almost down to his nose. His fancy was already wandering, and began to mingle up the present scene with the crater of Vesuvius, the French Opera, the Coliseum at Rome, Dolly's chop-house in London, and all the farrago of noted places with which the brain of a traveller is crammed,—in a word, he was just falling asleep.

Suddenly he was roused by the sound of footsteps, slowly pacing along the corridor. My uncle, as I have often heard him say himself, was a man not easily frightened. So he lay quiet, supposing this some other guest, or some servant on his way to bed. The footsteps, however, approached the door; the door gently opened; whether of its own accord, or whether pushed open, my uncle could not distinguish: a figure all in white glided in. It was a female, tall and stately, and of a commanding air. Her dress was of an ancient fashion, ample in volume, and sweeping the floor. She walked up to the fireplace, without regarding my uncle, who raised his nightcap with one hand, and stared earnestly at her. She remained for some time standing by the fire, which, flashing up at intervals, cast blue and white gleams of light, that enabled my uncle to remark her appearance minutely.

Her face was ghastly pale, and perhaps rendered still more so by the bluish light of the fire. It possessed beauty, but its beauty was saddened by care and anxiety. There was the look of one accustomed to trouble, but of one whom trouble could not cast down nor subdue; for there was still the predominating air of proud, unconquerable resolution. Such at least was the opinion formed by my uncle, and he considered himself a great physiognomist.

The figure remained, as I said, for some time by the fire, putting out first one hand, then the other; then each foot alternately, as if warming itself; for your ghosts, if ghost it really was, are apt to be cold. My uncle, furthermore, remarked that it wore high-heeled shoes, after an ancient fashion, with paste or diamond buckles, that sparkled as though they were alive. At length the figure turned gently round, casting a glassy look about the apartment, which, as it passed over my uncle, made his blood run cold, and chilled the very marrow in his bones. It then stretched its arms towards heaven, clasped its hands, and wringing them in a supplicating manner, glided slowly out of the room.

My uncle lay for some time meditating on this visitation, for (as he remarked when he told me the story) though a man of firmness, he was also a man of reflection, and did not reject a thing because it was out of the regular course of events. However, being, as I have before

said, a great traveller, and accustomed to strange adventures, he drew his nightcap resolutely over his eyes, turned his back to the door, hoisted the bedclothes high over his shoulders, and gradually fell asleep.

How long he slept he could not say, when he was awakened by the voice of some one at his bedside. He turned round, and beheld the old French servant, with his ear-locks in tight buckles on each side of a long lantern face, on which habit had deeply wrinkled an everlasting smile. He made a thousand grimaces, and asked a thousand pardons for disturbing Monsieur, but the morning was considerably advanced. While my uncle was dressing, he called vaguely to mind the visitor of the preceding night. He asked the ancient domestic what lady was in the habit of rambling about this part of the chateau at night. The old valet shrugged his shoulders as high as his head, laid one hand on his bosom, threw open the other with every finger extended, made a most whimsical grimace which he meant to be complimentary, and replied, that it was not for him to know anything of *les bonnes fortunes* of Monsieur.

My uncle saw there was nothing satisfactory to be learned in this quarter. After breakfast, he was walking with the Marquis through the modern apartments of the chateau, sliding over the well-waxed floors of silken saloons, amidst furniture rich in gilding and brocade, until they came to a long picture-gallery, containing many portraits, some in oil and some in chalks.

Here was an ample field for the eloquence of his host, who had all the pride of a nobleman of the *ancien régime*. There was not a grand name in Normandy, and hardly one in France, which was not, in some way or other, connected with his house. My uncle stood listening with inward impatience, resting sometimes on one leg, sometimes on the other, as the little Marquis descanted, with his usual fire and vivacity, on the achievements of his ancestors, whose portraits hung along the wall; from the martial deeds of the stern warriors in steel, to the gallantries and intrigues of the blue-eyed gentlemen, with fair smiling faces, powdered ear-locks, laced ruffles, and pink and blue silk coats and breeches;—not forgetting the conquests of the lovely shepherdesses, with hooped petticoats, and waists no thicker than an hour-glass, who appeared ruling over their sheep and their swains, with dainty crooks decorated with fluttering ribbons.

In the midst of his friend's discourse, my uncle was startled on beholding a full-length portrait, the very counterpart of his visitor of the preceding night.

"Methinks," said he, pointing to it, "I have seen the original of this portrait."

"*Pardonnez moi*," replied the Marquis politely, "that can hardly be, as the lady has been dead more than a hundred years. That was the beautiful Duchess de Longueville, who figured during the minority of Louis the Fourteenth."

"And was there anything remarkable in her history?"

Never was question more unlucky. The little Marquis immediately threw himself into the attitude of a man about to tell a long story. In fact, my uncle had pulled upon himself the whole history of the civil war of the Fronde, in which the beautiful Duchess had played so distinguished a part. Turenne, Coligni, Mazarin, were called up from their graves to grace his narration; nor were the affairs of the Barricadoes, nor the chivalry of the Port Cochères forgotten. My uncle began to wish himself a thousand leagues off from the Marquis and his merciless memory, when suddenly the little man's recollections took a more interesting turn. He was relating the imprisonment of the Duke de Longueville with the Princes Condé and Conti in the chateau of Vincennes, and the ineffectual efforts of the Duchess to rouse the sturdy Normans to their rescue. He had come to that part where she was invested by the royal forces in the Castle of Dieppe.

"The spirit of the Duchess," proceeded the Marquis, "rose from her trials. It was astonishing to see so delicate and beautiful a being buffet so resolutely with hardships. She determined on a desperate means of escape. You may have seen the château in which she was mewed up, —an old ragged wart of an edifice, standing on the knuckle of a hill, just above the rusty little town of Dieppe. One dark unruly night she issued secretly out of a small postern gate of the castle, which the enemy had neglected to guard. The postern gate is there to this very day; opening upon a narrow bridge over a deep fosse between the castle and the brow of the hill. She was followed by her female attendants, a few domestics, and some gallant cavaliers, who still remained faithful to her fortunes. Her object was to gain a small port about two leagues distant, where she had privately provided a vessel for her escape in case of emergency.

"The little band of fugitives were obliged to perform the distance on foot. When they arrived at the port the wind was high and stormy, the tide contrary, the vessel anchored far off in the road, and no means of getting on board but by a fishing-shallop which lay tossing like a cockle-shell on the edge of the surf. The Duchess determined to risk the attempt. The seamen endeavored to dissuade her, but the imminence of her danger on shore, and the magnanimity of her spirit, urged her on. She had to be borne to the shallop in the arms of a mariner.

Such was the violence of the wind and waves that he faltered, lost his foothold, and let his precious burden fall into the sea.

"The Duchess was nearly drowned, but partly through her own struggles, partly by the exertions of the seamen, she got to land. As soon as she had a little recovered strength, she insisted on renewing the attempt. The storm, however, had by this time become so violent as to set all efforts at defiance. To delay, was to be discovered and taken prisoner. As the only resource left, she procured horses, mounted with her female attendants, *en croupe*, behind the gallant gentlemen who accompanied her, and scoured the country to seek some temporary asylum.

"While the Duchess," continued the Marquis, laying his forefinger on my uncle's breast to arouse his flagging attention,—"while the Duchess, poor lady, was wandering amid the tempest in this disconsolate manner, she arrived at this chateau. Her approach caused some uneasiness; for the clattering of a troop of horse at dead of night up the avenue of a lonely chateau, in those unsettled times, and in a troubled part of the country, was enough to occasion alarm.

"A tall, broad-shouldered chasseur, armed to the teeth, galloped ahead, and announced the name of the visitor. All uneasiness was dispelled. The household turned out with flambeaux to receive her, and never did torches gleam on a more weather-beaten, travel-stained band than came tramping into the court. Such pale, careworn faces, such bedraggled dresses, as the poor Duchess and her females presented, each seated behind her cavalier: while the half-drenched, half-drowsy pages and attendants seemed ready to fall from their horses with sleep and fatigue.

"The Duchess was received with a hearty welcome by my ancestor. She was ushered into the hall of the chateau, and the fires soon crackled and blazed, to cheer herself and her train; and every spit and stew-pan was put in requisition to prepare ample refreshment for the wayfarers.

"She had a right to our hospitalities," continued the Marquis, drawing himself up with a slight degree of stateliness, "for she was related to our family. I'll tell you how it was. Her father, Henry de Bourbon, Prince of Condé——"

"But did the Duchess pass the night in the chateau?" said my uncle rather abruptly, terrified at the idea of getting involved in one of the Marquis's genealogical discussions.

"Oh, as to the Duchess, she was put into the very apartment you occupied last night, which at that time was a kind of state-apartment. Her followers were quartered in the chambers opening upon the neighboring corridor, and her favorite page slept in an adjoining closet. Up

and down the corridor walked the great chasseur who had announced
her arrival, and who acted as a kind of sentinel or guard. He was a
dark, stern, powerful-looking fellow; and as the light of a lamp in the
corridor fell upon his deeply marked face and sinewy form, he seemed
capable of defending the castle with his single arm.

"It was a rough, rude night; about this time of the year—apropos!—
now I think of it, last night was the anniversary of her visit. I may well
remember the precise date, for it was a night not to be forgotten by our
house. There is a singular tradition concerning it in our family." Here
the Marquis hesitated, and a cloud seemed to gather about his bushy
eyebrows. "There is a tradition—that a strange occurrence took place
that night.—A strange, mysterious, inexplicable occurrence——" Here he
checked himself, and paused.

"Did it relate to that lady?" inquired my uncle, eagerly.

"It was past the hour of midnight," resumed the Marquis,—"when
the whole chateau——" Here he paused again. My uncle made a movement of anxious curiosity.

"Excuse me," said the Marquis, a slight blush streaking his sallow
visage. "There are some circumstances connected with our family history which I do not like to relate. That was a rude period. A time of
great crimes among great men: for you know high blood, when it runs
wrong, will not run tamely, like blood of the canaille—poor lady!—But
I have a little family pride, that—excuse me—we will change the subject, if you please——"

My uncle's curiosity was piqued. The pompous and magnificent
introduction had led him to expect something wonderful in the story
to which it served as a kind of avenue. He had no idea of being cheated
out of it by a sudden fit of unreasonable squeamishness. Besides, being
a traveller in quest of information, he considered it his duty to inquire
into everything.

The Marquis, however, evaded every question.

"Well," said my uncle, a little petulantly, "whatever you may think
of it, I saw that lady last night."

The Marquis stepped back and gazed at him with surprise.

"She paid me a visit in my bedchamber."

The Marquis pulled out his snuff-box with a shrug and a smile;
taking this no doubt for an awkward piece of English pleasantry, which
politeness required him to be charmed with.

My uncle went on gravely, however, and related the whole circumstance. The Marquis heard him through with profound attention, holding his snuff-box unopened in his hand. When the story was finished,

he tapped on the lid of his box deliberately, took a long, sonorous pinch of snuff——

"Bah!" said the Marquis, and walked towards the other end of the gallery.——

Here the narrator paused. The company waited for some time for him to resume his narration; but he continued silent.

"Well," said the inquisitive gentleman,—"and what did your uncle say then?"

"Nothing," replied the other.

"And what did the Marquis say farther?"

"Nothing."

"And is that all?"

"That is all," said the narrator, filling a glass of wine.

"I surmise," said the shrewd old gentleman with the waggish nose,—"I surmise the ghost must have been the old housekeeper, walking her rounds to see that all was right."

"Bah!" said the narrator. "My uncle was too much accustomed to strange sights not to know a ghost from a housekeeper."

There was a murmur round the table, half of merriment, half of disappointment. I was inclined to think the old gentleman had really an after-part of his story in reserve; but he sipped his wine and said nothing more; and there was an odd expression about his dilapidated countenance which left me in doubt whether he were in drollery or earnest.

"Egad," said the knowing gentleman, with the flexible nose, "this story of your uncle puts me in mind of one that used to be told of an aunt of mine, by the mother's side; though I don't know that it will bear a comparison, as the good lady was not so prone to meet with strange adventures. But any rate you shall have it."

THE ADVENTURE OF MY AUNT

MY aunt was a lady of large frame, strong mind, and great resolution: she was what might be termed a very manly woman. My uncle was a thin, puny little man, very meek and acquiescent, and no match for my aunt. It was observed that he dwindled and dwindled gradually away, from the day of his marriage. His wife's powerful mind was too much for him; it wore him out. My aunt, however, took all possible care of him: had half the doctors in town to prescribe for him; made him take all their prescriptions, and dosed him with physic enough to cure a whole hospital. All was in vain. My uncle grew worse and worse the more dosing and nursing he underwent, until in the end he added another to the long list of matrimonial victims who have been killed with kindness.

"And was it his ghost that appeared to her?" asked the inquisitive gentleman, who had questioned the former story-teller.

"You shall hear," replied the narrator.—My aunt took on mightily for the death of her poor dear husband. Perhaps she felt some compunction at having given him so much physic, and nursed him into the grave. At any rate, she did all that a widow could do to honor his memory. She spared no expense in either the quantity or quality of her mourning weeds; wore a miniature of him about her neck as large as a little sun-dial, and had a full-length portrait of him always hanging in her bed-chamber. All the world extolled her conduct to the skies; and it was determined that a woman who behaved so well to the memory of one husband deserved soon to get another.

It was not long after this that she went to take up her residence in an old country-seat in Derbyshire, which had long been in the care of merely a steward and housekeeper. She took most of her servants with her, intending to make it her principal abode. The house stood in a lonely wild part of the country, among the gray Derbyshire hills, with a murderer hanging in chains on a bleak height in full view.

The servants from town were half frightened out of their wits at the idea of living in such a dismal, pagan-looking place; especially when they got together in the servants' hall in the evening, and compared notes on all the hobgoblin stories picked up in the course of the day. They were afraid to venture alone about the gloomy, black-looking

chambers. My lady's maid, who was troubled with nerves, declared she could never sleep alone in such a "gashly rummaging old building"; and the footman, who was a kind-hearted young fellow, did all in his power to cheer her up.

My aunt was struck with the lonely appearance of the house. Before going to bed, therefore, she examined well the fastnesses of the doors and windows; locked up the plate with her own hands, and carried the keys, together with a little box of money and jewels, to her own room; for she was a notable woman, and always saw to all things herself. Having put the keys under her pillow, and dismissed her maid, she sat by her toilet arranging her hair; for being, in spite of her grief for my uncle, rather a buxom widow, she was somewhat particular about her person. She sat for a little while looking at her face in the glass, first on one side, then on the other, as ladies are apt to do when they would ascertain whether they have been in good looks; for a roistering country squire of the neighborhood, with whom she had flirted when a girl, had called that day to welcome her to the country.

All of a sudden she thought she heard something move behind her. She looked hastily round, but there was nothing to be seen. Nothing but the grimly painted portrait of her poor dear man, hanging against the wall.

She gave a heavy sigh to his memory, as she was accustomed to do whenever she spoke of him in company, and then went on adjusting her night-dress, and thinking of the squire. Her sigh was re-echoed, or answered by a long-drawn breath. She looked round again, but no one was to be seen. She ascribed these sounds to the wind oozing through the ratholes of the old mansion, and proceeded leisurely to put her hair in papers, when, all at once, she thought she perceived one of the eyes of the portrait move.

"The back of her head being towards it!" said the story-teller with the ruined head,—"good!"

"Yes, sir!" replied dryly the narrator, "her back being towards the portrait, but her eyes fixed on its reflection in the glass."—Well, as I was saying, she perceived one of the eyes of the portrait move. So strange a circumstance, as you may well suppose, gave her a sudden shock. To assure herself of the fact, she put one hand to her forehead as if rubbing it; peeped through her fingers, and moved the candle with the other hand. The light of the taper gleamed on the eye, and was reflected from it. She was sure it moved. Nay, more, it seemed to give her a wink, as she had sometimes known her husband to do when living! It struck

a momentary chill to her heart; for she was a lone woman, and felt herself fearfully situated.

The chill was but transient. My aunt, who was almost as resolute a personage as your uncle, sir, (turning to the old story-teller,) became instantly calm and collected. She went on adjusting her dress. She even hummed an air, and did not make even a single false note. She casually overturned a dressing-box; took a candle and picked up the articles one by one from the floor; pursued a rolling pin-cushion that was making the best of its way under the bed; then opened the door; looked for an instant into the corridor, as if in doubt whether to go; and then walked quietly out.

She hastened down-stairs, ordered the servants to arm themselves with the weapons first at hand, placed herself at their head, and returned almost immediately.

Her hastily levied army presented a formidable force. The steward had a rusty blunder-buss, the coachman a loaded whip, the footman a pair of horse-pistols, the cook a huge chopping-knife, and the butler a bottle in each hand. My aunt led the van with a red-hot poker, and in my opinion she was the most formidable of the party. The waiting-maid, who dreaded to stay alone in the servants' hall, brought up the rear, smelling to a broken bottle of volatile salts, and expressing her terror of the ghostesses. "Ghosts!" said my aunt, resolutely. "I'll singe their whiskers for them!"

They entered the chamber. All was still and undisturbed as when she had left it. They approached the portrait of my uncle.

"Pull down that picture!" cried my aunt. A heavy groan, and a sound like the chattering of teeth, issued from the portrait. The servants shrunk back; the maid uttered a faint shriek, and clung to the footman for support.

"Instantly!" added my aunt, with a stamp of the foot.

The picture was pulled down, and from a recess behind it, in which had formerly stood a clock, they hauled forth a round-shouldered, black-bearded varlet, with a knife as long as my arm, but trembling all over like an aspen-leaf.

"Well, and who was he? No ghost, I suppose," said the inquisitive gentleman.

"A Knight of the Post," replied the narrator, "who had been smitten with the worth of the wealthy widow; or rather a marauding Tarquin, who had stolen into her chamber to violate her purse, and rifle her strong box, when all the house should be asleep. In plain terms," continued he, "the vagabond was a loose idle fellow of the neighborhood, who had once been a servant in the house, and had been employed to

assist in arranging it for the reception of its mistress. He confessed that he had contrived this hiding-place for his nefarious purpose, and had borrowed an eye from the portrait by way of a reconnoitring-hole."

"And what did they do with him?—did they hang him?" resumed the questioner.

"Hang him!—how could they?" exclaimed a beetle-browed barrister, with a hawk's nose. "The offence was not capital. No robbery, no assault had been committed. No forcible entry or breaking into the premises——"

"My aunt," said the narrator, "was a woman of spirit, and apt to take the law in her own hands. She had her own notions of cleanliness also. She ordered the fellow to be drawn through the horse-pond, to cleanse away all offences, and then to be well rubbed down with an oaken towel."

"And what became of him afterwards?" said the inquisitive gentleman."

"I do not exactly know. I believe he was sent on a voyage of improvement to Botany Bay."

"And your aunt," said the inquisitive gentleman; "I'll warrant she took care to make her maid sleep in the room with her after that."

"No, sir, she did better; she gave her hand shortly after to the roistering squire; for she used to observe, that it was a dismal thing for a woman to sleep alone in the country."

"She was right," observed the inquisitive gentleman, nodding sagaciously; "but I am sorry they did not hang that fellow."

It was agreed on all hands that the last narrator had brought his tale to the most satisfactory conclusion, though a country clergyman present regretted that the uncle and aunt, who figured in the different stories, had not been married together; they certainly would have been well matched.

"But I don't see, after all," said the inquisitive gentleman, "that there was any ghost in this last story."

"Oh! If it's ghosts you want, honey," cried the Irish Captain of Dragoons, "if it's ghosts you want, you shall have a whole regiment of them. And since these gentlemen have given the adventures of their uncles and aunts, faith, and I'll even give you a chapter out of my own family-history."

THE BOLD DRAGOON;

or The Adventure of My Grandfather

M Y grandfather was a bold dragoon, for it's a profession, d' ye see, that has run in the family. All my forefathers have been dragoons, and died on the field of honor, except myself, and I hope my posterity may be able to say the same; however, I don't mean to be vainglorious. Well, my grandfather, as I said, was a bold dragoon, and had served in the Low Countries. In fact, he was one of that very army, which according to my uncle Toby, swore so terribly in Flanders. He could swear a good stick himself; and moreover was the very man that introduced the doctrine Corporal Trim mentions of radical heat and radical moisture, or, in other words, the mode of keeping out the damps of ditchwater by burnt brandy. Be that as it may, it's nothing to the purport of my story. I only tell it to show you that my grandfather was a man not easily to be humbugged. He had seen service, or, according to his own phrase, he had seen the devil—and that's saying everything.

Well, gentlemen, my grandfather was on his way to England, for which he intended to embark from Ostend—bad luck to the place! for one where I was kept by storms and headwinds for three long days, and the devil of a jolly companion or pretty girl to comfort me. Well, as I was saying, my grandfather was on his way to England, or rather to Ostend—no matter which, it's all the same. So one evening, towards night fall, he rode jollily into Bruges.—Very like you all know Bruges, gentlemen; a queer old-fashioned Flemish town, once, they say, a great place for trade and money-making in old times, when the Mynheers were in their glory; but almost as large and as empty as an Irishman's pocket at the present day.—Well, gentlemen, it was at the time of the annual fair. All Bruges was crowded; and the canals swarmed with Dutch boats, and the streets swarmed with Dutch merchants; and there was hardly any getting along for goods, wares, and merchandises, and peasants in big breeches, and women in half a score of petticoats.

My grandfather rode jollily along, in his easy, slashing way, for he was a saucy, sun-shiny fellow—staring about him at the motley crowd, the old houses with gable ends to the street, and storks' nests in the chimneys; winking at the yafrows who showed their faces at the win-

dows and joking the women right and left in the street; all of whom laughed, and took it in amazing good part; for though he did not know a word of the language, yet he had always a knack of making himself understood among the women.

Well, gentlemen, it being the time of the annual fair, all the town was crowded, every inn and tavern full, and my grandfather applied in vain from one to the other for admittance. At length he rode up to an old rickety inn, that looked ready to fall to pieces, and which all the rats would have run away from, if they could have found room in any other house to put their heads. It was just such a queer building as you see in Dutch pictures, with a tall roof that reached up into the clouds, and as many garrets, one over the other, as the seven heavens of Mahomet. Nothing had saved it from tumbling down but a stork's nest on the chimney, which always brings good luck to a house in the Low Countries; and at the very time of my grandfather's arrival, there were two of these long-legged birds of grace standing like ghosts on the chimney-top. Faith, but they've kept the house on its legs to this very day, for you may see it any time you pass through Bruges, as it stands there yet, only it is turned into a brewery of strong Flemish beer,—at least it was so when I came that way after the battle of Waterloo.

My grandfather eyed the house curiously as he approached. It might not have altogether struck his fancy, had he not seen in large letters over the door,

HEER VERKOOPT MAN GOEDEN DRANK

My grandfather had learnt enough of the language to know that the sign promised good liquor. "This is the house for me," said he, stopping short before the door.

The sudden appearance of a dashing dragoon was an event in an old inn frequented only by the peaceful sons of traffic. A rich burgher of Antwerp, a stately ample man in a broad Flemish hat, and who was the great man and great patron of the establishment, sat smoking a clean long pipe on one side of the door; a fat little distiller of Geneva, from Schiedam, sat smoking on the other; and the bottle-nosed host stood in the door, and the comely hostess, in crimped cap, beside him; and the hostess's daughter, a plump Flanders lass, with long gold pendants in her ears, was at a side-window.

"Humph!" said the rich burgher of Antwerp, with a sulky glance at the stranger.

"De duyvel!" said the fat little distiller of Schiedam.

The landlord saw, with the quick glance of a publican, that the new

guest was not at all to the taste of the old ones; and, to tell the truth, he did not like my grandfather's saucy eye. He shook his head. "Not a garret in the house but was full."

"Not a garret!" echoed the landlady.

"Not a garret!" echoed the daughter.

The burgher of Antwerp, and the little distiller of Schiedam, continued to smoke their pipes sullenly, eying the enemy askance from under their broad hats, but said nothing.

My grandfather was not a man to be browbeaten. He threw the reins on his horse's neck, cocked his head on one side, stuck one arm akimbo, —"Faith and troth!" said he, "but I'll sleep in this house this very night." —As he said this he gave a slap on his thigh, by way of emphasis—the slap went to the landlady's heart.

He followed up the vow by jumping off his horse, and making his way past the staring Mynheers into the public room.—Maybe you've been in the bar-room of an old Flemish inn—faith, but a handsome chamber it was as you'd wish to see; with a brick floor, and a great fireplace, with the whole Bible history in glazed tiles; and then the mantelpiece, pitching itself head foremost out of the wall, with a whole regiment of cracked tea-pots and earthen jugs paraded on it; not to mention half a dozen great Delft platters, hung about the room by way of pictures; and the little bar in one corner, and the bouncing bar-maid inside of it, with a red calico cap, and yellow ear-drops.

My grandfather snapped his fingers over his head, as he cast an eye round the room,—"Faith, this is the very house I've been looking after," said he.

There was some further show of resistance on the part of the garrison; but my grandfather was an old soldier, and an Irishman to boot, and not easily repulsed, especially after he had got into the fortress. So he blarneyed the landlord, kissed the landlord's wife, tickled the landlord's daughter, chucked the bar-maid under the chin; and it was agreed on all hands that it would be a thousand pities, and a burning shame into the bargain, to turn such a bold dragoon into the streets. So they laid their heads together, that is to say, my grandfather and the landlady, and it was at length agreed to accommodate him with an old chamber that had been for some time shut up.

"Some say it's haunted," whispered the landlord's daughter; "but you are a bold dragoon, and I dare say don't fear ghosts."

"The devil a bit!" said my grandfather, pinching her plump cheek. "But if I should be troubled by ghosts, I've been to the Red Sea in my time, and have a pleasant way of laying them, my darling."

And then he whispered something to the girl which made her laugh,

and give him a good-humored box on the ear. In short, there was nobody knew better how to make his way among the petticoats than my
grandfather.

In a little while, as was his usual way, he took complete possession
of the house, swaggering all over it; into the stable to look after his
horse, into the kitchen to look after his supper. He had something to
say or do with every one; smoked with the Dutchmen, drank with the
Germans, slapped the landlord on the shoulder, romped with his daughter and the bar-maid;—never, since the days of Alley Croaker, had such
a rattling blade been seen. The landlord stared at him with astonishment; the landlord's daughter hung her head and giggled whenever
he came near; and as he swaggered along the corridor, with his sword
trailing by his side, the maids looked after him, and whispered to one
another, "What a proper man!"

At supper, my grandfather took command of the *table-d' hôte* as
though he had been at home; helped everybody, not forgetting himself; talked with every one, whether he understood their language or
not; and made his way into the intimacy of the rich burgher of Antwerp, who had never been known to be sociable with any one during
his life. In fact, he revolutionized the whole establishment, and gave it
such a rouse, that the very house reeled with it. He outsat every one at
table, excepting the little fat distiller of Schiedam, who sat soaking a
long time before he broke forth; but when he did, he was a very devil
incarnate. He took a violent affection for my grandfather; so they sat
drinking and smoking, and telling stories, and singing Dutch and Irish
songs, without understanding a word each other said, until the little
Hollander was fairly swamped with his own gin and water, and carried
off to bed, whooping and hickuping, and trolling the burden of a Low
Dutch love-song.

Well, gentlemen, my grandfather was shown to his quarters up a
large staircase, composed of loads of hewn timber; and through long
rigmarole passages, hung with blackened paintings of fish, and fruit,
and game, and country frolics, and huge kitchens, and portly burgo-
masters, such as you see about old-fashioned Flemish inns, till at length
he arrived at his room.

An old-times chamber it was, sure enough, and crowded with all
kinds of trumpery. It looked like an infirmary for decayed and superannuated furniture, where everything diseased or disabled was sent to
nurse or to be forgotten. Or rather it might be taken for a general congress of old legitimate movables, where every kind and country had a
representative. No two chairs were alike. Such high backs and low
backs, and leather bottoms, and worsted bottoms, and straw bottoms,

and no bottoms; and cracked marble tables with curiously carved legs, holding balls in their claws, as though they were going to play at nine-pins.

My grandfather made a bow to the motley assemblage as he entered, and, having undressed himself, placed his light in the fireplace, asking pardon of the tongs, which seemed to be making love to the shovel in the chimney-corner, and whispering soft nonsense in its ear.

The rest of the guests were by this time sound asleep, for your Myn-heers are huge sleepers. The housemaids, one by one, crept up yawn-ing to their attics; and not a female head in the inn was laid on a pil-low that night without dreaming of the bold dragoon.

My grandfather, for his part, got into bed, and drew over him one of those great bags of down, under which they smother a man in the Low Countries; and there he lay, melting between two feather beds, like an anchovy sandwich between two slices of toast and butter. He was a warm-complexioned man, and this smothering played the very deuce with him. So, sure enough, in a little time it seemed as if a legion of imps were twitching at him, and all the blood in his veins was in a fever-heat.

He lay still, however, until all the house was quiet excepting the snoring of the Mynheers from the different chambers; who answered one another in all kinds of tones and cadences, like so many bull-frogs in a swamp. The quieter the house became, the more unquiet became my grandfather. He waxed warmer and warmer, until at length the bed became too hot to hold him.

"Maybe the maid had warmed it too much?" said the curious gentle-man, inquiringly.

"I rather think the contrary," replied the Irishman. "But, be that as it may, it grew too hot for my grandfather."

"Faith, there's no standing this any longer," says he. So he jumped out of bed, and went strolling about the house.

"What for?" said the inquisitive gentleman.

"Why, to cool himself, to be sure—or perhaps to find a more com-fortable bed—or perhaps— But no matter what he went for—he never mentioned—and there's no use in taking up our time in conjecturing."

Well, my grandfather had been for some time absent from his room, and was returning, perfectly cool, when just as he reached the door, he heard a strange noise within. He paused and listened. It seemed as if some one were trying to hum a tune in defiance of the asthma. He recollected the report of the room being haunted; but he was no be-liever in ghosts, so he pushed the door gently open and peeped in.

Egad, gentlemen, there was a gambol carrying on within enough to

have astonished St. Anthony himself. By the light of the fire he saw a pale weazen-faced fellow, in a long flannel gown and a tall white night-cap with a tassel to it, who sat by the fire with a bellows under his arm by way of bagpipe, from which he forced the asthmatical music that had bothered my grandfather. As he played, too, he kept twitching about with a thousand queer contortions, nodding his head, and bobbing about his tasselled night-cap.

My grandfather thought this very odd and mighty presumptuous, and was about to demand what business he had to play his wind-instrument in another gentleman's quarters, when a new cause of as-tonishment met his eye. From the opposite side of the room a long-backed, bandy-legged chair, covered with leather, and studded all over in a coxcombical fashion with little brass nails, got suddenly into mo-tion, thrust out first a claw-foot, then a crooked arm, and at length, making a leg, slided gracefully up to an easy-chair of tarnished brocade, with a hole in its bottom, and led it gallantly out in a ghostly minuet about the floor.

The musician now played fiercer and fiercer, and bobbed his head and his night-cap about like mad. By degrees the dancing mania seemed to seize upon all the other pieces of furniture. The antique, long-bodied chairs paired off in couples and led down a country-dance; a three-legged stool danced a hornpipe, though horribly puzzled by its supernumerary limb; while the amorous tongs seized the shovel round the waist, and whirled it about the room in a German waltz. In short, all the movables got in motion; pirouetting hands across, right and left, like so many devils; all except a great clothes-press, which kept courte-sying and courtesying in a corner, like a dowager, in exquisite time to the music; being rather too corpulent to dance, or perhaps at a loss for a partner.

My grandfather concluded the latter to be the reason; so being, like a true Irishman, devoted to the sex, and at all times ready for a frolic, he bounced into the room, called to the musician to strike up Paddy O'Raf-ferty, capered up to the clothes-press, and seized upon the two handles to lead her out:——when-whirr! the whole revel was at an end. The chairs, tables, tongs and shovel, slunk in an instant as quietly into their places as if nothing had happened, and the musician vanished up the chimney, leaving the bellows behind him in his hurry. My grandfather found himself seated in the middle of the floor with the clothes-press sprawling before him, and the two handles jerked off, and in his hands.

"Then, after all, this was a mere dream," said the inquisitive gentle-men.

"The divil a bit of a dream!" replied the Irishman. "There never was

a truer fact in this world. Faith, I should have liked to see any man tell my grandfather it was a dream."

Well, gentlemen, as the clothes-press was a mighty heavy body, and my grandfather likewise, particularly in rear, you may easily suppose that two such heavy bodies coming to the ground would make a bit of a noise. Faith, the old mansion shook as though it had mistaken it for an earthquake. The whole garrison was alarmed. The landlord, who slept below, hurried up with a candle to inquire the cause, but with all his haste his daughter had arrived at the scene of uproar before him. The landlord was followed by the landlady, who was followed by the bouncing bar-maid, who was followed by the simpering chamber-maids, all holding together, as well as they could, such garments as they first laid hands on; but all in a terrible hurry to see what the deuce was to pay in the chamber of the bold dragoon.

My grandfather related the marvellous scene he had witnessed, and the broken handles of the prostrate clothes-press bore testimony to the fact. There was no contesting such evidence; particularly with a lad of my grandfather's complexion, who seemed able to make good every word either with sword or shillelah. So the landlord scratched his head and looked silly, as he was apt to do when puzzled. The landlady scratched—no, she did not scratch her head, but she knit her brow, and did not seem half pleased with the explanation. But the landlady's daughter corroborated it by recollecting that the last person who had dwelt in that chamber was a famous juggler who died of St. Vitus's dance, and had no doubt infected all the furniture.

This set all things to rights, particularly when the chambermaids declared that they had all witnessed strange carryings on in that room; and as they declared this "upon their honors," there could not remain a doubt upon this subject.

"And did your grandfather go to bed again in that room?" said the inquisitive gentleman.

"That's more than I can tell. Where he passed the rest of the night was a secret he never disclosed. In fact, though he had seen much service, he was but indifferently acquainted with geography, and apt to make blunders in his travels about inns at night, which it would have puzzled him sadly to account for in the morning."

"Was he ever apt to walk in his sleep?" said the knowing old gentleman.

"Never that I heard of."

There was a little pause after this rigmarole Irish romance, when the old gentleman with the haunted head observed, that the stories hitherto

related had rather a burlesque tendency. "I recollect an adventure however," added he, "which I heard of during a residence in Paris, for the truth of which I can undertake to vouch, and which is of a very grave and singular nature."

ADVENTURE OF THE GERMAN STUDENT

O N a stormy night, in the tempestuous times of the French revolution, a young German was returning to his lodgings, at a late
hour, across the old part of Paris. The lightning gleamed, and the loud
claps of thunder rattled through the lofty narrow streets—but I should
first tell you something about this young German.

Gottfried Wolfgang was a young man of good family. He had studied
for some time at Göttingen, but being of a visionary and enthusiastic
character, he had wandered into those wild and speculative doctrines
which have so often bewildered German students. His secluded life, his
intense application, and the singular nature of his studies, had an effect
on both mind and body. His health was impaired; his imagination
diseased. He had been indulging in fanciful speculations on spiritual
essences, until, like Swedenborg, he had an ideal world of his own
around him. He took up a notion, I do not know from what cause, that
there was an evil influence hanging over him; an evil genius or spirit
seeking to ensnare him and ensure his perdition. Such an idea working
on his melancholy temperament, produced the most gloomy effects. He
became haggard and desponding. His friends discovered the mental
malady preying upon him, and determined that the best cure was a
change of scene; he was sent, therefore, to finish his studies amidst the
splendors and gayeties of Paris.

Wolfgang arrived at Paris at the breaking out of the revolution. The
popular delirium at first caught his enthusiastic mind, and he was captivated by the political and philosophical theories of the day: but the
scenes of blood which followed shocked his sensitive nature, disgusted
him with society and the world, and made him more than ever a recluse. He shut himself up in a solitary apartment in the *Pays Latin*, the
quarter of students. There, in a gloomy street not far from the monastic
walls of the Sorbonne, he pursued his favorite speculations. Sometimes
he spent hours together in the great libraries of Paris, those catacombs
of departed authors, rummaging among their hordes of dusty and obsolete works in quest of food for his unhealthy appetite. He was, in a
manner, a literary ghoul, feeding in the charnel-house of decayed literature.

Wolfgang, though solitary and recluse, was of an ardent temperament, but for a time it operated merely upon his imagination. He was too shy and ignorant of the world to make any advances to the fair, but he was a passionate admirer of female beauty, and in his lonely chamber would often lose himself in reveries on forms and faces which he had seen, and his fancy would deck out images of loveliness far surpassing the reality.

While his mind was in this excited and sublimated state, a dream produced an extraordinary effect upon him. It was of a female face of transcendent beauty. So strong was the impression made, that he dreamt of it again and again. It haunted his thoughts by day, his slumbers by night; in fine, he became passionately enamoured of this shadow of a dream. This lasted so long that it became one of those fixed ideas which haunt the minds of melancholy men, and are at times mistaken for madness.

Such was Gottfried Wolfgang, and such his situation at the time I mentioned. He was returning home late one stormy night, through some of the old and gloomy streets of the *Marais*, the ancient part of Paris. The loud claps of thunder rattled among the high houses of the narrow streets. He came to the Place de Grève, the square where public executions are performed. The lightning quivered about the pinnacles of the ancient Hôtel de Ville, and shed flickering gleams over the open space in front. As Wolfgang was crossing the square, he shrank back with horror at finding himself close by the guillotine. It was the height of the reign of terror, when this dreadful instrument of death stood ever ready, and its scaffold was continually running with the blood of the virtuous and the brave. It had that very day been actively employed in the work of carnage, and there it stood in grim array, amidst a silent and sleeping city, waiting for fresh victims.

Wolfgang's heart sickened within him, and he was turning shuddering from the horrible engine, when he beheld a shadowy form, cowering as it were at the foot of the steps which led up to the scaffold. A succession of vivid flashes of lightning revealed it more distinctly. It was a female figure, dressed in black. She was seated on one of the lower steps of the scaffold, leaning forward, her face hid in her lap; and her long dishevelled tresses hanging to the ground, streaming with the rain which fell in torrents. Wolfgang paused. There was something awful in this solitary monument of woe. The female had the appearance of being above the common order. He knew the times to be full of vicissitude, and that many a fair head, which had once been pillowed on down, now wandered houseless. Perhaps this was some poor mourner whom the dreadful axe had rendered desolate, and who sat here heart-

broken on the strand of existence, from which all that was dear to her had been launched into eternity.

He approached, and addressed her in the accents of sympathy. She raised her head and gazed wildly at him. What was his astonishment at beholding, by the bright glare of the lightning, the very face which had haunted him in his dreams. It was pale and disconsolate, but ravishingly beautiful.

Trembling with violent and conflicting emotions, Wolfgang again accosted her. He spoke something of her being exposed at such an hour of the night, and to the fury of such a storm, and offered to conduct her to her friends. She pointed to the guillotine with a gesture of dreadful signification.

"I have no friend on earth!" said she.

"But you have a home," said Wolfgang.

"Yes—in the grave!"

The heart of the student melted at the words.

"If a stranger dare make an offer," said he, "without danger of being misunderstood, I would offer my humble dwelling as a shelter; myself as a devoted friend. I am friendless myself in Paris, and a stranger in the land; but if my life could be of service, it is at your disposal, and should be sacrificed before harm or indignity should come to you."

There was an honest earnestness in the young man's manner that had its effect. His foreign accent, too, was in his favor; it showed him not to be a hackneyed inhabitant of Paris. Indeed, there is an eloquence in true enthusiasm that is not to be doubted. The homeless stranger confided herself implicitly to the protection of the student.

He supported her faltering steps across the Pont Neuf, and by the place where the statue of Henry the Fourth had been overthrown by the populace. The storm had abated, and the thunder rumbled at a distance. All Paris was quiet; that great volcano of human passion slumbered for a while, to gather fresh strength for the next day's eruption. The student conducted his charge through the ancient streets of the *Pays Latin*, and by the dusky walls of the Sorbonne, to the great dingy hotel which he inhabited. The old portress who admitted them stared with surprise at the unusual sight of the melancholy Wolfgang with a female companion.

On entering his apartment, the student, for the first time, blushed at the scantiness and indifference of his dwelling. He had but one chamber—an old-fashioned saloon—heavily carved, and fantastically furnished with the remains of former magnificence, for it was one of those hotels in the quarter of the Luxembourg palace, which had once belonged to

nobility. It was lumbered with books and papers, and all the usual apparatus of a student, and his bed stood in a recess at one end.

When lights were brought, and Wolfgang had a better opportunity of contemplating the stranger, he was more than ever intoxicated by her beauty. Her face was pale, but of a dazzling fairness, set off by a profusion of raven hair that hung clustering about it. Her eyes were large and brilliant, with a singular expression approaching almost to wildness. As far as her black dress permitted her shape to be seen, it was of perfect symmetry. Her whole appearance was highly striking, though she was dressed in the simplest style. The only thing approaching to an ornament which she wore, was a broad black band round her neck, clasped by diamonds.

The perplexity now commenced with the student how to dispose of the helpless being thus thrown upon his protection. He thought of abandoning his chamber to her, and seeking shelter for himself elsewhere. Still he was so fascinated by her charms, there seemed to be such a spell upon his thoughts and senses, that he could not tear himself from her presence. Her manner, too, was singular and unaccountable. She spoke no more of the guillotine. Her grief had abated. The attentions of the student had first won her confidence, and then, apparently, her heart. She was evidently an enthusiast like himself, and enthusiasts soon understand each other.

In the infatuation of the moment, Wolfgang avowed his passion for her. He told her the story of his mysterious dream, and how she had possessed his heart before he had even seen her. She was strangely affected by his recital, and acknowledged to have felt an impulse towards him equally unaccountable. It was the time for wild theory and wild actions. Old prejudices and superstitions were done away; everything was under the sway of the "Goddess of Reason." Among other rubbish of the old times, the forms and ceremonies of marriage began to be considered superfluous bonds for honorable minds. Social compacts were the vogue. Wolfgang was too much of a theorist not to be tainted by the liberal doctrines of the day.

"Why should we separate?" said he; "our hearts are united; in the eye of reason and honor we are as one. What need is there of sordid forms to bind high souls together?"

The stranger listened with emotion: she had evidently received illumination at the same school.

"You have no home or family," continued he, "let me be everything to you, or rather let us be everything to one another. If form is necessary, form shall be observed—there is my hand. I pledge myself to you forever."

"Forever?" said the stranger, solemnly.

"Forever!" repeated Wolfgang.

The stranger clasped the hand extended to her: "Then I am yours," murmured she, and sank upon his bosom.

The next morning the student left his bride sleeping, and sallied forth at an early hour to seek more spacious apartments suitable to the change in his situation. When he returned, he found the stranger lying with her head hanging over the bed, and one arm thrown over it. He spoke to her, but received no reply. He advanced to awaken her from her uneasy posture. On taking her hand, it was cold—there was no pulsation—her face was pallid and ghastly. In a word, she was a corpse.

Horrified and frantic, he alarmed the house. A scene of confusion ensued. The police was summoned. As the officer of police entered the room, he started back on beholding the corpse.

"Great heaven!" cried he, "how did this woman come here?"

"Do you know anything about her?" said Wolfgang eagerly.

"Do I?" exclaimed the officer: "she was guillotined yesterday."

He stepped forward; undid the black collar round the neck of the corpse, and the head rolled on the floor!

The student burst into a frenzy. "The fiend! the fiend has gained possession of me!" shrieked he; "I am lost forever."

They tried to soothe him, but in vain. He was possessed with the frightful belief that an evil spirit had reanimated the dead body to ensnare him. He went distracted, and died in a mad-house.

Here the old gentleman with the haunted head finished his narrative.

"And is this really a fact?" said the inquisitive gentleman.

"A fact not to be doubted," replied the other. "I had it from the best authority. The student told it me himself. I saw him in a mad-house in Paris."

ADVENTURE OF THE MYSTERIOUS PICTURE

A S one story of the kind produces another and as all the company seemed fully engrossed with the subject, and disposed to bring their relatives and ancestors upon the scene, there is no knowing how many more strange adventures we might have heard, had not a corpulent old fox-hunter, who had slept soundly through the whole, now suddenly awakened, with a loud and long-drawn yawn. The sound broke the charm: the ghosts took to flight, as though it had been cockcrowing, and there was a universal move for bed.

"And now for the haunted chamber," said the Irish Captain, taking his candle.

"Ay, who's to be the hero of the night?" said the gentleman with the ruined head.

"That we shall see in the morning," said the old gentleman with the nose; "whoever looks pale and grizzly will have seen the ghost."

"Well, gentlemen," said the Baronet, "there's many a true thing said in jest—in fact, one of you will sleep in the room tonight——"

"What—a haunted room?—a haunted room—I claim the adventure—and I—and I—and I," said a dozen guests, talking and laughing at the same time.

"No, no," said mine host, "there is a secret about one of my rooms on which I feel disposed to try an experiment: so, gentlemen, none of you shall know who has the haunted chamber until circumstances reveal it. I will not even know it myself, but will leave it to chance and the allotment of the housekeeper. At the same time, if it will be any satisfaction to you, I will observe, for the honor of my paternal mansion, that there's scarcely a chamber in it but is well worthy of being haunted."

We now separated for the night, and each went to his allotted room. Mine was in one wing of the building, and I could not but smile at its resemblance in style to those eventful apartments described in the tales of the supper-table. It was spacious and gloomy, decorated with lampblack portraits; a bed of ancient damask, with a tester sufficiently lofty to grace a couch of state, and a number of massive pieces of old-fashioned furniture. I drew a great claw-footed arm-chair before the wide fireplace; stirred up the fire; sat looking into it, and musing upon the

odd stories I had heard, until, partly overcome by the fatigue of the day's hunting and partly by the wine and wassail of mine host, I fell asleep in my chair.

The uneasiness of my position made my slumber troubled, and laid me at the mercy of all kinds of wild and fearful dreams. Now it was that my perfidious dinner and supper rose in rebellion against my peace. I was hag-ridden by a fat saddle of mutton; a plum-pudding weighed like lead upon my conscience; the merry thought of a capon filled me with horrible suggestions; and a devilled leg of a turkey stalked in all kinds of diabolical shapes through my imagination. In short, I had a violent fit of the nightmare. Some strange, indefinite evil seemed hanging over me which I could not avert; something terrible and loathsome oppressed me which I could not shake off. I was conscious of being asleep, and strove to rouse myself, but every effort redoubled the evil; until gasping, struggling, almost strangling, I suddenly sprang bolt upright in my chair, and awoke.

The light on the mantel-piece had burnt low, and the wick was divided; there was a great winding-sheet made by the dripping wax on the side towards me. The disordered taper emitted a broad flaring flame, and threw a strong light on a painting over the fire-place which I had not hitherto observed. It consisted merely of a head, or rather a face, staring full upon me, with an expression that was startling. It was without a frame, and at the first glance I could hardly persuade myself that it was not a real face thrusting itself out of the dark oaken panel. I sat in my chair gazing at it, and the more I gazed, the more it disquieted me. I had never before been affected in the same way by any painting. The emotions it caused were strange and indefinite. They were something like what I have heard ascribed to the eyes of the basilisk, or like that mysterious influence in reptiles termed fascination. I passed my hand over my eyes several times, as if seeking instinctively to brush away the illusion—in vain. They instantly reverted to the picture, and its chilling, creeping influence over my flesh and blood was redoubled. I looked round the room on other pictures, either to divert my attention, or to see whether the same effect would be produced by them. Some of them were grim enough to produce the effect, if the mere grimness of the painting produced it.—No such thing—my eye passed over them all with perfect indifference, but the moment it reverted to this visage over the fireplace, it was as if an electric shock darted through me. The other pictures were dim and faded, but this one protruded from a plain background in the strongest relief, and with wonderful truth of coloring. The expression was that of agony—the agony of intense bodily pain; but a menace scowled upon the brow, and a few sprinklings of blood

added to its ghastliness. Yet it was not all these characteristics; it was some horror of the mind, some inscrutable antipathy awakened by this picture, which harrowed up my feelings.

I tried to persuade myself that this was chimerical, that my brain was confused by the fumes of mine host's good cheer, and in some measure by the odd stories about paintings which had been told at supper. I determined to shake off these vapors of the mind; rose from my chair; walked about the room; snapped my fingers; rallied myself; laughed aloud.—It was a forced laugh, and the echo of it in the old chamber jarred upon my ear.—I walked to the window, and tried to discern the landscape through the glass. It was pitch darkness, and a howling storm without; and as I heard the wind moan among the trees, I caught a reflection of this accursed visage in the pane of glass, as though it were staring through the window at me. Even the reflection of it was thrilling.

How was this vile nervous fit, for such I now persuaded myself it was, to be conquered? I determined to force myself not to look at the painting, but to undress quickly and get into bed. I began to undress, but in spite of every effort I could not keep myself from stealing a glance every now and then at the picture; and a glance was sufficient to distress me. Even when my back was turned to it, the idea of this strange face behind me, peeping over my shoulder, was insupportable. I threw off my clothes and hurried into bed, but still this visage gazed upon me. I had a full view of it in my bed, and for some time could not take my eyes from it. I had grown nervous to a dismal degree. I put out the light, and tried to force myself to sleep—all in vain. The fire gleaming up a little, threw an uncertain light about the room, leaving, however, the region of the picture in deep shadow. What, thought I, if this be the chamber about which mine host spoke as having a mystery reigning over it? I had taken his words merely as spoken in jest; might they have a real import? I looked around. The faintly lighted apartment had all the qualifications requisite for a haunted chamber. It began in my infected imagination to assume strange appearances—the old portraits turned paler and paler, and blacker and blacker; the streaks of light and shadow thrown among the quaint articles of furniture gave them more singular shapes and characters. There was a huge dark clothes-press of antique form, gorgeous in brass and lustrous with wax, that began to grow oppressive to me.

"Am I then," thought I, "indeed the hero of the haunted room? Is there really a spell laid upon me, or is this all some contrivance of mine host to raise a laugh at my expense?" The idea of being hag-ridden by my own fancy all night, and then bantered on my haggard looks the

next day, was intolerable; but the very idea was sufficient to produce the effect, and to render me still more nervous. "Pish," said I, "it can be no such thing. How could my worthy host imagine that I, or any man, would be so worried by a mere picture? It is my own diseased imagination that torments me."

I turned in bed, and shifted from side to side, to try to fall asleep; but all in vain; when one cannot get asleep by lying quiet, it is seldom that tossing about will effect the purpose. The fire gradually went out, and left the room in total darkness. Still I had the idea of that inexplicable countenance gazing and keeping watch upon me through the gloom —nay, what was worse, the very darkness seemed to magnify its terrors. It was like having an unseen enemy hanging about one in the night. Instead of having one picture now to worry me, I had a hundred. I fancied it in every direction—"There it is," thought I, "and there! and there! with its horrible and mysterious expression still gazing and gazing on me! No—if I must suffer the strange and dismal influence, it were better face a single foe than thus be haunted by a thousand images of it."

Whoever has been in a state of nervous agitation, must know that the longer it continues the more uncontrollable it grows. The very air of the chamber seemed at length infected by the baleful presence of this picture. I fancied it hovering over me. I almost felt the fearful visage from the wall approaching my face—it seemed breathing upon me. "This is not to be borne," said I, at length, springing out of bed: "I can stand this no longer—I shall only tumble and toss about here all night; make a very spectre of myself, and become the hero of the haunted chamber in good earnest. Whatever be the ill consequences, I'll quit this cursed room and seek a night's rest elsewhere—they can but laugh at me, at all events, and they'll be sure to have the laugh upon me if I pass a sleepless night, and show them a haggard and woe-begone visage in the morning."

All this was half-muttered to myself as I hastily slipped on my clothes, which having done, I groped my way out of the room and downstairs to the drawing-room. Here after tumbling over two or three pieces of furniture, I made out to reach a sofa, and stretching myself upon it, determined to bivouac there for the night. The moment I found myself out of the neighborhood of that strange picture, it seemed as if the charm were broken. All its influence was at an end. I felt assured that it was confined to its own dreary chamber, for I had, with a sort of instinctive caution, turned the key when I closed the door. I soon calmed down, therefore, into a state of tranquillity; from that into a drowsiness, and finally into a deep sleep; out of which I did not awake until the housemaid, with her besom and her matin-song, came to put

the room in order. She stared at finding me stretched upon the sofa, but I presume circumstances of the kind were not uncommon after hunting-dinners in her master's bachelor establishment, for she went on with her song and her work, and took no further heed of me.

I had an unconquerable repugnance to return to my chamber; so I found my way to the butler's quarters, made my toilet in the best way circumstances would permit, and was among the first to appear at the breakfast-table. Our breakfast was a substantial fox-hunter's repast, and the company generally assembled at it. When ample justice had been done to the tea, coffee, cold meats, and humming ale, for all these were furnished in abundance, according to the tastes of the different guests, the conversation began to break out with all the liveliness and freshness of morning mirth.

"But who is the hero of the haunted chamber—who has seen the ghost last night?" said the inquisitive gentleman, rolling his lobster-eyes about the table.

The question set every tongue in motion; a vast deal of bantering, criticising of countenances, of mutual accusation and retort took place. Some had drunk deep, and some were unshaven, so that there were suspicious faces enough in the assembly. I alone could not enter with ease and vivacity into the joke—I felt tongue-tied, embarrassed. A recollection of what I had seen and felt the preceding night still haunted my mind. It seemed as if the mysterious picture still held a thrall upon me. I thought also that our host's eye was turned on me with an air of curiosity. In short, I was conscious that I was the hero of the night, and felt as if every one might read it in my looks. The joke, however, passed over, and no suspicion seemed to attach to me. I was just congratulating myself on my escape, when a servant came in, saying, that the gentleman who had slept on the sofa in the drawing-room had left his watch under one of the pillows. My repeater was in his hand.

"What!" said the inquisitive gentleman, "did any gentleman sleep on the sofa?"

"Soho! Soho! a hare—a hare!" cried the old gentleman with the flexible nose.

I could not avoid acknowledging the watch, and was rising in great confusion, when a boisterous old squire who sat beside me exclaimed, slapping me on the shoulder, "'Sblood, lad, thou art the man as has seen the ghost!"

The attention of the company was immediately turned on me: if my face had been pale the moment before, it now glowed almost to burning. I tried to laugh, but could only make a grimace, and found the

muscles of my face twitching at sixes and sevens, and totally out of all control.

It takes but little to raise a laugh among a set of fox-hunters; there was a world of merriment and joking on the subject, and as I never relished a joke overmuch when it was at my own expense, I began to feel a little nettled. I tried to look cool and calm, and to restrain my pique; but the coolness and calmness of a man in a passion are confounded treacherous.

"Gentlemen," said I, with a slight cocking of the chin and a bad attempt at a smile, "this is all very pleasant—ha! ha!—very pleasant—but I'd have you know, I am as little superstitious as any of you—ha! ha!—and as to anything like timidity—you may smile, gentlemen, but I trust there's no one here means to insinuate that—as to a room's being haunted—I repeat, gentlemen, (growing a little warm at seeing a cursed grin breaking out round me) as to a room being haunted, I have as little faith in such silly stories as any one. But, since you put the matter home to me, I will say that I have met with something in my room strange and inexplicable to me. (A shout of laughter.) Gentlemen, I am serious; I know well what I am saying; I am calm, gentlemen, (striking my fist upon the table) by Heaven, I am calm. I am neither trifling, nor do I wish to be trifled with. (The laughter of the company suppressed, and with ludicrous attempts at gravity.) There is a picture in the room in which I was put last night, that has had an effect upon me the most singular and incomprehensible."

"A picture?" said the old gentleman with the haunted head. "A picture!" cried the narrator with the nose. "A picture! a picture!" echoed several voices. Here there was an ungovernable peal of laughter. I could not contain myself. I started up from my seat; looked round on the company with fiery indignation; thrust both of my hands into my pockets, and strode up to one of the windows as though I would have walked through it. I stopped short, looked out upon the landscape without distinguishing a feature of it, and felt my gorge rising almost to suffocation.

Mine host saw it was time to interfere. He had maintained an air of gravity through the whole of the scene; and now stepped forth, as if to shelter me from the overwhelming merriment of my companions.

"Gentlemen," said he, "I dislike to spoil sport, but you have had your laugh, and the joke of the haunted chamber has been enjoyed. I must now take the part of my guest. I must not only vindicate him from your pleasantries, but I must reconcile him to himself, for I suspect he is a little out of humor with his own feelings; and, above all, I must crave his pardon for having made him the subject of a kind of experiment.

Yes, gentlemen, there is something strange and peculiar in the chamber to which our friend was shown last night; there is a picture in my house which possesses a singular and mysterious influence, and with which there is connected a very curious story. It is a picture to which I attach a value from a variety of circumstances; and though I have often been tempted to destroy it, from the odd and uncomfortable sensations which it produces in every one that beholds it, yet I have never been able to prevail upon myself to make the sacrifice. It is a picture I never like to look upon myself, and which is held in awe by all my servants. I have therefore banished it to a room but rarely used, and should have had it covered last night, had not the nature of our conversation, and the whimsical talk about a haunted chamber, tempted me to let it remain, by way of experiment, to see whether a stranger, totally unacquainted with its story, would be affected by it."

The words of the Baronet had turned every thought into a different channel. All were anxious to hear the story of the mysterious picture; and, for myself, so strangely were my feelings interested, that I forgot to feel piqued at the experiment my host had made upon my nerves, and joined eagerly in the general entreaty. As the morning was stormy, and denied all egress, my host was glad of any means of entertaining his company; so, drawing his arm-chair towards the fire, he began.

ADVENTURE OF THE MYSTERIOUS STRANGER

MANY years since, when I was a young man, and had just left Oxford, I was sent on the grand tour to finish my education. I believe my parents had tried in vain to inoculate me with wisdom; so they sent me to mingle with society, in hopes that I might take it the natural way. Such, at least, appears the reason for which nine tenths of our youngsters are sent abroad. In the course of my tour I remained some time at Venice. The romantic character of that place delighted me; I was very much amused by the air of adventure and intrigue prevalent in this region of masks and gondolas; and I was exceedingly smitten by a pair of languishing black eyes, that played upon my heart from under an Italian mantle; so I persuaded myself that I was lingering at Venice to study men and manners; at least I persuaded my friends so, and that answered all my purposes.

I was a little prone to be struck by peculiarities in character and conduct, and my imagination was so full of romantic associations with Italy that I was always on the look-out for adventure. Everything chimed in with such a humor in this old mermaid of a city. My suite of apartments was in a proud, melancholy palace on the grand canal, formerly the residence of a magnifico, and sumptuous with the traces of decayed grandeur. My gondolier was one of the shrewdest of his class, active, merry, intelligent, and, like his brethren, secret as the grave; that is to say, secret to all the world except his master. I had not had him a week before he put me behind all the curtains in Venice. I liked the silence and the mystery of the place, and when I sometimes saw from my window a black gondola gliding mysteriously along in the dusk of the evening, with nothing visible but its little glimmering lantern, I would jump into my own *zendeletta*, and give a signal for pursuit—"But I am running away from my subject with the recollection of youthful follies," said the Baronet, checking himself. "Let us come to the point."

Among my familiar resorts was a casino under the arcades on one side of the grand square of St. Mark. Here I used frequently to lounge and take my ice, on those warm summer-nights, when in Italy everybody lives abroad until morning. I was seated here one evening, when

a group of Italians took their seat at a table on the opposite side of the saloon. Their conversation was gay and animated, and carried on with Italian vivacity and gesticulation. I remarked among them one young man, however, who appeared to take no share, and to find no enjoyment in the conversation, though he seemed to force himself to attend to it. He was tall and slender, and of extremely prepossessing appearance. His features were fine, though emaciated. He had a profusion of black glossy hair, that curled lightly about his head, and contrasted with the extreme paleness of his countenance. His brow was haggard; deep furrows seemed to have been ploughed into his visage by care, not by age, for he was evidently in the prime of youth. His eye was full of expression and fire, but wild and unsteady. He seemed to be tormented by some strange fancy or apprehension. In spite of every effort to fix his attention on the conversation of his companions, I noticed that every now and then he would turn his head slowly round, give a glance over his shoulder, and then withdraw it with a sudden jerk, as if something painful met his eye. This was repeated at intervals of about a minute, and he appeared hardly to have recovered from one shock, before I saw him slowly preparing to encounter another.

After sitting some time in the casino, the party paid for the refreshment they had taken, and departed. The young man was the last to leave the saloon, and I remarked him glancing behind him in the same way, just as he passed out of the door. I could not resist the impulse to rise and follow him; for I was at an age when a romantic feeling of curiosity is easily awakened. The party walked slowly down the arcades, talking and laughing as they went. They crossed the Piazetta, but paused in the middle of it to enjoy the scene. It was one of those moonlight nights, so brilliant and clear in the pure atmosphere of Italy. The moonbeams streamed on the tall tower of St. Mark, and lighted up the magnificent front and swelling domes of the cathedral. The party expressed their delight in animated terms. I kept my eye upon the young man. He alone seemed abstracted and self-occupied. I noticed the same singular and, as it were, furtive glance over the shoulder, which had attracted my attention in the casino. The party moved on, and I followed; they passed along the walk called the Broglio, turned the corner of the Ducal Palace, and getting into the gondola, glided swiftly away.

The countenance and conduct of this young man dwelt upon my mind, and interested me exceedingly. I met him a day or two afterwards in a gallery of paintings. He was evidently a connoisseur, for he always singled out the most masterly productions, and a few remarks drawn from him by his companions showed an intimate acquaintance

with the art. His own taste, however, ran on singular extremes. On Salvator Rosa, in his most savage and solitary scenes; or Raphael, Titian, and Correggio, in their softest delineations of female beauty; on these he would occasionally gaze with transient enthusiasm. But this seemed only a momentary forgetfulness. Still would recur that cautious glance behind, and always quickly withdrawn, as though something terrible met his view.

I encountered him frequently afterwards at the theatre, at balls, at concerts; at promenades in the gardens of San Georgia; at the grotesque exhibitions in the square of St. Mark; among the throng of merchants on the exchange by the Rialto. He seemed, in fact, to seek crowds; to hunt after bustle and amusement; yet never to take any interest in either the business or the gayety of the scene. Ever an air of painful thought, of wretched abstraction; and ever that strange and recurring movement of glancing fearfully over the shoulder. I did not know at first but this might be caused by apprehension of arrest; or, perhaps, from dread of assassination. But if so, why should he go thus continually abroad? why expose himself at all times and in all places?

I became anxious to know this stranger. I was drawn to him by that romantic sympathy which sometimes draws young men towards each other. His melancholy threw a charm about him, no doubt heightened by the touching expression of his countenance, and the manly graces of his person; for manly beauty has its effect even upon men. I had an Englishman's habitual diffidence and awkwardness to contend with; but from frequently meeting him in the casinos, I gradually edged myself into his acquaintance. I had no reserve on his part to contend with. He seemed, on the contrary, to court society; and, in fact, to seek anything rather than be alone.

When he found that I really took an interest in him, he threw himself entirely on my friendship. He clung to me like a drowning man. He would walk with me for hours up and down the place of St. Mark —or would sit, until night was far advanced, in my apartments. He took rooms under the same roof with me; and his constant request was that I would permit him, when it did not incommode me, to sit by me in my saloon. It was not that he seemed to take a particular delight in my conversation, but rather that he craved the vicinity of a human being; and, above all, of a being that sympathized with him. "I have often heard," said he, "of the sincerity of Englishmen—thank God I have one at length for a friend!"

Yet he never seemed disposed to avail himself of my sympathy other than by mere companionship. He never sought to unbosom himself to

me: there appeared to be a settled, corroding anguish in his bosom that neither could be soothed "by silence nor by speaking."

A devouring melancholy preyed upon his heart, and seemed to be drying up the very blood in his veins. It was not a soft melancholy, the disease of the affections, but a parching, withering agony. I could see at times that his mouth was dry and feverish; he panted rather than breathed; his eyes were bloodshot; his cheeks pale and livid; with now and then faint streaks of red athwart them, baleful gleams of the fire that was consuming his heart. As my arm was within his, I felt him press it at times with a convulsive motion to his side; his hands would clinch themselves involuntarily, and a kind of shudder would run through his frame.

I reasoned with him about his melancholy, sought to draw from him the cause; he shrunk from all confiding: "Do not seek to know it," said he, "you could not relieve it if you knew it; you would not even seek to relieve it. On the contrary, I should lose your sympathy, and that," said he, pressing my hand convulsively, "that I feel has become too dear to me to risk."

I endeavored to awaken hope within him. He was young; life had a thousand pleasures in store for him; there was a healthy reaction in the youthful heart; it medicines all its own wounds; "Come, come," said I, "there is no grief so great that youth cannot outgrow it."—"No! no!" said he, clinching his teeth, and striking repeatedly, with the energy of despair, on his bosom,—"it is here! here! deep-rooted; draining my heart's blood. It grows and grows, while my heart withers and withers. I have a dreadful monitor that gives me no repose—that follows me step by step—and will follow me step by step, until it pushes me into my grave!"

As he said this he involuntarily gave one of those fearful glances over his shoulder, and shrunk back with more than usual horror. I could not resist the temptation to allude to this movement, which I supposed to be some mere malady of the nerves. The moment I mentioned it, his face became crimsoned and convulsed; he grasped me by both hands—

"For God's sake," exclaimed he, with a piercing voice, "never allude to that again.—Let us avoid this subject, my friend; you cannot relieve me, indeed you cannot relieve me, but you may add to the torments I suffer.—At some future day you shall know all."

I never resumed the subject; for however much my curiosity might be roused, I felt too true a compassion for his sufferings to increase them by my intrusion. I sought various ways to divert his mind, and to arouse him from the constant meditations in which he was plunged.

He saw my efforts, and seconded them as far as in his power, for there was nothing moody or wayward in his nature. On the contrary, there was something frank, generous, unassuming, in his whole deportment. All the sentiments he uttered were noble and lofty. He claimed no indulgence, asked no toleration, but seemed content to carry his load of misery in silence, and only sought to carry it by my side. There was a mute beseeching manner about him, as if he craved companionship as a charitable boon; and a tacit thankfulness in his looks, as if he felt grateful to me for not repulsing him.

I felt this melancholy to be infectious. It stole over my spirits; interfered with all my gay pursuits, and gradually saddened my life; yet I could not prevail upon myself to shake off a being who seemed to hang upon me for support. In truth, the generous traits of character which beamed through all his gloom penetrated to my heart. His bounty was lavish and open-handed; his charity melting and spontaneous; not confined to mere donations, which humiliate as much as they relieve. The tone of his voice, the beam of his eye, enhanced every gift, and surprised the poor suppliant with that rarest and sweetest of charities, the charity not merely of the hand, but of the heart. Indeed his liberality seemed to have something in it of self-abasement and expiation. He, in a manner, humbled himself before the mendicant. "What right have I to ease and affluence"—would he murmur to himself—"when innocence wanders in misery and rags?"

The carnival-time arrived. I hoped the gay scenes then presented might have some cheering effect. I mingled with him in the motley throng that crowded the place of St. Mark. We frequented operas, masquerades, balls—all in vain. The evil kept growing on him. He became more and more haggard and agitated. Often, after we had returned from one of these scenes of revelry, I have entered his room and found him lying on his face on the sofa; his hands clinched in his fine hair, and his whole countenance bearing traces of the convulsions of his mind.

The carnival passed away; the time of Lent succeeded; passion-week arrived; we attended one evening a solemn service in one of the churches, in the course of which a grand piece of vocal and instrumental music was performed relating to the death of our Saviour.

I had remarked that he was always powerfully affected by music; on this occasion he was so in an extraordinary degree. As the pealing notes swelled through the lofty aisles, he seemed to kindle with fervor; his eyes rolled upwards, until nothing but the whites were visible; his hands were clasped together, until the fingers were deeply imprinted in the flesh. When the music expressed the dying agony, his face gradu-

ally sank upon his knees; and at the touching words resounding through the church, *"Jesu mori,"* sobs burst from him uncontrolled—I had never seen him weep before. His had always been agony rather than sorrow. I augered well from the circumstance, and let him weep on uninterrupted. When the service was ended, we left the church. He hung on my arm as we walked homewards with something of a softer and more subdued manner, instead of that nervous agitation I had been accustomed to witness. He alluded to the service we had heard. "Music," said he, "is indeed the voice of heaven; never before have I felt more impressed by the story of the atonement of our Saviour.—Yes, my friend," said he, clasping his hands with a kind of transport, "I know that my Redeemer liveth!"

We parted for the night. His room was not far from mine, and I heard him for some time busied in it. I fell asleep, but was awakened before daylight. The young man stood by my bedside, dressed for travelling. He held a sealed packet and a large parcel in his hand, which he laid on the table.

"Farewell, my friend," said he, "I am about to set forth on a long journey; but, before I go, I leave with you these remembrances. In this packet you will find the particulars of my story. When you read them I shall be far away; do not remember me with aversion.—You have been indeed a friend to me.—You have poured oil into a broken heart, but you could not heal it. Farewell! let me kiss your hand—I am unworthy to embrace you." He sank on his knees, seized my hand in despite of my efforts to the contrary, and covered it with kisses. I was so surprised by all the scene, that I had not been able to say a word—"But we shall meet again," said I, hastily, as I saw him hurrying towards the door. "Never, never, in this world!" said he solemnly.—He sprang once more to my bedside—seized my hand, pressed it to his heart and to his lips, and rushed out of the room.

Here the Baronet paused. He seemed lost in thought, and sat looking upon the floor, and drumming with his fingers on the arm of his chair.

"And did this mysterious personage return?" said the inquisitive gentleman.

"Never!" replied the Baronet, with a pensive shake of the head,—"I never saw him again."

"And pray what has all this to do with the picture?" inquired the old gentleman with the nose.

"True," said the questioner; "is it the portrait of that crack-brained Italian?"

"No," said the Baronet, dryly, not half liking the appellation given to his hero; "but this picture was enclosed in the parcel he left with me.

The sealed packet contained its explanation. There was a request on the outside that I would not open it until six months had elapsed. I kept my promise in spite of my curiosity. I have a translation of it by me, and had meant to read it by way of accounting for the mystery of the chamber; but I fear I have already detained the company too long."

Here there was a general wish expressed to have the manuscript read, particularly on the part of the inquisitive gentleman; so the worthy Baronet drew out a fairly-written manuscript, and, wiping his spectacles, read aloud the following story.

THE STORY OF THE YOUNG ITALIAN

I WAS born at Naples. My parents, though of noble rank, were limited, in fortune, or rather, my father was ostentatious beyond his means, and expended so much on his palace, his equipage, and his retinue, that he was continually straitened in his pecuniary circumstances. I was a younger son, and looked upon with indifference by my father, who, from a principle of family pride, wished to leave all his property to my elder brother. I showed, when quite a child, an extreme sensibility. Everything affected me violently. While yet an infant in my mother's arms, and before I had learned to talk, I could be wrought upon to a wonderful degree of anguish or delight by the power of music. As I grew older, my feelings remained equally acute, and I was easily transported into paroxysms of pleasure or rage. It was the amusement of my relations and of the domestics to play upon this irritable temperament. I was moved to tears, tickled to laughter, provoked to fury, for the entertainment of company, who were amused by such a tempest of mighty passion in a pigmy frame;—they little thought, or perhaps little heeded the dangerous sensibilities they were fostering. I thus became a little creature of passion before reason was developed. In a short time I grew too old to be a plaything, and then I became a torment. The tricks and passions I had been teased into became irksome, and I was disliked by my teachers for the very lessons they had taught me. My mother died; and my power as a spoiled child was at an end. There was no longer any necessity to humor or tolerate me, for there was nothing to be gained by it, as I was no favorite of my father. I therefore experienced the fate of a spoiled child in such a situation, and was neglected, or noticed only to be crossed and contradicted. Such was the early treatment of a heart which, if I can judge of it at all, was naturally disposed to the extremes of tenderness and affection.

My father, as I have already said, never liked me—in fact, he never understood me; he looked upon me as wilful and wayward, as deficient in natural affection. It was the stateliness of his own manner, the loftiness and grandeur of his own look, which had repelled me from his arms. I always pictured him to myself as I had seen him, clad in his senatorial robes, rustling with pomp and pride. The magnificence of

his person daunted my young imagination. I could never approach him with the confiding affection of a child.

My father's feelings were wrapt up in my elder brother. He was to be the inheritor of the family title and the family dignity, and everything was sacrificed to him—I, as well as everything else. It was determined to devote me to the Church, that so my humors and myself might be removed out of the way, either of tasking my father's time and trouble, or interfering with the interests of my brother. At an early age, therefore, before my mind had dawned upon the world and its delights, or known anything of it beyond the precincts of my father's palace, I was sent to a convent, the superior of which was my uncle, and was confided entirely to his care.

My uncle was a man totally estranged from the world: he had never relished, for he had never tasted its pleasures; and he regarded rigid self-denial as the great basis of Christian virtue. He considered every one's temperament like his own; or at least he made them conform to it. His character and habits had an influence over the fraternity of which he was superior: a more gloomy, saturnine set of beings were never assembled together. The convent, too, was calculated to awaken sad and solitary thoughts. It was situated in a gloomy gorge of those mountains away south of Vesuvius. All distant views were shut out by sterile volcanic heights. A mountain-stream raved beneath its walls, and eagles screamed about its turrets.

I had been sent to this place at so tender an age as soon to lose all distinct recollection of the scenes I had left behind. As my mind expanded, therefore, it formed its idea of the world from the convent and its vicinity, and a dreary world it appeared to me. An early tinge of melancholy was thus infused into my character; and the dismal stories of the monks, about devils and evil spirits, with which they affrighted my young imagination, gave me a tendency to superstition which I could never effectually shake off. They took the same delight to work upon my ardent feelings, that had been so mischievously executed by my father's household. I can recollect the horrors with which they fed my heated fancy during an eruption of Vesuvius. We were distant from that volcano, with mountains between us; but its convulsive throes shook the solid foundations of nature. Earthquakes threatened to topple down our convent-towers. A lurid, baleful light hung in the heavens at night, and showers of ashes, borne by the wind, fell in our narrow valley. The monks talked of the earth being honey-combed beneath us; of streams of molten lava raging through its veins; of caverns of sulphurous flames roaring in the centre, the abodes of demons and the damned; of fiery gulfs ready to yawn beneath our feet. All these tales were told

to the doleful accompaniment of the mountain's thunders, whose low bellowing made the walls of our convent vibrate.

One of the monks had been a painter, but had retired from the world, and embraced this dismal life in expiation of some crime. He was a melancholy man, who pursued his art in the solitude of his cell, but made it a source of penance to him. His employment was to portray, either on canvas or in waxen models, the human face and human form, in the agonies of death, and in all the stages of dissolution and decay. The fearful mysteries of the charnel-house were unfolded in his labors; the loathesome banquet of the beetle and the worm. I turn with shuddering even from the recollection of his works; yet, at the time, my strong but ill-directed imagination seized with ardor upon his instructions in his art. Anything was a variety from the dry studies and monotonous duties of the cloister. In a little while I became expert with my pencil, and my gloomy productions were thought worthy of decorating some of the altars of the chapel.

In this dismal way was a creature of feeling and fancy brought up. Everything genial and amiable in my nature was repressed, and nothing brought out but what was unprofitable and ungracious. I was ardent in my temperament; quick, mercurial, impetuous, formed to be a creature all love and adoration; but a leaden hand was laid on all my finer qualities. I was taught nothing but fear and hatred. I hated my uncle. I hated the monks. I hated the convent in which I was immured. I hated the world; and I almost hated myself for being, as I supposed, so hating and hateful an animal.

When I had nearly attained the age of sixteen, I was suffered, on one occasion, to accompany one of the brethren on a mission to a distant part of the country. We soon left behind us the gloomy valley in which I had been pent up for so many years, and after a short journey among the mountains, emerged upon the voluptuous landscape that spreads itself about the Bay of Naples. Heavens! how transported was I, when I stretched my gaze over a vast reach of delicious sunny country, gay with groves and vineyards; with Vesuvius rearing its forked summit to my right; the blue Mediterranean to my left, with its enchanting coast, studded with shining towns and sumptuous villas; and Naples, my native Naples, gleaming far, far in the distance.

Good God! was this the lovely world from which I had been excluded! I had reached that age when the sensibilities are in all their bloom and freshness. Mine had been checked and chilled. They now burst forth with the suddenness of a retarded spring-time. My heart, hitherto unnaturally shrunk up, expanded into a riot of vague but delicious emotions. The beauty of nature intoxicated—bewildered me.

The song of the peasants, their cheerful looks, their happy avocations, the picturesque gayety of their dresses, their rustic music, their dances, all broke upon me like witchcraft. My soul responded to the music, my heart danced in my bosom. All the men appeared amiable,—all the women lovely.

I returned to the convent; that is to say, my body returned, but my heart and soul never entered there again. I could not forget this glimpse of a beautiful and a happy world—a world so suited to my natural character. I had felt so happy while in it; so different a being from what I felt myself when in the convent—that tomb of the living. I contrasted the countenances of the beings I had seen, full of fire and freshness and enjoyment, with the pallid, leaden, lack-lustre visages of the monks: the dance with the droning chant of the chapel. I had before found the exercises of the cloister wearisome—they now became intolerable. The dull round of duties wore away my spirit; my nerves became irritated by the fretful tinkling of the convent-bell, evermore dinging among the mountain-echoes, evermore calling me from my repose at night, my pencil by day, to attend to some tedious and mechanical ceremony of devotion.

I was not of a nature to meditate long without putting my thoughts into action. My spirit had been suddenly aroused, and was now all awake within me. I watched an opportunity, fled from the convent, and made my way on foot to Naples. As I entered its gay and crowded streets, and beheld the variety and stir of life around me, the luxury of palaces, the splendor of equipages, and the pantomimic animation of the motley populace, I seemed as if awakened to a world of enchantment, and solemnly vowed that nothing should force me back to the monotony of the cloister.

I had to inquire my way to my father's palace, for I had been so young on leaving it that I knew not its situation. I found some difficulty in getting admitted to my father's presence; for the domestics scarcely knew that there was such a being as myself in existence, and my monastic dress did not operate in my favor. Even my father entertained no recollection of my person. I told him my name, threw myself at his feet, implored his forgiveness, and entreated that I might not be sent back to the convent.

He received me with the condescension of a patron, rather than the fondness of a parent; listened patiently, but coldly, to my tale of monastic grievances and disgusts, and promised to think what else could be done for me. This coldness blighted and drove back all the frank affection of my nature, that was ready to spring forth at the least warmth of parental kindness. All my early feelings towards my father

revived. I again looked up to him as the stately, magnificent being that had daunted my childish imagination, and felt as if I had no pretensions to his sympathies. My brother engrossed all his care and love; he inherited his nature, and carried himself towards me with a protecting rather than a fraternal air. It wounded my pride, which was great. I could brook condescension from my father, for I looked up to him with awe, as a superior being; but I could not brook patronage from a brother, who I felt was intellectually my inferior. The servants perceived that I was an unwelcome intruder in the paternal mansion, and, menial-like, they treated me with neglect. Thus baffled at every point, my affections outraged wherever they would attach themselves, I became sullen, silent, and desponding. My feelings, driven back upon myself, entered and preyed upon my own heart. I remained for some days an unwelcome guest rather than a restored son in my father's house. I was doomed never to be properly known there. I was made, by wrong treatment, strange even to myself, and they judged of me from my strangeness.

I was startled one day at the sight of one of the monks of my convent gliding out of my father's room. He saw me, but pretended not to notice me, and this very hypocrisy made me suspect something. I had become sore and susceptible in my feelings—everything inflicted a wound on them. In this state of mind, I was treated with marked disrespect by a pampered minion, the favorite servant of my father. All the pride and passion of my nature rose in an instant, and I struck him to the earth. My father was passing by; he stopped not to inquire the reason, nor indeed could he read the long course of mental sufferings which were the real cause. He rebuked me with anger and scorn; summoning all the haughtiness of his nature and grandeur of his look to give weight to the contumely with which he treated me. I felt that I had not deserved it. I felt that I was not appreciated. I felt that I had that within me which merited better treatment. My heart swelled against a father's injustice. I broke through my habitual awe of him—I replied to him with impatience. My hot spirit flushed in my cheek and kindled in my eye; but my sensitive heart swelled as quickly, and before I had half vented my passion, I felt it suffocated and quenched in my tears. My father was astonished and incensed at this turning of the worm, and ordered me to my chamber. I retired in silence, choking with contending emotions.

I had not been long there when I overheard voices in an adjoining apartment. It was a consultation between my father and the monk about the means of getting me back quietly to the convent. My resolution was taken. I had no longer a home nor a father. That very night

I left the paternal roof. I got on board a vessel about making sail from the harbor, and abandoned myself to the wide world. No matter to what port she steered; any part of so beautiful a world was better than my convent. No matter where I was cast by fortune; any place would be more a home to me than the home I had left behind. The vessel was bound to Genoa. We arrived there after a voyage of a few days.

As I entered the harbor between the moles which embrace it, and beheld the amphitheatre of palaces and churches and splendid gardens rising one above another, I felt at once its title to the appellation of Genoa the Superb. I landed on the mole an utter stranger, without knowing what to do, or whither to direct my steps. No matter: I was released from the thraldom of the convent and the humiliations of home. When I traversed the Strada Balbi and the Strada Nuova, those streets of palaces, and gazed at the wonders of architecture around me; when I wandered at close of day amid a gay throng of the brilliant and the beautiful, through the green alleys of the Aqua Verde, or among the colonnades and terraces of the magnificent Doria gardens; I thought it impossible to be ever otherwise than happy in Genoa. A few days sufficed to show me my mistake. My scanty purse was exhausted, and for the first time in my life I experienced the sordid distress of penury. I had never known the want of money, and had never adverted to the possibility of such an evil. I was ignorant of the world and all its ways; and when first the idea of destitution came over my mind, its effect was withering. I was wandering penniless through the streets which no longer delighted my eyes, when chance led my steps into the magnificent church of the Annunciata.

A celebrated painter of the day was at that moment superintending the placing of one of his pictures over an altar. The proficiency which I had acquired in his art during my residence in the convent, had made me an enthusiastic amateur. I was struck, at the first glance, with the painting. It was the face of a Madonna. So innocent, so lovely, such a divine expression of maternal tenderness! I lost, for the moment, all recollection of myself in the enthusiasm of my art. I clasped my hands together, and uttered an ejaculation of delight. The painter perceived my emotion. He was flattered and gratified by it. My air and manner pleased him, and he accosted me. I felt too much the want of friendship to repel the advances of a stranger; and there was something in this one so benevolent and winning that in a moment he gained my confidence.

I told him my story and my situation, concealing only my name and rank. He appeared strongly interested by my recital, invited me to his house, and from that time I became his favorite pupil. He thought he

perceived in me extraordinary talents for the art, and his encomiums awakened all my ardor. What a blissful period of my existence was it that I passed beneath his roof! Another being seemed created within me; or rather, all that was amiable and excellent was drawn out. I was as recluse as ever I had been at the convent, but how different was my seclusion! My time was spent in storing my mind with lofty and poetical ideas; in meditating on all that was striking and noble in history and fiction; in studying and tracing all that was sublime and beautiful in nature. I was always a visionary, imaginative being, but now my reveries and imaginings all elevated me to rapture. I looked up to my master as to a benevolent genius that had opened to me a region of enchantment. He was not a native of Genoa, but had been drawn thither by the solicitations of several of the nobility, and had resided there but a few years for the completion of certain works. His health was delicate, and he had to confide much of the filling up of his designs to the pencils of his scholars. He considered me as particularly happy in delineating the human countenance; in seizing upon characteristic though fleeting expressions, and fixing them powerfully upon my canvas. I was employed continually, therefore, in sketching faces, and often, when some particular grace or beauty of expression was wanted in a countenance, it was intrusted to my pencil. My benefactor was fond of bringing me forward; and partly, perhaps, through my actual skill, and partly through his partial praises, I began to be noted for the expressions of my countenances.

Among the various works which he had undertaken was an historical piece for one of the palaces of Genoa, in which were to be introduced the likenesses of several of the family. Among these was one intrusted to my pencil. It was that of a young girl, as yet in a convent for her education. She came out for the purpose of sitting for the picture. I first saw her in an apartment of one of the sumptuous palaces of Genoa. She stood before a casement that looked out upon the bay; a stream of vernal sunshine fell upon her, and shed a kind of glory round her, as it lit up the rich crimson chamber. She was but sixteen years of age—and oh, how lovely! The scene broke upon me like a mere vision of spring and youth and beauty. I could have fallen down and worshipped her. She was like one of those fictions of poets and painters, when they would express the *beau ideal* that haunts their minds with shapes of indescribable perfection. I was permitted to watch her countenance in various positions, and I fondly protracted the study that was undoing me. The more I gazed on her, the more I became enamoured; there was something almost painful in my intense admiration. I was but nineteen years of age, shy, diffident, and inexperienced.

I was treated with attention by her mother; for my youth and my enthusiasm in my art had won favor for me; and I am inclined to think something in my air and manner inspired interest and respect. Still the kindness with which I was treated could not dispel the embarrassment into which my own imagination threw me when in the presence of this lovely being. It elevated her into something almost more than mortal. She seemed too exquisite for earthly use; too delicate and exalted for human attainment. As I sat tracing her charms on my canvas, with my eyes occasionally riveted on her features, I drank in delicious poison that made me giddy. My heart alternately gushed with tenderness and ached with despair. Now I became more than ever sensible of the violent fires that had lain dormant at the bottom of my soul. You who were born in a more temperate climate, and under a cooler sky, have little idea of the violence of passion in southern bosoms.

A few days finished my task. Bianca returned to her convent, but sensible of the violent fires that had lain dormant at the bottom of my imagination; it became my pervading idea of beauty. It had an effect even upon my pencil. I became noted for my felicity in depicting female loveliness: it was but because I multiplied the image of Bianca. I soothed and yet fed my fancy by introducing her in all the productions of my master. I have stood, with delight, in one of the chapels of the Annunciata, and heard the crowd extol the seraphic beauty of a saint which I had painted. I have seen them bow down in adoration before the painting; they were bowing before the loveliness of Bianca.

I existed in this kind of dream, I might almost say delirium, for upwards of a year. Such is the tenacity of my imagination, that the image formed in it continued in all its power and freshness. Indeed, I was a solitary, meditative being, much given to reverie, and apt to foster ideas which had once taken strong possession of me. I was roused from this fond, melancholy, delicious dream by the death of my worthy benefactor. I cannot describe the pangs his death occasioned me. It left me alone, and almost broken-hearted. He bequeathed to me his little property, which, from the liberality of his disposition, and his expensive style of living, was indeed but small; and he most particularly recommended me, in dying, to the protection of a nobleman who had been his patron.

The latter was a man who passed for munificent. He was a lover and an encourager of the arts, and evidently wished to be thought so. He fancied he saw in me indications of future excellence; my pencil had already attracted attention; he took me at once under his protection. Seeing that I was overwhelmed with grief, and incapable of exerting my-

self in the mansion of my late benefactor, he invited me to sojourn for a time at a villa which he possessed on the border of the sea, in the picturesque neighborhood of Sestri di Ponente.

I found at the villa the count's only son, Filippo. He was nearly of my age; prepossessing in his appearance and fascinating in his manners, he attached himself to me, and seemed to court my good opinion. I thought there was something of profession in his kindness, and of caprice in his disposition; but I had nothing else near me to attach myself to, and my heart felt the need of something to repose upon. His education had been neglected; he looked upon me as his superior in mental powers and acquirements, and tacitly acknowledged my superiority. I felt that I was his equal in birth, and that gave independence to my manners, which had its effect. The caprice and tyranny I saw sometimes exercised on others, over whom he had power, were never manifested towards me. We became intimate friends and frequent companions. Still I loved to be alone, and to indulge in the reveries of my own imagination among the scenery by which I was surrounded. The villa commanded a wide view of the Mediterranean, and of the picturesque Ligurian coast. It stood alone in the midst of ornamented grounds, finely decorated with statues and fountains, and laid out in groves and alleys and shady lawns. Everything was assembled here that could gratify the taste or agreeably occupy the mind. Soothed by the tranquillity of this elegant retreat, the turbulence of my feelings gradually subsided, and blending with the romantic spell which still reigned over my imagination, produced a soft, voluptuous melancholy.

I had not been long under the roof of the count, when our solitude was enlivened by another inhabitant. It was a daughter of a relative of the count, who had lately died in reduced circumstances, bequeathing this only child to his protection. I had heard much of her beauty from Filippo, but my fancy had become so engrossed by one idea of beauty, as not to admit of any other. We were in the central saloon of the villa when she arrived. She was still in mourning, and approached, leaning on the count's arm. As they ascended the marble portico, I was struck by the grace with which the *mezzaro*, the bewitching veil of Genoa, was folded about her slender form. They entered. Heavens! what was my surprise when I beheld Bianca before me! It was herself; pale with grief, but still more matured in loveliness than when I had last beheld her. The time that had elapsed had developed the graces of her person, and the sorrow she had undergone had diffused over her countenance an irresistible tenderness.

She blushed and trembled at seeing me, and tears rushed into her eyes, for she remembered in whose company she had been accustomed

to behold me. For my part, I cannot express what were my emotions. By degrees I overcame the extreme shyness that had formerly paralyzed me in her presence. We were drawn together by sympathy of situation. We had each lost our best friend in the world; we were each, in some measure, thrown upon the kindness of others. When I came to know her intellectually all my ideal picturings of her were confirmed. Her newness to the world, her delightful susceptibility to everything beautiful and agreeable in nature, reminded me of my own emotions when first I escaped from the convent. Her rectitude of thinking delighted my judgment; the sweetness of her nature wrapped itself round my heart; and then her young, and tender, and budding loveliness, lent a delicious madness to my brain.

I gazed upon her with a kind of idolatry, as something more than mortal; and I felt humiliated at the idea of my comparative unworthiness. Yet she was mortal; and one of mortality's most susceptible and loving compounds,—for she loved me!

How first I discovered the transporting truth I cannot recollect. I believe it stole upon me by degrees as a wonder past hope or belief. We were both at such a tender and loving age; in constant intercourse with each other; mingling in the same elegant pursuits,—for music, poetry, and painting were our mutual delights, and we were almost separated from society among lovely and romantic scenery. Is it strange that two young hearts, thus brought together, should readily twine round each other?

Oh, gods! what a dream—a transient dream of unalloyed delight—then passed over my soul! Then it was that the world around me was indeed a paradise; for I had woman—lovely, delicious woman, to share it with me! How often have I rambled along the picturesque shores of Sestri, or climbed its wild mountains, with the coast gemmed with villas, and the blue sea far below me, and the slender Faro of Genoa on its romantic promontory in the distance; and as I sustained the faltering steps of Bianca, have thought there could no unhappiness enter into so beautiful a world! How often have we listened together to the nightingale, as it poured forth its rich notes among the moonlight bowers of the garden, and have wondered that poets could ever have fancied anything melancholy in its song! Why, oh why is this budding season of life and tenderness so transient! why is this rosy cloud of love, that sheds such a glow over the morning of our days, so prone to brew up into the whirlwind and storm!

I was the first to awaken from this blissful delirium of the affections. I had gained Bianca's heart, what was I to do with it? I had no wealth nor prospect to entitle me to her hand; was I to take advantage of her

ignorance of the world, of her confiding affection, and draw her down to my own poverty? Was this requiting the hospitality of the count? was this requiting the love of Bianca?

Now first I began to feel that even successful love may have its bitterness. A corroding care gathered about my heart. I moved about the palace like a guilty being. I felt as if I had abused its hospitality, as if I were a thief within its walls. I could no longer look with unembarrassed mien in the countenance of the count. I accused myself of perfidy to him, and I thought he read it in my looks, and began to distrust and despise me. His manner had always been ostentatious and condescending; it now appeared cold and haughty. Filippo, too, became reserved and distant; or at least I suspected him to be so. Heavens! was this the mere coinage of my brain? Was I to become suspicious of all the world? a poor, surmising wretch; watching looks and gestures; and torturing myself with misconstructions? Or, if true, was I to remain beneath a roof where I was merely tolerated, and linger there on sufferance? "This is not to be endured!" exclaimed I: "I will tear myself from this state of self-abasement—I will break through this fascination, and fly—fly!— Whither? from the world? for where is the world when I leave Bianca behind me?"

My spirit was naturally proud, and swelled within me at the idea of being looked upon with contumely. Many times I was on the point of declaring my family and rank, and asserting my equality in the presence of Bianca, when I thought her relations assumed an air of superiority. But the feeling was transient. I considered myself discarded and condemned by my family; and had solemnly vowed never to own relationship to them until they themselves should claim it.

The struggle of my mind preyed upon my happiness and my health. It seemed as if the uncertainty of being loved would be less intolerable than thus to be assured of it, and yet not dare to enjoy the conviction. I was no longer the enraptured admirer of Bianca; I no longer hung in ecstasy on the tones of her voice, nor drank in with insatiate gaze the beauty of her countenance. Her very smiles ceased to delight me, for I felt culpable in having won them.

She could not but be sensible of the change in me, and inquired the cause with her usual frankness and simplicity. I could not evade the inquiry, for my heart was full to aching. I told her all the conflict of my soul; my devouring passion, my bitter self-upbraiding. "Yes," said I, "I am unworthy of you. I am an offcast from my family—a wanderer—a nameless, homeless wanderer—with nothing but poverty for my portion; and yet I have dared to love you—have dared to aspire to your love."

My agitation moved her to tears, but she saw nothing in my situation

so hopeless as I had depicted it. Brought up in a convent, she knew nothing of the world—its wants—its cares: and indeed what woman is a worldly casuist in the matters of the heart? Nay, more, she kindled into sweet enthusiasm when she spoke of my fortunes and myself. We had dwelt together on the works of the famous masters. I related to her their histories; the high reputation, the influence, the magnificence to which they had attained. The companions of princes, the favorites of kings, the pride and boast of nations. All this she applied to me. Her love saw nothing in all their great productions that I was not able to achieve; and when I beheld the lovely creature glow with fervor, and her whole countenance radiant with visions of my glory, I was snatched up for the moment into the heaven of her own imagination.

I am dwelling too long upon this part of my story; yet I cannot help lingering over a period of my life on which, with all its cares and conflicts, I look back with fondness, for as yet my soul was unstained by a crime. I do not know what might have been the result of this struggle between pride, delicacy, and passion, had I not read in a Neapolitan gazette an account of the sudden death of my brother. It was accompanied by an earnest inquiry for intelligence concerning me, and a prayer, should this meet my eye, that I would hasten to Naples to comfort an infirm and afflicted father.

I was naturally of an affectionate disposition, but my brother had never been as a brother to me. I had long considered myself as disconnected from him, and his death caused me but little emotion. The thoughts of my father, infirm and suffering, touched me, however, to the quick; and when I thought of him, that lofty, magnificent being, now bowed down and desolate, and suing to me for comfort, all my resentment for past neglect was subdued, and a glow of filial affection was awakened within me.

The predominant feeling, however, that overpowered all others, was transport at the sudden change in my whole fortunes. A home, a name, rank, wealth, awaited me; and love painted a still more rapturous prospect in the distance. I hastened to Bianca, and threw myself at her feet. "Oh, Bianca!" exclaimed I, "at length I can claim you for my own. I am no longer a nameless adventurer, a neglected, rejected outcast. Look—read—behold the tidings that restore me to my name and to myself!"

I will not dwell on the scene that ensued. Bianca rejoiced in the reverse of my situation because she saw it lightened my heart of a load of care; for her own part, she had loved me for myself, and had never doubted that my own merits would command both fame and fortune.

I now felt all my native pride buoyant within me. I no longer walked

with my eyes bent to the dust; hope elevated them to the skies—my soul was lit up with fresh fires, and beamed from my countenance.

I wished to impart the change in my circumstances to the count; to let him know who and what I was—and to make formal proposals for the hand of Bianca; but he was absent on a distant estate. I opened my whole soul to Filippo. Now first I told him of my passion, of the doubts and fears that had distracted me, and of the tidings that had suddenly dispelled them. He overwhelmed me with congratulations, and with the warmest expressions of sympathy; I embraced him in the fulness of my heart,—I felt compunctions for having suspected him of coldness, and asked his forgiveness for ever having doubted his friendship.

Nothing is so warm and enthusiastic as a sudden expansion of the heart between young men. Filippo entered into our concerns with the most eager interest. He was our confidant and counsellor. It was determined that I should hasten at once to Naples, to re-establish myself in my father's affections and my paternal home; and the moment the reconciliation was effected, and my father's consent insured, I should return and demand Bianca of the count. Filippo engaged to secure his father's acquiescence; indeed, he undertook to watch over our interest, and to be the channel through which we might correspond.

My parting with Bianca was tender—delicious—agonizing. It was in a little pavilion of the garden which had been one of our favorite resorts. How often and often did I return to have one more adieu, to have her look once more on me in speechless emotion; to enjoy once more the rapturous sight of those tears streaming down her lovely cheeks; to seize once more on that delicate hand, the frankly accorded pledge of love, and cover it with tears and kisses! Heavens! there is a delight even in the parting agony of two lovers, worth a thousand tame pleasures of the world. I have her at this moment before my eyes, at the window of the pavilion, putting aside the vines which clustered about the casement, her form beaming forth in virgin light, her countenance all tears and smiles, sending a thousand and a thousand adieus after me, as hesitating, in a delirium of fondness and agitation, I faltered my way down the avenue.

As the bark bore me out of the harbor of Genoa, how eagerly my eye stretched along the coast of Sestri till it discovered the villa gleaming from among the trees at the foot of the mountain. As long as day lasted I gazed and gazed upon it, till it lessened and lessened to a mere white speck in the distance; and still my intense and fixed gaze discerned it, when all other objects of the coast had blended into indistinct confusion, or were lost in the evening gloom.

On arriving at Naples, I hastened to my paternal home. My heart

yearned for the long-withheld blessing of a father's love. As I entered
the proud portal of the ancestral palace, my emotions were so great that
I could not speak. No one knew me,—the servants gazed at me with
curiosity and surprise. A few years of intellectual elevation and development had made a prodigious change in the poor fugitive stripling from
the convent. Still, that no one should know me in my rightful home
was overpowering. I felt like the prodigal son returned. I was a stranger
in the house of my father. I burst into tears and wept aloud. When I
made myself known, however, all was changed. I, who had once been
almost repulsed from its walls, and forced to fly as an exile, was welcomed back with acclamation, with servility. One of the servants hastened to prepare my father for my reception; my eagerness to receive the
paternal embrace was so great that I could not await his return, but
hurried after him. What a spectacle met my eyes as I entered the chamber! My father, whom I had left in the pride of vigorous age, whose
noble and majestic bearing had so awed my young imagination, was
bowed down and withered into decrepitude. A paralysis had ravaged
his stately form, and left it a shaking ruin. He sat propped up in his
chair, with pale, relaxed visage, and glassy, wandering eye. His intellects had evidently shared in the ravages of his frame. The servant was
endeavoring to make him comprehend that a visitor was at hand. I
tottered up to him, and sank at his feet. All his past coldness and neglect were forgotten in his present sufferings. I remembered only that he
was my parent, and that I had deserted him. I clasped his knee; my
voice was almost filled with convulsive sobs.

"Pardon! oh! my father!" was all that I could utter. His apprehension
seemed slowly to return to him. He gazed at me for some moments
with a vague, inquiring look; a convulsive tremor quivered about his
lips: he feebly extended a shaking hand; laid it upon my head, and
burst into an infantine flow of tears.

From that moment he would scarcely spare me from his sight. I appeared the only object that his heart responded to in the world; all else
was as a blank to him. He had almost lost the power of speech, and the
reasoning faculty seemed at an end. He was mute and passive, excepting
that fits of childlike weeping would sometimes come over him without
any immediate cause. If I left the room at any time, his eye was incessantly fixed on the door till my return, and on my entrance there was
another gush of tears.

To talk with him of all my concerns, in this ruined state of mind,
would have been worse than useless; to have left him for ever so short
a time would have been cruel, unnatural. Here, then, was a new trial
for my affections. I wrote to Bianca an account of my return, and of my

actual situation, painting in colors vivid, for they were true, the torments I suffered at our being thus separated; for the youthful lover
every day of absence is an age of love lost. I enclosed the letter in one
to Filippo, who was the channel of our correspondence. I received a
reply from him full of friendship and sympathy; from Bianca, full of
assurances of affection and constancy. Week after week, and month after month elapsed, without making any change in my circumstances.
The vital flame which had seemed nearly extinct when first I met my
father, kept fluttering on without any apparent diminution. I watched
him constantly, faithfully,—I had almost said patiently. I knew that his
death alone would set me free—yet I never at any moment wished it. I
felt too glad to be able to make any atonement for past disobedience;
and denied, as I had been, all endearments of relationship in my early
days, my heart yearned towards a father, who, in his age and helplessness, had thrown himself entirely on me for comfort.

My passion for Bianca gained daily more force from absence: by
constant meditation it wore itself a deeper and deeper channel. I made
no new friends nor acquaintances; sought none of the pleasures of
Naples, which my rank and fortune threw open to me. Mine was a
heart that confined itself to few objects, but dwelt upon them with the
intenser passion. To sit by my father, administer to his wants, and to
meditate on Bianca in the silence of his chamber, was my constant
habit. Sometimes I amused myself with my pencil, in portraying the
image ever present to my imagination. I transferred to canvas every
look and smile of hers that dwelt in my heart. I showed them to my
father, in hopes of awakening an interest in his bosom for the mere
shadow of my love; but he was too far sunk in intellect to take any notice of them. When I received a letter from Bianca, it was a new source
of solitary luxury. Her letters, it is true, were less and less frequent, but
they were always full of assurances of unabated affection. They
breathed not the frank and innocent warmth with which she expressed
herself in conversation, but I accounted for it from the embarrassment
which inexperienced minds have often to express themselves upon paper. Filippo assured me of her unaltered constancy. They both lamented, in the strongest terms, our continued separation, though they
did justice to the filial piety that kept me by my father's side.

Nearly two years elapsed in this protracted exile. To me they were so
many ages. Ardent and impetuous by nature, I scarcely know how I
should have supported so long an absence, had I not felt assured that
the faith of Bianca was equal to my own. At length my father died. Life
went out from him almost imperceptibly. I hung over him in mute affliction, and watched the expiring spasms of nature. His last faltering ac-

cents whispered repeatedly a blessing on me. Alas! how has it been fulfilled!

When I had paid due honors to his remains and laid them in the
tomb of our ancestors, I arranged briefly my affairs, put them in a posture to be easily at my command from a distance, and embarked once
more with a bounding heart for Genoa.

Our voyage was propitious, and oh! what was my rapture, when first,
in the dawn of morning I saw the shadowy summits of the Apennines
rising almost like clouds above the horizon! The sweet breath of summer just moved us over the long wavering billows that were rolling us
on towards Genoa. By degrees the coast of Sestri rose like a creation of
enchantment from the silver bosom of the deep. I beheld the line of villages and palaces studding its borders. My eye reverted to a well-known
point, and at length, from the confusion of distant objects, it singled
out the villa which contained Bianca. It was a mere speck in the landscape, but glimmering from afar, the polar star of my heart.

Again I gazed at it for a livelong summer's day, but oh! how different
the emotion between departure and return. It now kept growing and
growing, instead of lessening and lessening on my sight. My heart
seemed to dilate with it. I looked at it through a telescope. I gradually
defined one feature after another. The balconies of the central saloon
where first I met Bianca beneath its roof; the terrace where we so often
had passed the delightful summer evenings; the awning which shaded
her chamber-window; I almost fancied I saw her beneath it. Could she
but know her lover was in the bark whose white sail now gleamed on
the sunny bosom of the sea! My fond impatience increased as we neared
the coast; the ship seemed to lag lazily over the billows; I could almost
have sprang into the sea, and swam to the desired shore.

The shadows of evening gradually shrouded the scene; but the moon
arose in all her fulness and beauty, and shed the tender light, so dear to
lovers, over the romantic coast of Sestri. My soul was bathed in unut-
terable tenderness. I anticipated the heavenly evenings I should pass in
once more wandering with Bianca by the light of that blessed moon.

It was late at night before we entered the harbor. As early next morning as I could get released from the formalities of landing, I threw myself on horseback, and hastened to the villa. As I galloped round the
rocky promontory on which stands the Faro, and saw the coast of Sestri
opening upon me, a thousand anxieties and doubts suddenly sprang up
in my bosom. There is something fearful in returning to those we love,
while yet uncertain what ills or changes absence may have effected. The
turbulence of my agitation shook my very frame. I spurred my horse to
redoubled speed; he was covered with foam when we both arrived pant-

ing at the gateway that opened to the grounds around the villa. I left my horse at a cottage, and walked through the grounds, that I might regain tranquillity for the approaching interview. I chid myself for having suffered mere doubts and surmises thus suddenly to overcome me; but I was always prone to be carried away by gusts of the feelings.

On entering the garden, everything bore the same look as when I had left it; and this unchanged aspect of things reassured me. There were the alleys in which I had so often walked with Bianca, as we listened to the song of the nightingale; the same shades under which we had so often sat during the noontide heat. There were the same flowers of which she was so fond; and which appeared still to be under the ministry of her hand. Everything looked and breathed of Bianca; hope and joy flushed in my bosom at every step. I passed a little arbor, in which we had often sat and read together;—a book and glove lay on the bench —it was Bianca's glove; it was a volume of the *Metastasio* I had given her. The glove lay in my favorite passage. I clasped them to my heart with rapture. "All is safe!" exclaimed I; "she loves me, she is still my own!"

·I bounded lightly along the avenue, down which I had faltered at my departure. I beheld her favorite pavilion, which had witnessed our parting scene. The window was open, with the same vine clambering about it, precisely as when she waved and wept me an adieu. Oh how transporting was the contrast in my situation! As I passed near the pavilion, I heard the tones of a female voice: they thrilled through me with an appeal to my heart not to be mistaken. Before I could think I *felt* they were Bianca's. For an instant I paused, overpowered with agitation. I feared to break so suddenly upon her. I softly ascended the steps of the pavilion. The door was open. I saw Bianca seated at a table; her back was towards me; she was warbling a soft melancholy air, and was occupied in drawing. A glance sufficed to show me that she was copying one of my own paintings. I gazed on her for a moment in a delicious tumult of emotions. She paused in her singing: a heavy sigh, almost a sob, followed. I could no longer contain myself. "Bianca!" exclaimed I, in a half-smothered voice. She started at the sound, brushed back the ringlets that hung clustering about her face, darted a glance at me, uttered a piercing shriek, and would have fallen to the earth, had I not caught her in my arms.

"Bianca! my own Bianca!" exclaimed I, folding her to my bosom, my voice stifled in sobs of convulsive joy. She lay in my arms without sense or motion. Alarmed at the effects of my precipitation, I scarce knew what to do. I tried by a thousand endearing words to call her back to consciousness. She slowly recovered, and half opened her eyes.—

"Where am I?" murmured she faintly. "Here!" exclaimed I, pressing her close to my bosom, "close to the heart that adores you—in the arms of your faithful Ottavio!" "Oh, no! no! no!" shrieked she, starting into sudden life and terror,—"away! away! leave me! leave me!"

She tore herself from my arms; rushed to a corner of the saloon and covered her face with her hands, as if the very sight of me were baleful. I was thunderstruck. I could not believe my senses. I followed her, trembling—confounded. I endeavored to take her hand; but she shrunk from my very touch with horror.

"Good heavens, Bianca!" exclaimed I, "what is the meaning of this? Is this my reception after so long an absence? Is this the love you professed for me?"

At the mention of love, a shuddering ran through her. She turned to me a face wild with anguish: "No more of that—no more of that!" gasped she; "talk not of love—I—I—am married!"

I reeled as if I had received a mortal blow—a sickness struck to my very heart. I caught at a window-frame for support. For a moment or two everything was chaos around me. When I recovered, I beheld Bianca lying on a sofa, her face buried in the pillow, and sobbing convulsively. Indignation for her fickleness for a moment overpowered every other feeling.

"Faithless! perjured!" cried I, striding across the room. But another glance at that beautiful being in distress checked all my wrath. Anger could not dwell together with her idea in my soul.

"Oh! Bianca," exclaimed I, in anguish, "could I have dreamt of this? Could I have suspected you would have been false to me?"

She raised her face all streaming with tears, all disordered with emotion, and gave me one appealing look. "False to you? They told me you were dead!"

"What," said I, "in spite of our constant correspondence?"

She gazed wildly at me; "Correspondence? what correspondence?"

"Have you not repeatedly received and replied to my letters?"

She clasped her hands with solemnity and fervor. "As I hope for mercy—never!"

A horrible surmise shot through my brain. "Who told you I was dead?"

"It was reported that the ship in which you embarked for Naples perished at sea."

"But who told you the report?"

She paused for an instant, and trembled;—"Filippo!"

"May the God of heaven curse him!" cried I, extending my clinched fists aloft.

"Oh, do not curse him, do not curse him!" exclaimed she; "he is—he is—my husband!"

This was all that was wanting to unfold the perfidy that had been practised upon me. My blood boiled like liquid fire in my veins. I gasped with rage too great for utterance—I remained for a time bewildered by the whirl of horrible thoughts that rushed through my mind. The poor victim of deception before me thought it was with her I was incensed. She faintly murmured forth her exculpation. I will not dwell upon it. I saw in it more than she meant to reveal. I saw with a glance how both of us had been betrayed.

" 'Tis well," muttered I to myself in smothered accents of concentrated fury. "He shall render an account of all this."

Bianca overheard me. New terror flashed in her countenance. "For mercy's sake, do not meet him!—say nothing of what has passed—for my sake say nothing to him—I only shall be the sufferer!"

A new suspicion darted across my mind.—"What!" exclaimed I, "do you then *fear* him? is he *unkind* to you? Tell me," reiterated I, grasping her hand and looking her eagerly in the face, "tell me—*dares* he to use you harshly?"

"No! no! no!" cried she, faltering and embarrassed; but the glance at her face had told volumes. I saw in her pallid and wasted features, in the prompt terror and subdued agony of her eye, a whole history of a mind broken down by tyranny. Great God! and was this beauteous flower snatched from me to be thus trampled upon? The idea roused me to madness. I clinched my teeth and hands; I foamed at the mouth; every passion seemed to have resolved itself into the fury that like a lava boiled within my heart. Bianca shrunk from me in speechless affright. As I strode by the window, my eye darted down the alley. Fatal moment! I beheld Filippo at a distance! my brain was in delirium—I sprang from the pavilion, and was before him with the quickness of lightning. He saw me as I came rushing upon him—he turned pale, looked wildly to right and left, as if he would have fled, and trembling, drew his sword.

"Wretch!" cried I, "well may you draw your weapon!"

I spoke not another word—I snatched forth a stiletto, put by the sword which trembled in his hand, and buried my poniard in his bosom. He fell with the blow, but my rage was unsated. I sprang upon him with the blood-thirsting feeling of a tiger; redoubled my blows; mangled him in my frenzy, grasped him by the throat until, with reiterated wounds and strangling convulsions, he expired in my grasp. I remained glaring on the countenance, horrible in death, that seemed to

stare back with its protruded eyes upon me. Piercing shrieks roused me from my delirium. I looked round and beheld Bianca flying distractedly towards us. My brain whirled—I waited not to meet her; but fled from the scene of horror. I fled forth from the garden like another Cain,—a hell within my bosom, and a curse upon my head. I fled without knowing whither, almost without knowing why. My only idea was to get farther and farther from the horrors I had left behind; as if I could throw space between myself and my conscience. I fled to the Apennines, and wandered for days and days among their savage heights. How I existed, I cannot tell; what rocks and precipices I braved, and how I braved them, I know not. I kept on and on, trying to out-travel the curse that clung to me. Alas! the shrieks of Bianca rung forever in my ears. The horrible countenance of my victim was forever before my eyes. The blood of Filippo cried to me from the ground. Rocks, trees, and torrents, all resounded with my crime. Then it was I felt how much more insupportable is the anguish of remorse than every other mental pang. Oh! could I but have cast off this crime that festered in my heart—could I but have regained the innocence that reigned in my breast as I entered the garden at Sestri—could I have but restored my victim to life, I felt as if I could look on with transport, even though Bianca were in his arms.

By degrees this frenzied fever of remorse settled into a permanent malady of the mind—into one of the most horrible that ever poor wretch was cursed with. Wherever I went, the countenance of him I had slain appeared to follow me. Whenever I turned my head, I beheld it behind me, hideous with the contortions of the dying moment. I have tried in every way to escape from this horrible phantom, but in vain. I know not whether it be an illusion of the mind, the consequence of my dismal education at the convent, or whether a phantom really sent by Heaven to punish me, but there it ever is—at all times—in all places. Nor has time nor habit had any effect in familiarizing me with its terrors. I have travelled from place to place—plunged into amusements—tried dissipation and distraction of every kind—all—all in vain. I once had recourse to my pencil, as a desperate experiment. I painted an exact resemblance of this phantom-face. I placed it before me, in hopes that by constantly contemplating the copy I might diminish the effect of the original. But I only doubled instead of diminishing the misery. Such is the curse that has clung to my footsteps—that has made my life a burden, but the thought of death terrible. God knows what I have suffered—what days and days, and nights and nights of sleepless torment—what a never-dying worm has preyed upon my

heart—what an unquenchable fire has burned within my brain! He knows the wrongs that wrought upon my poor weak nature; that converted the tenderest of affections into the deadliest of fury. He knows best whether a frail erring creature has expiated by long-enduring torture and measureless remorse the crime of a moment of madness. Often, often have I prostrated myself in the dust, and implored that He would give me a sign of His forgiveness, and let me die—

Thus far had I written some time since. I had meant to leave this record of misery and crime with you, to be read when I should be no more.

My prayer to Heaven has at length been heard. You were witness to my emotions last evening at the church, when the vaulted temple resounded with the words of atonement and redemption. I heard a voice speaking to me from the midst of the music; I heard it rising above the pealing of the organ and the voices of the choir—it spoke to me in tones of celestial melody—it promised mercy and forgiveness, but demanded from me full expiation. I go to make it. To-morrow I shall be on my way to Genoa to surrender myself to justice. You who have pitied my sufferings, who have poured the balm of sympathy into my wounds, do not shrink from my memory with abhorrence now that you know my story. Recollect, that when you read of my crime I shall have atoned for it with my blood!

When the Baronet had finished, there was a universal desire expressed to see the painting of this frightful visage. After much entreaty the Baronet consented, on condition that they should only visit it one by one. He called his housekeeper, and gave her charge to conduct the gentlemen, singly, to the chamber. They all returned varying in their stories: some affected in one way, some in another; some more, some less; but all agreeing that there was a certain something about the painting that had a very odd effect upon the feelings.

I stood in a deep bow-window with the Baronet, and could not help but expressing my wonder. "After all," said I, "there are certain mysteries in our nature, certain inscrutable impulses and influences, which warrant one in being superstitious. Who can account for so many persons of different characters being thus strangely affected by a mere painting?"

"And especially when not one of them has seen it?" said the Baronet, with a smile.

"How!" exclaimed I, "not seen it?"

"Not one of them!" replied he, laying his finger on his lips, in sign of

secrecy. "I saw that some of them were in a bantering vein, and did not choose that the memento of the poor Italian should be made a jest of. So I gave the housekeeper a hint to show them all to a different chamber!"

Thus ends the stories of the Nervous Gentleman.

From *Tales of a Traveller*

Buckthorne and His Friends

This world is the best that we live in,
To lend, or to spend, or to give in;
But to beg, or to borrow, or get a man's own,
'T is the very worst world, sir, that ever was known.
Lines from an Inn Window

The following ten tales, which comprise one narrative, are taken from *Tales of a Traveller.*—C.N.

LITERARY LIFE

A MONG other subjects of a traveller's curiosity, I had at one time a great craving after anecdotes of literary life; and being at London, one of the most noted places for the production of books, I was excessively anxious to know something of the animals which produced them. Chance fortunately threw me in the way of a literary man by the name of Buckthorne, an eccentric personage, who had lived much in the metropolis, and could give me the natural history of every odd animal to be met with in that wilderness of men. He readily imparted to me some useful hints upon the subject of my inquiry.

"The literary world," said he, "is made up of little confederacies, each looking upon its own members as the lights of the universe; and considering all others as mere transient meteors, doomed soon to fall and be forgotten, while its own luminaries are to shine steadily on to immortality."

"And pray," said I, "how is a man to get a peep into those confederacies you speak of? I presume an intercourse with authors is a kind of intellectual exchange, where one must bring his commodities to barter, and always give a *quid pro quo*."

"Pooh, pooh! how you mistake," said Buckthorne, smiling; "you must never think to become popular among wits by shining. They go into society to shine themselves, not to admire the brilliancy of others. I once thought as you do, and never went into literary society without studying my part beforehand; the consequence was, that I soon got the name of an intolerable proser, and should in a little while have been completely excommunicated, had I not changed my plan of operations. No, sir, no character succeeds so well among wits as that of a good listener; or if ever you are eloquent, let it be when tête-à-tête with an author, and then in praise of his own works, or, what is nearly as acceptable, in disparagement of the works of his contemporaries. If ever he speaks favorably of the productions of a particular friend, dissent boldly from him; pronounce his friend to be a blockhead; never fear his being vexed. Much as people speak of the irritability of authors, I never found one to take offence at such contradictions. No, no, sir, authors are particularly candid in admitting the faults of their friends.

"Indeed, I would advise you to be exceedingly sparing of remarks on all modern works, except to make sarcastic observations on the most distinguished writers of the day."

"Faith," said I, "I'll praise none that have not been dead for at least half a century."

"Even then," observed Mr. Buckthorne, "I would advise you to be rather cautious; for you must know that many old writers have been enlisted under the banners of different sects, and their merits have become as completely topics of party discussion as the merits of living statesmen and politicians. Nay, there have been whole periods of literature absolutely taboo'd, to use a South Sea phrase. It is, for example, as much as a man's critical reputation is worth in some circles, to say a word in praise of any of the writers of the reign of Charles the Second, or even of Queen Anne, they being all declared Frenchmen in disguise."

"And pray," said I, "when am I then to know that I am on safe grounds, being totally unacquainted with the literary landmarks, and the boundary-line of fashionable taste."

"Oh!" replied he, "there is fortunately one tract of literature which forms a kind of neutral ground, on which all the literary meet amicably, and run riot in the excess of their good-humor; and this is in the reigns of Elizabeth and James. Here you may praise away at random. Here it is 'cut and come again'; and the more obscure the author, and the more quaint and crabbed his style, the more your admiration will smack of the real relish of the connoisseur; whose taste, like that of an epicure, is always for game that has an antiquated flavor.

"But," continued he, "as you seem anxious to know something of literary society, I will take an opportunity to introduce you to some coterie where the talents of the day are assembled. I cannot promise you, however, that they will all be of the first order. Somehow or other, our great geniuses are not gregarious; they do not go in flocks, but fly singly in general society. They prefer mingling like common men with the multitude, and are apt to carry nothing of the author about them but the reputation. It is only the inferior orders that herd together, acquire strength and importance by their confederacies, and bear all the distinctive characteristics of their species."

A LITERARY DINNER

A FEW days after this conversation with Mr. Buckthorne, he called upon me, and took me with him to a regular literary dinner. It was given by a great bookseller, or rather a company of booksellers, whose firm surpassed in length that of Shadrach, Meshech, and Abednego.

I was surprised to find between twenty and thirty guests assembled, most of whom I had never seen before. Mr. Buckthorne explained this to me, by informing me that this was a business-dinner, or kind of field-day which the house gave twice a year to its authors. It is true they did occasionally give snug dinners to three or four literary men at a time; but then these were generally select authors, favorites of the public, such as had arrived at their sixth or seventh editions. "There are," said he, "certain geographical boundaries in the land of literature, and you may judge tolerably well of an author's popularity by the wine his bookseller gives him. An author crosses the port line about the third edition, and gets into claret; and when he has reached the sixth or seventh, he may revel in champagne and burgundy."

"And pray," said I, "how far may these gentlemen have reached that I see around me? are any of these claret-drinkers?"

"Not exactly—not exactly. You find at these great dinners the common steady run of authors, one or two edition men; or if any others are invited, they are aware that it is a kind of republican meeting—you understand me—a meeting of the republic of letters; and that they must expect nothing but plain, substantial fare."

These hints enabled me to comprehend more fully the arrangement of the table. The two ends were occupied by two partners of the house; and the host seemed to have adopted Addison's idea as to the literary precedence of his guests. A popular poet had the post of honor; opposite to whom was a hot-pressed traveller in quarto with plates. A grave-looking antiquarian, who had produced several solid works, that were much quoted and little read, was treated with great respect, and seated next to a neat, dressy gentleman in black, who had written a thin, genteel, hot-pressed octavo on political economy, that was getting into fashion. Several three-volumed duodecimo men, of fair currency, were placed about the centre of the table; while the lower end was

taken up with small poets, translators, and authors who had not as yet risen into much notoriety.

The conversation during dinner was by fits and starts; breaking out here and there in various parts of the table in small flashes, and ending in smoke. The poet who had the confidence of a man on good terms with the world, and independent of his bookseller, was very gay and brilliant, and said many clever things which set the partner next him in a roar, and delighted all the company. The other partner, however, maintained his sedateness, and kept carving on, with the air of a thorough man of business, intent upon the occupation of the moment. His gravity was explained to me by my friend Buckthorne. He informed me that the concerns of the house were admirably distributed among the partners. "Thus, for instance," said he, "the grave gentleman is the carving partner, who attends to the joints; and the other is the laughing partner, who attends to the jokes."

The general conversation was chiefly carried on at the upper end of the table, as the authors there seemed to possess the greatest courage of the tongue. As to the crew at the lower end of the table, if they did not make much figure in talking, they did in eating. Never was there a more determined, inveterate, thoroughly sustained attack on the trencher than by this phalanx of masticators. When the cloth was removed, and wine began to circulate, they grew very merry and jocose among themselves. Their jokes, however, if by chance any of them reached the upper end of the table, seldom produced much effect. Even the laughing partner did not think it necessary to honor them with a smile; which my neighbor Buckthorne accounted for, by informing me that there was a certain degree of popularity to be obtained before a bookseller could afford to laugh at an author's jokes.

Among this crew of questionable gentlemen thus seated below the salt, my eye singled out one in particular. He was rather shabbily dressed; though he had evidently made the most of a rusty black coat, and wore his shirt-frill plaited and puffed out voluminously at the bosom. His face was dusky, but florid, perhaps a little too florid, particularly about the nose; though the rosy hue gave the greater lustre to a twinkling black eye. He had a little the look of a boon companion, with that dash of the poor devil in it which gives an inexpressible mellow tone to a man's humor. I had seldom seen a face of richer promise; but never was promise so ill kept. He said nothing, ate and drank with the keen appetite of a garreteer, and scarcely stopped to laugh, even at the good jokes from the upper end of the table. I inquired who he was. Buckthorne looked at him attentively: "Gad," said he, "I have seen that face before, but where I cannot recollect. He cannot be an author of

any note. I suppose some writer of sermons, or grinder of foreign travels."

After dinner we retired to another room to take tea and coffee, where we were reinforced by a cloud of inferior guests,—authors of small volumes in boards, and pamphlets stitched in blue paper. These had not as yet arrived to the importance of a dinner-invitation, but were invited occasionally to pass the evening in a friendly way. They were very respectful to the partners, and, indeed, seemed to stand a little in awe of them; but they paid devoted court to the lady of the house, and were extravagantly fond of the children. Some few, who did not feel confidence enough to make such advances, stood shyly off in corners, talking to one another; or turned over the portfolios of prints which they had not seen above five thousand times, or moused over the music on the forte-piano.

The poet and the thin octavo gentleman were the persons most current and at their ease in the drawing-room; being men evidently of circulation in the West End. They got on each side of the lady of the house, and paid her a thousand compliments and civilities, at some of which I thought she would have expired with delight. Everything they said and did had the odor of fashionable life. I looked round in vain for the poor devil author in the rusty black coat; he had disappeared immediately after leaving the table, having a dread, no doubt, of the glaring light of a drawing-room. Finding nothing further to interest my attention, I took my departure soon after coffee had been served, leaving the poet, and the thin, genteel, hot-pressed octavo gentleman, masters of the field.

THE CLUB OF QUEER FELLOWS

I THINK it was the very next evening that, in coming out of Covent Garden Theatre with my eccentric friend Buckthorne, he proposed to give me another peep at life and character. Finding me willing for any research of the kind, he took me through a variety of the narrow courts and lanes about Covent Garden, until we stopped before a tavern, from which we heard the bursts of merriment of a jovial party. There would be a loud peal of laughter, then an interval, then another peal, as if a prime wag were telling a story. After a little while there was a song, and at the close of each stanza a hearty roar, and a vehement thumping on the table.

"This is the place," whispered Buckthorne; "it is the club of Queer Fellows, a great resort of the small wits, third-rate actors, and newspaper critics of the theatres. Any one can go in on paying a sixpence at the bar for the use of the club."

We entered, therefore, without ceremony, and took our seats at a lone table, in a dusky corner of the room. The club was assembled round a table on which stood beverages of various kinds, according to the tastes of the individuals. The members were a set of queer fellows indeed; but what was my surprise on recognizing, in the prime wit of the meeting, the poor-devil author whom I had remarked at the booksellers' dinner for his promising face and his complete taciturnity. Matters, however, were entirely changed with him. There he was a mere cipher; here he was lord of the ascendant, the choice spirit, the dominant genius. He sat at the head of the table with his hat on, and an eye beaming even more luminously than his nose. He had a quip and a fillip for every one, and a good thing on every occasion. Nothing could be said or done without eliciting a spark from him: and I solemnly declare I have heard much worse wit even from noblemen. His jokes, it must be confessed, were rather wet, but they suited the circle over which he presided. The company were in that maudlin mood, when a little wit goes a great way. Every time he opened his lips there was sure to be a roar; and even sometimes before he had time to speak.

We were fortunate enough to enter in time for a glee composed by him expressly for the club, and which he sung with two boon com-

panions, who would have been worthy subjects for Hogarth's pencil. As they were each provided with a written copy, I was enabled to procure the reading of it.

> "Merrily, merrily, push round the glass,
>   And merrily troll the glee,
> For he who won't drink till he wink is an ass,
>   So, neighbor, I drink to thee.

> "Merrily, merrily, fuddle thy nose,
>   Until it right rosy shall be;
> For a jolly red nose, I speak under the rose,
>   Is a sign of good company."

We waited until the party broke up, and no one but the wit remained. He sat at the table with his legs stretched under it, and wide apart; his hands in his breeches-pockets; his head drooped upon his breast; and gazing with lack-lustre countenance on an empty tankard. His gaiety was gone, his fire completely quenched.

My companion approached, and startled him from his fit of brown study, introducing himself on the strength of their having dined together at the booksellers.

"By the way," said he, "it seems to me I have seen you before; your face is surely that of an old acquaintance, though for the life of me I cannot tell where I have known you."

"Very likely," replied he, with a smile; "many of my old friends have forgotten me. Though, to tell the truth, my memory in this instance is as bad as your own. If, however, it will assist your recollection in any way, my name is Thomas Dribble, at your service."

"What! Tom Dribble, who was at old Birchell's school in Warwickshire?"

"The same," said the other, coolly.

"Why, then, we are old schoolmates, though it's no wonder you don't recollect me. I was your junior by several years; don't you recollect little Jack Buckthorne?"

Here there ensued a scene of school-fellow recognition, and a world of talk about old school-times and school-pranks. Mr. Dribble ended by observing, with a heavy sigh, "that times were sadly changed since those days."

"Faith, Mr. Dribble," said I, "you seem quite a different man here from what you were at dinner. I had no idea that you had so much stuff in you. There you were all silence, but here you absolutely keep the table in a roar."

"Ah! my dear sir," replied he, with a shake of the head, and a shrug of the shoulder, "I am a mere glow-worm. I never shine by daylight. Besides, it's a hard thing for a poor devil of an author to shine at the table of a rich bookseller. Who do you think would laugh at anything I could say, when I had some of the current wits of the day about me? But here, though a poor devil, I am among still poorer devils than myself; men who look up to me as a man of letters, and a *belle-esprit*, and all my jokes pass as sterling gold from the mint."

"You surely do yourself injustice, sir," said I; "I have certainly heard more good things from you this evening than from any of those *beaux-esprits* by whom you appear to have been so daunted."

"Ah, sir! but they have luck on their side; they are in the fashion—there's nothing like being in fashion. A man that has once got his character up for a wit is always sure of a laugh, say what he may. He may utter as much nonsense as he pleases, and all will pass current. No one stops to question the coin of a rich man; but a poor devil cannot pass off either a joke or a guinea, without its being examined on both sides. Wit and coin are always doubted with a threadbare coat.

"For my part," continued he, giving his hat a twitch a little more on one side,—"for my part, I hate your fine dinners; there's nothing, sir, like the freedom of a chop-house. I'd rather, any time, have my steak and tankard among my own set, than drink claret and eat venison with your cursed civil, elegant company, who never laugh at a good joke from a poor devil for fear of its being vulgar. A good joke grows in a wet soil; it flourishes in low places, but wither on your d—d high, dry grounds. I once kept high company, sir, until I nearly ruined myself; I grew so dull, and vapid, and genteel. Nothing saved me but being arrested by my landlady, and thrown into prison; where a course of catch-clubs, eight-penny ale, and poor-devil company, manured my mind, and brought it back to itself again."

As it was now growing late, we parted for the evening, though I felt anxious to know more of this practical philosopher. I was glad, therefore, when Buckthorne proposed to have another meeting, to talk over old school-times, and inquired his schoolmate's address. The latter seemed at first a little shy of naming his lodgings; but suddenly, assuming an air of hardihood—"Green-arbor Court, sir," exclaimed he—"Number —— in Green-arbor Court. You must know the place. Classic ground, sir, classic ground! It was there Goldsmith wrote his *Vicar of Wakefield*—I always like to live in literary haunts."

I was amused with this whimsical apology for shabby quarters. On our way homeward, Buckthorne assured me that this Dribble had been the prime wit and great wag of the school in their boyish days, and one

of those unlucky urchins denominated bright geniuses. As he perceived me curious respecting his old schoolmate, he promised to take me with him in his proposed visit to Green-arbor Court.

A few mornings afterward he called upon me, and we set forth on our expedition. He led me through a variety of singular alleys, and courts, and blind passages; for he appeared to be perfectly versed in all the intricate geography of the metropolis. At length we came out upon Fleet Market, and traversing it, turned up a narrow street to the bottom of a long, steep flight of stone steps, called Break-neck Stairs. These, he told me, led up to Green-arbor Court, and that down them poor Goldsmith might many a time have risked his neck. When we entered the court, I could not but smile to think in what out-of-the-way corners genius produces her bantlings! And the muses, those capricious dames, who, forsooth, so often refuse to visit palaces, and deny a single smile to votaries in splendid studies, and gilded drawing-rooms,—what holes and burrows will they frequent to lavish their favors on some ragged disciple!

This Green-arbor Court I found to be a small square, surrounded by tall and miserable houses, the very intestines of which seemed turned inside out, to judge from the old garments and frippery fluttering from every window. It appeared to be a region of washerwomen, and lines were stretched about the little square, on which clothes were dangling to dry.

Just as we entered the square, a scuffle took place between two viragoes about a disputed right to a wash-tub, and immediately the whole community was in a hubbub. Heads in mob-caps popped out of every window, and such a clamor of tongues ensued, that I was fain to stop my ears. Every amazon took part with one or other of the disputants, and brandished her arms, dripping with soap-suds, and fired away from her window as from the embrazure of a fortress; while the swarms of children nestled and cradled in every procreant chamber of this hive, waking with the noise, set up their shrill pipes to swell the general concert.

Poor Goldsmith! what a time he must have had of it, with his quiet disposition and nervous habits, penned up in this den of noise and vulgarity! How strange that, while every sight and sound was sufficient to embitter the heart, and fill it with misanthropy, his pen should be dropping the honey of Hybla! Yet it is more than probable that he drew many of his inimitable pictures of low life from the scenes which surrounded him in this abode. The circumstance of Mrs. Tibbs being obliged to wash her husband's two shirts in a neighbor's house, who refused to lend her wash-tub, may have been no sport of fancy, but a fact

passing under his own eye. His landlady may have sat for the picture, and Beau Tibbs's scanty wardrobe have been a *fac-simile* of his own.

It was with some difficulty that we found our way to Dribble's lodgings. They were up two pair of stairs, in a room that looked upon the court; and when we entered, he was seated on the edge of his bed, writing at a broken table. He received us, however, with a free, open, poor-devil air, that was irresistible. It is true he did at first appear slightly confused; buttoned up his waistcoat a little higher, and tucked in a stray frill of linen. But he recollected himself in an instant; gave a half-swagger, half-leer, as he stepped forth to receive us; drew a three-legged stool for Mr. Buckthorne; pointed me to a lumbering old damask chair, that looked like a dethroned monarch in exile; and bade us welcome to his garret.

We soon got engaged in conversation. Buckthorne and he had much to say about early school-scenes; and as nothing opens a man's heart more than recollections of the kind, we soon drew from him a brief outline of his literary career.

THE POOR-DEVIL AUTHOR

I BEGAN life unluckily by being the wag and bright fellow at school; and I had the further misfortune of becoming the great genius of my native village. My father was a country attorney, and intended I should succeed him in business; but I had too much genius to study, and he was too fond of my genius to force it into the traces; so I fell into bad company, and took to bad habits. Do not mistake me. I mean that I fell into the company of village-literati, and village-blues, and took to writing village-poetry.

It was quite the fashion in the village to be literary. There was a little knot of choice spirits of us, who assembled frequently together, formed ourselves into a Literary, Scientific, and Philosophical Society, and fancied ourselves the most learned Philos in existence. Every one had a great character assigned him, suggested by some casual habit or affectation. One heavy fellow drank an enormous quantity of tea, rolled in his arm-chair, talked sententiously, pronounced dogmatically, and was considered a second Dr. Johnson; another, who happened to be a curate, uttered coarse jokes, wrote doggerel rhymes, and was the Swift of our association. Thus we had also our Popes, and Goldsmiths and Addisons; and a blue-stocking lady, whose drawing-room we frequented, who corresponded about nothing with all the world, who wrote letters with the stiffness and formality of a printed book, was cried up as another Mrs. Montagu. I was, by common consent, the juvenile prodigy, the poetical youth, the great genius, the pride and hope of the village, through whom it was to become one day as celebrated as Stratford-on-Avon.

My father died, and left me his blessing and his business. His blessing brought no money into my pocket; and as to his business, it soon deserted me; for I was busy writing poetry, and could not attend to law, and my clients, though they had great respect for my talents, had no faith in a poetical attorney.

I lost my business, therefore, spent my money, and finished my poem. It was the *Pleasures of Melancholy,* and was cried up to the skies by the whole circle. The *Pleasures of Imagination,* the *Pleasures of Hope,* and the *Pleasures of Memory,* though each had placed its author in the first rank of poets, were blank prose in comparison. Our Mrs.

Montagu would cry over it from beginning to end. It was pronounced by all the members of the Literary, Scientific, and Philosophical Society the greatest poem of the age, and all anticipated the noise it would make in the great world. There was no doubt but the London booksellers would be mad after it; and the only fear of my friends was, that I would make a sacrifice by selling it too cheap. Every time they talked the matter over, they increased the price. They reckoned up the great sums given for the poems of certain popular writers, and determined that mine was worth more than all put together, and ought to be paid for accordingly. For my part, I was modest in my expectations, and determined that I would be satisfied with a thousand guineas. So I put my poem in my pocket, and set off for London.

My journey was joyous. My heart was light as my purse, and my head was full of anticipations of fame and fortune. With what swelling pride did I cast my eyes upon old London from the heights of Highgate! I was like a general, looking down upon a place he expects to conquer. The great metropolis lay stretched before me, buried under a home-made cloud of murky smoke, that wrapped it from the brightness of a sunny day, and formed for it a kind of artificial bad weather. At the outskirts of the city, away to the west, the smoke gradually decreased until all was clear and sunny, and the view stretched uninterrupted to the blue line of the Kentish hills.

My eye turned fondly to where the mighty cupola of St. Paul's swelled dimly through this misty chaos, and I pictured to myself the solemn realm of learning that lies about its base. How soon should the *Pleasures of Melancholy* throw this world of booksellers and printers into a bustle of business and delight! How soon should I hear my name repeated by printers' devils throughout Paternoster Row, and Angel Court, and Ave-Maria Lane, until Amen Corner should echo back the sound!

Arrived in town, I repaired at once to the most fashionable publisher. Every new author patronizes him, of course. In fact, it had been determined in the village circle that he should be the fortunate man. I cannot tell you how vain-gloriously I walked the streets. My head was in the clouds. I felt the airs of heaven playing about it, and fancied it already encircled by a halo of literary glory. As I passed by the windows of book-shops, I anticipated the time when my work would be shining among the hot-pressed wonders of the day; and my face, scratched on copper, or cut on wood, figuring in fellowship with those of Scott, and Byron, and Moore.

When I applied at the publisher's house, there was something in the loftiness of my air, and the dinginess of my dress, that struck the clerks

with reverence. They doubtless took me for some person of conse-quence; probably a digger of Greek roots, or a penetrater of pyramids. A proud man in a dirty shirt is always an imposing character in the world of letters; one must feel intellectually secure before he can venture to dress shabbily; none but a great genius, or a great scholar, dares to be dirty; so I was ushered at once to the sanctum sanctorum of this high-priest of Minerva.

The publishing of books is a very different affair nowadays from what it was in the time of Bernard Lintot. I found the publisher a fash-ionably dressed man, in an elegant drawing-room, furnished with sofas, and portraits of celebrated authors, and cases of splendidly bound books. He was writing letters at an elegant table. This was transacting business in style. The place seemed suited to the magnificent publica-tions that issued from it. I rejoiced at the choice I had made of a pub-lisher, for I always liked to encourage men of taste and spirit.

I stepped up to the table with the lofty poetical port I had been ac-customed to maintain in our village circle; though I threw in it some-thing of a patronizing air, such as one feels when about to make a man's fortune. The publisher paused with his pen in hand, and seemed waiting in mute suspense to know what was to be announced by so singular an apparition.

I put him at his ease in a moment, for I felt that I had but to come, see, and conquer. I made known my name, and the name of my poem; produced my precious roll of blotted manuscript; laid it on the table with an emphasis; and told him at once, to save time, and come directly to the point, the price was one thousand guineas.

I had given him no time to speak, nor did he seem so inclined. He continued looking at me for a moment with an air of whimsical perplex-ity; scanned me from head to foot; looked down at the manuscript, then up again at me, then pointed to a chair; and whistling softly to himself, went on writing his letter.

I sat for some time waiting his reply, supposing he was making up his mind; but he only paused occasionally to take a fresh dip of ink, to stroke his chin, or the tip of his nose, and then resumed his writing. It was evident his mind was intently occupied upon some other subject; but I had no idea that any other subject could be attended to, and my poem lie unnoticed on the table. I had supposed that everything would make way for the *Pleasures of Melancholy*.

My gorge at length rose within me. I took up my manuscript, thrust it into my pocket, and walked out of the room; making some noise as I went out, to let my departure be heard. The publisher, however, was too much buried in minor concerns to notice it. I was suffered to walk

down-stairs without being called back. I sallied forth into the street, but no clerk was sent after me; nor did the publisher call after me from the drawing-room window. I have been told since that he considered me either a madman or a fool. I leave you to judge how much he was in the wrong in his opinion.

When I turned the corner, my crest fell. I cooled down in my pride and my expectations, and reduced my terms with the next bookseller to whom I applied. I had no better success, nor with a third, nor with a fourth. I then desired the booksellers to make an offer themselves; but the deuce an offer would they make. They told me poetry was a mere drug; everybody wrote poetry; the market was overstocked with it. And then they said, the title of my poem was not taking; that pleasures of all kinds were worn threadbare, nothing but horrors did nowadays, and even those were almost worn out. Tales of Pirates, Robbers, and bloody Turks, might answer tolerably well; but then they must come from some established, well-known name, or the public would not look at them.

At last I offered to leave my poem with a bookseller to read it, and judge for himself. "Why, really, my dear Mr.——, a—a—I forget your name," said he, casting his eye at my rusty coat and shabby gaiters; "really, sir, we are so pressed with business just now, and have so many manuscripts on hand to read, that we have not time to look at any new productions; but if you can call again in a week or two, or say the middle of next month, we may be able to look over your writings, and give you an answer. Don't forget, the month after next; good morning, sir; happy to see you any time you are passing this way." So saying, he bowed me out in the civilest way imaginable. In short, sir, instead of an eager competition to secure my poem, I could not even get it read! In the mean time I was harassed by letters from my friends, wanting to know when the work was to appear; who was to be my publisher; and, above all things, warning me not to let it go too cheap.

There was but one alternative left. I determined to publish the poem myself; and to have my triumph over the booksellers when it should become the fashion of the day. I accordingly published the *Pleasures of Melancholy*,—and ruined myself. Excepting the copies sent to the reviews, and to my friends in the country, not one, I believe, ever left the bookseller's warehouse. The printer's bill drained my purse; and the only notice that was taken of my work was contained in the advertisements paid for by myself.

I could have borne all this, and have attributed it, as usual, to the mismanagement of the publisher, or the want of taste in the public; and could have made the usual appeal to posterity; but my village friends

would not let me rest in quiet. They were picturing me to themselves feasting with the great, communing with the literary, and in the high career of fortune and renown. Every little while, some one would call on me with a letter of introduction from the village circle, recommending him to my attentions, and requesting that I would make him known in society; with a hint, that an introduction to a celebrated literary nobleman would be extremely agreeable. I determined, therefore, to change my lodgings, drop my correspondence, and disappear altogether from the view of my village admirers. Besides, I was anxious to make one more poetic attempt. I was by no means disheartened by the failure of my first. My poem was evidently too didactic. The public was wise enough. It no longer read for instruction. "They want horrors, do they?" said I: "I'faith! then they shall have enough of them." So I looked out for some quiet, retired place, where I might be out of the reach of my friends, and have leisure to cook up some delectable dish of poetical "hell-broth."

I had some difficulty in finding a place to my mind, when chance threw me in the way of Canonbury Castle. It is an ancient brick tower, hard by "merry Islington"; the remains of a hunting-seat of Queen Elizabeth, where she took the pleasure of the country when the neighborhood was all woodland. What gave it particular interest in my eyes was the circumstance that it had been the residence of a poet.

It was here Goldsmith resided when he wrote his "Deserted Village." I was shown the very apartment. It was a relic of the original style of the castle, with panelled wainscots and Gothic windows. I was pleased with its air of antiquity, and with its having been the residence of poor Goldy.

"Goldsmith was a pretty poet," said I to myself, "a very pretty poet, though rather of the old school. He did not think and feel so strongly as is the fashion nowadays; but had he lived in these times of hot hearts and hot heads, he would no doubt have written quite differently."

In a few days I was quietly established in my new quarters; my books all arranged; my writing-desk placed by a window looking out into the fields; and I felt as snug as Robinson Crusoe, when he had finished his bower. For several days I enjoyed all the novelty of the change and the charms which grace new lodgings, before one has found out their defects. I rambled about the fields where I fancied Goldsmith had rambled. I explored merry Islington; ate my solitary dinner at the Black Bull, which, according to tradition, was a country-seat of Sir Walter Raleigh; and would sit and sip my wine, and muse on old times, in a quaint old room, where many a council had been held.

All this did very well for a few days. I was stimulated by novelty; in-

spired by the associations awakened in my mind by these curious haunts; and began to think I felt the spirit of composition stirring within me. But Sunday came, and with it the whole city world, swarming about Canonbury Castle. I could not open my window but I was stunned with shouts and noises from the cricket-ground; the late quiet road beneath my window was alive with the tread of feet and clack of tongues; and, to complete my misery, I found that my quiet retreat was absolutely a "show-house," the tower and its contents being shown to strangers at sixpence a head.

There was a perpetual tramping up-stairs of citizens and their families, to look about the country from the top of the tower, and to take a peep at the city through the telescope, to try if they could discern their own chimneys. And then, in the midst of a vein of thought, or a moment of inspiration, I was interrupted, and all my ideas put to flight, by my intolerable landlady's tapping at the door, and asking me if I would "just please to let a lady and gentlemen come in, to take a look at Mr. Goldsmith's room." If you know anything of what an author's study is, and what an author is himself, you must know that there was no standing this. I put positive interdict on my room's being exhibited; but then it was shown when I was absent, and my papers put in confusion; and, on returning home one day, I absolutely found a cursed tradesman and his daughters gaping over my manuscripts, and my landlady in a panic at my appearance. I tried to make out a little longer, by taking the key in my pocket; but it would not do. I overheard mine hostess one day telling some of her customers on the stairs, that the room was occupied by an author, who was always in a tantrum if interrupted; and I immediately perceived, by a slight noise at the door, that they were peeping at me through the key-hole. By the head of Apollo, but this was quite too much! With all my eagerness for fame, and my ambition of the stare of the million, I had no idea of being exhibited by retail, at sixpence a head, and that through a key-hole. So I bid adieu to Canonbury Castle, merry Islington, and the haunts of poor Goldsmith, without having advanced a single line in my labors.

My next quarters were at a small, white-washed cottage, which stands not far from Hampstead, just on the brow of a hill; looking over Chalk Farm and Camden Town, remarkable for the rival houses of Mother Red Cap and Mother Black Cap; and so across Crackskull Common to the distant city.

The cottage was in nowise remarkable in itself; but I regarded it with reverence, for it had been the asylum of a persecuted author. Hither poor Steele had retreated, and laid *perdu*, when persecuted by creditors and bailiffs—those immemorial plagues of authors and free-

spirited gentlemen; and here he had written many numbers of the *Spectator*. It was hence, too, that he had dispatched those little notes to his lady, so full of affection and whimsicality, in which the fond husband, the careless gentleman, and the shifting spendthrift, were so oddly blended. I thought, as I first eyed the window of his apartment, that I could sit within it and write volumes.

No such thing! It was haymaking season, and, as ill luck would have it, immediately opposite the cottage was a little ale-house, with the sign of the Load of Hay. Whether it was there in Steele's time, I cannot say; but it set all attempts at conception or inspiration at defiance. It was the resort of all the Irish haymakers who mow the broad fields in the neighborhood; and of drovers and teamsters who travel that road. Here they would gather in the endless summer twilight, or by the light of the harvest moon, and sit around a table at the door; and tipple, and laugh, and quarrel, and fight, and sing drowsy songs, and dawdle away the hours, until the deep solemn notes of St. Paul's clock would warn the varlets home.

In the daytime I was less able to write. It was broad summer. The haymakers were at work in the fields, and the perfume of the new-mown hay brought with it the recollection of my native fields. So instead of remaining in my room to write, I went wandering about Primrose Hill, and Hampstead Heights, and Shepherd's Fields, and all those Arcadian scenes so celebrated by London bards. I cannot tell you how many delicious hours I have passed, lying on the cocks of the new-mown hay, on the pleasant slopes of some of those hills, inhaling the fragrance of the fields, while the summer-fly buzzed about me, or the grasshopper leaped into my bosom; and how I have gazed with half-shut eye upon the smoky mass of London, and listened to the distant sound of its population, and pitied the poor sons of earth, toiling in its bowels, like gnomes in the "dark gold mines."

People may say what they please about cockney pastorals, but, after all, there is a vast deal of rural beauty about the western vicinity of London; and any one that has looked down upon the valley of the West End, with its soft bosom of green pasturage lying open to the south, and dotted with cattle; the steeple of Hampstead rising among rich groves on the brow of the hill; and the learned height of Harrow in the distance; will confess that never has he seen a more absolutely rural landscape in the vicinity of a great metropolis.

Still, however, I found myself not a whit the better off for my frequent change of lodgings; and I began to discover, that in literature, as in trade, the old proverb holds good, "a rolling stone gathers no moss."

The tranquil beauty of the country played the very vengeance with

me. I could not mount my fancy into the termagant vein. I could not conceive, amidst the smiling landscape, a scene of blood and murder; and the smug citizens in breeches and gaiters put all ideas of heroes and bandits out of my brain. I could think of nothing but dulcet subjects, "the Pleasures of Spring"—"the Pleasures of Solitude"—"the Pleasures of Tranquillity"—"the Pleasures of Sentiment"—nothing but pleasures; and I had the painful experience of "the *Pleasures of Melancholy*" too strongly in my recollection to be beguiled by them.

Chance at length befriended me. I had frequently, in my ramblings, loitered about Hampstead Hill, which is a kind of Parnassus of the metropolis. At such times I occasionally took my dinner at Jack Straw's Castle. It is a country inn so named; the very spot where that notorious rebel and his followers held their council of war. It is a favorite resort of citizens when rurally inclined, as it commands fine fresh air, and a good view of the city. I sat one day in the public room of this inn, ruminating over a beefsteak and a pint of porter, when my imagination kindled up with ancient and heroic images. I had long wanted a theme and a hero; both suddenly broke upon my mind. I determined to write a poem on the history of Jack Straw. I was so full of the subject, that I was fearful of being anticipated. I wondered that none of the poets of the day in their search after ruffian heroes, had never thought of Jack Straw. I went to work pellmell, blotted several sheets of paper with choice floating thoughts, and battles, and descriptions, to be ready at a moment's warning. In a few days' time I sketched out the skeleton of my poem, and nothing was wanting but to give it flesh and blood. I used to take my manuscript and stroll about Caen Wood, and read aloud; and would dine at the Castle, by way of keeping up the vein of thought.

I was there one day, at rather a late hour, in the public room. There was no other company but one man, who sat enjoying his pint of porter at the window, and noticing the passers-by. He was dressed in a green shooting-coat. His countenance was strongly marked: he had a hooked nose; a romantic eye, excepting that it had something of a squint; and altogether, as I thought, a poetical style of head. I was quite taken with the man, for you must know I am a little of a physiognomist; I set him down at once for either a poet or a philosopher.

As I like to make new acquaintances, considering every man a volume of human nature, I soon fell into conversation with the stranger, who, I was pleased to find, was by no means difficult of access. After I had dined, I joined him at the window, and we became so sociable that I proposed a bottle of wine together, to which he most cheerfully assented.

I was too full of my poem to keep long quiet on the subject, and be-

gan to talk about the origin of the tavern, and the history of Jack
Straw. I found my new acquaintance to be perfectly at home on the
topic, and to jump exactly with my humor in every respect. I became
elevated by the wine and the conversation. In the fulness of an author's
feelings, I told him of my projected poem, and repeated some passages,
and he was in raptures. He was evidently of a strong poetical turn.

"Sir," said he, filling my glass at the same time, "our poets don't look
at home. I don't see why we need go out of old England for robbers and
rebels to write about. I like your Jack Straw, sir,—he's a home-made
hero. I like him, sir,—I like him exceedingly. He's English to the backbone—damme—Give me honest old England after all! Them's my sentiments, sir."

"I honor your sentiment," cried I, zealously; "it is exactly my own. An
English ruffian is as good a ruffian for poetry as any in Italy, or Germany, or the Archipelago; but it is hard to make our poets think so."

"More shame for them!" replied the man in green. "What a plague
would they have? What have we to do with their Archipelagos of Italy
and Germany? Haven't we heaths and commons and highways on our
own little island—ay, and stout fellows to pad the hoof over them too?
Stick to home, I say,—them's my sentiments. Come, sir, my service to
you—I agree with you perfectly."

"Poets, in old times, had right notions on this subject," continued I;
"witness the fine old ballads about Robin Hood, Allan a'Dale, and other
stanch blades of yore."

"Right, sir, right," interrupted he; "Robin Hood! he was the lad to
cry stand! to a man and never flinch."

"Ah, sir," said I, "they had famous bands of robbers in the good old
times; those were glorious poetical days. The merry crew of Sherwood
Forest, who led such a roving picturesque life, 'under the greenwood
tree.' I have often wished to visit their haunts, and tread the scenes of
the exploits of Friar Tuck, and Clymm of the Clough, and Sir William of Cloudeslie."

"Nay, sir," said the gentleman in green, "we have had several very
pretty gangs since that day. Those gallant dogs that kept about the
great heaths in the neighborhood of London, about Bagshot, and
Hounslow, and Blackheath, for instance. Come, sir, my service to you.
You don't drink."

"I suppose," cried I, emptying my glass, "I suppose you have heard of
the famous Turpin, who was born in this very village of Hampstead,
and who used to lurk with his gang in Epping Forest about a hundred
years since?"

"Have I?" cried he, "to be sure I have! A hearty old blade that. Sound

as pitch. Old Turpentine! as we used to call him. A famous fine fellow, sir."

"Well, sir," continued I, "I have visited Woltham Abbey and Chingford Church merely from the stories I heard when a boy of his exploits there, and I have searched Epping Forest for the cavern where he used to conceal himself. You must know," added I, "that I am a sort of amateur of highwaymen. They were dashing, daring fellows: the best apologies that we had for the knights-errant of yore. Ah, sir! the country has been sinking gradually into tameness and commonplace. We are losing the old English spirit. The bold knights of the Post have all dwindled down into lurking footpads, and sneaking pickpockets; there's no such thing as a dashing, gentleman-like robbery committed nowadays on the King's highway; a man may roll from one end of England to the other in a drowsy coach, or jingling post-chaise, without any other adventure than that of being occasionally overturned, sleeping in damp sheets, or having an ill-cooked dinner. We hear no more of public coaches being stopped and robbed by a well-mounted gang of resolute fellows, with pistols in their hands, and crapes over their faces. What a pretty poetical incident was it, for example, in domestic life, for a family-carriage, on its way to a country seat, to be attacked about dark; the old gentleman eased of his purse and watch, the ladies of their necklaces and ear-rings, by a politely-spoken highwayman on a blood-mare, who afterwards leaped the hedge and galloped across the country, the admiration of Miss Caroline, the daughter, who would write a long and romantic account of the adventure to her friend, Miss Juliana, in town. Ah, sir! we meet with nothing of such incidents nowadays."

"That, sir," said my companion, taking advantage of a pause, when I stopped to recover breath, and to take a glass of wine which he had just poured out, "that, sir, craving your pardon is not owing to any want of old English pluck. It is the effect of this cursed system of banking. People do not travel with bags of gold as they did formerly. They have post-notes and drafts on bankers. To rob a coach is like catching a crow, where you have nothing but carrion flesh and feathers for your pains. But a coach in old times, sir, was as rich as a Spanish galleon. It turned out the yellow boys bravely. And a private carriage was a cool hundred or two at least."

I cannot express how much I was delighted with the sallies of my new acquaintance. He told me that he often frequented the Castle, and would be glad to know more of me; and I proposed myself many a pleasant afternoon with him, when I should read him my poem as it proceeded, and benefit by his remarks; for it was evident he had the true poetical feeling.

"Come, sir," said he, pushing the bottle: "Damme, I like you! you're a man after my own heart. I'm cursed slow in making new acquaintances. One must be on the reserve, you know. But when I meet with a man of your kidney, damme, my heart jumps at once to him. Them's my sentiments, sir. Come, sir, here's Jack Straw's health! I presume one can drink it nowadays without treason!"

"With all my heart," said I, gayly, "and Dick Turpin's into the bargain!"

"Ah, sir," said the man in green, "those are the kind of men for poetry. The *Newgate Calendar*, sir! the *Newgate Calendar* is your only reading! There's the place to look for bold deeds and dashing fellows."

We were so much pleased with each other that we sat until a late hour. I insisted upon paying the bill, for both my purse and my heart were full, and I agreed that he should pay the score at our next meeting. As the coaches had all gone that run between Hampstead and London, we had to return on foot. He was so delighted with the idea of my poem, that he could talk of nothing else. He made me repeat such passages as I could remember; and though I did it in a very mangled manner, having a wretched memory, yet he was in raptures.

Every now and then he would break out with some scrap which he would misquote most terribly, would rub his hands and exclaim, "By Jupiter, that's fine, that's noble! Damme, sir, if I can conceive how you hit upon such ideas!"

I must confess I did not always relish his misquotations, which sometimes made absolute nonsense of the passages; but what author stands upon trifles when he is praised?

Never had I spent a more delightful evening. I did not perceive how the time flew. I could not bear to separate, but continued walking on, arm in arm, with him, past my lodgings, through Camden Town, and across Crackskull Common, talking the whole way about my poem.

When we were half-way across the common, he interrupted me in the midst of a quotation, by telling me that this had been a famous place for footpads, and was still occasionally infested by them; and that a man had recently been shot there in attempting to defend himself.—"The more fool he!" cried I; "a man is an idiot to risk life, or even limb, to save a paltry purse of money. It's quite a different case from that of a duel, where one's honor is concerned. For my part," added I, "I should never think of making resistance against one of these desperadoes."

"Say you so?" cried my friend in green, turning suddenly upon me, and putting a pistol to my breast; "why, then, have at you, my lad!—come—disburse! empty! unsack!"

In a word, I found that the muse had played me another of her tricks,

and had betrayed me into the hands of a footpad. There was no time to parley; he made me turn my pockets inside out; and hearing the sound of distant footsteps, he made one fell swoop upon purse, watch, and all; gave me a thwack on my unlucky pate that laid me sprawling on the ground, and scampered away with his booty.

I saw no more of my friend in green until a year or two afterwards; when I caught sight of his poetical countenance among a crew of scape-graces heavily ironed, who were on the way for transportation. He recognized me at once, tipped me an impudent wink, and asked me how I came on with the history of Jack Straw's Castle.

The catastrophe at Crackskull Common put an end to my summer's campaign. I was cured of my poetical enthusiasm for rebels, robbers, and highwaymen. I was put out of conceit of my subject, and, what was worse, I was lightened of my purse, in which was almost every farthing I had in the world. So I abandoned Sir Richard Steele's cottage in despair, and crept into less celebrated, though no less poetical and airy lodgings in a garret in town.

I now determined to cultivate the society of the literary, and to enroll myself in the fraternity of authorship. It is by the constant collision of mind, thought I, that authors strike out the sparks of genius, and kindle up with glorious conceptions. Poetry is evidently a contagious complaint. I will keep company with poets; who knows but I may catch it as others have done?

I found no difficulty in making a circle of literary acquaintances, not having the sin of success lying at my door: indeed, the failure of my poem was a kind of recommendation to their favor. It is true my new friends were not of the most brilliant names in literature; but then if you would take their words for it, they were like the prophets of old, men of whom the world was not worthy; and who were to live in future ages, when the ephemeral favorites of the day should be forgotten.

I soon discovered, however, that the more I mingled in literary society the less I felt capable of writing: that poetry was not so catching as I imagined; and that in familiar life there was often nothing less poetical than a poet. Besides, I wanted the *esprit du corps* to turn these literary fellowships to any account. I could not bring myself to enlist in any particular sect. I saw something to like in them all, but found that would never do, for that the tacit condition on which a man enters into one of these sects is, that he abuses all the rest.

I perceived that there were little knots of authors who lived with, and for, and by one another. They considered themselves the salt of the earth. They fostered and kept up a conventional vein of thinking and talking, and joking on all subjects; and they cried each other up to the

skies. Each sect had its particular creed; and set up certain authors as divinities, and fell down and worshipped them; and considered every one who did not worship them, or who worshipped any other, as a heretic and an infidel.

In quoting the writers of the day, I generally found them extolling names of which I had scarcely heard, and talking slightingly of others who were favorites of the public. If I mentioned any recent work from the pen of a first-rate author, they had not read it; they had not time to read all that was spawned from the press, he wrote too much to write well;—and then they would break out into raptures about some Mr. Timson, or Tonson, or Jackson, whose works were neglected at the present day, but who was to be the wonder and delight of posterity! Alas! what heavy debts is this neglectful world daily accumulating on the shoulders of poor posterity!

But, above all, it was edifying to hear with what contempt they would talk of the great. Ye gods! how immeasurably the great are despised by the small fry of literature! It is true, an exception was now and then made of some nobleman, with whom, perhaps, they had casually shaken hands at an election, or hobnobbed at a public dinner, and was pronounced a "devilish good fellow," and "no humbug;" but, in general, it was enough for a man to have a title, to be the object of their sovereign disdain: you have no idea how poetically and philosophically they would talk of nobility.

For my part, this affected me but little; for though I had no bitterness against the great, and did not think the worse of a man for having innocently been born to a title, yet I did not feel myself at present called upon to resent the indignities poured upon them by the little. But the hostility to the great writers of the day went sore against the grain with me. I could not enter into such feuds, nor participate in such animosities. I had not become author sufficiently to hate other authors. I could still find pleasure in the novelties of the press, and could find it in my heart to praise a contemporary, even though he were successful. Indeed, I was miscellaneous in my taste, and could not confine it to any age or growth of writers. I could turn with delight from the glowing pages of Byron to the cool and polished raillery of Pope; and after wandering among the sacred groves of *Paradise Lost*, I could give myself up to voluptuous abandonment in the enchanted bowers of *Lalla Rookh*.

"I would have my authors," said I, "as various as my wines, and, in relishing the strong and the racy, would never decry the sparkling and exhilarating. Port and Sherry are excellent standbys, and so is Madeira; but Claret and Burgundy may be drunk now and then without dis-

paragement to one's palate, and Champagne is a beverage by no means to be despised."

Such was the tirade I uttered one day when a little flushed with ale at a literary club. I uttered it, too, with something of a flourish, for I thought my simile a clever one. Unluckily, my auditors were men who drank beer and hated Pope; so my figure about wines went for nothing, and my critical toleration was looked upon as downright heterodoxy. In a word, I soon became a freethinker in religion, an outlaw from every sect, and fair game for all. Such are the melancholy consequences of not hating in literature.

I see you are growing weary, so I will be brief with the residue of my literary career. I will not detain you with a detail of my various attempts to get astride of Pegasus; of the poems I have written which were never printed, the plays I have presented which were never performed, and the tracts I have published which were never purchased. It seemed as if booksellers, managers, and the very public, had entered into a conspiracy to starve me. Still I could not prevail upon myself to give up the trial, nor abandon those dreams of renown in which I had indulged. How should I be able to look the literary circle of my native village in the face, if I were so completely to falsify their predictions? For some time longer, therefore, I continued to write for fame, and was, of course, the most miserable dog in existence, besides being in continual risk of starvation. I accumulated loads of literary treasure on my shelves—loads which were to be treasures to posterity; but, alas! they put not a penny into my purse. What was all this wealth to my present necessities? I could not patch my elbows with an ode; nor satisfy my hunger with blank verse. "Shall a man fill his belly with the east wind?" says the proverb. He may as well do so as with poetry.

I have many a time strolled sorrowfully along, with a sad heart and an empty stomach, about five o'clock, and looked wistfully down the areas in the west end of the town, and seen through the kitchen-windows the fires gleaming, and the joints of meat turning on the spits and dripping with gravy, and the cook-maids beating up pudding, or trussing turkeys, and felt for the moment that if I could but have the run of one of those kitchens, Apollo and the Muses might have the hungry heights of Parnassus for me. Oh, sir! talk of meditations among the tombs,—they are nothing so melancholy as the meditations of a poor devil without penny in pouch, along a line of kitchen-windows towards dinnertime.

At length, when almost reduced to famine and despair, the idea all at once entered my head, that perhaps I was not so clever a fellow as the village and myself had supposed. It was the salvation of me. The mo-

A PRACTICAL PHILOSOPHER

THE anecdotes I had heard of Buckthorne's early schoolmate, together with a variety of peculiarities which I remarked in himself, gave me a strong curiosity to know something of his own history. I am a traveller of the good old school, and am fond of the custom laid down in books, according to which, whenever travellers met, they sat down forthwith, and gave a history of themselves and their adventures. This Buckthorne, too, was a man much to my taste; he had seen the world, and mingled with society, yet retained the strong eccentricities of a man who had lived much alone. There was a careless dash of good-humor about him, which pleased me exceedingly; and at times an odd tinge of melancholy mingled with his humor, and gave it an additional zest. He was apt to run into long speculations upon society and manners, and to indulge in whimsical views of human nature; yet there was nothing ill-tempered in his satire. It ran more upon the follies than the vices of mankind; and even the follies of his fellow-man were treated with the leniency of one who felt himself to be but frail. He had evidently been a little chilled and buffeted by fortune, without being soured thereby; as some fruits become mellower and more generous in their flavor from having been bruised and frost-bitten.

I have always had a great relish for the conversation of practical philosophers of this stamp, who have profited by the "sweet uses" of adversity without imbibing its bitterness; who have learnt to estimate the world rightly, yet good-humoredly; and who, while they perceive the truth of the saying, that "all is vanity," are yet able to do so without vexation of spirit.

Such a man was Buckthorne. In general a laughing philosopher; and if at any time a shade of sadness stole across his brow, it was but transient; like a summer cloud, which soon goes by, and freshens and revives the fields over which it passes.

I was walking with him one day in Kensington Gardens,—for he was a knowing epicure in all the cheap pleasures and rural haunts within reach of the metropolis. It was a delightful warm morning in spring; and he was in the happy mood of a pastoral citizen, when just turned loose into grass and sunshine. He had been watching a lark, which, ris-

whirl through ambition, however tormenting; as it is doubly irksome to be obliged to join in the game without being interested in the stake.

"There is a constant demand in the fashionable world for novelty; every nine days must have its wonder, no matter of what kind. At one time it is an author; at another, a fire-eater; at another, a composer, an Indian juggler, or an Indian chief; a man from the North Pole or the Pyramids; each figures through his brief term of notoriety, and then makes way for the succeeding wonder. You must know that we have oddity fanciers among our ladies of rank, who collect about them all kinds of remarkable beings; fiddlers, statesmen, singers, warriors, artists, philosophers, actors, and poets; every kind of personage, in short, who is noted for something peculiar; so that their routs are like fancy-balls, where every one comes 'in character.'

"I have had infinite amusement at these parties in noticing how industriously every one was playing a part, and acting out of his natural line. There is not a more complete game at cross purposes than the intercourse of the literary and the great. The fine gentleman is always anxious to be thought a wit, and the wit a fine gentleman.

· "I have noticed a lord endeavoring to look wise and talk learnedly with a man of letters, who was aiming at a fashionable air, and the tone of a man who had lived about town. The peer quoted a score or two of learned authors, with whom he would fain be thought intimate, while the author talked of Sir John this, and Sir Harry that, and extolled the Burgundy he had drunk at Lord Such-a-one's. Each seemed to forget that he could only be interesting to the other in his proper character. Had the peer been merely a man of erudition, the author would never have listened to his prosing; and had the author known all the nobility in the *Court Calendar* it would have given him no interest in the eyes of the peer.

"In the same way I have seen a fine lady, remarkable for beauty, weary a philosopher with flimsy metaphysics, while the philosopher put on an awkward air of gallantry, played with her fan, and prattled about the Opera. I have heard a sentimental poet talk very stupidly with a statesman about the national debt; and on joining a knot of scientific old gentlemen conversing in a corner, expecting to hear the discussion of some valuable discovery, I found they were only amusing themselves with a fat story.

NOTORIETY

WHEN we had emerged from the literary nest of honest Dribble and had passed safely through the dangers of Breakneck Stairs, and the labyrinths of Fleet Market, Buckthorne indulged in many comments upon the peep into literary life which he had furnished me.

I expressed my surprise at finding it so different a world from what I had imagined. "It is always so," said he, "with strangers. The land of literature is a fairy-land to those who view it at a distance, but, like all other landscapes, the charm fades on a nearer approach, and the thorns and briars become visible. The republic of letters is the most factious and discordant of all republics, ancient or modern."

"Yet," said I, smiling, "you would not have me take honest Dribble's experience as a view of the land. He is but a mousing owl; a mere groundling. We should have quite a different strain from one of those fortunate authors whom we see sporting about the empyreal heights of fashion, like swallows in the blue sky of a summer's day."

"Perhaps we might," replied he, "but I doubt it, I doubt whether, if any one, even of the most successful, were to tell his actual feeling; you would not find the truth of friend Dribble's philosophy with respect to reputation. One you would find carrying a gay face to the world, while some vulture critic was preying upon his very liver. Another, who was simple enough to mistake fashion for fame, you would find watching countenances, and cultivating invitations, more ambitious to figure in the *beau monde* than the world of letters, and apt to be rendered wretched by the neglect of an illiterate peer, or a dissipated duchess. Those who were rising to fame, you would find tormented with anxiety to get higher; and those who had gained the summit, in constant apprehension of a decline.

"Even those who are indifferent to the buzz of notoriety, and the farce of fashion, are not much better off, being incessantly harassed by intrusions on their leisure, and interruptions of their pursuits; for, whatever may be his feelings, when once an author is launched into notoriety, he must go the rounds until the idle curiosity of the day is satisfied, and he is thrown aside to make way for some new caprice. Upon the whole, I do not know but he is most fortunate who engages in the

ment the idea popped into my brain it brought conviction and comfort with it. I awoke as from a dream. I gave up immortal fame to those who could live on air; took to writing for mere bread; and have ever since had a very tolerable life of it. There is no man of letters so much at his ease, sir, as he who has no character to gain or lose. I had to train myself to it a little, and to clip my wings short at first, or they would have carried me up into poetry in spite of myself. So I determined to begin by the opposite extreme, and abandoning the higher regions of the craft, I came plump down to the lowest and turned creeper.

"Creeper! and pray what is that?" said I.

"Oh, sir, I see you are ignorant of the language of the craft; a creeper is one who furnishes the newspapers with paragraphs at so much a line; and who goes about in quest of misfortunes; attends the Bow Street Office; the Courts of Justice, and every other den of mischief and iniquity. We are paid at the rate of a penny a line, and as we can sell the same paragraph to almost every paper, we sometimes pick up a very decent day's work. Now and then the Muse is unkind, or the day uncommonly quiet, and then we rather starve; and sometimes the unconscionable editors will clip our paragraphs when they are a little too rhetorical, and snip off twopence or threepence at a go. I have many a time had my pot of porter snipped off my dinner in this way, and have had to dine with dry lips. However, I cannot complain. I rose gradually in the lower ranks of the craft, and am now, I think, in the most comfortable region of literature."

"And pray," said I, "what may you be at present?"

"At present," said he, "I am a regular job-writer, and turn my hand to anything. I work up the writings of others at so much a sheet; turn off translations; write second-rate articles to fill up reviews and magazines; compile travels and voyages, and furnish theatrical criticisms for the newspapers. All this authorship, you perceive, is anonymous; it gives me no reputation except among the trade; where I am considered an author of all work, and am always sure of employ. That's the only reputation I want. I sleep soundly, without dread of duns or critics, and leave immortal fame to those that choose to fret and fight about it. Take my word for it, the only happy author in this world is he who is below the care of reputation."

Books by Charles Neider

FICTION

THE LEFT EYE CRIES FIRST
OVERFLIGHT
A VISIT TO YAZOO
MOZART AND THE ARCHBOOBY
NAKED EYE
THE AUTHENTIC DEATH OF HENDRY JONES
THE WHITE CITADEL

NONFICTION

BEYOND CAPE HORN: TRAVELS IN THE ANTARCTIC
EDGE OF THE WORLD: ROSS ISLAND, ANTARCTICA
SUSY: A CHILDHOOD
MARK TWAIN
THE FROZEN SEA: A STUDY OF FRANZ KAFKA

Some Books Edited by Charles Neider

THE COMPLETE TALES OF WASHINGTON IRVING
THE COMPLETE SHORT STORIES OF ROBERT LOUIS STEVENSON
THE COMPLETE HUMOROUS SKETCHES AND TALES OF MARK TWAIN
THE AUTOBIOGRAPHY OF MARK TWAIN
THE COMPLETE SHORT STORIES OF MARK TWAIN
SHORT NOVELS OF THE MASTERS
GREAT SHORT STORIES FROM THE WORLD'S LITERATURE
THE GREAT WEST: A TREASURY OF FIRSTHAND ACCOUNTS
THE COMPLETE ESSAYS OF MARK TWAIN
GEORGE WASHINGTON: A BIOGRAPHY BY WASHINGTON IRVING
MAN AGAINST NATURE: TALES OF ADVENTURE AND EXPLORATION

FICTION

WITHDRAWN IRVING

THE COMPLET
WASHINGTO

Contents

Strange Stories by a Nervous Gentleman

To my daughter Susy
and to her daughter
Annie Donnelly
with admiration and love

Library of Congress Cataloging-in-Publication Data
Irving, Washington, 1783–1859.
  [Short stories]
  The complete tales of Washington Irving / edited with an introduc-
tion by Charles Neider.
      p.   cm.
  ISBN-10: 0-306-80840-4   ISBN-13: 978-0-306-80840-1 (alk. paper)
  1. Fantastic fiction, American. I. Neider, Charles, 1915– . II. Title.
PS2050   1998
813'.2—dc21   97-34555
                                                                    CIP

First Da Capo Press edition 1998

This Da Capo Press paperback edition of *The Complete Tales
of Washington Irving* is an unabridged republication of the
edition first published in New York in 1975. It is reprinted
by arrangement with the editor.

Published by Da Capo Press, Inc.
A member of the Perseus Books Group

Manufactured in the United States of America

The Complete Tales

of

WASHINGTON IRVING

EDITED WITH AN INTRODUCTION BY

Charles Neider

DA CAPO PRESS

ing from a bed of daisies and yellow-cups, had sung his way up to a
bright snowy cloud floating in the deep blue sky.

"Of all birds," said he, "I should like to be a lark. He revels in the
brightest time of the day in the happiest season of the year, among fresh
meadows and opening flowers; and when he has sated himself with the
sweetness of earth, he wings his flight up to heaven as if he would drink
in the melody of the morning stars. Hark to that note! How it comes
thrilling down upon the ear! What a stream of music, note falling over
note in delicious cadence! Who would trouble his head about operas
and concerts when he could walk in the fields and hear such music for
nothing? These are the enjoyments which set riches at scorn, and make
even a poor man independent:

" 'I care not, Fortune, what you do deny:
    You cannot rob me of free nature's grace;
  You cannot shut the windows of the sky,
    Through which Aurora shows her bright'ning
      face;
  You cannot bar my constant feet to trace
  The woods and lawns by living streams at eve'—

"Sir, there are homilies in nature's works worth all the wisdom of the
schools, if we could but read them rightly, and one of the pleasantest
lessons I ever received in time of trouble, was from hearing the notes of
the lark."

I profited by this communicative vein to intimate to Buckthorne a
wish to know something of the events of his life, which I fancied must
have been an eventful one.

He smiled when I expressed my desire. "I have no great story," said
he, "to relate. A mere tissue of errors and follies. But, such as it is, you
shall have one epoch of it, by which you may judge of the rest." And so,
without any further prelude, he gave me the following anecdotes of his
early adventures.

BUCKTHORNE:

or, the Young Man of Great Expectations

I WAS born to very little property, but to great expectations—which is, perhaps, one of the most unlucky fortunes a man can be born to. My father was a country gentleman, the last of a very ancient and honorable, but decayed family, and resided in an old hunting-lodge in Warwickshire. He was a keen sportsman, and lived to the extent of his moderate income, so that I had little to expect from that quarter; but then I had a rich uncle by the mother's side, a penurious, accumulating curmudgeon, who it was confidently expected would make me his heir, because he was an old bachelor, because I was named after him, and because he hated all the world except myself.

He was, in fact, an inveterate hater, a miser even in misanthropy, and hoarded up a grudge as he did a guinea. Thus, though my mother was an only sister, he had never forgiven her marriage with my father, against whom he had a cold, still, immovable pique, which had lain at the bottom of his heart, like a stone in a well, ever since they had been school-boys together. My mother, however, considered me as the intermediate being that was to bring everything again into harmony, for she looked upon me as a prodigy—God bless her! my heart overflows whenever I recall her tenderness. She was the most excellent, the most indulgent of mothers. I was her only child: it was a pity she had no more, for she had fondness of heart enough to have spoiled a dozen!

I was sent at an early age to a public school, sorely against my mother's wishes; but my father insisted that it was the only way to make boys hardy. The school was kept by a conscientious prig of the ancient system who did his duty by the boys intrusted to his care,—that is to say, we were flogged soundly when we did not get our lessons. We were put in classes, and thus flogged on in droves along the highway of knowledge, in much the same manner as cattle are driven to market; where those that are heavy in gait, or short in leg, have to suffer for the superior alertness or longer limbs of their companions.

For my part, I confess it with shame, I was an incorrigible laggard. I have always had the poetical feeling, that is to say, I have always been an idle fellow, and prone to play the vagabond. I used to get away from

my books and school whenever I could, and ramble about the fields. I
was surrounded by seductions for such a temperament. The school-house
was an old-fashioned whitewashed mansion, of wood and plaster, standing on the skirts of a beautiful village: close by it was the venerable
church, with a tall Gothic spire; before it spread a lovely green valley,
with a little stream glistening along through the willow groves; while a
line of blue hills bounding the landscape gave rise to many a summer
day-dream as to the fairy-land that lay beyond.

In spite of all the scourgings I suffered at that school to make me love
my book, I cannot but look back upon the place with fondness. Indeed,
I considered this frequent flagellation as the common lot of humanity,
and the regular mode in which scholars were made.

My kind mother used to lament over my details of the sore trials I
underwent in the cause of learning; but my father turned a deaf ear to
her expostulations. He had been flogged through school himself, and he
swore there was no other way of making a man of parts; though, let me
speak it with all due reverence, my father was an indifferent illustration
of his theory, for he was considered a grievous blockhead.

· My poetical temperament evinced itself at a very early period. The
village church was attended every Sunday by a neighboring squire, the
lord of the manor, whose park stretched quite to the village, and whose
spacious country-seat seemed to take the church under its protection. Indeed, you would have thought the church had been consecrated to him
instead of to the Deity. The parish clerk bowed low before him, and the
vergers humbled themselves unto the dust in his presence. He always
entered a little late, and with some stir; striking his cane emphatically
on the ground, swaying his hat in his hand, and looking loftily to the
right and left as he walked slowly up the aisle; and the parson, who always ate his Sunday dinner with him, never commenced service until
he appeared. He sat with his family in a large pew gorgeously lined,
humbling himself devoutly on velvet cushions, and reading lessons of
meekness and lowliness of spirit out of splendid gold and morocco
prayer-books. Whenever the parson spoke of the difficulty of a rich
man's entering the kingdom of heaven, the eyes of the congregation
would turn towards the "grand pew," and I thought the squire seemed
pleased with the application.

The pomp of this pew, and the aristocratical air of the family struck
my imagination wonderfully; and I fell desperately in love with a little
daughter of the squire's, about twelve years of age. This freak of fancy
made me more truant from my studies than ever. I used to stroll about
the squire's park, and lurk near the house, to catch glimpses of this

damsel at the windows, or playing about the lawn, or walking out with her governess.

I had not enterprise nor impudence enough to venture from my concealment. Indeed I felt like an arrant poacher, until I read one or two of Ovid's Metamorphoses, when I pictured myself as some sylvan deity, and she a coy wood-nymph of whom I was in pursuit. There is something extremely delicious in these early awakenings of the tender passion. I can feel even at this moment the throbbing in my boyish bosom, whenever by chance I caught a glimpse of her white frock fluttering among the shrubbery. I carried about in my bosom a volume of Waller, which I had purloined from my mother's library; and I applied to my little fair one all the compliments lavished upon Sacharissa.

At length I danced with her at a school ball. I was so awkward a booby, that I dared scarcely speak to her; I was filled with awe and embarrassment in her presence; but I was so inspired, that my poetical temperament for the first time broke out in verse, and I fabricated some glowing rhymes, in which I berhymed the little lady under the favorite name of Sacharissa. I slipped the verses, trembling and blushing, into her hand the next Sunday as she came out of church. The little prude handed them to her mamma; the mamma handed them to the squire; the squire, who had no soul for poetry, sent them in dudgeon to the school-master; and the school-master, with a barbarity worthy of the Dark Ages, gave me a sound and peculiarly humiliating flogging for thus trespassing upon Parnassus. This was a sad outset for a votary of the Muse; it ought to have cured me of my passion for poetry; but it only confirmed it, for I felt the spirit of a martyr rising within me. What was as well, perhaps, it cured me of my passion for the young lady; for I felt so indignant at the ignominious horsing I had incurred in celebrating her charms, that I could not hold up my head in church. Fortunately for my wounded sensibility, the Mid-summer holidays came on, and I returned home. My mother, as usual, inquired into all my school concerns, my little pleasures, and cares, and sorrows; for boyhood has its share of the one as well as of the other. I told her all, and she was indignant at the treatment I had experienced. She fired up at the arrogance of the squire, and the prudery of the daughter; and as to the school-master, she wondered where was the use of having school-masters, and why boys could not remain at home, and be educated by tutors, under the eye of their mothers. She asked to see the verses I had written, and she was delighted with them; for, to confess the truth, she had a pretty taste for poetry. She even showed them to the parson's wife, who protested they were charming; and the parson's three daughters insisted on each having a copy of them.

All this was exceedingly balsamic; and I was still more consoled and encouraged when the young ladies, who were the bluestockings of the neighborhood, and had read Dr. Johnson's Lives quite through, assured my mother that great geniuses never studied, but were always idle; upon which I began to surmise that I was myself something out of the common run. My father, however, was of a very different opinion; for when my mother, in the pride of her heart, showed him my copy of verses he threw them out of the window, asking her "if she meant to make a ballad-monger of the boy?" But he was a careless, common-thinking man, and I cannot say that I ever loved him much; my mother absorbed all my filial affection.

I used occasionally, on holidays, to be sent on short visits to the uncle who was to make me his heir; they thought it would keep me in his mind, and render him fond of me. He was a withered, anxious-looking, old fellow, and lived in a desolate old country-seat, which he suffered to go to ruin from absolute niggardliness. He kept but one man-servant, who had lived, or rather starved with him for years. No woman was allowed to sleep in the house. A daughter of the old servant lived by the gate, in what had been a porter's lodge, and was permitted to come into the house about an hour each day, to make the beds, and cook a morsel of provisions. The park that surrounded the house was all run wild; the trees were grown out of shape; the fish-ponds stagnant; the urns and statues fallen from their pedestals, and buried among the rank grass. The hares and pheasants were so little molested, except by poachers, that they bred in great abundance, and sported about the rough lawns and weedy avenues. To guard the premises, and frighten off robbers, of whom he was somewhat apprehensive, and visitors, of whom he was in almost equal awe, my uncle kept two or three bloodhounds, who were always prowling round the house, and were the dread of the neighboring peasantry. They were gaunt and half-starved, seemed ready to devour one from mere hunger, and were an effectual check on any stranger's approach to this wizard castle.

Such was my uncle's house, which I used to visit now and then during the holidays. I was, as I before said, the old man's favorite; that is to say, he did not hate me so much as he did the rest of the world. I had been apprised of his character, and cautioned to cultivate his good-will; but I was too young and careless to be a courtier, and, indeed, have never been sufficiently studious of my interests to let them govern my feelings. However, we jogged on very well together, and as my visits cost him almost nothing, they did not seem to be very unwelcome. I brought with me my fishing-rod, and half supplied the table from the fish-ponds.

Our meals were solitary and unsocial. My uncle rarely spoke; he pointed to whatever he wanted, and the servant perfectly understood him. Indeed, his man John, or Iron John, as he was called in the neighborhood, was a counterpart of his master. He was a tall, bony old fellow, with a dry wig, that seemed made of cow's tail, and a face as tough as though it had been made of cow's hide. He was generally clad in a long, patched livery coat, taken out of the wardrobe of the house, and which bagged loosely about him, having evidently belonged to some corpulent predecessor, in the more plenteous days of the mansion. From long habits of taciturnity the hinges of his jaws seemed to have grown absolutely rusty, and it cost him as much effort to set them ajar, and to let out a tolerable sentence, as it would have done to set open the iron gates of the park, and let out the old family carriage, that was dropping to pieces in the coach-house.

I cannot say, however, but that I was for some time amused with my uncle's peculiarities. Even the very desolateness of the establishment had something in it that struck my fancy. When the weather was fine, I used to amuse myself in a solitary way, by rambling about the park, and coursing like a colt across its lawns. The hares and pheasants seemed to stare with surprise to see a human being walking these forbidden grounds by daylight. Sometimes I amused myself by jerking stones, or shooting at birds with a bow and arrows; for to have used a gun would have been treason. Now and then my path was crossed by a little redheaded, ragged-tailed urchin, the son of the woman at the lodge, who ran wild about the premises. I tried to draw him into familiarity, and to make a companion of him, but he seemed to have imbibed the strange unsociable character of everything around him, and always kept aloof; so I considered him as another Orson, and amused myself with shooting at him with my bow and arrows, and he would hold up his breeches with one hand, and scamper away like a deer.

There was something in all this loneliness and wildness strangely pleasing to me. The great stables, empty and weather-broken, with the names of favorite horses over the vacant stalls; the windows bricked and boarded up; the broken roofs, garrisoned by rooks and jack-daws, all had a singularly forlorn appearance. One would have concluded the house to be totally uninhabited, were it not for the little thread of blue smoke which now and then curled up, like a corkscrew, from the centre of one of the wide chimneys where my uncle's starveling meal was cooking.

My uncle's room was in a remote corner of the building, strongly secured, and generally locked. I was never admitted into this stronghold, where the old man would remain for the greater part of the time, drawn up, like a veteran spider, in the citadel of his web. The rest of the mansion, however, was open to me, and I wandered about it un-constrained. The damp and rain which beat in through the broken windows, crumbled the paper from the walls, mouldered the pictures, and gradually destroyed the furniture. I loved to roam about the wide waste chambers in bad weather, and listen to the howling of the wind, and the banging about of the doors and window-shutters. I pleased my-self with the idea how completely, when I came to the estate, I would renovate all things, and make the old building ring with merriment, till it was astonished at its own jocundity.

The chambers which I occupied on these visits had been my mother's when a girl. There was still the toilet-table of her own adorning, the landscapes of her own drawing. She had never seen it since her mar-riage but would often ask me if everything was still the same. All was just the same, for I loved that chamber on her account, and had taken pains to put everything in order, and to mend all the flaws in the windows with my own hands. I anticipated the time when I should once more welcome her to the house of her fathers, and restore her to this little nestling-place of her childhood.

· At length my evil genius, or what, perhaps, is the same thing, the Muse, inspired me with the notion of rhyming again. My uncle, who never went to church, used on Sundays to read chapters out of the Bible; and Iron John, the woman from the lodge, and myself were his congregation. It seemed to be all one to him what he read, so long as it was something from the Bible. Sometimes, therefore, it would be the Song of Solomon, and this withered anatomy would read about being "stayed with flagons, and comforted with apples, for he was sick of love." Sometimes he would hobble, with spectacles on nose, through whole chapters, of hard Hebrew names in Deuteronomy, at which the poor woman would sigh and groan, as if wonderfully moved. His favorite book, however, was *The Pilgrim's Progress;* and when he came to that part which treats of Doubting Castle and Giant Despair, I thought invariably of him and his desolate old country-seat. So much did the idea amuse me, that I took to scribbling about it under the trees in the park; and in a few days had made some progress in a poem, in which I had given a description of the place, under the name of Doubting Castle, and personified my uncle as Giant Despair.

I lost my poem somewhere about the house, and I soon suspected that my uncle had found it, as he harshly intimated to me that I could return home, and that I need not come and see him again till he should send for me.

Just about this time my mother died. I cannot dwell upon the cir-cumstance. My heart, careless and wayward as it is, gushes with the recollection. Her death was an event that perhaps gave a turn to all that made home attractive. I had no longer anybody whom I was ambitious to please, or fearful to offend. My father was a good kind of a man in his way, but he had bad maxims in education, and we differed in material points. It makes a vast difference in opinion about the utility of the rod, which end happens to fall to one's share. I never could be brought into my father's way of thinking on the subject.

I now, therefore, began to grow very impatient of remaining at school, to be flogged for things that I did not like. I longed for variety, especially now that I had not my uncle's house to resort to, by way of diversifying the dulness of school with the dreariness of his country-seat.

I was now almost seventeen, tall for my age, and full of idle fancies. I had a roving, inextinguishable desire to see different kinds of life, and different orders of society; and this vagrant humor had been fostered in me by Tom Dribble, the prime wag and great genius of the school, who had all the rambling propensities of a poet.

I used to sit at my desk in the school, on a fine summer's day, and instead of studying the book which lay open before me, my eye was gazing through the windows on the green fields and blue hills. How I envied the happy groups on the tops of stage-coaches, chatting, and joking, and laughing, as they whirled by the school-house on their way to the metropolis. Even the wagoners, trudging along beside their ponderous teams, and traversing the kingdom from one end to the other, were objects of envy to me: I fancied to myself what adventures they must experience, and what odd scenes of life they must witness. All this was, doubtless, the poetical temperament working within me, and tempting me forth into a world of its own creation, which I mistook for the world of real life.

While my mother lived, this strong propensity to rove was counteracted by the stronger attractions of home, and by the powerful ties of affection which drew me to her side; but now that she was gone, the attraction had ceased; the ties were severed. I had no longer an anchorage-ground for my heart, but was at the mercy of every vagrant impulse. Nothing but the narrow allowance on which my father kept me, and the consequent penury of my purse, prevented me from mounting to the top of a stage-coach, and launching myself adrift on the great ocean of life.

Just about this time the village was agitated for a day or two, by the passing through of several caravans, containing wild beasts, and other spectacles, for a great fair annually held at a neighboring town.

I had never seen a fair of any consequence, and my curiosity was powerfully awakened by this bustle of preparation. I gazed with respect and wonder at the vagrant personages who accompanied these caravans. I loitered about the village inn, listening with curiosity and delight to the slang talk and cant jokes of the showmen and their followers; and I felt an eager desire to witness this fair, which my fancy decked out as something wonderfully fine.

A holiday afternoon presented, when I could be absent from noon until evening. A wagon was going from the village to the fair; I could not resist the temptation, nor the eloquence of Tom Dribble, who was a truant to the very heart's core. We hired seats, and set off full of boyish expectation. I promised myself that I would but take a peep at the land of promise, and hasten back again before my absence should be noticed.

Heavens! how happy I was on arriving at the fair! How I was enchanted with the world of fun and pageantry around me! The humors of Punch, the feats of the equestrians, the magical tricks of the conjurors! But what principally caught my attention was an itinerant theatre, where a tragedy, pantomime, and farce were all acted in the course of half an hour, and more of the dramatis personæ murdered than at either Drury Lane or Covent Garden in the course of a whole evening. I have since seen many a play performed by the best actors in the world, but never have I derived half the delight from any that I did from this first representation.

There was a ferocious tyrant in a skullcap like an inverted porringer, and a dress of red baize, magnificently embroidered with gilt leather; with his face so bewhiskered, and his eyebrows so knit and expanded with burnt cork, that he made my heart quake within me, as he stamped about the little stage. I was enraptured too with the surpassing beauty of a distressed damsel in a faded pink silk, and dirty white muslin, whom he held in cruel captivity by way of gaining her affections, and who wept, and wrung her hands, and flourished a ragged white handkerchief, from the top of an impregnable tower of the size of a bandbox.

Even after I had come out from the play, I could not tear myself from the vicinity of the theatre, but lingered, gazing and wondering, and laughing at the dramatis personæ as they performed their antics, or danced upon a stage in front of the booth, to decoy a new set of spectators.

I was so bewildered by the scene, and so lost in the crowd of sensations that kept swarming upon me, that I was like one entranced. I lost my companion, Tom Dribble, in a tumult and scuffle that took place near one of the shows; but I was too much occupied in mind to think long about him. I strolled about until dark, when the fair was lighted up, and a new scene of magic opened upon me. The illumination of the tents and booths, the brilliant effect of the stages decorated with lamps, with dramatic groups flaunting about them in gaudy dresses, contrasted splendidly with the surrounding darkness; while the uproar of drums, trumpets, fiddles, hautboys, and cymbals, mingled with the harangues of the showmen, the squeaking of Punch, and the shouts and laughter of the crowd, all united to complete my giddy distraction.

Time flew without my perceiving it. When I came to myself and thought of the school, I hastened to return. I inquired for the wagon in which I had come: it had been gone for hours! I asked the time: it was almost midnight! A sudden quaking seized me. How was I to get back to school? I was too weary to make the journey on foot, and I knew not where to apply for a conveyance. Even if I should find one, could I venture to disturb the school-house long after midnight—to arouse that sleeping lion, the usher, in the very midst of his night's rest?—the idea was too dreadful for a delinquent school-boy. All the horrors of return rushed upon me. My absence must long before this have been re-marked;—and absent for a whole night!—a deed of darkness not easily to be expiated. The rod of the pedagogue budded forth into tenfold terrors before my affrighted fancy. I pictured to myself punishment and humiliation in every variety of form, and my heart sickened at the picture. Alas! how often are the petty ills of boyhood as painful to our tender natures as are the sterner evils of manhood to our robuster minds.

I wandered about among the booths, and I might have derived a lesson from my actual feelings, how much the charms of this world depend upon ourselves; for I no longer saw anything gay or delightful in the revelry around me. At length I lay down, wearied and perplexed, behind one of the large tents, and covering myself with the margin of the tent-cloth, to keep off the night chill, I soon fell asleep.

I had not slept long, when I was awakened by the noise of merriment within an adjoining booth. It was the itinerant theatre, rudely constructed of boards and canvas. I peeped through an aperture, and saw the whole dramatis personæ, tragedy, comedy, and pantomime, all refreshing themselves after the final dismissal of their auditors. They were merry and gamesome, and made the flimsy theatre ring with their laughter. I was astonished to see the tragedy tyrant in red baize and fierce whiskers, who had made my heart quake as he strutted about the boards, now transformed into a fat, good-humored fellow; the beaming porringer laid aside from his brow, and his jolly face washed from all the terrors of burnt cork. I was delighted, too, to see the distressed damsel, in faded silk and dirty muslin, who had trembled under his tyranny, and afflicted me so much by her sorrows, now seated familiarly on his knee, and quaffing from the same tankard. Harlequin lay asleep on one of the benches; and monks, satyrs, and vestal virgins were grouped together, laughing outrageously at a broad story told by an unhappy count, who had been barbarously murdered in the tragedy.

This was, indeed, novelty to me. It was a peep into another planet. I gazed and listened with intense curiosity and enjoyment. They had a thousand odd stories and jokes about the events of the day, and burlesque descriptions and mimickings of the spectators who had been admiring them. Their conversation was full of allusions to their adventures at different places where they had exhibited; the characters they had met with in different villages and the ludicrous difficulties in which they had occasionally been involved. All past cares and troubles were now turned, by these thoughtless beings, into matters of merriment, and made to contribute to the gayety of the moment. They had been moving from fair to fair about the kingdom, and were the next morning to set out on their way to London. My resolution was taken. I stole from my nest, and crept through a hedge into a neighboring field, where I went to work to make a tatterdemalion of myself. I tore my clothes; soiled them with dirt; begrimed my face and hands and crawling near one of the booths, purloined an old hat, and left my new one in its place. It was an honest theft, and I hope may not hereafter rise up in judgment against me.

I now ventured to the scene of merry-making, and presenting myself before the dramatic corps, offered myself as a volunteer. I felt terribly agitated and abashed, for never before "stood I in such a presence." I had addressed myself to the manager of the company. He was a fat man, dressed in dirty white, with a red sash fringed with tinsel swathed round his body; his face was smeared with paint; and a majestic plume towered from an old spangled black bonnet. He was the Jupiter Tonans of this Olympus, and was surrounded by the inferior gods and goddesses of his court. He sat on the end of a bench, by a table, with one arm akimbo, and the other extended to the handle of a tankard, which he had slowly set down from his lips, as he surveyed me from head to foot. It was a moment of awful scrutiny; and I fancied the groups around, all watching as in silent suspense, and waiting for the imperial nod.

He questioned me as to who I was; what were my qualifications; and what terms I expected. I passed myself off for a discharged servant from a gentleman's family; and as, happily, one does not require a special recommendation to get admitted into bad company, the questions on that head were easily satisfied. As to my accomplishments, I could spout a little poetry, and knew several scenes of plays, which I had learnt at school exhibitions; I could dance—That was enough. No further questions were asked me as to accomplishments; it was the very thing they wanted; and as I asked no wages but merely meat and drink, and safe conduct about the world, a bargain was struck in a moment.

Behold me, therefore, transformed in a sudden from a gentleman student to a dancing buffoon; for such, in fact, was the character in which I made my debut. I was one of those who formed the groups in the dramas, and was principally employed on the stage in front of the booth to attract company. I was equipped as a satyr, in a dress of drab frieze that fitted to my shape, with a great laughing mask ornamented with huge ears and short horns. I was pleased with the disguise, because it kept me from the danger of being discovered, whilst we were in that part of the country; and as I had merely to dance and make antics, the character was favorable to a debutant—being almost on a par with Simon Smug's part of the lion, which required nothing but roaring.

I cannot tell you how happy I was at this sudden change in my situation. I felt no degradation, for I had seen too little of society to be thoughtful about the difference of rank; and a boy of sixteen is seldom aristocratical. I had given up no friend, for there seemed to be no one in the world that cared for me, now that my poor mother was dead; I had given up no pleasure, for my pleasure was to ramble about and indulge the flow of a poetical imagination, and I now enjoyed it in perfection. There is no life so truly poetical as that of a dancing buffoon.

It may be said that all this argued grovelling inclinations. I do not think so. Not that I mean to vindicate myself in any great degree: I know too well what a whimsical compound I am. But in this instance I was seduced by no love of low company, nor disposition to indulge in low vices. I have always despised the brutally vulgar, and had a disgust at vice, whether in high or low life. I was governed merely by a sudden and thoughtless impulse. I had no idea of resorting to this profession as a mode of life, or of attaching myself to these people, as my future class of society. I thought merely of a temporary gratification to my curiosity, and an indulgence of my humors. I had already a strong relish for the peculiarities of character and the varieties of situation, and I have always been fond of the comedy of life, and desirous of seeing it through all its shifting scenes.

In mingling, therefore, among mountebanks and buffoons, I was protected by the very vivacity of imagination which had led me among them; I moved about, enveloped, as it were, in a protecting delusion, which my fancy spread around me. I assimilated to these people only as they struck me poetically; their whimsical ways and a certain picturesqueness in their mode of life entertained me; but I was neither amused nor corrupted by their vices. In short, I mingled among them, as Prince Hal did among his graceless associates, merely to gratify my humor.

I did not investigate my motives in this manner, at the time, for I was too careless and thoughtless to reason about the matter; but I do so now, when I look back with trembling to think of the ordeal to which I unthinkingly exposed myself, and the manner in which I passed through it. Nothing, I am convinced, but the poetical temperament, that hurried me into the scrape, brought me out of it without my becoming an arrant vagabond.

Full of the enjoyment of the moment, giddy with the wildness of animal spirits, so rapturous in a boy, I capered, I danced, I played a thousand fantastic tricks about the stage, in the villages in which we exhibited; and I was universally pronounced the most agreeable monster that had ever been seen in those parts. My disappearance from school had awakened my father's anxiety; for I one day heard a description of myself cried before the very booth in which I was exhibiting, with the offer of a reward for any intelligence of me. I had no great scruple about letting my father suffer a little uneasiness on my account: it would punish him for past indifference, and would make him value me the more when he found me again.

I have wondered that some of my comrades did not recognize me in the stray sheep that was cried; but they were all, no doubt, occupied by their own concerns. They were all laboring seriously in their antic vocation; for folly was a mere trade with most of them, and they often grinned and capered with heavy hearts. With me, on the contrary, it was all real. I acted *con amore*, and rattled and laughed from the irrepressible gayety of my spirits. It is true that, now and then, I started and looked grave on receiving a sudden thwack from the wooden sword of Harlequin in the course of my gambols, as it brought to mind the birch of my schoolmaster. But I soon got accustomed to it, and bore all the cuffing, and kicking, and tumbling about, which form the practical wit of your itinerant pantomime, with a good humor that made me a prodigious favorite.

The country campaign of the troop was soon at an end, and we set off for the metropolis, to perform at the fairs which are held in its vicinity. The greater part of our theatrical property was sent on direct, to be in a state of preparation for the opening of the fairs; while a detachment of the company travelled slowly on, foraging among the villages. I was amused with the desultory, hap-hazard kind of life we led; here to-day and gone to-morrow. Sometimes revelling in ale-houses, sometimes feasting under hedges in the green fields. When audiences were crowded, and business profitable, we fared well; and when otherwise, we fared scantily, consoled ourselves, and made up with anticipations of the next day's success.

At length the increasing frequency of coaches hurrying past us, covered with passengers; the increasing number of carriages, carts, wagons, gigs, droves of cattle and flocks of sheep, all thronging the road; the snug country boxes with trim flower-gardens, twelve feet square, and their trees twelve feet high, all powdered with dust, and the innumerable seminaries for young ladies and gentlemen situated along the road for the benefit of country air and rural retirement; all these insignia announced that the mighty London was at hand. The hurry, and the crowd, and the bustle, and the noise, and the dust, increased as we proceeded, until I saw the great cloud of smoke hanging in the air, like a canopy of state, over this queen of cities.

In this way, then, did I enter the metropolis, a strolling vagabond, on the top of a caravan, with a crew of vagabonds about me; but I was as happy as a prince; for, like Prince Hal, I felt myself superior to my situation, and knew that I could at any time cast it off, and emerge into my proper sphere.

How my eyes sparkled as we passed Hyde Park Corner, and I saw splendid equipages rolling by; with powdered footmen behind, in rich liveries, with fine nosegays, and gold-headed canes; and with lovely women within, so sumptuously dressed, and so surpassingly fair! I was always extremely sensible to female beauty, and here I saw it in all its powers of fascination: for whatever may be said of "beauty unadorned," there is something almost awful in female loveliness decked out in jewelled state. The swanlike neck encircled with diamonds; the raven locks clustered with pearls; the ruby glowing on the snowy bosom, are objects which I could never contemplate without emotion; and a dazzling white arm clasped with bracelets, and taper, transparent fingers, laden with sparkling rings, are to me irresistible.

My very eyes ached as I gazed at the high and courtly beauty before me. It surpassed all that my imagination had conceived of the sex. I shrank, for a moment, into shame at the company in which I was placed, and repined at the vast distance that seemed to intervene between me and these magnificent beings.

I forbear to give a detail of the happy life I led about the skirts of the metropolis, playing at the various fairs held there during the latter part of spring and the beginning of summer. This continued change from place to place, and scene to scene, fed my imagination with novelties, and kept my spirits in a perpetual state of excitement. As I was tall of my age, I aspired, at one time, to play heroes in tragedy; but, after two or three trials, I was pronounced by the manager totally unfit for the line; and our first tragic actress, who was a large woman, and held a small hero in abhorrence, confirmed his decision.

The fact is, I had attempted to give point to language which had no point, and nature to scenes which had no nature. They said I did not fill out my characters; and they were right. The characters had all been prepared for a different sort of man. Our tragedy hero was a round, robustious fellow, with an amazing voice; who stamped and slapped his breast until his wig shook again; and who roared and bellowed out his bombast until every phrase swelled upon the ear like the sound of a kettle-drum. I might as well have attempted to fill out his clothes as his characters. When we had a dialogue together, I was nothing before him, with my slender voice and discriminating manner. I might as well have attempted to parry a cudgel with a small-sword. If he found me in any way gaining ground upon him, he would take refuge in his mighty voice, and throw his tones like peals of thunder at me, until they were drowned in the still louder thunder of applause from the audience.

To tell the truth, I suspect that I was not shown fair play, and that there was management at the bottom; for without vanity I think I was a better actor than he. As I had not embarked in the vagabond line through ambition, I did not repine at lack of preferment; but I was grieved to find that a vagrant life was not without its cares and anxieties; and that jealousies, intrigues, and mad ambition, were to be found even among vagabonds.

Indeed, as I became more familiar with my situation, and the delusions of fancy gradually faded away, I began to find that my associates were not the happy careless creatures I had at first imagined them. They were jealous of each other's talents; they quarrelled about parts, the same as the actors on the grand theatres; they quarrelled about dresses; and there was one robe of yellow silk, trimmed with red, and a head-dress of three rumpled ostrich-feathers, which were continually setting the ladies of the company by the ears. Even those who had attained the highest honors were not more happy than the rest; for Mr. Flimsey himself, our first tragedian, and apparently a jovial good-humored fellow, confessed to me one day, in the fulness of his heart, that he was a miserable man. He had a brother-in-law, a relative by marriage, though not by blood, who was manager of a theatre in a small country town. And this same brother ("little more than kin but less than kind") looked down upon him, and treated him with contumely, because, forsooth, he was but a strolling player. I tried to console him with the thoughts of the vast applause he daily received, but it was all in vain. He declared that it gave him no delight, and that he should never be a happy man, until the name of Flimsey rivalled the name of Crimp.

How little do those before the scenes know of what passes behind! how little can they judge, from the countenance of actors, of what is passing in their hearts! I have known two lovers quarrel like cats behind the scenes, who were, the moment after, to fly into each other's embraces. And I had dreaded, when our Belvidera was to take her farewell kiss of her Jaffier, lest she should bite a piece out of his cheek. Our tragedian was a rough joker off the stage; our prime clown the most peevish mortal living. The latter used to go about snapping and snarling, with a broad laugh painted on his countenance; and I can assure you, that, whatever may be said of the gravity of a monkey, or the melancholy of a gibed cat, there is no more melancholy creature in existence than a mountebank off duty.

The only thing in which all parties agreed, was to backbite the manager, and cabal against his regulations. This, however, I have since discovered to be a common trait of human nature, and to take place in all communities. It would seem to be the main business of man to repine at government. In all situations of life, into which I have looked, I have found mankind divided into two grand parties: those who ride, and those who are ridden. The great struggle of life seems to be which shall keep in the saddle. This, it appears to me, is the fundamental principle of politics, whether in great or little life. However, I do not mean to moralize—but one cannot always sink the philosopher.

Well, then, to return to myself, it was determined, as I said, that I was not fit for tragedy, and, unluckily, as my study was bad, having a very poor memory, I was pronounced unfit for comedy also; besides, the line of young gentlemen was already engrossed by an actor with whom I could not pretend to enter into competition, he having filled it for almost half a century. I came down again, therefore, to pantomime. In consequence, however, of the good offices of the manager's lady, who had taken a liking to me, I was promoted from the part of the satyr to that of the lover; and with my face patched and painted, a huge cravat of paper, a steepled-crowned hat, and dangling long-skirted sky-blue coat, was metamorphosed into the lover of Columbine. My part did not call for much of the tender and sentimental. I had merely to pursue the fugitive fair one; to have a door now and then slammed in my face; to run my head occasionally against a post; to tumble and roll about with Pantaloon and the Clown; and to endure the hearty thwacks of Harlequin's wooden sword.

As ill luck would have it, my poetical temperament began to ferment within me, and to work out new troubles. The inflammatory air of a great metropolis, added to the rural scenes in which the fairs were held, such as Greenwich Park, Epping Forest, and the lovely valley of the West End, had a powerful effect upon me. While in Greenwich Park, I was witness to the old holiday games of running down-hill, and kissing in the ring; and then the firmament of blooming faces and blue eyes that would be turned towards me, as I was playing antics on the stage; all these set my young blood and my poetical vein in full flow. In short, I played the character to the life, and became desperately enamoured of Columbine. She was a trim, well-made, tempting girl, with a roguish dimpling face, and fine chestnut hair clustering all about it. The moment I got fairly smitten, there was an end to all playing. I was such a creature of fancy and feeling, that I could not put on a pretended, when I was powerfully affected by a real emotion. I could not sport with a fiction that came so near to the fact. I became too natural in my acting to succeed. And then what a situation for a lover! I was a mere stripling, and she played with my passion; for girls soon grow more adroit and knowing in these matters than your awkward youngsters. What agonies had I to suffer! Every time that she danced in front of the booth, and made such liberal displays of her charms, I was in torment. To complete my misery, I had a real rival in Harlequin, an active, vigorous, knowing varlet, of six-and-twenty. What had a raw, inexperienced youngster like me to hope from such a competition?

I had still, however, some advantages in my favor. In spite of my change of life, I retained that indescribable something which always distinguishes the gentleman: that something which dwells in a man's air and deportment, and not in his clothes; and which is as difficult for a gentleman to put off as for a vulgar fellow to put on. The company generally felt it, and used to call me Little Gentleman Jack. The girl felt it too, and, in spite of her predilection for my powerful rival, she liked to flirt with me. This only aggravated my troubles, by increasing my passion, and awakening the jealousy of her party-colored lover.

Alas! think what I suffered at being obliged to keep up an ineffectual chase after my Columbine through whole pantomimes; to see her carried off in the vigorous arms of the happy Harlequin; and to be obliged, instead of snatching her from him, to tumble sprawling with Pantaloon and the Clown, and bear the infernal and degrading thwacks of my rival's weapon of lath, which, may heaven confound him! (excuse my passion), the villain laid on with a malicious good-will: nay, I could absolutely hear him chuckle and laugh beneath his accursed mask;—I beg pardon for growing a little warm in my narrative—I wish to be cool, but these recollections will sometimes agitate me. I have heard and read of many desperate and deplorable situations of lovers, but none, I think, in which true love was ever exposed to so severe and peculiar a trial.

This could not last long; flesh and blood, at least such flesh and blood as mine, could not bear it. I had repeated heart-burnings and quarrels with my rival, in which he treated me with the mortifying forbearance of a man towards a child. Had he quarrelled outright with me, I could have stomached it, at least I should have known what part to take; but to be humored and treated as a child in the presence of my mistress, when I felt all the bantam spirit of a little man swelling within me—Gods! it was insufferable!

At length, we were exhibiting one day at West End fair, which was at that time a very fashionable resort, and often beleaguered with gay equipages from town. Among the spectators that filled the first row of our little canvas theatre one afternoon, when I had to figure in a pantomime, were a number of young ladies from a boarding-school, with their governess. Guess my confusion, when, in the midst of my antics, I beheld among the number my quondam flame; her whom I had berhymed at school, her for whose charms I had smarted so severely, the cruel Sacharissa! What was worse, I fancied she recollected me, and was repeating the story of my humiliating flagellation, for I saw her whispering to her companions and her governess. I lost consciousness of the part I was acting, and of the place where I was. I felt shrunk to nothing, and could have crept into a rat-hole,—unluckily, none was open to receive me. Before I could recover from my confusion, I was tumbled over by Pantaloon and the Clown, and I felt the sword of Harlequin making vigorous assaults in a manner most degrading to my dignity.

Heaven and earth! was I again to suffer martyrdom in this ignominious manner, in the knowledge, and even before the very eyes of this most beautiful, but most disdainful of fair ones? All my long-smothered wrath broke out at once; the dormant feelings of the gentleman arose within me. Stung to the quick by intolerable mortification, I sprang on my feet in an instant; leaped upon Harlequin like a young tiger; tore off his mask; buffeted him in the face; and soon shed more blood on the stage than had been spilt upon it during a whole tragic campaign of battles and murders.

As soon as Harlequin recovered from his surprise, he returned my assault with interest. I was nothing in his hands. I was game, to be sure, for I was a gentleman; but he had the clownish advantage of bone and muscle. I felt as if I could have fought even unto the death; and I was likely to do so, for he was, according to the boxing phrase, "putting my head into chancery," when the gentle Columbine flew to my assistance. God bless the women; they are always on the side of the weak and the oppressed!

The battle now became general; the dramatis personæ ranged on either side. The manager interposed in vain; in vain were his spangled black bonnet and towering white feathers seen whisking about, and nodding and bobbing in the thickest of the fight. Warriors, ladies, priests, satyrs, kings, queens, gods, and goddesses, all joined pell-mell in the affray; never, since the conflict under the walls of Troy, had there been such a chance-medley warfare of combatants, human and divine. The audience applauded, the ladies shrieked, and fled from the theatre; and a scene of discord ensued that baffles all description.

Nothing but the interference of the peace-officers restored some degree of order. The havoc, however, among dresses and decorations, put an end to all further acting for that day. The battle over, the next thing was to inquire why it was begun: a common question among politicians after a bloody and unprofitable war, and one not always easy to be answered. It was soon traced to me, and my unaccountable transport of passion, which they could only attribute to my having *run a muck*. The manager was judge and jury, and plaintiff into the bargain; and in such cases justice is always speedily administered. He came out of the fight as sublime a wreck as the *Santissima Trinidada*. His gallant plumes, which once towered aloft, were drooping about his ears; his robe of state hung in ribbons from his back, and but ill concealed the ravages he had suffered in the rear. He had received kicks and cuffs from all sides during the tumult; for every one took the opportunity of slyly gratifying some lurking grudge on his fat carcass. He was a discreet man, and did not choose to declare war with all his company, so he swore all those kicks and cuffs had been given by me, and I let him enjoy the opinion. Some wounds he bore, however, which were the incontestable traces of a woman's warfare: his sleek rosy cheek was scored by trickling furrows, which were ascribed to the nails of my intrepid and devoted Columbine. The ire of the monarch was not to be appeased; he had suffered in his person, and he had suffered in his purse; his dignity, too, had been insulted, and that went for something; for dignity is always more irascible, the more petty the potentate. He wreaked his wrath upon the beginners of the affray, and Columbine and myself were discharged, at once, from the company.

Figure me, then, to yourself, a stripling of little more than sixteen, a gentleman by birth, a vagabond by trade, turned adrift upon the world, making the best of my way through the crowd of West End fair; my mountebank dress fluttering in rags about me; the weeping Columbine hanging upon my arm, in splendid but tattered finery; the tears coursing one by one down her face, carrying off the red paint in torrents, and literally "preying upon her damask cheek."

The crowd made way for us as we passed, and hooted in our rear. I felt the ridicule of my situation, but had too much gallantry to desert this fair one, who had sacrificed everything for me. Having wandered through the fair, we emerged, like another Adam and Eve, into unknown regions, and "had the world before us where to choose." Never was a more disconsolate pair seen in the soft valley of West End. The luckless Columbine cast many a lingering look at the fair, which seemed to put on a more than usual splendor: its tents, and booths, and party-colored groups, all brightening in the sunshine, and gleaming among the trees; and its gay flags and streamers fluttering in the light summer airs. With a heavy sigh she would lean on my arm and proceed. I had no hope for consolation to give her; but she had linked herself to my fortunes, and she was too much of a woman to desert me.

Pensive and silent, then, we traversed the beautiful fields which lie behind Hampstead, and wandered on, until the fiddle, and the hautboy, and the shout, and the laugh, were swallowed up in the deep sound of the big bass-drum, and even that died away into a distant rumble. We passed along the pleasant, sequestered walk of Nightingale Lane. For a pair of lovers, what scene could be more propitious?— But such a pair of lovers! Not a nightingale sang to soothe us: the very gypsies, who were encamped there during the fair, made no offer to tell the fortunes of such an ill-omened couple, whose fortunes, I suppose, they thought too legibly written to need an interpreter; and the gypsy children crawled into their cabins, and peeped out fearfully at us as we went by. For a moment I paused, and was almost tempted to turn gypsy, but the poetical feeling, for the present, was fully satisfied, and I passed on. Thus we travelled and travelled, like a prince and princess in a nursery tale, until we had traversed a part of Hampstead Heath, and arrived in the vicinity of Jack Straw's Castle. Here, wearied and dispirited, we seated ourselves on the margin of the hill, hard by the very mile-stone where Whittington of yore heard the Bowbells ring out the presage of his future greatness. Alas! no bell rung an invitation to us, as we looked disconsolately upon the distant city. Old London seemed to wrap itself unsociably in its mantle of brown smoke, and to offer no encouragement to such a couple of tatterdemalions.

For once, at least, the usual course of the pantomime was reversed,

Harlequin was jilted, and the lover had carried off Columbine in good earnest. But what was I to do with her? I could not take her in my hand, return to my father, throw myself on my knees, and crave his forgiveness and blessing, according to dramatic usage. The very dogs would have chased such a draggled-tailed beauty from the grounds.

In the midst of my doleful dumps, some one tapped me on the shoulder, and, looking up, I saw a couple of rough sturdy fellows standing behind me. Not knowing what to expect, I jumped on my legs, and was preparing again to make battle, but was tripped up and secured in a twinkling.

"Come, come, young master," said one of the fellows in a gruff but good-humored tone, "don't let's have any of your tantrums; one would have thought you had had swing enough for this bout. Come; it's high time to leave off harlequinading, and go home to your father."

In fact, I had fallen into the hands of remoreseless men. The cruel Sacharissa had proclaimed who I was, and that a reward had been offered throughout the country for any tidings of me; and they had seen a description of me which had been inserted in the public papers. Those harpies, therefore, for the mere sake of filthy lucre, were resolved to deliver me over into the hands of my father, and the clutches of my pedagogue.

In vain I swore I would not leave my faithful and afflicted Columbine. In vain I tore myself from their grasp, and flew to her, and vowed to protect her; and wiped the tears from her cheek, and with them a whole blush that might have vied with the carnation for brilliancy. My persecutors were inflexible; they even seemed to exult in our distress; and to enjoy this theatrical display of dirt, and finery, and tribulation. I was carried off in despair, leaving my Columbine destitute in the wide world; but many a look of agony did I cast back at her as she stood gazing piteously after me from the brink of Hampstead Hill; so forlorn, so fine, so ragged, so bedraggled, yet so beautiful.

Thus ended my first peep into the world. I returned home, rich in good-for-nothing experience, and dreading the reward I was to receive for my improvement. My reception, however, was quite different from what I had expected. My father had a spice of the devil in him, and did not seem to like me the worse for my freak, which he termed "sowing my wild oats." He happened to have some of his sporting friends to dine the very day of my return; they made me tell some of my adventures, and laughed heartily at them.

One old fellow, with an outrageously red nose, took to me hugely. I heard him whisper to my father that I was a lad of mettle, and might make something clever; to which my father replied, that I had good points, but was an ill-broken whelp, and required a great deal of the whip. Perhaps this conversation raised me a little in his esteem, for I found the red-nosed old gentleman was a veteran fox-hunter of the neighborhood, for whose opinion my father had vast deference. Indeed, I believe he would have pardoned anything in me more readily than poetry, which he called a cursed, sneaking, puling, housekeeping employment, the bane of all fine manhood. He swore it was unworthy of a youngster of my expectations, who was one day to have so great an estate, and would be able to keep horses and hounds, and hire poets to write songs for him into the bargain.

I had now satisfied, for a time, my roving propensity. I had exhausted the poetical feeling. I had been heartily buffeted out of my love for theatrical display. I felt humiliated by my exposure, and willing to hide my head anywhere for a season, so that I might be out of the way of the ridicule of the world; for I found folks not altogether so indulgent abroad as they were at my father's table. I could not stay at home; the house was intolerably doleful now that my mother was no longer there to cherish me. Everything around spoke mournfully of her. The little flower garden in which she delighted was all in disorder and overrun with weeds. I attempted for a day or two to arrange it, but my heart grew heavier and heavier as I labored. Every little broken-down flower, that I had seen her rear so tenderly, seemed to plead in mute eloquence to my feelings. There was a favorite honeysuckle which I had seen her often training with assiduity, and had heard her say it would be the pride of her garden. I found it grovelling along the ground, tangled and wild, and twining round every worthless weed; and it struck me as an emblem of myself, a mere scatterling, running to waste and uselessness. I could work no longer in the garden.

My father sent me to pay a visit to my uncle, by way of keeping the old gentleman in mind of me. I was received, as usual, without any expression of discontent, which we always considered equivalent to a hearty welcome. Whether he had ever heard of my strolling freak or not, I could not discover, he and his man were both so taciturn. I spent a day or two roaming about the dreary mansion and neglected park, and felt at one time, I believe, a touch of poetry, for I was tempted to drown myself in a fish-pond; I rebuked the evil spirit, however, and it left me. I found the same red-headed boy running wild about the park, but I felt in no humor to hunt him at present. On the contrary, I tried to coax him to me, and to make friends with him; but the young savage was untamable.

When I returned from my uncle's, I remained at home for some time, for my father was disposed, he said, to make a man of me. He took me out hunting with him, and I became a great favorite of the red-nosed squire, because I rode at everything, never refused the boldest leap, and was always sure to be in at the death. I used often, however, to offend my father at hunting-dinners, by taking the wrong side in politics. My father was amazingly ignorant, so ignorant, in fact, as not to know that he knew nothing. He was stanch, however, to church and king, and full of old-fashioned prejudices. Now I had picked up a little knowledge in politics and religion during my rambles with the strollers, and found myself capable of setting him right as to many of his antiquated notions. I felt it my duty to do so; we were apt, therefore, to differ occasionally in the political discussions which sometimes arose at those hunting-dinners.

I was at that age when a man knows least, and is most vain of his knowledge, and when he is extremely tenacious in defending his opinion upon subjects about which he knows nothing. My father was a hard man for any one to argue with, for he never knew when he was refuted. I sometimes posed him a little, but then he had one argument that always settled the question; he would threaten to knock me down. I believe he at last grew tired of me, because I both out-talked and out-rode him. The red-nosed squire, too, got out of conceit with me, because, in the heat of the chase, I rode over him one day as he and his horse lay sprawling in the dirt: so I found myself getting into disgrace with all the world, and would have got heartily out of humor with myself, had I not been kept in tolerable self-conceit by the parson's three daughters.

They were the same who had admired my poetry on a former occasion, when it had brought me into disgrace at school; and I had ever since retained an exalted idea of their judgment. Indeed, they were young ladies not merely of taste, but of science. Their education had been superintended by their mother, who was a blue-stocking. They knew enough of botany to tell the technical names of all the flowers in the garden, and all their secret concerns into the bargain. They knew music, too, not mere commonplace music, but Rossini and Mozart, and they sang Moore's Irish melodies to perfection. They had pretty little work-tables, covered with all kinds of objects of taste: specimens of lava, and painted eggs, and work-boxes, painted and varnished by themselves. They excelled in knotting and netting, and painted in water colors; and made feather fans, and fire screens, and worked in silks and worsteds; and talked French and Italian, and knew Shakspeare by heart. They even knew something of geology and mineralogy; and went about the neighborhood knocking stones to pieces, to the great admiration and perplexity of the country folk.

I am a little too minute, perhaps, in detailing their accomplishments, but I wish to let you see that these were not commonplace young ladies, but had pretensions quite above the ordinary run. It was some consolation to me, therefore, to find favor in such eyes. Indeed, they had always marked me out for a genius, and considered my late vagrant freak as fresh proof of the fact. They observed that Shakspeare himself had been a mere pickle in his youth; that he had stolen a deer, as every one knew, and kept loose company, and consorted with actors: so I comforted myself marvellously with the idea of having so decided a Shakspearian trait in my character.

The youngest of the three, however, was my grand consolation. She was a pale, sentimental girl, with long "hyacinthine" ringlets hanging about her face. She wrote poetry herself, and we kept up a poetical correspondence. She had a taste for the drama, too, and I taught her how to act several of the scenes in *Romeo and Juliet*. I used to rehearse the garden scene under her lattice, which looked out from among woodbine and honeysuckles into the churchyard. I began to think her amazingly pretty as well as clever, and I believe I should have finished by falling in love with her, had not her father discovered our theatrical studies. He was a studious, abstracted man, generally too much absorbed in his learned and religious labors to notice the little foibles of his daughters, and perhaps blinded by a father's fondness; but he unexpectedly put his head out of his study window one day in the midst of a scene, and put a stop to our rehearsals. He had a vast deal of that prosaic good sense which I forever found a stumbling-block in my poetical path. My rambling freak had not struck the good man as poetically as it had his daughters. He drew his comparison from a different manual. He looked upon me as a prodigal son, and doubted whether I should ever arrive at the happy catastrophe of the fatted calf.

I fancy some intimation was given to my father of this new breaking out of my poetical temperament, for he suddenly intimated that it was high time I should prepare for the university. I dreaded a return to the school whence I had eloped; the ridicule of my fellow-scholars, and the glance from the squire's pew, would have been worse than death to me. I was fortunately spared the humiliation. My father sent me to board with a country clergyman, who had three or four boys under his care. I went to him joyfully, for I had often heard my mother mention him with esteem. In fact, he had been an admirer of hers in his younger days, though too humble in fortune and modest in pretensions to aspire to her hand; but he had ever retained a tender regard for her. He was a good man; a worthy specimen of that valuable body of our country clergy who silently and unostentatiously do a vast deal of good;

who are, as it were, woven into the whole system of rural life, and operate upon it with the steady yet unobtrusive influence of temperate piety and learned good sense. He lived in a small village not far from Warwick, one of those little communities where the scanty flock is, in a manner, folded into the bosom of the pastor. The venerable church, in its grass-grown cemetery, was one of those rural temples scattered about our country as if to sanctify the land.

I have the worthy pastor before my mind's eye at this moment, with his mild, benevolent countenance, rendered still more venerable by his silver hairs. I have him before me, as I saw him on my arrival, seated in the embowered porch of his small parsonage, with a flower garden before it, and his pupils gathered round him like his children. I shall never forget his reception of me; for I believe he thought of my poor mother at the time, and his heart yearned towards her child. His eye glistened when he received me at the door, and he took me into his arms as the adopted child of his affections. Never had I been so fortunately placed. He was one of those excellent members of our church, who help out their narrow salaries by instructing a few gentleman's sons. I am convinced those little seminaries are among the best nurseries of talent and virtue in the land. Both heart and mind are cultivated and improved. The preceptor is the companion and the friend of his pupils. His sacred character gives him dignity in their eyes, and his solemn functions produce that elevation of mind and sobriety of conduct necessary to those who are to teach youth to think and act worthily.

I speak from my own random observation and experience; but I think I speak correctly. At any rate, I can trace much of what is good in my own heterogeneous compound to the short time I was under the instruction of that good man. He entered into the cares and occupations and amusements of his pupils; and won his way into our confidence, and studied our hearts and minds more intently than we did our books.

He soon sounded the depth of my character. I had become, as I have already hinted, a little liberal in my notions, and apt to philosophize on both politics and religion; having seen something of men and things, and learnt, from my fellow philosophers, the strollers, to despise all vulgar prejudices. He did not attempt to cast down my vainglory, nor to question my right view of things; he merely instilled into my mind a little information on these topics; though in a quiet, unobtrusive way, that never ruffled a feather of my self-conceit. I was astonished to find what a change a little knowledge makes in one's mode of viewing matters; and how different a subject is when one thinks, or when one only talks about it. I conceived a vast deference for my teacher, and was ambitious of his good opinion. In my zeal to make a favorable impression, I presented him with a whole ream of my poetry. He read it attentively, smiled, and pressed my hand when he returned it to me, but said nothing. The next day he set me at mathematics.

Somehow or other the process of teaching seemed robbed by him of all its austerity. I was not conscious that he thwarted an inclination or opposed a wish; but I felt that, for the time, my inclinations were entirely changed. I became fond of study, and zealous to improve myself. I made tolerable advances in studies which I had before considered as unattainable, and I wondered at my own proficiency. I thought, too, I astonished my preceptor; for I often caught his eyes fixed upon me with a peculiar expression. I suspect, since, that he was pensively tracing in my countenance the early lineaments of my mother.

Education was not apportioned by him into tasks and enjoined as a labor, to be abandoned with joy the moment the hour of study was expired. We had, it is true, our allotted hours of occupation, to give us habits of method, and of the distribution of time; but they were made pleasant to us, and our feelings were enlisted in the cause. When they were over, education still went on. It pervaded all our relaxations and amusements. There was a steady march of improvement. Much of his instruction was given during pleasant rambles, or when seated on the margin of the Avon; and information received in that way, often makes a deeper impression than when acquired by poring over books. I have many of the pure and eloquent precepts that flowed from his lips associated in my mind with lovely scenes in nature, which makes the recollection of them indescribably delightful.

I do not pretend to say that any miracle was effected with me. After all said and done, I was but a weak disciple. My poetical temperament still wrought within me and wrestled hard with wisdom, and, I fear, maintained the mastery. I found mathematics an intolerable task in fine weather. I would be prone to forget my problems, to watch the birds hopping about the windows, or the bees humming about the honeysuckles; and whenever I could steal away, I would wander about the grassy borders of the Avon, and excuse this truant propensity to myself with the idea that I was treading classic ground, over which Shakspeare had wandered. What luxurious idleness have I indulged, as I lay under the trees and watched the silver waves rippling through the arches of the broken bridge, and laving the rocky bases of old Warwick Castle; and how often have I thought of sweet Shakspeare, and in my boyish enthusiasm have kissed the waves which had washed his native village.

My good preceptor would often accompany me in these desultory rambles. He sought to get hold of this vagrant mood of mind and turn it to some account. He endeavored to teach me to mingle thought with mere sensation; to moralize on the scenes around; and to make the beauties of nature administer to the understanding of the heart. He endeavored to direct my imagination to high and noble objects, and to fill it with lofty images. In a word, he did all he could to make the best of a poetical temperament, and to counteract the mischief which had been done to me by my great expectations.

Had I been earlier put under the care of the good pastor, or remained with him a longer time, I really believe he would have made something of me. He had already brought a great deal of what had been flogged into me into tolerable order, and had weeded out much of the unprofitable wisdom which had sprung up in my vagabondizing. I already began to find that with all my genius a little study would be no disadvantage to me; and, in spite of my vagrant freaks, I began to doubt my being a second Shakspeare.

Just as I was making these precious discoveries, the good parson died. It was a melancholy day throughout the neighborhood. He had his little flock of scholars, his children, as he used to call us, gathered round him in his dying moments; and he gave us the parting advice of a father, now that he had to leave us, and we were to be separated from each other, and scattered about in the world. He took me by the hand, and talked with me earnestly and affectionately, and called to my mind my mother, and used her name to enforce his dying exhortations; for I rather think he considered me the most erring and heedless of his flock. He held my hand in his, long after he had done speaking, and kept his eye fixed on me tenderly and almost piteously: his lips moved as if he were silently praying for me; and he died away, still holding me by the hand.

There was not a dry eye in the church when the funeral service was read from the pulpit from which he had so often preached. When the body was committed to the earth, our little band gathered round it, and watched the coffin as it was lowered into the grave. The parishioners looked at us with sympathy; for we were mourners not merely in dress but in heart. We lingered about the grave, and clung to one another for a time, weeping and speechless, and then parted, like a band of brothers parting from the paternal hearth, never to assemble there again.

How had the gentle spirit of that good man sweetened our natures, and linked our young hearts together by the kindest ties! I have always had a throb of pleasure at meeting with an old schoolmate, even though one of my truant associates; but whenever, in the course of my life, I have encountered one of that little flock with which I was folded on the banks of the Avon, it has been with a gush of affection, and a glow of virtue, that for the moment have made me a better man.

I was now sent to Oxford, and was wonderfully impressed on first entering it as a student. Learning here puts on all its majesty. It is lodged in palaces; it is sanctified by the sacred ceremonies of religion; it has a pomp and circumstance which powerfully affect the imagination. Such, at least, it had in my eyes, thoughtless as I was. My previous studies with the worthy pastor had prepared me to regard it with deference and awe. He had been educated here, and always spoke of the University with filial fondness and classic veneration. When I beheld the clustering spires and pinnacles of this most august of cities rising from the plain, I hailed them in my enthusiasm as the points of a diadem, which the nation had placed upon the brows of science.

For a time old Oxford was full of enjoyment for me. There was a charm about its monastic buildings; its great Gothic quadrangles; its solemn halls, and shadowy cloisters. I delighted, in the evenings, to get in places surrounded by the colleges, where all modern buildings were screened from the sight; and to see the professors and students sweeping along in the dusk in their antiquated caps and gowns. I seemed for a time to be transported among the people and edifices of the old times. I was a frequent attendant, also, of the evening service in the New College Hall; to hear the fine organ, and the choir swelling an anthem in that solemn building, where painting, music, and architecture are in such admirable unison.

A favorite haunt, too, was the beautiful walk bordered by lofty elms along the river, behind the gray walls of Magdalen College, which goes by the name of Addison's Walk, from being his favorite resort when an Oxford student. I became also a lounger in the Bodleian library, and a great dipper into books, though I cannot say that I studied them; in fact, being no longer under direction or control, I was gradually relapsing into mere indulgence of the fancy. Still this would have been pleasant and harmless enough, and I might have awakened from mere literary dreaming to something better. The chances were in my favor, for the riotous times of the University were past. The days of hard drinking were at an end. The old feuds of "Town and Gown," like the civil wars of the White and Red Rose, had died away; and student and citizen slept in peace and whole skins, without risk of being summoned in the night to bloody brawl. It had become the fashion to study at the University, and the odds were always in favor of my following the fashion. Unluckily, however, I fell in company with a special knot of young fellows, of lively parts and ready wit, who had lived occasionally upon town, and become initiated into the *Fancy.* They voted study to be the toil of dull minds, by which they slowly crept up the hill, while genius arrived at it at a bound. I felt ashamed to play the owl among such gay birds; so I threw by my books, and became a man of spirit.

As my father made me a tolerable allowance, notwithstanding the narrowness of his income, having an eye always to my great expectations, I was enabled to appear to advantage among my companions. I cultivated all kinds of sport and exercises. I was one of the most expert oarsmen that rowed on the Isis. I boxed, fenced, angled, shot, and hunted, and my rooms in college were always decorated with whips of all kinds, spurs, fowling pieces, fishing rods, foils, and boxing gloves. A pair of leather breeches would seem to be throwing one leg out of the half-open drawers, and empty bottles lumbered the bottom of every closet.

My father came to see me at college when I was in the height of my career. He asked me how I came on with my studies, and what kind of hunting there was in the neighborhood. He examined my various sporting apparatus with a curious eye; wanted to know if any of the professors were fox-hunters, and whether they were generally good shots, for he suspected their studying so much must be hurtful to the sight. We had a day's shooting together: I delighted him with my skill, and astonished him by my learned disquisitions on horse-flesh, and on Manton's guns; so, upon the whole, he departed highly satisfied with my improvement at college.

I do not know how it is, but I cannot be idle long without getting in love. I had not been a very long time a man of spirit, therefore, before I became deeply enamoured of a shopkeeper's daughter in the High Street, who, in fact, was the admiration of many of the students. I wrote several sonnets in praise of her, and spent half of my pocket money at the shop, in buying articles which I did not want, that I might have an opportunity of speaking to her. Her father, a severe-looking old gentleman, with bright silver buckles and a crisp-curled wig, kept a strict guard on her, as the fathers generally do upon their daughters in Oxford; and well they may. I tried to get into his good graces, and to be sociable with him, but all in vain. I said several good things in his shop, but he never laughed: he had no relish for wit and humor. He was one of those dry gentlemen who keep youngsters at bay. He had already brought up two or three daughters, and was experienced in the ways of students. He was as knowing and wary as a gray old badger that has often been hunted. To see him on Sunday, so stiff and starched in his demeanor, so precise in his dress, with his daughter under his arm, was enough to deter all graceless youngsters from approaching.

I managed, however, in spite of his vigilance, to have several conversations with the daughter, as I cheapened articles in the shop. I made terrible long bargains, and examined the articles over and over before I purchased. In the meantime, I would convey a sonnet or an acrostic under cover of a piece of cambric, or slipped into a pair of stockings; I would whisper soft nonsense into her ear as I haggled about the price; and would squeeze her hand tenderly as I received my halfpence of change in a bit of whity-brown paper. Let this serve as a hint to all haberdashers who have pretty daughters for shop-girls, and young students for customers. I do not know whether my words and looks were very eloquent, but my poetry was irresistible; for, to tell the truth, the girl had some literary taste, and was seldom without a book from the circulating library.

By the divine power of poetry, therefore, which is so potent with the lovely sex, did I subdue the heart of this fair little haberdasher. We carried on a sentimental correspondence for a time across the counter, and I supplied her with rhyme by the stocking-full. At length I prevailed on her to grant an assignation. But how was this to be effected? Her father kept her always under his eye; she never walked out alone; and the house was locked up the moment that the shop was shut. All these difficulties served but to give zest to the adventure. I proposed that the assignation should be in her own chamber, into which I would climb at night. The plan was irresistible—A cruel father, a secret lover, and a clandestine meeting! All the little girl's studies from the circulating library seemed about to be realized.

But what had I in view in making this assignation? Indeed, I know not. I had no evil intentions, nor can I say that I had any good ones. I liked the girl, and wanted to have an opportunity of seeing more of her; and the assignation was made, as I have done many things else, heedlessly and without forethought. I asked myself a few questions of the kind, after all my arrangements were made, but the answers were very unsatisfactory. "Am I to ruin this poor thoughtless girl?" said I to myself. "No!" was the prompt and indignant answer. "Am I to run away with her?"—"whither, and to what purpose?"—"Well, then, am I to marry her?"—"Poh! a man of my expectations marry a shopkeeper's daughter!" "What then am I to do with her?" "Hum—why—let me get into the chamber first, and then consider"—and so the self-examination ended.

Well, sir, "come what come might," I stole under cover of the darkness to the dwelling of my dulcinea. All was quiet. At the concerted signal her window was gently opened. It was just above the projecting bow-window of her father's shop, which assisted me in mounting. The house was low, and I was enabled to scale the fortress with tolerable ease. I clambered with a beating heart; I reached the casement; I hoisted my body half into the chamber; and was welcomed, not by the embraces of my expecting fair one, but by the grasp of the crabbed-looking old father in the crisp-curled wig.

I extricated myself from his clutches, and endeavored to make my retreat; but I was confounded by his cries of thieves! and robbers! I was bothered too by his Sunday cane, which was amazingly busy about my head as I descended, and against which my hat was but a poor protection. Never before had I an idea of the activity of an old man's arm, and the hardness of the knob of an ivory-headed cane. In my hurry and confusion I missed my footing, and fell sprawling on the pavement. I was immediately surrounded by myrmidons, who, I doubt not, were on the watch for me. Indeed, I was in no situation to escape, for I had sprained my ankle in the fall, and could not stand. I was seized as a house-breaker; and to exonerate myself of a great crime, I had to accuse myself of a less. I made known who I was, and why I came there. Alas! the varlets knew it already, and were only amusing themselves at my expense. My perfidious Muse had been playing me one of her slippery tricks. The old curmudgeon of a father had found my sonnets and acrostics hid away in holes and corners of his shop; he had no taste for poetry like his daughter, and had instituted a rigorous though silent observation. He had moused upon our letters, detected our plans, and prepared everything for my reception. Thus was I ever doomed to be led into scrapes by the Muse. Let no man henceforth carry on a secret amour in poetry!

The old man's ire was in some measure appeased by the pommelling of my head and the anguish of my sprain; so he did not put me to death on the spot. He was even humane enough to furnish a shutter, on which I was carried back to college like a wounded warrior. The porter was roused to admit me. The college gate was thrown open for my entry. The affair was blazed about the next morning, and became the joke of the college from the buttery to the hall.

I had leisure to repent during several weeks' confinement by my sprain, which I passed in translating Boethius's *Consolations of Philosophy*. I received a most tender and ill-spelled letter from my mistress, who had been sent to a relation in Coventry. She protested her innocence of my misfortune, and vowed to be true to me "till deth." I took no notice of the letter, for I was cured for the present, both of love and poetry. Women, however, are more constant in their attachments than men, whatever philosophers may say to the contrary. I am assured that she actually remained faithful to her vow for several months; but she had to deal with a cruel father, whose heart was as hard as the knob of his cane. He was not to be touched by tears nor poetry, but absolutely compelled her to marry a reputable young tradesman, who made her a happy woman in spite of herself and of all the rules of romance, and, what is more, the mother of several children. They are at this very day a thriving couple, and keep a snug corner-shop, just opposite the figure of Peeping Tom, at Coventry.

I will not fatigue you by any more details of my studies at Oxford; though they were not always as severe as these, nor did I always pay as dear for my lessons. To be brief, then, I lived on in my usual miscellaneous manner, gradually getting knowledge of good and evil, until I had attained my twenty-first year. I had scarcely come of age when I heard of the sudden death of my father. The shock was severe, for though he had never treated me with much kindness, still he was my father, and at his death I felt alone in the world.

I returned home, and found myself the solitary master of the paternal mansion. A crowd of gloomy feelings came thronging upon me. It was a place that always sobered me, and brought me to reflection, now especially; it looked so deserted and melancholy. I entered the little breakfasting-room. There were my father's whip and spurs, hanging by the fireplace; the *Stud-Book, Sporting Magazine,* and *Racing Calendar,* his only reading. His favorite spaniel lay on the hearth-rug. The poor animal, who had never before noticed me, now came fondling about me, licked my hand, then looked round the room, whined, wagged his tail slightly, and gazed wistfully in my face. I felt the full force of the appeal. "Poor Dash," said I, "we are both alone in the world, with nobody to care for us, and will take care of one another."—The dog never quitted me afterwards.

I could not go into my mother's room—my heart swelled when I passed within sight of the door. Her portrait hung in the parlor, just over the place where she used to sit. As I cast my eyes on it, I thought that it looked at me with tenderness, and I burst into tears. I was a careless dog, it is true, hardened a little, perhaps, by living in public schools, and buffeting about among strangers, who cared nothing for me; but the recollection of a mother's tenderness was overcoming.

I was not of an age or a temperament to be long depressed. There was a reaction in my system that always brought me up again after every pressure; and, indeed, my spirits were always most buoyant after a temporary prostration. I settled the concerns of the estate as soon as possible; realized my property, which was not very considerable, but which appeared a vast deal to me, having a poetical eye that magnified everything; and finding myself, at the end of a few months, free of all further business or restraint, I determined to go to London and enjoy myself. Why should I not? I was young, animated, joyous; had plenty of funds for present pleasures, and my uncle's estate in the perspective. Let those mope at college, and pore over books, thought I, who have their way to make in the world; it would be ridiculous drudgery in a youth of my expectations. Away to London, therefore, I rattled in a tandem, determined to take the town gayly. I passed through several of the villages where I had played the Jack Pudding a few years before; and I visited the scenes of many of my adventures and follies merely from that feeling of melancholy pleasure which we have in stepping again the footprints of foregone existence, even when they have passed among weeds and briers. I made a circuit in the latter part of my journey, so as to take in West End and Hampstead, the scenes of my last dramatic exploit, and of the battle royal of the booth. As I drove along the ridge of Hampstead Hill, by Jack Straw's Castle, I paused at the spot where Columbine and I had sat down so disconsolately in our ragged finery, and had looked dubiously on London. I almost expected to see her again, standing on the hill's brink, "like Niobe, all tears"—mournful as Babylon in ruins!

"Poor Columbine!" said I, with a heavy sigh, "thou wert a gallant, generous girl—a true woman;—faithful to the distressed, and ready to sacrifice thyself in the cause of worthless man!"

I tried to whistle off the recollection of her, for there was always something of self-reproach with it. I drove gayly along the road, enjoying the stare of hostlers and stable-boys, as I managed my horses knowingly down the steep street of Hampstead; when just at the skirts of the village, one of the traces of my leader came loose. I pulled up, and as the animal was restive, and my servant a bungler, I called for assistance to the robustious master of a snug alehouse, who stood at his door with a tankard in his hand. He came readily to assist me, followed by his wife, with her bosom half open, a child in her arms, and two more at her heels. I stared for a moment, as if doubting my eyes. I could not be mistaken; in the fat, beer-blown landlord of the alehouse I recollected my old rival Harlequin, and in his slattern spouse the once trim and dimpling Columbine.

The change of my looks from youth to manhood, and the change in my circumstances, prevented them from recognizing me. They could not suspect in the dashing young buck, fashionably dressed and driving his own equipage, the painted beau, with old peaked hat, and long flimsy, sky-blue coat. My heart yearned with kindness towards Columbine, and I was glad to see her establishment a thriving one. As soon as the harness was adjusted, I tossed a small purse of gold into her ample bosom; and then, pretending to give my horse a hearty cut of the whip, I made the lash curl with a whistling about the sleek sides of ancient Harlequin. The horses dashed off like lightning, and I was whirled out of sight before either of the parties could get over their surprise at my liberal donations. I have always considered this as one of the greatest proofs of my poetical genius; it was distributing poetical justice in perfection.

I now entered London *en cavalier*, and became a blood upon town. I took fashionable lodgings, in the West End; employed the first tailor; frequented the regular lounges; gambled a little; lost my money good-humoredly; and gained a number of fashionable, good-for-nothing acquaintances. I gained some reputation also for a man of science, having become an expert boxer in the course of my studies at Oxford. I was distinguished, therefore, among the gentlemen of the Fancy; became hand and glove with certain boxing noblemen, and was the admiration of the Fives Court. A gentleman's science, however, is apt to get him into bad scrapes; he is too prone to play the knight-errant, and to pick up quarrels which less scientifical gentlemen would quietly avoid. I undertook one day to punish the insolence of a porter. He was a Hercules of a fellow, but then I was so secure in my science! I gained the victory of course. The porter pocketed his humiliation, bound up his broken head, and went about his business as unconcernedly as though nothing had happened; while I went to bed with my victory, and did not dare to show my battered face for a fortnight: by which I discovered that a gentleman may have the worst of the battle even when victorious.

I am naturally a philosopher, and no one can moralize better after a misfortune has taken place; so I lay on my bed and moralized on this sorry ambition, which levels the gentleman with the clown. I know it is the opinion of many sages, who have thought deeply on these matters, that the noble science of boxing keeps up the bull-dog courage of the nation; and far be it from me to decry the advantage of becoming a nation of bull-dogs; but I now saw clearly that it was calculated to keep up the breed of English ruffians. "What is the Fives Court," said I to myself, as I turned uncomfortably in bed, "but a college of scoundrelism, where every bully-ruffian in the land may gain a fellowship? What is the slang language of the Fancy but a jargon by which fools and knaves commune and understand each other, and enjoy a kind of superiority over the uninitiated? What is a boxing match but an arena, where the noble and the illustrious are jostled into familiarity with the infamous and the vulgar? What, in fact, is the Fancy itself, but a chain of easy communication, extending from the peer down to the pick-pocket, through the medium of which a man of rank may find he has shaken hands, at three removes, with the murderer on the gibbet?—

"Enough!" ejaculated I, thoroughly convinced through the force of my philosophy, and the pain of my bruises,—"I'll have nothing more to do with the Fancy." So when I had recovered from my victory, I turned my attention to softer themes, and became a devoted admirer of the ladies. Had I more industry and ambition in my nature, I might have worked my way to the very height of fashion, as I saw many laborious gentlemen doing around me. But it is a toilsome, an anxious, and an unhappy life; there are few things so sleepless and miserable as your cultivators of fashionable smiles. I was quite content with that kind of society which forms the frontiers of fashion, and may be easily taken possession of. I found it a light, easy, productive soil. I had but to go about and sow visiting-cards, and I reaped a whole harvest of invitations. Indeed, my figure and address were by no means against me. It was whispered, too, among the young ladies, that I was prodigiously clever, and wrote poetry; and the old ladies had ascertained that I was a young gentleman of good family, handsome fortune, and "great expectations."

I now was carried away by the hurry of gay life, so intoxicating to a young man, and which a man of poetical temperament enjoys so highly on his first tasting of it; that rapid variety of sensations; that whirl of brilliant objects; that succession of pungent pleasures! I had no time for thought. I only felt. I never attempted to write poetry; my poetry seemed all to go off by transpiration. I lived poetry; it was all a poetical dream to me. A mere sensualist knows nothing of the delights of a splendid metropolis. He lives in a round of animal gratifications and heartless habits. But to a young man of poetical feelings, it is an ideal world, a scene of enchantment and delusion; his imagination is in perpetual excitement, and gives a spiritual zest to every pleasure.

A season of town life, however, somewhat sobered me of my intoxication; or rather I was rendered more serious by one of my old complaints—I fell in love. It was with a very pretty, though a very haughty fair one, who had come to London under the care of an old maiden aunt to enjoy the pleasures of a winter in town, and to get married. There was not a doubt of her commanding a choice of lovers; for she had long been the belle of a little cathedral city, and one of the poets of the place had absolutely celebrated her beauty in a copy of Latin verses. The most extravagant anticipations were formed by her friends of the sensation she would produce. It was feared by some that she might be precipitate in her choice, and take up with some inferior title. The aunt was determined nothing should gain her under a lord.

Alas! with all her charms, the young lady lacked the one thing needful—she had no money. So she waited in vain for duke, marquis, or earl, to throw himself at her feet. As the season waned, so did the lady's expectations; when, just towards the close, I made my advances.

I was most favorably received by both the young lady and her aunt. It is true, I had no title; but then such great expectations. A marked preference was immediately shown me over two rivals, the younger son of a needy baronet, and a captain of dragoons on half-pay. I did not absolutely take the field in form, for I was determined not to be precipitate; but I drove my equipage frequently through the street in which she lived, and was always sure to see her at the window, generally with a book in her hand. I resumed my knack at rhyming, and sent her a long copy of verses; anonymously, to be sure, but she knew my handwriting. Both aunt and niece, however, displayed the most delightful ignorance on the subject. The young lady showed them to me; wondered who they could be written by; and declared there was nothing in this world she loved so much as poetry; while the maiden aunt would put her pinching spectacles on her nose, and read them, with blunders in sense and sound, excruciating to an author's ears; protesting there was nothing equal to them in the whole Elegant Extracts.

The fashionable season closed without my adventuring to make a declaration, though I certainly had encouragement. I was not perfectly sure that I had effected a lodgment in the young lady's heart; and, to tell the truth, the aunt overdid her part, and was a little too extravagant in her liking of me. I knew that maiden aunts were not to be captivated by the mere personal merits of their nieces' admirers; and I wanted to ascertain how much of all this favor I owed to driving an equipage, and having great expectations.

I had received many hints how charming their native place was during the summer months; what pleasant society they had; and what beautiful drives about the neighborhood. They had not, therefore, returned home long, before I made my appearance in dashing style, driving down the principal street. The very next morning I was seen at prayers, seated in the same pew with the reigning belle. Questions were whispered about the aisles, after service, "Who is he?" and "What is he?" And the replies were as usual, "A young gentleman of good family and fortune, and great expectations."

I was much struck with the peculiarities of this reverend little place. A cathedral, with its dependencies and regulations, presents a picture of other times, and of a different order of things. It is a rich relic of a more poetical age. There still linger about it the silence and solemnity of the cloister. In the present instance especially, where the cathedral was large, and the town small, its influence was the more apparent. The solemn pomp of the service, performed twice a day, with the grand intonations of the organ, and the voices of the choir swelling through the magnificent pile, diffused, as it were, a perpetual Sabbath over the place. This routine of solemn ceremony continually going on, independent, as it were, of the world; this daily offering of melody and praise, ascending like incense from the altar, had a powerful effect upon my imagination.

The aunt introduced me to her coterie, formed of families connected with the cathedral, and others of moderate fortune, but high respectability, who had nestled themselves under the wings of the cathedral to enjoy good society at moderate expense. It was a highly aristocratical little circle; scrupulous in its intercourse with others, and jealously cautious about admitting anything common or unclean.

It seemed as if the courtesies of the old school had taken refuge here. There were continual interchanges of civilities, and of small presents of fruits and delicacies, and of complimentary crow-quill billets; for in a quiet, well-bred community like this, living entirely at ease, little duties, and little amusements, and little civilities, filled up the day. I have seen, in the midst of a warm day, a corpulent, powdered footman, issuing from the iron gateway of a stately mansion, and traversing the little place with an air of mighty import, bearing a small tart on a large silver salver.

Their evening amusements were sobered and primitive. They assembled at a moderate hour; the young ladies played music, and the old ladies, whist; and at an early hour they dispersed. There was no parade on these social occasions. Two or three old sedan chairs were in constant activity, though the greater part made their exit in clogs and pattens, with a footman or waiting-maid carrying a lantern in advance; and long before midnight the clank of pattens and gleam of lanterns about the quiet little place told that the evening party had dissolved.

Still I did not feel myself altogether so much at my ease as I had anticipated considering the smallness of the place. I found it very different from the other country places, and that it was not so easy to make a dash there. Sinner that I was! the very dignity and decorum of the little community was rebuking to me. I feared my past idleness and folly would rise in judgment against me. I stood in awe of the dignitaries of the cathedral, whom I saw mingling familiarly in society. I became nervous on this point. The creak of a prebendary's shoes, sounding from one end of a quiet street to another, was appalling to me; and the sight of a shovel hat was sufficient at any time to check me in the midst of my boldest poetical soarings.

And then the good aunt could not be quiet, but would cry me up for a genius, and extol my poetry to every one. So long as she confined this to the ladies it did well enough, because they were able to feel and appreciate poetry of the new romantic school. Nothing would content the good lady, however, but she must read my verses to a prebendary, who had long been the undoubted critic of the place. He was a thin, delicate old gentleman, of mild, polished manners, steeped to the lips in classic lore, and not easily put in a heat by any hot-blooded poetry of the day. He listened to my most fervid thoughts and fervid words without a glow; shook his head with a smile, and condemned them as not being according to Horace, as not being legitimate poetry.

Several old ladies, who had heretofore been my admirers, shook their heads at hearing this: they could not think of praising any poetry that was not according to Horace; and as to anything illegitimate, it was not to be countenanced in good society. Thanks to my stars, however, I had youth and novelty on my side: so the young ladies persisted in admiring my poetry in despite of Horace and illegitimacy.

I consoled myself with the good opinion of the young ladies, whom I had always found to be the best judges of poetry. As to these old scholars, said I, they are apt to be chilled by being steeped in the cold fountains of the classics. Still I felt that I was losing ground, and that it was necessary to bring matters to a point. Just as this time there was a public ball, attended by the best society of the place, and by the gentry of the neighborhood: I took great pains with my toilet on the occasion, and I had never looked better. I had determined that night to make my grand assault on the heart of the young lady, to battle it with all my forces, and the next morning to demand a surrender in due form.

I entered the ball-room amidst a buzz and flutter, which generally took place among the young ladies on my appearance. I was in fine spirits; for, to tell the truth, I had exhilarated myself by a cheerful glass of wine on the occasion. I talked, and rattled, and said a thousand silly things, slap-dash, with all the confidence of a man sure of his auditors,—and everything had its effect.

In the midst of my triumph I observed a little knot gathering together in the upper part of the room. By degrees it increased. A tittering broke out here and there, and glances were cast round at me, and then there would be fresh tittering. Some of the young ladies would hurry away to distant parts of the room, and whisper to their friends. Wherever they went, there was still this tittering and glancing at me. I did not know what to make of all this. I looked at myself from head to foot, and peeped at my back in a glass, to see if anything was odd about my person; any awkward exposure, any whimsical tag hanging out;—no—everything was right—I was a perfect picture. I determined that it must be some choice saying of mine that was bandied about in this knot of merry beauties, and I determined to enjoy one of my good things in the rebound. I stepped gently, therefore, up the room, smiling at every one as I passed, who, I must say, all smiled and tittered in return. I approached the group, smirking and perking my chin, like a man who is full of pleasant feeling, and sure of being well received. The cluster of little belles opened as I advanced.

Heavens and earth! whom should I perceive in the midst of them but my early and tormenting flame, the everlasting Sacharissa! She was grown, it is true, into the full beauty of womanhood; but showed, by the provoking merriment of her countenance, that she perfectly recollected me, and the ridiculous flagellations of which she had twice been the cause.

I saw at once the exterminating cloud of ridicule bursting over me. My crest fell. The flame of love went suddenly out, or was extinguished by overwhelming shame. How I got down the room I know not; I fancied every one tittering at me. Just as I reached the door, I caught a glance of my mistress and her aunt listening to the whispers of Sacharissa, the old lady raising her hands and eyes, and the face of the young one lighted up, as I imagined, with scorn ineffable. I paused to see no more, but made two steps from the top of the stairs to the bottom. The next morning, before sunrise, I beat a retreat, and did not feel the blushes cool from my tingling cheeks, until I had lost sight of the old towers of the cathedral.

I now returned to town thoughtful and crestfallen. My money was nearly spent, for I had lived freely and without calculation. The dream of love was over, and the reign of pleasure at an end. I determined to retrench while I had yet a trifle left: so, selling my equipage and horses for half their value, I quietly put the money in my pocket, and turned pedestrian. I had not a doubt that, with my great expectations, I could at any time raise funds, either on usury or by borrowing; but I was principled against both, and resolved by strict economy to make my slender purse hold out until my uncle should give up the ghost, or rather the estate. I stayed at home therefore and read, and would have written, but I had already suffered too much from my poetical productions, which had generally involved me in some ridiculous scrape. I gradually acquired a rusty look, and had a straightened money-borrowing air, upon which the world began to shy me. I have never felt disposed to quarrel with the world for its conduct; it has always used me well. When I have been flush and gay, and disposed for society, it has caressed me; and when I have been pinched and reduced, and wished to be alone, why, it has left me alone; and what more could a man desire? Take my word for it, this world is a more obliging world than people generally represent it.

Well, sir, in the midst of my entrenchment, my retirement, and my studiousness, I received news that my uncle was dangerously ill. I hastened on the wings of an heir's affections to receive his dying breath and his last testament. I found him attended by his faithful valet, old Iron John; by the woman who occasionally worked about the house, and by the foxy-headed boy, young Orson, whom I had occasionally hunted about the park. Iron John gasped a kind of asthmatical salutation as I entered the room, and received me with something almost like a smile of welcome. The woman sat blubbering at the foot of the bed; and the foxy-headed Orson, who had now grown up to be a lubberly lout, stood gazing in stupid vacancy at a distance.

My uncle lay stretched upon his back. The chamber was without fire, or any of the comforts of a sick-room. The cobwebs flaunted from the ceiling. The tester was covered with dust, and the curtains were tattered. From underneath the bed peeped out one end of his strong box. Against the wainscot were suspended rusty blunderbusses, horse-pistols, and a cut-and-thrust sword, with which he had forfeited his room to defend his life and treasure. He had employed no physician during his illness; and from the scanty relics lying on the table, seemed almost to have denied himself the assistance of a cook.

When I entered the room, he was lying motionless; his eyes fixed and his mouth open: at the first look I thought him a corpse. The noise of my entrance made him turn his head. At the sight of me a ghastly smile came over his face, and his glazing eye gleamed with satisfaction. It was the only smile he had ever given me, and it went to my heart. "Poor old man!" thought I, "Why should you force me to leave you thus desolate, when I see that my presence has the power to cheer you?"

"Nephew," said he, after several efforts, and in a low gasping voice, —"I am glad you are come. I shall now die with satisfaction. Look," said he, raising his withered hand, and pointing,—"look in that box on the table: you will find that I have not forgotten you."

I pressed his hand to my heart, and the tears stood in my eyes. I sat down by his bedside, and watched him, but he never spoke again. My presence, however, gave him evident satisfaction; for every now and then, as he looked to me, a vague smile would come over his visage, and he would feebly point to the sealed box on the table. As the day wore away, his life appeared to wear away with it. Towards sunset his head sank on the bed, and lay motionless, his eyes grew glazed, his mouth remained open, and thus he gradually died.

I could not but feel shocked at this absolute extinction of my kindred. I dropped a tear of real sorrow over this strange old man, who had thus reserved the smile of kindness to his death-bed,—like an evening sun after a gloomy day, just shining out to set in darkness. Leaving the corpse in charge of the domestics, I retired for the night.

It was a rough night. The winds seemed as if singing my uncle's requiem about the mansion, and the bloodhounds howled without, as if they knew of the death of their old master. Iron John almost grudged me the tallow candle to burn in my apartment, and light up its dreariness, so accustomed had he been to starveling economy. I could not sleep. The recollection of my uncle's dying-scene, and the sounds about the house, affected my mind. These, however, were succeeded by plans for the future, and I lay awake the greater part of the night, indulging the poetical anticipation how soon I should make these old walls ring with cheerful life, and restore the hospitality of my mother's ancestors.

My uncle's funeral was decent, but private. I knew that nobody respected his memory, and I was determined none should be summoned to sneer over his funeral, and make merry at his grave. He was buried in the church of the neighboring village, though it was not the burying-place of his race; but he had expressly enjoined that he should not be buried with his family: he had quarrelled with most of them when living, and he carried his resentments even into the grave.

I defrayed the expenses of the funeral out of my own purse, that I might have done with the undertakers at once, and clear the ill-omened birds from the premises. I invited the parson of the parish, and the lawyer from the village, to attend at the house the next morning, and hear the reading of the will. I treated them to an excellent breakfast, a profusion that had not been seen at the house for many a year. As soon as the breakfast things were removed, I summoned Iron John, the woman, and the boy, for I was particular in having every one present, and proceeding regularly. The box was placed on the table—all was silence—I broke the seal—raised the lid, and beheld—not the will—but my accursed poem of Doubting Castle and Giant Despair!

Could any mortal have conceived that this old withered man, so taciturn, and apparently so lost to feeling, could have treasured up for years the thoughtless pleasantry of a boy, to punish him with such cruel ingenuity? I now could account for his dying smile, the only one he had ever given me. He had been a grave man all his life, it was strange that he should die in the enjoyment of a joke, and it was hard that that joke should be at my expense.

The lawyer and the parson seemed at a loss to comprehend the matter. "Here must be some mistake," said the lawyer; "there is no will here."

"Oh!" said Iron John, creaking forth his rusty jaws, "if it is a will you are looking for, I believe I can find one."

He retired with the same singular smile with which he had greeted me on my arrival, and which I now apprehended boded me no good. In a little while he returned with a will perfect at all points, properly signed and sealed, and witnessed and worded with horrible correctness; in which the deceased left large legacies to Iron John and his daughter, and the residue of his fortune to the foxy-headed boy, who, to my utter astonishment, was his son by this very woman; he having married her privately, and, as I verily believe, for no other purpose than to have an heir, and so balk my father and his issue of the inheritance. There was one proviso, in which he mentioned, that, having discovered his nephew to have a pretty turn for poetry, he presumed he had no occasion for wealth; he recommended him, however, to the patronage of his heir, and requested that he might have a garret, rent-free, in Doubting Castle.

GRAVE REFLECTIONS OF A
DISAPPOINTED MAN

M R. BUCKTHORNE had paused at the death of his uncle, and the downfall of his great expectations, which formed, as he said, an epoch in his history; and it was not until some little time afterwards, and in a very sober mood, that he resumed his party-colored narrative.

After leaving the remains of my defunct uncle, said he, when the gate closed between me and what was once to have been mine, I felt thrust out naked into the world, and completely abandoned to fortune. What was to become of me? I had been brought up to nothing but expectations, and they had all been disappointed. I had no relations to look to for counsel or assistance. The world seemed all to have died away from me. Wave after wave of relationship had ebbed off, and I was left a mere hulk upon the strand. I am not apt to be greatly cast down, but at this time I felt sadly disheartened. I could not realize my situation, nor form a conjecture how I was to get forward. I was now to endeavor to make money. The idea was new and strange to me. It was like being asked to discover the philosopher's stone. I had never thought about money otherwise than to put my hand into my pocket and find it; or, if there were none there, to wait until a new supply came from home. I had considered life as a mere space of time to be filled up with enjoyments; but to have it portioned out into long hours and days of toil, merely that I might gain bread to give me strength to toil on— to labor but for the purpose of perpetuating a life of labor, was new and appalling to me. This may appear a very simple matter to some; but it will be understood by every unlucky wight in my predicament, who has had the misfortune of being born to great expectations.

I passed several days in rambling about the scenes of my boyhood; partly because I absolutely did not know what to do with myself, and partly because I did not know that I should ever see them again. I clung to them as one clings to a wreck, though he knows he must eventually cast himself loose and swim for his life. I sat down on a little hill within sight of my paternal home, but I did not venture to approach it, for I felt compunction at the thoughtlessness with which I had dissipated my patrimony; yet was I to blame, when I had the rich possessions of my curmudgeon of an uncle in expectation?

The new possessor of the place was making great alterations. The house was almost rebuilt. The trees which stood about it were cut down; my mother's flower-garden was thrown into a lawn,—all was undergoing a change. I turned my back upon it with a sigh, and rambled to another part of the country.

How thoughtful a little adversity makes one! As I came within sight of the schoolhouse where I had so often been flogged in the cause of wisdom, you would hardly have recognized the truant boy, who, but a few years since, had eloped so heedlessly from its walls. I leaned over the paling of the play-ground, and watched the scholars at their games, and looked to see if there might not be some urchin among them like I was once, full of gay dreams about life and the world. The play-ground seemed smaller than when I used to sport about it. The house and park, too, of the neighboring squire, the father of the cruel Sacharissa, had shrunk in size and diminished in magnificence. The distant hills no longer appeared so far off, and, alas! no longer awakened ideas of a fairy land beyond.

As I was rambling pensively through a neighboring meadow, in which I had many a time gathered primroses, I met the very pedagogue who had been the tyrant and dread of my boyhood. I had sometimes vowed to myself, when suffering under his rod, that I would have my revenge if ever I met him when I had grown to be a man. The time had come; but I had no disposition to keep my vow. The few years which had matured me into a vigorous man had shrunk him into decrepitude. He appeared to have had a paralytic stroke. I looked at him, and wondered that this poor helpless mortal could have been an object of terror to me; that I should have watched with anxiety the glance of that failing eye, or dreaded the power of that trembling hand. He tottered feebly along the path, and had some difficulty in getting over a stile. I ran and assisted him. He looked at me with surprise, but did not recognize me, and made a low bow of humility and thanks. I had no disposition to make myself known, for I felt that I had nothing to boast of. The pains he had taken, and the pains he had inflicted, had been equally useless. His repeated predictions were fully verified, and I felt that little Jack Buckthorne, the idle boy, had grown to be a good-for-nothing man.

This is all very comfortless detail; but as I have told you of my follies, it is meet that I show you how for once I was schooled for them. The most thoughtless of mortals will some time or other have his day of gloom, when he will be compelled to reflect.

I felt on this occasion as if I had a kind of penance to perform, and I made a pilgrimage in expiation of my past levity. Having passed a night at Leamington, I set off by a private path, which leads up a hill through a grove and across quiet fields, till I came to the small village, or rather hamlet, of Lenington. I sought the village church. It is an old low edifice of gray stone, on the brow of a small hill, looking over fertile fields, towards where the proud towers of Warwick castle lift themselves against the distant horizon.

A part of the churchyard is shaded by large trees. Under one of them my mother lay buried. You have no doubt thought me a light, heartless being. I thought myself so; but there are moments of adversity which let us into some feelings of our nature to which we might otherwise remain perpetual strangers.

I sought my mother's grave; the weeds were already matted over it, and the tombstone was half hid among nettles. I cleared them away, and they stung my hands; but I was heedless of the pain, for my heart ached too severely. I sat down on the grave, and read over and over again the epitaph on the stone.

It was simple,—but it was true. I had written it myself. I had tried to write a poetical epitaph, but in vain; my feelings refused to utter themselves in rhyme. My heart had gradually been filling during my lonely wanderings; it was now charged to the brim, and overflowed. I sank upon the grave, and buried my face in the tall grass, and wept like a child. Yes, I wept in manhood upon the grave, as I had in infancy upon the bosom of my mother. Alas! how little do we appreciate a mother's tenderness while living! how heedless are we in youth of all her anxieties and kindness! But when she is dead and gone; when the cares and coldness of the world come withering to our hearts; when we find how hard it is to meet with true sympathy; how few love us for ourselves; how few will befriend us in our misfortunes; then it is that we think of the mother we have lost. It is true I had always loved my mother, even in my most heedless days; but I felt how inconsiderate and ineffectual had been my love. My heart melted as I retraced the days of infancy, when I was led by a mother's hand, and rocked to sleep in a mother's arms, and was without care or sorrow. "O my mother!" exclaimed I, burying my face again in the grass of the grave; "oh that I were once more by your side; sleeping never to wake again on the cares and troubles of this world."

I am not naturally of a morbid temperament, and the violence of my emotion gradually exhausted itself. It was a hearty, honest, natural discharge of grief which had been slowly accumulating, and gave me wonderful relief. I rose from the grave as if I had been offering up a sacrifice, and I felt as if that sacrifice had been accepted.

I sat down again on the grass, and plucked, one by one, the weeds from her grave: the tears trickled more slowly down my cheeks, and ceased to be bitter. It was a comfort to think that she had died before sorrow and poverty came upon her child and all his great expectations were blasted.

I leaned my cheek upon my hand, and looked upon the landscape. Its quiet beauty soothed me. The whistle of a peasant from an adjoining field came cheerily to my ear. I seemed to respire hope and comfort with the free air that whispered through the leaves, and played through my hair, and dried the tears upon my cheek. A lark, rising from the field before me, and leaving as it were a stream of song behind him as he rose, lifted my fancy with him. He hovered in the air just above the place where the towers of Warwick castle marked the horizon, and seemed as if fluttering with delight at his own melody. "Surely," thought I, "if there was such a thing as transmigration of souls, this might be taken for some poet let loose from the earth, but still revelling in song, and carolling about fair fields and lordly towers."

At this moment the long-forgotten feeling of poetry rose within me. A thought sprang at once into my mind.—"I will become an author!" said I. "I have hitherto indulged in poetry as a pleasure, and it has brought me nothing but pain; let me try what it will do when I cultivate it with devotion as a pursuit."

The resolution thus suddenly aroused within me heaved a load from off my heart. I felt a confidence in it from the very place where it was formed. It seemed as though my mother's spirit whispered it to me from the grave. "I will henceforth," said I, "endeavor to be all that she fondly imagined me. I will endeavor to act as if she were witness of my actions; I will endeavor to acquit myself in such a manner that, when I revisit her grave, there may at least be no compunctious bitterness with my tears."

I bowed down and kissed the turf in solemn attestation of my vow. I plucked some primroses that were growing there, and laid them next my heart. I left the churchyard with my spirits once more lifted up, and set out a third time for London in the character of an author.—

Here my companion made a pause and I waited in anxious suspense, hoping to have a whole volume of literary life unfolded to me. He seemed, however, to have sunk into a fit of pensive musing, and when, after some time, I gently roused him by a question or two as to his literary career,

"No," said he, smiling, "over that part of my story I wish to leave a cloud. Let the mysteries of the craft rest sacred for me. Let those who have never ventured into the republic of letters still look upon it as a fairy land. Let them suppose the author the very being they picture him from his works—I am not the man to mar their illusion. I am not the man to hint, while one is admiring the silken web of Persia, that it has been spun from the entrails of a miserable worm."

"Well," said I, "if you will tell me nothing of your literary history, let me know at least if you have had any further intelligence from Doubting Castle."

"Willingly," replied he, "though I have but little to communicate."

THE BOOBY SQUIRE

A LONG time elapsed, said Buckthorne, without my receiving any accounts of my cousin and his estate. Indeed, I felt so much soreness on the subject, that I wished, if possible, to shut it from my thoughts. At length, chance took me to that part of the country, and I could not refrain from making some inquiries.

I learnt that my cousin had grown up ignorant, self-willed, and clownish. His ignorance and clownishness had prevented his mingling with the neighboring gentry: in spite of his great fortune, he had been unsuccessful in an attempt to gain the hand of the daughter of the parson, and had at length shrunk into the limits of such a society as a mere man of wealth can gather in a country neighborhood.

He kept horses and hounds, and a roaring table, at which were collected the loose livers of the country round, and the shabby gentlemen of a village in the vicinity. When he could get no other company, he would smoke and drink with his own servants, who in turn fleeced and despised him. Still, with all his apparent prodigality, he had a leaven of the old man in him, which showed that he was his trueborn son. He lived far within his income, was vulgar in his expenses, and penurious in many points wherein a gentleman would be extravagant. His house-servants were obliged occasionally to work on his estate, and part of the pleasure-grounds were ploughed up and devoted to husbandry.

His table, though plentiful, was coarse; his liquors were strong and bad; and more ale and whisky were expended in his establishment than generous wine. He was loud and arrogant at his own table, and exacted a rich man's homage from his vulgar and obsequious guests.

As to Iron John, his old grandfather, he had grown impatient of the tight hand his own grandson kept over him, and quarrelled with him soon after he came to the estate. The old man had retired to the neighboring village, where he lived on the legacy of his late master, in a small cottage, and was as seldom seen out of it as a rat out of his hole in daylight.

The cub, like Calaban, seemed to have an instinctive attachment to his mother. She resided with him, but from long habit, she acted more as a servant than as a mistress of the mansion; for she toiled in all the domestic drudgery, and was oftener in the kitchen than the parlor. Such was the information which I collected of my rival cousin, who had so unexpectedly elbowed me out of my expectations.

I now felt an irresistible hankering to pay a visit to this scene of my boyhood, and to get a peep at the odd kind of life that was passing within the mansion of my maternal ancestors. I determined to do so in disguise. My booby cousin had never seen enough of me to be very familiar with my countenance, and a few years make a great difference between youth and manhood. I understood he was a breeder of cattle, and proud of his stock; I dressed myself therefore as a substantial farmer, and with the assistance of a red scratch that came low down on my forehead, made a complete change in my physiognomy.

It was past three o'clock when I arrived at the gate of the park, and was admitted by an old woman who was washing in a dilapidated building, which had once been a porter's lodge. I advanced up the remains of a noble avenue, many of the trees of which had been cut down and sold for timber. The grounds were in scarcely better keeping than during my uncle's lifetime. The grass was overgrown with weeds, and the trees wanted pruning and clearing of dead branches. Cattle were grazing about the lawns, and ducks and geese swimming in the fish-ponds. The road to the house bore very few traces of carriage-wheels, as my cousin received few visitors but such as came on foot or horseback, and never used a carriage himself. Once, indeed, as I was told, he had the old family carriage drawn out from among the dust and cobwebs of the coach-house, and furbished up, and driven, with his mother, to the village church, to take formal possession of the family pew; but there was such hooting and laughing after them as they passed through the village, and such giggling and bantering about the church-door, that the pageant had never made a reappearance.

As I approached the house, a legion of whelps sallied out, barking at me, accompanied by the low howling, rather than barking, of two old worn-out bloodhounds, which I recognized for the ancient lifeguards of my uncle. The house had still a neglected, random appearance, though much altered for the better since my last visit. Several of the windows were broken and patched up with boards, and others had been bricked up to save taxes. I observed smoke, however, rising from the chimneys, a phenomenon rarely witnessed in the ancient establishment. On passing that part of the house where the dining-room was situated, I heard the sound of boisterous merriment, where three or four voices were talking at once, and oaths and laughter were horribly mingled.

The uproar of the dogs had brought a servant to the door, a tall hard-fisted country clown, with a livery coat put over the under garments of a ploughman. I requested to see the master of the house, but was told that he was at dinner with some "gemmen" of the neighborhood. I made known my business, and sent in to know if I might talk with the master about his cattle, for I felt a great desire to have a peep at him in his orgies.

Word was returned that he was engaged with company, and could not attend to business, but that if I would step in and take a drink of something, I was heartily welcome. I accordingly entered the hall, where whips and hats of all kinds and shapes were lying on an oaken table; two or three clownish servants were lounging about; everything had a look of confusion and carelessness.

The apartments through which I passed had the same air of departed gentility and sluttish housekeeping. The once rich curtains were faded and dusty; the furniture greased and tarnished. On entering the dining-room, I found a number of odd, vulgar-looking, rustic gentlemen, seated round a table, on which were bottles, decanters, tankards, pipes, and tobacco. Several dogs were lying about the room, or sitting and watching their masters, and one was gnawing a bone under a side-table. The master of the feast sat at the head of the board. He was greatly altered. He had grown thickset and rather gummy, with a fiery foxy head of hair. There was a singular mixture of foolishness, arrogance, and conceit in his countenance. He was dressed in a vulgarly fine style, with leather breeches, a red waist-coat, and green coat, and was evidently, like his guests, a little flushed with drinking. The whole company stared at me with a whimsical muzzy look, like men whose senses were a little obfuscated by beer rather than wine.

My cousin (God forgive me! the appellation sticks in my throat), my cousin invited me with awkward civility, or, as he intended it, condescension, to sit to the table and drink. We talked, as usual, about the weather, the crops, politics, and hard times. My cousin was a loud politician, and evidently accustomed to talk without contradiction at his own table. He was amazingly loyal, and talked of standing by the throne to the last guinea, "as every gentleman of fortune should do." The village exciseman, who was half asleep, could just ejaculate "very true" to everything he said. The conversation turned upon cattle; he boasted of his breed, his mode of crossing it, and of the general management of his estate. This unluckily drew out a history of the place and of the family. He spoke of my late uncle with the greatest irreverence, which I could easily forgive. He mentioned my name, and my blood began to boil. He described my frequent visits to my uncle, when I was a lad, and I found the varlet, even at that time, imp as he was, had known that he was to inherit the estate. He described the scene of my uncle's death, and the opening of the will, with a degree of coarse humor that I had not expected from him; and, vexed as I was, I could not help joining in the laugh, for I have always relished a joke, even though made at my own expense. He went on to speak of my various pursuits, my strolling freak; and that somewhat nettled me; at length he talked of my parents. He ridiculed my father; I stomached even that, though with great difficulty. He mentioned my mother with a sneer, and in an instant he lay sprawling at my feet.

Here a tumult succeeded; the table was nearly overturned; bottles, glasses, and tankards rolled crashing and clattering about the floor. The company seized hold of both of us, to keep us from doing any further mischief. I struggled to get loose, for I was boiling with fury. My cousin defied me to strip and fight him on the lawn. I agreed, for I felt the strength of a giant in me, and I longed to pommel him soundly.

Away then we were borne. A ring was formed. I had a second assigned me in true boxing style. My cousin, as he advanced to fight, said something about his generosity in showing me such fair play, when I had made such an unprovoked attack upon him at his own table. "Stop there," cried I, in a rage. "Unprovoked? know that I am John Buckthorne, and you have insulted the memory of my mother."

The lout was suddenly struck by what I said; he drew back, and thought for a moment.

"Nay, damn it," said he, "that's too much—that's clean another thing —I've a mother myself—and no one shall speak ill of her, bad as she is."

He paused again: and nature seemed to have a rough struggle in his rude bosom.

"Damn it, cousin," cried he, "I'm sorry for what I said. Thou'st served me right in knocking me down, and I like thee the better for it. Here's my hand: come and live with me, and damn me but the best room in the house, and the best horse in the stable, shall be at thy service."

I declare to you I was strongly moved at this instance of nature breaking her way through such a lump of flesh. I forgave the fellow in a moment his two heinous crimes, of having been born in wedlock, and inheriting my estate. I shook the hand he offered me, to convince him that I bore him no ill-will; and then making my way through the gaping crowd of toad-eaters, bade adieu to my uncle's domains forever.— This is the last I have seen or heard of my cousin or of the domestic concerns of Doubting Castle.

THE STROLLING MANAGER

A S I was walking one morning with Buckthorne near one of the principal theatres, he directed my attention to a group of those equivocal beings that may often be seen hovering about the stage-doors of theatres. They were marvellously ill-favored in their attire, their coats buttoned up to their chins; yet they wore their hats smartly on one side, and had a certain knowing, dirty-gentleman-like air, which is common to the subalterns of the drama. Buckthorne knew them well by early experience.

"These," said he, "are the ghosts of departed kings and heroes; fellows who sway sceptres and truncheons; command kingdoms and armies; and after giving away realms and treasures over night, have scarce a shilling to pay for a breakfast in the morning. Yet they have the true vagabond abhorrence of all useful and industrious employment; and they have their pleasures, too; one of which is to lounge in this way in the sunshine, at the stage-door, during rehearsals, and make hackneyed theatrical jokes on all passers-by. Nothing is more traditional and legitimate than the stage. Old scenery, old clothes, old sentiments, old ranting, and old jokes, are handed down from generation to generation; and will probably continue to be so until time shall be no more. Every hanger-on of a theatre becomes a wag by inheritance, and flourishes about at tap-rooms and sixpenny clubs with the property jokes of the green-room."

While amusing ourselves with reconnoitring this group, we noticed one in particular who appeared to be the oracle. He was a weather-beaten veteran, a little bronzed by time and beer, who had no doubt grown gray in the parts of robbers, cardinals, Roman senators, and walking noblemen.

"There is something in the set of that hat, and the turn of that physiognomy, extremely familiar to me," said Buckthorne. He looked a little closer,—"I cannot be mistaken, that must be my old brother of the truncheon, Flimsey, the tragic hero of the Strolling Company."

It was he in fact. The poor fellow showed evident signs that times went hard with him, he was so finely and shabbily dressed. His coat was somewhat threadbare, and of the Lord Townly cut; single breasted, and scarcely capable of meeting in the front of his body, which, from long intimacy, had acquired the symmetry and robustness of a beer-barrel. He wore a pair of dingy-white stockinet pantaloons, which had much ado to reach his waistcoat, a great quantity of dirty cravat; and a pair of old russet-colored tragedy boots.

When his companions had dispersed, Buckthorne drew him aside, and made himself known to him. The tragic veteran could scarcely recognize him, or believe that he was really his quondam associate, "little Gentleman Jack." Buckthorne invited him to a neighboring coffee-house to talk over old times; and in the course of a little while we were put in possession of his history in brief.

He had continued to act the heroes in the strolling company for some time after Buckthorne had left it, or rather had been driven from it so abruptly. At length the manager died, and the troop was thrown into confusion. Every one aspired to the crown, every one was for taking the lead; and the manager's widow, although a tragedy queen, and a brimstone to boot, pronounced it utterly impossible for a woman to keep any control over such a set of tempestuous rascallions.

"Upon this hint, I spoke," said Flimsey. I stepped forward, and offered my services in the most effectual way. They were accepted. In a week's time I married the widow, and succeeded to the throne. "The funeral baked meats did coldly furnish forth the marriage table," as Hamlet says. But the ghost of my predecessor never haunted me; and I inherited crowns, sceptres, bowls, daggers, and all the stage trappings and trumpery, not omitting the widow, without the least molestation.

I now led a flourishing life of it; for our company was pretty strong and attractive, and as my wife and I took the heavy parts of tragedy, it was a great saving to the treasury. We carried off the palm from all the rival shows at country fairs; and I assure you we have even drawn full houses, and been applauded by the critics at Batlemy Fair itself, though we had Astley's troop, the Irish giant, and "the death of Nelson" in wax-work, to contend against.

I soon began to experience, however, the cares of command. I discovered that there were cabals breaking out in the company, headed by the clown, who you may recollect was a terribly peevish, fractious fellow, and always in ill-humor. I had a great mind to turn him off at once, but I could not do without him, for there was not a droller scoundrel on the stage. His very shape was comic, for he had but to turn his back upon the audience, and all the ladies were ready to die with laughing. He felt his importance, and took advantage of it. He would keep the audience in a continual roar, and then come behind the scenes, and fret and fume, and play the very devil. I excused a great deal in him, however, knowing that comic actors are a little prone to this infirmity of temper.

I had another trouble of a nearer and dearer nature to struggle with, which was the affection of my wife. As ill-luck would have it, she took it into her head to be very fond of me, and became intolerably jealous. I could not keep a pretty girl in the company, and hardly dared embrace an ugly one, even when my part required it. I have known her reduce a fine lady to tatters, "to very rags," as Hamlet says, in an instant, and destroy one of the very best dresses in the wardrobe, merely because she saw me kiss her at the side scenes; though I give you my honor it was done merely by way of rehearsal.

This was doubly annoying, because I have a natural liking to pretty faces, and wish to have them about me; and because they are indispensable to the success of a company at a fair, where one has to vie with so many rival theatres. But when once a jealous wife gets a freak in her head, there's no use in talking of interest or anything else. Egad, sir, I have more than once trembled when, during a fit of her tantrums, she was playing high tragedy, and flourishing her tin dagger on the stage, lest she should give way to her humor, and stab some fancied rival in good earnest.

I went on better, however, than could be expected, considering the weakness of my flesh, and the violence of my rib. I had not a much worse time of it than old Jupiter, whose spouse was continually ferreting out some new intrigue, and making the heavens almost too hot to hold him.

At length, as luck would have it, we were performing at a country fair, when I understood the theatre of a neighboring town to be vacant. I had always been desirous to be enrolled in a settled company, and the height of my desire was to get on a par with a brother-in-law, who was manager of a regular theatre, and who had looked down upon me. Here was an opportunity not to be neglected. I concluded an agreement with the proprietors, and in a few days opened the theatre with great éclat.

Behold me now at the summit of my ambition, "the high top-gallant of my joy," as Romeo says. No longer a chieftain of a wandering tribe, but a monarch of a legitimate throne, and entitled to call even the great potentates of Covent Garden and Drury Lane cousins. You, no doubt, think my happiness complete. Alas, sir! I was one of the most uncomfortable dogs living. No one knows, who has not tried, the miseries of a manager; but above all of a country manager. No one can conceive the contentions and quarrels within doors, the oppressions and vexations from without. I was pestered with the bloods and loungers of a country town, who infested my green-room, and played the mischief among my actresses. But there was no shaking them off. It would have been ruin to affront them; for though troublesome friends, they would have been dangerous enemies. Then there was the village critics and village amateurs, who were continually tormenting me with advice, and getting into a passion if I would not take it; especially the village doctor and the village attorney, who had both been to London occasionally, and knew what acting should be.

I had also to manage as arrant a crew of scapegraces as ever were collected together within the walls of a theatre. I had been obliged to combine my original troop with some of the former troop of the theatre, who were favorites of the public. Here was a mixture that produced perpetual ferment. They were all the time either fighting or frolicking with each other, and I scarcely know which mood was least troublesome. If they quarrelled, everything went wrong, and if they were friends, they were continually playing off some prank upon each other, or upon me; for I had unhappily acquired among them the character of an easy, good-natured fellow,—the worst character that a manager can possess.

Their waggery at times drove me almost crazy, for there is nothing so vexatious as the hackneyed tricks and hoaxes and pleasantries of a veteran band of theatrical vagabonds. I relished them well enough, it is true, while I was merely one of the company, but as a manager I found them detestable. They were incessantly bringing some disgrace upon the theatre by their tavern frolics and their pranks about the country town. All my lectures about the importance of keeping up the dignity of the profession and the respectability of the company were in vain. The villains could not sympathize with the delicate feelings of a man in station. They even trifled with the seriousness of stage business. I have had the whole piece interrupted, and a crowded audience of at least twenty-five pounds kept waiting, because the actors had hid away the breeches of Rosalind; and have known Hamlet to stalk solemnly on to deliver his soliloquy with a dish-clout pinned to his skirts. Such are the baleful consequences of a manager's getting a character for good-nature.

I was intolerably annoyed, too, by the great actors who came down starring, as it is called, from London. Of all baneful influences, keep me from that of a London star. A first-rate actress going the rounds of the country theatres is as bad as a blazing comet whisking about the heavens, and shaking fire and plagues and discord from its tail.

The moment one of these "heavenly bodies" appeared in my horizon, I was sure to be in hot water. My theatre was overrun by provincial dandies, copper-washed counterfeits of Bond Street loungers, who are always proud to be in the train of an actress from town, and anxious to be thought on exceeding good terms with her. It was really a relief to me when some random young nobleman would come in pursuit of the bait, and awe all this small fry at a distance. I have always felt myself more at ease with a nobleman than with the dandy of a country town.

And then the injuries I suffered in my personal dignity and my managerial authority from the visits of these great London actors! 'Sblood, sir, I was no longer master of myself on my throne. I was hectored and lectured in my own green-room, and made an absolute nincompoop on my own stage. There is no tyrant so absolute and capricious as a London star at a country theatre. I dreaded the sight of all of them, and yet if I did not engage them, I was sure of having the public clamorous against me. They drew full houses, and appeared to be making my fortune; but they swallowed up all the profits by their insatiable demands. They were absolute tape-worms to my little theatre; the more it took in the poorer it grew. They were sure to leave me with an exhausted public, empty benches, and a score or two of affronts to settle among the townsfolk, in consequence of misunderstanding about the taking of places.

But the worst thing I had to undergo in my managerial career was patronage. Oh, sir! of all things deliver me from the patronage of the great people of a country town. It was my ruin. You must know that this town, though small, was filled with feuds, and parties, and great folks; being a busy little trading and manufacturing town. The mischief was that their greatness was of a kind not to be settled by reference to the court calendar, or college of heraldry; it was therefore the most quarrelsome kind of greatness in existence. You smile, sir, but let me tell you there are no feuds more furious than the frontier feuds which take place in these "debatable lands" of gentility. The most violent dispute that I ever knew in high life was one which occurred at a country town, on a question of precedence between the ladies of a manufacturer of pins and a manufacturer of needles.

At the town where I was situated there were perpetual altercations of the kind. The head manufacturer's lady, for instance, was at daggers-drawings with the head shopkeeper's, and both were too rich and had too many friends to be treated lightly. The doctor's and lawyer's ladies held their heads still higher: but they in turn were kept in check by the wife of a country banker, who kept her own carriage; while a masculine widow of cracked character and second-handed fashion, who lived in a large house and claimed to be in some way related to nobility looked down upon them all. To be sure, her manners were not over-elegant nor her fortune over large; but then, sir, her blood—oh, her blood carried it all hollow: there was no withstanding a woman with such blood in her veins.

After all, her claims to high connection were questioned, and she had frequent battles for precedence at balls and assemblies with some of the sturdy dames of the neighborhood, who stood upon their wealth and their virtue; but then she had two dashing daughters, who dressed as fine as dragoons, and had as high blood as their mother, and seconded her in everything; so they carried their point with high heads, and everybody hated, abused, and stood in awe of the Fantadlins.

Such was the state of the fashionable world in this self-important little town. Unluckily, I was not as well acquainted with its politics as I should have been. I had found myself a stranger and in great perplexities during my first season; I determined, therefore, to put myself under the patronage of some powerful name, and thus to take the field with the prejudices of the public in my favor. I cast around my thoughts for that purpose, and in an evil hour they fell upon Mrs. Fantadlin. No one seemed to me to have a more absolute sway in the world of fashion. I· had always noticed that her party slammed the box-door the loudest at the theatre; and had the most beaux attending on them, and talked and laughed loudest during the performance; and then the Miss Fantadlins wore always more flowers than any other ladies; and used quizzing-glasses incessantly. The first evening of my theatre's reopening, therefore, was announced in staring capitals on the play-bills, as under the patronage of "The Honorable Mrs. Fantadlin."

Sir, the whole community flew to arms! the banker's wife felt her dignity grievously insulted at not having the preference; her husband being high bailiff and the richest man in the place. She immediately issued invitations for a large party, for the night of the performance, and asked many a lady to it whom she never had noticed before. Presume to patronize the theatre! insufferable! And then for me to dare to term her "The Honorable!" What claim had she to the title forsooth? The fashionable world had long groaned under the tyranny of the Fantadlins, and were glad to make a common cause against this new instance of assumption. Those, too, who had never before been noticed by the banker's lady were ready to enlist in any quarrel for the honor of her acquaintance. All minor feuds were forgotten. The doctor's lady and the lawyer's lady met together, and the manufacturer's lady and the shopkeeper's lady kissed each other; and all, headed by the banker's lady, voted the theatre a *bore*, and determined to encourage nothing but the Indian Jugglers and Mr. Walker's Eidouranion.

Alas for poor Pillgarlick! I knew little the mischief that was brewing against me. My book remained blank; the evening arrived; but no audience. The music struck up to a tolerable pit and gallery, but no fashionables! I peeped anxiously from behind the curtain, but the time passed away; the play was retarded until pit and gallery became furious; and I had to raise the curtain, and play my greatest part in tragedy to "a beggarly account of empty boxes."

It is true the Fantadlins came late, as was their custom, and entered like a tempest, with a flutter of feathers and red shawls; but they were evidently disconcerted at finding they had no one to admire and envy them, and were enraged at this glaring defection of their fashionable followers. All the *beau-monde* were engaged at the banker's lady's rout. They remained for some time in solitary and uncomfortable state; and though they had the theatre almost to themselves, yet, for the first time, they talked in whispers. They left the house at the end of the first piece, and I never saw them afterwards.

Such was the rock on which I split. I never got over the patronage of the Fantadlin family. My house was deserted; my actors grew discontented because they were ill-paid; my door became a hammering place for every bailiff in the country; and my wife became more and more shrewish and tormenting the more I wanted comfort.

I tried for a time the usual consolation of a harassed and henpecked man; I took to the bottle, and tried to tipple away my cares, but in vain. I don't mean to decry the bottle; it is no doubt an excellent remedy in many cases, but it did not answer in mine. It cracked my voice, coppered my nose, but neither improved my wife nor my affairs. My establishment became a scene of confusion and peculation. I was considered a ruined man, and of course fair game for every one to pluck at, as every one plunders a sinking ship. Day after day some of the troop deserted, and, like deserting soldiers, carried off their arms and accoutrements with them. In this manner my wardrobe took legs and walked away, my finery strolled all over the country, my swords and daggers glittered in every barn, until, at last, my tailor made "one fell swoop," and carried off three dress-coats, half a dozen doublets, and nineteen pair of flesh-colored pantaloons. This was the "be all and the end of all" of my fortune. I no longer hesitated what to do. Egad, thought I, since stealing is the order of the day, I'll steal too; so I secretly gathered together the jewels of my wardrobe, packed up a hero's dress in a handkerchief, slung it on the end of a tragedy sword, and quietly stole off at dead of night, "the bell then beating one," leaving my queen and kingdom to the mercy of my rebellious subjects, and my merciless foes the bum-bailiffs.

Such, sir, was the "end of all my greatness." I was heartily cured of all passion for governing, and returned once more into the ranks. I had for some time the usual run of an actor's life. I played in various country theatres, at fairs, and in barns; sometimes hard pushed, sometimes flush, until, on one occasion, I came within an ace of making my fortune, and becoming one of the wonders of the age.

I was playing the part of Richard the Third in a country barn, and in my best style; for, to tell the truth, I was a little in liquor, and the critics of the company always observed that I played with most effect when I had a glass too much. There was a thunder of applause when I came to that part where Richard cries for "a horse! a horse!" My cracked voice had always a wonderful effect here; it was like two voices run into one; you would have thought two men had been calling for a horse, or that Richard had called for two horses. And when I flung the taunt at Richmond, "Richard is *hoarse* with calling thee to arms," I thought the barn would have come down about my ears with the raptures of the audience.

The very next morning a person waited upon me at my lodgings. I saw at once he was a gentleman by his dress; for he had a large brooch in his bosom, thick rings on his fingers, and used a quizzing-glass. And a gentleman he proved to be; for I soon ascertained that he was a kept author, or kind of literary tailor to one of the great London theatres; one who worked under the manager's directions, and cut up and cut down plays, and patched and pieced, and new faced, and turned them inside out; in short, he was one of the readiest and greatest writers of the day.

He was now on a foraging excursion in quest of something that might be got up for a prodigy. The theatre, it seems, was in desperate condition—nothing but a miracle could save it. He had seen me act Richard the night before, and had pitched upon me for that miracle. I had a remarkable bluster in my style and swagger in my gait. I certainly differed from all other heroes of the barn: so the thought struck the agent to bring me out as a theatrical wonder, as the restorer of natural and legitimate acting, as the only one who could understand and act Shakspeare rightly.

When he opened his plan I shrunk from it with becoming modesty, for well as I thought of myself, I doubted my competency to such an undertaking.

I hinted at my imperfect knowledge of Shakspeare, having played his characters only after mutilated copies, interlarded with a great deal of my own talk by way of helping memory or heightening the effect.

"So much the better!" cried the gentleman with rings on his fingers;

"so much the better! New readings, sir!—new readings! Don't study a line—let us have Shakspeare after your own fashion."

"But then my voice was cracked; it could not fill a London theatre."

"So much the better! so much the better! The public is tired of intonation—the *ore rotundo* has had its day. No, sir, your cracked voice is the very thing;—spit and splutter, and snap and snarl, and 'play the very dog' about the stage, and you'll be the making of us."

"But then,"—I could not help blushing to the end of my very nose as I said it, but I was determined to be candid,—"but then," added I, "there is one awkward circumstance: I have an unlucky habit—my misfortunes, and the exposures to which one is subjected in country barns, have obliged me now and then to—to—take a drop of something comfortable—and so—and so——"

"What! you drink?" cried the agent, eagerly.

I bowed my head in blushing acknowledgment.

"So much the better! so much the better! The irregularities of genius! A sober fellow is commonplace. The public like an actor that drinks. Give me your hand, sir. You're the very man to make a dash with."

I still hung back with lingering diffidence, declaring myself unworthy of such praise.

" 'Sblood, man," cried he, "no praise at all. You don't imagine *I* think you a wonder; I only want the public to think so. Nothing is so easy as to gull the public, if you only set up a prodigy. Common talent anybody can measure by common rule; but a prodigy sets all rule and measurement at defiance."

These words opened my eyes in an instant: we now came to a proper understanding, less flattering, it is true, to my vanity, but much more satisfactory to my judgment.

It was agreed that I should make my appearance before a London audience, as a dramatic sun just bursting from behind the clouds: one that was to banish all the lesser lights and false fires of the stage. Every precaution was to be taken to possess the public mind at every avenue. The pit was to be packed with sturdy clappers; the newspapers secured by vehement puffers; every theatrical resort to be haunted by hireling talkers. In a word, every engine of theatrical humbug was to be put in action. Wherever I differed from former actors, it was to be maintained that I was right and they were wrong. If I ranted, it was to be pure passion; if I were vulgar, it was to be pronounced a familiar touch of nature; if I made any queer blunder, it was to be a new reading. If my voice cracked, or I got out in my part, I was only to bounce, and grin, and snarl at the audience, and make any horrible grimace that came into my head, and my admirers were to call it "a great point," and to fall back and shout and yell with rapture.

"In short," said the gentleman with the quizzing-glass, "strike out boldly and bravely: no matter how or what you do, so that it be but odd and strange. If you do but escape pelting the first night, your fortune and the fortune of the theatre is made."

I set off for London, therefore, in company with the kept author, full of new plans and new hopes. I was to be the restorer of Shakspeare and Nature, and the legitimate drama; my very swagger was to be heroic, and my cracked voice the standard of elocution. Alas, sir, my usual luck attended me: before I arrived at the metropolis a rival wonder had appeared; a woman who could dance the slack rope, and run up a cord from the stage to the gallery with fireworks all round her. She was seized on by the manager with avidity. She was the saving of the great national theatre for the season. Nothing was talked of but Madame Saqui's fireworks and flesh-colored pantaloons; and Nature, Shakspeare, the legitimate drama, and poor Pillgarlick, were completely left in the lurch.

· When Madame Saqui's performance grew stale, other wonders succeeded: horses, and harlequinades, and mummery of all kinds; until another dramatic prodigy was brought forward to play the very game for which I had been intended. I called upon the kept author for an explanation, but he was deeply engaged in writing a melodrama or a pantomime, and was extremely testy on being interrupted in his studies. However, as the theatre was in some measure pledged to provide for me, the manager acted, according to the usual phrase, "like a man of honor," and I received an appointment in the corps. It had been a turn of a die whether I should be Alexander the Great or Alexander the coppersmith—the latter carried it. I could not be put at the head of the drama, so I was put at the tail of it. In other words, I was enrolled among the number of what are called *useful men;* those who enact soldiers, senators, and Banquo's shadowy line. I was perfectly satisfied with my lot; for I have always been a bit of a philosopher. If my situation was not splendid, it at least was secure; and in fact I have seen half a dozen prodigies appear, dazzle, burst like bubbles, and pass away, and yet here I am, snug, unenvied, and unmolested, at the foot of the profession.

You may smile; but let me tell you, we "useful men" are the only comfortable actors on the stage. We are safe from hisses, and below the hope of applause. We fear not the success of rivals, nor dread the critic's pen. So long as we get the words of our parts, and they are not often many, it is all we care for. We have our own merriment, our own friends, and our own admirers,—for every actor has his friends and admirers, from the highest to the lowest. The first-rate actor dines with the noble amateur, and entertains, a fashionable table with scraps and songs and theatrical slip-slop. The second-rate actors have their second-rate friends and admirers, with whom they likewise spout tragedy and talk slip-slop;—and so down even to us; who have our friends and admirers among spruce clerks and aspiring apprentices—who treat us to a dinner now and then, and enjoy at tenth hand the same scraps and songs and slip-slop that have been served up by our more fortunate brethren at the tables of the great.

I now, for the first time in my theatrical life, experience what true pleasure is. I have known enough of notoriety to pity the poor devils who are called favorites of the public. I would rather be a kitten in the arms of a spoiled child, to be one moment patted and pampered and the next moment thumped over the head with the spoon. I smile to see our leading actors fretting themselves with envy and jealousy about a trumpery renown, questionable in its quality, and uncertain in its duration. I laugh, too, though of course in my sleeve, at the bustle and importance, and trouble and perplexities of our manager—who is harassing himself to death in the hopeless effort to please everybody.

I have found among my fellow-subalterns two or three quondam managers, who like myself have wielded the sceptres of country theatres, and we have many a sly joke together at the expense of the manager and the public. Sometimes, too, we meet, like deposed and exiled kings, talk over the events of respective reigns, moralize over a tankard of ale, and laugh at the humbug of the great and little world; which, I take it, is the essence of practical philosophy.

Thus end the anecdotes of Buckthorne and his friends. It grieves me much that I could not procure from him further particulars of his history, and especially of that part of it which passed in town. He had evidently seen much of literary life; and, as he had never risen to eminence in letters, and yet was free from the gall of disappointment, I had hoped to gain some candid intelligence concerning his contemporaries. The testimony of such an honest chronicler would have been particularly valuable at the present time; when, owing to the extreme fecundity of the press, and the thousand anecdotes, criticisms, and biographical sketches that are daily poured forth concerning public characters, it is extremely difficult to get at any truth concerning them.

He was always, however, excessively reserved and fastidious on this point, at which I very much wondered, authors in general appearing to think each other fair game, and being ready to serve each other up for the amusement of the public.

A few mornings after hearing the history of the ex-manager, I was surprised by a visit from Buckthorne before I was out of bed. He was dressed for travelling.

"Give me joy! give me joy!" said he, rubbing his hands with the utmost glee, "my great expectations are realized!"

I gazed at him with a look of wonder and inquiry.

"My booby cousin is dead!" cried he; "may he rest in peace! he nearly broke his neck in a fall from his horse in a fox-chase. By good luck, he lived long enough to make his will. He has made me his heir, partly out of an odd feeling of retributive justice, and partly because, as he says, none of his own family nor friends know how to enjoy such an estate. I'm off to the country to take possession. I've done with authorship. That for the critics!" said he, snapping his finger. "Come down to Doubting Castle, when I get settled, and, egad, I'll give you a rouse." So saying, he shook me heartily by the hand, and bounded off in high spirits.

· A long time elapsed before I heard from him again. Indeed, it was but lately that I received a letter, written in the happiest of moods. He was getting the estate in fine order; everything went to his wishes; and what was more, he was married to Sacharissa, who it seems had always entertained an ardent though secret attachment for him, which he fortunately discovered just after coming to his estate.

"I find," said he, "you are a little given to the sin of authorship, which I renounce: if the anecdotes I have given you of my story are of any interest, you may make use of them; but come down to Doubting Castle, and see how we live, and I'll give you my whole London life over a social glass; and a rattling history it shall be about authors and reviewers."

If ever I visit Doubting Castle and get the history he promises, the public shall be sure to hear of it.

From *Tales of a Traveller*

The Italian Banditti

The following eight tales form one narrative. They are drawn from *Tales of a Traveller.*—C.N.

THE INN AT TERRACINA

CRACK! crack! crack! crack! crack! "Here comes the estafette from Naples," said mine host of the inn at Terracina; "bring out the relay."

The estafette came galloping up the road according to custom, brandishing over his head a short-handled whip, with a long, knotted lash, every smack of which made a report like a pistol. He was a tight, square-set young fellow, in the usual uniform: a smart blue coat, ornamented with facings and gold lace, but so short behind as to reach scarcely below his waistband, and cocked up not unlike the tail of a wren; a cocked hat edged with gold lace; a pair of stiff riding-boots: but, instead of the usual leathern breeches, he had a fragment of a pair of drawers, that scarcely furnished an apology to hide behind.

The estafette galloped up to the door, and jumped from his horse.

"A glass of rosolio, a fresh horse, and a pair of breeches," said he, "and quickly, *per l'amor di Dio*, I am behind my time, and must be off!"

"San Gennaro!" replied the host; "why, where hast thou left thy garment?"

"Among the robbers between this and Fondi."

"What, rob an estafette! I never heard of such folly. What could they hope to get from thee?"

"My leather breeches!" replied the estafette. "They were bran new, and shone like gold, and hit the fancy of the captain."

"Well, these robbers grow worse and worse. To meddle with an estafette! and that merely for the sake of a pair of leather breeches!"

The robbing of the government messenger seemed to strike the host with more astonishment than any other enormity that had taken place on the road; and, indeed, it was the first time so wanton an outrage had been committed; the robbers generally taking care not to meddle with anything belonging to the government.

The estafette was by this time equipped, for he had not lost an instant in making his preparations while talking. The relay was ready; the rosolio tossed off; he grasped the reins and the stirrup.

"Were there many robbers in the band?" said a handsome, dark young man, stepping forward from the door of the inn.

"As formidable a band as ever I saw," said the estafette, springing into the saddle.

"Are they cruel to travellers?" said a beautiful young Venetian lady, who had been hanging on the gentleman's arm.

"Cruel, Signora!" echoed the estafette, giving a glance at the lady as he put spurs to his horse. "Corpo di Bacco! They stiletto all the men; and, as to the women"—Crack! crack! crack! crack! crack!—The last words were drowned in the smacking of the whip, and away galloped the estafette along the road to the Pontine marshes.

"Holy Virgin!" ejaculated the fair Venetian, "what will become of us!"

The inn of which we are speaking stands just outside of the walls of Terracina, under a vast precipitous height of rocks, crowned with the ruins of the castle of Theodoric the Goth. The situation of Terracina is remarkable. It is a little ancient, lazy Italian town, on the frontiers of the Roman territory. There seems to be an idle pause in everything about the place. The Mediterranean spreads before it—that sea without flux or reflux. The port is without a sail, excepting that once in a while a solitary felucca may be seen disgorging its holy cargo of baccala, or codfish, the meagre provision for the quaresima, or Lent. The inhabitants are apparently a listless, heedless race, as people of soft sunny climates are apt to be; but under this passive, indolent exterior are said to lurk dangerous qualities. They are supposed by many to be little better than the banditti of the neighboring mountains, and indeed to hold a secret correspondence with them. The solitary watchtowers, erected here and there along the coast, speak of pirates and corsairs that hover about these shores; while the low huts, as stations for soldiers, which dot the distant road, as it winds up through an olive grove, intimate that in the ascent there is danger for the traveller, and facility for the bandit. Indeed, it is between this town and Fondi that the road to Naples is most infested by banditti. It has several windings and solitary places, where the robbers are enabled to see the traveller from a distance, from the brows of hills or impending precipices, and to lie in wait for him at lonely and difficult passes.

The Italian robbers are a desperate class of men, that have almost formed themselves into an order of society. They wear a kind of uniform, or rather costume, which openly designates their profession. This is probably done to diminish its skulking, lawless character, and to give it something of a military air in the eyes of the common people; or, perhaps, to catch by outward show and finery the fancies of the young men of the villages, and thus to gain recruits. Their dresses are often very rich and picturesque. They wear jackets and breeches of bright colors, sometimes gaily embroidered; their breasts are covered with medals and relics; their hats are broad-brimmed, with conical crowns, decorated with feathers, of variously-colored ribands; their hair is sometimes gathered in silk nets; they wear a kind of sandal of cloth or leather, bound round the legs with thongs, and extremely flexible, to enable them to scramble with ease and celerity among the mountain precipices; a broad belt of cloth, or a sash of silk net, is stuck full of pistols and stilettos; a carbine is slung at the back; while about them is generally thrown, in a negligent manner, a great dingy mantle, which serves as a protection in storms, or a bed in their bivouacs among the mountains.

They range over a great extent of wild country, along the chains of the Apennines, bordering on different states; they know all the difficult passes, the short cuts for retreat, and the impracticable forests of the mountain summits, where no force dare follow them. They are secure of the good-will of the inhabitants of those regions, a poor and semi-barbarous race, whom they never disturb and often enrich. Indeed, they are considered as a sort of illegitimate heroes among the mountain villages, and in certain frontier towns where they dispose of their plunder. Thus countenanced, and sheltered, and secure in the fastnesses of their mountains, the robbers have set the weak police of the Italian states at defiance. It is in vain that their names and descriptions are posted on the doors of country churches, and rewards offered for them alive or dead; the villagers are either too much awed by the terrible instances of vengeance inflicted by the brigands, or have too good an understanding with them to be their betrayers. It is true they are now and then hunted and shot down like beasts of prey by the gendarmes, their heads put in iron cages, and stuck upon posts by the roadside, or their limbs hung up to blacken in the trees near the places where they have committed their atrocities; but these ghastly spectacles only serve to make some dreary pass of the road still more dreary, and to dismay the traveller, without deterring the bandit.

At the time that the estafette made his sudden appearance almost *in cuerpo,* as has been mentioned, the audacity of the robbers had risen to an unparalleled height. They had laid villas under contribution; they had sent messages into country towns, to tradesmen and rich burghers, demanding supplies of money, of clothing, or even of luxuries, with menaces of vengeance in case of refusal. They had their spies and emissaries in every town, village, and inn along the principal roads, to give them notice of the movements and quality of travellers. They had plundered carriages, carried people of rank and fortune into the mountains, and obliged them to write for heavy ransoms, and had committed outrages on females who had fallen into their hands.

Such was briefly the state of the robbers, or rather such was the account of the rumors prevalent concerning them, when the scene took place at the inn of Terracina. The dark handsome young man and the Venetian lady, incidentally mentioned, had arrived early that afternoon in a private carriage drawn by mules, and attended by a single servant. They had been recently married, were spending the honeymoon in travelling through these delicious countries, and were on their way to visit a rich aunt of the bride at Naples.

The lady was young, and tender, and timid. The stories she heard along the road had filled her with apprehension, not more for herself than for her husband; for though she had been married almost a month, she still loved him almost to idolatry. When she reached Terracina the rumors of the road had increased to an alarming magnitude; and the sight of two robbers' skulls, grinning in iron cages, on each side of the old gateway of the town, brought her to a pause. Her husband had tried in vain to reassure her; they had lingered all the afternoon at the inn, until it was too late to think of starting that evening, and the parting words of the estafette completed her affright.

. "Let us return to Rome," said she, putting her arm within her husband's, and drawing towards him as if for protection.—"Let us return to Rome, and give up this visit to Naples."

"And give up the visit to your aunt, too?" said the husband.

"Nay—what is my aunt in comparison with your safety?" said she, looking up tenderly in his face.

There was something in her tone and manner that showed she really was thinking more of her husband's safety at the moment than of her own; and being so recently married, and a match of pure affection, too, it is very possible that she was; at least her husband thought so. Indeed, any one who has heard the sweet musical tone of a Venetian voice, and the melting tenderness of a Venetian phrase, and felt the soft witchery of a Venetian eye, would not wonder at the husband's believing what they professed. He clasped the white hand that had been laid within his, put his arm round her slender waist, and drawing her fondly to his bosom, "This night, at least," said he, "we will pass at Terracina."

Crack! crack! crack! crack! crack! Another apparition of the road attracted the attention of mine host and his guests. From the direction of the Pontine marshes, a carriage, drawn by half a dozen horses, came driving at a furious rate; the postilions smacking their whips like mad, as is the case when conscious of the greatness or of the munificence of their fare. It was a landaulet with a servant mounted on the dickey. The compact, highly finished, yet proudly simple construction of the carriage; the quantity of neat, well-arranged trunks and conveniences; the loads of box-coats on the dickey; the fresh, burly, bluff-looking face of the master at the window; and the ruddy, round-headed servant, in close-cropped hair, short coat, drab breeches, and long gaiters, all proclaimed at once that this was the equipage of an Englishman.

"Horses to Fondi," said the Englishman, as the landlord came bowing to the carriage door.

"Would not his Excellenza alight, and take some refreshments?"

"No—he did not mean to eat until he got to Fondi."

"But the horses will be some time in getting ready."

"Ah! that's always the way; nothing but delay in this cursed country!"

"If his Excellenza would only walk into the house——"

"No, no, no!—I tell you no!—I want nothing but horses, and as quick as possible. John, see that the horses are got ready, and don't let us be kept here an hour or two. Tell him if we're delayed over the time, I'll lodge a complaint with the postmaster."

John touched his hat, and set off to obey his master's orders with the taciturn obedience of an English servant.

In the meantime, the Englishman got out of the carriage, and walked up and down before the inn, with his hands in his pockets, taking no notice of the crowd of idlers who were gazing at him and his equipage. He was tall, stout, and well made; dressed with neatness and precision; wore a travelling cap of the color of gingerbread; and had rather an unhappy expression about the corners of his mouth; partly from not having yet made his dinner, and partly from not having been able to get on at a greater rate than seven miles an hour. Not that he had any other cause for haste than an Englishman's usual hurry to get to the end of a journey; or, to use the regular phrase, "to get on." Perhaps, too, he was a little sore from having been fleeced at every stage.

After some time, the servant returned from the stable with a look of some perplexity.

"Are the horses ready, John?"

"No, sir—I never saw such a place. There's no getting anything done. I think your honor had better step into the house and get something to eat; it will be a long while before we get to Fundy."

"D—n the house—it's a mere trick—I'll not eat anything, just to spite them," said the Englishman, still more crusty at the prospect of being so long without his dinner.

"They say your honor's very wrong," said John, "to set off at this late hour. The road's full of highwaymen."

"Mere tales to get custom."

"The estafette which passed us was stopped by a whole gang," said John, increasing his emphasis with each additional piece of information.

"I don't believe a word of it."

"They robbed him of his breeches," said John, giving at the same time a hitch to his own waistband.

"All humbug!"

Here the dark handsome young man stepped forward, and addressing the Englishman very politely, in broken English, invited him to partake of a repast he was about to make.

"Thank'ee," said the Englishman, thrusting his hands deeper into his pockets, and casting a slight side-glance of suspicion at the young man, as if he thought, from his civility, he must have a design upon his purse.

"We shall be most happy, if you will do us the favor," said the lady, in her soft Venetian dialect. There was a sweetness in her accents that was most persuasive. The Englishman cast a look upon her countenance; her beauty was still more eloquent. His features instantly relaxed. He made a polite bow. "With great pleasure, Signora," said he.

· In short, the eagerness to "get on" was suddenly slackened; the determination to famish himself as far as Fondi, by way of punishing the landlord, was abandoned; John chose an apartment in the inn for his master's reception; and preparations were made to remain there until morning.

The carriage was unpacked of such of its contents as were indispensable for the night. There was the usual parade of trunks and writing-desks, and portfolios and dressing-boxes, and those other oppressive conveniences which burden a comfortable man. The observant loiterers about the inn door, wrapped up in great dirt-colored cloaks, with only a hawk's-eye uncovered, made many remarks to each other on this quantity of luggage that seemed enough for an army. The domestics of the inn talked with wonder of the splendid dressing-case, with its gold and silver furniture, that was spread out on the toilet-table, and the bag of gold that clinked as it was taken out of the trunk. The strange *Milor's* wealth, and the treasures he carried about him, were the talk, that evening, over all Terracina.

The Englishman took some time to make his ablutions and arrange his dress for table; and, after considerable labor and effort in putting himself at his ease, made his appearance, with stiff white cravat, his clothes free from the least speck of dust, and adjusted with precision. He made a civil bow on entering in the unprofessing English way, which the fair Venetian, accustomed to the complimentary salutations of the Continent, considered extremely cold.

The supper, as it was termed by the Italian, or dinner, as the Englishman called it, was now served; heaven and earth, and the waters under the earth, had been moved to furnish it; for there were birds of the air, and beasts of the field, and fish of the sea. The Englishman's servant, too, had turned the kitchen topsy-turvey in his zeal to cook his master a beefsteak; and made his appearance, loaded with ketchup, and soy, and Cayenne pepper, and Harvey sauce, and a bottle of port wine, from that warehouse, the carriage, in which his master seemed desirous of carrying England about the world with him. Indeed the repast was one of those Italian farragoes which require a little qualifying. The tureen of soup was a black sea, with livers, and limbs, and fragments of all kinds of birds, and beasts floating like wrecks about it. A meagre-winged animal, which my host called a delicate chicken, had evidently died of a consumption. The macaroni was smoked. The beefsteak was tough buffalo's flesh. There was what appeared to be a dish of stewed eels, of which the Englishman ate with great relish; but had nearly refunded them when told that they were vipers, caught among the rocks of Terracina, and esteemed a great delicacy.

. Nothing, however, conquers a traveller's spleen sooner than eating, whatever may be the cookery; and nothing brings him into good-humor with his company sooner than eating together; the Englishman, therefore, had not half finished his repast and his bottle, before he began to think the Venetian a very tolerable fellow for a foreigner, and his wife almost handsome enough to be an Englishwoman.

In the course of the repast, the usual topics of travellers were discussed, and among others, the reports of robbers, which harassed the mind of the fair Venetian. The landlord and waiter dipped into the conversation with that familiarity permitted on the Continent, and served up so many bloody tales as they served up the dishes, that they almost frightened away the poor lady's appetite. The Englishman, who had a national antipathy to everything technically called "humbug," listened to them all with a certain screw of the mouth, expressive of incredulity. There was the well-known story of the school of Terracina, captured by the robbers; and one of the scholars cruelly massacred, in order to bring the parents to terms for the ransom of the rest. And another, of a gentleman of Rome, who received his son's ear in a letter, with information that his son would be remitted to him in this way, by instalments, until he paid the required ransom.

The fair Venetian shuddered as she heard these tales; and the landlord, like a true narrator of the terrible, doubled the dose when he saw how it operated. He was just proceeding to relate the misfortunes of a great English lord and his family, when the Englishman, tired of his volubility, interrupted him, and pronounced these accounts to be mere travellers' tales, or the exaggerations of ignorant peasants, and designing innkeepers. The landlord was indignant at the doubt levelled at his stories, and the innuendo leveled at his cloth; he cited, in corroboration, half a dozen tales still more terrible.

"I don't believe a word of them," said the Englishman.

"But the robbers have been tried and executed!"

"All a farce!"

"But their heads are stuck up along the road?"

"Old skulls accumulated during a century."

The landlord muttered to himself as he went out at the door, "San Gennaro! quanto sono singolari questi Inglesi!"

A fresh hubbub outside of the inn announced the arrival of more travellers; and, from the variety of voices, or rather of clamors, the clattering of hoofs, the rattling of wheels, and the general uproar both within and without, the arrival seemed to be numerous.

It was, in fact, the procaccio and its convoy: a kind of caravan which sets out on certain days for the transportation of merchandise, with an escort of soldiery to protect it from the robbers. Travellers avail themselves of its protection, and a long file of carriages generally accompanies it.

A considerable time elapsed before either landlord or waiter returned; being hurried hither and thither by that tempest of noise and bustle, which takes place in an Italian inn on the arrival of any considerable accession of custom. When mine host reappeared, there was a smile of triumph on his countenance.

"Perhaps," said he, as he cleared the table; "perhaps the signor has not heard of what has happened?"

"What?" said the Englishman, dryly.

"Why, the procaccio has brought accounts of fresh exploits of the robbers."

"Pish!"

"There's more news of the English Milor and his family," said the host exultingly.

"An English lord! What English lord?"

"Milor Popkin."

"Lord Popkins? I never heard of such a title!"

"O! sicuro a great nobleman, who passed through here lately with mi ladi and her daughters. A magnifico, one of the grand counsellors of London, an almanno!"

"Almanno—almanno?—tut—he means alderman."

"Sicuro—Aldermanno Popkin, and the Principessa Popkin, and the Signorine Popkin!" said mine host, triumphantly.

He now put himself into an attitude, and would have launched into a full detail, had he not been thwarted by the Englishman, who seemed determined neither to credit nor indulge him in his stories, but dryly motioned for him to clear away the table.

An Italian tongue, however, is not easily checked; that of mine host continued to wag with increasing volubility, as he conveyed the relics of the repast out of the room; and the last that could be distinguished of his voice, as it died away along the corridor, was the iteration of the favorite word, Popkin—Popkin—Popkin—pop—pop—pop—

The arrival of the procaccio had, indeed, filled the house with stories, as it had with guests. The Englishman and his companions walked after supper up and down the large hall, or common room of the inn, which ran through the centre of the building. It was spacious and somewhat dirty, with tables placed in various parts, at which groups of travellers were seated; while others strolled about, waiting in famished impatience, for their evening's meal.

It was a heterogeneous assemblage of people of all ranks and countries, who arrived in all kinds of vehicles. Though distinct knots of travellers, yet the travelling together under one common escort, had jumbled them into a certain degree of companionship on the road; besides, on the Continent travellers are always familiar, and nothing is more motley than the groups which gather casually together in sociable conversation in the public rooms of inns.

The formidable number, and formidable guard of the procaccio had prevented any molestation from banditti; but every party of travellers had its tale of wonder, and one carriage vied with another in its budget of assertions and surmises. Fierce, whiskered faces had been seen peering over the rocks; carbines and stilettos gleaming from among the bushes; suspicious-looking fellows, with flapped hats, and scowling eyes, had occasionally reconnoitred a straggling carriage, but had disappeared on seeing the guard.

The fair Venetian listened to all these stories with that avidity with which we always pamper any feeling of alarm; even the Englishman began to feel interested in the common topic, desirous of getting more correct information than mere flying reports. Conquering, therefore, that shyness which is prone to keep an Englishman solitary in crowds, he approached one of the talking groups, the oracle of which was a tall, thin Italian, with long aquiline nose, a high forehead, and lively prominent eye, beaming from under a green velvet travelling-cap, with gold tassel. He was of Rome, a surgeon by profession, a poet by choice, and something of an improvisatore.

In the present instance, however, he was talking in plain prose, but holding forth with the fluency of one who talks well, and likes to exert his talent. A question or two from the Englishman drew copious replies; for an Englishman sociable among strangers is regarded as a phenomenon on the Continent, and always treated with attention for the rarity's sake. The improvisatore gave much the same account of the banditti that I have already furnished.

"But why does not the police exert itself, and root them out?" demanded the Englishman.

"Because the police is too weak, and the banditti are too strong," replied the other. "To root them out would be a more difficult task than you imagine. They are connected and almost identified with the mountain peasantry and the people of the villages. The numerous bands have an understanding with each other, and with the country round. A gendarme cannot stir without their being aware of it. They have their scouts everywhere, who lurk about towns and villages, and inns, mingle in every crowd, and pervade every place of resort. I should not be surprised if some one should be supervising us at this moment."

The fair Venetian looked round fearfully, and turned pale.

Here the improvisatore was interrupted by a lively Neapolitan lawyer.

"By the way," said he, "I recollect a little adventure of a learned doctor, a friend of mine, which happened in this very neighborhood; not far from the ruins of Theodoric's Castle, which are on the top of those great rocky heights above the town."

A wish was, of course, expressed to hear the adventure of the doctor, by all excepting the improvisatore, who, being fond of talking and of hearing himself talk, and accustomed, moreover, to harangue without interruption, looked rather annoyed at being checked when in full career. The Neapolitan, however, took no notice of his chagrin, but related the following anecdote.

ADVENTURE OF THE LITTLE
ANTIQUARY

MY friend, the Doctor, was a thorough antiquary; a little rusty, musty old fellow, always groping among ruins. He relished a building as you Englishmen relish a cheese,—the more mouldy and crumbling it was, the more it suited his taste. A shell of an old nameless temple, or the cracked walls of a broken-down amphitheatre, would throw him into raptures; and he took more delight in these crusts and cheese-parings of antiquity than in the best conditioned modern palaces.

He was a curious collector of coins also, and had just gained an accession of wealth that almost turned his brain. He had picked up, for instance, several Roman Consulars, half a Roman As, two Punics, which had doubtless belonged to the soldiers of Hannibal, having been found on the very spot where they had encamped among the Apennines. He had, moreover, one Samnite, struck after the Social War, and a Philistis, a queen that never existed; but above all, he valued himself upon a coin, indescribable to any but the initiated in these matters, bearing a cross on one side, and a pegasus on the other, and which, by some antiquarian logic, the little man adduced as an historical document, illustrating the progress of Christianity.

All these precious coins he carried about him in a leathern purse, buried deep in a pocket of his little black breeches.

The last maggot he had taken into his brain was to hunt after the ancient cities of the Pelasgi, which are said to exist to this day among the mountains of the Abruzzi; but about which a singular degree of obscurity prevails.* He had made many discoveries concerning them, and

---

*Among the many fond speculations of antiquaries is that of the existence of traces of the ancient Pelasgian cities in the Apennines; and many a wistful eye is cast by the traveller, versed in antiquarian lore, at the richly wooded mountains of the Abruzzi, as a forbidden fairy land of research. These spots, so beautiful, yet so inaccessible, from the rudeness of their inhabitants and the hordes of banditti which infest them, are a region of fable to the learned. Sometimes a wealthy virtuoso, whose purse and whose consequence could command a military escort, has penetrated to some individual point among the mountains; and sometimes a wandering artist or student, under protection of poverty or insignificance, has brought

had recorded a great many valuable notes and memorandums on the subject, in a voluminous book which he always carried about with him; either for the purpose of frequent reference, or through fear lest the precious document should fall into the hands of antiquaries. He had, therefore, a large pocket in the skirt of his coat, where he bore about this inestimable tome, banging against his rear as he walked.

Thus heavily laden with the spoils of antiquity, the good little man, during a sojourn at Terracina, mounted one day the rocky cliffs which overhang the town, to visit the castle of Theodoric. He was groping about the ruins towards the hour of sunset, buried in his reflections, his wits no doubt wool-gathering among the Goths and Romans, when he heard footsteps behind him.

He turned, and beheld five or six young fellows, of rough, saucy demeanor, clad in a singular manner, half peasant, half huntsman, with carbines in their hands. Their whole appearance and carriage left him no doubt into what company he had fallen.

The Doctor was a feeble little man, poor in look, and poorer in purse. He had but little gold or silver to be robbed of; but, then, he had his curious ancient coin in his breeches-pocket. He had, moreover, certain other valuables, such as an old silver watch, thick as a turnip, with figures on it large enough for a clock; and a set of seals at the end of a steel chain, dangling half-way down to his knees. All these were of precious esteem, being family relics. He had also a seal ring, a veritable

---

away some vague account, only calculated to give a keener edge to curiosity and conjecture.

By those who maintain the existence of the Pelasgian cities, it is affirmed that the formation of the different kingdoms in the Peloponnesus gradually caused the expulsion thence of the Pelasgi; but that their great migration may be dated from the finishing the wall around Acropolis, and that at this period they came to Italy. To these, in the spirit of theory, they would ascribe the introduction of the elegant arts into the country. It is evident, however, that, as barbarians flying before the first dawn of civilization, they could bring little with them superior to the inventions of the aborigines, and nothing that would have survived to the antiquarian through such a lapse of ages. It would appear more probable, that these cities, improperly termed Pelasgian, were coeval with many that have been discovered. The romantic Aricia, built by Hippolytus before the siege of Troy, and the poetic Tibur, Æsculate and Proenes, built by Telegonus after the dispersion of the Greeks;—these, lying contiguous to inhabited and cultivated spots, have been discovered. There are others, too, on the ruins of which the latter and more civilized Grecian colonists have ingrafted themselves, and which have become known by their merits or their medals. But that there are many still undiscovered, imbedded in the Abruzzi, it is the delight of the antiquarians to fancy. Strange that such a virgin soil for research, such an unknown realm of knowledge, should at this day remain in the very centre of hackneyed Italy.

antique intaglio, that covered half his knuckles. It was a Venus, which the old man almost worshipped with the zeal of a voluptuary. But what he most valued was his inestimable collection of hints relative to the Pelasgian cities, which he would gladly have given all the money in his pocket to have had safe at the bottom of his trunk in Terracina.

However, he plucked up a stout heart, at least as stout a heart as he could, seeing that he was but a puny little man at the best of times. So he wished the hunters a "buon giorno." They returned his salutation, giving the old gentleman a sociable slap on the back that made his heart leap into his throat.

They fell into conversation, and walked for some time together among the heights, the Doctor wishing them all the while at the bottom of the crater of Vesuvius. At length they came to a small osteria on the mountain, where they proposed to enter and have a cup of wine together; the Doctor consented, though he would as soon have been invited to drink hemlock.

One of the gang remained sentinel at the door; the others swaggered into the house, stood their guns in the corner of the room, and each drawing a pistol or stiletto out of his belt, laid it upon the table. They now drew benches round the board, called lustily for wine, and, hailing the Doctor as though he had been a boon companion of long standing, insisted upon his sitting down and making merry.

The worthy man complied with forced grimace, but with fear and trembling; sitting uneasily on the edge of his chair; eying ruefully the black-muzzled pistols, and cold, naked stilettos; and supping down heartburn with every drop of liquor. His new comrades, however, pushed the bottle bravely, and plied him vigorously. They sang, they laughed; told excellent stories of their robberies and combats, mingled with many ruffian jokes; and the little Doctor was fain to laugh at all their cut-throat pleasantries, though his heart was dying away at the very bottom of his bosom.

By their own account, they were young men from the villages, who had recently taken up this line of life out of the wild caprice of youth. They talked of their murderous exploits as a sportsman talks of his amusements; to shoot down a traveller seemed of little more consequence to them than to shoot a hare. They spoke with rapture of the glorious roving life they led, free as birds; here to-day, gone to-morrow; ranging the forests, climbing the rocks, scouring the valleys; the world their own wherever they could lay hold of it; full purses—merry companions—pretty women. The little antiquary got fuddled with their talk and their wine, for they did not spare bumpers. He half forgot his fears, his seal-ring, and his family watch; even the treatise on the Pelasgian cities, which was warming under him, for a time faded from his memory in the glowing picture that they drew. He declares that he no longer wonders at the prevalence of this robber mania among the mountains; for he felt at the time, that, had he been a young man, and had there been no danger of the galleys in the background, he should have been half tempted himself to turn bandit.

At length the hour of separating arrived. The Doctor was suddenly called to himself and his fears by seeing the robbers resume their weapons. He now quaked for his valuables, and, above all, for his antiquarian treatise. He endeavored, however, to look cool and unconcerned; and drew from out his deep pocket a long, lank, leathern purse, far gone in consumption, at the bottom of which a few coin chinked with the trembling of his hand.

The chief of the party observed his movement, and laying his hand upon the antiquary's shoulder, "Harkee! Signore Dottore!" said he, "we have drunk together as friends and comrades; let us part as such. We understand you. We know who and what you are, for we know who everybody is that sleeps at Terracina, or that puts foot upon the road. You are a rich man, but you carry all your wealth in your head: we cannot get at it, and we should not know what to do with it if we could. I see you are uneasy about your ring; but don't worry yourself, it is not worth taking; you think it an antique, but it's a counterfeit—a mere sham."

Here the ire of the antiquary rose: the Doctor forgot himself in his zeal for the character of his ring. Heaven and earth! his Venus a sham. Had they pronounced the wife of his bosom "no better than she should be," he could not have been more indignant. He fired up in vindication of his intaglio.

"Nay, nay," continued the robber, "we have no time to dispute about it: value it as you please. Come, you're a brave little old signor—one more cup of wine, and we'll pay the reckoning. No compliments—you shall not pay a grain—you are our guest—I insist upon it. So—now make the best of your way back to Terracina, it's growing late. Buono viaggo! And harkee, take care how you wander among these mountains,—you may not always fall into such good company."

They shouldered their guns; sprang gayly up the rocks; and the little Doctor hobbled back to Terracina, rejoicing that the robbers had left his watch, his coins, and his treatise, unmolested; but still indignant that they should have pronounced his Venus an impostor.

The improvisatore had shown many symptoms of impatience during this recital. He saw his theme in danger of being taken out of his hands, which to an able talker is always a grievance, but to an improvisatore is an absolute calamity: and then for it to be taken away by a Neapolitan was still more vexatious; the inhabitants of the different Italian states having an implacable jealousy of each other in all things, great and small. He took advantage of the first pause of the Neapolitan to catch hold again of the thread of the conversation.

"As I observed before," said he, "the prowlings of the banditti are so extensive; they are so much in league with one another, and so interwoven with various ranks of society——"

"For that matter," said the Neapolitan, "I have heard that your government has had some understanding with those gentry! or, at least, has winked at their misdeeds."

"My government?" said the Roman, impatiently.

"Ay, they say that Cardinal Gonsalvi—"

"Hush!" said the Roman, holding up his finger, and rolling his large eyes about the room.

"Nay, I only repeat what I heard commonly rumored in Rome," replied the Neapolitan, sturdily. "It was openly said, that the Cardinal had been up to the mountains, and had an interview with some of the chiefs. And I have been told, moreover, that, while honest people have been kicking their heels in the Cardinal's antechamber, waiting by the hour for admittance, one of those stiletto-looking fellows has elbowed his way through the crowd and entered without ceremony into the Cardinal's presence."

"I know," observed the improvisatore, "that there have been such reports, and it is not impossible that government may have made use of these men at particular periods; such as at the time of your late abortive revolution, when your carbonari were so busy with their machinations all over the country. The information which such men could collect, who were familiar, not merely with the recesses and secret places of the mountains, but also with the dark and dangerous recesses of society; who knew every suspicious character, and all his movements and all his lurkings; in a word, who knew all that was plotting in a world of mischief;—the utility of such men as instruments in the hands of government was too obvious to be overlooked; and Cardinal Gonsalvi, as a politic statesman, may, perhaps, have made use of them. Besides, he knew that, with all their atrocities, the robbers were always respectful towards the Church, and devout in their religion."

"Religion! religion!" echoed the Englishman.

"Yes, religion," repeated the Roman. "They have each their patron saint. They will cross themselves and say their prayers, whenever, in their mountain haunts, they hear the matin or the Ave-Maria bells sounding from the valleys; and will often descend from their retreats, and run imminent risks to visit some favorite shrine. I recollect an instance in point.

"I was one evening in the village of Frascati, which stands on the beautiful brow of a hill rising from the Campagna, just below the Abruzzi Mountains. The people, as is usual in fine evenings in our Italian towns and villages, were recreating themselves in the open air, and chatting in groups in the public square. While I was conversing with a knot of friends, I noticed a tall fellow, wrapped in a great mantle, passing across the square, but skulking along in the dusk, as if anxious to avoid observation. The people drew back as he passed. It was whispered to me that he was a notorious bandit."

"But why was he not immediately seized?" said the Englishman.

"Because it was nobody's business; because nobody wished to incur the vengeance of his comrades; because there were not sufficient gendarmes near to insure security against the number of desperadoes he might have at hand; because the gendarmes might not have received particular instructions with respect to him, and might not feel disposed to·engage in a hazardous conflict without compulsion. In short, I might give you a thousand reasons rising out of the state of our government and manners, not one of which after all might appear satisfactory."

The Englishman shrugged his shoulders with an air of contempt.

"I have been told," added the Roman, rather quickly, "that even in your metropolis of London, notorious thieves, well known to the police as such, walk the streets at noonday in search of their prey, and are not molested unless caught in the very act of robbery."

The Englishman gave another shrug but with a very different expression.

"Well, sir, I fixed my eye on this daring wolf, thus prowling through the fold, and saw him enter a church. I was curious to witness his devotion. You know our spacious, magnificent churches. The one in which he entered was vast, and shrouded in the dusk of the evening. At the extremity of the long aisles a couple of tapers feebly glimmered on the grand altar. In one of the side chapels was a votive candle placed before the image of a saint. Before this image the robber had prostrated himself. His mantle partly falling off from his shoulders as he knelt, revealed a form of Herculean strength; a stiletto and pistol glittered in his belt; and the light falling on his countenance, showed features not unhandsome, but strongly and fiercely characterized. As he prayed, he became vehemently agitated; his lips quivered; sighs and murmurs, almost groans, burst from him; he beat his breast with vi-

ADVENTURE OF THE LITTLE ANTIQUARY 377

olence; then clasped his hands and wrung them convulsively, as he extended them towards the image. Never had I seen such a terrific picture of remorse. I felt fearful of being discovered watching him, and withdrew. Shortly afterwards I saw him issue from the church wrapped in his mantle. He recrossed the square, and no doubt returned to the mountains with a disburdened conscience, ready to incur a fresh arrear of crime."

Here the Neapolitan was about to get hold of the conversation, and had just preluded with the ominous remark: "That puts me in mind of a circumstance," when the improvisatore, too adroit to suffer himself to be again superseded, went on, pretending not to hear the interruption.

"Among the many circumstances connected with the banditti, which serve to tender the traveller uneasy and insecure, is the understanding which they sometimes have with the innkeepers. Many an isolated inn among the lonely parts of the Roman territories, and especially about the mountains, are of a dangerous and perfidious character. They are places where the banditti gather information, and where the unwary traveller, remote from hearing or assistance, is betrayed to the midnight dagger. The robberies committed at such inns are often accompanied by the most atrocious murders; for it is only by the complete extermination of their victims that the assassins can escape detection. I recollect an adventure," added he, "which occurred at one of these solitary mountain inns, which, as you all seem in a mood for robber anecdotes, may not be uninteresting."

Having secured the attention and awakened the curiosity of the bystanders, he paused for a moment, rolled up his large eyes as improvisatori are apt to do when they would recollect an impromptu, and then related with great dramatic effect the following story, which had, doubtless, been well prepared and digested beforehand.

THE BELATED TRAVELLERS

IT was late one evening that a carriage drawn by mules, slowly toiled
its way up one of the passes of the Apennines. It was through one of
the wildest defiles, where a hamlet occurred only at distant intervals,
perched on the summit of some rocky height, or the white towers of a
convent peeped out from among the thick mountain foliage. The carriage was of ancient and ponderous construction. Its faded embellishments spoke of former splendor, but its crazy springs and axle-trees
creaked out the tale of present decline. Within was seated a tall, thin
old gentleman, in a kind of military travelling-dress, and a foraging-
cap trimmed with fur, though the gray locks which stole from under
it hinted that his fighting days were over. Beside him was a pale, beautiful girl of eighteen, dressed in something of a northern or Polish costume. One servant was seated in front, a rusty, crusty looking fellow,
with a scar across his face, an orange-tawny *schnurbart* or pair of
moustaches, bristling from under his nose, and altogether the air of an
old soldier.

It was, in fact, the equipage of a Polish nobleman; a wreck of one
of those princely families once of almost oriental magnificence, but
broken down and impoverished by the disasters of Poland. The Count,
like many other generous spirits, had been found guilty of the crime of
patriotism, and was, in a manner, an exile from his country. He had resided for some time in the first cities of Italy, for the education of his
daughter, in whom all his cares and pleasures were now centred. He
had taken her into society, where her beauty and her accomplishments
gained her many admirers; and had she not been the daughter of a
poor broken-down Polish nobleman, it is more than probable many
would have contended for her hand. Suddenly, however, her health
became delicate and drooping; her gayety fled with the roses of her
cheek, and she sank into silence and debility. The old Count saw the
change with the solicitude of a parent. "We must try a change of air
and scene," said he, and in a few days the old family carriage was rumbling among the Apennines.

Their only attendant was the veteran Caspar, who had been born in
the family, and grown rusty in its service. He had followed his master
in all his fortunes; had fought by his side; had stood over him when

fallen in battle; and had received, in his defence, the sabre-cut which added such grimness to his countenance. He was now his valet, his steward, his butler, his factotum. The only being that rivalled his master in his affections was his youthful mistress. She had grown up under his eye, he had led her by the hand when she was a child, and he now looked upon her with the fondness of a parent. Nay, he even took the freedom of a parent in giving his blunt opinion on all matters which he thought were for her good; and felt a parent's vanity at seeing her gazed at and admired.

The evening was thickening; they had been for some time passing through narrow gorges of the mountains, along the edges of a tumbling stream. The scenery was lonely and savage. The rocks often beetled over the road, with flocks of white goats browsing on their brinks, and gazing down upon the travellers. They had between two or three leagues yet to go before they could reach any village; yet the muleteer, Pietro, a tippling old fellow, who had refreshed himself at the last halting-place with a more than ordinary quantity of wine, sat singing and talking alternately to his mules, and suffering them to lag on at a snail's pace, in spite of the frequent entreaties of the Count and maledictions of Caspar.

The clouds began to roll in heavy masses along the mountains, shrouding their summits from view. The air was damp and chilly. The Count's solicitude on his daughter's account overcame his usual patience. He leaned from the carriage, and called to old Pietro in an angry tone.

"Forward!" said he. "It will be midnight before we arrive at our inn."

"Yonder it is, Signor," said the muleteer.

"Where?" demanded the Count.

"Yonder," said Pietro, pointing to a desolate pile about a quarter of a league distant.

"That the place?—why, it looks more like a ruin than an inn. I thought we were to put up for the night at a comfortable village."

Here Pietro uttered a string of piteous exclamations and ejaculations, such as are ever at the tip of the tongue of a delinquent muleteer. "Such roads! and such mountains! and then his poor animals were way-worn, and leg-weary; they would fall lame; they would never be able to reach the village. And then what could His Excellenza wish for better than the inn; a perfect castella—a palazza—and such people!— and such a larder!—and such beds!—His Excellenza might fare as sumptuously, and sleep as soundly there as a prince!"

The Count was easily persuaded, for he was anxious to get his daughter out of the night air; so in a little while the old carriage rattled and jingled into the great gateway of the inn.

The building did certainly in some measure answer to the muleteer's description. It was large enough for either castle or palace; built in a strong, but simple and almost rude style; with a great quantity of waste room. It had in fact been, in former times, a hunting-seat of one of the Italian princes. There was space enough within its walls and out-buildings to have accommodated a little army. A scanty household seemed now to people this dreary mansion. The faces that presented themselves on the arrival of the travellers were begrimed with dirt, and scowling in their expression. They all knew old Pietro, however, and gave him a welcome as he entered, singing and talking, and almost whooping, into the gateway.

The hostess of the inn waited, herself, on the Count and his daughter, to show them the apartments. They were conducted through a long gloomy corridor, and then through a suite of chambers opening into each other, with lofty ceilings, and great beams extending across them. Everything, however, had a wretched, squalid look. The walls were damp and bare, excepting that here and there hung some great painting, large enough for a chapel, and blackened out of all distinction.

They chose two bedrooms, one within another; the inner one for the daughter. The bedsteads were massive and misshapen; but on examining the beds so vaunted by old Pietro, they found them stuffed with fibres of hemp knotted in great lumps. The Count shrugged his shoulders, but there was no choice left.

The chilliness of the apartments crept to their bones; and they were glad to return to a common chamber or kind of hall, where was a fire burning in a huge cavern, miscalled a chimney. A quantity of green wood, just thrown on, puffed out volumes of smoke. The room corresponded to the rest of the mansion. The floor was paved and dirty. A great oaken table stood in the centre, immovable from its size and weight. The only thing that contradicted this prevalent air of indigence was the dress of the hostess. She was a slattern of course; yet her garments, though dirty and negligent, were of costly materials. She wore several rings of great value on her fingers, and jewels in her ears, and round her neck was a string of large pearls, to which was attached a sparkling crucifix. She had the remains of beauty, yet there was something in the expression of her countenance that inspired the young lady with singular aversion. She was officious and obsequious in her attentions, and both the Count and his daughter felt relieved, when she consigned them to the care of a dark, sullen-looking servant-maid, and went off to superintend the supper.

Caspar was indignant at the muleteer for having, either through negligence or design, subjected his master and mistress to such quarters; and vowed by his moustaches to have revenge on the old varlet the moment they were safe out from among the mountains. He kept up a continual quarrel with the sulky servant-maid, which only served to increase the sinister expression with which she regarded the travellers, from under her strong dark eyebrows.

As to the Count, he was a good-humored passive traveller. Perhaps real misfortunes had subdued his spirit, and rendered him tolerant of many of those petty evils which make prosperous men miserable. He drew a large broken arm-chair to the fireside for his daughter, and another for himself, and seizing an enormous pair of tongs, endeavored to rearrange the wood so as to produce a blaze. His efforts, however, were only repaid by thicker puffs of smoke, which almost overcame the good gentleman's patience. He would draw back, cast a look upon his delicate daughter, then upon the cheerless, squalid apartment, and, shrugging his shoulders, would give a fresh stir to the fire.

Of all the mysteries of a comfortless inn, however, there is none greater than sulky attendance; the good Count for some time bore the smoke in silence, rather than address himself to the scowling servant-maid. At length he was compelled to beg for drier firewood. The woman retired muttering. On re-entering the room hastily, with an armful of fagots, her foot slipped; she fell, and striking her head against the corner of a chair, cut her temple severely.

The blow stunned her for a time, and the wound bled profusely. When she recovered, she found the Count's daughter administering to her wound, and binding it up with her own handkerchief; but perhaps there was something in the appearance of the lovely being who bent over her, or in the tones of her voice, that touched the heart of the woman, unused to be administered to by such hands. Certain it is, she was strongly affected. She caught the delicate hand of the Polonaise, and pressed it fervently to her lips.

"May San Francesco watch over you, Signora!" exclaimed she.

A new arrival broke the stillness of the inn; it was a Spanish princess with a numerous retinue. The courtyard was in an uproar; the house in a bustle. The landlady hurried to attend such distinguished guests; and the poor Count and his daughter, and their supper, were for a moment forgotten. The veteran Caspar muttered Polish maledictions enough to agnoize an Italian ear; but it was impossible to convince the hostess of the superiority of his old master and young mistress to the whole nobility of Spain.

The noise of the arrival had attracted the daughter to the window just as the new-comers had alighted. A young cavalier sprang out of the carriage and handed out the Princess. The latter was a little shrivelled old lady, with a face of parchment and sparkling black eye; she was richly and gayly dressed, and walked with the assistance of a golden-headed cane as high as herself. The young man was tall and elegantly formed. The Count's daughter shrank back at the sight of him, though the deep frame of the window screened her from observation. She gave a heavy sigh as she closed the casement. What that sigh meant I cannot say. Perhaps it was at the contrast between the splendid equipage of the Princess, and the crazy rheumatic-looking old vehicle of her father, which stood hard by. Whatever might be the reason, the young lady closed the casement with a sigh. She returned to her chair, —a slight shivering passed over her delicate frame: she rested her pale cheek in the palm of her hand, and looked mournfully into the fire.

The Count thought she appeared paler than usual.

"Does anything ail thee, my child?" said he.

"Nothing, dear father!" she said, laying her hand within his, and looking up smiling in his face; but as she said so, a treacherous tear rose suddenly to her eye, and she turned away her head.

"The air of the window has chilled thee," said the Count, fondly, "but a good night's rest will make all well again."

The supper-table was at length laid, and the supper about to be served, when the hostess appeared, with her usual obsequiousness, apologizing for showing in the new-comers; but the night air was cold, and there was no other chamber in the inn with a fire in it. She had scarcely made the apology when the Princess entered, leaning on the arm of the elegant young man.

The Count immediately recognized her for a lady whom he had met frequently in society, both at Rome and Naples; and at whose conversaziones, in fact, he had been constantly invited. The cavalier, too, was her nephew and heir, who had been greatly admired in the gay circles both for his merits and prospects, and who had once been on a visit at the same time with his daughter and himself at the villa of a nobleman near Naples. Report had recently affianced him to a rich Spanish heiress.

The meeting was agreeable to both the Count and the Princess. The former was a gentleman of the old school, courteous in the extreme; the Princess had been a belle in her youth, and a woman of fashion all her life, and liked to be attended to.

The young man approached the daughter, and began something of a complimentary observation; but his manner was embarrassed, and his compliment ended in an indistinct murmur; while the daughter bowed without looking up, moved her lips without articulating a word, and sank again into her chair, where she sat gazing into the fire, with a thousand varying expressions passing over her countenance.

This singular greeting of the young people was not perceived by the old ones, who were occupied at the time with their own courteous salutations. It was arranged that they should sup together; and as the Princess travelled with her own cook, a very tolerable supper soon smoked upon the board. This, too, was assisted by choice wines, and liquors, and delicate confitures brought from one of her carriages; for she was a veteran epicure, and curious in her relish for the good things of this world. She was, in fact, a vivacious little old lady, who mingled the woman of dissipation with the devotee. She was actually on her way to Loretto to expiate a long life of gallantries and peccadilloes by a rich offering at the holy shrine. She was, to be sure, rather a luxurious penitent, and a contrast to the primitive pilgrims, with scrip and staff, and cockle-shell; but then it would be unreasonable to expect such self-denial from people of fashion; and there was not a doubt of the ample efficacy of the rich crucifixes, and golden vessels, and jewelled ornaments, which she was bearing to the treasury of the blessed Virgin.

The Princess and the Count chatted much during supper about the scenes and society in which they had mingled, and did not notice that they had all the conversation to themselves; the young people were silent and constrained. The daughter ate nothing, in spite of the politeness of the Princess, who continually pressed her to taste of one or other of the delicacies. The Count shook his head.

"She is not well this evening," said he. "I thought she would have fainted just now as she was looking out of the window at your carriage on its arrival."

A crimson glow flushed to the very temples of the daughter; but she leaned over her plate, and her tresses cast a shade over her countenance.

When supper was over, they drew their chairs about the great fireplace. The flame and smoke had subsided, and a heap of glowing embers diffused a grateful warmth. A guitar, which had been brought from the Count's carriage, leaned against the wall; the Princess perceived it. "Can we not have a little music before parting for the night?" demanded she.

The Count was proud of his daughter's accomplishment, and joined in the request. The young man made an effort of politeness, and taking up the guitar, presented it, though in an embarrassed manner, to the fair musician. She would have declined it, but was too much confused to do so; indeed, she was so nervous and agitated that she dared not trust her voice to make an excuse. She touched the instrument with a faltering hand, and, after preluding a little, accompanied herself in several Polish airs. Her father's eyes glistened as he sat gazing on her. Even the crusty Caspar lingered in the room, partly through a fondness for the music of his native country, but chiefly through his pride in the musician. Indeed, the melody of the voice and the delicacy of the touch were enough to have charmed more fastidious ears. The little Princess nodded her head and tapped her hand to the music, though exceedingly out of time; while the nephew sat buried in profound contemplation of a black picture on the opposite wall.

"And now," said the Count, patting her cheek fondly, "one more favor. Let the Princess hear that little Spanish air you were so fond of. You can't think," added he, "what a proficiency she has made in your language; though she has been a sad girl, and neglected it of late."

The color flushed the pale cheek of the daughter. She hesitated, murmured something; but with sudden effort collected herself, struck the guitar boldly, and began. It was a Spanish romance, with something of love and melancholy in it. She gave the first stanza with great expression, for the tremulous, melting tones of her voice went to the heart; but her articulation failed, her lips quivered, the song died away, and she burst into tears.

The Count folded her tenderly in his arms. "Thou art not well, my child," said he, "and I am tasking thee cruelly. Retire to thy chamber, and God bless thee!" She bowed to the company without raising her eyes, and glided out of the room.

The Count shook his head as the door closed. "Something is the matter with that child," said he, "which I cannot divine. She has lost all health and spirits lately. She was always a tender flower, and I had much pains to rear her. Excuse a father's foolishness," continued he, "but I have seen much trouble in my family; and this poor girl is all that is now left to me; and she used to be so lively—"

"Maybe she's in love!" said the little Princess, with a shrewd nod of the head.

"Impossible!" replied the good Count, artlessly. "She has never mentioned a word of such a thing to me."

How little did the worthy gentleman dream of the thousand cares, and griefs, and mighty love concerns which agitate a virgin heart, and which a timid girl scarcely breathes unto herself.

The nephew of the Princess rose abruptly and walked about the room.

When she found herself alone in her chamber, the feelings of the young lady, so long restrained, broke forth with violence. She opened the casement that the cool air might blow upon her throbbing temples.

Perhaps there was some little pride or pique mingled with her emotions; though her gentle nature did not seem calculated to harbor any such angry inmate.

"He saw me weep!" said she, with a sudden mantling of the cheek, and a swelling of the throat,—"but no matter!—no matter!"

And so saying, she threw her white arms across the window-frame, buried her face in them, and abandoned herself to an agony of tears. She remained lost in a reverie, until the sound of her father's and Caspar's voices in the adjoining room gave token that the party had retired for the night. The lights gleaming from window to window, showed that they were conducting the Princess to her apartments, which were in the opposite wing of the inn; and she distinctly saw the figure of the nephew as he passed one of the casements.

She heaved a deep heart-drawn sigh, and was about to close the lattice, when her attention was caught by words spoken below her window by two persons who had just turned an angle of the building.

"But what will become of the poor young lady?" said a voice, which she recognized for that of the servant-woman.

"Pooh! she must take her chance," was the reply from old Pietro.

"But cannot she be spared?" asked the other, entreatingly; "she's so kind-hearted!"

"Cospetto! what has got into thee?" replied the other, petulantly: "would you mar the whole business for the sake of a silly girl?" By this time they had got so far from the window that the Polonaise could hear nothing further. There was something in this fragment of conversation calculated to alarm. Did it relate to herself?—and if so, what was this impending danger from which it was entreated that she might be spared? She was several times on the point of tapping at her father's door, to tell him what she had heard, but she might have been mistaken; she might have heard indistinctly; the conversation might have alluded to some one else; at any rate, it was too indefinite to lead to any conclusion. While in this state of irresolution, she was startled by a low knock against the wainscot in a remote part of her gloomy chamber. On holding up the light, she beheld a small door there, which she had not before remarked. It was bolted on the inside. She advanced, and demanded who knocked, and was answered in a voice of the female domestic. On opening the door, the woman stood before it pale and agitated. She entered softly, laying her finger on her lips as in sign of caution and secrecy.

"Fly!" said she: "leave this house instantly, or you are lost!"

The young lady, trembling with alarm, demanded an explanation.

"I have no time," replied the woman, "I dare not—I shall be missed if I linger here—but fly instantly, or you are lost."

"And leave my father?"

"Where is he?"

"In the adjoining chamber."

"Call him, then, but lose no time."

The young lady knocked at her father's door. He was not yet retired to bed. She hurried into his room, and told him of the fearful warnings she had received. The Count returned with her into the chamber, followed by Caspar. His questions soon drew the truth out of the embarrassed answers of the woman. The inn was beset by robbers. They were to be introduced after midnight, when the attendants of the Princess and the rest of the travellers were sleeping, and would be an easy prey.

"But we can barricade the inn, we can defend ourselves," said the Count.

"What! when the people of the inn are in league with the banditti?"

"How then are we to escape? Can we not order out the carriage and depart?"

. "San Francesco! for what? to give the alarm that the plot is discovered? That would make the robbers desperate, and bring them on you at once. They have had notice of the rich booty in the inn, and will not easily let it escape them."

"But how else are we to get off?"

"There is a horse behind the inn," said the woman, "from which the man has just dismounted who has been to summon the aid of part of the band at a distance."

"One horse; and there are three of us!" said the Count.

"And the Spanish Princess!" cried the daughter, anxiously. "How can she be extricated from the danger?"

"Diavolo? what is she to me?" said the woman, in sudden passion. "It is *you* I come to save, and you will betray me, and we shall all be lost! Hark!" continued she, "I am called—I shall be discovered—one word more. This door leads by a staircase to the courtyard. Under the shed, in the rear of the yard is a small door leading out to the fields. You will find a horse there; mount it; make a circuit under the shadow of a ridge of rocks that you will see; proceed cautiously and quietly until you cross a brook, and find yourself on the road just where there are three white crosses nailed against a tree; then put your horse to his speed, and make the best of your way to the village—but recollect, my life is in your hands—say nothing of what you have heard or seen, whatever may happen at this inn."

The woman hurried away. A short and agitated consultation took place between the Count, his daughter, and the veteran Caspar. The young lady seemed to have lost all apprehension for herself in her solicitude for the safety of the Princess. "To fly in selfish silence, and leave her to be massacred!"—A shuddering seized her at the very thought. The gallantry of the Count, too, revolted at the idea. He could not consent to turn his back upon a party of helpless travellers, and leave them in ignorance of the danger which hung over them.

"But what is to become of the young lady," said Caspar, "if the alarm is given, and the inn thrown in a tumult? What may happen to her in a chance-medley affray?"

Here the feelings of the father were aroused; he looked upon his lovely, helpless child, and trembled at the chance of her falling into the hands of ruffians.

The daughter, however, thought nothing of herself. "The Princess! the Princess!—only let the Princess know her danger." She was willing to share it with her.

At length Caspar interfered with the zeal of a faithful old servant. No time was to be lost—the first thing was to get the young lady out of danger. "Mount the horse," said he to the Count, "take her behind you and fly! Make for the village, rouse the inhabitants, and send assistance. Leave me here to give the alarm to the Princess and her people. I am an old soldier, and I think we shall be able to stand siege until you send us aid."

The daughter would again have insisted on staying with the Princess—

"For what?" said old Caspar, bluntly. "You could do no good—you would be in the way;—we should have to take care of you instead of ourselves."

There was no answering these objections; the Count seized his pistols, and taking his daughter under his arm, moved towards the staircase. The young lady paused, stepped back, and said, faltering with agitation—"There is a young cavalier with the Princess—her nephew—perhaps he may—"

"I understand you, Mademoiselle," replied old Caspar, with a significant nod; "not a hair of his head shall suffer harm if I can help it."

The young lady blushed deeper than ever; she had not anticipated being so thoroughly understood by the blunt old servant.

"That is not what I mean," said she, hesitating. She would have added something, or made some explanation, but the moments were precious and her father hurried her away.

They found their way through the courtyard to the small postern gate where the horse stood, fastened to a ring in the wall. The Count mounted, took his daughter behind him, and they proceeded as quietly as possible in the direction which the woman had pointed out. Many a fearful and anxious look did the daughter cast back upon the gloomy pile; the lights which had feebly twinkled through the dusty casements were one by one disappearing, a sign that the inmates were gradually sinking to repose; and she trembled with impatience, lest succor should not arrive until that repose had been fatally interrupted.

They passed silently and safely along the skirts of the rocks, protected from observation by their overhanging shadows. They crossed the brook, and reached the place where three white crosses nailed against a tree told of some murder that had been committed there. Just as they had reached this ill-omened spot they beheld several men in the gloom coming down a craggy defile among the rocks.

"Who goes there?" exclaimed a voice. The Count put spurs to his horse, but one of the men sprang forward and seized the bridle. The horse started back, and reared; and had not the young lady clung to her father, she would have been thrown off. The Count leaned forward, put a pistol to the very head of the ruffian, and fired. The latter fell dead. The horse sprang forward. Two or three shots were fired which whistled by the fugitives, but only served to augment their speed. They reached the village in safety.

The whole place was soon roused; but such was the awe in which the banditti were held, that the inhabitants shrunk at the idea of encountering them. A desperate band had for some time infested that pass through the mountains, and the inn had long been suspected of being one of those horrible places where the unsuspicious wayfarer is entrapped and silently disposed of. The rich ornaments worn by the slattern hostess of the inn had excited heavy suspicions. Several instances had occurred of small parties of travellers disappearing mysteriously on that road, who, it was supposed at first, had been carried off by the robbers for the purpose of ransom, but who had never been heard of more. Such were the tales buzzed in the ears of the Count by the villagers, as he endeavored to rouse them to the rescue of the Princess and her train from their perilous situation. The daughter seconded the exertions of her father with all the eloquence of prayers, and tears, and beauty. Every moment that elapsed increased her anxiety until it became agonizing. Fortunately there was a body of gendarmes resting at the village. A number of the young villagers volunteered to accompany them, and the little army was put in motion. The Count having deposited his daughter in a place of safety, was too much of the old soldier not to hasten to the scene of danger. It would be difficult to paint the anxious agitation of the young lady while awaiting the result.

The party arrived at the inn just in time. The robbers, finding their plans discovered, and the travellers prepared for their reception, had become open and furious in their attack. The Princess's party had barricaded themselves in one suite of apartments, and repulsed the robbers from the doors and windows. Caspar had shown the generalship of a veteran, and the nephew of the Princess the dashing valor of a young soldier. Their ammunition, however, was nearly exhausted, and they would have found it difficult to hold out much longer, when a discharge from the musketry of the gendarmes gave them the joyful tidings of succor.

A fierce fight ensued, for part of the robbers were surprised in the inn, and had to stand siege in their turn; while their comrades made desperate attempts to relieve them from under cover of the neighboring rocks and thickets.

I cannot pretend to give a minute account of the fight, as I have heard it related in a variety of ways. Suffice it to say, the robbers were defeated; several of them killed, and several taken prisoners; which last, together with the people of the inn, were either executed or sent to the galleys.

I picked up these particulars in the course of a journey which I made some time after the event had taken place. I passed by the very inn. It was then dismantled, excepting one wing, in which a body of gendarmes was stationed. They pointed out to me the shot-holes in the window-frames, the walls, and the panels of the doors. There were a number of withered limbs dangling from the branches of a neighboring tree, and blackening in the air, which I was told were the limbs of the robbers who had been slain, and the culprits who had been executed. The whole place had a dismal, wild, forlorn look.

"Were any of the Princess's party killed?" inquired the Englishman.

"As far as I can recollect, there were two or three."

"Not the nephew, I trust?" said the fair Venetian.

"Oh, no: he hastened with the Count to relieve the anxiety of the daughter by the assurances of victory. The young lady had been sustained through the interval of suspense by the very intensity of her feelings. The moment she saw her father returning in safety, accompanied by the nephew of the Princess, she uttered a cry of rapture, and fainted. Happily, however, she soon recovered, and what is more, was married shortly afterwards to the young cavalier; and the whole party accompanied the old Princess in her pilgrimage to Loretto, where her votive offerings may still be seen in the treasury of the Santa Casa."

It would be tedious to follow the devious course of the conversation as it wound through a maze of stories of the kind, until it was taken up by two other travellers who had come under convoy of the procaccio: Mr. Hobbs and Mr. Dobbs, a linen-draper and a green-grocer, just returning from a hasty tour in Greece and the Holy Land. They were full of the story of Alderman Popkins. They were astonished that the robbers should dare to molest a man of his importance on 'Change, he being an eminent dry-salter of Throgmorton Street, and a magistrate to boot.

In fact, the story of the Popkins family was but too true. It was attested by too many present to be for a moment doubted; and from the contradictory and concordant testimony of half a score, all eager to relate it, and all talking at the same time, the Englishman was enabled to gather the following particulars.

ADVENTURE OF THE POPKINS FAMILY

IT was but a few days before, that the carriage of Alderman Popkins had driven up to the inn of Terracina. Those who have seen an English family-carriage on the Continent must have remarked the sensation it produces. It is an epitome of England; a little morsel of the old Island rolling about the world. Everything about it compact, snug, finished, and fitting. The wheels turning on patent axles without rattling; the body, hanging so well on its springs, yielding to every motion, yet protecting from every shock; the ruddy faces gaping from the windows, —sometimes of a portly old citizen, sometimes of a voluminous dowager, and sometimes of a fine fresh hoyden just from boarding-school. And then the dickeys loaded with well-dressed servants, beef-fed and bluff; looking down from their heights with contempt on all the world around; profoundly ignorant of the country and the people, and devoutly certain that everything not English must be wrong.

Such was the carriage of Alderman Popkins as it made its appearance at Terracina. The courier who had preceded it to order horses, and who was a Neapolitan, had given a magnificent account of the richness and greatness of his master; blundering with an Italian's splendor of imagination about the Alderman's titles and dignities. The host had added his usual share of exaggeration; so that by the time the Alderman drove up to the door, he was a Milor—Magnitico—Principe—the Lord knows what!

The Alderman was advised to take an escort to Fondi and Itri, but he refused. It was as much as a man's life was worth, he said, to stop him on the king's highway: he would complain of it to the ambassador at Naples; he would make a national affair of it. The Principessa Popkins, a fresh, motherly dame, seemed perfectly secure in the protection of her husband, so omnipotent a man in the city. The Signorines Popkins, two fine bouncing girls, looked to their brother Tom, who had taken lessons in boxing; and as to the dandy himself, he swore no scaramouch of an Italian robber would dare to meddle with an Englishman. The landlord shrugged his shoulders, and turned out the palms of his hands with a true Italian grimace, and the carriage of Milor Popkins rolled on.

They passed through several very suspicious places without any molestation. The Misses Popkins, who were very romantic, and had learnt to draw in water-colors, were enchanted with the savage scenery around; it was so like what they had read in Mrs. Radcliff's romances; they should like, of all things, to make sketches. At length the carriage arrived at a place where the road wound up a long hill. Mrs. Popkins had sunk into a sleep; the young ladies were lost in the *Loves of the Angels*; and the dandy was hectoring the postilions from the coach-box. The Alderman got out, as he said, to stretch his legs up the hill. It was a long, winding ascent, and obliged him every now and then to stop and blow and wipe his forehead, with many a pish! and phew! being rather pursy and short of wind. As the carriage, however, was far behind him, and moved slowly under the weight of so many well-stuffed trunks, and well-stuffed travellers, he had plenty of time to walk at leisure.

On a jutting point of a rock that overhung the road, nearly at the summit of the hill, just where the road began to descend, he saw a solitary man seated, who appeared to be tending goats. Alderman Popkins was one of your shrewd travellers who always liked to be picking up small information along the road; so he thought he'd just scramble up to the honest man, and have a little talk by the way of learning the news and getting a lesson in Italian. As he drew near to the peasant, he did not half like his looks. He was partly reclining on the rocks, wrapped in the usual long mantle, which, with his slouched hat, only left a part of the swarthy visage, with a keen black eye, a beetle brow, and a fierce moustache to be seen. He had whistled several times to his dog, which was roving about the side of the hill. As the Alderman approached, he arose and greeted him. When standing erect, he seemed almost gigantic, at least in the eyes of Alderman Popkins, who, however, being a short man, might be deceived.

The latter would gladly now have been back in the carriage, or even on 'Change in London, for he was by no means well pleased with his company. However, he determined to put the best face on matters, and was beginning a conversation about the state of the weather, the baddishness of the crops, and the price of goats in that part of the country, when he heard a violent screaming. He ran to the edge of the rock, and looking over beheld his carriage surrounded by robbers. One held down the fat footman, another had the dandy by his starched cravat, with a pistol to his head; one was rummaging a portmanteau, another rummaging the Principessa's pockets; while the two Misses Popkins were screaming from each window of the carriage, and their waiting-maid squalling from the dickey.

Alderman Popkins felt all the ire of the parent and the magistrate roused within him. He grasped his cane, and was on the point of scrambling down the rocks either to assault the robbers or to read the riot act, when he was suddenly seized by the arm. It was by his friend the goatherd, whose cloak falling open, discovered a belt stuck full of pistols and stilettos. In short, he found himself in the clutches of the captain of the band, who had stationed himself on the rock to look out for travellers and to give notice to his men.

A sad ransacking took place. Trunks were turned inside out, and all the finery and frippery of the Popkins family scattered about the road. Such a chaos of Venice beads and Roman mosaics, and Paris bonnets of the young ladies, mingled with the Alderman's nightcaps and lambs'-wool stockings, and the dandy's hair-brushes, stays, and starched cravats.

The gentlemen were eased of their purses and their watches, and the ladies of their jewels; and the whole party were on the point of being carried up into the mountain, when fortunately the appearance of soldiers at a distance obliged the robbers to make off with the spoils they had secured, and leave the Popkins family to gather together the remnants of their effects, and make the best of their way to Fondi.

. When safe arrived, the Alderman made a terrible blustering at the inn; threatened to complain to the ambassador at Naples, and was ready to shake his cane at the whole country. The dandy had many stories to tell of his scuffles with the brigands, who overpowered him merely by numbers. As to the Misses Popkins, they were quite delighted with the adventure, and were occupied the whole evening in writing it in their journals. They declared the captain of the band to be a most romantic-looking man, they dared to say some unfortunate lover or exiled nobleman; and several of the band to be very handsome young men—"quite picturesque!"

"In verity," said mine host of Terracina, "they say the captain of the band is *un gallant uomo.*"

"A gallant man!" said the Englishman, indignantly: "I'd have your gallant man hanged like a dog!"

"To dare to meddle with Englishmen!" said Mr. Hobbs.

"And such a family as the Popkinses!" said Mr. Dobbs.

"They ought to come upon the country for damages!" said Mr. Hobbs.

"Our ambassador should make a complaint to the government of Naples," said Mr. Dobbs.

"They should be obliged to drive these rascals out of the country," said Hobbs.

"And if they did not we should declare war against them," said Dobbs.

"Pish!—humbug!" muttered the Englishman to himself, and walked away.

The Englishman had been a little wearied by this story, and by the ultra zeal of his countrymen, and was glad when a summons to their supper relieved him from the crowd of travellers. He walked out with his Venetian friends and a young Frenchman of an interesting demeanor, who had become sociable with them in the course of the conversation. They directed their steps towards the sea, which was lit up by the rising moon.

As they strolled along the beach they came to where a party of soldiers were stationed in a circle. They were guarding a number of galley slaves, who were permitted to refresh themselves in the evening breeze, and sport and roll upon the sand.

The Frenchman paused, and pointed to the group of wretches at their sports. "It is difficult," said he, "to conceive a more frightful mass of crime than is here collected. Many of these have probably been robbers, such as you have heard described. Such is, too often, the career of crime in this country. The parricide, the fratricide, the infanticide, the miscreant of every kind, first flies from justice and turns mountain bandit; and then when wearied of a life of danger, becomes traitor to his brother desperadoes; betrays them to punishment, and thus buys a commutation of his own sentence from death to the galleys; happy in the privilege of wallowing on the shore an hour a day, in this mere state of animal enjoyment."

The fair Venetian shuddered as she cast a look at the horde of wretches at their evening amusement. "They seemed," she said, "like so many serpents writhing together." And yet the idea that some of them had been robbers, those formidable beings that haunted her imagination, made her still cast another fearful glance, as we contemplate some terrible beast of prey, with a degree of awe and horror, even though caged and chained.

The conversation reverted to the tales of banditti which they had heard at the inn. The Englishman condemned some of them as fabrications, others as exaggerations. As to the story of the improvisatore, he pronounced it a mere piece of romance, originating in the heated brain of the narrator.

"And yet," said the Frenchman, "there is so much romance about the real life of those beings, and about the singular country they infest, that it is hard to tell what to reject on the ground of improbability. I have had an adventure happen to myself which gave me an opportunity of getting some insight into their manners and habits, which I found altogether out of the common run of existence."

There was an air of mingled frankness and modesty about the Frenchman which had gained the good will of the whole party, not even excepting the Englishman. They all eagerly inquired after the particulars of the circumstances he alluded to, and as they strolled slowly up and down the sea-shore, he related the following adventure.

THE PAINTER'S ADVENTURE

I AM an historical painter by profession, and resided for some time in the family of a foreign Prince at his villa, about fifteen miles from Rome, among some of the most interesting scenery of Italy. It is situated on the heights of ancient Tusculum. In its neighborhood are the ruins of the villas of Cicero, Scylla, Lucullus, Rufinus, and other illustrious Romans, who sought refuge here occasionally from their toils, in the bosom of a soft and luxurious repose. From the midst of delightful bowers, refreshed by the pure mountain breeze, the eye looks over a romantic landscape full of poetical and historical associations. The Albanian Mountains; Tivoli, once the favorite residence of Horace and Mæcenas; the vast, deserted, melancholy Campagna, with the Tiber winding through it, and St. Peter's dome swelling in the midst, the monument, as it were, over the grave of ancient Rome.

I assisted the Prince in researches which he was making among the classic ruins of his vicinity: his exertions were highly successful. Many wrecks of admirable statues and fragments of exquisite sculpture were dug up; monuments of the taste and magnificence that reigned in the ancient Tusculan abodes. He had studded his villa and its grounds with statues, relievos, vases, and sarcophagi, thus retrieved from the bosom of the earth.

The mode of life pursued at the villa was delightfully serene, diversified by interesting occupation and elegant leisure. Every one passed the day according to his pleasure or pursuits; and we all assembled in a cheerful dinner-party at sunset.

It was on the fourth of November, a beautiful, serene day, that we had assembled in the saloon at the sound of the first dinner-bell. The family were surprised at the absence of the Prince's confessor. They waited for him in vain, and at length placed themselves at table. They at first attributed his absence to his having prolonged his customary walk; and the early part of the dinner passed without any uneasiness. When the dessert was served, however, without his making his appearance, they began to feel anxious. They feared he might have been taken ill in some alley of the woods, or might have fallen into the hands of robbers. Not far from the villa, with the interval of a small valley, rose the mountains of the Abruzzi, the stronghold of banditti. Indeed, the neighborhood had for some time past been infested by them; and Barbone, a notorious bandit chief, had often been met prowling about the solitudes of Tusculum. The daring enterprises of these ruffians were well known: the objects of their cupidity or vengeance were insecure even in palaces. As yet they had respected the possessions of the Prince; but the idea of such dangerous spirits hovering about the neighborhood was sufficient to occasion alarm.

The fears of the company increased as evening closed in. The Prince ordered out forest guards and domestics with flambeaux to search for the confessor. They had not departed long when a slight noise was heard in the corridor of the ground-floor. The family were dining on the first floor, and the remaining domestics were occupied in attendance. There was no one on the ground-floor at this moment but the house-keeper, the laundress, and three field-laborers, who were resting themselves, and conversing with the women.

I heard the noise from below, and presuming it to be occasioned by the return of the absentee, I left the table and hastened down-stairs, eager to gain intelligence that might relieve the anxiety of the Prince and Princess. I had scarcely reached the last step, when I beheld before me a man dressed as a bandit; a carbine in his hand, and a stiletto and pistols in his belt. His countenance had a mingled expression of ferocity and trepidation: he sprang upon me, and exclaimed exultingly, "Ecco il principe!"

I saw at once into what hands I had fallen, but endeavored to summon up coolness and presence of mind. A glance towards the lower end of the corridor showed me several ruffians, clothed and armed in the same manner with the one who had seized me. They were guarding the two females and the field-laborers. The robber, who held me firmly by the collar, demanded repeatedly whether or not I were the Prince: his object evidently was to carry off the Prince, and extort an immense ransom. He was enraged at receiving none but vague replies, for I felt the importance of misleading him.

A sudden thought struck me how I might extricate myself from his clutches. I was unarmed, it is true, but I was vigorous. His companions were at a distance. By a sudden exertion I might wrest myself from him, and spring up the staircase, whither he would not dare to follow me singly. The idea was put in practice as soon as conceived. The ruffian's throat was bare; with my right hand I seized him by it, with my left hand I grasped the arm which held the carbine. The suddenness of my attack took him completely unawares, and the strangling nature of my grasp paralyzed him. He choked and faltered. I felt his hand relaxing its hold, and was on the point of jerking myself away, and darting up the staircase, before he could recover himself, when I was suddenly seized by some one from behind.

I had to let go my grasp. The bandit, once released, fell upon me with fury, and gave me several blows with the butt end of his carbine, one of which wounded me severely in the forehead and covered me with blood. He took advantage of my being stunned to rifle me of my watch, and whatever valuables I had about my person.

When I recovered from the effect of the blow, I heard the voice of the chief of the banditti who exclaimed: "Quello e il principe; siamo contente; andiamo!" (It is the Prince; enough, let us be off.) The band immediately closed around me and dragged me out of the palace, bearing off the three laborers likewise.

I had no hat on, and the blood flowed from my wound; I managed to stanch it, however, with my pocket-handkerchief, which I bound round my forehead. The captain of the band conducted me in triumph, supposing me to be the Prince. We had gone some distance before he learnt his mistake from one of the laborers. His rage was terrible. It was too late to return to the villa and endeavor to retrieve his error, for by this time the alarm must have been given, and every one in arms. He darted at me a ferocious look,—swore I had deceived him, and caused him to miss his fortune,—and told me to prepare for death. The rest of the robbers were equally furious. I saw their hands upon their poniards, and I knew that death was seldom an empty threat with these ruffians. The laborers saw the peril into which their information had betrayed me, and eagerly assured the captain that I was a man for whom the Prince would pay a great ransom. This produced a pause. For my part, I cannot say that I had been much dismayed by their menaces. I mean not to make any boast of courage; but I have been so schooled to hardship during the late revolutions, and have beheld death around me in so many perilous and disastrous scenes, that I have become in some measure callous to its terrors. The frequent hazard of life makes a man at length as reckless of it as a gambler of his money. To their threat of death, I replied, "that the sooner it was executed the better." This reply seemed to astonish the captain; and the prospect of ransom held out by the laborers had, no doubt, a still greater effect on him. He considered for a moment, assumed a calmer manner, and made a sign to his companions, who had remained waiting for my death-warrant. "Forward!" said he, "we will see about this matter by and by!"

We descended rapidly towards the road of La Molara, which leads to Rocca Priori. In the midst of this road is a solitary inn. The captain ordered the troop to halt at the distance of a pistol-shot from it, and enjoined profound silence. He approached the threshold alone, with noiseless steps. He examined the outside of the door very narrowly, and then returning precipitately, made a sign for the troop to continue its march in silence. It has since been ascertained, that this was one of those infamous inns which are the secret resorts of banditti. The innkeeper had an understanding with the captain as he most probably had with the chiefs of the different bands. When any of the patrols and gendarmes were quartered at his house, the brigands were warned of it by a preconcerted signal on the door; when there was no such signal, they might enter with safety, and be sure of welcome.

After pursuing our road a little further, we struck off towards the woody mountains which envelop Rocca Priori. Our march was long and painful; with many circuits and windings, at length we clambered a steep ascent, covered with a thick forest; and when we had reached the centre, I was told to seat myself on the ground. No sooner had I done so than, at a sign from their chief, the robbers surrounded me, and spreading their great cloaks from one to the other, formed a kind of pavilion of mantles, to which their bodies might be said to serve as columns. The captain then struck a light, and a flambeau was lit immediately. The mantles were extended to prevent the light of the flambeau from being seen through the forest. Anxious as was my situation, I could not look around upon this screen of dusky drapery, relieved by the bright colors of the robber's garments, the gleaming of their weapons, and the variety of strongly marked countenances, lit up by the flambeau, without admiring the picturesque effects of the scene. It was quite theatrical.

The captain now held an inkhorn, and giving me pen and paper, ordered me to write what he should dictate. I obeyed. It was a demand, couched in the style of robber eloquence, "that the Prince should send three thousand dollars for my ransom; or that my death should be the consequence of a refusal."

I knew enough of the desperate character of these beings to feel assured this was not an idle menace. Their only mode of insuring attention to their demands is to make the infliction of the penalty inevitable. I saw at once, however, that the demand was preposterous, and made in improper language.

I told the captain so, and assured him that so extravagant a sum would never be granted.

That I was neither a friend nor relative of the Prince, but a mere artist, employed to execute certain paintings. That I had nothing to offer as a ransom, but the price of my labors; if this were not sufficient, my life was at their disposal; it was a thing on which I set but little value.

I was the more hardy in my reply, because I saw that coolness and hardihood had an effect upon the robbers. It is true, as I finished speaking, the captain laid his hand upon his stiletto; but he restrained himself, and snatching the letter folded it, and ordered me, in a peremptory tone, to address it to the Prince. He then dispatched one of the laborers with it to Tusculum, who promised to return with all possible speed.

The robbers now prepared themselves for sleep, and I was told that I might do the same. They spread their great cloaks on the ground, and lay down around me. One was stationed at a little distance to keep watch, and was relieved every two hours. The strangeness and wildness of this mountain bivouac among lawless beings, whose hands seemed ever ready to grasp the stiletto, and with whom life was so trivial and insecure, was enough to banish repose. The coldness of the earth, and the dew, however, had a still greater effect than mental causes in disturbing my rest. The air wafted to these mountains from the distant Mediterranean diffused a great chilliness as the night advanced. An expedient suggested itself. I called one of my fellow-prisoners, the laborers, and made him lie down beside me. Whenever one of my limbs became chilled, I approached it to the robust limb of my neighbor, and borrowed some of his warmth. In this way I was able to obtain a little sleep.

Day at length dawned, and I was aroused from my slumber by the voice of my chieftain. He desired me to rise and follow him. I obeyed. On considering his physiognomy attentively, it appeared a little softened. He even assisted me in scrambling up the steep forest, among rocks and brambles. Habit had made him a vigorous mountaineer; but I found it excessively toilsome to climb these rugged heights. We arrived at length at the summit of the mountain.

Here it was that I felt all the enthusiasm of my art suddenly awakened; and I forgot in an instant all my perils and fatigues at this magnificent view of the sunrise in the midst of the mountains of the Abruzzi. It was on these heights that Hannibal first pitched his camp, and pointed out Rome to his followers. The eye embraces a vast extent of country. The minor height of Tusculum, with its villas and its sacred ruins, lies below; the Sabine Hills and the Albanian Mountains stretch on either hand; and beyond Tusculum and Frascati spreads out the immense Campagna, with its lines of tombs, and here and there a broken aqueduct stretching across it, and the towers and domes of the eternal city in the midst.

Fancy this scene lit up by the glories of a rising sun, and bursting upon my sight as I looked forth from among the majestic forests of the Abruzzi. Fancy, too, the savage foreground, made still more savage by groups of banditti, armed and dressed in their wild picturesque manner, and you will not wonder that the enthusiasm of a painter for a moment overpowered all his other feelings.

The banditti were astonished at my admiration of a scene which familiarity had made so common in their eyes. I took advantage of their halting at this spot, drew forth a quire of drawing-paper, and began to sketch the features of the landscape. The height on which I was seated was wild and solitary, separated from the ridge of Tusculum by a valley nearly three miles wide, though the distance appeared less from the purity of the atmosphere. This height was one of the favorite retreats of the banditti, commanding a look-out over the country; while at the same time it was covered with forests, and distant from the populous haunts of men.

While I was sketching, my attention was called off for a moment by the cries of birds, and the bleatings of sheep. I looked around, but could see nothing of the animals which uttered them. They were repeated, and appeared to come from the summits of the trees. On looking more narrowly, I perceived six of the robbers perched in the tops of oaks, which grew on the breezy crest of the mountain, and commanded an uninterrupted prospect. They were keeping a look-out like so many vultures; casting their eyes into the depths of the valley below us; communicating with each other by signs, or holding discourse in sounds which might be mistaken by the wayfarer for the cries of hawks and crows, or the bleating of the mountain flocks. After they had reconnoitred the neighborhood, and finished their singular discourse, they descended from their airy perch, and returned to their prisoners. The captain posted three of them at three naked sides of the mountain, while he remained to guard us with what appeared his most trusty companion.

I had my book of sketches in my hand; he requested to see it, and after having run his eye over it, expressed himself convinced of the truth of my assertion that I was a painter. I thought I saw a gleam of good feeling dawning in him, and determined to avail myself of it. I knew that the worst of men have their good points and their accessible sides, if one would but study them carefully. Indeed, there is a singular mixture in the character of the Italian robber. With reckless ferocity he often mingles traits of kindness and good-humor. He is not always radically bad; but driven to his course of life by some unpremeditated crime, the effect of those sudden bursts of passion to which the Italian temperament is prone. This has compelled him to take to the mountains, or, as it is technically termed among them, "andare in campagna." He has become a robber by profession; but, like a soldier, when not in action he can lay aside his weapon and his fierceness, and become like other men.

I took occasion, from the observations of the captain on my sketchings, to fall into conversation with him, and found him sociable and communicative. By degrees I became completely at my ease with him. I had fancied I perceived about him a degree of self-love, which I determined to make use of. I assumed an air of careless frankness, and told him, that, as an artist, I pretended to the power of judging of the physiognomy; that I thought I perceived something in his features and demeanor which announced him worthy of higher fortunes; that he was not formed to exercise the profession to which he had abandoned himself; that he had talents and qualities fitted for a nobler sphere of action; that he had but to change his course of life, and, in a legitimate career, the same courage and endowments which now made him an object of terror, would assume him the applause and admiration of society.

I had not mistaken my man; my discourse both touched and excited him. He seized my hand, pressed it, and replied with strong emotion, "You have guessed the truth; you have judged of me rightly." He remained for a moment silent; then, with a kind of effort, he resumed,— "I will tell you some particulars of my life, and you will perceive that it was the oppression of others, rather than my own crimes, which drove me to the mountains. I sought to serve my fellow-men, and they have persecuted me from among them." We seated ourselves on the grass, and the robber gave me the following anecdotes of his history.

THE STORY OF THE BANDIT
CHIEFTAIN

I AM a native of the village of Prossedi. My father was easy enough in circumstances, and we lived peaceably and independently, cultivating our fields. All went on well with us, until a new chief of the Sbirri was sent to our village to take command of the police. He was an arbitrary fellow, prying into everything, and practising all sorts of vexations and oppressions in the discharge of his office. I was at that time eighteen years of age, and had a natural love of justice and good neighborhood. I had also a little education, and knew something of history, so as to be able to judge a little of men and their actions. All this inspired me with hatred for this paltry despot. My own family, also, became the object of his suspicion or dislike, and felt more than once the arbitrary abuse of his power. These things worked together in my mind, and I gasped after vengeance. My character was always ardent and energetic, and, acted upon by the love of justice, determined, by one blow, to rid the country of the tyrant.

Full of my project, I rose one morning before peep of day, and concealing a stiletto under my waistcoat,—here you see it!—(and he drew forth a long, keen poniard), I lay in wait for him in the outskirts of the village. I knew all his haunts, and his habit of making his rounds and prowling about like a wolf in the gray of the morning. At length I met him, and attacked him with fury. He was armed, but I took him unawares, and was full of youth and vigor. I gave him repeated blows to make sure work, and laid him lifeless at my feet.

When I was satisfied that I had done for him, I returned with all haste to the village, but had the ill-luck to meet two of the Sbirri as I entered it. They accosted me, and asked if I had seen their chief. I assumed an air of tranquillity, and told them I had not. They continued on their way, and within a few hours brought back the dead body to Prossedi. Their suspicions of me being already awakened, I was arrested and thrown into prison. Here I lay several weeks, when the Prince, who was Seigneur of Prossedi, directed judicial proceedings against me. I was brought to trial, and a witness was produced, who pretended to have seen me flying with precipitation not far from the bleeding body; and so I was condemned to the galleys for thirty years.

"Curse on such laws!" vociferated the bandit, foaming with rage: "Curse on such a government! and ten thousand curses on the Prince who caused me to be adjudged so rigorously, while so many other Roman Princes harbor and protect assassins a thousand times more culpable! What had I done but what was inspired by a love of justice and my country? Why was my act more culpable than that of Brutus, when he sacrificed Cæsar to the cause of liberty and justice?"

There was something at once both lofty and ludicrous in the rhapsody of this robber chief, thus associating himself with one of the great names of antiquity. It showed, however, that he had at least the merit of knowing the remarkable facts in the history of his country. He became more calm, and resumed his narrative.

I was conducted to Civita Vecchia in fetters. My heart was burning with rage. I had been married scarce six months to a woman whom I passionately loved, and who was pregnant. My family was in despair. For a long time I made unsuccessful efforts to break my chain. At length I found a morsel of iron, which I hid carefully, and endeavored, with a pointed flint, to fashion it into a kind of file. I occupied myself in this work during the night-time, and when it was finished, I made out, after a long time, to sever one of the rings of my chain. My flight was successful.

I wandered for several weeks in the mountains which surround Prossedi, and found means to inform my wife of the place where I was concealed. She came often to see me. I had determined to put myself at the head of an armed band. She endeavored, for a long time, to dissuade me, but finding my resolution fixed, she at length united in my project of vengeance, and brought me, herself, my poniard. By her means I communicated with several brave fellows of the neighboring villages, whom I knew to be ready to take to the mountains, and only panting for an opportunity to exercise their daring spirits. We soon formed a combination, procured arms, and we have had ample opportunities of revenging ourselves for the wrongs and injuries which most of us have suffered. Everything has succeeded with us until now; and had it not been for our blunder in mistaking you for the Prince, our fortunes would have been made.

Here the robber concluded his story. He had talked himself into complete companionship, and assured me he no longer bore me any grudge for the error of which I had been the innocent cause. He even professed a kindness for me, and wished me to remain some time with them. He promised to give me a sight of certain grottos which they occupied beyond Villetri, and whither they resorted during the intervals of their expeditions.

He assured me that they led a jovial life there; had plenty of good cheer; slept on beds of moss; and were waited upon by young and beautiful females, whom I might take for models.

I confess I felt my curiosity roused by his descriptions of the grottos and their inhabitants: they realized those scenes in robber story which I had always looked upon as mere creations of the fancy. I should gladly have accepted his invitation, and paid a visit to these caverns, could I have felt more secure in my company.

I began to find my situation less painful. I had evidently propitiated the good-will of the chieftain, and hoped that he might release me for a moderate ransom. A new alarm, however, awaited me. While the captain was looking out with impatience for the return of the messenger, who had been sent to the Prince, the sentinel posted on the side of the mountain facing the plain of La Molara came running towards us. "We are betrayed!" exclaimed he. "The police of Frascati are after us. A party of carabineers have just stopped at the inn below the mountain." Then, laying his hand on his stiletto, he swore, with a terrible oath, that if they made the least movement towards the mountain, my life and the lives of my fellow-prisoners should answer for it.

The chieftain resumed all his ferocity of demeanor, and approved of what his companion said; but when the latter had returned to his post, he turned to me with a softened air: "I must act as chief," said he, "and humor my dangerous subalterns. It is a law with us to kill our prisoners rather than suffer them to be rescued; but do not be alarmed. In case we are surprised, keep by me; fly with us, and I will consider myself responsible for your life."

There was nothing very consolatory in this arrangement, which would have placed me between two dangers. I scarcely knew, in case of flight, from which I should have the most to apprehend, the carbines of the pursuers, or the stilettos of the pursued. I remained silent, however, and endeavored to maintain a look of tranquillity.

For an hour was I kept in this state of peril and anxiety. The robbers, crouching among their leafy coverts, kept an eagle watch upon the carabineers below, as they loitered about the inn; sometimes lolling about the portal; sometimes disappearing for several minutes; then sallying out, examining their weapons, pointing in different directions, and apparently asking questions about the neighborhood. Not a movement, a gesture, was lost upon the keen eyes of the brigands. At length we were relieved from our apprehensions. The carabineers having finished their refreshment, seized their arms, continued along the valley towards the great road, and gradually left the mountain behind them. "I felt almost certain," said the chief, "that they could not be sent after us. They know too well how prisoners have fared in our hands on similar occasions. Our laws in this respect are inflexible, and are necessary for our safety. If we once flinched from them, there would no longer be such a thing as a ransom procured."

There were no signs yet of the messenger's return. I was preparing to resume my sketching, when the captain drew a quire of paper from his knapsack. "Come," said he, laughing, "you are a painter,—take my likeness. The leaves of your portfolio are small,—draw it on this." I gladly consented, for it was a study that seldom presents itself to a painter. I recollected that Salvator Rosa in his youth had voluntarily sojourned for a time among the banditti of Calaoria, and had filled his mind with the savage scenery and savage associates by which he was surrounded. I seized my pencil with enthusiasm at the thought. I found the captain the most docile of subjects, and, after various shiftings of position, placed him in an attitude to my mind.

Picture to yourself a stern muscular figure, in fanciful bandit costume; with pistols and poniard in belt; his brawny neck bare; a handkerchief loosely thrown around it, and the two ends in front strung with rings of all kinds, the spoils of travellers; relics and medals hanging on his breast; his hat decorated with various colored ribbons; his vest and short breeches of bright colors, and finely embroidered; his legs in buskins or leggins. Fancy him on a mountain height, among wild rocks and rugged oaks, leaning on his carbine, as if meditating some exploit; while far below are beheld villages and villas, the scenes of his maraudings, with the wide Campagna dimly extending in the distance.

The robber was pleased with the sketch, and seemed to admire himself upon paper. I had scarcely finished, when the laborer arrived who had been sent for my ransom. He had reached Tusculum two hours after midnight. He had brought me a letter from the Prince, who was in bed at the time of his arrival. As I had predicted, he treated the demand as extravagant, but offered five hundred dollars for my ransom. Having no money by him at the moment, he had sent a note for the amount, payable to whomsoever shall conduct me safe and sound to Rome. I presented the note of hand to the chieftain; he received it with a shrug. "Of what use are notes of hand to us?" said he. "Who can we send with you to Rome to receive it?" We are all marked men; known and described at every gate, and military post, and village church-door. No, we must have gold and silver; let the sum be paid in cash, and you shall be restored to liberty."

The captain again placed a sheet of paper before me to communicate his determination to the Prince. When I had finished the letter, and took the sheet from the quire, I found on the opposite side of it the portrait which I had just been tracing. I was about to tear it off and give it to the chief.

"Hold!" said he, "let it go to Rome; let them see what kind of a looking fellow I am. Perhaps the Prince and his friends may form as good an opinion of me from my face as you have done."

This was said sportively, yet it was evident there was vanity lurking at the bottom. Even this wary, distrustful chief of banditti forgot for a moment his usual foresight and precaution, in the common wish to be admired. He never reflected what use might be made of this portrait in his pursuit and conviction.

The letter was folded and directed, and the messenger departed again for Tusculum. It was now eleven o'clock in the morning, and as yet we had eaten nothing. In spite of all my anxiety, I began to feel a craving appetite. I was glad, therefore, to hear the captain talk something about eating. He observed that for three days and nights they had been lurking about among rocks and woods, meditating their expedition to Tusculum, during which time all their provisions had been exhausted. He should now take measures to procure a supply. Leaving me, therefore, in charge of his comrade, in whom he appeared to have implicit confidence, he departed, assuring me that in less than two hours I should make a good dinner. Where it was to come from was an enigma to me, though it was evident these beings had their secret friends and agents throughout the country.

Indeed the inhabitants of these mountains, and of the valleys which they embosom, are a rude, half-civilized set. The towns and villages among the forests of the Abruzzi, shut up from the rest of the world, are almost like savage dens. It is wonderful that such rude abodes, so little known and visited, should be embosomed in the midst of one of the most travelled and civilized countries of Europe. Among these regions the robber prowls unmolested; not a mountaineer hesitates to give him secret harbor and assistance. The shepherds, however, who tend their flocks among the mountains, are the favorite emissaries of the robbers, when they would send messages down to the valley either for ransom or supplies.

The shepherds of the Abruzzi are as wild as the scenes they frequent. They are clad in a rude garb of black or brown sheepskin; they have high conical hats, and coarse sandals of cloth bound around their legs with thongs, similar to those worn by the robbers. They carry long staves, on which, as they lean, they form picturesque objects in the lonely landscape, and they are followed by their ever-constant companion, the dog. They are a curious, questioning set, glad at any time to relieve the monotony of their solitude by the conversation of the passer-by; and the dog will lend an attentive ear, and put on as sagacious and inquisitive a look as his master.

But I am wandering from my story. I was now left alone with one of the robbers, the confidential companion of the chief. He was the youngest and most vigorous of the band; and though his countenance had something of that dissolute fierceness which seems natural to this desperate, lawless mode of life, yet there were traces of manly beauty about it. As an artist I could not but admire it. I had remarked in him an air of abstraction and reverie, and at times a movement of inward suffering and impatience. He now sat on the ground, his elbows on his knees, his head resting between his clenched fists, and his eyes fixed on the earth with an expression of sadness and bitter rumination. I had grown familiar with him from repeated conversations, and had found him superior in mind to the rest of the band. I was anxious to seize any opportunity of sounding the feelings of these singular beings. I fancied I read in the countenance of this one traces of self-condemnation and remorse; and the ease with which I had drawn forth the confidence of the chieftain, encouraged me to hope the same with his follower.

After a little preliminary conversation, I ventured to ask him if he did not feel regret at having abandoned his family, and taken to this dangerous profession. "I feel," replied he, "but one regret, and that will end only with my life."

As he said this, he pressed his clenched fists upon his bosom, drew his breath through his set teeth, and added, with a deep emotion, "I have something within here that stifles me; it is like a burning iron consuming my very heart. I could tell you a miserable story—but not now—another time."

He relapsed into his former position, and sat with his head between his hands, muttering to himself in broken ejaculations, and what appeared at times to be curses and maledictions. I saw he was not in a mood to be disturbed, so I left him to himself. In a little while the exhaustion of his feelings, and probably the fatigues he had undergone in this expedition, began to produce drowsiness. He struggled with it for a time, but the warmth and stillness of midday made it irresistible, and he at length stretched himself upon the herbage and fell asleep.

I now beheld a chance of escape within my reach. My guard lay before me at my mercy. His vigorous limbs relaxed by sleep—his bosom open for the blow—his carbine slipped from his nerveless grasp, and lying by his side—his stiletto half out of his pocket in which it was usually carried. Two only of his comrades were in sight, and those at a considerable distance on the edge of the mountain, their backs turned to us and their attention occupied in keeping a lookout upon the plain.

Through a strip of intervening forest, and at the foot of a steep descent, I beheld the village of Rocca Priori. To have secured the carbine of the sleeping brigand; to have plunged it in his heart, would have been the work of an instant. Should he die without noise, I might dart through the forest, and down to Rocca Priori before my flight might be discovered. In case of alarm, I should still have a fair start of the robbers, and a chance of getting beyond the reach of their shot.

Here then was an opportunity for both escape and vengeance; perilous indeed, but powerfully tempting. Had my situation been more critical, I could not have resisted it. I reflected, however, for a moment. The attempt, if successful, would be followed by the sacrifice of my two fellow-prisoners, who were sleeping profoundly, and could not be awakened in time to escape. The laborer who had gone after the ransom might also fall a victim to the rage of the robbers, without the money which he brought being saved. Besides, the conduct of the chief towards me made me feel confident of speedy deliverance. These reflections overcame the first powerful impulse, and I calmed the turbulent agitation which it had awakened.

·I again took out my materials for drawing, and amused myself with sketching the magnificent prospect. It was now about noon, and everything had sunk into repose, like the sleeping bandit before me. The noontide stillness that reigned over these mountains, the vast landscape below gleaming with distant towns, and dotted with various habitations and signs of life, yet all so silent, had a powerful effect upon my mind. The intermediate valleys, too, which lie among the mountains, have a peculiar air of solitude. Few sounds are heard at mid-day to break the quiet of the scene. Sometimes the whistle of a solitary muleteer, lagging with his lazy animal along the road which winds through the centre of the valley; sometimes the faint piping of a shepherd's reed from the side of the mountain, or sometimes the bell of an ass slowly pacing along, followed by a monk with bare feet, and bare, shining head, and carrying provisions to his convent.

I had continued to sketch for some time among my sleeping companions, when at length I saw the captain of the band approaching followed by a peasant leading a mule, on which was a well-filled sack. I at first apprehended that this was some new prey fallen into the hands of the robber; but the contented look of the peasant soon relieved me, and I was rejoiced to hear that it was our promised repast. The brigands now came running from the three sides of the mountain, having the quick scent of vultures. Every one busied himself in unloading the mule, and relieving the sack of its contents.

The first thing that made its appearance was an enormous ham, of a colour and plumpness that would have inspired the pencil of Teniers; it was followed by a large cheese, a bag of boiled chestnuts, a little barrel of wine, and a quantity of good household bread. Everything was arranged on the grass with a degree of symmetry; and the captain, presenting me with his knife, requested me to help myself. We all seated ourselves around the viands, and nothing was heard for a time but the sound of vigorous mastication, or the gurgling of the barrel of wine as it revolved briskly about the circle. My long fasting, and mountain air and exercise, had given me a keen appetite; and never did repast appear to me more excellent or picturesque.

From time to time one of the band was dispatched to keep a lookout upon the plain. No enemy was at hand, and the dinner was undisturbed. The peasant received nearly three times the value of his provisions, and set off down the mountain highly satisfied with his bargain. I felt invigorated by the hearty meal I had made, and notwithstanding that the wound I had received the evening before was painful, yet I could not but feel extremely interested and gratified by the singular scenes continually presented to me. Everything was picturesque about these wild beings and their haunts. Their bivouacs; their groups on guard; their indolent noontide repose on the mountain-brow; their rude repast on the herbage among rocks and trees; everything presented a study for a painter; but it was towards the approach of evening that I felt the highest enthusiasm awakened.

The setting sun, declining beyond the vast Campagna, shed its rich yellow beams on the woody summit of the Abruzzi. Several mountains crowned with snow shone brilliantly in the distance, contrasting their brightness with others, which, thrown into shade, assumed deep tints of purple and violet. As the evening advanced, the landscape darkened into a sterner character. The immense solitude around; the wild mountains broken into rocks and precipices, intermingled with vast oaks, corks, and chestnuts; and the groups of banditti in the foreground, reminded me of the savage scenes of Salvator Rosa.

To beguile the time, the captain proposed to his comrades to spread before me their jewels and cameos, as I must doubtless be a judge of such articles, and able to form an estimate of their value. He set the example, the others followed it; and in a few moments I saw the grass before me sparkling with jewels and gems that would have delighted the eyes of an antiquary or a fine lady.

Among them were several precious jewels and antique intaglios and cameos of great value, the spoils, doubtless, of travellers of distinction. I found that they were in the habit of selling their booty in the frontier town; but as these, in general, were thinly and poorly peopled, and little frequented by travellers, they could offer no market for such valuable articles of taste and luxury. I suggested to them the certainty of their readily obtaining great prices for these gems among the rich strangers with whom Rome was thronged.

The impression made upon their greedy minds was immediately apparent. One of the band, a young man, and the least known, requested permission of the captain to depart the following day, in disguise, for Rome, for the purpose of traffic, promising, on the faith of a bandit (a sacred pledge among them), to return in two days to any place that he might appoint. The captain consented, and a curious scene took place; the robbers crowded round him eagerly, confiding to him such of their jewels as they wished to dispose of, and giving him instructions what to demand. There was much bargaining and exchanging and selling of trinkets among them, and I beheld my watch, which had a chain and valuable seals, purchased by the young robber-merchant of the ruffian who had plundered me, for sixty dollars. I now conceived a faint hope, that if it went to Rome, I might somehow or other regain possession of it.*

In the meantime day declined, and no messenger returned from Tusculum. The idea of passing another night in the woods was extremely disheartening, for I began to be satisfied with what I had seen of robber-life. The chieftain now ordered his men to follow him, that he might station them at their posts; adding, that, if the messenger did not return before night, they must shift their quarters to some other place.

I was again left alone with the young bandit who before guarded me; he had the same gloomy air and haggard eye, with now and then a bitter sardonic smile. I determined to probe this ulcerated heart, and reminded him of a kind promise he had given me to tell me the cause of his suffering. It seemed to me as if these troubled spirits were glad of any opportunity to disburden themselves, and of having some fresh, undiseased mind, with which they could communicate. I had hardly made the request when he seated himself by my side, and gave me his story in, as near as I can recollect, the following words.

---

* The hopes of the artist were not disappointed: the robber was stopped at one of the gates of Rome. Something in his looks or deportment had excited suspicion. He was searched, and the valuable trinkets found on him sufficiently evinced his character. On applying to the police, the artist's watch was returned to him.

THE STORY OF THE YOUNG
ROBBER

I WAS born in the little town of Frosinone, which lies at the skirts of the Abruzzi. My father had made a little property in trade, and gave me some education, as he intended me for the Church; but I had kept gay company too much to relish the cowl, so I grew up a loiterer about the place. I was a heedless fellow, a little quarrelsome on occasion, but good-humored in the main; so I made my way very well for a time, until I fell in love. There lived in our town a surveyor or land-bailiff of the Prince, who had a young daughter, a beautiful girl of sixteen; she was looked upon as something better than the common run of our townsfolk, and was kept almost entirely at home. I saw her occasionally, and became madly in love with her—she looked so fresh and tender, and so different from the sunburnt females to whom I had been accustomed.

As my father kept me in money, I always dressed well, and took all opportunities of showing myself off to advantage in the eyes of the little beauty. I used to see her at church; and as I could play a little on the guitar, I gave a tune sometimes under her window of an evening; and I tried to have interviews with her in her father's vineyard, not far from the town, where she sometimes walked. She was evidently pleased with me, but she was young and shy; and her father kept a strict eye upon her, and took alarm at my attentions, for he had a bad opinion of me, and looked for a better match for his daughter. I became furious at the difficulties thrown in my way, having been accustomed always to easy success among the women, being considered one of the smartest young fellows of the place.

Her father brought home a suitor for her,—a rich farmer from a neighboring town. The wedding-day was appointed, and preparations were making. I got sight of her at the window, and I thought she looked sadly at me. I determined the match should not take place, cost what it might. I met her intended bridegroom in the market-place, and could not restrain the expression of my rage. A few hot words passed between us, when I drew my stiletto and stabbed him to the heart. I fled to a neighboring church for refuge, and with a little money I obtained absolution, but I did not dare to venture from my asylum.

At that time our captain was forming his troop. He had known me from boyhood; and hearing of my situation, came to me in secret, and made such offers, that I agreed to enroll myself among his followers. Indeed, I had more than once thought of taking to this mode of life, having known several brave fellows of the mountains, who used to spend their money freely among us youngsters of the town. I accordingly left my asylum late one night, repaired to the appointed place of meeting, took the oaths prescribed, and became one of the troop. We were for some time in a distant part of the mountains, and our wild, adventurous kind of life hit my fancy wonderfully, and diverted my thoughts. At length they returned with all their violence to the recollection of Rosetta; the solitude in which I often found myself gave me time to brood over her image; and, as I have kept watch at night over our sleeping camp in the mountains, my feelings have been aroused almost to a fever.

At length we shifted our ground, and determined to make a descent upon the road between Terracina and Naples. In the course of our expedition we passed a day or two in the woody mountains which rise above Frosinone. I cannot tell you how I felt when I looked down upon the place, and distinguished the residence of Rosetta. I determined to have an interview with her;—but to what purpose? I could not expect that she would quit her home, and accompany me in my hazardous life among the mountains. She had been brought up too tenderly for that; when I looked upon the women who were associated with some of our troops, I could not have borne the thoughts of her being their companion. All return to my former life was likewise hopeless, for a price was set upon my head. Still I determined to see her; the very hazard and fruitlessness of the thing made me furious to accomplish it.

About three weeks since, I persuaded our captain to draw down to the vicinity of Frosinone, suggesting the chance of entrapping some of its principal inhabitants, and compelling them to a ransom. We were lying in ambush towards evening, not far from Rosetta's father. I stole quietly from my companions, and drew near to reconnoiter the place of her frequent walks. How my heart beat when among the vines I beheld the gleamings of a white dress! I knew it must be Rosetta's; it being rare for any female of that place to dress in white. I advanced secretly and without noise, until, putting aside the vines, I stood suddenly before her. She uttered a piercing shriek, but I seized her in my arms, put my hand upon her mouth, and conjured her to be silent. I poured out all the frenzy of my passion; offered to renounce my mode of life; to put my fate in her hands; to fly where we might live in safety together. All that I could say or do would not pacify her. Instead of love, horror and affright seemed to have taken possession of her breast. She struggled partly from my grasp, and filled the air with her cries.

In an instant the captain and the rest of my companions were around us. I would have given anything at that moment had she been safe out of our hands, and in her father's house. It was too late. The captain pronounced her a prize, and ordered that she should be borne to the mountains. I represented to him that she was my prize; that I had a previous claim to her; and I mentioned my former attachment. He sneered bitterly in reply; observed that brigands had no business with village intrigues, and that, according to the laws of the troop, all spoils of the kind were determined by lot. Love and jealousy were raging in my heart, but I had to choose between obedience and death. I surrendered her to the captain, and we made for the mountains.

She was overcome by affright, and her steps were so feeble and faltering that it was necessary to support her. I could not endure the idea that my comrades should touch her, and assuming a forced tranquillity, begged she might be confided to me, as one to whom she was more accustomed. The captain regarded me, for a moment, with a searching look, but I bore it without flinching, and he consented. I took her in my arms; she was almost senseless. Her head rested on my shoulder; I felt her breath on my face, and it seemed to fan the flame which devoured me. O God! to have this glowing treasure in my arms, and yet to think it was not mine!

We arrived at the foot of the mountain; I ascended it with difficulty, particularly where the woods were thick, but I would not relinquish my delicious burden. I reflected with rage, however, that I must soon do so. The thoughts that so delicate a creature must be abandoned to my rude companions maddened me. I felt tempted, the stiletto in my hand, to cut my way through them all, and bear her off in triumph. I scarcely conceived the idea before I saw its rashness; but my brain was fevered with the thought that any but myself should enjoy her charms. I endeavored to outstrip my companions by the quickness of my movements, and to get a little distance ahead, in case any favorable opportunity of escape should present. Vain effort! The voice of the captain suddenly ordered a halt. I trembled, but had to obey. The poor girl partly opened a liquid eye, but was without strength or motion. I laid her upon the grass. The captain darted upon me a terrible look of suspicion, and ordered me to scour the woods with my companions in search of some shepherd, who might be sent to her father's to demand a ransom.

I saw at once the peril. To resist with violence was certain death, but to leave her alone, in the power of the captain!—I spoke out then with a fervor inspired by my passion and despair. I reminded the captain that I was the first to seize her; that she was my prize; and that my previous attachment to her ought to make her sacred among my companions. I insisted, therefore, that he should pledge me his word to respect her, otherwise I would refuse obedience to his orders. His only reply was to cock his carbine, and at the signal my comrades did the same. They laughed with cruelty at my impotent rage. What could I do? I felt the madness of resistance. I was menaced on all hands, and my companions obliged me to follow them. She remained alone with the chief—yes, alone—and almost lifeless!—

Here the robber paused in his recital, overpowered by his emotions. Great drops of sweat stood on his forehead; he panted rather than breathed; his brawny bosom rose and fell like the waves of the troubled sea. When he had become a little calm, he continued his recital.

I was not long in finding a shepherd, said he. I ran with the rapidity of a deer, eager, if possible, to get back before what I dreaded might take place. I had left my companions far behind, and I rejoined them before they had reached one-half the distance I had made. I hurried them back to the place where we had left the captain. As we approached, I beheld him seated by the side of Rosetta. His triumphant look, and the desolate condition of the unfortunate girl, left me no doubt of her fate. I know not how I restrained my fury.

It was with extreme difficulty, and by guiding her hand, that she was made to trace a few characters, requesting her father to send three hundred dollars as her ransom. The letter was dispatched by the shepherd. When he was gone, the chief turned sternly to me. "You have set an example," said he, "of mutiny and self-will, which, if indulged, would be ruinous to the troop. Had I treated you as our laws require, this bullet would have been driven through your brain. But you are an old friend. I have borne patiently with your fury and your folly. I have even protected you from a foolish passion that would have unmanned you. As to this girl, the laws of our association must have their course." So saying, he gave his commands: lots were drawn, and the helpless girl was abandoned to the troop.

Here the robber paused again, panting with fury, and it was some moments before he could resume his story.

Hell, said he, was raging in my heart. I beheld the impossibility of avenging myself; and I felt that, according to the articles in which we stood bound to one another, the captain was in the right. I rushed with frenzy from the place; I threw myself upon the earth; tore up the grass with my hands; and beat my head and gnashed my teeth in agony and rage. When at length I returned, I beheld the wretched victim, pale, dishevelled, her dress torn and disordered. An emotion of pity, for a moment, subdued my fiercer feelings. I bore her to the foot of a tree, and leaned her gently against it. I took my gourd, which was filled with wine, and applying it to her lips, endeavored to make her swallow a little. To what a condition was she reduced! she, whom I had once seen the pride of Frosinone, whom but a short time before I had beheld sporting in her father's vineyard, so fresh, and beautiful, and happy! Her teeth were clenched; her eyes fixed on the ground; her form without motion, and in a state of absolute insensibility. I hung over her in an agony of recollection at all that she had been, and of anguish at what I now beheld her. I darted around a look of horror at my companions, who seemed like so many fiends exulting in the downfall of an angel; and I felt a horror at being myself their accomplice.

The captain, always suspicious, saw, with his usual penetration, what was passing within me, and ordered me to go upon the ridge of the woods, to keep a look-out over the neighborhood, and await the return of the shepherd. I obeyed, of course, stifling the fury that raged within me, though I felt, for the moment, that he was my most deadly foe.

On my way, however, a ray of reflection came across my mind. I perceived that the captain was but following, with strictness, the terrible laws to which we had sworn fidelity; that the passion by which I had been blinded might, with justice, have been fatal to me, but for his forbearance; that he had penetrated my soul, and had taken precautions, by sending me out of the way, to prevent my committing any excess in my anger. From that instant I felt that I was capable of pardoning him.

Occupied with these thoughts, I arrived at the foot of the mountain. The country was solitary and secure, and in a short time I beheld the shepherd at a distance crossing the plain. I hastened to meet him. He had obtained nothing. He had found the father plunged in the deepest distress. He had read the letter with violent emotion, and then, calming himself with a sudden exertion, he had replied coldly: "My daughter has been dishonored by those wretches; let her be returned without ransom,—or let her die!"

I shuddered at his reply. I knew that, according to the laws of our troop, her death was inevitable. Our oaths required it. I felt, nevertheless, that, not having been able to have her to myself, I could be her executioner!

The robber again paused with agitation. I sat musing upon his last frightful words, which proved to what excess the passions may be carried when escaped from all moral restraint. There was a horrible verity in this story that reminded me of some of the tragic fictions of Dante.

We now come to a fatal moment, resumed the bandit. After the report of the shepherd, I returned with him, and the chieftain received from his lips the refusal of her father. At a signal which we all understood, we followed him to some distance from the victim. He there pronounced her sentence of death. Every one stood ready to execute his orders, but I interfered. I observed that there was something due to pity as well as to justice; that I was as ready as any one to approve the implacable law, which was to serve as a warning to all those who hesitated to pay the ransoms demanded for our prisoners; but though the sacrifice was proper, it ought to be made without cruelty. The night is approaching, continued I; she will soon be wrapped in sleep; let her then be dispatched. All I now claim on the score of former kindness is, let me strike the blow. I will do it as surely, though more tenderly than another. Several raised their voices against my proposition, but the captain imposed silence on them. He told me I might conduct her into a thicket at some distance, and he relied upon my promise.

I hastened to seize upon my prey. There was a forlorn kind of triumph at having at length become her exclusive possessor. I bore her off into the thickness of the forest. She remained in the same state of insensibility or stupor. I was thankful that she did not recollect me, for had she once murmured my name, I should have been overcome. She slept at length in the arms of him who was to poniard her. Many were the conflicts I underwent before I could bring myself to strike the blow. But my heart had become sore by the recent conflicts it had undergone, and I dreaded lest, by procrastination, some other should become her executioner. When her repose had continued for some time, I separated myself gently from her, that I might not disturb her sleep, and seizing suddenly my poniard, plunged it into her bosom. A painful and concentrated murmur, but without any convulsive movement, accompanied her last sigh.—So perished this unfortunate!

He ceased to speak. I sat, horror-struck, covering my face with my hands, seeking, as it were, to hide from myself the frightful images he had presented to my mind. I was roused from this silence by the voice of the captain: "You sleep," said he, "and it is time to be off. Come, we must abandon this height, as night is settling in, and the messenger is not returned. I will post some one on the mountain edge to conduct him to the place where we shall pass the night."

This was no agreeable news to me. I was sick at heart with the dismal story I had heard. I was harassed and fatigued, and the sight of the banditti began to grow insupportable to me.

The captain assembled his comrades. We rapidly descended the forest, which we had mounted with so much difficulty in the morning, and soon arrived in what appeared to be a frequented road. The robbers proceeded with great caution, carrying their guns cocked, and looking on every side with wary and suspicious eyes. They were apprehensive of encountering the civic patrol. We left Rocca Priori behind us. There was a fountain near by, and as I was excessively thirsty, I begged permission to stop and drink. The captain himself went and brought me water in his hat. We pursued our route, when, at the extremity of an alley which crossed the road, I perceived a female on horseback, dressed in white. She was alone. I recollected the fate of the poor girl in the story, and trembled for her safety.

One of the brigands saw her at the same instant, and plunging into the bushes, he ran precipitately in the direction towards her. Stopping on the border of the alley, he put one knee to the ground, presented his carbine ready to menace her, or to shoot her horse if she attempted to fly, and in this way awaited her approach. I kept my eyes fixed on her with intense anxiety. I felt tempted to shout and warn her of her danger, though my own destruction would have been the consequence. It was awful to see this tiger crouching ready for a bound, and the poor innocent victim unconsciously near him. Nothing but a mere chance could save her. To my joy the chance turned in her favor. She seemed almost accidently to take an opposite path which led outside of the woods, where the robber dared not venture. To this casual deviation she owed her safety.

I could not imagine why the captain of the band had ventured to such a distance from the height on which he had placed the sentinel to watch the return of the messenger. He seemed himself anxious at the risk to which he exposed himself. His movements were rapid and uneasy; I could scarce keep pace with him. At length, after three hours of what might be termed a forced march, we mounted the extremity of the same woods, the summit of which we had occupied during the day; and I learnt with satisfaction that we had reached our quarters for the night. "You must be fatigued," said the chieftain; "but it was necessary to survey the environs so as not to be surprised during the night. Had we met with the famous civic guard of Rocca Priori, you would have seen fine sport." Such was the indefatigable precaution and fore-thought of this robber chief, who really gave continual evidence of military talent.

The night was magnificent. The moon, rising above the horizon in a cloudless sky, faintly lit up the grand features of the mountain, while lights twinkling here and there, like terrestrial stars in the wide dusky expanse of the landscape, betrayed the lonely cabins of the shepherds.

Exhausted by fatigue, and by the many agitations I had experienced, I prepared to sleep, soothed by the hope of approaching deliverance. The captain ordered his companions to collect some dry moss; he arranged with his own hands a kind of mattress and pillow of it, and gave me his ample mantle as a covering. I could not but feel both surprised and gratified by such unexpected attentions on the part of this benevolent cut-throat; for there is nothing more striking than to find the ordinary charities, which are matters of course in common life, flourishing by the side of such stern and sterile crime. It is like finding tender flowers and fresh herbage of the valley growing among the rocks and cinders of the volcano.

Before I fell asleep I had some further discourse with the captain, who seemed to feel great confidence in me. He referred to our previous conversation of the morning; told me he was weary of his hazardous profession; that he had acquired sufficient property, and was anxious to return to the world, and lead a peaceful life in the bosom of his family. He wished to know whether it was not in my power to procure for him a passport to the United States of America. I applauded his good intentions, and promised to do everything in my power to promote its success. We then parted for the night. I stretched myself upon my couch of moss, which, after my fatigues, felt like a bed of down; and, sheltered by the robber-mantle from all humidity, I slept soundly, without waking, until the signal to arise.

It was nearly six o'clock, and the day was just dawning. As the place where we had passed the night was too much exposed, we moved up into the thickness of the woods. A fire was kindled. While there was any flame, the mantles were again extended round it: but when nothing remained but glowing cinders, they were lowered, and the robbers seated themselves in a circle.

The scene before me reminded me of some of those described by Homer. There wanted only the victim on the coals, and the sacred knife to cut off the succulent parts, and distribute them around. My companions might have rivalled the grim warriors of Greece. In place of the noble repasts, however, of Achilles and Agamemnon, I beheld displayed on the grass the remains of the ham which had sustained so vigorous an attack on the preceding evening, accompanied by the relics of the bread, cheese, and wine. We had scarcely commenced our frugal breakfast, when I heard again an imitation of the bleating of sheep, similar to what I had heard the day before. The captain answered it in the same tone. Two men were soon after seen descending from the woody height, where we had passed the preceding evening. On nearer approach, they proved to be the sentinel and the messenger. The captain rose, and went to meet them. He made a signal for his comrades to join him. They had a short conference, and then returning to me with great eagerness, "Your ransom is paid," said he; "you are free!"

Though I had anticipated deliverance, I cannot tell you what a rush of delight these tidings gave me. I cared not to finish my repast, but prepared to depart. The captain took me by the hand, requested permission to write to me, and begged me not to forget the passport. I replied, that I hoped to be of effectual service to him, and that I relied on his honor to return the Prince's note for five hundred dollars, now that the cash was paid. He regarded me for a moment with surprise, then seeming to recollect himself, "E giusto," said he, "eccoto—adio!"* He delivered me the note, pressed my hand once more, and we separated. The laborers were permitted to follow me, and we resumed with joy our road toward Tusculum.

The Frenchman ceased to speak. The party continued, for a few moments, to pace the shore in silence. The story had made a deep impression, particularly on the Venetian lady. At the part which related to the young girl of Trosinone, she was violently affected. Sobs broke from her; she clung closer to her husband, and as she looked up to him as if for protection, the moonbeams shining on her beautifully fair countenance, showed it paler than usual, while tears glittered in her fine dark eyes.

"Corragio, mia vita!" said he, as he gently and fondly tapped the white hand that lay upon his arm.

The party now returned to the inn, and separated for the night. The fair Venetian, though of the sweetest temperament, was half out of humor with the Englishman, for certain slowness of faith which he had evinced throughout the whole evening. She could not understand this dislike to "humbug," as he termed it, which held a kind of sway over him, and seemed to control his opinions and his very actions.

"I'll warrant," said she to her husband, as they retired for the night, —"I'll warrant, with all his affected indifference, this Englishman's heart would quake at the very sight of a bandit."

Her husband gently, and good-humoredly, checked her.

"I have no patience with these Englishmen," said she, as she got into bed,—"they are so cold and insensible!"

---

* It is just—there it is—adieu!

THE ADVENTURE OF THE
ENGLISHMAN

IN the morning all was bustle in the inn at Terracina. The procaccio
had departed at daybreak on its route towards Rome, but the Englishman was yet to start, and the departure of an English equipage is always enough to keep an inn in a bustle. On this occasion there was
more than usual stir, for the Englishman having much property about
him, and having been convinced of the real danger of the road, had applied to the police, and obtained by dint of liberal pay, an escort of
eight dragoons and twelve foot-soldiers, as far as Fondi.

Perhaps, too, there might have been a little ostentation at bottom,
though, to say the truth, he had nothing of it in his manner. He moved
about, taciturn and reserved as usual, among the gaping crowd, gave
laconic orders to John, as he packed away the thousand and one indispensable conveniences of the night; double loaded his pistols with
great *sang froid*, and deposited them in the pockets of the carriage; taking no notice of a pair of keen eyes gazing on him from among the herd
of loitering idlers.

The fair Venetian now came up with a request, made in her dulcet
tones, that he would permit their carriage to proceed under protection
of his escort. The Englishman, who was busy loading another pair of
pistols for his servant, and held the ramrod between his teeth, nodded
assent, as a matter of course, but without lifting up his eyes. The fair
Venetian was a little piqued at what she supposed indifference: "O
Dio!" ejaculated she softly as she retired; "Quanto sono insensibili questi
Inglesi."

At length, off they set in gallant style. The eight dragoons prancing
in front, the twelve foot-soldiers marching in rear, and the carriage moving slowly in the centre, to enable the infantry to keep pace with them.
They had proceeded but a few hundred yards, when it was discovered
that some indispensable article had been left behind. In fact, the Englishman's purse was missing, and John was dispatched to the inn to
search for it. This occasioned a little delay, and the carriage of the
Venetians drove slowly on. John came back out of breath and out of
humor. The purse was not to be found. His master was irritated; he
recollected the very place where it lay; he had not a doubt the Italian

servant had pocketed it. John was again sent back. He returned once more without the purse, but with the landlord and the whole household at his heels. A thousand ejaculations and protestations, accompanied by all sorts of grimaces and contortions—"No purse had been seen —his excellenza must be mistaken."

"No—his excellenza was not mistaken—the purse lay on the marble table, under the mirror—a green purse, half full of gold and silver." Again a thousand grimaces and contortions, and vows by San Gennaro, that no purse of the kind had been seen.

The Englishman became furious. "The waiter had pocketed it—the landlord was a knave—the inn a den of thieves—it was a vile country— he had been cheated and plundered from one end of it to the other— but he'd have satisfaction—he'd drive right off to the police."

He was on the point of ordering the postilions to turn back, when on rising, he displaced the cushion of the carriage, and the purse of money fell chinking to the floor.

All the blood in his body seemed to rush into his face.—"Curse the purse," said he, as he snatched it up. He dashed a handful of money on the ground before the pale cringing waiter,—"There, be off!" cried he. "John, order the postilions to drive on."

About half an hour had been exhausted in this altercation. The Venetian carriage had loitered along; its passengers looking out from time to time, and expecting the escort every moment to follow. They had gradually turned an angle of the road that shut them out of sight. The little army was again in motion, and made a very picturesque appearance as it wound along at the bottom of the rocks; the morning sunshine beaming upon the weapons of the soldiers.

The Englishman lolled back in his carriage, vexed with himself at what had passed, and consequently out of humor with all the world. As this, however, is no uncommon case with gentlemen who travel for their pleasure, it is hardly worthy of remark. They had wound up from the coast among the hills, and came to a part of the road that admitted of some prospect ahead.

"I see nothing of the lady's carriage, sir," said John, leaning down from the coach-box.

"Pish!" said the Englishman, testily; "don't plague me about the lady's carriage; must I be continually pestered with the concerns of strangers?" John said not another word, for he understood his master's mood.

The road grew more wild and lonely; they were slowly proceeding on a foot-pace up a hill; the dragoons were some distance ahead, and had just reached the summit of the hill, when they uttered an exclamation, or rather shout, and galloped forward. The Englishman was roused from his sulky reverie. He stretched his head from the carriage, which had attained the brow of the hill. Before him extended a long hollow defile, commanded on one side by rugged precipitous heights, covered with bushes of scanty forest. At some distance he beheld the carriage of the Venetians overturned. A numerous gang of desperadoes were rifling it; the young man and his servant were overpowered, and partly stripped; and the lady was in the hands of two of the ruffians. The Englishman seized his pistols, sprang from the carriage, and called upon John to follow him.

In the meantime, as the dragoons came forward, the robbers, who were busy with the carriage, quitted their spoil, formed themselves in the middle of the road, and taking a deliberate aim, fired. One of the dragoons fell, another was wounded, and the whole were for a moment checked and thrown into confusion. The robbers loaded again in an instant. The dragoons discharged their carbines, but without apparent effect. They received another volley, which, though none fell, threw them again into confusion. The robbers were loading a second time when they saw the foot-soldiers at hand. "*Scampa via!*" was the word: they abandoned their prey, and retreated up the rocks, the soldiers after them. They fought from cliff to cliff, and bush to bush, the robbers turning every now and then to fire upon their pursuers; the soldiers scrambling after them, and discharging their muskets whenever they could get a chance. Sometimes a soldier or a robber was shot down, and came tumbling among the cliffs. The dragoons kept firing from below, whenever a robber came in sight.

The Englishman had hastened to the scene of action, and the balls discharged at the dragoons had whistled past him as he advanced. One object, however, engrossed his attention. It was the beautiful Venetian lady in the hands of two of the robbers, who, during the confusion of the fight, carried her shrieking up the mountain. He saw her dress gleaming among the bushes, and he sprang up the rocks to intercept the robbers, as they bore off their prey. The ruggedness of the steep, and the entanglements of the bushes, delayed and impeded him. He lost sight of the lady, but was still guided by her cries, which grew fainter. They were off to the left, while the reports of muskets showed that the battle was raging to the right. At length he came upon what appeared to be a rugged footpath, faintly worn in a gully of the rocks, and beheld the ruffians at some distance hurrying the lady up the defile. One of them hearing his approach, let go his prey, advanced towards him, and levelling the carbine which had been slung on his back, fired. The ball whizzed through the Englishman's hat, and carried with it some of his hair. He returned the fire with one of his pistols, and the robber fell. The other brigand now dropped the lady, and drawing a long pistol from his belt, fired on his adversary with deliberate aim. The ball passed between his left arm and his side, slightly wounding the arm. The Englishman advanced, and discharged his remaining pistol, which wounded the robber, but not severely.

The brigand drew a stiletto and rushed upon his adversary, who eluded the blow, receiving merely a slight wound, and defended himself with his pistol, which had a spring bayonet. They closed with one another, and a desperate struggle ensued. The robber was a square-built, thickset man, powerful, muscular, and active. The Englishman, though of larger frame and greater strength, was less active, and less accustomed to athletic exercises and feats of hardihood, but he showed himself practised and skilled in the art of defence. They were on a craggy height, and the Englishman perceived that his antagonist was striving to press him to the edge. A side-glance showed him also the robber whom he had first wounded, scrambling up to the assistance of his comrade, stiletto in hand. He had in fact attained the summit of the cliff; he was within a few steps, and the Englishman felt that his case was desperate, when he heard suddenly the report of a pistol, and the ruffian fell. The shot came from John, who had arrived just in time to save his master.

The remaining robber, exhausted by loss of blood and the violence of the contest, showed signs of faltering. The Englishman pursued his advantage, pressed on him, and as his strength relaxed, dashed him headlong from the precipice. He looked after him, and saw him lying motionless among the rocks below.

The Englishman now sought the fair Venetian. He found her senseless on the ground. With his servant's assistance he bore her down to the road, where her husband was raving like one distracted. He had sought her in vain, and had given her over for lost; and when he beheld her thus brought back in safety, his joy was equally wild and ungovernable. He would have caught her insensible form to his bosom had not the Englishman restrained him. The latter, now really aroused, displayed a true tenderness and manly gallantry, which one would not have expected from his habitual phlegm. His kindness, however, was practical, not wasted in words. He dispatched John to the carriage for restoratives of all kinds, and, totally thoughtless of himself, was anxious only about his lovely charge. The occasional discharge of firearms along the height, showed that a retreating fight was still kept up by the robbers. The lady gave signs of reviving animation. The Englishman, eager to get her from this place of danger, conveyed her to his own carriage, and, committing her to the care of her husband, ordered the dragoons to escort them to Fondi. The Venetian would have insisted on the Englishman's getting into the carriage; but the latter refused. He poured forth a torrent of thanks and benedictions; but the Englishman beckoned to the postilions to drive on.

John now dressed his master's wounds, which were found not to be serious, though he was faint with the loss of blood. The Venetian carriage had been righted, and the baggage replaced; and, getting into it, they set out on their way towards Fondi, leaving the foot-soldiers still engaged in ferreting out the banditti.

Before arriving at Fondi, the fair Venetian had completely recovered from her swoon. She made the usual question,—

"Where was she?"

"In the Englishman's carriage."

"How had she escaped from the robbers?"

"The Englishman had rescued her."

Her transports were unbounded; and mingled with them were enthusiastic ejaculations of gratitude to her deliverer. A thousand times did she reproach herself for having accused him of coldness and insensibility. The moment she saw him she rushed into his arms with the vivacity of her nation, and hung about his neck in a speechless transport of gratitude. Never was man more embarrassed by the embraces of a fine woman.

"Tut!—tut!" said the Englishman.

"You are wounded!" shrieked the fair Venetian as she saw blood upon his clothes.

"Pooh! nothing at all!"

"My deliverer!—my angel!" exclaimed she, clasping him again round the neck, and sobbing on his bosom.

"Pish!" said the Englishman, with a good-humored tone, but looking somewhat foolish, "this is all humbug."

The fair Venetian, however, has never since accused the English of insensibility.

From *Tales of a Traveller*

The Money-Diggers

FOUND AMONG THE PAPERS OF THE LATE DIEDRICH
KNICKERBOCKER

"Now I remember those old women's words,
Who in my youth would tell me winter's tales;
And speak of sprites and ghosts that glide by night
About the place where treasure hath been hid."
MARLOW's *Jew of Malta*

The following group of five tales is taken from *Tales of a Traveller.*—C.N.

HELL GATE

ABOUT six miles from the renowned city of the Manhattoes, in that Sound or arm of the sea which passes between the mainland and Nassau, or Long Island, there is a narrow strait, where the current is violently compressed between shouldering promontories, and horribly perplexed by rocks and shoals. Being, at the best of times, a very violent, impetuous current, it takes these impediments in mighty dudgeon; being in whirlpools; brawling and fretting in ripples; raging and roaring in rapids and breakers; and, in short, indulging in all kinds of wrongheaded paroxysms. At such times, woe to an unlucky vessel, that ventures within its clutches.

This termagant humor, however, prevails only at certain times of tide. At low water, for instance, it is as pacific a stream as you would wish to see; but as the tide rises, it begins to fret; at half-tide it roars with might and main, like a bull bellowing for more drink; but when the tide is full, it relapses into quiet, and for a time, sleeps as soundly as an alderman after dinner. In fact, it may be compared to a quarrelsome toper, who is a peaceful fellow enough when he has no liquor at all, or when he has a skinfull; but who, when half-seas-over, plays the very devil.

This mighty, blustering, bullying, hard-drinking little strait was a place of great danger and perplexity to the Dutch navigators of ancient days; hectoring their tub-built barks in a most unruly style; whirling them about in a manner to make any but a Dutchman giddy, and not unfrequently stranding them upon rocks and reefs, as it did the famous squadron of Oloffe the Dreamer, when seeking a place to found the city of the Manhattoes. Whereupon, out of sheer spleen, they denominated it *Helle-gat*, and solemnly gave it over to the devil. This appellation has since been aptly rendered into English by the name of Hell Gate, and into nonsense by the name of *Hurl* Gate, according to certain foreign intruders, who neither understood Dutch nor English—may St. Nicholas confound them!

This strait of Hell Gate was a place of great awe and perilous enterprise to me in my boyhood, having been much of a navigator on those small seas, and having more than once run the risk of shipwreck and drowning in the course of certain holiday voyages, to which, in common with other Dutch urchins, I was rather prone. Indeed, partly from the name, and partly from various strange circumstances connected with it, this place had far more terrors in the eyes of my truant companions and myself than had Scylla and Charybdis for the navigators of yore.

In the midst of this strait, and hard by a group of rocks called the Hen and Chickens, there lay the wreck of a vessel which had been entangled in the whirlpools and stranded during a storm. There was a wild story told to us of this being the wreck of a pirate, and some tale of bloody murder which I cannot now recollect, but which made us regard it with great awe, and keep far from it in our cruisings. Indeed, the desolate look of the forlorn hulk, and the fearful place where it lay rotting, were enough to awaken strange notions. A row of timber-heads, blackened by time, just peered above the surface at high water; but at low tide a considerable part of the hull was bare, and its great ribs or timbers, partly stripped of their planks, and dripping with sea-weeds, looked like the huge skeleton of some sea-monster. There was also the stump of a mast, with a few ropes and blocks swinging about and whistling in the wind, while the sea-gull wheeled and screamed around the melancholy carcass. I have a faint recollection of some hob-goblin tale of sailors' ghosts being seen about his wreck at night, with bare skulls, and blue lights in their sockets instead of eyes, but I have forgotten all the particulars.

In fact, the whole of this neighborhood was like the straits of Pelorus of yore, a region of fable and romance to me. From the strait to the Manhattoes, the borders of the Sound are greatly diversified, being broken and indented by rocky nooks overhung with trees, which give them a wild and romantic look. In the time of my boyhood, they abounded with traditions about pirates, ghosts, smugglers, and buried money which had a wonderful effect upon the young minds of my companions and myself.

As I grew to more mature years, I made diligent research after the truth of these strange traditions; for I have always been a curious investigator of the valuable but obscure branches of the history of my native province. I found infinite difficulty, however, in arriving at any precise information. In seeking to dig up one fact, it is incredible the number of fables that I unearthed. I will say nothing of the devil's stepping-stones, by which the arch-fiend made his retreat from Connecticut to Long Island, across the Sound; seeing the subject is likely to be learnedly treated by a worthy friend and contemporary historian, whom I have furnished with particulars thereof.* Neither will I say anything of the black man in a three-cornered hat, seated in the stern of a jolly-boat, who used to be seen about Hell Gate in stormy weather, who went by the name of the pirate's *spuke*, (*i.e.* pirate's ghost,) and whom, it is said, old Governor Stuyvesant once shot with a silver bullet; because I never could meet with any person of stanch credibility who professed to have seen this spectrum, unless it were the widow of Manus Conklen, the blacksmith, of Frogsneck; but then, poor woman, she was a little purblind, and might have been mistaken; though they say she saw farther than other folks in the dark.

All this, however, was but little satisfactory in regard to the tales of pirates and their buried money, about which I was most curious; and the following is all that I could, for a long time, collect, that had anything like an air of authenticity.

---

* For a very interesting and authentic account of the devil and his stepping-stones, see the valuable Memoir read before the New York Historical Society, since the death of Mr. Knickerbocker, by his friend, an eminent jurist of the place.

KIDD THE PIRATE

IN old times, just after the territory of the New Netherlands had been wrested from the hands of their High Mightinesses, the Lords States-General of Holland, by King Charles the Second, and while it was as yet in an unquiet state, the province was a great resort of random adventurers, loose livers, and all that class of hap-hazard fellows who live by their wits, and dislike the old-fashioned restraint of law and gospel. Among these, the foremost were the buccaneers. These were rovers of the deep, who perhaps in time of war had been educated in those schools of piracy, the privateers; but having once tasted the sweets of plunder, had ever retained a hankering after it. There is but a slight step from the privateersman to the pirate; both fight for the love of plunder; only that the latter is the bravest, as he dares both the enemy and the gallows.

But in whatever school they had been taught, the buccaneers that kept about the English colonies were daring fellows, and made sad work in times of peace among the Spanish settlements and Spanish merchantmen. The easy access to the harbor of the Manhattoes, the number of hiding-places about its waters, and the laxity of its scarcely organized government, made it a great rendezvous of the pirates; where they might dispose of their booty, and concert new depredations. As they brought home with them wealthy lading of all kinds, the luxuries of the tropics, and the sumptuous spoils of the Spanish provinces, and disposed of them with the proverbial carelessness of freebooters, they were welcome visitors to the thrifty traders of the Manhattoes. Crews of these desperadoes, therefore, the runagates of every country and every clime, might be seen swaggering in the open day about the streets of the little burgh, elbowing its quiet mynheers; trafficking away their rich outlandish plunder at half or quarter price to the wary merchant; and then squandering their prize money in taverns, drinking, gambling, singing, swearing, shouting, and astounding the neighborhood with midnight brawl and ruffian revelry.

At length these excesses rose to such a height as to become a scandal to the provinces, and to call loudly for the interposition of government. Measures were accordingly taken to put a stop to the widely extended evil, and to ferret this vermin brood out of the colonies.

Among the agents employed to execute this purpose was the notorious Captain Kidd. He had long been an equivocal character; one of those nondescript animals of the ocean that are neither fish, flesh, nor fowl. He was somewhat of a trader, something more of a smuggler, with a considerable dash of the picaroon. He had traded for many years among the pirates, in a little rakish, mosquito-built vessel, that could run into all kinds of waters. He knew all their haunts and lurking-places; was always hooking about on mysterious voyages, and was as busy as Mother Cary's chicken in a storm.

This nondescript personage was pitched upon by the government as the very man to hunt the pirates by sea, upon the good old maxim of "setting a rogue to catch a rogue"; or as otters are sometimes used to catch their cousins-german, the fish.

Kidd accordingly sailed for New York, in 1695, in a gallant vessel called the *Adventure Galley*, well armed and duly commissioned. On arriving at his old haunts, however, he shipped his crew on new terms; enlisted a number of his old comrades, lads of the knife and the pistol; and then set sail for the East. Instead of cruising against pirates, he turned pirate, himself; steered to the Madeiras, to Bonavista, and Madagascar, and cruised about the entrance of the Red Sa. Here, among other maritime robberies, he captured a rich Quedah merchantman, manned by Moors, though commanded by an Englishman. Kidd would fain have passed this off for a worthy exploit, as being a kind of crusade against the infidels; but government had long since lost all relish for such Christian triumphs.

After roaming the seas, trafficking his prizes, and changing from ship to ship, Kidd had the hardihood to return to Boston, laden with booty, with a crew of swaggering companions at his heels.

Times, however, were changed. The buccaneers could no longer show a whisker in the colonies with impunity. The new governor, Lord Bellamont, had signalized himself by his zeal in extirpating these offenders; and was doubly exasperated against Kidd, having been instrumental in appointing him to the trust which he had betrayed. No sooner, therefore, did he show himself in Boston, than the alarm was given of his reappearance, and measures were taken to arrest this cutpurse of the ocean. The daring character which Kidd had acquired, however, and the desperate fellows who followed like bull-dogs at his heels, caused a little delay in his arrest. He took advantage of this, it is said, to bury the greater part of his treasures, and then carried a high head about the streets of Boston. He even attempted to defend himself when arrested, but was secured and thrown into prison, with his followers. Such was the formidable character of this pirate and his crew, that it was thought advisable to dispatch a frigate to bring them to England. Great exertions were made to screen him from justice, but in vain; he and his comrades were tried, condemned, and hanged at Execution Dock in London. Kidd died hard, for the rope with which he was first tied up broke with his weight, and he tumbled to the ground. He was tied up a second time, and more effectually; hence came, doubtless, the story of Kidd's having a charmed life, and that he had to be twice hanged.

Such is the main outline of Kidd's history; but it has given birth to an innumerable progeny of traditions. The report of his having buried great treasures of gold and jewels before his arrest, set the brains of all the good people along the coast in a ferment. There were rumors on rumors of great sums of money found here and there, sometimes in one part of the country, sometimes in another; of coins with Moorish inscriptions, doubtless the spoils of his eastern prizes, but which the common people looked upon with superstitious awe, regarding the Moorish letters as diabolical or magical characters.

Some reported the treasure to have been buried in solitary, unsettled places, about Plymouth and Cape Cod; but by degrees various other parts, not only on the eastern coast, but along the shores of the Sound, and even of Manhattan and Long Island, were gilded by these rumors. In fact, the rigorous measures of Lord Bellamont spread sudden consternation among the buccaneers in every part of the provinces: they secreted their money and jewels in lonely out-of-the-way places, about the wild shores of the rivers and sea-coast, and dispersed themselves over the face of the country. The hand of justice prevented many of them from returning to regain their buried treasures, which remained, and remain probably to this day, objects of enterprise for the money-digger.

This is the cause of those frequent reports of trees and rocks bearing mysterious marks, supposed to indicate the spots where treasures lay hidden; and many have been the ransackings after the pirate's booty. In all the stories which once abounded of these enterprises, the devil played a conspicuous part. Either he was conciliated by ceremonies and invocations, or some solemn compact was made with him. Still he was ever prone to play some slippery trick. Some would dig so far as to come to an iron chest, when some baffling circumstance was sure to take place. Either the earth would fall in and fill up the pit, or some direful noise or apparition would frighten the party from the place: sometimes the devil himself would appear, and bear off the prize when within their very grasp; and if they revisited the place the next day, not a trace would be found of their labors of the preceding night.

All these rumors, however, were extremely vague, and for a long time tantalized, without gratifying, my curiosity. There is nothing in this world so hard to get at as truth, and there is nothing in this world but truth that I care for. I sought among all my favorite sources of authentic information, the oldest inhabitants, and particularly the old Dutch wives of the province; but though I flatter myself that I am better versed than most men in the curious history of my native province, yet for a long time my inquiries were unattended with any substantial result.

At length it happened that, one calm day in the latter part of summer, I was relaxing myself from the toils of severe study, by a day's amusement in fishing in those waters which had been the favorite resort of my boyhood. I was in company with several worthy burghers of my native city, among whom were more than one illustrious member of the corporation, whose names, did I dare to mention them, would do honor to my humble page. Our sport was indifferent. The fish did not bite freely, and we frequently changed our fishing-ground without bettering our luck. We were at length anchored close under a ledge of rocky coast, on the eastern side of the Island of Manhatta. It was a still, warm day. The stream whirled and dimpled by us, without a wave or even a ripple; and everything was so calm and quiet, that it was almost startling when the kingfisher would pitch himself from the branch of some high tree, and after suspending himself for a moment in the air, to take his aim, would souse into the smooth water after his prey. While we were lolling in our boat, half drowsy with the warm stillness of the day, and the dulness of our sport, one of our party, a worthy alderman, was overtaken by a slumber, and as he dozed, suffered the sinker of his drop-line to lie upon the bottom of the river. On waking, he found he had caught something of importance from the weight. On drawing it to the surface, we were much surprised to find it a long pistol of very curious and outlandish fashion, which, from its rusted condition, and its stock being worm-eaten and covered with barnacles, appeared to have lain a long time under water. The unexpected appearance of this document of warfare occasioned much speculation among my pacific companions. One supposed it to have fallen there during the revolutionary war; another, from the peculiarity of its fashion, attributed it to the voyagers in the earliest days of the settlement; perchance to the renowned Adrian Block, who explored the Sound, and discovered Block Island, since so noted for its cheese. But a third, after regarding it for some time, pronounced it to be of veritable Spanish workmanship.

"I'll warrant," said he, "if this pistol could talk, it would tell strange stories of hard fights among the Spanish Dons. I've no doubt but it is a relic of the buccaneers of old times,—who knows but it belonged to Kidd himself?"

"Ah! that Kidd was a resolute fellow," cried an old iron-faced Cape-Cod whaler.—"There's a fine old song about him, all to the tune of—

> My name is Captain Kidd,
> As I sailed, as I sailed;—

and then it tells about how he gained the devil's good graces by burying the Bible:—

> I had the Bible in my hand,
> As I sailed, as I sailed,
> And I buried it in the sand,
> As I sailed.—

"Odsfish, if I thought that pistol had belonged to Kidd, I should set great store by it, for curiosity's sake. By the way, I recollect a story about a fellow who once dug up Kidd's buried money, which was written by a neighbor of mine and which I learnt by heart. As the fish don't bite just now, I'll tell it to you, by way of passing away the time."—And so saying, he gave us the following narration.

THE DEVIL AND TOM WALKER

A FEW miles from Boston in Massachusetts, there is a deep inlet, winding several miles into the interior of the country from Charles Bay, and terminating in a thickly-wooded swamp or morass. On one side of this inlet is a beautiful dark grove; on the opposite side the land rises abruptly from the water's edge into a high ridge, on which grow a few scattered oaks of great age and immense size. Under one of these gigantic trees, according to old stories, there was a great amount of treasure buried by Kidd the pirate. The inlet allowed a facility to bring the money in a boat secretly and at night to the very foot of the hill; the elevation of the place permitted a good lookout to be kept that no one was at hand; while the remarkable trees formed good landmarks by which the place might easily be found again. The old stories add, moreover, that the devil presided at the hiding of the money, and took it under his guardianship; but this, it is well known, he always does with buried treasure, particularly when it has been ill-gotten. Be that as it may, Kidd never returned to recover his wealth; being shortly after seized at Boston, sent out to England, and there hanged for a pirate.

About the year 1727, just at the time that earthquakes were prevalent in New England, and shook many tall sinners down upon their knees, there lived near this place a meagre, miserly fellow, of the name of Tom Walker. He had a wife as miserly as himself: they were so miserly that they even conspired to cheat each other. Whatever the woman could lay hands on, she hid away; a hen could not cackle but she was on the alert to secure the new-laid egg. Her husband was continually prying about to detect her secret hoards, and many and fierce were the conflicts that took place about what ought to have been common property. They lived in a forlorn-looking house that stood alone, and had an air of starvation. A few straggling savin-trees, emblems of sterility, grew near it; no smoke ever curled from its chimney; no traveller stopped at its door. A miserable horse, whose ribs were as articulate as the bars of a gridiron, stalked about a field, where a thin carpet of moss, scarcely covering the ragged beds of pudding-stone, tantalized and balked his hunger; and sometimes he would lean his head over the fence, look piteously at the passer-by, and seem to petition deliverance from this land of famine.

The house and its inmates had altogether a bad name. Tom's wife was a tall termagant, fierce of temper, loud of tongue, and strong of arm. Her voice was often heard in wordy warfare with her husband; and his face sometimes showed signs that their conflicts were not confined to words. No one ventured, however, to interfere between them. The lonely wayfarer shrunk within himself at the horrid clamor and clapper-clawing; eyed the den of discord askance; and hurried on his way, rejoicing, if a bachelor, in his celibacy.

One day that Tom Walker had been to a distant part of the neighborhood, he took what he considered a short cut homeward, through the swamp. Like most short cuts, it was an ill-chosen route. The swamp was thickly grown with great gloomy pines and hemlocks, some of them ninety feet high, which made it dark at noonday, and a retreat for all the owls of the neighborhood. It was full of pits and quagmires, partly covered with weeds and mosses, where the green surface often betrayed the traveller into a gulf of black, smothering mud: there were also dark and stagnant pools, the abodes of the tadpole, the bull-frog, and the water-snake; where the trunks of pines and hemlocks lay half drowned, half rotting, looking like alligators sleeping in the mire.

Tom had long been picking his way cautiously through this treacherous forest; stepping from tuft to tuft of rushes and roots, which afforded precarious footholds among deep sloughs; or pacing carefully, like a cat, along the prostrate trunks of trees; startled now and then by the sudden screaming of the bittern, or the quacking of wild duck rising on the wing from some solitary pool. At length he arrived at a firm piece of ground, which ran out like a peninsula into the deep bosom of the swamp. It had been one of the strongholds of the Indians during their wars with the first colonists. Here they had thrown up a kind of fort, which they had looked upon as almost impregnable, and had used as a place of refuge for their squaws and children. Nothing remained of the old Indian fort but a few embankments, gradually sinking to the level of the surrounding earth, and already overgrown in part by oaks and other forest trees, the foliage of which formed a contrast to the dark pines and hemlocks of the swamp.

It was late in the dusk of evening when Tom Walker reached the old fort, and he paused there awhile to rest himself. Any one but he would have felt unwilling to linger in this lonely, melancholy place, for the common people had a bad opinion of it, from the stories handed down from the time of the Indian wars; when it was asserted that the savages held incantations here, and made sacrifices to the evil spirit.

Tom Walker, however, was not a man to be troubled with any fears of the kind. He reposed himself for some time on the trunk of a fallen hemlock, listening to the boding cry of the tree-toad, and delving with his walking-staff into a mound of black mould at his feet. As he turned up the soil unconsciously, his staff struck against something hard. He raked it out of the vegetable mould, and lo! a cloven skull, with an Indian tomahawk buried deep in it, lay before him. The rust on the weapon showed the time that had elapsed since this death-blow had been given. It was a dreary memento of the fierce struggle that had taken place in this last foothold of the Indian warriors.

"Humph!" said Tom Walker, as he gave it a kick to shake the dirt from it.

"Let that skull alone!" said a gruff voice. Tom lifted up his eyes, and beheld a great black man seated directly opposite him, on the stump of a tree. He was exceedingly surprised, having neither heard nor seen any one approach; and he was still more perplexed on observing, as well as the gathering gloom would permit, that the stranger was neither negro nor Indian. It is true he was dressed in a rude half Indian garb, and had a red belt or sash swathed round his body; but his face was neither black nor copper-color, but swarthy and dingy, and begrimed with soot, as if he had been accustomed to toil among fires and forges. He had a shock of coarse black hair, that stood out from his head in all directions, and bore an axe on his shoulder.

He scowled for a moment at Tom with a pair of great red eyes.

"What are you doing on my grounds?" said the black man, with a hoarse, growling voice.

"Your grounds!" said Tom, with a sneer, "no more your grounds than mine; they belong to Deacon Peabody."

"Deacon Peabody be d——d," said the stranger, "as I flatter myself he will be, if he does not look more to his own sins and less to those of his neighbors. Look yonder, and see how Deacon Peabody is faring."

Tom looked in the direction that the stranger pointed, and beheld one of the great trees, fair and flourishing without, but rotten at the core, and saw that it had been nearly hewn through, so that the first high wind was likely to blow it down. On the bark of the tree was scored the name of Deacon Peabody, an eminent man, who had waxed wealthy by driving shrewd bargains with the Indians. He now looked around, and found most of the tall trees marked with the name of some great man of the colony, and all more or less scored by the axe. The one on which he had been seated, and which had evidently just been hewn down, bore the name of Crowninshield; and he recollected a mighty rich man of that name, who made a vulgar display of wealth, which it was whispered he had acquired by buccaneering.

"He's just ready for burning!" said the black man, with a growl of triumph. "You see I am likely to have a good stock of firewood for winter."

"But what right have you," said Tom, "to cut down Deacon Peabody's timber?"

"The right of a prior claim," said the other. "This woodland belonged to me long before one of your white-faced race put foot upon the soil."

"And pray, who are you, if I may be so bold?" said Tom.

"Oh, I go by various names. I am the wild huntsman in some countries; the black miner in others. In this neighborhood I am known by the name of the black woodsman. I am he to whom the red men consecrated this spot, and in honor of whom they now and then roasted a white man, by way of sweet-smelling sacrifice. Since the red men have been exterminated by you white savages, I amuse myself by presiding at the persecutions of Quakers and Anabaptists; I am the great patron and prompter of slave-dealers, and the grand-master of the Salem witches."

"The upshot of all which is, that, if I mistake not," said Tom, sturdily, "you are he commonly called Old Scratch."

"The same, at your service!" replied the black man, with a half civil nod.

Such was the opening of this interview, according to the old story; though it has almost too familiar an air to be credited. One would think that to meet with such a singular personage, in this wild, lonely place, would have shaken any man's nerves; but Tom was a hard-minded fellow, not easily daunted, and he had lived so long with a termagant wife, that he did not even fear the devil.

It is said that after this commencement they had a long and earnest conversation together, as Tom returned homeward. The black man told him of great sums of money buried by Kidd the pirate, under the oak-trees on the high ridge, not far from the morass. All these were under his command, and protected by his power, so that none could find them but such as propitiated his favor. These he offered to place within Tom Walker's reach, having conceived an especial kindness for him; but they were to be had only on certain conditions. What these conditions were may be easily surmised, though Tom never disclosed them publicly. They must have been very hard, for he required time to think of them, and he was not a man to stick at trifles when money was in view. When they had reached the edge of the swamp, the stranger paused. "What proof have I that all you have been telling me is true?" said Tom. "There's my signature," said the black man, pressing his finger on Tom's forehead. So saying, he turned off among the thickest of the swamp, and seemed, as Tom said, to go down, down, down, into the earth, until nothing but his head and shoulders could be seen, and so on, until he totally disappeared.

When Tom reached home, he found the black print of a finger burnt, as it were, into his forehead, which nothing could obliterate.

The first news his wife had to tell him was the sudden death of Absalom Crowninshield, the rich buccaneer. It was announced in the papers with the usual flourish, that "A great man had fallen in Israel."

Tom recollected the tree which his black friend had just hewn down, and which was ready for burning. "Let the freebooter roast," said Tom; "who cares!" He now felt convinced that all he had heard and seen was no illusion.

He was not prone to let his wife into his confidence; but as this was an uneasy secret, he willingly shared it with her. All her avarice was awakened at the mention of hidden gold, and she urged her husband to comply with the black man's terms, and secure what would make them wealthy for life. However Tom might have felt disposed to sell himself to the devil, he was determined not to do so to oblige his wife; so he flatly refused, out of the mere spirit of contradiction. Many and bitter were the quarrels they had on the subject; but the more she talked, the more resolute was Tom not to be damned to please her.

At length she determined to drive the bargain on her own account, and if she succeeded, to keep all the gain to herself. Being of the same fearless temper as her husband, she set off for the old Indian fort towards the close of a summer's day. She was many hours absent. When she came back, she was reserved and sullen in her replies. She spoke something of a black man, whom she met about twilight hewing at the root of a tall tree. He was sulky, however, and would not come to terms: she was to go again with a propitiatory offering, but what it was she forbore to say.

The next evening she set off again for the swamp, with her apron heavily laden. Tom waited and waited for her, but in vain; midnight came, but she did not make her appearance: morning, noon, night returned, but still she did not come. Tom now grew uneasy for her safety, especially as he found she had carried off in her apron the silver tea-pot and spoons, and every portable article of value. Another night elapsed, another morning came; but no wife. In a word, she was never heard of more.

What was her real fate nobody knows, in consequence of so many pretending to know. It is one of those facts which have become confounded by a variety of historians. Some asserted that she lost her way among the tangled mazes of the swamp, and sank into some pit or slough; others, more uncharitable, hinted that she had eloped with the household booty, and made off to some other province; while others surmised that the tempter had decoyed her into a dismal quagmire, on the top of which her hat was found lying. In confirmation of this, it was said a great black man, with an axe on his shoulder, was seen late that very evening coming out of the swamp, carrying a bundle tied in a check apron, with an air of surly triumph.

The most current and probable story, however, observes, that Tom Walker grew so anxious about the fate of his wife and his property, that he set out at length to seek them both at the Indian fort. During a long summer's afternoon he searched about the gloomy place, but no wife was to be seen. He called her name repeatedly, but she was nowhere to be heard. The bittern alone responded to his voice, as he flew screaming by; or the bull-frog croaked dolefully from a neighboring pool. At length, it is said, just in the brown hour of twilight, when the owls began to hoot, and the bats to flit about, his attention was attracted by the clamor of carrion crows hovering about a cypress-tree. He looked up, and beheld a bundle tied in a check apron, and hanging in the branches of the tree, with a great vulture perched hard by, as if keeping watch upon it. He leaped with joy; for he recognized his wife's apron, and supposed it to contain the household valuables.

"Let us get hold of the property," said he, consolingly to himself, "and we will endeavor to do without the woman."

As he scrambled up the tree, the vulture spread its wide wings, and sailed off screaming, into the deep shadows of the forest. Tom seized the checked apron, but, woful sight! found nothing but a heart and liver tied up in it!

Such, according to this most authentic old story, was all that was to be found of Tom's wife. She had probably attempted to deal with the black man as she had been accustomed to deal with her husband; but though a female scold is generally considered a match for the devil, yet in this instance she appears to have had the worst of it. She must have died game, however; for it is said Tom noticed many prints of cloven feet deeply stamped upon the tree, and found handfuls of hair, that looked as if they had been plucked from the coarse black shock of the woodman. Tom knew his wife's prowess by experience. He shrugged his shoulders, as he looked at the signs of a fierce clapper-clawing.

"Egad," said he to himself, "Old Scratch must have had a tough time of it!"

Tom consoled himself for the loss of his property, with the loss of his wife, for he was a man of fortitude. He even felt something like gratitude towards the black woodman, who, he considered, had done him a kindness. He sought, therefore, to cultivate a further acquaintance with him, but for some time without success; the old black-legs played shy, for whatever people may think, he is not always to be had for calling for: he knows how to play his cards when pretty sure of his game.

At length, it is said, when delay had whetted Tom's eagerness to the quick, and prepared him to agree to anything rather than not gain the promised treasure, he met the black man one evening in his usual woodman's dress, with his axe on his shoulder, sauntering along the swamp, and humming a tune. He affected to receive Tom's advances with great indifference, made brief replies, and went on humming his tune.

By degrees, however, Tom brought him to business, and they began to haggle about the terms on which the former was to have the pirate's treasure. There was one condition which need not be mentioned, being generally understood in all cases where the devil grants favors; but there were others about which, though of less importance, he was inflexibly obstinate. He insisted that the money found through his means should be employed in his service. He proposed, therefore, that Tom should employ it in the black traffic; that is to say, that he should fit out a slave-ship. This, however, Tom resolutely refused: he was bad enough in all conscience; but the devil himself could not tempt him to turn slave-trader.

Finding Tom so squeamish on this point, he did not insist upon it, but proposed, instead, that he should turn usurer; the devil being extremely anxious for the increase of usurers, looking upon them as his peculiar people.

To this no objections were made, for it was just to Tom's taste.

"You shall open a broker's shop in Boston next month," said the black man.

"I'll do it to-morrow, if you wish," said Tom Walker.

"You shall lend money at two per cent a month."

"Egad, I'll charge four!" replied Tom Walker.

"You shall extort bonds, foreclose mortgages, drive the merchants to bankruptcy"—

"I'll drive them to the d——l," cried Tom Walker.

"You are the usurer for my money!" said black-legs with delight. "When will you want the rhino?"

"This very night."

"Done!" said the devil.

"Done!" said Tom Walker.—So they shook hands and struck a bargain.

A few days' time saw Tom Walker seated behind his desk in a counting-house in Boston.

His reputation for a ready-moneyed man, who would lend money out for a good consideration, soon spread abroad. Everybody remembers the time of Governor Belcher, when money was particularly scarce. It was a time of paper credit. The country had been deluged with government bills, the famous Land Bank had been established; there had been a rage for speculating; the people had run mad with schemes for new settlements; for building cities in the wilderness; land-jobbers went about with maps of grants, and townships, and Eldorados, lying nobody knew where, but which everybody was ready to purchase. In a word, the great speculating fever which breaks out every now and then in the country, had raged to an alarming degree, and every body was dreaming of making sudden fortunes from nothing. As usual the fever had subsided; the dream had gone off, and the imaginary fortunes with it; the patients were left in doleful plight, and the whole country resounded with the consequent cry of "hard times."

At this propitious time of public distress did Tom Walker set up as usurer in Boston. His door was soon thronged by customers. The needy and adventurous; the gambling speculator; the dreaming land-jobber; the thriftless tradesman; the merchant with cracked credit; in short, every one driven to raise money by desperate means and desperate sacrifices, hurried to Tom Walker.

Thus Tom was the universal friend of the needy, and acted like a "friend in need"; that is to say, he always exacted good pay and good security. In proportion to the distress of the applicant was the hardness of his terms. He accumulated bonds and mortgages; gradually squeezed his customers closer and closer: and sent them at length, dry as a sponge, from his door.

In this way he made money hand over hand; became a rich and mighty man, and exalted his cocked hat upon 'Change. He built himself, as usual, a vast house, out of ostentation; but left the greater part of it unfinished and unfurnished, out of parsimony. He even set up a carriage in the fulness of his vainglory, though he nearly starved the horses which drew it; and as the ungreased wheels groaned and screeched on the axle-trees, you would have thought you heard the souls of the poor debtors he was squeezing.

As Tom waxed old, however, he grew thoughtful. Having secured the good things of this world, he began to feel anxious about those of the next. He thought with regret on the bargain he had made with his black friend, and set his wits to work to cheat him out of the conditions. He became, therefore, all of a sudden, a violent church-goer. He prayed loudly and strenuously, as if heaven were to be taken by force of lungs. Indeed, one might always tell when he had sinned most during the week, by the clamor of his Sunday devotion. The quiet Christians who had been modestly and steadfastly travelling Zionward, were struck with self-reproach at seeing themselves so suddenly outstripped in their career by this new-made convert. Tom was as rigid in religious as in money matters; he was a stern supervisor and censurer of his neighbors, and seemed to think every sin entered up to their account became a credit on his own side of the page. He even talked of the expediency of reviving the persecution of Quakers and Anabaptists. In a word, Tom's zeal became as notorious as his riches.

Still, in spite of all this strenuous attention to forms, Tom had a lurking dread that the devil, after all, would have his due. That he might not be taken unawares, therefore, it is said he always carried a small Bible in his coat-pocket. He had also a great folio Bible on his counting-house desk, and would frequently be found reading it when people called on business; on such occasions he would lay his green spectacles in the book, to mark the place, while he turned round to drive some usurious bargain.

Some say that Tom grew a little crack-brained in his old days, and that, fancying his end approaching, he had his horse new shod, saddled and bridled, and buried with his feet uppermost; because he supposed that at the last day the world would be turned upside-down; in which case he should find his horse standing ready for mounting, and he was determined at the worst to give his old friend a run for it. This, however, is probably a mere old wives' fable. If he really did take such a precaution, it was totally superfluous; at least so says the authentic old legend, which closes his story in the following manner:

One hot summer afternoon in the dog-days, just as a terrible black thunder gust was coming up, Tom sat in his counting-house, in his white cap and India silk morning-gown. He was on the point of foreclosing a mortgage, by which he would complete the ruin of an unlucky land-speculator for whom he had professed the greatest friendship. The poor land-jobber begged him to grant a few months' indulgence. Tom had grown testy and irritated, and refused another day.

"My family will be ruined and brought upon the parish," said the land-jobber. "Charity begins at home," replied Tom; "I must take care of myself in these hard times."

"You have made so much money out of me," said the speculator.

Tom lost his patience and his piety. "The devil take me," said he, "if I have made a farthing!"

Just then there were three loud knocks at the street door. He stepped out to see who was there. A black man was holding a black horse, which neighed and stamped with impatience.

"Tom, you're come for," said the black fellow, gruffly. Tom shrank back, but too late. He had left his little Bible at the bottom of his coat-pocket, and his big Bible on the desk buried under the mortgage he was about to foreclose: never was sinner taken more unawares. The black man whisked him like a child into the saddle, gave the horse the lash, and away he galloped, with Tom on his back, in the midst of the thunder-storm. The clerks stuck their pens behind their ears, and stared after him from the windows. Away went Tom Walker, dashing down the streets; his white cap bobbing up and down; his morning-gown fluttering in the wind, and his steed striking fire out of the pavement at every bound. When the clerks turned to look for the black man, he had disappeared.

Tom Walker never returned to foreclose the mortgage. A country-man, who lived on the border of the swamp, reported that in the height of the thunder-gust he had heard a great clattering of hoofs and a howling along the road, and running to the window caught sight of a figure, such as I have described, on a horse that galloped like mad across the fields, over the hills, and down into the black hemlock swamp towards the old Indian fort; and that shortly after a thunder-bolt falling in that direction seemed to set the whole forest in a blaze.

The good people of Boston shook their heads and shrugged their shoulders, but had been so much accustomed to witches and goblins, and tricks of the devil, in all kinds of shapes, from the first settlement of the colony, that they were not so much horror-struck as might have been expected. Trustees were appointed to take charge of Tom's effects. There was nothing, however, to administer upon. On searching his coffers, all his bonds and mortgages were found reduced to cinders. In place of gold and silver, his iron chest was filled with chips and shavings; two skeletons lay in his stable instead of his half-starved horses, and the very next day his great house took fire and burnt to the ground.

Such was the end of Tom Walker and his ill-gotten wealth. Let all griping money-brokers lay this story to heart. The truth of it is not to be doubted. The very hole under the oak-trees whence he dug Kidd's

money is to be seen to this day; and the neighboring swamp and old
Indian fort are often haunted in stormy nights by a figure on horseback,
in morning-gown and white cap, which is doubtless the troubled spirit
of the usurer. In fact the story has resolved itself into a proverb, and is
the origin of that popular saying, so prevalent throughout New England, of "The Devil and Tom Walker."

Such, as nearly as I can recollect, was the purport of the tale told by
the Cape-Cod whaler. There were divers trivial particulars which I
have omitted, and which whiled away the morning very pleasantly, until the time of tide favorable to fishing being passed, it was proposed to
land, and refresh ourselves under the trees, till the noontide heat should
have abated.

We accordingly landed on a delectable part of the island of Manhatta, in that shady and embowered tract formerly under the domain of
the ancient family of the Hardenbrooks. It was a spot well known to
me in the course of the aquatic expeditions of my boyhood. Not far
from where we landed there was an old Dutch family vault, constructed
in the side of a bank, which had been an object of great awe and fable
among my schoolboy associates. We had peered into it during one of
our coasting voyages, and been startled by the sight of mouldering
coffins and musty bones within; but what had given it the most fearful
interest in our eyes, was its being in some way connected with the pirate
wreck which lay rotting among the rocks of Hell Gate. There were
stories also of smuggling connected with it, particularly relating to a
time when this retired spot was owned by a noted burgher, called
Ready Money Provost; a man of whom it was whispered that he had
many mysterious dealings with parts beyond the seas. All these things,
however, had been jumbled together in our minds in that vague way in
which such themes are mingled up in the tales of boyhood.

While I was pondering upon these matters, my companions had
spread a repast, from the contents of our well-stored pannier, under a
broad chestnut, on the greensward which swept down to the water's
edge. Here we solaced ourselves on the cool grassy carpet during the
warm sunny hours of mid-day. While lolling on the grass, indulging in
that kind of musing reverie of which I am fond, I summoned up the
dusky recollections of my boyhood respecting this place, and repeated
them like the imperfectly remembered traces of a dream, for the amusement of my companions. When I had finished, a worthy old burgher,
John Josse Vandermoere, the same who once related to me the adventures of Dolph Heyliger, broke silence, and observed, that he recollected

a story of money-digging, which occurred in this very neighborhood, and might account for some of the traditions which I had heard in my boyhood. As we knew him to be one of the most authentic narrators in the province, we begged him to let us have the particulars, and accordingly, while we solaced ourselves with a clean long pipe of Blase Moore's best tobacco, the authentic John Josse Vandermoere related the following tale.

WOLFERT WEBBER, OR GOLDEN DREAMS

IN the year of grace one thousand seven hundred and—blank—for I do not remember the precise date; however, it was somewhere in the early part of the last century, there lived in the ancient city of the Manhattoes a worthy burgher, Wolfert Webber by name. He was descended from old Cobus Webber of the Brille in Holland, one of the original settlers, famous for introducing the cultivation of cabbages, and who came over to the province during the protectorship of Oloffe Van Kortlandt, otherwise called the Dreamer.

The field in which Cobus Webber first planted himself and his cabbages had remained ever since in the family, who continued in the same line of husbandry, with that praiseworthy perseverance for which our Dutch burghers are noted. The whole family genius, during several generations, was devoted to the study and development of this one noble vegetable; and to this concentration of intellect may doubtless be ascribed the prodigious renown to which the Webber cabbages attained.

The Webber dynasty continued in uninterrupted succession; and never did a line give more unquestionable proofs of legitimacy. The eldest son succeeded to the looks, as well as the territory of his sire; and had the portraits of this line of tranquil potentates been taken, they would have presented a row of heads marvellously resembling in shape and magnitude the vegetables over which they reigned.

The seat of government continued unchanged in the family mansion —a Dutch-built house, with a front, or rather gable-end of yellow brick, tapering to a point, with the customary iron weathercock at the top. Everything about the building bore the air of long-settled ease and security. Flights of martins peopled the little coops nailed against its walls, and swallows built their nests under the eaves; and every one knows that these house-loving birds bring good luck to the dwelling where they take up their abode. In a bright summer morning in early summer, it was delectable to hear their cheerful notes, as they sported about in the pure sweet air, chirping forth, as it were, the greatness and prosperity of the Webbers.

Thus quietly and comfortably did this excellent family vegetate under the shade of a mighty button-wood tree, which, by little and little, grew so great as entirely to overshadow their palace. The city gradually spread its suburbs round their domain. Houses sprang up to interrupt their prospects. The rural lanes in the vicinity began to grow into the bustle and populousness of streets; in short, with all the habits of rustic life they began to find themselves the inhabitants of a city. Still, however, they maintained their hereditary character and their hereditary possessions, with all the tenacity of petty German princes in the midst of the empire. Wolfert was the last of the line, and succeeded to the patriarchal bench at the door, under the family tree, and swayed the sceptre of his fathers, a kind of rural potentate in the midst of the metropolis.

To share the cares and sweets of sovereignty, he had taken unto himself a helpmate, one of that excellent kind called stirring women; that is to say, she was one of those notable little house-wives who are always busy where there is nothing to do. Her activity, however, took one particular direction: her whole life seemed devoted to intense knitting; whether at home or abroad, walking or sitting, her needles were continually in motion, and it is even affirmed that by her unwearied industry she very nearly supplied her household with stockings throughout the year. This worthy couple were blessed with one daughter, who was brought up with great tenderness and care; uncommon pains had been taken with her education, so that she could stitch in every variety of way; make all kinds of pickles and preserves, and mark her own name on a sampler. The influence of her taste was seen also in the family garden, where the ornamental began to mingle with the useful; whole rows of fiery marigolds and splendid hollyhocks bordered the cabbage-beds; and gigantic sunflowers lolled their broad jolly faces over the fences, seeming to ogle most affectionately the passers-by.

Thus reigned and vegetated Wolfert Webber over his paternal acres, peacefully and contentedly. Not but that, like all other sovereigns, he had his occasional cares and vexations. The growth of his native city sometimes caused him annoyance. His little territory gradually became hemmed in by streets and houses, which intercepted air and sunshine. He was now and then subjected to the irruptions of the border population that infest the streets of a metropolis; who would make midnight forays into his dominions, and carry off captive whole platoons of his noblest subjects. Vagrant swine would make a descent, too, now and then, when the gate was left open, and lay all waste before them; and mischievous urchins would decapitate the illustrious sunflowers, the glory of the garden, as they lolled their heads so fondly over the walls. Still all these were petty grievances, which might now and then ruffle the surface of his mind, as a summer breeze will ruffle the surface of a mill-pond; but they could not disturb the deep-seated quiet of his soul. He would but seize a trusty staff, that stood behind the door, issue suddenly out, and anoint the back of the aggressor, whether pig or urchin, and then return within doors, marvellously refreshed and tranquillized.

The chief cause of anxiety to honest Wolfert, however, was the growing prosperity of the city. The expense of living doubled and trebled; but he could not double and treble the magnitude of his cabbages; and the number of competitors prevented the increase of price; thus, therefore, while every one around him grew richer, Wolfert grew poorer, and he could not, for the life of him, perceive how the evil was to be remedied.

This growing care, which increased from day to day, had its gradual effect upon our worthy burgher; insomuch, that it at length implanted two or three wrinkles in his brow; things unknown before in the family of the Webbers; and it seemed to pinch up the corners of his cocked hat into an expression of anxiety, totally opposite to the tranquil, broadbrimmed, low-crowned beavers of his illustrious progenitors.

· Perhaps even this would not have materially disturbed the serenity of his mind, had he had only himself and his wife to care for; but there was his daughter gradually growing to maturity; and all the world knows that when daughters begin to ripen, no fruit nor flower requires so much looking after. I have no talent at describing female charms, else fain would I depict the progress of this little Dutch beauty. How her blue eyes grew deeper and deeper, and her cherry lips redder and redder; and how she ripened and ripened, and rounded and rounded in the opening breath of sixteen summers, until, in her seventeenth spring, she seemed ready to burst out of her bodice, like a half-blown rose-bud.

Ah, well-a-day! could I but show her as she was then, tricked out on a Sunday morning, in the hereditary finery of the old Dutch clothespress, of which her mother had confided to her the key. The weddingdress of her grandmother, modernized for use, with sundry ornaments, handed down as heirlooms in the family. Her pale brown hair smoothed with buttermilk in flat waving lines on each side of her fair forehead. The chain of yellow virgin gold, that encircled her neck; the little cross, that just rested at the entrance of a soft valley of happiness, as if it would sanctify the place. The—but, pooh!—it is not for an old man like me to be prosing about female beauty; suffice it to say, Amy had attained her seventeenth year. Long since had her sampler exhibited hearts in couples desperately transfixed with arrows, and true lovers' knots worked in deep blue silk; and it was evident she began to languish for some more interesting occupation than the rearing of sunflowers or pickling of cucumbers.

At this critical period of female existence, when the heart within a damsel's bosom, like its emblem, the miniature which hangs without, is apt to be engrossed by a single image, a new visitor began to make his appearance under the roof of Wolfert Webber. This was Dick Waldron, the only son of a poor widow, but who could boast of more fathers than any lad in the province; for his mother had had four husbands, and this only child; so that though born in her last wedlock, he might fairly claim to be the tardy fruit of a long course of cultivation. This son of four fathers united the merits and the vigors of all his sires. If he had not had a great family before him, he seemed likely to have a great one after him; for you had only to look at the fresh bucksome youth, to see that he was formed to be the founder of a mighty race.

This youngster gradually became an intimate visitor of the family. He talked little, but he sat long. He filled the father's pipe when it was empty, gathered up the mother's knitting-needle, or ball of worsted when it fell to the ground; stroked the sleek coat of the tortoise-shell cat, and replenished the tea-pot for the daughter from the bright copper kettle that sang before the fire. All these quiet little offices may seem of trifling import; but when true love is translated into Low Dutch, it is in this way that it eloquently expresses itself. They were not lost upon the Webber family. The winning youngster found marvellous favor in the eyes of the mother; the tortoise-shell cat, albeit the most staid and demure of her kind, gave indubitable signs of approbation of his visits; the tea-kettle seemed to sing out a cheering note of welcome at his approach; and if the sly glances of the daughter might be rightly read, as she sat bridling and dimpling, and sewing by her mother's side, she was not a whit behind Dame Webber, or grimalkin, or the tea-kettle, in good-will.

Wolfert alone saw nothing of what was going on. Profoundly wrapt up in meditation on the growth of the city and his cabbages, he sat looking in the fire, and puffing his pipe in silence. One night, however, as the gentle Amy, according to custom, lighted her lover to the outer door, and he, according to custom, took his parting salute, the smack resounded so vigorously through the long silent entry, as to startle even the dull ear of Wolfert. He was slowly roused to a new source of anxiety. It had never entered into his head that this mere child, who, as it seemed, but the other day had been climbing about his knees, and playing with dolls and baby-houses, could all at once be thinking of lovers and matrimony. He rubbed his eyes, examined into the fact, and really found that, while he had been dreaming of other matters, she had actually grown to be a woman, and, what was worse, had fallen in love. Here arose new cares for Wolfert. He was a kind father, but he was a prudent man. The young man was a lively, stirring lad; but then he had neither money nor land. Wolfert's ideas all ran in one channel; and he saw no alternative in case of a marriage but to portion off the young couple with a corner of his cabbage-garden, the whole of which was barely sufficient for the support of his family.

Like a prudent father, therefore, he determined to nip this passion in the bud, and forbade the youngster the house; though sorely did it go against his fatherly heart, and many a silent tear did it cause in the bright eye of his daughter. She showed herself, however, a pattern of filial piety and obedience. She never pouted and sulked; never flew in the face of parental authority; she never flew into a passion, nor fell into hysterics, as many romantic novel-read young ladies would do. Not she, indeed! She was none such heroical, rebellious trumpery, I'll warrant ye. On the contrary, she acquiesced like an obedient daughter, shut the street-door in her lover's face, and if ever she did grant him an interview, it was either out of the kitchen-window, or over the garden-fence.

Wolfert was deeply cogitating these matters in his mind, and his brow wrinkled with unusual care, as he wended his way one Saturday afternoon to a rural inn, about two miles from the city. It was a favorite resort of the Dutch part of the community, from being always held by a Dutch line of landlords, and retaining an air and relish of the good old times. It was a Dutch-built house, that had probably been a country seat of some-opulent burgher in the early time of the settlement. It stood near a point of land called Corlear's Hook, which stretches out into the Sound, and against which the tide, at its flux and reflux, sets with extraordinary rapidity. The venerable and somewhat crazy mansion was distinguished from afar by a grove of elms and sycamores that seemed to wave a hospitable invitation, while a few weeping-willows, with their dank, drooping foliage, resembling falling waters, gave an idea of coolness, that rendered it an attractive spot during the heat of the summer.

Here, therefore, as I said, resorted many of the old inhabitants of the Manhattoes, where, while some played at shuffle-board and quoits and nine-pins, others smoked a deliberate pipe, and talked over public affairs.

It was on a blustering autumnal afternoon that Wolfert made his visit to the inn. The grove of elms and willows was stripped of its leaves, which whirled in rustling eddies about the fields. The nine-pin alley was deserted, for the premature chilliness of the day had driven the company within doors. As it was Saturday afternoon, the habitual club was in session, composed principally of regular Dutch burghers, though mingled occasionally with persons of various character and country, as is natural in a place of such motley population.

Beside the fireplace, in a huge leather-bottomed arm-chair, sat the dictator of this little world, the venerable Rem, or, as it was pronounced, Ramm Rapelye. He was a man of Walloon race, and illustrious for the antiquity of his line; his great-grandmother having been the first white child born in the province. But he was still more illustrious for his wealth and dignity: he had long filled the noble office of alderman, and was a man to whom the governor himself took off his hat. He had maintained possession of the leather-bottomed chair from time immemorial, and had gradually waxed in bulk as he sat in his seat of government, until in the course of years he filled its whole magnitude. His word was decisive with his subjects; for he was so rich a man that he was never expected to support any opinion by argument. The landlord waited on him with peculiar officiousness; not that he paid better than his neighbors, but then the coin of a rich man seems always to be so much more acceptable. The landlord had ever a pleasant word and a joke to insinuate in the ear of the august Ramm. It is true, Ramm never laughed, and, indeed, ever maintained a mastiff-like gravity, and even surliness of aspect; yet he now and then rewarded mine host with a token of approbation; which, though nothing more nor less than a kind of a grunt, still delighted the landlord more than a broad laugh from a poorer man.

"This will be a rough night for the money-diggers," said mine host, as a gust of wind howled round the house, and rattled at the windows.

"What, are they at their works again?" said an English half-pay captain, with one eye, who was a very frequent attendant at the inn.

"Aye, are they," said the landlord, "and well may they be. They've had luck of late. They say a great pot of money has been dug up in the fields, just behind Stuyvesant's orchard. Folks think it must have been buried there in old times, by Peter Stuyvesant, the Dutch governor."

"Fudge!" said the one-eyed man of war, as he added a small portion of water to a bottom of brandy.

"Well, you may believe it or not, as you please," said mine host, somewhat nettled; "but everybody knows that the old governor buried a great deal of his money at the time of the Dutch troubles, when the English red-coats seized on the province. They say, too, the old gentleman walks; aye, and in the very same dress that he wears in the picture that hangs up in the family house."

"Fudge!" said the half-pay officer.

"Fudge, if you please!—But didn't Corney Van Zandt see him at midnight, stalking about in the meadow with his wooden leg, and a drawn sword in his hand, that flashed like fire? And what can he be walking for, but because people have been troubling the place where he buried his money in old times?"

Here the landlord was interrupted by several guttural sounds from Ramm Rapelye, betokening that he was laboring with the unusual production of an idea. As he was too great a man to be slighted by a prudent publican, mine host respectfully paused until he should deliver himself. The corpulent frame of this mighty burgher now gave all the symptoms of a volcanic mountain on the point of an eruption. First, there was a certain heaving of the abdomen, not unlike an earthquake; then was emitted a cloud of tobacco-smoke from that crater, his mouth; then there was a kind of rattle in the throat, as if the idea were working its way up through a region of phlegm; then there were several disjointed members of a sentence thrown out, ending in a cough; at length his voice forced its way into a slow, but absolute tone of a man who feels the weight of his purse, if not his ideas; every portion of his speech being marked by a testy puff of tobacco smoke.

"Who talks of old Peter Stuyvesant's walking?—puff—Have people no respect for persons?—puff—puff—Peter Stuyvesant knew better what to do with his money than to bury it—puff—I know the Stuyvesant family —puff—every one of them—puff—not a more respectable family in the province—puff—old standards—puff—warm householders—puff—none of your upstarts—puff—puff—puff—. Don't talk to me of Peter Stuyvesant's walking—puff—puff—puff—puff."

Here the redoubtable Ramm contracted his brow, clasped up his mouth, till it wrinkled at each corner, and redoubled his smoking with such vehemence, that the cloudy volumes soon wreathed round his head, as the smoke envelopes the awful summit of Mount Ætna.

A general silence followed the sudden rebuke of this very rich man. The subject, however, was too interesting to be readily abandoned. The conversation soon broke forth again from the lips of Peechy Prauw Van Hook, the chronicler of the club, one of those prosing, narrative old men who seem to be troubled with an incontinence of words, as they grow old.

Peechy could, at any time, tell as many stories in an evening as his hearers could digest in a month. He now resumed the conversation, by affirming that, to his knowledge, money had, at different times, been digged up in various parts of the island. The lucky persons who had discovered them had always dreamt of them three times beforehand,

and what was worthy of remark, those treasures had never been found but by some descendant of the good old Dutch families, which clearly proved that they had been buried by Dutchmen in the olden time.

"Fiddlestick with your Dutchmen!" cried the half-pay officer. "The Dutch had nothing to do with them. They were all buried by Kidd the pirate, and his crew."

Here a key-note was touched that roused the whole company. The name of Captain Kidd was like a talisman in those times, and was associated with a thousand marvellous stories.

The half-pay officer took the lead, and in his narrations fathered upon Kidd all the plunderings and exploits of Morgan, Blackbeard, and the whole list of bloody buccaneers.

The officer was a man of great weight among the peaceable members of the club, by reason of his warlike character and gunpowder tales. All his golden stories of Kidd, however, and of the booty he had buried, were obstinately rivalled by the tales of Peechy Prauw, who, rather than suffer his Dutch progenitors to be eclipsed by a foreign freebooter, enriched every field and shore in the neighborhood with the hidden wealth of Peter Stuyvesant and his contemporaries.

Not a word of this conversation was lost upon Wolfert Webber. He returned pensively home, full of magnificent ideas. The soil of his native island seemed to be turned into gold dust; and every field to teem with treasure. His head almost reeled at the thought how often he must have heedlessly rambled over places where countless sums lay, scarcely covered by the turf beneath his feet. His mind was in an uproar with this whirl of new ideas. As he came in sight of the venerable mansion of his forefathers, and the little realm where the Webbers had so long, and so contentedly flourished, his gorge rose at the narrowness of his destiny.

"Unlucky Wolfert!" exclaimed he; "others can go to bed and dream themselves into whole mines of wealth; they have but to seize a spade in the morning, and turn up doubloons like potatoes; but thou must dream of hardships, and rise to poverty,—must dig thy field from year's end to year's end, and yet raise nothing but cabbages!"

Wolfert Webber went to bed with a heavy heart; and it was long before the golden visions that disturbed his brain permitted him to sink into repose. The same visions, however, extended into his sleeping thoughts, and assumed a more definite form. He dreamt that he had discovered an immense treasure in the centre of his garden. At every stroke of the spade he laid bare a golden ingot; diamond crosses sparkled out of the dust; bags of money turned up their bellies, corpulent with pieces-of-eight, or venerable doubloons; and chests, wedged close with moidores, ducats, and pistareens, yawned before his ravished eyes, and vomited forth their glittering contents.

Wolfert awoke a poorer man than ever. He had no heart to go about his daily concerns, which appeared so paltry and profitless; but sat all day long in the chimney-corner, picturing to himself ingots and heaps of gold in the fire. The next night his dream was repeated. He was again in his garden, digging, and laying open stores of hidden wealth. There was something very singular in this repetition. He passed another day of reverie, and though it was cleaning-day, and the house, as usual in Dutch households, completely topsy-turvy, yet he sat unmoved amidst the general uproar.

The third night he went to bed with a palpitating heart. He put on his red night-cap wrong-side outwards, for good luck. It was deep midnight before his anxious mind could settle itself into sleep. Again the golden dream was repeated, and again he saw his garden teeming with ingots and money-bags.

Wolfert rose the next morning in complete bewilderment. A dream, three times repeated, was never known to lie; and if so, his fortune was made.

In his agitation he put on his waistcoat with the hind part before, and this was a corroboration of good luck. He no longer doubted that a huge store of money lay buried somewhere in his cabbage-field, coyly waiting to be sought for; and he repined at having so long been scratching about the surface of the soil instead of digging to the centre.

He took his seat at the breakfast-table full of these speculations; asked his daughter to put a lump of gold into his tea, and on handing his wife a plate of slap-jacks, begged her to help herself to a doubloon.

His grand care now was how to secure this immense treasure without its being known. Instead of his working regularly in his grounds in the daytime, he now stole from his bed at night, and with spade and pick-axe went to work to rip up and dig about his paternal acres, from one end to the other. In a little time the whole garden, which had presented such a goodly and regular appearance, with its phalanx of cabbages, like a vegetable army in battle array, was reduced to a scene of devastation; while the relentless Wolfert, with night-cap on head, and lantern and spade in hand, stalked through the slaughtered ranks, the destroying angel of his own vegetable world.

Every morning bore testimony to the ravages of the preceding night in cabbages of all ages and conditions, from the tender sprout to the full-grown head, piteously rooted from their quiet beds like worthless weeds, and left to wither in the sunshine. In vain Wolfert's wife remonstrated; in vain his darling daughter wept over the destruction of some favorite marigold. "Thou shalt have gold of another guess sort," he would say, chucking her under the chin; "thou shalt have a string of crooked ducats for thy wedding necklace, my child." His family began really to fear that the poor man's wits were diseased. He muttered in his sleep at night about mines of wealth, about pearls and diamonds, and bars of gold. In the daytime he was moody and abstracted, and walked about as if in a trance. Dame Webber held frequent councils with all the old women of the neighborhood; scarce an hour in the day but a knot of them might be seen wagging their white caps together round her door, while the poor woman made some piteous recital. The daughter, too, was fain to seek for more frequent consolation from the stolen interviews of her favored swain, Dick Waldron. The delectable little Dutch songs, with which she used to dulcify the house, grew less and less frequent, and she would forget her sewing, and look wistfully in her father's face as he sat pondering by the fireside. Wolfert caught her eye one day fixed on him thus anxiously, and for a moment was roused from his golden reveries.—"Cheer up, my girl," said he, exultingly; "why dost thou droop?—thou shalt hold up thy head one day with the Brinckerhoffs, and the Schermerhorns, the Van Hornes, and the Van Dams. By Saint Nicholas, but the patroon himself shall be glad to get thee for his son!"

Amy shook her head at his vainglorious boast, and was more than ever in doubt of the soundness of the good man's intellect.

In the meantime Wolfert went on digging and digging; but the field was extensive, and as his dream had indicated no precise spot, he had to dig at random. The winter set in before one tenth of the scene of promise had been explored.

The ground became frozen hard, and the nights too cold for the labors of the spade.

No sooner, however, did the returning warmth of spring loosen the soil, and the small frogs begin to pipe in the meadows, but Wolfert resumed his labors with renovated zeal. Still, however, the hours of industry were reversed.

Instead of working cheerily all day, planting and setting out his vegetables, he remained thoughtfully idle, until the shades of night summoned him to his secret labors. In this way he continued to dig from night to night, and week to week, and month to month, but not a stiver did he find. On the contrary, the more he digged, the poorer he grew. The rich soil of his garden was digged away, and the sand and gravel from beneath was thrown to the surface, until the whole field presented an aspect of sandy barrenness.

In the meantime, the seasons gradually rolled on. The little frogs which had piped in the meadows in early spring, croaked as bull-frogs during the summer heats, and then sank into silence. The peach-tree budded, blossomed, and bore its fruit. The swallows and martins came, twitted about the roof, built their nests, reared their young, held their congress along the eves, and then winged their flight in search of another spring. The caterpillar spun its winding-sheet, dangled it from the great button-wood tree before the house; turned into a moth, fluttered with the last sunshine of summer, and disappeared; and finally the leaves of the button-wood tree turned yellow, then brown, then rustled one by one to the ground, and whirling about in little eddies of wind and dust, whispered that winter was at hand.

Wolfert gradually woke from his dream of wealth as the year declined. He had reared no crop for the supply of his household during the sterility of winter. The season was long and severe, and for the first time the family was really straitened in its comforts. By degrees a revulsion of thought took place in Wolfert's mind, common to those whose golden dreams have been disturbed by pinching realities. The idea gradually stole upon him that he should come to want. He already considered himself one of the most unfortunate men in the province, having lost such an incalculable amount of undiscovered treasure, and now, when thousands of pounds had eluded his search, to be perplexed for shillings and pence, was cruel in the extreme.

Haggard care gathered about his brow; he went about with a money-seeking air, his eyes bent downwards into the dust, and carrying his hands in his pockets, as men are apt to do when they have nothing else to put into them. He could not even pass the city almshouse without giving it a rueful glance, as if destined to be his future abode.

The strangeness of his conduct and of his looks occasioned much speculation and remark. For a long time he was suspected of being crazy, and then everybody pitied him, and at length it began to be suspected that he was poor, and then everybody avoided him.

The rich old burghers of his acquaintance met him outside of the door when he called, entertained him hospitably on the threshold, pressed him warmly by the hand at parting, shook their heads as he walked away, with the kind-hearted expression of "poor Wolfert," and turned a corner nimbly if by chance they saw him approaching as they walked the streets. Even the barber and the cobbler of the neighborhood, and a tattered tailor in an alley hard by, three of the poorest and merriest rogues in the world, eyed him with that abundant sympathy which usually attends a lack of means; and there is not a doubt but their pockets would have been at his command, only that they happened to be empty.

Thus everybody deserted the Webber mansion, as if poverty were contagious, like the plague; everybody but honest Dick Waldron, who still kept up his stolen visits to the daughter, and indeed seemed to wax more affectionate as the fortunes of his mistress were in the wane.

Many months had elapsed since Wolfert had frequented his old resort, the rural inn. He was taking a long lonely walk one Saturday afternoon, musing over his wants and disappointments, when his feet took instinctively their wonted direction, and on awaking out of a reverie, he found himself before the door of the inn. For some moments he hesitated whether to enter, but his heart yearned for companionship; and where can a ruined man find better companionship than at a tavern, where there is neither sober example nor sober advice to put him out of countenance?

Wolfert found several of the old frequenters of the inn at their usual places; but one was missing, the great Ramm Rapelye, who for many years had filled the leather-bottomed chair of state. His place was supplied by a stranger, who seemed, however, completely at home in the chair and the tavern. He was rather under size, but deep-chested, square, and muscular. His broad shoulders, double joints, and bow knees, gave tokens of prodigious strength. His face was dark and weather-beaten; a deep scar, as if from the slash of a cutlass, had almost divided his nose, and made a gash in his upper lip, through which his teeth shone like a bull-dog's. A mop of iron-gray hair gave a grisly finish to this hard-favored visage. His dress was of an amphibious character. He wore an old hat edged with tarnished lace, and cocked in martial style, on one side of his head; a rusty blue military coat with brass buttons, and a wide pair of short petticoat trousers, or rather breeches, for they were gathered up at the knees. He ordered everybody about him with an authoritative air; talking in a brattling voice, that sounded like the crackling of thorns under a pot; d——d the landlord and servants with perfect impunity, and was waited upon with greater obsequiousness than had ever been shown to the mighty Ramm himself.

Wolfert's curiosity was awakened to know who and what was this stranger, who had thus usurped absolute sway in this ancient domain. Peechy Prauw took him aside, into a remote corner of the hall, and there, in an under voice, and with great caution, imparted to him all that he knew on the subject. The inn had been aroused several months before, on a dark night, by repeated long shouts, that seemed like the howling of a wolf. They came from the water-side and at length were distinguished to be hailing the house in the seafaring manner, "House-a-hoy!" The landlord turned out with his head waiter, tapster, hostler, and errand-boy,—that is to say, with his old negro Cuff. On approaching the place whence the voice proceeded, they found this amphibious-looking personage at the water's edge, quite alone, and seated on a great oaken sea-chest. How he came there, whether he had been set on shore from some boat, or had floated to land on his chest, nobody could tell, for he did not seem disposed to answer questions; and there was something in his looks and manners that put a stop to all questioning. Suffice it to say, he took possession of a corner-room of the inn, to which his chest was removed with great difficulty. Here he had remained ever since, keeping about the inn and its vicinity. Sometimes, it is true, he disappeared for one, two, or three days at a time, going and returning without giving any notice or account of his movements. He always appeared to have plenty of money, though often of very strange, outlandish coinage; and he regularly paid his bill every evening before turning in.

He had fitted up his room to his own fancy, having slung a hammock from the ceiling instead of a bed, and decorated the walls with rusty pistols and cutlasses of foreign workmanship. A greater part of his time was passed in this room, seated by the window, which commanded a wide view of the Sound, a short old-fashioned pipe in his mouth, a glass of rum-toddy at his elbow, and a pocket-telescope in his hand, with which he reconnoitered every boat that moved upon the water. Large, square-rigged vessels seemed to excite but little attention; but the moment he descried anything with a shoulder-of-mutton sail, or that a barge, or yawl, or jolly-boat hove in sight, up went the telescope, and he examined it with the most scrupulous attention.

All this might have passed without much notice, for in those times the province was so much the resort of adventurers of all characters and climes, that any oddity in dress or behavior attracted but small attention. In a little while, however, this strange sea-monster, thus strangely cast upon dry land, began to encroach upon the long-established customs and customers of the place, and to interfere in a dictatorial manner in the affairs of the nine-pin alley and the bar-room, until in the end he usurped an absolute command over the whole inn. It was all in vain to attempt to withstand his authority. He was not exactly quarrelsome, but boisterous and peremptory, like one accustomed to tyrannize on a quarter-deck; and there was a dare-devil air about everything he said and did, that inspired wariness in all by-standers. Even the half-pay officer, so long the hero of the club, was soon silenced by him; and the quiet burghers stared with wonder at seeing their inflammable man-of-war so readily and quietly extinguished.

And then the tales that he would tell were enough to make a peaceable man's hair stand on end. There was not a sea-fight, nor marauding nor freebooting adventure that had happened within the last twenty years, but he seemed perfectly versed in it. He delighted to talk of the exploits of the buccaneers in the West Indies, and on the Spanish Main. How his eyes would glisten, as he described the waylaying of treasure-ships, the desperate fights, yard-arm and yard-arm—broadside and broadside—the boarding and capturing huge Spanish galleons! With what chuckling relish would he describe the descent upon some rich Spanish colony; the rifling of a church; the sacking of a convent! You would have thought you heard some gormandizer dilating upon the roasting of a savory goose at Michaelmas as he described the roasting of some Spanish Don to make him discover his treasure—a detail given with a minuteness that made every rich old burgher present turn uncomfortably in his chair. All this would be told with infinite glee, as if he considered it an excellent joke; and then he would give such a tyrannical leer in the face of his next neighbor, that the poor man would be fain to laugh out of sheer faint-heartedness. If any one, however, pretended to contradict him in any of his stories, he was on fire in an instant. His very cocked hat assumed a momentary fierceness, and seemed to resent the contradiction. "How the devil should you know as well as I?—I tell you it was as I say"; and he would at the same time let slip a broadside of thundering oaths and tremendous sea-phrases, such as had never been heard before within these peaceful walls.

Indeed, the worthy burghers began to surmise that he knew more of those stories than mere hearsay. Day after day their conjectures concerning him grew more and more wild and fearful. The strangeness of his arrival, the strangeness of his manners, the mystery that surrounded him, all made him something incomprehensible in their eyes. He was a kind of monster of the deep to them—he was a merman—he was a behemoth—he was a leviathan—in short, they knew not what he was.

The domineering spirit of this boisterous sea-urchin at length grew quite intolerable. He was no respecter of persons; he contradicted the richest burghers without hesitation; he took possession of the sacred elbow-chair, which, time out of mind, had been the seat of sovereignty of the illustrious Ramm Rapelye. Nay, he even went so far, in one of his rough jocular moods, as to slap that mighty burgher on the back, drink his toddy, and wink in his face, a thing scarcely to be believed. From this time Ramm Rapelye appeared no more at the inn; his example was followed by several of the most eminent customers, who were too rich to tolerate being bullied out of their opinions, or being obliged to laugh at another man's jokes. The landlord was almost in despair; but he knew not how to get rid of this sea-monster and his sea-chest, who seemed both to have grown like fixtures, or excrescences, on his establishment.

Such was the account whispered cautiously in Wolfert's ear, by the narrator, Peechy Prauw, as he held him by the button in a corner of the hall, casting a wary glance now and then towards the door of the bar-room, lest he should be overheard by the terrible hero of his tale.

Wolfert took his seat in a remote part of the room in silence; impressed with profound awe of this unknown, so versed in freebooting history. It was to him a wonderful instance of the revolutions of mighty empires, to find the venerable Ramm Rapelye thus ousted from the throne, and a rugged tarpauling dictating from his elbow-chair, hectoring the patriarchs, and filling this tranquil little realm with brawl and bravado.

The stranger was on this evening in a more than usually communicative mood, and was narrating a number of astounding stories of plunderings and burnings on the high seas. He dwelt upon them with peculiar relish, heightening the frightful particulars in proportion to their effect on his peaceful auditors. He gave a swaggering detail of the capture of a Spanish merchantman. She was lying becalmed during a long summer's day, just off from the island which was one of the lurking-places of the pirates. They had reconnoitered her with their spy-glasses from the shore, and ascertained her character and force. At night a picked crew of daring fellows set off for her in a whale-boat. They approached with muffled oars, as she lay rocking idly with the undulations of the sea, and her sails flapping against the masts. They were close under the stern before the guard on deck was aware of their approach. The alarm was given; the pirates threw hand-grenades on deck, and sprang up the main chains, sword in hand.

The crew flew to arms, but in great confusion; some were shot down, others took refuge in the tops; others were driven overboard and drowned, while others fought hand to hand from the main-deck to the quarter-deck, disputing gallantly every inch of ground. There were three Spanish gentlemen on board with their ladies, who made the most desperate resistance. They defended the companion-way, cut down several of their assailants, and fought like very devils, for they were maddened by the shrieks of the ladies from the cabin. One of the Dons was old, and soon dispatched. The other two kept their ground vigorously, even though the captain of the pirates was among their assailants. Just then there was a shout of victory from the main-deck. "The ship is ours!" cried the pirates.

One of the Dons immediately dropped his sword and surrendered; the other, who was a hot-headed youngster, and just married, gave the captain a slash in the face that laid it all open. The captain just made out to articulate the words "no quarter."

"And what did they do with their prisoners?" said Peechy Prauw, eagerly.

"Threw them all overboard," was the answer. A dead pause followed the reply. Peechy Prauw sunk quietly back, like a man who had unwarily stolen upon the lair of a sleeping lion. The honest burghers cast fearful glances at the deep scar slashed across the visage of the stranger, and moved their chairs a little farther off. The seaman, however, smoked on without moving a muscle, as though he either did not perceive or did not regard the unfavorable effect he had produced upon his hearers.

The half-pay officer was the first to break the silence; for he was continually tempted to make ineffectual head against this tyrant of the seas, and to regain his lost consequence in the eyes of his ancient companions. He now tried to match the gunpowder tales of the stranger by others equally tremendous. Kidd, as usual, was his hero, concerning whom he seemed to have picked up many of the floating traditions of the province. The seaman had always evinced a settled pique against the one-eyed warrior. On this occasion he listened with peculiar impatience. He sat with arm akimbo, the other elbow on the table, the hand holding on to the small pipe he was pettishly puffing; his legs crossed; drumming with one foot on the ground, and casting every now and then the side-glance of a basilisk at the prosing captain. At length the latter spoke of Kidd's having ascended the Hudson with some of his crew, to land his plunder in secrecy.

"Kidd up the Hudson!" burst forth the seaman, with a tremendous oath,—"Kidd never was up the Hudson!"

"I tell you he was," said the other. "Aye, and they say he buried a quantity of treasure on the little flat that runs out into the river, called the Devil's Dans Kammer."

"The Devil's Dans Kammer in your teeth!" cried the seaman. "I tell you Kidd never was up the Hudson. What a plague do you know of Kidd and his haunts?"

"What do I know?" echoed the half-pay officer. "Why, I was in London at the time of his trial; aye, and I had the pleasure of seeing him hanged at Execution Dock."

"Then, sir, let me tell you that you saw as pretty a fellow hanged as ever trod shoe-leather. Aye!" putting his face nearer to that of the officer, "and there was many a land-lubber looked on that might much better have swung in his stead."

The half-pay officer was silenced; but the indignation thus pent up in his bosom glowed with intense vehemence in his single eye, which kindled like a coal.

Peechy Prauw, who never could remain silent, observed that the gentleman certainly was in the right. Kidd never did bury money up the Hudson, nor indeed in any of those parts, though many affirmed such to be the fact. It was Bradish and others of the buccaneers who had buried money; some said in Turtle Bay, others in Long Island, others in the neighborhood of Hell Gate. "Indeed," added he, "I recollect an adventure of Sam, the negro fisherman, many years ago, which some think had something to do with the buccaneers. As we are all friends here, and as it will go no further, I'll tell it to you.

"Upon a dark night many years ago, as Black Sam was returning from fishing in Hell Gate—"

Here the story was nipped in the bud by a sudden movement from the unknown, who laying his iron fist on the table, knuckles downward, with a quiet force that indented the very boards, and looking grimly over his shoulder, with the grin of an angry bear,—"Heark'ee, neighbor," said he, with a significant nodding of the head, "you'd better let the buccaneers and their money alone,—they're not for old men and old women to meddle with. They fought hard for their money; they gave body and soul for it; and wherever it lies buried, depend upon it he must have a tug with the devil who gets it!"

This sudden explosion was succeeded by a blank silence throughout the room. Peechy Prauw shrunk within himself, and even the one-eyed officer turned pale. Wolfert, who from a dark corner of the room had listened with intense eagerness to all this talk about buried treasure, looked with mingled awe and reverence at this bold buccaneer; for such he really suspected him to be. There was a chinking of gold and a sparkling of jewels in all his stories about the Spanish Main that gave a value to every period; and Wolfert would have given anything for the rummaging of the ponderous sea-chest, which his imagination crammed full of golden chalices, crucifixes, and jolly round bags of doubloons.

The dead stillness that had fallen upon the company was at length interrupted by the stranger, who pulled out a prodigious watch of curious and ancient workmanship, and which in Wolfert's eyes had a decidedly Spanish look. On touching a spring it struck ten o'clock; upon which the sailor called for his reckoning, and having paid it out of a handful of outlandish coin, he drank off the remainder of his beverage, and without taking leave of any one, rolled out of the room, muttering to himself, as he stamped upstairs to his chamber.

It was some time before the company could recover from the silence into which they had been thrown. The very footsteps of the stranger, which were heard now and then as he traversed his chamber, inspired awe.

Still the conversation in which they had been engaged was too interesting not to be resumed. A heavy thunder-gust had gathered up unnoticed while they were lost in talk, and the torrents of rain that fell forbade all thoughts of setting off for home until the storm should subside. They drew nearer together, therefore, and entreated the worthy Peechy Prauw to continue the tale which had been so discourteously interrupted. He readily complied, whispering, however, in a tone scarcely above his breath, and drowned occasionally by the rolling of the thunder; and he would pause every now and then, and listen with evident awe, as he heard the heavy footsteps of the stranger pacing overhead.

The following is the purport of his story.

Adventure of the Black Fisherman

EVERYBODY knows Black Sam, the old negro fisherman, or, as he is commonly called, Mud Sam, who has fished about the Sound for the last half century. It is now many years since Sam, who was then as active a young negro as any in the province, and worked on the farm of Killian Suydam on Long Island, having finished his day's work at an early hour, was fishing, one still summer evening, just about the neighborhood of Hell Gate.

He was in a light skiff; and being well acquainted with the currents and eddies, had shifted his station according to the shifting of the tide, from the Hen and Chickens to the Hog's Back, from the Hog's Back to the Pot, and from the Pot to the Frying-Pan; but in the eagerness of his sport he did not see that the tide was rapidly ebbing, until the roaring of the whirlpools and eddies warned him of his danger; and he had some difficulty in shooting his skiff from among the rocks and breakers, and getting to the point of Blackwell's Island. Here he cast anchor for some time, waiting the turn of the tide to enable him to return homewards. As the night set in, it grew blustering and gusty. Dark clouds came bundling up in the west; and now and then a growl of thunder or a flash of lightning told that a summer storm was at hand. Sam pulled over, therefore, under the lee of Manhattan Island, and coasting along, came to a snug nook, just under a steep beetling rock, where he fastened his skiff to the root of a tree that shot out from a cleft, and spread its broad branches like a canopy over the water. The gust came scouring along; the wind threw up the river in white surges; the rain rattled among the leaves; the thunder bellowed worse than that which is now bellowing; the lightning seemed to lick up the surges of the stream; but Sam, snugly sheltered under rock and tree, lay crouching in his skiff, rocking upon the billows until he fell asleep. When he awoke all was quiet. The gust had passed away, and only now and then a faint gleam of lightning in the east showed which way it had gone. The night was dark and moonless; and from the state of the tide Sam concluded it was near midnight. He was on the point of making loose his skiff to return homewards, when he saw a light gleaming along the water from a distance, which seemed rapidly approaching. As it drew near he perceived it came from a lantern in the bow of a boat gliding along under shadow of the land. It pulled up in a small cove, close to where he was. A man jumped on shore, and searching about with the lantern, exclaimed, "This is the place—here's the iron ring." The boat was then made fast, and the man returning on board, assisted his comrades in conveying something heavy on shore. As the light gleamed among them, Sam saw that they were five stout desperate-looking fellows, in red woollen caps, with a leader in a three-cornered hat, and that some of them were armed with dirks, or long knives, and pistols. They talked low to one another, and occasionally in some outlandish tongue which he could not understand.

On landing they made their way among the bushes, taking turns to relieve each other in lugging their burden up the rocky bank. Sam's curiosity was now fully aroused; so leaving his skiff he clambered silently up a ridge that overlooked their path. They had stopped to rest for a moment, and the leader was looking about among the bushes with his lantern. "Have you brought the spades?" said one. "They are here," replied another, who had them on his shoulder. "We must dig deep, where there will be no risk of discovery," said a third.

A cold chill ran through Sam's veins. He fancied he saw before him a gang of murderers, about to bury their victim. His knees smote together. In his agitation he shook the branch of a tree with which he was supporting himself as he looked over the edge of the cliff.

"What's that?" cried one of the gang.—"Some one stirs among the bushes!"

The lantern was held up in the direction of the noise. One of the red-caps cocked a pistol, and pointed it towards the very place where Sam was standing. He stood motionless—breathless; expecting the next moment to be his last. Fortunately his dingy complexion was in his favor, and made no glare among the leaves.

" 'Tis no one," said the man with the lantern. "What a plague! you would not fire off your pistol and alarm the country!"

The pistol was uncocked; the burden was resumed, and the party slowly toiled along the bank. Sam watched them as they went; the light sending back fitful gleams through the dripping bushes, and it was not until they were fairly out of sight that he ventured to draw breath freely. He now thought of getting back to his boat, and making his escape out of the reach of such dangerous neighbors; but curiosity was all-powerful. He hesitated and lingered and listened. By and by he heard the strokes of spades.—"They are digging the grave!" said he to himself; and the cold sweat started upon his forehead. Every stroke of a spade, as it sounded through the silent groves, went to his heart; it was evident there was as little noise made as possible; everything had an air of terrible mystery and secrecy. Sam had a great relish for the horrible,—a tale of murder was a treat for him; and he was a constant attendant at executions. He could not resist an impulse, in spite of every danger, to steal nearer to the scene of mystery, and overlook the midnight fellows at their work. He crawled along cautiously, therefore, inch by inch; stepping with the utmost care among the dry leaves, lest their rustling should betray him. He came at length to where a steep rock intervened between him and the gang; for he saw the light of their lantern shining up against the branches of the trees on the other side. Sam slowly and silently clambered up the surface of the rock, and raising his head above its naked edge, beheld the villains immediately below him, and so near, that though he dreaded discovery, he dared not withdraw lest the least movement should be heard. In this way he remained, with his round black face peering above the edge of the rock, like the sun just emerging above the edge of the horizon, or the round-cheeked moon on the dial of a clock.

The red-caps had nearly finished their work; the grave was filled up, and they were carefully replacing the turf. This done, they scattered dry leaves over the place. "And now," said the leader, "I defy the devil himself to find it out."

"The murderers!" exclaimed Sam, involuntarily.

The whole gang started, and looking up, beheld the round black head of Sam just above them. His white eyes strained half out of their orbits; his white teeth chattering, and his whole visage shining with cold perspiration.

"We're discovered!" cried one.

"Down with him!" cried another.

Sam heard the cocking of a pistol, but did not pause for the report. He scrambled over rock and stone, through brush and brier; rolled down banks like a hedge-hog; scrambled up others like a catamount. In every direction he heard some one or other of the gang hemming him in. At length he reached the rocky ridge along the river; one of the red-caps was hard behind him. A steep rock like a wall rose directly in his way; it seemed to cut off all retreat, when fortunately he espied the strong cord-like branch of a grape-vine reaching half-way down it. He sprang at it with the force of a desperate man, seized it with both hands, and being young and agile, succeeded in swinging himself to the summit of the cliff. Here he stood in full relief against the sky, when the red-cap cocked his pistol and fired. The ball whistled by Sam's head. With the lucky thought of a man in an emergency, he uttered a yell, fell to the ground, and detached at the same time a fragment of the rock, which tumbled with a loud splash into the river.

"I've done his business," said the red-cap to one or two of his comrades as they arrived panting. "He'll tell no tales, except to the fishes in the river."

His pursuers now turned to meet their companions. Sam, sliding silently down the surface of the rock, let himself quietly into his skiff, cast loose the fastening, and abandoned himself to the rapid current, which in that place runs like a mill-stream, and soon swept him off from the neighborhood. It was not, however, until he had drifted a great distance that he ventured to ply his oars, when he made his skiff dart like an arrow through the strait of Hell Gate, never heeding the danger of Pot, Frying-Pan, nor Hog's Back itself: nor did he feel himself thoroughly secure until safely nestled in bed in the cockloft of the ancient farm-house of the Suydams.

Here the worthy Peechy Prauw paused to take breath, and to take a sip of the gossip tankard that stood at his elbow. His auditors remained with open mouths and outstretched necks, gaping like a nest of swallows for an additional mouthful.

"And is that all?" exclaimed the half-pay officer.

"That's all that belongs to the story," said Peechy Prauw.

"And did Sam never find out what was buried by the red-caps?" said Wolfert, eagerly, whose mind was haunted by nothing but ingots and doubloons.

"Not that I know of," said Peechy; "he had no time to spare from his work, and, to tell the truth, he did not like to run the risk of another race among the rocks. Besides, how should he recollect the spot where the grave had been digged? everything would look so different by daylight. And then, where was the use of looking for a dead body, when there was no chance of hanging the murderers?"

"Aye, but are you sure it was a dead body they buried?" said Wolfert.

"To be sure," cried Peechy Prauw, exultingly. "Does it not haunt in the neighborhood to this very day?"

"Haunts!" exclaimed several of the party, opening their eyes still wider, and edging their chairs still closer.

"Aye, haunts," repeated Peechy; "have none of you heard of father Red-cap, who haunts the old burnt farm-house in the woods, on the border of the Sound, near Hell Gate?"

"Oh, to be sure, I've heard tell of something of the kind, but then I took it for some old wives' fable."

"Old wives' fable or not," said Peechy Prauw, "that farm-house stands hard by the very spot. It's been unoccupied time out of mind, and stands in a lonely part of the coast; but those who fish in the neighborhood have often heard strange noises there; and lights have been seen about the wood at night; and an old fellow in a red cap has been seen at the windows more than once, which people take to be the ghost of the body buried there. Once upon a time three soldiers took shelter in the building for the night, and rummaged it from top to bottom, when they found old father Red-cap astride of a cider-barrel in the cellar, with a jug in one hand and a goblet in the other. He offered them a drink out of his goblet, but just as one of the soldiers was putting it to his mouth—whew!—a flash of fire blazed through the cellar, blinded every mother's son of them for several minutes, when they recovered their eye-sight, jug, goblet, and Red-cap had vanished, and nothing but the empty cider-barrel remained."

Here the half-pay officer, who was growing very muzzy and sleepy, and nodding over his liquor, with half-extinguished eye, suddenly gleamed up like an expiring rushlight.

"That's all fudge!" said he, as Peechy finished his last story.

"Well, I don't vouch for the truth of it myself," said Peechy Prauw, "though all the world knows that there's something strange about that house and grounds; but as to the story of Mud Sam, I believe it just as well as if it had happened to myself."

The deep interest taken in this conversation by the company had made them unconscious of the uproar abroad among the elements, when suddenly they were electrified by a tremendous clap of thunder. A lumbering crash followed instantaneously, shaking the building to its very foundation. All started from their seats, imagining it the shock of an earthquake, or that old father Red-cap was coming among them in all his terrors. They listened for a moment, but only heard the rain pelting against the windows, and the wind howling among the trees. The explosion was soon explained by the apparition of an old negro's bald head thrust in at the door, his white goggle eyes contrasting with his jetty poll, which was wet with rain, and shone like a bottle. In a jargon but half intelligible, he announced that the kitchen-chimney had been struck with lightning.

A sullen pause of the storm, which now rose and sunk in gusts, produced a momentary stillness. In this interval the report of a musket was heard, and a long shout, almost like a yell, resounded from the shores. Every one crowded to the window; another musket-shot was heard, and another long shout, mingled wildly with a rising blast of wind. It seemed as if the cry came up from the bosom of the waters; for though incessant flashes of lightning spread a light about the shore, no one was to be seen.

Suddenly the window of the room overhead was opened, and a loud halloo uttered by the mysterious stranger. Several hailings passed from one party to the other, but in a language which none of the company in the bar-room could understand; and presently they heard the window closed, and a great noise overhead, as if all the furniture were pulled and hauled about the room. The negro servant was summoned, and shortly afterwards was seen assisting the veteran to lug the ponderous sea-chest downstairs.

The landlord was in amazement. "What, you are not going on the water in such a storm?"

"Storm!" said the other, scornfully, "do you call such a sputter of weather a storm?"

"You'll get drenched to the skin,—you'll catch your death!" said Peechy Prauw, affectionately.

"Thunder and lightning!" exclaimed the veteran, "don't preach about weather to a man that has cruised in whirlwinds and tornadoes."

The obsequious Peechy was again struck dumb. The voice from the water was heard once more in a tone of impatience; the bystanders stared with redoubled awe at this man of storms, who seemed to have come up out of the deep, and to be summoned back to it again.

As, with the assistance of the negro, he slowly bore his ponderous sea-chest towards the shore, they eyed it with a superstitious feeling,—half doubting whether he were not really about to embark upon it and launch forth upon the wild waves. They followed him at a distance with a lantern.

"Dowse the light!" roared the horse voice from the water. "No one wants light here!"

"Thunder and lightning!" exclaimed the veteran, turning short upon them; "back to the house with you!"

Wolfert and his companions shrunk back in dismay. Still their curiosity would not allow them entirely to withdraw. A long sheet of light-ning now flickered across the waves, and discovered a boat, filled with men, just under a rocky point, rising and sinking with the heaving surges, and swashing the waters at every heave. It was with difficulty held to the rocks by a boat-hook, for the current rushed furiously round the point. The veteran hoisted one end of the lumbering sea-chest on the gunwale of the boat, and seized the handle at the other end to lift it in, when the motion propelled the boat from the shore; the chest slipped off from the gunwale, and, sinking into the waves, pulled the veteran headlong after it. A loud shriek was uttered by all on shore, and a volley of execrations by those on board; but boat and man were hurried away by the rushing swiftness of the tide. A pitchy darkness succeeded; Wolfert Webber indeed fancied that he distinguished a cry for help, and that he beheld the drowning man beckoning for assist-ance; but when the lightning again gleamed along the water, all was void; neither man nor boat was to be seen; nothing but the dashing and weltering of the waves as they hurried past.

The company returned to the tavern to await the subsiding of the storm. They resumed their seats, and gazed on each other with dismay. The whole transaction had not occupied five minutes, and not a dozen words had been spoken. When they looked at the oaken chair, they could scarcely realize the fact that the strange being who had so lately tenanted it, full of life and Herculean vigor, should already be a corpse. There was the very glass he had just drunk from; there lay the ashes from the pipe which he had smoked, as it were, with his last breath. As the worthy burghers pondered on these things, they felt a terrible con-viction of the uncertainty of existence, and each felt as if the ground on which he stood was rendered less stable by his awful example.

As, however, the most of the company were possessed of that valuable philosophy which enables a man to bear up with fortitude against the misfortunes of his neighbors, they soon managed to console themselves for the tragic end of the veteran. The landlord was particularly happy that the poor dear man had paid his reckoning before he went; and made a kind of farewell speech on the occasion.

"He came," said he, "in a storm, and he went in a storm; he came in the night, and he went in the night; he came nobody knows whence, and he has gone nobody knows where. For aught I know he has gone to sea once more on his chest, and may land to bother some people on the other side of the world! Though it's a thousand pities, added he, "if he has gone to Davy Jones's locker that he had not left his own locker behind him."

"His locker! St. Nicholas preserve us!" cried Peechy Prauw. "I'd not have had that sea-chest in the house for any money; I'll warrant he'd come racketing after it at nights, and making a haunted house of the inn. And, as to his going to sea in his chest, I recollect what happened to Skipper Onderdonk's ship on his voyage from Amsterdam.

"The boatswain died during a storm: so they wrapped him up in a sheet, and put him in his own sea-chest, and threw him overboard; but they neglected in their hurry-skurry to say prayers over him—and the storm raged and roared louder than ever, and they saw the dead man seated in his chest, with his shroud for a sail, coming hard after the ship; and the sea breaking before him in great sprays like fire; and there they kept scudding day after day, and night after night, expecting every moment to go to wreck: and every night they saw the dead boatswain in his sea-chest trying to get up with them, and they heard his whistle above the blasts of wind, and he seemed to send great seas mountain-high after them, that would have swamped the ship if they had not put up the dead-lights. And so it went on till they lost sight of him in the fogs off Newfoundland, and supposed he had veered ship and stood for Dead Man's Isle. So much for burying a man at sea without saying prayers over him."

The thunder-gust which had hitherto detained the company was now at an end. The cuckoo clock in the hall told midnight; every one pressed to depart, for seldom was such a late hour of the night trespassed on by these quiet burghers. As they sallied forth, they found the heavens once more serene. The storm which had lately obscured them had rolled away, and lay piled up in fleecy masses on the horizon, lighted up by the bright crescent of the moon, which looked like a little silver lamp hung up in a palace of clouds.

The dismal occurrence of the night, and the dismal narrations they had made, had left a superstitious feeling in every mind. They cast a fearful glance at the spot where the buccaneer had disappeared, almost expecting to see him sailing on his chest in the cool moonshine. The trembling rays glittered along the waters, but all was placid; and the current dimpled over the spot where he had gone down. The party huddled together in a little crowd as they repaired homewards; particularly when they passed a lonely field where a man had been murdered; and even the sexton, who had to complete his journey alone, though accustomed, one would think, to ghosts and goblins, went a long way round, rather than pass by his own churchyard.

Wolfert Webber had now carried home a fresh stock of stories and notions to ruminate upon. These accounts of pots of money and Spanish treasures, buried here and there and everywhere, about the rocks and bays of these wild shores, made him almost dizzy. "Blessed St.

Nicholas!" ejaculated he, half aloud, "is it not possible to come upon one of these golden hoards, and to make one's self rich in a twinkling? How hard that I must go on delving and delving, day in and day out, merely to make a morsel of bread, when one lucky stroke of a spade might enable me to ride in my carriage for the rest of my life!"

As he turned over in his thoughts all that had been told of the singular adventure of the negro fisherman, his imagination gave a totally different complexion to the tale. He saw in the gang of red-caps nothing but a crew of pirates burying their spoils, and his cupidity was once more awakened by the possibility of at length getting on the traces of some of this lurking wealth. Indeed, his infected fancy tinged everything with gold. He felt like the greedy inhabitant of Bagdad, when his eyes had been greased with the magic ointment of the dervise, that gave him to see all the treasures of the earth. Caskets of buried jewels, chests of ingots, and barrels of outlandish coins, seemed to court him from their concealments, and supplicate him to relieve them from their untimely graves.

On making private inquiries about the grounds said to be haunted by Father Red-cap, he was more and more confirmed in his surmise. He learned that the place had several times been visited by experienced money-diggers, who had heard black Sam's story, though none of them had met with success. On the contrary, they had always been dogged with ill-luck of some kind or other, in consequence, as Wolfert concluded, of not going to work at the proper time, and with the proper ceremonials. The last attempt had been made by Cobus Quackenbos, who dug for a whole night, and met with incredible difficulty, for as fast as he threw one shovelful of earth out of the hole, two were thrown in by invisible hands. He succeeded so far, however, as to uncover an iron chest, when there was a terrible roaring, ramping, and raging of uncouth figures about the hole, and at length a shower of blows, dealt by invisible cudgels, fairly belabored him off the forbidden ground. This Cobus Quackenbos had declared on his death-bed, so that there could not be any doubt of it. He was a man that had devoted many years of his life to money-digging, and it was thought would have ultimately succeeded, had he not died recently of a brain-fever in the almshouse.

Wolfert Webber was now in a worry of trepidation and impatience; fearful lest some rival adventurer should get a scent of the buried gold. He determined privately to seek out the black fisherman, and get him to serve as guide to the place where he had witnessed the mysterious scene of interment. Sam was easily found; for he was one of those old habitual beings that live about a neighborhood until they wear themselves a place in the public mind, and become, in a manner, public characters. There was not an unlucky urchin about town that did not know Sam the fisherman, and think that he had a right to play his tricks upon the old negro. Sam had led an amphibious life for more than half a century, about the shores of the bay, and the fishing-grounds of the Sound. He passed the greater part of his time on and in the water, particularly about Hell Gate; and might have been taken, in bad weather, for one of the hobgoblins that used to haunt that strait. There would he be seen, at all times, and in all weathers; sometimes in his skiff, anchored among the eddies, or prowling like a shark about some wreck, where the fish are supposed to be most abundant. Sometimes seated on a rock from hour to hour, looking, in the mist and drizzle, like a solitary heron watching for its prey. He was well acquainted with every hole and corner of the Sound; from the Wallabout to Hell Gate, and from Hell Gate unto the Devil's Stepping-Stones; and it was even affirmed that he knew all the fish in the river by their Christian names.

Wolfert found him at his cabin, which was not much larger than a tolerable dog-house. It was rudely constructed of fragments of wrecks and drift-wood, and built on the rocky shore, at the root of the old fort, just about what at present forms the point of the Battery. A "most ancient and fishlike smell" pervaded the place. Oars, paddles, and fishing-rods were leaning against the wall of the fort; a net was spread on the sand to dry; a skiff was drawn up on the beach; and at the door of his cabin was Mud Sam himself, indulging in the true negro luxury of sleeping in the sunshine.

Many years had passed away since the time of Sam's youthful adventure, and the snows of many a winter had grizzled the knotty wool upon his head. He perfectly recollected the circumstances, however, for he had often been called upon to relate them, though in his version of the story he differed in many points from Peechy Prauw; as is not unfrequently the case with authentic historians. As to the subsequent researches of money-diggers, Sam knew nothing about them; they were matters quite out of his line; neither did the cautious Wolfert care to disturb his thoughts on that point. His only wish was to secure the old fisherman as a pilot to the spot; and this was readily effected. The long time that had intervened since his nocturnal adventure had effaced all Sam's awe of the place, and the promise of a trifling reward roused him at once from his sleep and his sunshine.

The tide was adverse to making the expedition by water, and Wolfert was too impatient to get to the land of promise to wait for its turning; they set off, therefore, by land. A walk of four or five miles brought them to the edge of the wood, which at that time covered the greater part of the eastern side of the island. It was just beyond the pleasant region of Bloomen-dael. Here they struck into a long lane, straggling among trees and bushes, very much overgrown with weeds and mullein-stalks, as if but seldom used, and so completely overshadowed as to en-joy but a kind of twilight. Wild vines entangled the trees and flaunted in their faces; brambles and briers caught their clothes as they passed; the garter-snake glided across their path; the spotted toad hopped and waddled before them, and the restless cat-bird mewed at them from every thicket. Had Wolfert Webber been deeply read in romantic leg-end, he might have fancied himself entering upon forbidden, en-chanted ground; or that these were some of the guardians set to keep watch upon buried treasure. As it was, the loneliness of the place, and the wild stories connected with it, had their effect upon his mind.

On reaching the lower end of the lane, they found themselves near the shore of the Sound in a kind of amphitheatre, surrounded by forest-trees. The area had once been a grass-plot, but was now shagged with briers and rank weeds. At one end, and just on the river bank, was a ruined building, little better than a heap of rubbish, with a stack of chimneys rising like a solitary tower out of the centre. The current of the Sound rushed along just below it; with wildly grown trees drooping their branches into its waves.

Wolfert had not a doubt that this was the haunted house of Father Red-cap, and called to mind the story of Peechy Prauw. The evening was approaching, and the light falling dubiously among the woody places, gave a melancholy tone to the scene, well calculated to foster any lurking feeling of awe or superstition. The night-hawk, wheeling about in the highest regions of the air, emitted his peevish, boding cry. The woodpecker gave a lonely tap now and then on some hollow tree, and the fire-bird* streamed by them with his deep-red plumage.

They now came to an enclosure that had once been a garden. It ex-tended along the foot of a rocky ridge, but was little better than a wilderness of weeds, with here and there a matted rose-bush, or a peach or plum tree grown wild and ragged and covered with moss. At the lower end of the garden they passed a kind of vault in the side of a bank, facing the water. It had the look of a root-house. The door, though decayed, was still strong, and appeared to have been recently patched up. Wolfert pushed it open. It gave a harsh grating upon its hinges, and striking against something like a box, a rattling sound en-sued, and a skull rolled on the floor. Wolfert drew back shuddering, but was reassured on being informed by the negro that this was a family vault, belonging to one of the old Dutch families that owned this

---

* Orchard oriole.

estate; an assertion corroborated by the sight of coffins of various sizes piled within. Sam had been familiar with all these scenes when a boy, and now knew that he could not be far from the place of which they were in quest.

They now made their way to the water's edge, scrambling along ledges of rocks that overhung the waves, and obliged often to hold by shrubs and grape-vines to avoid slipping into the deep and hurried stream. At length they came to a small cove, or rather indent of the shore. It was protected by steep rocks, and overshadowed by a thick copse of oaks and chestnuts, so as to be sheltered and almost concealed. The beach shelved gradually within the cove, but the current swept deep, and black, and rapid, along its jutting points. The negro paused, raised his remnant of a hat, and scratched his grizzled poll for a moment, as he regarded this nook; then suddenly clapping his hands, he stepped exultingly forward, and pointed to a large iron ring, stapled firmly in the rock, just where a broad shelf of stone furnished a commodious landing-place. It was the very spot where the red-caps had landed. Years had changed the more perishable features of the scene; but rock and iron yield slowly to the influence of time. On looking more closely, Wolfert remarked three crosses cut in the rock just above the ring, which had no doubt some mysterious signification. Old Sam now readily recognized the overhanging rock under which his skiff had been sheltered during the thunder-gust. To follow up the course which the midnight gang had taken, however, was a harder task. His mind had been so much taken up on that eventful occasion by the persons of the drama, as to pay but little attention to the scenes; and these places look so different by night and day. After wandering about for some time, however, they came to an opening among the trees which Sam thought resembled the place. There was a ledge of rock of moderate height like a wall on one side, which he thought might be the very ridge whence he had overlooked the diggers. Wolfert examined it narrowly, and at length discovered three crosses similar to those on the above ring, cut deeply into the face of the rock, but nearly obliterated by moss that had grown over them. His heart leaped with joy, for he doubted not they were the private marks of the buccaneers. All now that remained was to ascertain the precise spot where the treasure lay buried; for otherwise he might dig at random in the neighborhood of the crosses, without coming upon the spoils, and he had already had enough of such profitless labor. Here, however, the old negro was perfectly at a loss, and indeed perplexed him by a variety of opinions; for his recollections were all confused. Sometimes he declared it must have been at the foot of a mulberry-tree hard by; then beside a great white stone;

then under a small green knoll, a short distance from the ledge of rocks; until at length Wolfert became as bewildered as himself.

The shadows of evening were now spreading themselves over the woods, and rock and tree began to mingle together. It was evidently too late to attempt anything further at present; and, indeed, Wolfert had come unprovided with implements to prosecute his researches. Satisfied, therefore, with having ascertained the place, he took note of all its landmarks, that he might recognize it again, and set out on his return homewards, resolved to prosecute this golden enterprise without delay.

The leading anxiety which had hitherto absorbed every feeling, being now in some measure appeased, fancy began to wander, and to conjure up a thousand shapes and chimeras as he returned through this haunted region. Pirates hanging in chains seemed to swing from every tree, and he almost expected to see some Spanish Don, with his throat cut from ear to ear, rising slowly out of the ground, and shaking the ghost of a money-bag.

Their way back lay through the desolate garden, and Wolfert's nerves had arrived at so sensitive a state that the flitting of a bird, the rustling of a leaf, or the falling of a nut, was enough to startle him. As they entered the confines of the garden, they caught sight of a figure at a distance advancing slowly up one of the walks, and bending under the weight of a burden. They paused and regarded him attentively. He wore what appeared to be a woollen cap, and, still more alarming, of a most sanguinary red.

The figure moved slowly on, ascended the bank, and stopped at the very door of the sepulchral vault. Just before entering it he looked around. What was the affright of Wolfert when he recognized the grizzly visage of the drowned buccaneer! He uttered an ejaculation of horror. The figure slowly raised his iron fist, and shook it with a terrible menace. Wolfert did not pause to see any more, but hurried off as fast as his legs could carry him, nor was Sam slow in following at his heels, having all his ancient terrors revived. Away, then, did they scramble through bush and brake, horribly frightened at every bramble that tugged at their skirts, nor did they pause to breathe, until they had blundered their way through this perilous wood, and fairly reached the high-road to the city.

Several days elapsed before Wolfert could summon courage enough to prosecute the enterprise, so much had he been dismayed by the apparition, whether living or dead, of the grisly buccaneer. In the meantime, what a conflict of mind did he suffer! He neglected all his concerns, was moody and restless all day, lost his appetite, wandered in his thoughts and words, and committed a thousand blunders. His rest was broken; and when he fell asleep, the nightmare, in shape of a huge money-bag, sat squatted upon his breast. He babbled about incalculable sums; fancied himself engaged in money-digging; threw the bed-clothes right and left, in the idea that he was shovelling away the dirt; groped under the bed in quest of the treasure, and lugged forth, as he supposed, an inestimable pot of gold.

Dame Webber and her daughter were in despair at what they conceived a returning touch of insanity. There are two family oracles, one or other of which Dutch housewives consult in all cases of great doubt and perplexity—the dominie and the doctor. In the present instance they repaired to the doctor. There was at that time a little dark mouldy man of medicine, famous among the old wives of the Manhattoes for his skill, not only in the healing art, but in all matters of strange and mysterious nature. His name was Dr. Knipperhausen, but he was more commonly known by the appellation of the High-German Doctor.* To him did the poor woman repair for counsel and assistance touching the mental vagaries of Wolfert Webber.

·They found the doctor seated in his little study, clad in his dark camlet robe of knowledge, with his black velvet cap; after the manner of Boorhaave, Van Helmont, and other medical sages; a pair of green spectacles set in black horn upon his clubbed nose, and poring over a German folio that reflected back the darkness of his physiognomy. The doctor listened to their statement of the symptoms of Wolfert's malady with profound attention; but when they came to mention his raving about buried money, the little man pricked up his ears. Alas, poor women! they little knew the aid they had called in.

Dr. Knipperhausen had been half his life engaged in seeking the short cuts to fortune, in quest of which so many a long lifetime is wasted. He had passed some years of his youth among the Harz mountains of Germany, and had derived much valuable instruction from the miners, touching the mode of seeking treasure buried in the earth. He had prosecuted his studies also under a travelling sage who united the mysteries of medicine with magic and legerdemain. His mind therefore had become stored with all kinds of mystic lore: he had dabbled a little in astrology, alchemy, divination; knew how to detect stolen money, and to tell where springs of water lay hidden; in a word, by the dark nature of his knowledge he had acquired the name of the High-German Doctor, which is pretty nearly equivalent to that of necromancer. The

* The same, no doubt, of whom mention is made in the history of Dolph Heyliger.

doctor had often heard rumors of treasure being buried in various parts of the island, and had long been anxious to get on the traces of it. No sooner were Wolfert's waking and sleeping vagaries confided to him, than he beheld in them the confirmed symptoms of a case of money-digging, and lost no time in probing it to the bottom. Wolfert had long been sorely oppressed in mind by the golden secret, and as a family physician is a kind of father confessor, he was glad of any opportunity of unburdening himself. So far from curing, the doctor caught the malady from his patient. The circumstances unfolded to him awakened all his cupidity: he had not a doubt of money being buried somewhere in the neighborhood of the mysterious crosses, and offered to join Wolfert in the search. He informed him that much secrecy and caution must be observed in enterprises of that kind; that money is only to be digged for at night; with certain forms and ceremonies, and burning of drugs, the repeating of mystic words; and above all, that the seekers must first be provided with a divining rod, which had the wonderful property of pointing to the very spot on the surface of the earth under which treasure lay hidden. As the doctor had given much of his mind to these matters, he charged himself with all the necessary preparations, and, as the quarter of the moon was propitious, he undertook to have the divining rod ready by a certain night.*

---

* The following note was found appended to this passage in the handwriting of Mr. Knickerbocker. "There has been much written against the divining rod by those light minds who are ever ready to scoff at the mysteries of nature; but I fully join with Dr. Knipperhausen in giving it my faith. I shall not insist upon its efficacy in discovering the concealment of stolen goods, the boundary stones of fields, the traces of robbers and murderers, or even the existence of subterraneous springs and streams of water: albeit, I think these properties not to be readily discredited; but of its potency in discovering veins of precious metal, and hidden sums of money and jewels, I have not the least doubt. Some said that the rod turned only in the hands of persons who had been born in particular months of the year; hence astrologers had recourse to planetary influence when they would procure a talisman. Others declared that the properties of the rod were either an effect of chance, or the fraud of the holder, or the work of the devil. Thus saith the reverend father Gaspard Sebett in his Treatise on Magic: 'Propter hæc et similia argumenta audacter ego promisero vim conversivam virgulæ bifurcatæ nequaquam naturalem esse, sed vel casu vel fraude virgulam tractantis vel ope diaboli,' etc.

"Georgius Agricola also was of opinion that it was a mere delusion of the devil to inveigle the avaricious and unwary into his clutches, and in his treatise 'de re Metallica,' lays particular stress on the mysterious words pronounced by those persons who employed the divining rod during his time. But I make not a doubt that the divining rod is one of those secrets of natural magic, the mystery of which is to be explained by the sympathies existing between physical things operated upon

Wolfert's heart leaped with joy at having met with so learned and able a coadjutor. Everything went on secretly, but swimmingly. The doctor had many consultations with his patient, and the good woman of the household lauded the comforting effect of his visits. In the meantime the wonderful divining rod, that great key to nature's secrets, was duly prepared. The doctor had thumbed over all his books of knowledge for the occasion; and the black fisherman was engaged to take them in his skiff to the scene of enterprise; to work with spade and pickaxe in unearthing the treasure; and to freight his bark with the weighty spoils they were certain of finding.

At length the appointed night arrived for this perilous undertaking. Before Wolfert left his home he counselled his wife and daughter to go to bed, and feel no alarm if he should not return during the night. Like reasonable women, on being told not to feel alarm they fell immediately into a panic. They saw at once by his manner that something unusual was in agitation; all their fears about the unsettled state of his mind were revived with tenfold force: they hung about him, entreating him not to expose himself to the night air, but all in vain. When once Wolfert was mounted on his hobby, it was no easy matter to get him out of the saddle. It was a clear starlight night, when he issued out of the portal of the Webber palace. He wore a large flapped hat tied under the chin with a handkerchief of his daughter's, to secure him from the night damp, while Dame Webber threw her long red cloak about his shoulders, and fastened it round his neck.

The doctor had been no less carefully armed and accoutred by his housekeeper, the vigilant Frau Ilsy; and sallied forth in his camlet robe by way of surcoat; his black velvet cap under his cocked hat, a thick clasped book under his arm, a basket of drugs and dried herbs in one hand, and in the other the miraculous rod of divination.

The great church-clock struck ten as Wolfert and the doctor passed by the churchyard, and the watchman bawled in a hoarse voice a long and doleful "All's well!" A deep sleep had already fallen upon this primitive burgh: nothing disturbed this awful silence, excepting now and then the bark of some poor profligate night-walking dog, or the serenade of some romantic cat. It is true, Wolfert fancied more than

---

by the planets, and rendered efficacious by the strong faith of the individual. Let the divining rod be properly gathered at the proper time of the moon, cut into the proper form, used with the proper ceremonies, and with a perfect faith in its efficacy, and I can confidently recommend it to my fellow-citizens as an infallible means of discovering the places on the Island of the Manhattoes where treasure hath been buried in the olden time. D.K."

once that he heard the sound of a stealthy footfall at a distance behind them; but it might have been merely the echo of their own steps along the quiet streets. He thought also at one time that he saw a tall figure skulking after them—stopping when they stopped, and moving on as they proceeded; but the dim and uncertain lamp-light threw such vague gleams and shadows, that this might all have been mere fancy.

They found the old fisherman waiting for them, smoking his pipe in the stern of the skiff, which was moored just in front of his little cabin. A pickaxe and spade were lying in the bottom of the boat, with a dark lantern, and a stone bottle of good Dutch courage, in which honest Sam no doubt put even more faith than Dr. Knipperhausen in his drugs.

Thus then did these three worthies embark in their cockle-shell of a skiff upon this nocturnal expedition, with a wisdom and valor equalled only by the three wise men of Gotham, who adventured to sea in a bowl. The tide was rising and running rapidly up the Sound. The current bore them along, almost without the aid of an oar. The profile of the town lay all in shadow. Here and there a light feebly glimmered from some sick-chamber, or from the cabin-window of some vessel at anchor in the stream. Not a cloud obscured the deep starry firmament, the lights of which wavered on the surface of the placid river; and a shooting meteor, streaking its pale course in the very direction they were taking, was interpreted by the doctor into a most propitious omen.

In a little while they glided by the point of Corlaer's Hook with the rural inn which had been the scene of such night adventures. The family had retired to rest, and the house was dark and still. Wolfert felt a chill pass over him as they passed the point where the buccaneer had disappeared. He pointed it out to Dr. Knipperhausen. While regarding it, they thought they saw a boat actually lurking at the very place; but the shore cast such a shadow over the border of the water that they could discern nothing distinctly. They had not proceeded far when they heard the low sounds of distant oars, as if cautiously pulled. Sam plied his oars with redoubled vigor, and knowing all the eddies and currents of the stream, soon left their followers, if such they were, far astern. In a little while they stretched across Turtle Bay and Kip's Bay, then shrouded themselves in the deep shadows of Manhattan shore, and glided swiftly along, secure from observation. At length the negro shot his skiff into a little cove, darkly embowered by trees, and made it fast to the well-known iron ring. They now landed, and lighting the lantern, gathered their various implements and proceeded slowly through the bushes. Every sound startled them, even that of their own footsteps among the dry leaves; and the hooting of a screech-owl, from the shattered chimney of the neighboring ruin, made their blood run cold.

In spite of all Wolfert's caution in taking note of the landmarks, it was some time before they could find the open place among the trees, where the treasure was supposed to be buried. At length they came to the ledge of rock; and on examining its surface by the aid of the lantern, Wolfert recognized the three mystic crosses. Their hearts beat quick, for the momentous trial was at hand that was to determine their hopes.

The lantern was now held by Wolfert Webber, while the doctor produced the divining rod. It was a forked twig, one end of which was grasped firmly in each hand, while the centre, forming the stem, pointed perpendicularly upwards. The doctor moved this wand about, within a certain distance of the earth, from place to place, but for some time without any effect, while Wolfert kept the light of the lantern turned full upon it, and watched it with the most breathless interest. At length the rod began slowly to turn. The doctor grasped it with greater earnestness, his hands trembling with the agitation of his mind. The wand continued to turn gradually, until at length the stem had reversed its position, and pointed perpendicularly downward, and remained pointing to one spot as fixedly as the needle to the pole.

"This is the spot!" said the doctor, in an almost inaudible tone.

Wolfert's heart was in his throat.

"Shall I dig?" said the negro, grasping the spade.

"Pots tausend, no!" replied the little doctor, hastily. He now ordered his companions to keep close by him, and to maintain the most inflexible silence. That certain precautions must be taken and ceremonies used to prevent the evil spirits which kept about buried treasure from doing them any harm. He then drew a circle about the place, enough to include the whole party. He next gathered dry twigs and leaves and made a fire, upon which he threw certain drugs and dried herbs which he had brought in his basket. A thick smoke rose, diffusing a potent odor, savoring marvellously of brimstone and assafœtida, which, however grateful it might be to the olfactory nerves of spirits, nearly strangled poor Wolfert, and produced a fit of coughing and wheezing that made the whole grove resound. Dr. Knipperhausen then unclasped the volume which he had brought under his arm, which was printed in red and black characters in German text. While Wolfert held the lantern, the doctor, by the aid of his spectacles, read off several forms of conjuration in Latin and German. He then ordered Sam to seize the pickaxe and proceed to work. The close-bound soil gave obstinate signs of not having been disturbed for many a year. After having picked his way through the surface, Sam came to a bed of sand and gravel, which he threw briskly to right and left with the spade.

"Hark!" said Wolfert, who fancied he heard a trampling among the dry leaves, and a rustling through the bushes. Sam paused for a moment, and they listened. No footstep was near. The bat flitted by them in silence; a bird, roused from its roost by the light which glared up among the trees, flew circling about the flame. In the profound stillness of the woodland, they could distinguish the current rippling along the rocky shore, and the distant murmuring and roaring of Hell Gate.

The negro continued his labors, and had already digged a considerable hole. The doctor stood on the edge, reading formulæ every now and then from his black-letter volume, or throwing more drugs and herbs upon the fire; while Wolfert bent anxiously over the pit, watching every stroke of the spade. Any one witnessing the scene thus lighted up by fire, lantern, and the reflection of Wolfert's red mantle, might have mistaken the little doctor for some foul magician, busied in his incantations, and the grizzly-headed negro for some swart goblin, obedient to his commands.

· At length the spade of the fisherman struck upon something that sounded hollow. The sound vibrated to Wolfert's heart. He struck his spade again.—

" 'Tis a chest," said Sam.

"Full of gold, I'll warrant it!" cried Wolfert, clasping his hands with rapture.

Scarcely had he uttered the words when a sound from above caught his ear. He cast up his eyes, and lo! by the expiring light of the fire he beheld, just over the disk of the rock, what appeared to be the grim visage of the drowned buccaneer, grinning hideously down upon him.

Wolfert gave a loud cry, and let fall the lantern. His panic communicated itself to his companions. The negro leaped out of the hole; the doctor dropped his book and basket, and began to pray in German. All was horror and confusion. The fire was scattered about, the lantern extinguished. In their hurry-scurry they ran against and confounded one another. They fancied a legion of hobgoblins let loose upon them, and that they saw, by the fitful gleams of the scattered embers, strange figures, in red caps, glibbering and ramping around them. The doctor ran one way, the negro another, and Wolfert made for the water side. As he plunged struggling onwards through brush and brake, he heard the tread of some one in pursuit. He scrambled frantically forward. The footsteps gained upon him. He felt himself grasped by his cloak, when suddenly his pursuer was attacked in turn; a fierce fight and struggle ensued—a pistol was discharged that lit up rock and bush for a second, and showed two figures grappling together—all was then darker than ever. The contest continued—the combatants clinched each other, and panted and groaned, and rolled among the rocks. There was snarling and growling as of a cur, mingled with curses, in which Wolfert fancied he could recognize the voice of the buccaneer. He would fain have fled, but he was on the brink of a precipice, and could go no farther.

Again the parties were on their feet; again there was a tugging and struggling, as if strength alone could decide the combat, until one was precipitated from the brow of the cliff, and sent headlong into the deep stream that whirled below. Wolfert heard the plunge, and a kind of strangling, bubbling murmur, but the darkness of the night hid every- thing from him, and the swiftness of the current swept everything in- stantly out of hearing. One of the combatants was disposed of, but whether friend or foe, Wolfert could not tell, nor whether they might not both be foes. He heard the survivor approach, and his terror re- vived. He saw, where the profile of the rocks rose against the horizon, a human form advancing. He could not be mistaken: it must be the buccaneer. Whither should he fly!—a precipice was on one side—a murderer on the other. The enemy approached—he was close at hand. Wolfert attempted to let himself down the face of the cliff. His cloak caught in a thorn that grew on the edge. He was jerked from off his feet, and held dangling in the air, half-choked by the string with which his careful wife had fastened the garment around his neck. Wolfert thought his last moment was arrived; already had he com- mitted his soul to St. Nicholas, when the string broke, and he tumbled down the bank, bumping from rock to rock, and bush to bush, and leaving the red cloak fluttering like a bloody banner in the air.

It was a long while before Wolfert came to himself. When he opened his eyes, the ruddy streaks of morning were already shooting up the sky. He found himself grievously battered, and lying in the bottom of a boat. He attempted to sit up, but was too sore and stiff to move. A voice requested him in friendly accents to lie still. He turned his eyes towards the speaker: it was Dirk Waldron. He had dogged the party, at the earnest request of Dame Webber and her daughter, who, with the laudable curiosity of their sex, had pried into the secret consulta- tions of Wolfert and the doctor. Dirk had been completely distanced in following the light skiff of the fisherman, and had just come in to res- cue the poor money-digger from his pursuer.

Thus ended this perilous enterprise. The doctor and Black Sam sev- erally found their way back to the Manhattoes, each having some dreadful tale of peril to relate. As to poor Wolfert, instead of returning in triumph laden with bags of gold, he was borne home on a shutter, followed by a rabble-rout of curious urchins. His wife and daughter saw the dismal pageant from a distance, and alarmed the neighborhood with their cries; they thought the poor man had suddenly settled the great debt of nature in one of his wayward moods. Finding him, however, still living, they had him speedily to bed, and a jury of old matrons of the neighborhood assembled, to determine how he should be doctored. The whole town was in a buzz with the story of the money-diggers. Many repaired to the scene of the previous night's adventures: but though they found the very place of the digging, they discovered nothing that compensated them for their trouble. Some say they found the fragments of an oaken chest, and an iron pot-lid, which savored strongly of hidden money; and that in the old family vault there were traces of bales and boxes; but this is all very dubious.

In fact, the secret of all this story has never to this day been discovered: whether any treasure were ever actually buried at that place; whether, if so, it were carried off at night by those who had buried it; or whether it still remains there under the guardianship of gnomes and spirits until it shall be properly sought for, is all matter of conjecture. For my part, I incline to the latter opinion; and make no doubt that great sums lie buried, both there and in other parts of this island and its neighborhood, ever since the times of the buccaneers and the Dutch colonists; and I would earnestly recommend the search after them to such of my fellow-citizens as are not engaged in any other speculations.

There were many conjectures formed, also, as to who and what was the strange man of the seas who had domineered over the little fraternity at Corlaer's Hook for a time, disappeared so strangely, and reappeared so fearfully.

Some supposed him a smuggler stationed at that place to assist his comrades in landing their goods among the rocky coves of the island. Others, that he was one of the ancient comrades of Kidd or Bradish, returned to convey away treasures formerly hidden in the vicinity. The only circumstance that throws anything like a vague light on this mysterious matter, is a report which prevailed of a strange foreign-built shallop, with much the look of a picaroon, having been seen hovering about the Sound for several days without landing or reporting herself, though boats were seen going to and from her at night; and that she was seen standing out of the mouth of the harbor, in the gray of the dawn, after the catastrophe of the money-diggers.

I must not omit to mention another report, also, which I confess is rather apocryphal, of the buccaneer, who was supposed to have been drowned, being seen before daybreak, with a lantern in his hand, seated astride of his great sea-chest, and sailing through Hell Gate, which just then began to roar and bellow with redoubled fury.

While all the gossip world was thus filled with talk and rumor, poor Wolfert lay sick and sorrowfully in his bed, bruised in body and sorely beaten down in mind. His wife and daughter did all they could to bind up his wounds, both corporal and spiritual. The good old dame never stirred from his bedside, where she sat knitting from morning till night; while his daughter busied herself about him with the fondest care. Nor did they lack assistance from abroad. Whatever may be said of the desertion of friends in distress, they had no complaint of the kind to make. Not an old wife of the neighborhood but abandoned her work to crowd to the mansion of Wolfert Webber, to inquire after his health, and the particulars of his story. Not one came moreover without her little pipkin of pennyroyal, sage, balm, or other herb tea, delighted at an opportunity of signalizing her kindness and her doctorship. What drenchings did not the poor Wolfert undergo, and all in vain! It was a moving sight to behold him wasting away day by day; growing thinner and thinner, and ghastlier and ghastlier, and staring with rueful visage from under an old patchwork counterpane, upon the jury of matrons kindly assembled to sigh and groan and look unhappy around him.

Dirk Waldron was the only being that seemed to shed a ray of sunshine into this house of mourning. He came in with a cheery look and manly spirit, and tried to reanimate the expiring heart of the poor money-digger, but it was all in vain. Wolfert was completely done over. If anything was wanting to complete his despair, it was a notice served upon him in the midst of his distress, that the corporation were about to run a new street through the very centre of his cabbage-garden. He now saw nothing before him but poverty and ruin; his last reliance, the garden of his forefathers, was to be laid waste, and what then was to become of his poor wife and child?

His eyes filled with tears as they followed the dutiful Amy out of the room one morning. Dirk Waldron was seated beside him; Wolfert grasped his hand, pointed after his daughter, and for the first time since his illness, broke the silence he had maintained.

"I am going!" said he, shaking his head feebly, "and when I am gone —my poor daughter——"

"Leave her to me, father!" said Dirk, manfully,—"I'll take care of her!"

Wolfert looked up in the face of the cheery, strapping youngster, and saw there was none better able to take care of a woman.

"Enough," said he,—"she is yours!—and now fetch me a lawyer—let me make my will and die."

The lawyer was brought—a dapper, bustling, round-headed little man, Roorback (or Rollebuck as it was pronounced) by name. At the sight of him the women broke into loud lamentations, for they looked upon the signing of a will as the signing of a death-warrant. Wolfert made a feeble motion for them to be silent. Poor Amy buried her face and her grief in the bed-curtain. Dame Webber resumed her knitting to hide her distress, which betrayed itself however in a pellucid tear, which trickled silently down, and hung at the end of her peaked nose; while the cat, the only unconcerned member of the family, played with the good dame's ball of worsted, as it rolled about the floor.

Wolfert lay on his back, his night-cap drawn over his forehead; his eyes closed; his whole visage the picture of death. He begged the lawyer to be brief, for he felt his end approaching, and that he had no time to lose. The lawyer nibbed his pen, spread out his paper, and prepared to write.

"I give and bequeath," said Wolfert, faintly, "my small farm——"

."What—all!" exclaimed the lawyer.

Wolfert half opened his eyes and looked upon the lawyer.

"Yes—all," said he.

"What! all that great patch of land with cabbages and sun-flowers, which the corporation is just going to run a main street through?"

"The same," said Wolfert, with a heavy sigh, and sinking back upon his pillow.

"I wish him joy that inherits it!" said the little lawyer, chuckling, and rubbing his hands involuntarily.

"What do you mean?" said Wolfert, again opening his eyes.

"That he'll be one of the richest men in the place!" cried little Rollebuck.

The expiring Wolfert seemed to step back from the threshold of existence: his eyes again lighted up; he raised himself in his bed, shoved back his red worsted night-cap, and stared broadly at the lawyer.

"You don't say so!" exclaimed he.

"Faith, but I do!" rejoined the other.—"Why, when that great field and that huge meadow come to be laid out in streets, and cut up into snug building-lots—why, whoever owns it need not pull off his hat to the patroon!"

"Say you so?" cried Wolfert, half thrusting one leg out of bed, "why, then I think I'll not make my will yet!"

To the surprise of everybody the dying man actually recovered. The vital spark, which had glimmered faintly in the socket, received fresh fuel from the oil of gladness, which the little lawyer poured into his soul. It once more burnt up into a flame.

Give physic to the heart, ye who would revive the body of a spirit-broken man! In a few days Wolfert left his room; in a few days more his table was covered with deeds, plans of streets, and building-lots. Little Rollebuck was constantly with him, his right-hand man and adviser; and instead of making his will, assisted in the more agreeable task of making his fortune. In fact, Wolfert Webber was one of those worthy Dutch burghers of the Manhattoes whose fortunes have been made, in a manner, in spite of themselves; who have tenaciously held on to their hereditary acres, raising turnips and cabbages about the skirts of the city, hardly able to make both ends meet, until the corporation has cruelly driven streets through their abodes, and they have suddenly awakened out of their lethargy, and, to their astonishment, found themselves rich men.

Before many months had elapsed, a great bustling street passed through the very centre of the Webber garden, just where Wolfert had dreamed of finding a treasure. His golden dream was accomplished; he did indeed find an unlooked-for source of wealth; for, when his paternal lands were distributed into building lots, and rented out to safe tenants, instead of producing a paltry crop of cabbages, they returned him an abundant crop of rent; insomuch that on quarter-day it was a goodly sight to see his tenants knocking at the door, from morning till night, each with a little round-bellied bag of money, a golden produce of the soil.

The ancient mansion of his forefathers was still kept up; but instead of being a little yellow-fronted Dutch house in a garden, it now stood boldly in the midst of a street, the grand home of the neighborhood; for Wolfert enlarged it with a wing on each side, and a cupola or tea-room on top, where he might climb up and smoke his pipe in hot weather; and in the course of time the whole mansion was overrun by the chubby-faced progeny of Amy Webber and Dirk Waldron.

As Wolfert waxed old, and rich, and corpulent, he also set up a great gingerbread-colored carriage, drawn by a pair of black Flanders mares with tails that swept the ground; and to commemorate the origin of his greatness, he had for his crest a full-blown cabbage painted on the pannels, with the pithy motto *Alles Kopf*, that is to say, ALL HEAD; meaning thereby that he had risen by sheer head-work.

To fill the measure of his greatness, in the fulness of time the renowned Ramm Rapelye slept with his fathers, and Wolfert Webber succeeded to the leather-bottomed arm-chair, in the inn-parlor at Corlaer's Hook; where he long reigned greatly honored and respected, insomuch that he was never known to tell a story without its being believed, nor to utter a joke without its being laughed at.

From Tales of a Traveller

THE ADVENTURE OF THE MASON

I was one evening seated in the balcony, enjoying the light breeze that came rustling along the side of the hill, among the tree-tops, when my humble historiographer Mateo, who was at my elbow, pointed out a spacious house, in an obscure street of the Albaycin, about which he related, as nearly as I can recollect, the following anecdote.

THERE was once upon a time a poor mason, or bricklayer, in Granada, who kept all the saints' days and holidays, and Saint Monday into the bargain, and yet, with all his devotion, he grew poorer and poorer, and could scarcely earn bread for his numerous family. One night he was roused from his first sleep by a knocking at his door. He opened it, and beheld before him a tall, meagre, cadaverous-looking priest.

"Hark ye, honest friend!" said the stranger; "I have observed that you are a good Christian, and one to be trusted; will you undertake a job this very night?"

"With all my heart, Señor Padre, on condition that I am paid accordingly."

"That you shall be; but you must suffer yourself to be blindfolded."

To this the mason made no objection. So, being hoodwinked, he was led by the priest through various rough lanes and winding passages, until they stopped before the portal of a house. The priest then applied a key, turned a creaking lock, and opened what sounded like a ponderous door. They entered, the door was closed and bolted, and the mason was conducted through an echoing corridor and a spacious hall to an interior part of the building. Here the bandage was removed from his eyes, and he found himself in a *patio*, or court, dimly lighted by a single lamp. In the centre was the dry basin of an old Moorish fountain, under which the priest requested him to form a small vault, bricks and mortar being at hand for the purpose. He accordingly worked all night, but without finishing the job. Just before daybreak the priest put a

---

I have deleted the innumerable, old-fashioned and unnecessary quotation marks that clutter the tale as it appears in *The Alhambra.*—C.N.

piece of gold into his hand, and having again blindfolded him, conducted him back to his dwelling.

"Are you willing," said he, "to return and complete your work?"

"Gladly, Señor Padre, provided I am so well paid."

"Well, then, to-morrow at midnight I will call again."

He did so, and the vault was completed.

"Now," said the priest, "you must help me to bring forth the bodies that are to be buried in this vault."

The poor mason's hair rose on his head at these words: he followed the priest, with trembling steps, into a retired chamber of the mansion, expecting to behold some ghastly spectacle of death, but was relieved on perceiving three or four portly jars standing in one corner. They were evidently full of money, and it was with great labor that he and the priest carried them forth and consigned them to their tomb. The vault was then closed, the pavement replaced, and all traces of the work were obliterated. The mason was again hoodwinked and led forth by a route different from that by which he had come. After they had wandered for a long time through a perplexed maze of lanes and alleys, they halted. The priest then put two pieces of gold into his hand: "Wait here," said he, "until you hear the cathedral bell toll for matins. If you presume to uncover your eyes before that time, evil will befall you": so saying, he departed. The mason waited faithfully, amusing himself by weighing the gold pieces in his hand, and clinking them against each other. The moment the cathedral bell rang its matin peal, he uncovered his eyes, and found himself on the banks of the Xenil, whence he made the best of his way home, and revelled with his family for a whole fortnight on the profits of his two nights' work; after which he was as poor as ever.

He continued to work a little, and pray a good deal, and keep saints' days and holidays, from year to year, while his family grew up as gaunt and ragged as a crew of gypsies. As he was seated one evening at the door of his hovel, he was accosted by a rich old curmudgeon, who was noted for owning many houses, and being a griping landlord. The man of money eyed him for a moment from beneath a pair of anxious shagged eyebrows.

"I am told, friend, that you are very poor."

"There is no denying the fact, señor,—it speaks for itself."

"I presume, then, that you will be glad of a job, and will work cheap."

"As cheap, my master, as any mason in Granada."

"That's what I want. I have an old house fallen into decay, which costs me more money than it is worth to keep it in repair, for nobody will live in it; so I must contrive to patch it up and keep it together at as small expense as possible."

The mason was accordingly conducted to a large deserted house that seemed going to ruin. Passing through several empty halls and chambers, he entered an inner court, where his eye was caught by an old Moorish fountain. He paused for a moment, for a dreaming recollection of the place came over him.

"Pray," said he, "who occupied this house formerly?"

"A pest upon him!" cried the landlord; "it was an old miserly priest, who cared for nobody but himself. He was said to be immensely rich, and, having no relations, it was thought he would leave all his treasures to the Church. He died suddenly, and the priests and friars thronged to take possession of his wealth, but nothing could they find but a few ducats in a leathern purse. The worst luck has fallen on me, for, since his death, the old fellow continues to occupy my house without paying rent, and there is no taking the law of a dead man. The people pretend to hear the clinking of gold all night in the chamber where the old priest slept, as if he were counting over his money, and sometimes a groaning and moaning about the court. Whether true or false, these stories have brought a bad name on my house, and not a tenant will remain in it."

"Enough," said the mason sturdily; "let me live in your house rent-free until some better tenant present, and I will engage to put it in repair, and to quiet the troubled spirit that disturbs it. I am a good Christian and a poor man, and am not to be daunted by the Devil himself, even though he should come in the shape of a big bag of money!"

The offer of the honest mason was gladly accepted; he moved with his family into the house, and fulfilled all his engagements. By little and little he restored it to its former state; the clinking of gold was no more heard at night in the chamber of the defunct priest, but began to be heard by day in the pocket of the living mason. In a word, he increased rapidly in wealth, to the admiration of all his neighbors, and became one of the richest men in Granada: he gave large sums to the Church, by way, no doubt, of satisfying his conscience, and never revealed the secret of the vault until on his death-bed to his son and heir.

From *The Alhambra*

LEGEND OF THE ARABIAN ASTROLOGER

Local Traditions

THE common people of Spain have an Oriental passion for story-telling, and are fond of the marvellous. They will gather round the doors of their cottages in summer evenings, or in the great cavernous chimney-corners of the *ventas* in the winter, and listen with insatiable delight to miraculous legends of saints, perilous adventures of travellers, and daring exploits of robbers and *contrabandistas*. The wild and solitary character of the country, the imperfect diffusion of knowledge, the scarceness of general topics of conversation, and the romantic adventurous life that every one leads in a land where travelling is yet in its primitive state, all contribute to cherish this love of oral narration, and to produce a strong infusion of the extravagant and incredible. There is no theme, however, more prevalent and popular than that of treasures buried by the Moors; it pervades the whole country. In traversing the wild sierras, the scenes of ancient foray and exploit, you cannot see a Moorish *atalaya*, or watch-tower, perched among the cliffs, or beetling above its rock-built village, but your muleteer, on being closely questioned, will suspend the smoking of his *cigarillo* to tell some tale of Moslem gold buried beneath its foundations; nor is there a ruined *alcazar* in a city but has its golden tradition, handed down from generation to generation among the poor people of the neighborhood.

These, like most popular fictions, have sprung from some scanty groundwork of fact. During the wars between Moor and Christian, which distracted this country for centuries, towns and castles were liable frequently and suddenly to change owners, and the inhabitants, during sieges and assaults, were fain to bury their money and jewels in the earth, or hide them in vaults and wells, as is often done at the present day in the despotic and belligerent countries of the East. At the time of the expulsion of the Moors also, many of them concealed their

---

I have included two chapters from *The Alhambra* which are prefatory to this tale.—C.N.

most precious effects, hoping that their exile would be but temporary, and that they would be enabled to return and retrieve their treasures at some future day. It is certain that from time to time hoards of gold and silver coin have been accidentally digged up, after a lapse of centuries, from among the ruins of Moorish fortresses and habitations; and it requires but a few facts of the kind to give birth to a thousand fictions.

The stories thus originating have generally something of an Oriental tinge, and are marked with that mixture of the Arabic and the Gothic which seems to me to characterize everything in Spain, and especially in its southern provinces. The hidden wealth is always laid under magic spell, and secured by charm and talisman. Sometimes it is guarded by uncouth monsters or fiery dragons, sometimes by enchanted Moors, who sit by it in armor, with drawn swords, but motionless as statues, maintaining a sleepless watch for ages.

The Alhambra of course, from the peculiar circumstances of its history, is a stronghold for popular fictions of the kind; and various relics, digged up from time to time, have contributed to strengthen them. At one time an earthen vessel was found containing Moorish coins and the skeletons of a cock, which, according to the opinion of certain shrewd inspectors, must have been buried alive. At another time a vessel was dug up containing a great *scarabæus* or beetle of baked clay, covered with Arabic inscriptions, which was pronounced a prodigious amulet of occult virtues. In this way the wits of the ragged brood who inhabit the Alhambra have been set wool-gathering, until there is not a hall, nor tower, nor vault, of the old fortress, that has not been made the scene of some marvellous tradition. Having, I trust, in the preceding papers made the reader in some degree familiar with the localities of the Alhambra, I shall now launch out more largely into the wonderful legends connected with it, and which I have diligently wrought into shape and form, from various legendary scraps and hints picked up in the course of my perambulations,—in the same manner that an antiquary works out a regular historical document from a few scattered letters of an almost defaced inscription.

If anything in these legends should shock the faith of the over-scrupulous reader, he must remember the nature of the place and make due allowances. He must not expect here the same laws of probability that govern commonplace scenes and every-day life; he must remember that he treads the halls of an enchanted palace, and that all is "haunted ground."

The House of the Weathercock

ON the brow of the lofty hill of the Albaycin, the highest part of Granada, and which rises from the narrow valley of the Darro, directly opposite to the Alhambra, stands all that is left of what was once a royal palace of the Moors. It has, in fact, fallen into such obscurity, that it cost me much trouble to find it, though aided in my researches by the sagacious and all-knowing Mateo Ximenes. This edifice has borne for centuries the name of "The House of the Weathercock" (La Casa del Gallo de Viento), from a bronze figure on one of its turrets, in ancient times, of a warrior on horseback, and turning with every breeze. This weathercock was considered by the Moslems of Granada, a portentous talisman. According to some traditions, it bore the following Arabic inscription:

.

>Calet el Bedici Aben Habuz,
>Quidet ehahet Lindabuz.

Which has been rendered into Spanish:

>Dice el sabio Aben Habuz,
>Que asi se defiende el Anduluz.

And into English:

>In this way, says Aben Habuz the Wise,
>Andaluz guards against surprise.

This Aben Habuz, according to some of the Moorish chronicles, was a captain in the invading army of Taric, one of the conquerors of Spain, who left him as Alcayde of Granada. He is supposed to have intended this effigy as a perpetual warning to the Moslems of Andaluz, that, surrounded by foes, their safety depended upon their being always on their guard and ready for the field.

Others, among whom is the Christian historian Marmol, affirm "Badis Aben Habus" to have been a Moorish Sultan of Granada, and that the weathercock was intended as a perpetual admonition of the instability of Moslem power, bearing the following words in Arabic:

"Thus Ibn Habus al badise predicts Andalus shall one day vanish and pass away."*

Another version of this portentous inscription is given by a Moslem historian, on the authority of Sidi Hasan, a faquir who flourished about the time of Ferdinand and Isabella, and who was present at the taking down of the weathercock, when the old Kassaba was undergoing repairs.

" 'I saw it," says the venerable faquir, "with my own eyes; it was of a heptagonal shape, and had the following inscription in verse:

" 'The palace at fair Granda presents a talisman.'

" 'The horseman, though a solid body, turns with every wind.'

" 'This to a wise man reveals a mystery. In a little while comes a calamity to ruin both the palace and its owner.' "

In effect it was not long after this meddling with the portentous weathercock that the following event occurred. As old Muley Abul Hassan, the king of Granada, was seated under a sumptuous pavilion, reviewing his troops, who paraded before him in armor of polished steel and gorgeous silken robes, mounted on fleet steeds, and equipped with swords, spears, and shields embossed with gold and silver,—suddenly a tempest was seen hurrying from the southwest. In a little while black clouds overshadowed the heavens and burst forth with a deluge of rain. Torrents came roaring down from the mountains, bringing with them rocks and trees; the Darro overflowed its banks; mills were swept away, bridges destroyed, gardens laid waste; the inundation rushed into the city, undermining houses, drowning their inhabitants, and overflowing even the square of the Great Mosque. The people rushed in affright to the mosques to implore the mercy of Allah, regarding this uproar of the elements as the harbinger of dreadful calamities; and, indeed, according to the Arabian historian Al Makkari, it was but a type and prelude of the direful war which ended in the downfall of the Moslem kingdom of Granada.

I have thus given historic authorities sufficient to show the portentous mysteries connected with the House of the Weathercock, and its talismanic horseman.

I now proceed to relate still more surprising things about Aben Habuz and his palace; for the truth of which, should any doubt be entertained, I refer the dubious reader to Mateo Ximenes and his fellow-historiographers of the Alhambra.

---

* Marmol, "Hist. Rebellion of the Moors."

IN old times, many hundred years ago, there was a Moorish king named Aben Habuz, who reigned over the kingdom of Granada. He was a retired conqueror—that is to say, one who, having in his more youthful days led a life of constant foray and depredation, now that he was grown feeble and superannuated, "languished for repose," and desired nothing more than to live at peace with all the world, to husband his laurels, and to enjoy in quiet the possessions he had wrested from his neighbors.

It so happened, however, that this most reasonable and pacific old monarch had young rivals to deal with; princes full of his early passion for fame and fighting, and who were disposed to call him to account for the scores he had run up with their fathers. Certain distant districts of his own territories, also, which during the days of his vigor he had treated with a high hand, were prone, now that he languished for repose, to rise in rebellion and threaten to invest him in his capital. Thus he had foes on every side; and as Granada is surrounded by wild and craggy mountains, which hide the approach of an enemy, the unfortunate Aben Habuz was kept in a constant state of vigilance and alarm, not knowing in what quarter hostilities might break out.

It was in vain that he built watch-towers on the mountains, and stationed guards at every pass with orders to make fires by night and smoke by day, on the approach of an enemy. His alert foes, baffling every precaution, would break out of some unthought-of defile, ravage his lands beneath his very nose, and then make off with prisoners and booty to the mountains. Was ever peaceable and retired conqueror in a more uncomfortable predicament?

While Aben Habuz was harassed by these perplexities and molestations, an ancient Arabian physician arrived at his court. His gray beard descended to his girdle, and he had every mark of extreme age, yet he had travelled almost the whole way from Egypt on foot, with no other aid than a staff, marked with hieroglyphics. His fame had preceded him. His name was Ibrahim Ebn Abu Ayub; he was said to have lived ever since the days of Mahomet, and to be the son of Abu Ayub, the last of the companions of the Prophet. He had, when a child, followed the conquering army of Amru into Egypt, where he had remained many years studying the dark sciences, and particularly magic, among the Egyptian priests.

It was, moreover, said that he had found out the secret of prolonging life, by means of which he had arrived to the great age of upwards of two centuries, though, as he did not discover the secret until well stricken in years, he could only perpetuate his gray hairs and wrinkles.

This wonderful old man was honorably entertained by the king, who, like most superannuated monarchs, began to take physicians into great favor. He would have assigned him an apartment in his palace, but the astrologer preferred a cave in the side of the hill which rises above the city of Granada, being the same on which the Alhambra has since been built. He caused the cave to be enlarged so as to form a spacious and lofty hall, with a circular hole at the top, through which, as through a well, he could see the heavens and behold the stars even at mid-day. The walls of this hall were covered with Egyptian hieroglyphics with cabalistic symbols, and with the figures of the stars in their signs. This hall he furnished with many implements, fabricated under his directions by cunning artificers of Granada, but the occult properties of which were known only to himself.

In a little while the sage Ibrahim became the bosom counsellor of the king, who applied to him for advice in every emergency. Aben Habuz was once inveighing against the injustice of his neighbors, and bewailing the restless vigilance he had to observe to guard himself against their invasions; when he had finished, the astrologer remained silent for a moment, and then replied, "Know, O king, that when I was in Egypt, I beheld a great marvel devised by a pagan priestess of old. On a mountain above the city of Borsa, and overlooking the great valley of the Nile, was a figure of a ram, and above it a figure of a cock, both of molten brass, and turning upon a pivot. Whenever the country was threatened with invasion, the ram would turn in the direction of the enemy, and the cock would crow; upon this the inhabitants of the city knew of the danger, and of the quarter from which it was approaching, and could take timely means to guard against it."

"God is great!" exclaimed the pacific Aben Habuz, "what a treasure would be such a ram to keep an eye upon these mountains around me; and then such a cock, to crow in time of danger! Allah Akbar! how securely I might sleep in my palace with such sentinels on the top!"

The astrologer waited until the ecstasies of the king had subsided, and then proceeded.

"After the victorious Amru (may he rest in peace!) had finished his conquest of Egypt, I remained among the priests of the land, studying the rites and ceremonies of their idolatrous faith, and seeking to make myself master of the hidden knowledge for which they are renowned. I was one day seated on the banks of the Nile, conversing with an ancient priest, when he pointed to the mighty pyramids which rose like mountains out of the neighboring desert. 'All that we can teach thee,' said he, 'is nothing to the knowledge locked up in those mighty piles. In the centre of the central pyramid is a sepulchral chamber, in which is enclosed the mummy of the high-priest who aided in rearing that stupendous pile; and with him is buried a wondrous book of knowledge, containing all the secrets of magic and art. This book was given to Adam after his fall, and was handed down from generation to generation to King Solomon the Wise, and by its aid he built the Temple of Jerusalem. How it came into the possession of the builder of the pyramids is known to Him alone who knows all things.'

"When I heard these words of the Egyptian priest, my heart burned to get possession of that book. I could command the services of many of the soldiers of our conquering army, and of a number of the native Egyptians. With these I set to work, and pierced the solid mass of the pyramid, until, after great toil, I came upon one of its interior and hidden passages. Following this up, and threading a fearful labyrinth, I penetrated into the very heart of the pyramids, even to the sepulchral chamber, where the mummy of the high-priest had lain for ages. I broke through the outer cases of the mummy, unfolded its many wrappers and bandages, and at length found the precious volume on its bosom. I seized it with a trembling hand, and groped my way out of the pyramid, leaving the mummy in its dark and silent sepulchre, there to await the final day of resurrection and judgment."

"Son of Abu Ayub," exclaimed Aben Habuz, "thou hast been a great traveller, and seen marvellous things; but of what avail to me is the secret of the pyramid, and the volume of knowledge of the wise Solomon?"

"This it is, O king! By the study of that book I am instructed in all magic arts, and can command the assistance of genii to accomplish my plans. The mystery of the Talisman of Borsa is therefore familiar to me, and such a talisman can I make, nay, one of greater virtues."

"O wise son of Abu Ayub," cried Aben Habuz, "better were such a talisman than all the watch-towers on the hills, and sentinels upon the borders. Give me such a safeguard, and the riches of my treasury are at thy command."

The astrologer immediately set to work to gratify the wishes of the monarch. He caused a great tower to be erected upon the top of the royal palace, which stood on the brow of the hill of the Albaycin. The tower was built of stones brought from Egypt, and taken, it is said, from one of the pyramids. In the upper part of the tower was a circular hall, with windows looking towards every point of the compass, and before each window was a table, on which was arranged, as on a chessboard, a mimic army of horse and foot, with the effigy of the potentate that ruled in that direction, all carved of wood. To each of these tables there was a small lance, no bigger than a bodkin, on which were engraved certain Chaldaic characters. This hall was kept constantly closed, by a gate of brass, with a great lock of steel, the key of which was in possession of the king.

On the top of the tower was a bronze figure of a Moorish horseman, fixed on a pivot, with a shield on one arm, and his lance elevated perpendicularly. The face of this horseman was towards the city, as if keeping guard over it; but if any foe were at hand, the figure would turn in that direction, and would level the lance as if for action.

When this talisman was finished, Aben Habuz was all impatient to try its virtues, and longed as ardently for an invasion as he had ever sighed after repose. His desire was soon gratified. Tidings were brought, early one morning, by the sentinel appointed to watch the tower, that the face of the bronze horseman was turned towards the mountains of Elvira, and that his lance pointed directly against the Pass of Lope.

"Let the drums and trumpets sound to arms, and all Granada be put on the alert," said Aben Habuz.

"O king," said the astrologer, "let not your city be disquieted, nor your warriors called to arms; we need no aid of force to deliver you from your enemies. Dismiss your attendants, and let us proceed alone to the secret hall of the tower."

The ancient Aben Habuz mounted the staircase of the tower, leaning on the arm of the still more ancient Ibrahim Ebn Abu Ayub. They unlocked the brazen door and entered. The window that looked towards the Pass of Lope was open. "In this direction," said the astrologer, "lies the danger; approach, O king, and behold the mystery of the table."

King Aben Habuz approached the seeming chess-board, on which were arranged the small wooden effigies, when, to his surprise, he perceived that they were all in motion. The horses pranced and curveted, the warriors brandished their weapons, and there was a faint sound of drums and trumpets, and the clang of arms, and neighing of steeds; but all no louder, nor more distinct, than the hum of the bee, or the summer-fly, in the drowsy ear of him who lies at noontide in the shade.

"Behold, O king," said the astrologer, "a proof that thy enemies are even now in the field. They must be advancing through yonder mountains, by the Pass of Lope. Would you produce a panic and confusion amongst them, and cause them to retreat without loss of life, strike these effigies with the but-end of this magic lance; would you cause bloody feud and carnage, strike with the point."

A livid streak passed across the countenance of Aben Habuz; he seized the lance with trembling eagerness; his gray beard wagged with exultation as he tottered toward the table: "Son of Abu Ayub," exclaimed he, in chuckling tone, "I think we will have a little blood!"

So saying, he thrust the magic lance into some of the pigmy effigies, and belabored others with the but-end, upon which the former fell as dead upon the board, and the rest, turning upon each other, began, pellmell, a chance-medley fight.

It was with difficulty the astrologer could stay the hand of the most pacific of monarchs, and prevent him from absolutely exterminating his foes. At length he prevailed upon him to leave the tower, and to send out scouts to the mountains by the Pass of Lope.

They returned with the intelligence that a Christian army had advanced through the heart of the Sierra, almost within sight of Granada, where a dissension had broken out among them; they had turned their weapons against each other, and after much slaughter had retreated over the border.

Aben Habuz was transported with joy on thus proving the efficacy of the talisman. "At length," said he, "I shall lead a life of tranquillity, and have all my enemies in my power. O wise son of Abu Ayub, what can I bestow on thee in reward for such a blessing?"

"The wants of an old man and a philosopher, O king, are few and simple; grant me but the means of fitting up my cave as a suitable hermitage, and I am content."

"How noble is the moderation of the truly wise!" exclaimed Aben Habuz, secretly pleased at the cheapness of the recompense. He summoned his treasurer, and bade him dispense whatever sums might be required by Ibrahim to complete and furnish his hermitage.

The astrologer now gave orders to have various chambers hewn out of the solid rock, so as to form ranges of apartments connected with his astrological hall; these he caused to be furnished with luxurious ottomans and divans, and the walls to be hung with the richest silks of Damascus. "I am an old man," said he, "and can no longer rest my bones on stone couches, and these damp walls require covering."

He had baths too constructed, and provided with all kinds of perfumes and aromatic oils. "For a bath," said he, "is necessary to counteract the rigidity of age, and to restore freshness and suppleness to the frame withered by study."

He caused the apartments to be hung with innumerable silver and crystal lamps, which he filled with a fragrant oil prepared according to a receipt discovered by him in the tombs of Egypt. This oil was perpetual in its nature, and diffused a soft radiance like the tempered light of day. "The light of the sun," said he, "is too garish and violent for the eyes of an old man, and the light of the lamp is more congenial to the studies of a philosopher."

The treasurer of King Aben Habuz groaned at the sums daily demanded to fit up this hermitage, and he carried his complaints to the king. The royal word, however, had been given; Aben Habuz shrugged his shoulders: "We must have patience," said he; "this old man has taken his idea of a philosophic retreat from the interior of the pyramids, and of the vast ruins of Egypt; but all things have an end, and so will the furnishing of his cavern."

The king was in the right; the hermitage was at length complete, and formed a sumptuous subterranean palace. The astrologer expressed himself perfectly content, and, shutting himself up, remained for three whole days buried in study. At the end of that time he appeared again before the treasurer. "One thing more is necessary," said he, "one trifling solace for the intervals of mental labor."

"O wise Ibrahim, I am bound to furnish everything necessary for thy solitude; what more dost thou require?"

"I would fain have a few dancing-women."

"Dancing-women!" echoed the treasurer, with surprise.

"Dancing-women," replied the sage, gravely; "and let them be young and fair to look upon; for the sight of youth and beauty is refreshing. A few will suffice, for I am a philosopher of simple habits and easily satisfied."

While the philosophic Ibrahim Ebn Abu Ayub passed his time thus sagely in his hermitage, the pacific Aben Habuz carried on furious campaigns in effigy in his tower. It was a glorious thing for an old man, like himself, of quiet habits, to have war made easy, and to be enabled to amuse himself in his chamber by brushing away whole armies like so many swarms of flies.

For a time he rioted in the indulgence of his humors, and even taunted and insulted his neighbors, to induce them to make incursions; but by degrees they grew wary from repeated disasters, until no one ventured to invade his territories. For many months the bronze horseman remained on the peace establishment, with his lance elevated in the air; and the worthy old monarch began to repine at the want of his accustomed sport, and to grow peevish at his monotonous tranquillity.

At length, one day, the talismanic horseman veered suddenly round, and lowering his lance, made a dead point towards the mountains of Gaudix. Aben Habuz hastened to his tower, but the magic table in that direction remained quiet. Not a single warrior was in motion. Perplexed at the circumstance, he sent forth a troop of horse to scour the mountains and reconnoitre. They returned after three days' absence.

"We have searched every mountain pass," said they, "but not a helm or a spear was stirring. All that we have found in the course of our foray was a Christian damsel of surpassing beauty, sleeping at noontide beside a fountain, whom we have brought away captive."

"A damsel of surpassing beauty!" exclaimed Aben Habuz, his eyes gleaming with animation; "let her be conducted into my presence."

The beautiful damsel was accordingly conducted into his presence. She was arrayed with all the luxury of ornament that had prevailed among the Gothic Spaniards at the time of the Arabian Conquest. Pearls of dazzling whiteness were entwined with her raven tresses; and jewels sparkled on her forehead, rivalling the lustre of her eyes. Around her neck was a golden chain, to which was suspended a silver lyre, which hung by her side.

The flashes of her dark refulgent eye were like sparks of fire on the withered, yet combustible, heart of Aben Habuz; the swimming voluptuousness of her gait made his senses reel. "Fairest of women," cried he, with rapture, "who and what art thou?"

"The daughter of one of the Gothic princes, who but lately ruled over this land. The armies of my father have been destroyed, as if by magic, among these mountains; he has been driven into exile, and his daughter is a captive."

"Beware, O king!" whispered Ibrahim Ebn Abu Ayub, "this may be one of those northern sorceresses of whom we have heard, who assume the most seductive forms to beguile the unwary. Methinks I read witchcraft in her eye, and sorcery in every movement. Doubtless this is the enemy pointed out by the talisman."

"Son of Abu Ayub," replied the king, "thou art a wise man, I grant, a conjurer for aught I know; but thou art little versed in the ways of woman. In that knowledge will I yield to no man; no, not to the wise Solomon himself, notwithstanding the number of his wives and concubines. As to this damsel, I see no harm in her; she is fair to look upon, and finds favor in my eyes."

"Hearken, O king!" replied the astrologer. "I have given thee many victories by means of my talisman, but have never shared any of the spoil. Give me then this stray captive, to solace me in my solitude with her silver lyre. If she be indeed a sorceress, I have counter spells that set her charms at defiance."

"What! more women!" cried Aben Habuz. "Hast thou not already dancing-women enough to solace thee?"

"Dancing-women have I, it is true, but no singing-women. I would fain have a little minstrelsy to refresh my mind when weary with the toils of study."

"A truce with thy hermit cravings," said the king, impatiently. "This damsel have I marked for my own. I see much comfort in her: even such comfort as David, the father of Solomon the Wise, found in the society of Abishag the Shunamite."

Further solicitations and remonstrances of the astrologer only pro-voked a more peremptory reply from the monarch, and they parted in high displeasure. The sage shut himself up in his hermitage to brood over his disappointment; ere he departed, however, he gave the king one more warning to beware of his dangerous captive. But where is the old man in love that will listen to counsel? Aben Habuz resigned himself to the full sway of his passion. His only study was how to render himself amiable in the eyes of the Gothic beauty. He had not youth to recom-mend him, it is true, but then he had riches; and when a lover is old, he is generally generous. The Zacatin of Granada was ransacked for the most precious merchandise of the East; silks, jewels, precious gems, ex-quisite perfumes, all that Asia and Africa yielded of rich and rare, were lavished upon the princess. All kinds of spectacles and festivities were devised for her entertainment; minstrelsy, dancing, tournaments, bull-fights;—Granada for a time was a scene of perpetual pageant. The Gothic princess regarded all this splendor with the air of one accus-tomed to magnificence. She received everything as a homage due to her rank, or rather to her beauty; for beauty is more lofty in its exactions even than rank. Nay, she seemed to take a secret pleasure in exciting the monarch to expenses that made his treasury shrink, and then treat-ing his extravagant generosity as a mere matter of course. With all his assiduity and munificence, also, the venerable lover could not flatter himself that he had made any impression on her heart. She never frowned on him, it is true, but then she never smiled. Whenever he be-gan to plead his passion, she struck her silver lyre. There was a mystic charm in the sound. In an instant the monarch began to nod; a drowsi-ness stole over him, and he gradually sank into a sleep, from which he awoke wonderfully refreshed, but perfectly cooled, for the time, of his passion. This was very baffling to his suit; but then these slumbers were accompanied by agreeable dreams, which completely enthralled the senses of the drowsy lover; so he continued to dream on, while all Gra-nada scoffed at his infatuation, and groaned at the treasures lavished for a song.

At length a danger burst on the head of Aben Habuz, against which his talisman yielded him no warning. An insurrection broke out in his very capital; his palace was surrounded by an armed rabble, who men-aced his life and the life of his Christian paramour. A spark of his an-cient warlike spirit was awakened in the breast of the monarch. At the head of a handful of his guards he sallied forth, put the rebels to flight, and crushed the insurrection in the bud.

When quiet was again restored, he sought the astrologer, who still re-mained shut up in his hermitage, chewing the bitter cud of resentment.

Aben Habuz approached him with a conciliatory tone. "O wise son of Abu Ayub," said he, "well didst thou predict dangers to me from this captive beauty; tell me then, thou who art so quick at foreseeing peril, what I should do to avert it."

"Put from thee the infidel damsel who is the cause."

"Sooner would I part with my kingdom," cried Aben Habuz.

"Thou art in danger of losing both," replied the astrologer.

"Be not harsh and angry, O most profound of philosophers; consider the double distress of a monarch and a lover, and devise some means of protecting me from the evils by which I am menaced. I care not for grandeur, I care not for power, I languish only for repose; would that I had some quiet retreat where I might take refuge from the world, and all its cares, and pomps, and troubles, and devote the remainder of my days to tranquillity and love.

The astrologer regarded him for a moment from under his bushy eyebrows.

"And what wouldst thou give, if I could provide thee such a retreat?"

"Thou shouldst name thy own reward, and whatever it might be, if within the scope of my power, as my soul liveth, it should be thine."

"Thou hast heard, O king, of the garden of Irem, one of the prodigies of Arabia the happy."

"I have heard of that garden; it is recorded in the Koran, even in the chapter entitled 'The Dawn of Day.' I have, moreover, heard marvellous things related of it by pilgrims who had been to Mecca; but I considered them wild fables, such as travellers are wont to tell who have visited remote countries."

"Discredit not, O king, the tales of travellers," rejoined the astrologer, gravely, "for they contain precious rarities of knowledge brought from the ends of the earth. As to the palace and garden of Irem, what is generally told of them is true. I have seen them with mine own eyes;—listen to my adventure, for it has a bearing upon the object of your request.

"In my younger days, when a mere Arab of the desert, I tended my father's camels. In traversing the desert of Aden, one of them strayed from the rest, and was lost. I searched after it for several days, but in vain, until, wearied and faint, I laid myself down at noontide, and slept under a palm-tree by the side of a scanty well. When I awoke I found myself at the gate of a city. I entered, and beheld noble streets, and squares, and market-places; but all were silent and without an inhabitant. I wandered on until I came to a sumptuous palace, with a garden adorned with fountains and fish-ponds, and groves and flowers, and orchards laden with delicious fruit; but still no one was to be seen. Upon which, appalled at this loneliness, I hastened to depart; and, after issuing forth at the gate of the city, I turned to look upon the place, but it was no longer to be seen: nothing but the silent desert extended before my eyes.

"In the neighborhood I met with an aged dervise, learned in the traditions and secrets of the land, and related to him what had befallen me. 'This,' said he, 'is the far-famed garden of Irem, one of the wonders of the desert. It only appears at times to some wanderer like thyself, gladdening him with the sight of towers and palaces and garden walls overhung with richly laden fruit-trees, and then vanishes, leaving nothing but a lonely desert. And this is the story of it. In old times, when this country was inhabited by the Addites, King Sheddad, the son of Ad, the great grandson of Noah, founded here a splendid city. When it was finished, and he saw its grandeur, his heart was puffed up with pride and arrogance, and he determined to build a royal palace, with gardens which should rival all related in the Koran of the celestial paradise. But the curse of heaven fell upon him for his presumption. He and his subjects were swept from the earth, and his splendid city, and palace, and gardens, were laid under a perpetual spell, which hides them from human sight, excepting that they are seen at intervals, by way of keeping his sin in perpetual remembrance.'"

"This story, O king, and the wonders I had seen, ever dwelt in my mind; and in after-years, when I had been in Egypt, and was possessed of the book of knowledge of Solomon the Wise, I determined to return and revisit the garden of Irem. I did so, and found it revealed to my instructed sight. I took possession of the palace of Sheddad, and passed several days in his mock paradise. The genii who watch over the place were obedient to my magic power, and revealed to me the spells by which the whole garden had been, as it were, conjured into existence, and by which it was rendered invisible. Such a palace and garden, O king, can I make for thee, even here, on the mountain above thy city. Do I not know all the secret spells? and am I not in possession of the book of knowledge of Solomon the Wise?"

"O wise son of Abu Ayub!" exclaimed Aben Habuz, trembling with eagerness, "thou art a traveller indeed, and hast seen and learned marvellous things! Contrive me such a paradise, and ask any reward, even to the half of my kingdom."

"Alas!" replied the other, "thou knowest I am an old man, and a philosopher, and easily satisfied; all the reward I ask is the first beast of burden, with its load, which shall enter the magic portal of the palace."

The monarch gladly agreed to so moderate a stipulation, and the astrologer began his work. On the summit of the hill, immediately above his subterranean hermitage, he caused a great gateway or barbican to be erected, opening through the centre of a strong tower.

There was an outer vestibule or porch, with a lofty arch, and within it a portal secured by massive gates. On the keystone of the portal the astrologer, with his own hand, wrought the figure of a huge key; and on the keystone of the outer arch of the vestibule, which was loftier than that of the portal, he carved a gigantic hand. These were potent talismans, over which he repeated many sentences in an unknown tongue.

When this gateway was finished, he shut himself up for two days in his astrological hall, engaged in secret incantations; on the third he ascended the hill, and passed the whole day on its summit. At a late hour of the night he came down, and presented himself before Aben Habuz. "At length, O king," said he, "my labor is accomplished. On the summit of the hill stands one of the most delectable palaces that ever the head of man devised, or the heart of man desired. It contains sumptuous halls and galleries, delicious gardens, cool fountains, and fragrant baths; in a word, the whole mountain is converted into a paradise. Like the garden of Irem, it is protected by a mighty charm, which hides it from the view and search of mortals, excepting such as possess the secret of its talismans."

"Enough!" cried Aben Habuz, joyfully, "to-morrow morning with the first light we will ascend and take possession." The happy monarch slept but little that night. Scarcely had the rays of the sun begun to play about the snowy summit of the Sierra Nevada, when he mounted his steed, and, accompanied only by a few chosen attendants, ascended a steep and narrow road leading up the hill. Beside him, on a white palfrey, rode the Gothic princess, her whole dress sparkling with jewels, while round her neck was suspended her silver lyre. The astrologer walked on the other side of the king, assisting his steps with his hieroglyphic staff, for he never mounted steed of any kind.

Aben Habuz looked to see the towers of the palace brightening above him, and the embowered terraces of its gardens stretching along the heights; but as yet nothing of the kind was to be descried. "That is the mystery and safeguard of the place," said the astrologer; "nothing can be discerned until you have passed the spell-bound gateway, and been put in possession of the place."

As they approached the gateway, the astrologer paused, and pointed out to the king the mystic hand and key carved upon the portal of the arch. "These," said he, "are the talismans which guard the entrance to this paradise. Until yonder hand shall reach down and seize that key, neither mortal power nor magic artifice can prevail against the lord of this mountain."

While Aben Habuz was gazing, with open mouth and silent wonder, at these mystic talismans, the palfrey of the princess proceeded, and bore her in at the portal, to the very centre of the barbican.

"Behold," cried the astrologer, "my promised reward; the first animal with its burden which should enter the magic gateway."

Aben Habuz smiled at what he considered a pleasantry of the ancient man; but when he found him to be in earnest, his gray beard trembled with indignation.

"Son of Abu Ayub," said he, sternly, "what equivocation is this? Thou knowest the meaning of my promise: the first beast of burden, with its load, that should enter this portal. Take the strongest mule in my stables, load it with the most precious things of my treasury, and it is thine; but dare not raise thy thoughts to her who is the delight of my heart."

"What need I of wealth?" cried the astrologer, scornfully; "have I not the book of knowledge of Solomon the Wise, and through it the command of the secret treasures of the earth? The princess is mine by right; thy royal word is pledged; I claim her as my own."

The princess looked down haughtily from her palfrey, and a light smile of scorn curled her rosy lip at this dispute between two gray-beards for the possession of youth and beauty. The wrath of the monarch got the better of his discretion. "Base son of the desert," cried he, "thou mayst be master of many arts, but know me for thy master, and presume not to juggle with thy king."

"My master! my king!" echoed the astrologer,—"the monarch of a mole-hill to claim sway over him who possesses the talismans of Solomon! Farewell, Aben Habuz; reign over thy petty kingdom, and revel in thy paradise of fools; for me, I will laugh at thee in my philosophic retirement."

So saying, he seized the bridle of the palfrey, smote the earth with his staff, and sank with the Gothic princess through the centre of the barbican. The earth closed over them, and no trace remained of the opening by which they had descended.

Aben Habuz was struck dumb for a time with astonishment. Recovering himself, he ordered a thousand workmen to dig, with pickaxe and spade, into the ground where the astrologer had disappeared. They digged and digged, but in vain; the flinty bosom of the hill resisted their implements; or if they did penetrate a little way, the earth filled in again as fast as they threw it out. Aben Habuz sought the mouth of the cavern at the foot of the hill, leading to the subterranean palace of the astrologer; but it was nowhere to be found. Where once had been an entrance, was now a solid surface of primeval rock. With the disappearance of Ibrahim Ebn Abu Ayub ceased the benefit of his talismans. The bronze horseman remained fixed, with his face turned toward the hill, and his spear pointed to the spot where the astrologer had descended, as if there still lurked the deadliest foe of Aben Habuz.

From time to time the sound of music, and the tones of a female voice, could be faintly heard from the bosom of the hill; and a peasant one day brought word to the king, that in the preceding night he had found a fissure in the rock, by which he had crept in, until he looked down into a subterranean hall, in which sat the astrologer, on a magnificent divan, slumbering and nodding to the silver lyre of the princess, which seemed to hold a magic sway over his senses.

Aben Habuz sought the fissure in the rock, but it was again closed. He renewed the attempt to unearth his rival, but all in vain. The spell of the hand and key was too potent to be counteracted by human power. As to the summit of the mountain, the site of the promised palace and garden, it remained a naked waste; either the boasted elysium was hidden from sight by enchantment, or was a mere fable of the astrologer. The world charitably supposed the latter, and some used to call the place "The King's Folly"; while others named it "The Fool's Paradise."

To add to the chagrin of Aben Habuz, the neighbors whom he had defied and taunted, and cut up at his leisure while master of the talismanic horseman, finding him no longer protected by magic spell, made inroads into his territories from all sides, and the remainder of the life of the most pacific of monarchs was a tissue of turmoils.

At length Aben Habuz died, and was buried. Ages have since rolled away. The Alhambra has been built on the eventful mountain, and in some measure realizes the fabled delights of the garden of Irem. The spellbound gateway still exists entire, protected no doubt by the mystic hand and key, and now forms the Gate of Justice, the grand entrance to the fortress. Under that gateway, it is said, the old astrologer remains in his subterranean hall, nodding on his divan, lulled by the silver lyre of the princess.

The old invalid sentinels who mount guard at the gate hear the strains occasionally in the summer nights; and, yielding to their soporific power, doze quietly at their posts. Nay, so drowsy an influence pervades the place, that even those who watch by day may generally be seen nodding on the stone benches of the barbican, or sleeping under the neighboring trees; so that in fact it is the drowsiest military post in all Christendom. All this, say the ancient legends, will endure from age to age. The princess will remain captive to the astrologer; and the astrologer, bound up in magic slumber by the princess, until the last day, unless the mystic hand shall grasp the fated key, and dispel the whole charm of this enchanted mountain.

NOTE TO THE ARABIAN ASTROLOGER

Al Makkari, in his "History of the Mohammedan Dynasties in Spain," cites from another Arabian writer an account of a talismanic effigy somewhat similar to the one in the foregoing legend.

In Cadiz, says he, there formerly stood a square tower upwards of one hundred cubits high, built of huge blocks of stone, fastened together with clamps of brass. On the top was the figure of a man, holding a staff in his right hand, his face turned to the Atlantic, and pointing with the forefinger of his left hand to the Straits of Gibraltar. It was said to have been set up in ancient times by the Gothic kings of Andalus, as a beacon or guide to navigators. The Moslems of Barbary and Andalus considered it a talisman which exercised a spell over the seas. Under it guidance, swarms of piratical people of a nation called Majus, appeared on the coast in large vessels with a square sail in the bow, and another in the stern. They came every six or seven years; captured everything they met with on the sea;— guided by the statue, they passed through the Straits into the Mediterranean, landed on the coasts of Andalus, laid everything waste with fire and sword; and sometimes carried their depredations on the opposite coasts even as far as Syria.

At length it came to pass in the time of the civil wars, a Moslem admiral who had taken possession of Cadiz, hearing that the statue on top of the tower was of pure gold, had it lowered to the ground and broken to pieces, when it proved to be of gilded brass. With the destruction of the idol, the spell over the sea was at an end. From that time forward nothing more was seen of the piratical people of the ocean, excepting that two of their barks were wrecked on the coast, one at Marsu-l-Majus (the port of the Majus), the other close to the promontory of Al-Aghan.

The maritime invaders above mentioned by Al Makkari must have been the Northmen.

From *The Alhambra*

LEGEND OF PRINCE AHMED AL KAMEL

or,

THE PILGRIM OF LOVE

The Generalife

HIGH above the Alhambra, on the breast of the mountain, amidst embowered gardens and stately terraces, rise the lofty towers and white walls of the Generalife; a fairy palace, full of storied recollections. Here are still to be seen the famous cypresses of enormous size which flourished in the time of the Moors, and which tradition has connected with the fabulous story of Boabdil and his sultana.

Here are preserved the portraits of many who figured in the romantic drama of the Conquest. Ferdinand and Isabella, Ponce de Leon, the gallant Marquis of Cadiz, and Garcilaso de la Vega, who slew in desperate fight Tarfe the Moor, a champion of Herculean strength. Here too hangs a portrait which has long passed for that of the unfortunate Boabdil, but which is said to be that of Aben Hud, the Moorish king from whom descended the princes of Almeria. From one of these princes, who joined the standard of Ferdinand and Isabella towards the close of the Conquest, and was Christianized by the name of Don Pedro de Granada Venegas, was descended the present proprietor of the palace, the Marquis of Campotejar. The proprietor, however, dwells in a foreign land, and the palace has no longer a princely inhabitant.

Yet here is everything to delight a southern voluptuary: fruits, flowers, fragrance, green arbors and myrtle hedges, delicate air and gushing waters. Here I had an opportunity of witnessing those scenes which painters are fond of depicting about southern palaces and gardens. It was the saint's day of the count's daughter, and she had brought up several of her youthful companions from Granada, to sport away a long summer's day among the breezy halls and bowers of the Moorish palaces. A visit to the Generalife was the morning's entertainment. Here

---

I have included a prefatory chapter from *The Alhambra* inasmuch as I consider it to be an integral part of the tale.—C.N.

some of the gay company dispersed itself in groups about the green walks, the bright fountains, the flights of Italian steps, the noble terraces and marble balustrades. Others, among whom I was one, took their seats in an open gallery or colonnade commanding a vast prospect; with the Alhambra, the city, and the Vega, far below, and the distant horizon of mountains—a dreamy world, all glimmering to the eye in summer sunshine. While thus seated, the all-pervading tinkling of the guitar and click of the castanets came stealing up from the valley of the Darro, and half-way down the mountain we descried a festive party under the trees, enjoying themselves in true Andalusian style; some lying on the grass, others dancing to the music.

All these sights and sounds, together with the princely seclusion of the place, the sweet quiet which prevailed around, and the delicious serenity of the weather, had a witching effect upon the mind, and drew from some of the company, versed in local story, several of the popular fancies and traditions connected with this old Moorish palace; they were "such stuff as dreams are made of," but out of them I have shaped the following legend, which I hope may have the good fortune to prove acceptable to the reader.

THERE was once a Moorish king of Granada, who had but one son, whom he named Ahmed, to which his courtiers added the surname of Al Kamel, or The Perfect, from the indubitable signs of superexcellence which they perceived in him in his very infancy. The astrologers countenanced them in their foresight, predicting everything in his favor that could make a perfect prince and a prosperous sovereign. One cloud only rested upon his destiny, and even that was of a roseate hue: he would be of an amorous temperament, and run great perils from the tender passion. If, however, he could be kept from the allurements of love until of mature age, these dangers would be averted, and his life thereafter be one uninterrupted course of felicity.

To prevent all danger of the kind, the king wisely determined to rear the prince in a seclusion where he would never see a female face, nor hear even the name of love. For this purpose he built a beautiful palace on the brow of the hill above the Alhambra, in the midst of delightful gardens, but surrounded by lofty walls, being, in fact, the same palace known at the present day by the name of the Generalife. In this palace the youthful prince was shut up, and intrusted to the guardianship and instruction of Eben Bonabben, one of the wisest and dryest of Arabian sages, who had passed the greatest part of his life in Egypt, studying hieroglyphics, and making researches among the tombs and pyramids, and who saw more charms in an Egyptian mummy than in the most tempting of living beauties. The sage was ordered to instruct the prince in all kinds of knowledge but one,—he was to be kept utterly ignorant of love. "Use every precaution for the purpose you may think proper," said the king, "but remember, O Eben Bonabben, if my son learns aught of that forbidden knowledge while under your care, your head shall answer for it." A withered smile came over the dry visage of the wise Bonabben at the menace. "Let your majesty's heart be as easy about your son, as mine is about my head: am I a man likely to give lessons in the idle passion?"

Under the vigilant care of the philosopher, the prince grew up in the seclusion of the palace and its gardens. He had black slaves to attend upon him—hideous mutes who knew nothing of love, or if they did, had not words to communicate it. His mental endowments were the peculiar care of Eben Bonabben, who sought to initiate him into the abstruse lore of Egypt; but in this the prince made little progress, and it was soon evident that he had no turn for philosophy.

He was, however, amazingly ductile for a youthful prince, ready to follow any advice, and always guided by the last counsellor. He suppressed his yawns, and listened patiently to the long and learned discourses of Eben Bonabben, from which he imbibed a smattering of various kinds of knowledge, and thus happily attained his twentieth year, a miracle of princely wisdom—but totally ignorant of love.

About this time, however, a change came over the conduct of the prince. He completely abandoned his studies, and took to strolling about the gardens, and musing by the side of the fountains. He had been taught a little music among his various accomplishments; it now engrossed a great part of his time, and a turn for poetry became apparent. The sage Eben Bonabben took the alarm, and endeavored to work these idle humors out of him by a severe course of algebra; but the prince turned from it with distaste. "I cannot endure algebra," said he; "it is an abomination to me. I want something that speaks more to the heart."

The sage Eben Bonabben shook his dry head at the words. "Here is an end to philosophy," thought he. "The prince has discovered he has a heart!" He now kept anxious watch upon his pupil, and saw that the latent tenderness of his nature was in activity, and only wanted an object. He wandered about the gardens of the Generalife in an intoxication of feelings of which he knew not the cause. Sometimes he would sit plunged in a delicious reverie; then he would seize his lute and draw from it the most touching notes, and then throw it aside, and break forth into sighs and ejaculations.

By degrees this loving disposition began to extend to inanimate objects; he had his favorite flowers, which he cherished with tender assiduity; then he became attached to various trees, and there was one in particular, of a graceful form and drooping foliage, on which he lavished his armorous devotion, carving his name on its bark, hanging garlands on its branches, and singing couplets in its praise, to the accompaniment of his lute.

Eben Bonabben was alarmed at this excited state of his pupil. He saw him on the very brink of forbidden knowledge—the least hint might reveal to him the fatal secret. Trembling for the safety of the prince and the security of his own head, he hastened to drawn him from the seductions of the garden, and shut him up in the highest tower of the Generalife. It contained beautiful apartments, and commanded an almost boundless prospect, but was elevated far above the atmosphere of sweets and those witching bowers so dangerous to the feelings of the too susceptible Ahmed.

What was to be done, however, to reconcile him to this restraint and to beguile the tedious hours? He had exhausted almost all kinds of agreeable knowledge; and algebra was not to be mentioned. Fortunately Eben Bonabben had been instructed, when in Egypt, in the language of birds by a Jewish Rabbin, who had received it in lineal transmission from Solomon the Wise, who had been taught it by the Queen of Sheba. At the very mention of such a study, the eyes of the prince sparkled with animation, and he applied himself to it with such avidity, that he soon became as great and adept as his master.

The tower of the Generalife was no longer a solitude; he had companions at hand with whom he could converse. The first acquaintance he formed was with a hawk, who built his nest in a crevice of the lofty battlements, whence he soared far and wide in quest of prey. The prince, however, found little to like or esteem in him. He was a mere pirate of the air, swaggering and boastful, whose talk was all about rapine and carnage, and desperate exploits.

His next acquaintance was an owl, a mighty wise-looking bird, with a huge head and staring eyes, who sat blinking and goggling all day in a hole in the wall, but roamed forth at night. He had great pretensions to wisdom, talked something of astrology and the moon, and hinted at the dark sciences; he was grievously given to metaphysics, and the prince found his prosings even more ponderous than those of the sage Eben Bonabben.

Then there was a bat, that hung all day by his heels in the dark corner of a vault, but sallied out in slipshod style at twilight. He, however, had but twilight ideas on all subjects, derided things of which he had taken but an imperfect view, and seemed to take delight in nothing.

Besides these there was a swallow, with whom the prince was at first much taken. He was a smart talker, but restless, bustling, and forever on the wing; seldom remaining long enough for any continued conversation. He turned out in the end to be a mere smatterer, who did but skim over the surface of things, pretending to know everything, but knowing nothing thoroughly.

These were the only feathered associates with whom the prince had any opportunity of exercising his newly acquired language; the tower was too high for any other birds to frequent it. He soon grew weary of his new acquaintances, whose conversation spoke so little to the head and nothing to the heart, and gradually relapsed into his loneliness. A winter passed away, spring opened with all its bloom and verdure and breathing sweetness, and the happy time arrived for birds to pair and build their nests. Suddenly, as it were, a universal burst of song and melody broke forth from the groves and gardens of the Generalife, and reached the prince in the solitude of his tower. From every side he heard the same universal theme—love—love—love—chanted forth, and responded to in every variety of note and tone. The prince listened in silence and perplexity. "What can be this love," thought he, "of which the world seems so full, and of which I know nothing?" He applied for information to his friend the hawk. The ruffian bird answered in a tone of scorn: "You must apply," said he, "to the vulgar peaceable birds of earth, who are made for the prey of us princes of the air. My trade is war, and fighting my delight. I am a warrior, and know nothing of this thing called love."

The prince turned from him with disgust, and sought the owl in his retreat. "This is a bird," said he, "of peaceful habits, and may be able to solve my question." So he asked the owl to tell him what was this love about which all the birds in the groves below were singing.

Upon this the owl put on a look of offended dignity. "My nights," said he, "are taken up in study and research, and my days in ruminating in my cell upon all that I have learnt. As to these singing birds of whom you talk, I never listen to them—I despise them and their themes. Allah be praised, I cannot sing; I am a philosopher, and know nothing of this thing called love."

The prince now repaired to the vault, where his friend the bat was hanging by the heels, and propounded the same question. The bat wrinkled up his nose into a most snappish expression. "Why do you disturb me in my morning's nap with such an idle question?" said he, peevishly. "I only fly by twilight, when all birds are asleep, and never trouble myself with their concerns. I am neither bird nor beast, and I thank heaven for it. I have found out the villainy of the whole of them, and hate them one and all. In a word, I am a misanthrope—and know nothing of this thing called love."

As a last resort, the prince now sought the swallow, and stopped him just as he was circling about the summit of the tower. The swallow, as usual, was in a prodigious hurry, and had scarce time to make a reply. "Upon my word," said he, "I have so much public business to attend to, and so many pursuits to follow, that I have had no time to think on the subject. I have every day a thousand visits to pay; a thousand affairs of importance to examine into, that leave me not a moment of leisure for these little sing-song matters. In a word, I am a citizen of the world—I know nothing of this thing called love." So saying, the swallow dived into the valley, and was out of sight in a moment.

The prince remained disappointed and perplexed, but with his curiosity still more piqued by the difficulty of gratifying it. While in this mood, his ancient guardian entered the tower. The prince advanced eagerly to meet him. "O Eben Bonabben," cried he, "thou hast revealed to me much of the wisdom of the earth; but there is one thing of which I remain in utter ignorance, and would fain be informed."

"My prince has but to make the inquiry, and everything within the limited range of his servant's intellect is at his command."

"Tell me, then, O most profound of sages, what is the nature of this thing called love?"

Eben Bonabben was struck as with a thunderbolt. He trembled and turned pale, and felt as if his head sat but loosely on his shoulders.

"What could suggest such a question to my prince,—where could he have learnt so idle a word?"

The prince led him to the window of the tower. "Listen, Eben Bonabben," said he. The sage listened. The nightingale sat in a thicket below the tower, singing to his paramour, the rose; from every blossomed spray and tufted grove rose a strain of melody; and love—love— love—was still the unvarying strain.

"Allah Akbar! God is great!" exclaimed the wise Bonabben. "Who shall pretend to keep this secret from the heart of man, when even the birds of the air conspire to betray it?"

Then turning to Ahmed—"O my prince," cried he, "shut thine ears to these seductive strains. Close thy mind against this dangerous knowledge. Know that this love is the cause of half the ills of wretched mortality. It is this which produces bitterness and strife between brethren and friends; which causes treacherous murder and desolating war. Care and sorrow, weary days and sleepless nights, are its attendants. It withers the bloom and blights the joy of youth, and brings on the ills and griefs of premature old age. Allah preserve thee, my prince, in total ignorance of this thing called love!"

The sage Eben Bonabben hastily retired, leaving the prince plunged in still deeper perplexity. It was in vain he attempted to dismiss the subject from his mind; it still continued uppermost in his thoughts, and teased and exhausted him with vain conjectures. Surely, said he to himself, as he listened to the tuneful strains of the birds, there is no sorrow in those notes; everything seems tenderness and joy. If love be a cause of such wretchedness and strife, why are not these birds drooping in solitude, or tearing each other in pieces, instead of fluttering cheerfully about the groves, or sporting with each other among the flowers?

He lay one morning on his couch, meditating on this inexplicable matter. The window of his chamber was open to admit the soft morning breeze, which came laden with the perfume of orange-blossoms from the valley of the Darro. The voice of the nightingale was faintly heard, still chanting the wonted theme. As the prince was listening and sighing, there was a sudden rushing noise in the air; a beautiful dove, pursued by a hawk, darted in at the window, and fell panting on the floor, while the pursuer, balked of his prey, soared off to the mountains.

The prince took up the gasping bird, smoothed its feathers, and nestled it in his bosom. When he had soothed it by his caresses, he put it in a golden cage, and offered it, with his own hands, the whitest and finest of wheat and the purest of water. The bird, however, refused food, and sat drooping and pining, and uttering piteous moans.

"What aileth thee?" said Ahmed. "Hast thou not everything thy heart can wish?"

"Alas, no!" replied the dove; "am I not separated from the partner of my heart, and that too in the happy spring-time, the very season of love!"

"Of love!" echoed Ahmed. "I pray thee, my pretty bird, canst thou then tell me what is love?"

"Too well can I, my prince. It is the torment of one, the felicity of two, the strife and enmity of three. It is a charm which draws two beings together, and unites them by delicious sympathies, making it happiness to be with each other, but misery to be apart. Is there no being to whom you are drawn by these ties of tender affection?"

"I like my old teacher Eben Bonabben better than any other being; but he is often tedious, and I occasionally feel myself happier without his society."

"That is not the sympathy I mean. I speak of love, the great mystery and principle of life: the intoxicating revel of youth; the sober delight of age. Look forth, my prince, and behold how at this blest season all nature is full of love. Every created being has its mate; the most insignificant bird sings to its paramour; the very beetle wooes its lady-beetle in the dust, and yon butterflies which you see fluttering high above the tower and toying in the air, are happy in each other's loves. Alas, my prince! hast thou spent so many of the precious days of youth without knowing anything of love? Is there no gentle being of another sex—no beautiful princess nor lovely damsel who has ensnared your heart, and filled your bosom with a soft tumult of pleasing pains and tender wishes?"

"I begin to understand," said the prince, sighing; "such a tumult I have more than once experienced, without knowing the cause; and where should I seek for an object such as you describe in this dismal solitude?"

A little further conversation ensued, and the first amatory lesson of the prince was complete.

"Alas!" said he, "if love be indeed such a delight, and its interruption such a misery, Allah forbid that I should mar the joy of any of its votaries." He opened the cage, took out the dove, and having fondly kissed it, carried it to the window. "Go, happy bird," said he, "rejoice with the partner of thy heart in the days of youth and spring-time. Why should I make thee a fellow-prisoner in this dreary tower, where love can never enter?"

The dove flapped its wings in rapture, gave one vault into the air, and then swooped downward on whistling wings to the blooming bowers of the Darro.

The prince followed him with his eyes, and then gave way to bitter repining. The singing of the birds, which once delighted him, now added to his bitterness. Love! love! love! Alas, poor youth! he now understood the strain.

His eyes flashed fire when next he beheld the sage Bonabben. "Why hast thou kept me in this abject ignorance?" cried he. "Why has the great mystery and principle of life been withheld from me, in which I find the meanest insect is so learned? Behold all nature is in a revel of delight. Every created being rejoices with its mate. This—this is the love about which I have sought instruction. Why has so much of my youth been wasted without a knowledge of its raptures?"

The sage Bonabben saw that all further reserve was useless; for the prince had acquired the dangerous and forbidden knowledge. He revealed to him, therefore, the predictions of the astrologers and the precautions that had been taken in his education to avert the threatened evils. "And now, my prince," added he, "my life is in your hands. Let the king, your father, discover that you have learned the passion of love while under my guardianship, and my head must answer for it."

The prince was as reasonable as most young men of his age, and easily listened to the remonstrances of his tutor, since nothing pleaded against them. Besides, he really was attached to Eben Bonabben, and being as yet but theoretically acquainted with the passion of love, he consented to confine the knowledge of it to his own bosom, rather than endanger the head of the philosopher.

His discretion was doomed, however, to be put to still further proofs. A few mornings afterward, as he was ruminating on the battlements of the tower, the dove which had been released by him came hovering in the air, and alighted fearlessly upon his shoulder.

The prince fondled it to his heart. "Happy bird," said he, "who can fly, as it were, with the wings of the morning to the uttermost parts of the earth. Where has thou been since we parted?"

"In a far country, my prince, whence I bring you tidings in reward for my liberty. In the wild compass of my flight, which extends over plain and mountain, as I was soaring in the air, I beheld below me a delightful garden with all kinds of fruits and flowers. It was in a green meadow, on the banks of a wandering stream, and in the centre of the garden was a stately palace. I alighted in one of the bowers to repose after my weary flight. On the green bank below me was a youthful princess, in the very sweetness and bloom of her years. She was surrounded by female attendants, young like herself, who decked her with garlands and coronets of flowers; but no flower of field or garden could compare with her for loveliness. Here, however, she bloomed in secret, for the garden was surrounded by high walls, and no mortal man was permitted to enter. When I beheld this beauteous maid, thus young and innocent and unspotted by the world, I thought, here is the being formed by heaven to inspire my prince with love."

The description was a spark of fire to the combustible heart of Ahmed; all the latent amorousness of his temperament had at once found an object, and he conceived an immeasurable passion for the princess. He wrote a letter, couched in the most impassioned language, breathing his fervent devotion, but bewailing the unhappy thraldom of his person, which prevented him from seeking her out and throwing himself at her feet. He added couplets of the most tender and moving eloquence, for he was a poet by nature, and inspired by love. He addressed his letter—"To the Unknown Beauty, from the captive Prince Ahmed;" then perfuming it with musk and roses, he gave it to the dove.

"Away, trustiest of messengers!" said he. "Fly over mountain, and valley, and river, and plain; rest not in bower, nor set foot on earth, until thou hast given this letter to the mistress of my heart."

The dove soared high in air, and taking his course darted away in one undeviating direction. The prince followed him with his eye until he was a mere speck on a cloud, and gradually disappeared behind a mountain.

Day after day he watched for the return of the messenger of love, but he watched in vain. He began to accuse him of forgetfulness, when towards sunset one evening the faithful bird fluttered into his apartment, and falling at his feet expired. The arrow of some wanton archer had pierced his breast, yet he had struggled with the lingerings of life to execute his mission. As the prince bent with grief over this gentle martyr to fidelity, he beheld a chain of pearls round his neck, attached to which, beneath his wing, was a small enameled picture. It represented a lovely princess in the very flower of her years. It was doubtless the unknown beauty of the garden; but who and where was she?—how had she received his letter? and was this picture sent as a token of her approval of his passion? Unfortunately the death of the faithful dove left everything in mystery and doubt.

The prince gazed on the picture till his eyes swam with tears. He pressed it to his lips and to his heart; he sat for hours contemplating it almost in an agony of tenderness. "Beautiful image!" said he, "alas, thou art but an image! Yet thy dewy eyes beam tenderly upon me; those rosy lips look as though they would speak encourgement: vain fancies! Have they not looked the same on some more happy rival? But where in this wide world shall I hope to find the original? Who knows what mountains, what realms may separate us; what adverse chances may intervene? Perhaps now, even now, lovers may be crowding around her, while I sit here a prisoner in a tower, wasting my time in adoration of a painted shadow."

The resolution of Prince Ahmed was taken. "I will fly from this palace," said he, "which has become an odious prison; and, a pilgrim of love, will seek this unknown princess throughout the world." To escape from the tower in the day, when every one was awake, might be a difficult matter; but at night the palace was slightly guarded; for no one apprehended any attempt of the kind from the prince, who had always been so passive in his captivity. How was he to guide himself, however, in his darkling flight, being ignorant of the country? He bethought him of the owl, who was accustomed to roam at night, and must know every by-lane and secret pass. Seeking him in his hermitage, he questioned him touching his knowledge of the land. Upon this the owl put on a mighty self-important look. "You must know, O prince," said he, "that we owls are of a very ancient and extensive family, though rather fallen to decay, and possess ruinous castles and palaces in all parts of Spain. There is scarcely a tower of the mountains, or a fortress of the plains, or an old citadel of a city, but has some brother, or uncle, or cousin quartered in it; and in going the rounds to visit this my numerous kindred, I have pried into every nook and corner, and made myself acquainted with every secret of the land."

The prince was overjoyed to find the owl so deeply versed in topography, and now informed him, in confidence, of his tender passion and his intended elopement, urging him to be his companion and counsellor.

"Go to!" said the owl, with a look of displeasure; "am I a bird to engage in a love-affair?—I, whose whole time is devoted to meditation and the moon?"

"Be not offended, most solemn owl," replied the prince; "abstract thyself for a time from meditation and the moon, and aid me in my flight, and thou shalt have whatever heart can wish."

"I have that already," said the owl; "a few mice are sufficient for my frugal table, and this hole in the wall is spacious enough for my studies; and what more does a philosopher like myself desire?"

"Bethink thee, most wise owl, that while moping in thy cell and gazing at the moon, all thy talents are lost to the world. I shall one day be a sovereign prince, and may advance thee to some post of honor and dignity."

The owl, though a philosopher and above the ordinary wants of life, was not above ambition, so he was finally prevailed on to elope with the prince, and be his guide and mentor in his pilgrimage.

The plans of a lover are promptly executed. The prince collected all his jewels, and concealed them about his person as travelling funds. That very night he lowered himself by his scarf from a balcony of the tower, clambered over the outer walls of the Generalife, and, guided by the owl, made good his escape before morning to the mountains.

He now held a council with his mentor as to his future course.

"Might I advise," said the owl, "I would recommend you to repair to Seville. You must know that many years since I was on a visit to an uncle, an owl of great dignity and power, who lived in a ruined wing of the Alcazar of that place. In my hoverings at night over the city I frequently remarked a light burning in a lonely tower. At length I alighted on the battlements, and found it to proceed from the lamp of an Arabian magician: he was surrounded by his magic books, and on his shoulder was perched his familiar, an ancient raven who had come with him from Egypt. I am acquainted with that raven, and owe to him a great part of the knowledge I possess. The magician is since dead, but the raven still inhabits the tower, for these birds are of wonderful long life. I would advise you, O prince, to seek that raven, for he is a soothsayer and a conjurer, and deals in the black art, for which all ravens, and especially those of Egypt, are renowned."

The prince was struck with the wisdom of this advice, and accordingly bent his course towards Seville. He travelled only in the night to accommodate his companion, and lay by during the day in some dark cavern or mouldering watch-tower, for the owl knew every hiding-hole of the kind, and had a most antiquarian taste for ruins.

At length one morning at breakfast they reached the city of Seville, where the owl, who hated the glare and bustle of crowded streets, halted without the gate, and took up his quarters in a hollow tree.

The prince entered the gate, and readily found the magic tower, which rose above the houses of the city, as a palm-tree rises above the shrubs of the desert; it was in fact the same tower standing at the present day, and known as the Giralda, the famous Moorish tower of Seville.

The prince ascended by a great winding staircase to the summit of the tower, where he found the cabalistic raven—an old, mysterious, gray-headed bird, ragged in feather, with a film over one eye that gave him the glare of a spectre. He was perched on one leg, with his head turned on one side, poring with his remaining eye on a diagram described on the pavement.

The prince approached him with the awe and reverence naturally inspired by his venerable appearance and supernatural wisdom. "Pardon me, most ancient and darkly wise raven," exclaimed he, "if for a moment I interrupt those studies which are the wonder of the world. You behold before you a votary of love, who would fain seek your counsel how to obtain the object of his passion."

"In other words," said the raven, with a significant look, "you seek to try my skill in palmistry. Come, show me your hand, and let me decipher the mysterious lines of fortune."

"Excuse me," said the prince, "I come not to pry into the decrees of fate, which are hidden by Allah from the eyes of mortals; I am a pilgrim of love, and seek but to find a clue to the object of my pilgrimage."

"And can you be at any loss for an object in amorous Andalusia?" said the old raven, leering upon him with his single eye; "above all, can you be at a loss in wanton Seville, where black-eyed damsels dance the *zambra* under every orange grove?"

The prince blushed, and was somewhat shocked at hearing an old bird with one foot in the grave talk thus loosely. "Believe me," said he, gravely, "I am on none such light and vagrant errand as thou dost insinuate. The black-eyed damsels of Andalusia who dance among the orange groves of the Guadalquivir are as naught to me. I seek one unknown but immaculate beauty, the original of this picture; and I beseech thee, most potent raven, if it be within the scope of thy knowledge or the reach of thy art, inform me where she may be found?"

The gray-headed raven was rebuked by the gravity of the prince.

"What know I," replied he, dryly, "of youth and beauty? My visits are to the old and withered, not to the fresh and fair; the harbinger of fate am I, who croak bodings of death from the chimney-top, and flap my wings at the sick man's window. You must seek elsewhere for tidings of your unknown beauty."

"And where can I seek if not among the sons of wisdom, versed in the book of destiny? Know that I am a royal prince, fated by the stars, and sent on a mysterious enterprise on which may hang the destiny of empires."

When the raven heard that it was a matter of vast moment, in which the stars took interest, he changed his tone and manner, and listened with profound attention to the story of the prince. When it was concluded, he replied: "Touching this princess, I can give thee no information of myself, for my flight is not among gardens, or around ladies' bowers; but hie thee to Cordova, seek the palm-tree of the great Abderahman, which stands in the court of the principal mosque; at the foot of it thou wilt find a great traveller who has visited all countries and courts, and been a favorite with queens and princesses. He will give thee tidings of the object of thy search."

"Many thanks for this precious information," said the prince. "Farewell, most venerable conjurer."

"Farewell, pilgrim of love," said the raven, dryly, and again fell to pondering on the diagram.

The prince sallied forth from Seville, sought his fellow-traveller the owl, who was still dozing in the hollow tree, and set off for Cordova.

He approached it along hanging gardens and orange and citron groves, overlooking the fair valley of the Guadalquivir. When arrived at its gates the owl flew up to a dark hole in the wall, and the prince proceeded in quest of the palm-tree planted in days of yore by the great Abderahman. It stood in the midst of the great court of the mosque, towering from amidst orange and cypress trees. Dervises and faquirs were seated in groups under the cloisters of the court, and many of the faithful were performing their ablutions at the fountains before entering the mosque.

At the foot of the palm-tree was a crowd listening to the words of one who appeared to be talking with great volubility. "This," said the prince to himself, "must be the great traveller who is to give me tidings of the unknown princess." He mingled in the crowd, but was astonished to perceive that they were all listening to a parrot, who, with his bright-green coat, pragmatical eye, and consequential top-knot, had the air of a bird on excellent terms with himself.

"How is this," said the prince to one of the by-standers, "that so many grave persons can be delighted with the garrulity of a chattering bird?"

"You know not whom you speak of," said the other; "this parrot is a descendant of the famous parrot of Persia, renowned for his story-telling talent. He has all the learning of the East at the tip of his tongue, and can quote poetry as fast as he can talk. He has visited various foreign courts, where he has been considered an oracle of erudition. He has been a universal favorite also with the fair sex, who have a vast admiration for erudite parrots that can quote poetry."

"Enough," said the prince, "I will have some private talk with this distinguished traveller."

· He sought a private interview, and expounded the nature of his errand. He had scarcely mentioned it when the parrot burst into a fit of dry rickety laughter, that absolutely brought tears into his eyes. "Excuse my merriment," said he, "but the mere mention of love always sets me laughing."

The prince was shocked at this ill-timed mirth. "Is not love," said he, "the great mystery of nature, the secret principle of life, the universal bond of sympathy?"

"A fig's end!" cried the parrot, interrupting him; "prithee where hast thou learned this sentimental jargon? Trust me, love is quite out of vogue; one never hears of it in the company of wits and people of refinement."

The prince sighed as he recalled the different language of his friend the dove. But this parrot, thought he, has lived about the court, he affects the wit and the fine gentleman, he knows nothing of the thing called love. Unwilling to provoke any more ridicule of the sentiment which filled his heart, he now directed his inquiries to the immediate purport of his visit.

"Tell me," said he, "most accomplished parrot, thou who hast everywhere been admitted to the most secret bowers of beauty, hast thou in the course of thy travels met with the original of this portrait?"

The parrot took the picture in his claw, turned his head from side to side, and examined it curiously with either eye. "Upon my honor," said he, "a very pretty face, very pretty; but then one sees so many pretty women in one's travels that one can hardly—but hold—bless me! now I look at it again—sure enough, this is the Princess Aldegonda: how could I forget one that is so prodigious a favorite with me!"

"The Princess Aldegonda!" echoed the prince; "and where is she to be found?"

"Softly, softly," said the parrot, "easier to be found than gained. She is the only daughter of the Christian king who reigns at Toledo, and is shut up from the world until her seventeenth birthday, on account of some prediction of those meddlesome fellows the astrologers. You'll not get a sight of her; no mortal man can see her. I was admitted to her presence to entertain her, and I assure you, on the word of a parrot who has seen the world, I have conversed with much sillier princesses in my time."

"A word in confidence, my dear parrot," said the prince. "I am heir to a kingdom, and shall one day sit upon a throne. I see that you are a bird of parts, and understand the world. Help me to gain possession of this princess, and I will advance you to some distinguished place about court."

"With all my heart," said the parrot; "but let it be a sinecure if possible, for we wits have a great dislike to labor."

Arrangements were promptly made: the prince sallied forth from Cordova through the same gate by which he had entered; called the owl down from the hole in the wall, introduced him to his new travelling companion as a brother savant, and away they set off on their journey.

They travelled much more slowly than accorded with the impatience of the prince; but the parrot was accustomed to high life, and did not like to be disturbed early in the morning. The owl, on the other hand, was for sleeping at mid-day, and lost a great deal of time by his long siestas. His antiquarian taste also was in the way; for he insisted on pausing and inspecting every ruin, and had long legendary tales to tell about every old tower and castle in the country. The prince had supposed that he and the parrot, being both birds of learning, would delight in each other's society, but never had he been more mistaken. They were eternally bickering. The one was a wit, the other a philosopher. The parrot quoted poetry, was critical on new readings and eloquent on small points of erudition, the owl treated all such knowledge as trifling, and relished nothing but metaphysics. Then the parrot would sing songs and repeat *bon mots* and crack jokes upon his solemn neighbor, and laugh outrageously at his own wit; all which proceedings the owl considered as a grievous invasion of his dignity, and would scowl and sulk and swell, and be silent for a whole day together.

The prince heeded not the wranglings of his companions, being wrapped up in the dreams of his own fancy and the contemplation of the portrait of the beautiful princess. In this way they journeyed through the stern passes of the Sierra Morena, across the sunburnt plains of La Mancha and Castile, and along the banks of the "Golden Tagus," which winds its wizard mazes over one half of Spain and Portugal. At length they came in sight of a strong city with walls and towers built on a rocky promontory, round the foot of which the Tagus circled with brawling violence.

"Behold," exclaimed the owl, "the ancient and renowned city of Toledo; a city famous for its antiquities. Behold those venerable domes and towers, hoary with time and clothed with legendary grandeur, in which so many of my ancestors have meditated."

"Pish!" cried the parrot, interrupting his solemn antiquarian rapture, "what have we to do with antiquities, and legends, and your ancestry? Behold what is more to the purpose—behold the abode of youth and beauty—behold at length, O prince, the abode of your long-sought princess."

The prince looked in the direction indicated by the parrot, and beheld, in a delightful green meadow on the banks of the Tagus, a stately palace rising from amidst the bowers of a delicious garden. It was just such a place as had been described by the dove as the residence of the original of the picture. He gazed at it with a throbbing heart; "perhaps at this moment," thought he, "the beautiful princess is sporting beneath those shady bowers, or pacing with delicate step those stately terraces, or reposing beneath those lofty roofs!" As he looked more narrowly, he perceived that the walls of the garden were of great height, so as to defy access, while numbers of armed guards patrolled around them.

The prince turned to the parrot. "O most accomplished of birds," said he, "thou hast the gift of human speech. Hie thee to yon garden; seek the idol of my soul, and tell her that Prince Ahmed, a pilgrim of love, and guided by the stars, has arrived in quest of her on the flowery banks of the Tagus."

The parrot, proud of his embassy, flew away to the garden, mounted above its lofty walls, and after soaring for a time over the lawns and groves, alighted on the balcony of a pavilion that overhung the river. Here, looking in at the casement, he beheld the princess reclining on a couch, with her eyes fixed on a paper, while tears gently stole after each other down her pallid cheek.

Pluming his wings for a moment, adjusting his bright-green coat, and elevating his top-knot, the parrot perched himself beside her with a gallant air; then assuming a tenderness of tone, "Dry thy tears, most beautiful of princesses," said he; "I come to bring solace to thy heart."

The princess was startled on hearing a voice, but turning, and seeing nothing but a little green-coated bird bobbing and bowing before her, "Alas! what solace canst thou yield," said she, "seeing thou art but a parrot?"

The parrot was nettled at the question. "I have consoled many beautiful ladies in my time," said he; "but let that pass. At present I come ambassador from a royal prince. Know that Ahmed, the Prince of Granada, has arrived in quest of thee, and is encamped even now on the flowery banks of the Tagus."

The eyes of the beautiful princess sparkled at these words, even brighter than the diamonds in her coronet. "O sweetest of parrots," cried she, "joyful indeed are thy tidings, for I was faint and weary, and sick almost unto death with doubt of the constancy of Ahmed. Hie thee back, and tell him that the words of his letter are engraven in my heart, and his poetry has been the food of my soul. Tell him, however, that he must prepare to prove his love by force of arms; to-morrow is my seventeenth birthday, when the king, my father, holds a great tournament; several princes are to enter the lists, and my hand is to be the prize of the victor."

The parrot again took wing, and rustling through the groves, flew back to where the prince awaited his return. The rapture of Ahmed on finding the original of his adored portrait, and finding her kind and true, can only be conceived by those favored mortals who have had the good fortune to realize day-dreams and turn a shadow into substance; still there was one thing that alloyed his transport—this impending tournament. In fact, the banks of the Tagus were already glittering with arms, and resounding with trumpets of the various knights, who, with proud retinues, were prancing on towards Toledo to attend the ceremonial. The same star that had controlled the destiny of the prince had governed that of the princess, and until her seventeenth birthday she had been shut up from the world, to guard her from the tender passion. The fame of her charms, however, had been enhanced rather than obscured by this seclusion. Several powerful princes had contended for her hand; and her father, who was a king of wondrous shrewdness, to avoid making enemies by showing partiality, had referred them to the arbitrament of arms. Among the rival candidates were several renowned for strength and prowess. What a predicament for the unfortunate Ahmed, unprovided as he was with weapons, and unskilled in the exercise of chivalry! "Luckless prince that I am!" said he, "to have been brought up in seclusion under the eye of a philosopher! Of what avail are algebra and philosophy in affairs of love? Alas, Eben Bonabben! why hast thou neglected to instruct me in the management of arms?" Upon this the owl broke silence, preluding his harangue with a pious ejaculation, for he was a devout Mussulman.

"Allah Akbar! God is great!" exclaimed he; "in his hands are all secret things—he alone governs the destiny of princes! Know, O prince, that this land is full of mysteries, hidden from all but those who, like myself, can grope after knowledge in the dark. Know that in the neighboring mountains there is a cave, and in that cave there is an iron table, and on that table there lies a suit of magic armor, and beside that table there stands a spell-bound steed, which have been shut up there for many generations."

The prince stared with wonder, while the owl, blinking his huge round eyes, and erecting his horns, proceeded.

"Many years since I accompanied my father to these parts on a tour of his estates, and we sojourned in that cave; and thus became I acquainted with the mystery. It is a tradition in our family which I have heard from my grandfather, when I was yet but a very little owlet, that this armor belonged to a Moorish magician, who took refuge in this cavern when Toledo was captured by the Christians, and died here, leaving his steed and weapons under a mystic spell, never to be used but by a Moslem, and by him only from sunrise to mid-day. In that interval, whoever uses them will overthrow every opponent."

"Enough: let us seek this cave!" exclaimed Ahmed.

Guided by his legendary mentor, the prince found the cavern, which was in one of the wildest recesses of those rocky cliffs which rise around Toledo; none but the mousing eye of an owl or an antiquary could have discovered the entrance to it. A sepulchral lamp of everlasting oil shed a solemn light through the place. On an iron table in the centre of the cavern lay the magic armor, against it leaned the lance, and beside it stood an Arabian steed, caparisoned for the field, but motionless as a statue. The armor was bright and unsullied as it had gleamed in days of old, the steed in as good condition as if just from the pasture, and when Ahmed laid his hand upon his neck, he pawed the ground and gave a loud neigh of joy that shook the walls of the cavern. Thus amply provided with "horse and rider and weapon to wear," the prince determined to defy the field in the impending tourney.

The eventful morning arrived. The lists for the combat were prepared in the *vega*, or plain, just before the cliff-built walls of Toledo, where stages and galleries were erected for the spectators, covered with rich tapestry, and sheltered from the sun by silken awnings. All the beauties of the land were assembled in those galleries, while below pranced plumed knights with their pages and esquires, among whom figured conspicuously the princes who were to contend in the tourney. All the beauties of the land, however, were eclipsed when the Princess Aldegonda appeared in the royal pavilion, and for the first time broke forth upon the gaze of an admiring world. A murmur of wonder ran through the crowd at her transcendent loveliness; and the princes who were candidates for her hand, merely on the faith of her reported charms, now felt tenfold ardor for the conflict.

The princess, however, had a troubled look. The color came and went from her cheek, and her eye wandered with a restless and unsatisfied expression over the plumed throng of knights. The trumpets were about sounding for the encounter, when the herald announced the arrival of a strange knight, and Ahmed rode into the field. A steel helmet studded with gems rose above his turban, his cuirass was embossed with gold, his cimeter and dagger were of the workmanship of Fez, and flamed with precious stones. A round shield was at his shoulder, and in his hand he bore the lance of charmed virtue. The caparison of his Arabian steed was richly embroidered and swept the ground, and the proud animal pranced and snuffed the air, and neighed with joy at once more beholding the array of arms. The lofty and graceful demeanor of the prince struck every eye, and when his appellation was announced, "The Pilgrim of Love," a universal flutter and agitation prevailed among the fair dames in the galleries.

When Ahmed presented himself at the lists, however, they were closed against him, none but princes, he was told, were admitted to the contest. He declared his name and rank. Still worse!—he was a Moslem, and could not engage in a tourney where the hand of a Christian princess was the prize.

The rival princes surrounded him with haughty and menacing aspects, and one of insolent demeanor and herculean frame sneered at his light and youthful form, and scoffed at his amorous appellation. The ire of the prince was roused. He defied his rival to the encounter. They took distance, wheeled, and charged: and at the first touch of the magic lance, the brawny scoffer was tilted from his saddle. Here the prince would have paused, but, alas! he had to deal with a demoniac horse and armor; once in action, nothing could control them. The Arabian steed charged into the thickest of the throng; the lance overturned everything that presented; the gentle prince was carried pell-mell about the field, strewing it with high and low, gentle and simple, and grieving at his own involuntary exploits. The king stormed and raged at this outrage on his subjects and his guests. He ordered out all his guards—they were unhorsed as fast as they came up. The king threw off his robes, grasped buckler and lance, and rode forth to awe the stranger with the presence of majesty itself. Alas! majesty fared no better than the vulgar; the steel and lance were no respecters of persons; to the dismay of Ahmed, he was borne full tilt against the king, and in a moment the royal heels were in the air, and the crown was rolling in the dust.

At this moment the sun reached the meridian; the magic spell resumed its power; the Arabian steed scoured across the plain, leaped the barrier, plunged into the Tagus, swam its raging current, bore the prince breathless and amazed to the cavern, and resumed his station, like a statue, beside the iron table. The prince dismounted right gladly, and replaced the armor, to abide the further decrees of fate. Then seating himself in the cavern, he ruminated on the desperate state to which this demoniac steed and armor had reduced him. Never should he dare to show his face at Toledo after inflicting such disgrace upon its chivalry, and such an outrage on its king. What, too, would the princess think of so rude and riotous an achievement? Full of anxiety, he sent forth his winged messengers to gather tidings. The parrot resorted to all the public places and crowded resorts of the city, and soon returned with a world of gossip. All Toledo was in consternation. The princess had been borne off senseless to the palace; the tournament had ended in confusion; every one was talking of the sudden apparition, prodigious exploits, and strange disappearance of the Moslem knight. Some pronounced him a Moorish magician, others thought him a demon who had assumed a human shape, while others related traditions of enchanted warriors hidden in the caves of the mountains, and thought it might be one of these, who had made a sudden irruption from his den. All agreed that no mere ordinary mortal could have wrought such wonders, or unhorsed such accomplished and stalwart Christian warriors.

The owl flew forth at night and hovered about the dusky city, perching on the roofs and chimneys. He then wheeled his flight up to the royal palace, which stood on a rocky summit of Toledo, and went prowling about its terraces and battlements, eavesdropping at every cranny, and glaring in with his big goggling eyes at every window where there was a light, so as to throw two or three maids of honor into fits. It was not until the gray dawn began to peer above the mountains that he returned from his mousing expedition, and related to the prince what he had seen.

"As I was prying about one of the loftiest towers of the palace," said he, "I beheld through a casement a beautiful princess. She was reclining on a couch with attendants and physicians around her, but she would none of their ministry and relief. When they retired, I beheld her draw forth a letter from her bosom, and read and kiss it, and give way to loud lamentations; at which, philosopher as I am, I could but be greatly moved."

The tender heart of Ahmed was distressed at these tidings. "Too true were thy words, O sage Eben Bonabben," cried he; "care and sorrow and sleepless nights are the lot of lovers. Allah preserve the princess from the blighting influence of this thing called love!"

Further intelligence from Toledo corroborated the report of the owl. The city was a prey to uneasiness and alarm. The princess was conveyed to the highest tower of the palace, every avenue to which was strongly guarded. In the meantime a devouring melancholy had seized upon her, of which no one could divine the cause—she refused food and turned a deaf ear to every consolation. The most skilful physicians had essayed their art in vain; it was thought some magic spell had been practised upon her, and the king made proclamation, declaring that whoever should effect her cure should receive the richest jewel in the royal treasury.

When the owl, who was dozing in a corner, heard of this proclamation, he rolled his large eyes and looked more mysterious than ever.

"Allah Akbar!" exclaimed he, "happy the man that shall effect that cure, should he but know what to choose from the royal treasury."

"What mean you, most reverend owl?" said Ahmed.

"Hearken, O prince, to what I shall relate. We owls, you must know, are a learned body, and much given to dark and dusty research. During my late prowling at night about the domes and turrets of Toledo, I discovered a college of antiquarian owls, who hold their meetings in a great vaulted tower where the royal treasury is deposited. Here they were discussing the forms and inscriptions and designs of ancient gems and jewels, and of golden and silver vessels, heaped up in the treasury, the fashion of every country and age; but mostly they were interested about certain relics and talismans that have remained in the treasury since the time of Roderick the Goth. Among these was a box of sandalwood secured by bands of steel of Oriental workmanship, and inscribed with mystic characters known only to the learned few. This box and its inscription had occupied the college for several sessions, and had caused much long and grave dispute. At the time of my visit a very ancient owl, who had recently arrived from Egypt, was seated on the lid of the box, lecturing upon the inscription, and he proved from it that the coffer contained the silken carpet of the throne of Solomon the

Wise; which doubtless had been brought to Toledo by the Jews who took refuge there after the downfall of Jerusalem."

When the owl had concluded his antiquarian harangue, the prince remained for a time absorbed in thought. "I have heard," said he, "from the sage Eben Bonabben, of the wonderful properties of that talisman, which disappeared at the fall of Jerusalem, and was supposed to be lost to mankind. Doubtless it remains a sealed mystery to the Christians of Toledo. If I can get possession of that carpet, my fortune is secure."

The next day the prince laid aside his rich attire, and arrayed himself in the simple garb of an Arab of the desert. He dyed his complexion to a tawny hue, and no one could have recognized in him the splendid warrior who had caused such admiration and dismay at the tournament. With staff in hand, and scrip by his side, and a small pastoral reed, he repaired to Toledo, and presenting himself at the gate of the royal palace, announced himself as a candidate for the reward offered for the cure of the princess. The guards would have driven him away with blows. "What can a vagrant Arab like thyself pretend to do," said they, "in a case where the most learned of the land have failed?" The king, however, overheard the tumult, and ordered the Arab to be brought into his presence.

"Most potent king," said Ahmed, "you behold before you a Bedouin Arab, the greater part of whose life has been passed in the solitudes of the desert. These solitudes, it is well known, are the haunts of demons and evil spirits, who beset us poor shepherds in our lonely watchings, enter into and possess our flocks and herds, and sometimes render even the patient camel furious; against these, our counter charm is music; and we have legendary airs handed down from generation to generation, that we chant and pipe, to cast forth these evil spirits. I am of a gifted line, and possess this power in its fullest force. If it be any evil influence of the kind that holds a spell over thy daughter, I pledge my head to free her from its sway."

The king, who was a man of understanding, and knew the wonderful secrets possessed by the Arabs, was inspired with hope by the confident language of the prince. He conducted him immediately to the lofty tower, secured by several doors, in the summit of which was the chamber of the princess. The windows opened upon a terrace with balustrades, commanding a view over Toledo and all the surrounding country. The windows were darkened, for the princess lay within, a prey to a devouring grief that refused all alleviation.

The prince seated himself on the terrace, and performed several wild Arabian airs on his pastoral pipe, which he had learnt from his attendants in the Generalife at Granada. The princess continued insensible, and the doctors who were present shook their heads and smiled with incredulity and contempt: at length the prince laid aside the reed, and, to a simple melody, chanted the amatory verses of the letter which had declared his passion.

The princess recognized the strain—a fluttering joy stole to her heart; she raised her head and listened; tears rushed to her eyes and streamed down her cheeks; her bosom rose and fell with a tumult of emotions. She would have asked for the minstrel to be brought into her presence, but maiden coyness held her silent. The king read her wishes, and at his command Ahmed was conducted into the chamber. The lovers were discreet: they but exchanged glances, yet those glances spoke volumes. Never was triumph of music more complete. The rose had returned to the soft cheek of the princess, the freshness to her lip, and the dewy light to her languishing eyes.

All the physicians present stared at each other with astonishment. The king regarded the Arab minstrel with admiration mixed with awe. "Wonderful youth!" exclaimed he, "thou shalt henceforth be the first physician of my court, and no other prescription will I take but thy melody. For the present receive thy reward, the most precious jewel in my treasury."

"O king," replied Ahmed, "I care not for silver or gold or precious stones. One relic hast thou in thy treasury, handed down from the Moslems who once owned Toledo—a box of sandal-wood containing a silken carpet: give me that box, and I am content."

All present were surprised at the moderation of the Arab, and still more when the box of sandal-wood was brought and the carpet drawn forth. It was of fine green silk, covered with Hebrew and Chaldaic characters. The court physicians looked at each other, shrugged their shoulders, and smiled at the simplicity of this new practitioner, who could be content with so paltry a fee.

"This carpet," said the prince, "once covered the throne of Solomon the Wise; it is worthy of being placed beneath the feet of beauty."

So saying, he spread it on the terrace beneath an ottoman that had been brought forth for the princess; then seating himself at her feet——

"Who," said he, "shall counteract what is written in the book of fate? Behold the prediction of the astrologers verified. Know, O king, that your daughter and I have long loved each other in secret. Behold in me the Pilgrim of Love!"

These words were scarcely from his lips when the carpet rose in the air, bearing off the prince and the princess. The king and the physicians gazed after it with open mouths and straining eyes until it became a little speck on the white bosom of a cloud, and then disappeared in the blue vault of heaven.

The king in a rage summoned his treasurer. "How is this," said he, "that thou hast suffered an infidel to get possession of such a talisman?"

"Alas, sir, we knew not its nature, nor could we decipher the inscription of the box. If it be indeed the carpet of the throne of the wise Solomon, it is possessed of magic power, and can transport its owner from place to place through the air."

The king assembled a mighty army, and set off for Granada in pursuit of the fugitives. His march was long and toilsome. Encamping in the Vega, he sent a herald to demand restitution of his daughter. The king himself came forth with all his court to meet him. In the king he beheld the real minstrel, for Ahmed had succeeded to the throne on the death of his father, and the beautiful Aldegonda was his sultana.

The Christian king was easily pacified when he found that his daughter was suffered to continue in her faith; not that he was particularly pious, but religion is always a point of pride and etiquette with princes. Instead of bloody battles, there was a succession of feasts and rejoicings, after which the king returned well pleased to Toledo, and the youthful couple continued to reign, as happily as wisely, in the Alhambra.

It is proper to add that the owl and the parrot had severally followed the prince by easy stages to Granada; the former travelling by night, and stopping at the various hereditary possessions of his family; the latter figuring in gay circles of every town and city on his route.

Ahmed gratefully requited the services which they had rendered on his pilgrimage. He appointed the owl his prime-minister, the parrot his master of ceremonies. It is needless to say that never was a realm more sagely administered, nor a court conducted with more exact punctilio.

From *The Alhambra*

LEGEND OF THE MOOR'S LEGACY

A Ramble Among the Hills

I USED frequently to amuse myself towards the close of the day, when the heat had subsided, with taking long rambles about the neighboring hills, and the deep umbrageous valleys, accompanied by my historiographic squire, Mateo, to whose passion for gossiping I on such occasions gave the most unbounded license; and there was scarce a rock, or ruin, or broken fountain, or lonely glen, about which he had not some marvellous story; or, above all, some golden legend; for never was poor devil so munificent in dispensing hidden treasures.

. In the course of one of these strolls Mateo was more than usually communicative. It was toward sunset that we sallied forth from the great Gate of Justice, and ascended an alley of trees until we came to a clump of figs and pomegranates at the foot of the Tower of the Seven Floors (de los Siéte Suelos), the identical tower whence Boabdil is said to have issued, when he surrendered his capital. Here, pointing to a low archway in the foundation, Mateo informed me of a monstrous sprite or hobgoblin, said to infest this tower, ever since the time of the Moors, and to guard the treasures of a Moslem king. Sometimes it issues forth in the dead of the night, and scours the avenues of the Alhambra, and the streets of Granada, in the shape of a headless horse, pursued by six dogs with terrible yells and howlings.

"But have you ever met with it yourself, Mateo, in any of your rambles?" demanded I.

"No, Señor, God be thanked! but my grandfather, the tailor, knew several persons that had seen it, for it went about much oftener in his time than at present; sometimes in one shape, sometimes in another. Everybody in Granada has heard of the Belludo, for the old women and the nurses frighten the children with it when they cry. Some say it is the spirit of a cruel Moorish king, who killed his six sons and buried them in these vaults, and that they hunt him at nights in revenge."

I have included a prefatory chapter from *The Alhambra* so that the reader may have the tale in its original setting.—C.N.

I forbear to dwell upon the marvellous details given by the simple-minded Mateo about this redoubtable phantom, which has, in fact, been time out of mind a favorite theme of nursery tales and popular tradition in Granada, and of which honorable mention is made by an ancient and learned historian and topographer of the place.

Leaving this eventful pile, we continued our course, skirting the fruitful orchards of the Generalife, in which two or three nightingales were pouring forth a rich strain of melody. Behind these orchards we passed a number of Moorish tanks, with a door cut into the rocky bosom of the hill, but closed up. These tanks, Mateo informed me, were favorite bathing-places of himself and his comrades in boyhood, until frightened away by a story of a hideous Moor, who used to issue forth from the door in the rock to entrap unwary bathers.

Leaving these haunted tanks behind us, we pursued our ramble up a solitary mule-path winding among the hills, and soon found ourselves amidst wild and melancholy mountains, destitute of trees, and here and there tinted with scanty verdure. Everything within sight was severe and sterile, and it was scarcely possible to realize the idea that but a·short distance behind us was the Generalife, with its blooming orchards and terraced gardens, and that we were in the vicinity of delicious Granada, that city of groves and fountains. But such is the nature of Spain; wild and stern the moment it escapes from cultivation; the desert and the garden are ever side by side.

The narrow defile up which we were passing is called, according to Mateo, El Barranco de la Tinaja, or the Ravine of the Jar, because a jar full of Moorish gold was found here in old times. The brain of poor Mateo was continually running upon these golden legends.

"But what is the meaning of the cross I see yonder upon a heap of stones, in that narrow part of the ravine?"

"Oh, that's nothing—a muleteer was murdered there some years since."

"So then, Mateo, you have robbers and murderers even at the gates of the Alhambra?"

"Not at present, Señor; that was formerly, when there used to be many loose fellows about the fortress; but they've all been weeded out. Not but that the gypsies who live in caves in the hillsides, just out of the fortress, are many of them fit for anything; but we have had no murder about here for a long time past. The man who murdered the muleteer was hanged in the fortress."

Our path continued up the *barranco*, with a bold, rugged height to our left, called the Silla del Moro, or Chair of the Moor, from the tradition already alluded to, that the unfortunate Boabdil fled thither during a popular insurrection, and remained all day seated on the rocky summit, looking mournfully down on his factious city.

We at length arrived on the highest part of the promontory above Granada, called the mountain of the sun. The evening was approaching; the setting sun just gilded the loftiest heights. Here and there a solitary shepherd might be descried driving his flock down the declivities, to be folded for the night; or a muleteer and his lagging animals threading some mountain path to arrive at the city gates before nightfall.

Presently the deep tones of the cathedral bell came swelling up the defiles, proclaiming the hour of "oration" or prayer. The note was responded to from the belfry of every church, and from the sweet bells of the convents among the mountains. The shepherd paused on the fold of the hill, the muleteer in the midst of the road; each took off his hat and remained motionless for a time, murmuring his evening prayer. There is always something pleasingly solemn in this custom, by which, at a melodious signal, every human being throughout the land unites at the same moment in a tribute of thanks to God for the mercies of the day. It spreads a transient sanctity over the land, and the sight of the sun sinking in all his glory adds not a little to the solemnity of the scene.

In the present instance the effect was heightened by the wild and lonely nature of the place. We were on the naked and broken summit of the haunted mountain of the sun, where ruined tanks and cisterns, and the mouldering foundations of extensive buildings, spoke of former populousness, but where all was now silent and desolate.

As we were wandering about among these traces of old times, we came to a circular pit, penetrating deep into the bosom of the mountain, which Mateo pointed out as one of the wonders and mysteries of the place. I supposed it to be a well dug by the indefatigable Moors, to obtain their favorite element in its greatest purity. Mateo, however, had a different story, and one much more to his humor. According to a tradition, in which his father and grandfather firmly believed, this was an entrance to the subterranean caverns of the mountain, in which Boabdil and his court lay bound in magic spell, and whence they sallied forth at night, at allotted times, to revisit their ancient abodes.

"Ah, Señor, this mountain is full of wonders of the kind. In another place there was a hole somewhat like this, and just within it hung an iron pot by a chain; nobody knew what was in that pot, for it was always covered up; but everybody supposed it full of Moorish gold. Many tried to draw it forth, for it seemed just within reach; but the moment it was touched it would sink far, far down, and not come up again for some time. At last one who thought it must be enchanted touched it with the cross, by way of breaking the charm; and faith he did break it, for the pot sank out of sight and never was seen any more.

"All this is fact, Señor, for my grandfather was an eye-witness."

"What! Mateo; did he see the pot?"

"No, Señor, but he saw the hole where the pot had hung."

"It's the same thing, Mateo."

The deepening twilight, which in this climate is of short duration, admonished us to leave this haunted ground. As we descended the mountain defile, there was no longer herdsman nor muleteer to be seen, nor anything to be heard but our own footsteps and the lonely chirping of the cricket. The shadows of the valley grew deeper and deeper, until all was dark around us. The lofty summit of the Sierra Nevada alone retained a lingering gleam of daylight; its snowy peaks glaring against the dark blue firmament, and seeming close to us from the extreme purity of the atmosphere.

"How near the Sierra looks this evening!" said Mateo; "it seems as if you could touch it with your hand; and yet it is many long leagues off." While he was speaking, a star appeared over the snowy summit of the mountain, the only one yet visible in the heavens, and so pure, so large, so bright and beautiful, as to call forth ejaculations of delight from honest Mateo.

"*Que estrella hermosa! que clara y limpia es! No pueda ser estrella mas brillante!*"

(What a beautiful star! how clear and lucid—a star could not be more brilliant!)

I have often remarked this sensibility of the common people of Spain to the charms of natural objects. The lustre of a star, the beauty or fragrance of a flower, the crystal purity of a fountain, will inspire them with a kind of poetical delight; and then, what euphonious words their magnificent language affords, with which to give utterance to their transports!

"But what lights are those, Mateo, which I see twinkling along the Sierra Nevada, just below the snowy region, and which might be taken for stars, only that they are ruddy, and against the dark side of the mountain?"

"Those, Señor, are fires, made by the men who gather snow and ice for the supply of Granada. They go up every afternoon with mules and asses, and take turns, some to rest and warm themselves by the fires, while others fill the panniers with ice. They then set off down the mountains, so as to reach the gates of Granada before sunrise. That

Sierra Nevada, Señor, is a lump of ice in the middle of Andalusia, to keep it all cool in summer."

It was now completely dark; we were passing through the *barranco*, where stood the cross of the murdered muleteer, when I beheld a number of lights moving at a distance, and apparently advancing up the ravine. On nearer approach, they proved to be torches borne by a train of uncouth figures arrayed in black. It would have been a procession dreary enough at any time, but was peculiarly so in this wild and solitary place.

Mateo drew near, and told me, in a low voice, that it was a funeral train bearing a corpse to the burying-ground among the hills.

As the procession passed by, the lugubrious light of the torches, falling on the rugged features and funeral weeds of the attendants, had the most fantastic effect, but was perfectly ghastly, as it revealed the countenance of the corpse, which, according to the Spanish custom, as borne uncovered on an open bier. I remained for some time gazing after the dreary train as it wound up the dark defile of the mountain. It put me in mind of the old story of a procession of demons bearing the body of a sinner up the crater of Stromboli.

"Ah! Señor," cried Mateo, "I could tell you a story of a procession once seen among these mountains, but then you'd laugh at me, and say it was one of the legacies of my grandfather the tailor."

"By no means, Mateo. There is nothing I relish more than a marvellous tale."

"Well, Señor, it is about one of those very men we have been talking of, who gather snow on the Sierra Nevada.

"You must know, that a great many years since, in my grandfather's time, there was an old fellow, Tio Nicolo [Uncle Nicholas] by name, who had filled the panniers of his mule with snow and ice, and was returning down the mountain. Being very drowsy, he mounted upon the mule, and soon falling asleep, went with his head nodding and bobbing about from side to side, while his sure-footed old mule stepped along the edge of precipices, and down steep and broken *barrancos*, just as safe and steady as if it had been on plain ground. At length Tio Nicolo awoke, and gazed about him, and rubbed his eyes—and, in good truth, he had reason. The moon shone almost as bright as day, and he saw the city below him, as plain as your hand, and shining with its white buildings, like a silver platter, in the moonshine; but, Lord! Señor, it was nothing like the city he had left a few hours before! Instead of the cathedral, with its great dome and turrets, and the churches with their spires, and the convents with their pinnacles, all surmounted with the blessed cross, he saw nothing but Moorish mosques, and minarets, and cupolas, all topped off with glittering crescents, such as you see on the Barbary flags. Well, Señor, as you may suppose, Tio Nicolo was mightily puzzled at all this, but while he was gazing down upon the city, a great army came marching up the mountains, winding along the ravines, sometimes in the moonshine, sometimes in the shade. As it drew nigh, he saw that there were horse and foot, all in Moorish armor. Tio Nicolo tried to scramble out of their way, but his old mule stood stock still, and refused to budge, trembling, at the same time, like a leaf,—for dumb beasts, Señor, are just as much frightened at such things as human beings. Well, Señor, the hobgoblin army came marching by; there were men that seemed to blow trumpets, and others to beat drums and strike cymbals, yet never a sound did they make; they all moved on without the least noise, just as I have seen painted armies move across the stage in the theatre of Granada, and all looked as pale as death. At last, in the rear of the army, between two black Moorish horsemen, rode the Grand Inquisitor of Granada, on a mule as white as snow. Tio Nicolo wondered to see him in such company, for the Inquisitor was famous for his hatred of Moors, and, indeed, of all kinds of infidels, Jews, and heretics, and used to hunt them out with fire and scourge. However, Tio Nicolo felt himself safe, now that there was a priest of such sanctity at hand. So, making the sign of the cross, he called out for his benediction, when, *hombre!* he received a blow that sent him and his old mule over the edge of a steep bank, down which they rolled, head-over-heels, to the bottom! Tio Nicolo did not come to his senses until long after sunrise, when he found himself at the bottom of a deep ravine, his mule grazing beside him, and his panniers of snow completely melted. He crawled back to Granada sorely bruised and battered, but was glad to find the city looking as usual, with Christian churches and crosses. When he told the story of his night's adventure, every one laughed at him; some said he had dreamed it all, as he dozed on his mule; others thought it all a fabrication of his own; but what was strange, Señor, and made people afterwards think more seriously of the matter, was, that the Grand Inquisitor died within the year. I have often heard my grandfather, the tailor, say, that there was more meant by that hobgoblin army bearing off the resemblance of the priest, than folks dared to surmise."

"Then you would insinuate, friend Mateo, that there is a kind of Moorish limbo, or purgatory, in the bowels of these mountains, to which the *padre* Inquisitor was borne off."

"God forbid, Señor! I know nothing of the matter. I only relate what I heard from my grandfather."

By the time Mateo had finished the tale, which I have more succinctly related, and which was interlarded with many comments, and spun out with minute details, we reached the gate of the Alhambra.

The marvellous stories hinted at by Mateo, in the early part of our ramble about the Tower of the Seven Floors, set me as usual upon my goblin researches. I found that the redoubtable phantom, the Belludo, had been time out of mind a favorite theme of nursery tales and popular traditions in Granada, and that honorable mention had been made of it by an ancient historian and topographer of the place. The scattered members of one of these popular traditions I have gathered together, collated them with infinite pains, and digested them into the following legend; which only wants a number of learned notes and references at bottom to take its rank among those concrete productions gravely passed upon the world for historical facts.

JUST within the fortress of the Alhambra, in front of the royal palace, is a broad open esplanade, called the Place or Square of the Cisterns (La Plaza de los Algibes), so called from being undermined by reservoirs of water, hidden from sight, and which have existed from the time of the Moors. At one corner of this esplanade is a Moorish well, cut through the living rock to a great depth, the water of which is cold as ice and clear as crystal. The wells made by the Moors are always in repute, for it is well known what pains they took to penetrate to the purest and sweetest springs and fountains. The one of which we now speak is famous throughout Granada, insomuch that water-carriers, some bearing great water-jars on their shoulders, others driving asses before them laden with earthen vessels, are ascending and descending the steep woody avenues of the Alhambra, from early dawn until a late hour of the night.

Fountains and wells, ever since the scriptural days, have been noted gossiping-places in hot climates; and at the well in question there is a kind of perpetual club kept up during the livelong day, by the invalids, old women, and other curious do-nothing folk of the fortress, who sit here on the stone benches, under an awning spread over the well to shelter the toll-gatherer from the sun, and dawdle over the gossip of the fortress, and question every water-carrier that arrives about the news of the city, and make long comments on everything they hear and see. Not an hour of the day but loitering housewives and idle maidservants may be seen, lingering, with pitcher on head or in hand, to hear the last of the endless tattle of these worthies.

Among the water-carriers who once resorted to this well, there was a sturdy, strong-backed, bandy-legged little fellow, named Pedro Gil, but called Peregil for shortness. Being a water-carrier, he was a Gallego, or native of Galicia, of course. Nature seems to have formed races of men, as she has of animals, for different kinds of drudgery. In France; the shoeblacks are all Savoyards, the porters of hotels all Swiss, and in the days of hoops and hair-powder in England, no man could give the regular swing to a sedan-chair but a bog-trotting Irishman. So in Spain, the carriers of water and bearers of burdens are all sturdy little natives of Galicia. No man says, "Get me a porter," but, "Call a Gallego."

To return from this digression, Peregil the Gallego had begun business with merely a great earthen jar which he carried upon his shoulder; by degrees he rose in the world, and was enabled to purchase an assistant of a correspondent class of animals, being a stout shaggy-haired donkey. On each side of this his long-eared aide-de-camp, in a kind of pannier, were slung his water-jars, covered with fig-leaves to protect them from the sun. There was not a more industrious water-carrier in all Granada, nor one more merry withal. The streets rang with his cheerful voice as he trudged after his donkey, singing forth the usual summer note that resounds through the Spanish towns: *"Quien quiere agua—agua mas fria que la nieve?"*—"Who wants water—water colder than snow? Who wants water from the well of the Alhambra, cold as ice and clear as crystal?" When he served a customer with a sparkling glass, it was always with a pleasant word that caused a smile; and if, perchance it was a comely dame or dimpling damsel, it was always with a sly leer and a compliment to her beauty that was irresistible. Thus Peregil the Gallego was noted throughout all Granada for being one of the civilest, pleasantest, and happiest of mortals. Yet it is not he who sings loudest and jokes most that has the lightest heart. Under all this air of merriment, honest Peregil had his cares and troubles. He had a large family of ragged children to support, who were hungry and clamorous as a nest of young swallows, and beset him with their outcries for food whenever he came home of an evening. He had a helpmate, too, who was anything but a help to him. She had been a village beauty before marriage, noted for her skill at dancing the *bolero* and rattling the castanets; and she still retained her early propensities, spending the hard earnings of honest Peregil in frippery, and laying the very donkey under requisition for junketing parties into the country on Sundays and saints' days, and those innumerable holidays, which are rather more numerous in Spain than the days of the week. With all this she was a little of a slattern, something more of a lie-abed, and, above all, a gossip of the first water; neglecting house, household, and everything else, to loiter slipshod in the houses of her gossip neighbors.

He, however, who tempers the wind to the shorn lamb, accommo-
dates the yoke of matrimony to the submissive neck. Peregil bore all
the heavy dispensations of wife and children with as meek a spirit as
his donkey bore the water-jars; and, however he might shake his ears
in private, never ventured to question the household virtues of his
slattern spouse.

He loved his children, too, even as an owl loves its owlets, seeing in
them his own image multiplied and perpetuated; for they were a
sturdy, long-backed, bandy-legged little brood. The great pleasure of
honest Peregil was, whenever he could afford himself a scanty holiday,
and had a handful of *maravedis* to spare, to take the whole litter forth
with him, some in his arms, some tugging at his skirts, and some trudging at his heels, and to treat them to a gambol among the orchards of
the Vega, while his wife was dancing with her holiday friends in the
Angosturas of the Darro.

It was a late hour one summer night, and most of the water-carriers
had desisted from their toils. The day had been uncommonly sultry; the
night was one of those delicious moonlights which tempt the inhabitants of southern climes to indemnify themselves for the heat and inac-
tion of the day, by lingering in the open air, and enjoying its tempered
sweetness until after midnight. Customers for water were therefore
still abroad. Peregil, like a considerate, painstaking father, thought
of his hungry children. "One more journey to the well," said he to
himself, "to earn a Sunday's *puchero* for the little ones." So saying,
he trudged manfully up the steep avenue of the Alhambra, singing as
he went, and now and then bestowing a hearty thwack with a cudgel
on the flanks of his donkey, either by way of cadence to the song, or
refreshment to the animal; for dry blows serve in lieu of provender
in Spain for all beasts of burden.

When arrived at the well, he found it deserted by every one except
a solitary stranger in Moorish garb, seated on a stone bench in the
moonlight. Peregil paused at first and regarded him with surprise,
not unmixed with awe, but the Moor feebly beckoned him to approach. "I am faint and ill," said he; "aid me to return to the city, and
I will pay thee double what thou couldst gain by the jars of water."

The honest heart of the little water-carrier was touched with compassion at the appeal of the stranger. "God forbid," said he, "that I
should ask fee or reward for doing a common act of humanity." He
accordingly helped the Moor on his donkey, and set off slowly for
Granada, the poor Moslem being so weak that it was necessary to hold
him on the animal to keep him from falling to the earth.

When they entered the city the water-carrier demanded whither he should conduct him. "Alas!" said the Moor, faintly, "I have neither home nor habitation; I am a stranger in the land. Suffer me to lay my head this night beneath thy roof, and thou shalt be amply repaid."

Honest Peregil thus saw himself unexpectedly saddled with an infidel guest, but he was too humane to refuse a night's shelter to a fellow-being in so forlorn a plight; so he conducted the Moor to his dwelling. The children, who had sallied forth open-mouthed as usual on hearing the tramp of the donkey, ran back with affright when they beheld the turbaned stranger, and hid themselves behind their mother. The latter stepped forth intrepidly, like a ruffling hen before her brood when a vagrant dog approaches.

"What infidel companion," cried she, "is this you have brought home at this late hour to draw upon us the eyes of the inquisition?"

"Be quiet, wife," replied the Gallego; "here is a poor sick stranger, without friend or home; wouldst thou turn him forth to perish in the streets?"

The wife would still have remonstrated, for although she lived in a hovel, she was a furious stickler for the credit of her house; the little water-carrier, however, for once was stiffnecked, and refused to bend beneath the yoke. He assisted the poor Moslem to alight, and spread a mat and a sheep-skin for him, on the ground, in the coolest part of the house; being the only kind of bed that his poverty afforded.

In a little while the Moor was seized with violent convulsions, which defied all the ministering skill of the simple water-carrier. The eye of the poor patient acknowledged his kindness. During an interval of his fits he called him to his side, and addressing him in a low voice: "My end," said he, "I fear is at hand. If I die, I bequeath you this box as a reward for your charity"; so saying, he opened his *albornoz*, or cloak, and showed a small box of sandal-wood, strapped round his body. "God grant, my friend," replied the worthy little Gallego, "that you may live many years to enjoy our treasure, whatever it may be." The Moor shook his head; he laid his hand upon the box, and would have said something more concerning it, but his convulsions returned with increasing violence, and in a little while he expired.

The water-carrier's wife was now as one distracted. "This comes," said she, "of your foolish good-nature, always running into scrapes to oblige others. What will become of us when this corpse is found in our house? We shall be sent to prison as murderers; and if we escape with our lives, we shall be ruined by notaries and *alguazils*."

Poor Peregil was in equal tribulation, and almost repented himself of having done a good deed. At length a thought struck him. "It is not yet day," said he; "I can convey the dead body out of the city, and bury it in the sands on the banks of the Xenil. No one saw the Moor enter our dwelling, and no one will know anything of his death."

So said, so done. The wife aided him; they rolled the body of the unfortunate Moslem in the mat on which he had expired, laid it across the ass, and Peregil set out with it for the banks of the river.

As ill-luck would have it, there lived opposite to the water-carrier a barber named Pedrillo Pedrugo, one of the most prying, tattling, and mischief-making of his gossip tribe. He was a weasel-faced, spider-legged varlet, supple and insinuating; the famous barber of Seville could not surpass him for his universal knowledge of the affairs of others, and he had no more power of retention than a sieve. It was said that he slept but with one eye at a time, and kept one ear uncovered, so that even in his sleep he might see and hear all that was going on. Certain it is, he was a sort of scandalous chronicle for the quidnuncs of Granada, and had more customers than all the rest of his fraternity.

This meddlesome barber heard Peregil arrive at an unusual hour at night, and the exclamations of his wife and children. His head was instantly popped out of a little window which served him as a look-out, and he saw his neighbor assist a man in Moorish garb into his dwelling. This was so strange an occurrence that Pedrillo Pedrugo slept not a wink that night. Every five minutes he was at his loophole, watching the lights that gleamed through the chinks of his neighbor's door, and before daylight he beheld Peregil sally forth with his donkey unusually laden.

The inquisitive barber was in a fidget; he slipped on his clothes, and, stealing forth silently, followed the water-carrier at a distance, until he saw him dig a hole in the sandy bank of the Xenil, and bury something that had the appearance of a dead body.

The barber hied him home, and fidgeted about his shop, setting everything upside down, until sunrise. He then took a basin under his arm, and sallied forth to the house of his daily customer the Alcalde.

The Alcalde had just risen. Pedrillo Pedrugo seated him in a chair, threw a napkin round his neck, put a basin of hot water under his chin, and began to mollify his beard with his fingers.

"Strange doings!" said Pedrugo, who played barber and newsmonger at the same time,—"strange doings! Robbery, and murder, and burial all in one night!"

"Hey!—how!—what is that you say," cried the Alcalde.

"I say," replied the barber, rubbing a piece of soap over the nose and mouth of the dignitary, for a Spanish barber disdains to employ a brush,—"I say that Peregil the Gallego has robbed and murdered a

Moorish Mussulman, and buried him, this blessed night. *Maldita sea la noche;*—Accursed be the night for the same!"

"But how do you know all this?" demanded the Alcalde.

"Be patient, Señor, and you shall hear all about it," replied Pedrillo, taking him by the nose and sliding a razor over his cheek. He then recounted all that he had seen, going through both operations at the same time, shaving his beard, washing his chin, and wiping him dry with a dirty napkin, while he was robbing, murdering, and burying the Moslem.

Now it so happened that this Alcalde was one of the most overbearing and at the same time most griping and corrupt curmudgeons in all Granada. It could not be denied, however, that he set a high value upon justice, for he sold it at its weight in gold. He presumed the case in point to be one of murder and robbery; doubtless there must be a rich spoil; how was it to be secured into the legitimate hands of the law? for as to merely entrapping the delinquent—that would be feeding the gallows; but entrapping the booty—that would be enriching the judge, and such, according to his creed, was the great end of justice. So thinking, he summoned to his presence his trustiest *alguazil* —a gaunt, hungry-looking varlet, clad, according to the custom of his order, in the ancient Spanish garb, a broad black beaver turned up at its sides; a quaint ruff; a small black cloak dangling from his shoulders; rusty black under-clothes that set off his spare wiry frame, while in his hand he bore a slender white wand, the dreaded insignia of his office. Such was the legal bloodhound of the ancient Spanish breed, that he put upon the traces of the unlucky water-carrier, and such was his speed and certainty, that he was upon the haunches of poor Peregil before he had returned to his dwelling, and brought both him and his donkey before the dispenser of justice.

The Alcalde bent upon him one of the most terrific frowns. "Hark ye, culprit!" roared he, in a voice that made the knees of the little Gallego smite together,—"hark ye, culprit! there is no need of denying thy guilt, everything is known to me. A gallows is the proper reward for the crime thou hast committed, but I am merciful, and readily listen to reason. The man that has been murdered in thy house was a Moor, an infidel, the enemy of our faith. It was doubtless in a fit of religious zeal that thou hast slain him. I will be indulgent, therefore; render up the property of which thou hast robbed him, and we will hush the matter up."

The poor water-carrier called upon all the saints to witness his innocence; alas! not one of them appeared; and if they had the Alcalde would have disbelieved the whole calendar. The water-carrier related

the whole story of the dying Moor with the straightforward simplicity of truth, but it was all in vain. "Wilt thou persist in saying,"
demanded the judge, "that this Moslem had neither gold nor jewels,
which were the object of thy cupidity?"

"As I hope to be saved, your worship," replied the water-carrier, "he
had nothing but a small box of sandal-wood, which he bequeathed
to me in reward for my services."

"A box of sandal-wood! a box of sandalwood!" exclaimed the Alcalde, his eyes sparkling at the idea of precious jewels. "And where is
this box? where have you concealed it?"

"An' it please your grace," replied the water-carrier, "it is in one of
the panniers of my mule, and heartily at the service of your worship."

He had hardly spoken the words, when the keen *alguazil* darted
off, and reappeared in an instant with the mysterious box of sandal-
wood. The Alcalde opened it with an eager and trembling hand; all
pressed forward to gaze upon the treasure it was expected to contain; when, to their disappointment, nothing appeared within, but a
parchment scroll, covered with Arabic characters, and an end of a
waxen taper.

When there is nothing to be gained by the conviction of a prisoner,
justice, even in Spain, is apt to be impartial. The Alcalde, having
recovered from his disappointment, and found that there was really
no booty in the case, now listened dispassionately to the explanation of
the water-carrier, which was corroborated by the testimony of his wife.
Being convinced, therefore, of his innocence, he discharged him
from arrest; nay, more, he permitted him to carry off the Moor's legacy,
the box of sandal-wood and its contents, as the well-merited reward of
his humanity; but he retained his donkey in payment of costs and
charges.

Behold the unfortunate little Gallego reduced once more to the
necessity of being his own water-carrier, and trudging up to the well of
the Alhambra with a great earthen jar upon his shoulder.

As he toiled up the hill in the heat of a summer noon, his usual
good-humor forsook him. "Dog of an Alcalde!" would he cry, "to rob a
poor man of the means of his subsistence, of the best friend he had
in the world!" And then at the remembrance of the beloved companion
of his labors, all the kindness of his nature would break forth. "Ah,
donkey of my heart!" would he exclaim, resting his burden on a stone,
and wiping the sweat from his brow—"ah, donkey of my heart! I warrant me thou thinkest of thy old master! I warant me thou missest the
water-jars—poor beast!"

To add to his afflictions, his wife received him, on his return home, with whimperings and repinings; she had clearly the vantage-ground of him, having warned him not to commit the egregious act of hospitality which had brought on him all these misfortunes; and, like a knowing woman, she took every occasion to throw her superior sagacity in his teeth. If her children lacked food, or needed a new garment, she could answer with a sneer, "Go to your father—he is heir to King Chico of the Alhambra: ask him to help you out of the Moor's strong box."

Was ever poor mortal so soundly punished for having done a good action? The unlucky Peregil was grieved in flesh and spirit, but still he bore meekly with the railings of his spouse. At length, one evening, when, after a hot day's toil, she taunted him in the usual manner, he lost all patience. He did not venture to retort upon her, but his eye rested upon the box of sandal-wood, which lay on a shelf with lid half open, as if laughing in mockery at his vexation. Seizing it up, he dashed it with indignation to the floor. "Unlucky was the day that I ever set eyes on thee," he cried, "or sheltered thy master beneath my roof!"

As the box struck the floor, the lid flew wide open, and the parchment scroll rolled forth.

Peregil sat regarding the scroll for some time in moody silence. At length rallying his ideas, "Who knows," thought he, "but this writing may be of some importance, as the Moor seems to have guarded it with such care?" Picking it up therefore, he put it in his bosom, and the next morning, as he was crying water through the streets, he stopped at the shop of a Moor, a native of Tangiers, who sold trinkets and perfumery in the Zacatin, and asked him to explain the contents.

The Moor read the scroll attentively, then stroked his beard and smiled. "This manuscript," said he, "is a form of incantation for the recovery of hidden treasure that is under the power of enchantment. It is said to have such virtue that the strongest bolts and bars, nay the adamantine rock itself, will yield before it!"

"Bah!" cried the little Gallego, "what is all that to me? I am no enchanter, and know nothing of buried treasure." So saying, he shouldered his water-jar, left the scroll in the hands of the Moor, and trudged forward on his daily rounds.

That evening, however, as he rested himself about twilight at the well of the Alhambra, he found a number of gossips assembled at the place, and their conversation, as is not unusual at that shadowy hour, turned upon old tales and traditions of a supernatural nature. Being all poor as rats, they dwelt with peculiar fondness upon the popular theme of enchanted riches left by the Moors in various parts of the Alhambra. Above all, they concurred in the belief that there were great treasures buried deep in the earth under the Tower of the Seven Floors.

These stories made an unusual impression on the mind of the honest Peregil, and they sank deeper and deeper into his thoughts as he returned alone down the darkling avenues. "If, after all, there should be treasure hid beneath that tower; and if the scroll I left with the Moor should enable me to get at it!" In the sudden ecstasy of the thought he had well-nigh let fall his water-jar.

That night he tumbled and tossed, and could scarcely get a wink of sleep for the thoughts that were bewildering his brain. Bright and early he repaired to the shop of the Moor, and told him all that was passing in his mind. "You can read Arabic," said he; "suppose we go together to the tower, and try the effect of the charm; if it fails, we are no worse off than before; but if it succeeds, we will share equally all the treasure we may discover."

"Hold," replied the Moslem; "this writing is not sufficient of itself; it must be read at midnight, by the light of a taper singularly compounded and prepared, the ingredients of which are not within my reach. Without such a taper the scroll is of no avail."

"Say no more!" cried the little Gallego; "I have such a taper at hand, and will bring it here in a moment." So saying, he hastened home, and soon returned with the end of yellow wax taper that he had found in the box of sandal-wood.

The Moor felt it and smelled of it. "Here are rare and costly perfumes," said he, "combined with this yellow wax. This is the kind of taper specified in the scroll. While this burns, the strongest walls and most secret caverns will remain open. Woe to him, however, who lingers within until it be extinguished. He will remain enchanted with the treasure."

It was now agreed between them to try the charm that very night. At a late hour, therefore, when nothing was stirring but bats and owls, they ascended the woody hill of the Alhambra, and approached that awful tower, shrouded by trees and rendered formidable by so many traditionary tales. By the light of a lantern they groped their way through bushes, and over fallen stones, to the door of a vault beneath the tower. With fear and trembling they descended a flight of steps cut into the rock. It led to an empty chamber, damp and drear, from which another flight of steps led to a deeper vault. In this way they descended four several flights, leading into as many vaults, one below the other, but the floor of the fourth was solid; and though, according to tradition, there remained three vaults still below, it was said to be impossible to penetrate farther, the residue being shut up by strong enchantment. The air of this vault was damp and chilly, and had an earthy smell, and the light scarce cast forth any rays. They paused here for a time, in breathless suspense, until they faintly heard the clock of the watch-tower strike midnight; upon this they lit the waxen taper, which diffused an odor of myrrh and frankincense and storax.

The Moor began to read in a hurried voice. He had scarce finished when there was a noise as of subterraneous thunder. The earth shook, and the floor, yawning open, disclosed a flight of steps. Trembling with awe, they descended, and by the light of the lantern found themselves in another vault covered with Arabic inscriptions. In the centre stood a great chest, secured with seven bands of steel, at each end of which sat an enchanted Moor in armor, but motionless as a statue, being controlled by the power of the incantation. Before the chest were several jars filled with gold and silver and precious stones. In the largest of these they thrust their arms up to the elbow, and at every dip hauled forth handfuls of broad yellow pieces of Moorish gold, or bracelets and ornaments of the same precious metal, while occasionally a necklace of Oriental pearl would stick to their fingers. Still they trembled and breathed short while cramming their pockets with the spoils; and cast many a fearful glance at the two enchanted Moors, who sat grim and motionless, glaring upon them with unwinking eyes. At length, struck with a sudden panic at some fancied noise, they both rushed up the staircase, tumbled over one another into the upper apartment, overturned and extinguished the waxen taper, and the pavement again closed with a thundering sound.

Filled with dismay, they did not pause until they had groped their way out of the tower, and beheld the stars shining through the trees. Then, seating themselves upon the grass, they divided the spoil, determining to content themselves for the present with this mere skimming of the jars, but to return on some future night and drain them to the bottom. To make sure of each other's good faith, also, they divided the talismans between them, one retaining the scroll and the other the taper; this done, they set off with light hearts and well-lined pockets for Granada.

As they wended their way down the hill, the shrewd Moor whispered a word of counsel in the ear of the simple little water-carrier.

"Friend Peregil," said he, "all this affair must be kept a profound secret until we have secured the treasure, and conveyed it out of harm's way. If a whisper of it gets to the ear of the Alcalde, we are undone!"

"Certainly," replied the Gallego, "nothing can be more true."

"Friend Peregil," said the Moor, "you are a discreet man, and I make no doubt can keep a secret; but you have a wife."

"She shall not know a word of it," replied the little water-carrier, sturdily.

"Enough," said the Moor, "I depend upon thy discretion and thy promise."

Never was promise more positive and sincere; but alas! what man can keep a secret from his wife? Certainly not such a one as Peregil the water-carrier, who was one of the most loving and tractable of husbands. On his return home, he found his wife moping in a corner. "Mighty well," cried she as he entered, "you've come at last, after rambling about until this hour of the night. I wonder you have not brought home another Moor as a house-mate." Then bursting into tears, she began to wring her hands and smite her breast. "Unhappy woman that I am!" exclaimed she, "what will become of me? My house stripped and plundered by lawyers and *alguazils*; my husband a do-no-good, that no longer brings home bread to his family, but goes rambling about day and night, with infidel Moors! O my children! my children! what what will become of us? We shall all have to beg in the streets!"

Honest Peregil was so moved by the distress of his spouse that he could not help whimpering also. His heart was as full as his pocket, and not to be restrained. Thrusting his hand into the latter he hauled forth three or four broad gold-pieces, and slipped them into her bosom. The poor woman stared with astonishment, and could not understand the meaning of this golden shower. Before she could recover her surprise, the little Gallego drew forth a chain of gold and dangled it before her, capering with exultation, his mouth distended from ear to ear.

"Holy Virgin protect us!" exclaimed the wife. "What hast thou been doing, Peregil? surely thou hast not been committing murder and robbery!"

The idea scarce entered the brain of the poor woman than it became a certainty with her. She saw a prison and a gallows in the distance, and a little bandy-legged Gallego hanging pendent from it; and, overcome by the horrors conjured up by imagination, fell into violent hysterics.

What could the poor man do? He had no other means of pacifying his wife, and dispelling the phantoms of her fancy, than by relating the whole story of his good fortune. This, however, he did not do until he had exacted from her the most solemn promise to keep it a profound secret from every living being.

To describe her joy would be impossible. She flung her arms round the neck of her husband, and almost strangled him with her caresses.

"Now, wife," exclaimed the little man, with honest exultation, "what say you now to the Moor's legacy? Henceforth never abuse me for helping a fellow-creature in distress."

The honest Gallego retired to his sheep-skin mat, and slept as soundly as if on a bed of down. Not so his wife. She emptied the whole contents of his pockets upon the mat, and sat counting gold pieces of Arabic coin, trying on necklaces and earrings, and fancying the figure she should one day make when permitted to enjoy her riches.

On the following morning the honest Gallego took a broad golden coin, and repaired with it to a jeweller's shop in the Zacatin to offer it for sale, pretending to have found it among the ruins of the Alhambra. The jeweller saw that it had an Arabic inscription, and was of the purest gold; he offered, however, but a third of its value, with which the water-carrier was perfectly content. Peregil now bought new clothes for his little flock, and all kinds of toys, together with ample provisions for a hearty meal, and returning to his dwelling, set all his children dancing around him, while he capered in the midst, the happiest of fathers.

The wife of the water-carrier kept her promise of secrecy with surprising strictness. For a whole day and a half she went about, with a look of mystery and a heart swelling almost to bursting; yet she held her peace, though surrounded by her gossips. It is true she could not help giving herself a few airs, apologized for her ragged dress, and talked of ordering a new *basquiña*, all trimmed with gold lace and bugles, and a new lace *mantilla*. She threw out hints of her husband's intention of leaving off his trade of water-carrying, as it did not altogether agree with his health. In fact, she thought they should all retire to the country for the summer, that the children might have the benefit of the mountain air, for there was no living in the city in this sultry season.

The neighbors stared at each other, and thought the poor woman had lost her wits; and her airs and graces and elegant pretensions were the theme of universal scoffing and merriment among her friends the moment her back was turned.

If she restrained herself abroad, however, she indemnified herself at home, and putting a string of rich Oriental pearls round her neck, Moorish bracelets on her arms, and an *aigrette* of diamonds on her head, sailed backwards and forwards in her slattern rags about the room, now and then stopping to admire herself in a broken mirror. Nay, in the impulse of her simple vanity, she could not resist, on one occasion, showing herself at the window, to enjoy the effect of her finery on the passers by.

As the fates would have it, Pedrillo Pedrugo, the meddlesome barber, was at this moment sitting idly in his shop on the opposite side of the street, when his ever-watchful eye caught the sparkle of a diamond. In an instant he was at his loophole reconnoitring the slattern spouse of the water-carrier, decorated with the splendor of an Eastern bride. No sooner had he taken an accurate inventory of her ornaments, than he posted off with all speed to the Alcalde. In a little while the hungry *alguazil* was again on the scent, and before the day was over the unfortunate Peregil was once more dragged into the presence of the judge. "How is this, villain!" cried the Alcalde, in a furious voice. "You told me that the infidel who died in your house left nothing behind but an empty coffer, and now I hear of your wife flaunting in her rags decked out with pearls and diamonds. Wretch that thou art! prepare to render up the spoils of thy miserable victim, and to swing on the gallows that is already tired of waiting for thee."

The terrified water-carrier fell on his knees, and made a full relation of the marvellous manner in which he had gained his wealth. The Alcalde, the *alguazil*, and the inquisitive barber listened with greedy ears to this Arabian tale of enchanted treasure. The *alguazil* was despatched to bring the Moor who had assisted in the incantation. The Moslem entered, half frightened out of his wits at finding himself in the hands of the harpies of the law. When he beheld the water-carrier standing with sheepish looks and downcast countenance, he comprehended the whole matter. "Miserable animal," said he, as he passed near him, "did I not warn thee against babbling to thy wife?"

The story of the Moor coincided exactly with that of his colleague; but the Alcalde affected to be slow of belief, and threw out menaces of imprisonment and rigorous investigation.

"Softly, good Señor Alcalde," said the Mussulman, who by this time had recovered his usual shrewdness and self-possession. "Let us not mar fortune's favors in the scramble for them. Nobody knows anything of this matter but ourselves; let us keep the secret. There is wealth enough in the cave to enrich us all. Promise a fair division, and all shall be produced; refuse, and the cave shall remain forever closed."

The Alcalde consulted apart with the *alguazil*. The latter was an old fox in his profession. "Promise anything," said he, "until you get possession of the treasure. You may then seize upon the whole, and if he and his accomplice dare to murmur, threaten them with the fagot and the stake as infidels and sorcerers."

The Alcalde relished the advice. Smoothing his brow and turning to the Moor: "This is a strange story," said he, "and may be true; but I must have ocular proof of it. This very night you must repeat the incantation in my presence. If there be really such treasure, we will share it amicably between us, and say nothing further of the matter; if ye have deceived me, expect no mercy at my hands. In the meantime you must remain in custody."

The Moor and the water-carrier cheerfully agreed to these conditions, satisfied that the event would prove the truth of their words.

Towards midnight the Alcalde sallied forth secretly, attended by the *alguazil* and the meddlesome barber, all strongly armed. They conducted the Moor and the water-carrier as prisoners, and were provided with the stout donkey of the latter to bear off the expected treasure. They arrived at the tower without being observed, and tying the donkey to a fig-tree, descended into the fourth vault of the tower.

The scroll was produced, the yellow waxen taper lighted, and the Moor read the form of incantation. The earth trembled as before, and the pavement opened with a thundering sound, disclosing the narrow flight of steps. The Alcalde, the *alguazil,* and the barber were struck aghast, and could not summon courage to descend. The Moor and the water-carrier entered the lower vault, and found the two Moors seated as before, silent and motionless. They removed two of the great jars, filled with golden coin and precious stones. The water-carrier bore them up one by one upon his shoulders, but though a strong-backed little man, and accustomed to carry burdens, he staggered beneath their weight, and found, when slung on each side of his donkey, they were as much as the animal could bear.

· "Let us be content for the present," said the Moor; "here is as much treasure as we can carry off without being perceived, and enough to make us all wealthy to our heart's desire."

"Is there more treasure remaining behind?" demanded the Alcalde.

"The greatest prize of all," said the Moor, "a huge coffer bound with bands of steel, and filled with pearls and precious stones."

"Let us have up the coffer by all means," cried the grasping Alcalde.

"I will descend for no more," said the Moor, doggedly; "enough is enough for a reasonable man—more is superfluous."

"And I," said the water-carrier, "will bring up no further burden to break the back of my poor donkey."

Finding commands, threats and entreaties equally vain, the Alcalde turned to his two adherents. "Aid me," said he, "to bring up the coffer, and its contents shall be divided between us." So saying, he descended the steps, followed with trembling reluctance by the *alguazil* and the barber.

No sooner did the Moor behold them fairly earthed than he extinguished the yellow taper; the pavement closed with its usual crash, and the three worthies remained buried in its womb.

He then hastened up the different flights of steps, nor stopped until in the open air. The little water-carrier followed him as fast as his short legs would permit.

"What hast thou done?" cried Peregil, as soon as he could recover breath. "The Alcalde and the other two are shut up in the vault."

"It is the will of Allah!" said the Moor, devoutly.

"And will you not release them?" demanded the Gallego.

"Allah forbid!" replied the Moor, smoothing his beard. "It is written in the book of fate that they shall remain enchanted until some future adventurer arrive to break the charm. The will of God be done!" so saying, he hurled the end of the waxen taper far among the gloomy thickets of the glen.

There was now no remedy; so the Moor and the water-carrier proceeded with the richly laden donkey towards the city, nor could honest Peregil refrain from hugging and kissing his long-eared fellow-laborer, thus restored to him from the clutches of the law; and, in fact, it is doubtful which gave the simple-hearted little man most joy at the moment, the gaining of the treasure, or the recovery of the donkey.

The two partners in good luck divided their spoil amicably and fairly, except that the Moor, who had a little taste for trinketry, made out to get into his heap the most of the pearls and precious stones and other baubles, but then he always gave the water-carrier in lieu magnificent jewels of massy gold, of five times the size, with which the latter was heartily content. They took care not to linger within reach of accidents, but made off to enjoy their wealth undisturbed in other countries. The Moor returned to Africa, to his native city of Tangiers, and the Gallego, with his wife, his children, and his donkey, made the best of his way to Portugal. Here, under the admonition and tuition of his wife, he became a personage of some consequence, for she made the worthy little man array his long body and short legs in doublet and hose, with a feather in his hat and a sword by his side, and laying aside his familiar appellation of Peregil, assume the more sonorous title of Don Pedro Gil: his progeny grew up a thriving and merry-hearted, though short and bandy-legged generation, while Señora Gil, befringed, belaced, and betasselled from her head to her heels, with glittering rings on every finger, became a model of slattern fashion and finery.

As to the Alcalde and his adjuncts, they remained shut up under the great Tower of the Seven Floors, and there they remain spellbound at the present day. Whenever there shall be a lack in Spain of pimping barbers, sharking *alguazils*, and corrupt *alcaldes*, they may be sought after; but if they have to wait until such time for their deliverance, there is danger of their enchantment enduring until doomsday.

From *The Alhambra*

LEGEND OF THE THREE
BEAUTIFUL PRINCESSES

IN old times there reigned a Moorish king in Granada, whose name
was Mohamed, to which his subjects added the appellation of El
Hayzari, or "The Left-handed." Some say he was so called on account
of his being really more expert with his sinister than his dexter hand;
others, because he was prone to take everything by the wrong end, or,
in other words, to mar wherever he meddled. Certain it is, either
through misfortune or mismanagement, he was continually in trouble;
thrice was he driven from his throne, and on one occasion barely escaped to Africa with his life, in the disguise of a fisherman.* Still he
was as brave as he was blundering; and though left-handed, wielded his
cimeter to such purpose, that he each time re-established himself upon
his throne by dint of hard fighting. Instead, however, of learning wisdom from adversity, he hardened his neck, and stiffened his left arm
in wilfulness. The evils of a public nature which he thus brought upon
himself and his kingdom may be learned by those who will delve into
the Arabian annals of Granada; the present legend deals but with his
domestic policy.

As this Mohamed was one day riding forth with a train of his courtiers, by the foot of the mountain of Elvira, he met a band of horsemen
returning from a foray into the land of the Christians. They were conducting a long string of mules laden with spoil, and many captives of
both sexes, among whom the monarch was struck with the appearance
of a beautiful damsel, richly attired, who sat weeping on a low palfrey,
and heeded not the consoling words of a *duenna* who rode beside her.

The monarch was struck with her beauty, and, on inquiring of the
captain of the troop, found that she was the daughter of the Alcalde
of a frontier fortress, that had been surprised and sacked in the course
of the foray. Mohamed claimed her as his royal share of the booty, and
had her conveyed to his harem in the Alhambra. There everything was
devised to soothe her melancholy; and the monarch, more and more
enamored, sought to make her his queen. The Spanish maid at first

---

* The reader will recognize the sovereign connected with the fortunes of the
Abencerrages. His story appears to be a little fictionized in the legend.—w.i.

repulsed his addresses; he was an infidel; he was the open foe of her country; what was worse, he was stricken in years!

The monarch, finding his assiduities of no avail, determined to enlist in his favor the *duenna*, who had been captured with the lady. She was an Andalusian by birth, whose Christian name is forgotten, being mentioned in Moorish legends by no other appellation than that of the discreet Kadiga; and discreet in truth she was, as her whole history makes evident. No sooner had the Moorish king held a little private conversation with her, than she saw at once the cogency of his reasoning, and undertook his cause with her young mistress.

"Go to, now!" cried she; "what is there in all this to weep and wail about? Is it not better to be mistress of this beautiful palace, with all its gardens and fountains, than to be shut up within your father's old frontier tower? As to this Mohamed being an infidel, what is that to the purpose? You marry him, not his religion; and if he is waxing a little old, the sooner will you be a widow, and mistress of yourself; at any rate, you are in his power, and must either be a queen or a slave. When in the hands of a robber, it is better to sell one's merchandise for a fair price, than to have it taken by main force."

The arguments of the discreet Kadiga prevailed. The Spanish lady dried her tears, and became the spouse of Mohamed the Left-handed; she even conformed, in appearance, to the faith of her royal husband; and her discreet *duenna* immediately became a zealous convert to the Moslem doctrines: it was then the latter received the Arabian name of Kadiga, and was permitted to remain in the confidential employ of her mistress.

In due process of time the Moorish king was made the proud and happy father of three lovely daughters, all born at a birth; he could have wished they had been sons, but consoled himself with the idea that three daughters at a birth were pretty well for a man somewhat stricken in years, and left-handed!

As usual with all Moslem monarchs, he summoned his astrologers on this happy event. They cast the nativities of the three princesses, and shook their heads. "Daughters, O king!" said they, "are always precarious property; but these will most need your watchfulness when they arrive at a marriageable age; at that time gather them under your wings, and trust them to no other guardianship."

Mohamed the Left-handed was acknowledged to be a wise king by his courtiers, and was certainly so considered by himself. The prediction of the astrologers caused him but little disquiet, trusting to his ingenuity to guard his daughters and outwit the Fates.

The threefold birth was the last matrimonial trophy of the monarch; his queen bore him no more children, and died within a few years, bequeathing her infant daughters to his love, and to the fidelity of the discreet Kadiga.

Many years had yet to elapse before the princesses would arrive at that period of danger—the marriageable age. "It is good, however, to be cautious in time," said the shrewd monarch; so he determined to have them reared in the royal castle of Salobreña. This was a sumptuous palace, incrusted, as it were, in a powerful Moorish fortress on the summit of a hill overlooking the Mediterranean Sea. It was a royal retreat, in which the Moslem monarchs shut up such of their relatives as might endanger their safety; allowing them all kinds of luxuries and amusements, in the midst of which they passed their lives in voluptuous indolence.

Here the princesses remained, immured from the world, but surrounded by enjoyment, and attended by female slaves who anticipated their wishes. They had delightful gardens for their recreation, filled with the rarest fruits and flowers, with aromatic groves and perfumed baths. On three sides the castle looked down upon a rich valley, enamelled with all kinds of culture, and bounded by the lofty Alpuxarra mountains; on the other side it overlooked the broad sunny sea.

In this delicious abode, in a propitious climate, and under a cloudless sky, the three princesses grew up into wondrous beauty; but though all reared alike, they gave early tokens of diversity of character. Their names were Zayda, Zorayda, and Zorahayda; and such was their order of seniority, for there had been precisely three minutes between their births.

Zayda, the eldest, was of an intrepid spirit, and took the lead of her sisters in everything, as she had done in entering into the world. She was curious and inquisitive, and fond of getting at the bottom of things.

Zorayda had a great feeling for beauty, which was the reason, no doubt, of her delighting to regard her own image in a mirror or a fountain, and of her fondness for flowers, and jewels, and other tasteful ornaments.

As to Zorahayda, the youngest, she was soft and timid, and extremely sensitive, with a vast deal of disposable tenderness, as was evident from her number of pet-flowers, and pet-birds, and pet-animals, all of which she cherished with the fondest care. Her amusements, too, were of a gentle nature, and mixed up with musing and reverie. She would sit for hours in a balcony, gazing on the sparkling stars of a summer's night, or on the sea when lit up by the moon; and at such times, the song of a fisherman, faintly heard from the beach, or the notes of a Moorish flute from some gliding bark, sufficed to elevate her feelings into ecstasy. The least uproar of the elements, however, filled her with dismay; and a clap of thunder was enough to throw her into a swoon.

Years rolled on smoothly and serenely; the discreet Kadiga, to whom the princesses were confided, was faithful to her trust, and attended them with unremitting care.

The castle of Salobreña, as has been said, was built upon a hill on the sea-coast. One of the exterior walls straggled down the profile of the hill, until it reached a jutting rock over-hanging the sea, with a narrow sandy beach at its foot, laved by the rippling billows. A small watch-tower on this rock had been fitted up as a pavilion, with latticed windows to admit the sea-breeze. Here the princesses used to pass the sultry hours of mid-day.

The curious Zayda was one day seated at a window of the pavilion, as her sisters, reclining on ottomans, were taking the siesta or noontide slumber. Her attention was attracted to a galley which came coasting along, with measured strokes of the oar. As it drew near, she observed that it was filled with armed men. The galley anchored at the foot of the tower. A number of Moorish soldiers landed on the narrow beach, conducting several Christian prisoners. The curious Zayda awakened her sisters, and all three peeped cautiously through the close *jalousies* of the lattice which screened them from sight. Among the prisoners were three Spanish cavaliers, richly dressed. They were in the flower of youth, and of noble presence; and the lofty manner in which they carried themselves, though loaded with chains and surrounded with enemies, bespoke the grandeur of their souls. The princesses gazed with intense and breathless interest. Cooped up as they had been in this castle among female attendants, seeing nothing of the male sex but black slaves, or the rude fishermen of the sea-coast, it is not to be wondered at that the appearance of three gallant cavaliers, in the pride of youth and manly beauty, should produce some commotion in their bosom.

"Did ever nobler being tread the earth than that cavalier in crimson?" cried Zayda, the eldest of the sisters. "See how proudly he bears himself, as though all around him were his slaves!"

"But notice that one in green!" exclaimed Zorayda. "What grace! what elegance! what spirit!"

The gentle Zorahayda said nothing, but she secretly gave preference to the cavalier in blue.

The princesses remained gazing until the prisoners were out of sight; then, heaving long-drawn sighs, they turned round, looked at each other for a moment, and sat down, musing and pensive, on their ottomans.

The discreet Kadiga found them in this situation. They related what they had seen; and even the withered heart of the *duenna* was warmed. "Poor youths!" exclaimed she, "I'll warrant their captivity makes many a fair and high-born lady's heart ache in their native land! Ah! my children, you have little idea of the life these cavaliers lead in their own country. Such prankling at tournaments! such devotion to the ladies! such courting and serenading!"

The curiosity of Zayda was fully aroused; she was insatiable in her inquiries, and drew from the *duenna* the most animated pictures of the scenes of her youthful days and native land. The beautiful Zorayda bridled up, and slyly regarded herself in a mirror, when the theme turned upon the charms of the Spanish ladies; while Zorahayda suppressed a struggling sigh at the mention of moonlight serenades.

Every day the curious Zayda renewed her inquiries, and every day the sage *duenna* repeated her stories, which were listened to with profound interest, though with frequent sighs, by her gentle auditors. The discreet old woman awoke at length to the mischief she might be doing. She had been accustomed to think of the princesses only as children; but they had imperceptibly ripened beneath her eye, and now bloomed before her three lovely damsels of the marriageable age. It is time, thought the *duenna*, to give notice to the king.

Mohamed the Left-handed was seated one morning on a divan in a cool hall of the Alhambra, when a slave arrived from the fortress of Salobreña, with a message from the sage Kadiga, congratulating him on the anniversary of his daughters' birthday. The slave at the same time presented a delicate little basket, decorated with flowers, within which, on a couch of vine and fig-leaves, lay a peach, an apricot, and a nectarine, with their bloom and down and dewy sweetness upon them, and all in the early stage of tempting ripeness. The monarch was versed in the Oriental language of fruits and flowers, and rapidly divined the meaning of this emblematical offering.

"So," said he, "the critical period pointed out by the astrologers is arrived: my daughters are at a marriageable age. What is to be done? They are shut up from the eyes of men; they are under the eyes of the discreet Kadiga,—all very good; but still they are not under my own eye, as was prescribed by the astrologers. I must gather them under my wing, and trust to no other guardianship."

So saying, he ordered that a tower of the Alhambra should be prepared for their reception, and departed at the head of his guards for the fortress of Salobreña, to conduct them home in person.

About three years had elapsed since Mohamed had beheld his daughters, and he could scarcely credit his eyes at the wonderful change which that small space of time had made in their appearance. During the interval, they had passed that wondrous boundary line in female life which separates the crude, unformed, and thoughtless girl from the blooming, blushing, meditative woman. It is like passing from the flat, bleak, uninteresting plains of La Mancha to the voluptuous valleys and swelling hills of Andalusia.

Zayda was tall and finely formed, with a lofty demeanor and a penetrating eye. She entered with a stately and decided step, and made a profound reverence to Mohamed, treating him more as her sovereign than her father. Zorayda was of the middle height, with an alluring look and swimming gait, and a sparkling beauty, heightened by the assistance of the toilette. She approached her father with a smile, kissed his hand, and saluted him with several stanzas from a popular Arabian poet, with which the monarch was delighted. Zorahayda was shy and timid, smaller than her sisters, and with a beauty of that tender, beseeching kind which looks for fondness and protection. She was little fitted to command, like her elder sister, or to dazzle, like the second, but was rather formed to creep to the bosom of manly affection, to nestle within it, and be content. She drew near to her father, with a timid and almost faltering step, and would have taken his hand to kiss; but on looking up into his face, and seeing it beaming with a paternal smile, the tenderness of her nature broke forth, and she threw herself upon his neck.

Mohamed the Left-handed surveyed his blooming daughters with mingled pride and perplexity, for while he exulted in their charms, he bethought himself of the prediction of the astrologers. "Three daughters! three daughters!" muttered he repeatedly to himself, "and all of a marriageable age! Here's tempting Hesperian fruit, that requires a dragon watch!"

He prepared for his return to Granada, by sending heralds before him, commanding every one to keep out of the road by which he was to pass, and that all doors and windows should be closed at the approach of the princesses. This done, he set forth, escorted by a troop of black horsemen of hideous aspect, and clad in shining armor.

The princesses rode beside the king, closely veiled, on beautiful white palfreys, with velvet caparisons, embroidered with gold, and sweeping the ground; the bits and stirrups were of gold, and the silken bridles adorned with pearls and precious stones. The palfreys were covered with little silver bells, which made the most musical tinkling as they ambled gently along. Woe to the unlucky wight, however, who lingered in the way when he heard the tinkling of these bells!—the guards were ordered to cut him down without mercy.

The cavalcade was drawing near to Granada, when it overtook, on the banks of the river Xenil, a small body of Moorish soldiers with a convoy of prisoners. It was too late for the soldiers to get out of the way, so they threw themselves on their faces on the earth, ordering their captives to do the like. Among the prisoners were the three identical cavaliers whom the princesses had seen from the pavilion. They either did not understand, or were too haughty to obey the order, and remained standing and gazing upon the cavalcade as it approached.

The ire of the monarch was kindled at this flagrant defiance of his orders. Drawing his cimeter, and pressing forward, he was about to deal a left-handed blow that might have been fatal to at least one of the gazers, when the princesses crowded round him, and implored mercy for the prisoners; even the timid Zorahayda forgot her shyness, and became eloquent in their behalf. Mohamed paused, with uplifted cimeter, when the captain of the guard threw himself at his feet. "Let not your highness," said he, "do a deed that may cause great scandal throughout the kingdom. These are three brave and noble Spanish knights, who have been taken in battle, fighting like lions; they are of high birth, and may bring great ransoms." "Enough!" said the king. "I will spare their lives, but punish their audacity—let them be taken to the Vermilion Towers, and put to hard labor."

Mohamed was making one of his usual left-handed blunders. In the tumult and agitation of this blustering scene, the veils of the three princesses had been thrown back, and the radiance of their beauty revealed; and in prolonging the parley, the king had given that beauty time to have its full effect. In those days people fell in love much more suddenly than at present, as all ancient stories make manifest. It is not a matter of wonder, therefore, that the hearts of the three cavaliers were completely captured; especially as gratitude was added to their admiration. It is a little singular, however, though no less certain, that each of them was enraptured with a several beauty. As to the princesses, they were more than ever struck with the noble demeanor of the captives, and cherished in their breasts all that they had heard of their valor and noble lineage.

The cavalcade resumed its march; the three princesses rode pensively along on their tinkling palfreys, now and then stealing a glance behind in search of the Christian captives, and the latter were conducted to their allotted prison in the Vermilion Towers.

The residence provided for the princesses was one of the most dainty that fancy could devise. It was in a tower somewhat apart from the main palace of the Alhambra, though connected with it by the wall which encircled the whole summit of the hill. On one side it looked into the interior of the fortress, and had, at its foot, a small garden filled with the rarest flowers. On the other side it overlooked a deep embowered ravine separating the grounds of the Alhambra from those of the Generalife. The interior of the tower was divided into small fairy apartments, beautifully ornamented in the light Arabian style, surrounding a lofty hall, the vaulted roof of which rose almost to the summit of the tower. The walls and ceilings of the hall were adorned with arabesque and fretwork, sparkling with gold and with brilliant pencilling. In the centre of the marble pavement was an alabaster fountain, set round with aromatic shrubs and flowers, and throwing up a jet of water that cooled the whole edifice and had a lulling sound. Round the hall were suspended cages of gold and silver wire, containing singing-birds of the finest plumage or sweetest note.

The princesses had been represented as always cheerful when in the castle of the Salobreña; the king had expected to see them enraptured with the Alhambra. To his surprise, however, they began to pine, and grow melancholy, and dissatisfied with everything around them. The flowers yielded them no fragrance, the song of the nightingale disturbed their night's rest, and they were out of all patience with the alabaster fountain, with its eternal drop-drop and splash-splash, from morning till night and from night till morning.

The king, who was somewhat of a testy, tyrannical disposition, took this at first in high dudgeon; but he reflected that his daughters had arrived at an age when the female mind expands and its desires augment. "They are no longer children," said he to himself, "they are women grown, and require suitable objects to interest them." He put in requisition, therefore, all the dressmakers, and the jewellers, and the artificers in gold and silver throughout the Zacatin of Granada, and the princesses were overwhelmed with robes of silk, and tissue, and brocade, and cashmere shawls, and necklaces of pearls and diamonds, and rings, and bracelets, and anklets, and all manner of precious things.

All, however, was of no avail; the princesses continued pale and languid in the midst of their finery, and looked like three blighted rose-buds, drooping from one stalk. The king was at his wits' end. He had in general a laudable confidence in his own judgment, and never took advice. "The whims and caprices of three marriageable damsels, however, are sufficient," said he, "to puzzle the shrewdest head." So for once in his life he called in the aid of counsel.

The person to whom he applied was the experienced *duenna*.

"Kadiga," said the king, "I know you to be one of the most discreet women in the whole world, as well as one of the most trustworthy; for these reasons I have always continued you about the persons of my daughters. Fathers cannot be too wary in whom they repose such confidence; I now wish you to find out the secret malady that is preying upon the princesses, and to devise some means of restoring them to health and cheerfulness."

Kadiga promised implicit obedience. In fact she knew more of the malady of the princesses than they themselves. Shutting herself up with them, however, she endeavored to insinuate herself into their confidence.

"My dear children, what is the reason you are so dismal and downcast in so beautiful a place, where you have everything that heart can wish?"

The princesses looked vacantly round the apartment, and sighed.

"What more, then, would you have? Shall I get you the wonderful parrot that talks all languages, and is the delight of Granada?"

"Odious!" exclaimed the princess Zayda. "A horrid, screaming bird, that chatters words without ideas: one must be without brains to tolerate such a pest."

"Shall I send for a monkey from the rock of Gibraltar, to divert you with his antics?"

"A monkey! faugh!" cried Zorayda; "the detestable mimic of man. I hate the nauseous animal."

"What say you to the famous black singer Casem, from the royal harem, in Morocco? They say he has a voice as fine as a woman's."

"I am terrified at the sight of these black slaves," said the delicate Zorahayda; "besides I have lost all relish for music."

"Ah! my child, you would not say so," replied the old woman, slyly, "had you heard the music I heard last evening, from the three Spanish cavaliers whom we met on our journey. But bless me, children! what is the matter that you blush so and are in such a flutter?"

"Nothing, nothing, good mother; pray proceed."

"Well; as I was passing by the Vermilion Towers last evening, I saw the three cavaliers resting after their day's labor. One was playing on the guitar, so gracefully, and the others sang by turns; and they did it in such style, that the very guards seemed like statues, or men enchanted. Allah forgive me! I could not help being moved at hearing the songs of my native country. And then to see three such noble and handsome youths in chains and slavery!"

Here the kind-hearted old woman could not restrain her tears.

"Perhaps, mother, you could manage to procure us a sight of these cavaliers," said Zayda.

"I think," said Zorayda, "a little music would be quite reviving."

The timid Zorahayda said nothing, but threw her arms round the neck of Kadiga.

"Mercy on me!" exclaimed the discreet old woman, "what are you talking of, my children? Your father would be the death of us all if he heard of such a thing. To be sure, these cavaliers are evidently well-bred and high-minded youths; but what of that? they are the enemies of our faith, and you must not even think of them but with abhorrence."

There is an admirable intrepidity in the female will, particularly when about the marriageable age, which is not to be deterred by dangers and prohibitions. The princesses hung round their old *duenna*, and coaxed, and entreated, and declared that a refusal would break their hearts.

What could she do? She was certainly the most discreet old woman in the whole world, and one of the most faithful servants to the king; but was she to see three beautiful princesses break their hearts for the mere tinkling of a guitar? Besides, though she had been so long among the Moors, and changed her faith in imitation of her mistress, like a trusty follower, yet she was a Spaniard born, and had the lingerings of Christianity in her heart. So she set about to contrive how the wish of the princesses might be gratified.

The Christian captives, confined in the Vermilion Towers, were under the charge of a big-whiskered, broad-shouldered *renegado*, called Hussein Baba, who was reputed to have a most itching palm. She went to him privately, and slipping a broad piece of gold into his hand, "Hussein Baba," said she, "my mistresses the three princesses, who are shut up in the tower, and in sad want of amusement, have heard of the musical talents of the three Spanish cavaliers, and are desirous of hearing a specimen of their skill. I am sure you are too kind-hearted to refuse them so innocent a gratification."

"What! and to have my head set grinning over the gate of my own tower! for that would be the reward, if the king should discover it."

"No danger of anything of the kind; the affair may be managed so that the whim of the princesses may be gratified, and their father be never the wiser. You know the deep ravine outside of the walls which passes immediately below the tower. Put the three Christians to work there, and at the intervals of their labor, let them play and sing, as if for their own recreation. In this way the princesses will be able to hear them from the windows of the tower, and you may be sure of their paying well for your compliance."

As the good old woman concluded her harangue, she kindly pressed the rough hand of the *renegado,* and left within it another piece of gold.

Her eloquence was irresistible. The very next day the three cavaliers were put to work in the ravine. During the noontide heat, when their fellow-laborers were sleeping in the shade, and the guard nodding drowsily at his post, they seated themselves among the herbage at the foot of the tower, and sang a Spanish roundelay to the accompaniment of the guitar.

The glen was deep, the tower was high, but their voices rose distinctly in the stillness of the summer noon. The princesses listened from their balcony; they had been taught the Spanish language by their *duenna,* and were moved by the tenderness of the song. The discreet Kadiga, on the contrary, was terribly shocked. "Allah preserve us!" cried she, "they are singing a love-ditty, addressed to yourselves. Did ever mortal hear of such audacity? I will run to the slave-master, and have them soundly bastinadoed."

"What! bastinado such gallant cavaliers, and for singing so charmingly!" The three beautiful princesses were filled with horror at the idea. With all her virtuous indignation, the good old woman was of a placable nature, and easily appeased. Besides, the music seemed to have a beneficial effect upon her young mistresses. A rosy bloom had already come to their cheeks, and their eyes began to sparkle. She made no further objection, therefore, to the amorous ditty of the cavaliers.

When it was finished, the princesses remained silent for a time; at length Zorayda took up a lute, and with a sweet, though faint and trembling voice, warbled a little Arabian air, the burden of which was, "The rose is concealed among her leaves, but she listens with delight to the song of the nightingale."

From this time forward the cavaliers worked almost daily in the ravine. The considerate Hussein Baba became more and more indulgent, and daily more prone to sleep at his post. For some time a vague intercourse was kept up by popular songs and romances, which in some measure responded to each other, and breathed the feelings of the parties. By degrees the princesses showed themselves at the balcony, when they could do so without being perceived by the guards. They conversed with the cavaliers also, by means of flowers, with the symbolical language of which they were mutually acquainted; the difficulties of their intercourse added to its charms, and strengthened the passion they had so singularly conceived; for love delights to struggle with difficulties, and thrives the most hardily on the scantiest soil.

The change effected in the looks and spirits of the princesses by this secret intercourse, surprised and gratified the left-handed king; but no one was more elated than the discreet Kadiga, who considered it all owing to her able management.

At length there was an interruption in this telegraphic correspondence; for several days the cavaliers ceased to make their appearance in the glen. The princesses looked out from the tower in vain. In vain they stretched their swan-like necks from the balcony; in vain they sang like captive nightingales in their cage: nothing was to be seen of their Christian lovers; not a note responded from the groves. The discreet Kadiga sallied forth in quest of intelligence, and soon returned with a face full of trouble. "Ah, my children!" cried she, "I saw what all this would come to, but you would have your way; you may now hang up your lutes on the willows. The Spanish cavaliers are ransomed by their families; they are down in Granada, and preparing to return to their native country."

The three beautiful princesses were in despair at the tidings. Zayda was indignant at the slight put upon them, in thus being deserted without a parting word. Zorayda wrung her hands and cried, and looked in the glass, and wiped away her tears, and cried afresh. The gentle Zorahayda leaned over the balcony and wept in silence, and her tears fell drop by drop among the flowers of the bank, where the faithless cavaliers had so often been seated.

The discreet Kadiga did all in her power to soothe their sorrow. "Take comfort, my children," said she, "this is nothing when you are used to it. This is the way of the world. Ah! when you are as old as I am, you will know how to value these men. I'll warrant these cavaliers have their loves among the Spanish beauties of Cordova and Seville, and will soon be serenading under their balconies, and thinking no more of the Moorish beauties in the Alhambra. Take comfort, therefore, my children, and drive them from your hearts."

The comforting words of the discreet Kadiga only redoubled the distress of the three princesses, and for two days they continued inconsolable. On the morning of the third the good old woman entered their apartment, all ruffling with indignation.

"Who would have believed such insolence in mortal man!" exclaimed she, as soon as she could find words to express herself; "but I am rightly served for having connived at this deception of your worthy father. Never talk more to me of your Spanish cavaliers."

"Why, what has happened, good Kadiga?" exclaimed the princesses in breathless anxiety.

"What has happened?—treason has happened! or, what is almost as bad, treason has been proposed; and to me, the most faithful of subjects, the trustiest of *duennas!* Yes, my children, the Spanish cavaliers have dared to tamper with me, that I should persuade you to fly with them to Cordova, and become their wives!"

Here the excellent old woman covered her face with her hands, and gave way to a violent burst of grief and indignation. The three beautiful princesses turned pale and red, pale and red, and trembled, and looked down, and cast shy looks at each other, but said nothing. Meantime the old woman sat rocking backward and forward in violent agitation, and now and then breaking out into exclamations: "That ever I should live to be so insulted!—I, the most faithful of servants!"

At length the eldest princess, who had most spirit and always took the lead, approached her, and laying her hand upon her shoulder, "Well, mother," said she, "supposing we were willing to fly with these Christian cavaliers—is such a thing possible?"

The good old woman paused suddenly in her grief, looking up, "Possible," echoed she; "to be sure it is possible. Have not the cavaliers already bribed Hussein Baba, the *renegado* captain of the guard, and arranged the whole plan? But then, to think of deceiving your father! your father, who has placed such confidence in me!" Here the worthy woman gave way to a fresh burst of grief, and began again to rock backward and forward, and to wring her hands.

"But our father has never placed any confidence in us," said the eldest princess, "but has trusted to bolts and bars, and treated us as captives."

"Why, that is true enough," replied the old woman, again pausing in her grief; "he has indeed treated you most unreasonably, keeping you shut up here, to waste your bloom in a moping old tower, like roses left to wither in a flower-jar. But, then, to fly from your native land!"

"And is not the land we fly to the native land of our mother, where we shall live in freedom? And shall we not each have a youthful husband in exchange for a severe old father?"

"Why, that again is all very true; and your father, I must confess, is rather tyrannical; but what then," relapsing into her grief, "would you leave me behind to bear the brunt of his vengeance?"

"By no means, my good Kadiga; cannot you fly with us?"

"Very true, my child; and to tell the truth, when I talked the matter over with Hussein Baba, he promised to take care of me, if I would accompany you in your flight; but then, bethink you, my children, are you willing to renounce the faith of your father?"

"The Christian faith was the original faith of our mother," said the eldest princess; "I am ready to embrace it, and so, I am sure, are my sisters."

"Right again," exclaimed the old woman, brightening up; "it was the original faith of your mother, and bitterly did she lament on her death-bed that she had renounced it. I promised her then to take care of your souls, and I rejoice to see that they are now in a fair way to be saved. Yes, my children, I too was born a Christian, and have remained a Christian in my heart, and am resolved to return to the faith. I have talked on the subject with Hussein Baba, who is a Spaniard by birth, and comes from a place not far from my native town. He is equally anxious to see his own country, and to be reconciled to the Church; and the cavaliers have promised that, if we are disposed to become man and wife, on returning to our native land, they will provide for us handsomely."

In a word, it appeared that this extremely discreet and provident old woman had consulted with the cavaliers and the *renegado*, and had concerted the whole plan of escape. The eldest princess immediately assented to it, and her example, as usual, determined the conduct of her sisters. It is true, the youngest hesitated, for she was gentle and timid of soul, and there was a struggle in her bosom between filial feeling and youthful passion; the latter, however, as usual, gained the victory, and with silent tears and stifled sighs she prepared herself for flight.

The rugged hill on which the Alhambra is built was, in old times, perforated with subterranean passages cut through the rock and leading from the fortress to various parts of the city and to distant sally-ports on the banks of the Darro and the Xenil. They had been constructed at different times by the Moorish kings as means of escape from sudden insurrections, or of secretly issuing forth on private enterprises. Many of them are now entirely lost, while others remain, partly choked with rubbish, and partly walled up,—monuments of the jealous precautions and warlike stratagems of the Moorish government. By one of these passages Hussein Baba had undertaken to conduct the princesses to a sally-port beyond the walls of the city, where the cavaliers were to be ready with fleet steeds, to bear the whole party over the borders.

The appointed night arrived; the tower of the princesses had been locked up as usual, and the Alhambra was buried in deep sleep. Towards midnight the discreet Kadiga listened from the balcony of a window that looked into the garden. Hussein Baba, the *renegado*, was already below, and gave the appointed signal. The *duenna* fastened the end of a ladder of ropes to the balcony, lowered it into the garden and descended. The two eldest princesses followed her with beating hearts; but when it came to the turn of the youngest princess, Zorahayda, she hesitated and trembled. Several times she ventured a delicate little foot upon the ladder, and as often drew it back, while her poor little heart fluttered more and more the longer she delayed. She cast a wistful look back into the silken chamber; she had lived in it, to be sure, like a bird in a cage; but within it she was secure; who could tell what dangers might beset her should she flutter forth into the wide world! Now she bethought her of her gallant Christian lover, and her little foot was instantly upon the ladder; and anon she thought of her father, and shrank back. But fruitless is the attempt to describe the conflict in the bosom of one so young and tender and loving, but so timid and so ignorant of the world.

In vain her sisters implored, the *duenna* scolded, and the *renegado* blasphemed beneath the balcony: the gentle little Moorish maid stood doubting and wavering on the verge of elopement; tempted by the sweetness of the sin, but terrified at its perils.

Every moment increased the danger of discovery. A distant tramp was heard. "The patrols are walking their rounds," cried the *renegado*; "if we linger, we perish. Princess, descend instantly, or we leave you."

Zorahayda was for a moment in fearful agitation; then loosening the ladder of ropes, with desperate resolution she flung it from the balcony. "It is decided!" cried she; "flight is now out of my power! Allah guide and bless ye, my dear sisters!"

The two eldest princesses were shocked at the thoughts of leaving her behind, and would fain have lingered, but the patrol was advancing; the *renegado* was furious, and they were hurried away to the subterraneous passage. They groped their way through a fearful labyrinth, cut through the heart of the mountain, and succeeded in reaching, undiscovered, an iron gate that opened outside of the walls. The Spanish cavaliers were waiting to receive them, disguised as Moorish soldiers of the guard, commanded by the *renegado*.

The lover of Zorahayda was frantic when he learned that she had refused to leave the tower; but there was no time to waste in lamentations. The two princesses were placed behind their lovers, the discreet Kadiga mounted behind the *renegado*, and they all set off at a round pace in the direction of the Pass of Lope, which leads through the mountains towards Cordova.

They had not proceeded far when they heard the noise of drums and trumpets from the battlements of the Alhambra.

"Our flight is discovered!" said the *renegado*.

"We have fleet steeds, the night is dark, and we may distance all pursuit," replied the cavaliers.

They put spurs to their horses, and scoured across the Vega. They attained the foot of the mountain of Elvira, which stretches like a promontory into the plain. The *renegado* paused and listened. "As yet," said he, "there is no one on our traces, we shall make good our escape to the mountains." While he spoke, a light blaze sprang up on the top of the watch-tower of the Alhambra.

"Confusion!" cried the *renegado*, "that bale fire will put all the guards of the passes on the alert. Away! away! Spur like mad,—there is no time to be lost."

Away they dashed—the clattering of their horses' hoofs echoed from rock to rock, as they swept along the road that skirts the rocky mountain of Elvira. As they galloped on, the bale fire of the Alhambra was answered in every direction; light after light blazed on the *atalayas*, or watch-towers of the mountains.

"Forward! forward!" cried the *renegado*, with many an oath, "to the bridge,—to the bridge, before the alarm has reached there!"

They doubled the promontory of the mountains, and arrived in sight of the famous Bridge of Pinos, that crosses a rushing stream often dyed with Christian and Moslem blood. To their confusion, the tower on the bridge blazed with lights and glittered with armed men. The *renegado* pulled up his steed, rose in his stirrups, and looked about him for a moment; then beckoning to the cavaliers, he struck off from the road, skirted the river for some distance, and dashed into its waters. The cavaliers called upon the princesses to cling to them, and did the same. They were borne for some distance down the rapid current, the surges roared round them, but the beautiful princesses clung to their Christian knights, and never uttered a complaint. The cavaliers attained the opposite bank in safety, and were conducted by the *renegado*, by rude and unfrequented paths and wild *barrancos*, through the heart of the mountains, so as to avoid all the regular passes. In a word, they succeeded in reaching the ancient city of Cordova; where their restoration to their country and friends was celebrated with great rejoicings, for they were of the noblest families. The beautiful princesses were forthwith received into the bosom of the Church, and, after being in all due form made regular Christians, were rendered happy wives.

In our hurry to make good the escape of the princesses across the river, and up the mountains, we forgot to mention the fate of the discreet Kadiga. She had clung like a cat to Hussein Baba in the scamper across the Vega, screaming at every bound, and drawing many an oath from the whiskered *renegado;* but when he prepared to plunge his steed into the river, her terror knew no bounds. "Grasp me not so tightly," cried Hussein Baba; "hold on by my belt and fear nothing." She held firmly with both hands by the leathern belt that girded the broad-backed *renegado;* but when he halted with the cavaliers to take breath on the mountain summit, the *duenna* was no longer to be seen.

"What has become of Kadiga?" cried the princesses in alarm.

"Allah alone knows!" replied the *renegado;* "my belt came loose when in the midst of the river, and Kadiga was swept with it down the stream. The will of Allah be done! but it was an embroidered belt, and of great price."

There was no time to waste in idle regrets; yet bitterly did the princesses bewail the loss of their discreet counsellor. That excellent old woman, however, did not lose more than half of her nine lives in the water; a fisherman, who was drawing his nets some distance down the stream, brought her to land, and was not a little astonished at his miraculous draught. What further became of the discreet Kadiga, the legend does not mention; certain it is that she evinced her discretion in never venturing within the reach of Mohamed the Left-handed.

Almost as little is known of the conduct of that sagacious monarch when he discovered the escape of his daughters, and the deceit practised upon him by the most faithful of servants. It was the only instance in which he had called in the aid of counsel, and he was never afterwards known to be guilty of a similar weakness. He took good care, however, to guard his remaining daughter, who had no disposition to elope; it is thought, indeed, that she secretly repented having remained behind: now and then she was seen leaning on the battlements of the tower, and looking mournfully towards the mountains in the direction of Cordova, and sometimes the notes of her lute were heard accompanying plaintive ditties, in which she was said to lament the loss of her sisters and her lover, and to bewail her solitary life. She died young, and, according to popular rumor, was buried in a vault beneath the tower, and her untimely fate has given rise to more than one traditionary fable.

The following legend, which seems in some measure to spring out of the foregoing story, is too closely connected with high historic names to be entirely doubted. The Count's daughter, and some of her young companions, to whom it was read in one of the evening *tertullias,* thought certain parts of it had much appearance of reality; and Dolores, who was much more versed than they in the improbable truths of the Alhambra, believed every word of it.

LEGEND OF THE ROSE OF THE ALHAMBRA

FOR some time after the surrender of Granada by the Moors, that delightful city was a frequent and favorite residence of the Spanish sovereigns, until they were frightened away by successive shocks of earthquakes, which toppled down various houses, and made the old Moslem towers rock to their foundation.

Many, many years then rolled away, during which Granada was rarely honored by a royal guest. The palaces of the nobility remained silent and shut up; and the Alhambra, like a slighted beauty, sat in mournful desolation among her neglected gardens. The Tower of the Infantas, once the residence of the three beautiful Moorish princesses, partook of the general desolation; the spider spun her web athwart the gilded vault, and bats and owls nestled in those chambers that had been graced by the presence of Zayda, Zorayda, and Zorahayda. The neglect of this tower may have been partly owing to some superstitious notions of the neighbors. It was rumored that the spirit of the youthful Zorahayda, who had perished in that tower, was often seen by moonlight seated beside the fountain in the hall, or moaning about the battlements, and that the notes of her silver lute would be heard at midnight by wayfarers passing along the glen.

At length the city of Granada was once more welcomed by the royal presence. All the world knows that Philip V. was the first Bourbon that swayed the Spanish sceptre. All the world knows that he married, in second nuptials, Elizabetta or Isabella (for they are the same), the beautiful princess of Parma; and all the world knows that by this chain of contingencies a French prince and an Italian princess were seated together on the Spanish throne. For a visit of this illustrious pair, the Alhambra was repaired and fitted up with all possible expedition. The arrival of the court changed the whole aspect of the lately deserted palace. The clangor of drum and trumpet, the tramp of steed about the avenues and outer court, the glitter of arms and display of banners about barbican and battlement, recalled the ancient and war-like glories of the fortress. A softer spirit, however, reigned within the royal palace. There was the rustling of robes and the cautious tread and murmuring voice of reverential courtiers about the ante-chambers, a loitering of pages and maids of honor about the gardens, and the sound of music stealing from open casements.

Among those who attended in the train of the monarchs was a favorite page of the queen, named Ruyz de Alarcon. To say that he was a favorite page of the queen was at once to speak his eulogium, for every one in the suite of the stately Elizabetta was chosen for grace, and beauty, and accomplishments. He was just turned of eighteen, light and lithe of form, and graceful as a young Antinous. To the queen he was all deference and respect, yet he was at heart a roguish stripling, petted and spoiled by the ladies about the court, and experienced in the ways of women far beyond his years.

This loitering page was one morning rambling about the groves of the Generalife, which overlook the grounds of the Alhambra. He had taken with him for his amusement a favorite gerfalcon of the queen. In the course of his rambles, seeing a bird rising from a thicket, he unhooded the hawk and let him fly. The falcon towered high in the air, made a swoop at his quarry, but missing it, soared away, regardless of the calls of the page. The latter followed the truant bird with his eye, in its capricious flight, until he saw it alight upon the battlements of a remote and lonely tower, in the outer wall of the Alhambra, built on the edge of a ravine that separated the royal fortress from the grounds of the Generalife. It was in fact the "Tower of the Princesses."

The page descended into the ravine and approached the tower, but it had no entrance from the glen, and its lofty height rendered any attempt to scale it fruitless. Seeking one of the gates of the fortress, therefore, he made a wide circuit to that side of the tower facing within the walls.

A small garden, enclosed by a trellis-work of reeds overhung with myrtle, lay before the tower. Opening a wicket, the page passed between beds of flowers and thickets of roses to the door. It was closed and bolted. A crevice in the door gave him a peep into the interior. There was a small Moorish hall with fretted walls, light marble columns, and an alabaster fountain surrounded with flowers. In the centre hung a gilt cage containing a singing-bird; beneath it, on a chair, lay a tortoise-shell cat among reels of silk and other articles of female labor, and a guitar decorated with ribbons leaned against the fountain.

Ruyz de Alarcon was struck with these traces of female taste and elegance in a lonely and, as he had supposed, deserted tower. They reminded him of the tales of enchanted halls current in the Alhambra; and the tortoise-shell cat might be some spell-bound princess.

He knocked gently at the door. A beautiful face peeped out from a little window above, but was instantly withdrawn. He waited, expecting that the door would be opened, but he waited in vain; no footstep was to be heard within—all was silent. Had his senses deceived him, or was this beautiful apparition the fairy of the tower? He knocked again, and more loudly. After a little while the beaming face once more peeped forth; it was that of a blooming damsel of fifteen.

The page immediately doffed his plumed bonnet, and entreated in the most courteous accents to be permitted to ascend the tower in pursuit of his falcon.

"I dare not open the door, Señor," replied the little damsel, blushing, "my aunt has forbidden it."

"I do beseech you, fair maid—it is the favorite falcon of the queen. I dare not return to the palace without it."

"Are you then one of the cavaliers of the court?"

"I am, fair maid; but I shall lose the queen's favor and my place, if I lose this hawk."

"*Santa Maria!* It is against you cavaliers of the court my aunt has charged me especially to bar the door."

"Against wicked cavaliers doubtless, but I am none of these, but a simple, harmless page, who will be ruined and undone if you deny me this small request."

The heart of the little damsel was touched by the distress of the page. It was a thousand pities he should be ruined for the want of so trifling a boon. Surely too he could not be one of those dangerous beings whom her aunt had described as a species of cannibal, ever on the prowl to make prey of thoughtless damsels; he was gentle and modest, and stood so entreatingly with cap in hand, and looked so charming.

The sly page saw that the garrison began to waver, and redoubled his entreaties in such moving terms that it was not in the nature of mortal maiden to deny him; so the blushing little warden of the tower descended, and opened the door with a trembling hand, and if the page had been charmed by a mere glimpse of her countenance from the window, he was ravished by the full-length portrait now revealed to him.

Her Andalusian bodice and trim *basquiña* set off the round but delicate symmetry of her form, which was as yet scarce verging into womanhood. Her glossy hair was parted on her forehead with scrupulous exactness, and decorated with a fresh-plucked rose, according to the universal custom of the country. It is true her complexion was tinged by the ardor of a southern sun, but it served to give richness to the mantling bloom of her cheek, and to heighten the lustre of her melting eyes.

Ruyz de Alarcon beheld all this with a single glance, for it became him not to tarry; he merely murmured his acknowledgments, and then bounded lightly up the spiral staircase in quest of his falcon.

He soon returned with the truant bird upon his fist. The damsel, in the meantime, had seated herself by the fountain in the hall, and was winding silk; but in her agitation she let fall the reel upon the pavement. The page sprang and picked it up, then dropping gracefully on one knee, presented it to her; but, seizing the hand extended to receive it, imprinted on it a kiss more fervent and devout than he had ever imprinted on the fair hand of his sovereign.

"*Ave Maria, Señor!*" exclaimed the damsel, blushing still deeper with confusion and surprise, for never before had she received such a salutation.

The modest page made a thousand apologies, assuring her it was the way at court of expressing the most profound homage and respect.

Her anger, if anger she felt, was easily pacified, but her agitation and embarrassment continued, and she sat blushing deeper and deeper, with her eyes cast down upon her work, entangling the silk which she attempted to wind.

· The cunning page saw the confusion in the opposite camp, and would fain have profited by it, but the fine speeches he would have uttered died upon his lips; his attempts at gallantry were awkward and ineffectual; and to his surprise, the adroit page, who had figured with such grace and effrontery among the most knowing and experienced ladies of the court, found himself awed and abased in the presence of a simple damsel of fifteen.

In fact, the artless maiden, in her own modesty and innocence, had guardians more effectual than the bolts and bars prescribed by her vigilant aunt. Still, where is the female bosom proof against the first whisperings of love? The little damsel, with all her artlessness, instinctively comprehended all that the faltering tongue of the page failed to express, and her heart was fluttered at beholding, for the first time, a lover at her feet—and such a lover!

The diffidence of the page, though genuine, was short-lived, and he was recovering his usual ease and confidence, when a shrill voice was heard at a distance.

"My aunt is returning from mass!" cried the damsel in affright; "I pray you, Señor, depart."

"Not until you grant me that rose from your hair as a remembrance."

She hastily untwisted the rose from her raven locks. "Take it," cried she, agitated and blushing, "but pray begone."

The page took the rose, and at the same time covered with kisses the fair hand that gave it. Then, placing the flower in his bonnet, and taking the falcon upon his fist, he bounded off through the garden, bearing away with him the heart of the gentle Jacinta.

When the vigilant aunt arrived at the tower, she remarked the agitation of her niece, and an air of confusion in the hall; but a word of explanation sufficed. "A gerfalcon had pursued his prey into the hall."

"Mercy on us! to think of a falcon flying into the tower. Did ever one hear of so saucy a hawk? Why, the very bird in the cage is not safe!"

The vigilant Fredegonda was one of the most wary of ancient spinsters. She had a becoming terror and distrust of what she denominated "the opposite sex," which had gradually increased through a long life of celibacy. Not that the good lady had ever suffered from their wiles, nature having set up a safeguard in her face that forbade all trespass upon her premises; but ladies who have least cause to fear for themselves are most ready to keep a watch over their more tempting neighbors.

The niece was the orphan of an officer who had fallen in the wars. She had been educated in a convent, and had recently been transferred from her sacred asylum to the immediate guardianship of her aunt, under whose overshadowing care she vegetated in obscurity, like an opening rose blooming beneath a brier. Nor indeed is this comparison entirely accidental; for, to tell the truth, her fresh and dawning beauty had caught the public eye, even in her seclusion, and, with that poetical turn common to the people of Andalusia, the peasantry of the neighborhood had given her the appellation of "the Rose of the Alhambra."

The wary aunt continued to keep a faithful watch over her tempting little niece as long as the court continued at Granada, and flattered herself that her vigilance had been successful. It is true the good lady was now and then discomposed by the tinkling of guitars and chanting of love-ditties from the moonlit groves beneath the tower; but she would exhort her niece to shut her ears against such idle minstrelsy, assuring her that it was one of the arts of the opposite sex, by which simple maids were often lured to their undoing. Alas! what chance with a simple maid has a dry lecture against a moonlight serenade?

At length King Philip cut short his sojourn at Granada, and suddenly departed with all his train. The vigilant Fredegonda watched the royal pageant as it issued forth from the Gate of Justice and descended the great avenue leading to the city. When the last banner disappeared from her sight, she returned exulting to her tower, for all her cares were over. To her surprise, a light Arabian steed pawed the ground at the wicket-gate of the garden;—to her horror she saw through the thickets of roses a youth in gayly embroidered dress, at the feet of her niece. At the sounds of her footsteps he gave a tender adieu, bounded lightly over the barrier of reeds and myrtles, sprang upon his horse, and was out of sight in an instant.

The tender Jacinta, in the agony of her grief, lost all thought of her aunt's displeasure. Throwing herself into her arms, she broke forth into sobs and tears.

"*Ay de mi!*" cried she; "he's gone! he's gone! and I shall never see him more!"

"Gone!—who is gone?—what youth is that I saw at your feet?"

"A queen's page, aunt, who came to bid me farewell."

"A queen's page, child!" echoed the vigilant Fredegonda, faintly, "and when did you become acquainted with the queen's page?"

"The morning that the gerfalcon came into the tower. It was the queen's gerfalcon, and he came in pursuit of it."

"Ah silly, silly girl! know that there are no gerfalcons half so dangerous as these young prankling pages, and it is precisely such simple birds as thee that they pounce upon."

The aunt was at first indignant at learning that in despite of her boasted vigilance, a tender intercourse had been carried on by the youthful lovers, almost beneath her eye; but when she found that her simple-hearted niece, though thus exposed, without the protection of bolt or bar, to all the machinations of the opposite sex, had come forth unsinged from the fiery ordeal, she consoled herself with the persuasion that it was owing to the chaste and cautious maxims in which she had, as it were, steeped her to the very lips.

While the aunt laid this soothing unction to her pride, the niece treasured up the oft-repeated vows of fidelity of the page. But what is the love of restless, roving man? A vagrant stream that dallies for a time with each flower upon its bank, then passes on, and leaves them all in tears.

Days, weeks, months, elapsed, and nothing more was heard of the page. The pomegranate ripened, the vine yielded up its fruit, the autumnal rains descended in torrents from the mountains; the Sierra Nevada became covered with a snowy mantle, and wintry blasts howled through the halls of the Alhambra—still he came not. The winter passed away. Again the genial spring burst forth with song and blossom and balmy zephyr; the snows melted from the mountains, until none remained but on the lofty summit of Nevada, glistening through the sultry summer air. Still nothing was heard of the forgetful page.

In the meantime the poor little Jacinta grew pale and thoughtful. Her former occupations and amusements were abandoned, her silk lay entangled, her guitar unstrung, her flowers were neglected, the notes of her bird unheeded, and her eyes, once so bright, were dimmed with secret weeping. If any solitude could be devised to foster the passion of a love-lorn damsel it would be such a place as the Alhambra, where everything seems disposed to produce tender and romantic reveries. It is a very paradise for lovers; how hard then to be alone in such a paradise—and not merely alone, but forsaken!

"Alas, silly child!" would the staid and immaculate Fredegonda say, when she found her niece in one of her desponding moods—"did I not warn thee against the wiles and deceptions of these men? What couldst thou expect, too, from one of a haughty and aspiring family—thou an orphan, the descendant of a fallen and impoverished line? Be assured, if the youth were true, his father, who is one of the proudest nobles about the court, would prohibit his union with one so humble and portionless as thou. Pluck up thy resolution therefore, and drive these idle notions from thy mind."

The words of the immaculate Fredegonda only served to increase the melancholy of her niece, but she sought to indulge it in private. At a late hour one midsummer night, after her aunt had retired to rest, she remained alone in the hall of the tower, seated beside the alabaster fountain. It was here that the faithless page had first knelt and kissed her hand; it was here that he had often vowed eternal fidelity. The poor little damsel's heart was overladen with sad and tender recollections, her tears began to flow, and slowly fell drop by drop into the fountain. By degrees the crystal water became agitated, and—bubble—bubble—bubble—boiled up and was tossed about, until a female figure, richly clad in Moorish robes, slowly rose to view.

Jacinta was so frightened that she fled from the hall and did not venture to return. The next morning she related what she had seen to her aunt, but the good lady treated it as a fantasy of her troubled mind, or supposed she had fallen asleep and dreamt beside the fountain. "Thou hast been thinking of the story of the three Moorish princesses that once inhabited this tower," continued she, "and it has entered into thy dreams."

"What story, aunt? I know nothing of it."

"Thou hast certainly heard of the three princesses, Zayda, Zorayda, and Zorahayda, who were confined in this tower by the king their father, and agreed to fly with three Christian cavaliers. The two first accomplished their escape, but the third failed in her resolution, and, it is said, died in this tower."

"I now recollect to have heard of it," said Jacinta, "and to have wept over the fate of the gentle Zorahayda."

"Thou mayest well weep over her fate," continued the aunt, "for the lover of Zorahayda was thy ancestor. He long bemoaned his Moorish love; but time cured him of his grief, and he married a Spanish lady, from whom thou art descended."

Jacinta ruminated over these words. "That which I have seen is no fantasy of the brain," said she to herself, "I am confident. If indeed it be the spirit of the gentle Zorahayda, which I have heard lingers about this tower, of what should I be afraid? I'll watch by the fountain to-night—perhaps the visit will be repeated."

Towards midnight, when everything was quiet, she again took her seat in the hall. As the bell in the distant watch-tower of the Alhambra struck the midnight hour, the fountain was again agitated; and bubble —bubble—bubble—it tossed about the waters until the Moorish female again rose to view. She was young and beautiful; her dress was rich with jewels, and in her hand she held a silver lute. Jacinta trembled and was faint, but was reassured by the soft and plaintive voice of the apparition, and the sweet expression of her pale, melancholy countenance.

"Daughter of mortality," said she, "what aileth thee? Why do thy tears trouble my fountain, and thy sighs and plaints disturb the quiet watches of the night?"

"I weep because of the faithlessness of man, and I bemoan my solitary and forsaken state."

"Take comfort; thy sorrows may yet have an end. Thou beholdest a Moorish princess, who, like thee, was unhappy in her love. A Christian knight, thy ancestor, won my heart, and would have borne me to his native land and to the bosom of his church. I was a convert in my heart, but I lacked courage equal to my faith, and lingered till too late. For this the evil genii are permitted to have power over me, and I remain enchanted in this tower until some pure Christian will deign to break the magic spell. Wilt thou undertake the task?"

"I will," replied the damsel, trembling.

"Come hither, then, and fear not; dip thy hand in the fountain, sprinkle the water over me, and baptize me after the manner of thy faith; so shall the enchantment be dispelled, and my troubled spirit have repose."

The damsel advanced with faltering steps, dipped her hand in the fountain, collected water in the palm, and sprinkled it over the pale face of the phantom.

The latter smiled with ineffable benignity. She dropped her silver lute at the feet of Jacinta, crossed her white arms upon her bosom, and melted from sight, so that it seemed merely as if a shower of dewdrops had fallen into the fountain.

Jacinta retired from the hall filled with awe and wonder. She scarcely closed her eyes that night; but when she awoke at daybreak out of a troubled slumber, the whole appeared to her like a distempered dream. On descending into the hall, however, the truth of the vision was established, for beside the fountain she beheld the silver lute glittering in the morning sunshine.

She hastened to her aunt, to relate all that had befallen her, and called her to behold the lute as a testimonial of the reality of her story. If the good lady had any lingering doubts, they were removed when Jacinta touched the instrument, for she drew forth such ravishing tones as to thaw even the frigid bosom of the immaculate Fredegonda, that region of eternal winter, into a genial flow. Nothing but supernatural melody could have produced such an effect.

The extraordinary power of the lute became every day more and more apparent. The wayfarer passing by the tower was detained, and, as it were, spellbound in breathless ecstasy. The very birds gathered in the neighboring trees, and hushing their own strains, listened in charmed silence.

Rumor soon spread the news abroad. The inhabitants of Granada thronged to the Alhambra to catch a few notes of the transcendent music that floated about the Tower of Las Infantas.

The lovely little minstrel was at length drawn forth from her retreat. The rich and powerful of the land contended who should entertain and do honor to her; or rather, who should secure the charms of her lute to draw fashionable throngs to their saloons. Wherever she went her vigilant aunt kept a dragon watch at her elbow, awing the throngs of impassioned admirers who hung in raptures on her strains. The report of her wonderful powers spread from city to city. Malaga, Seville, Cordova, all became successively mad on the theme; nothing was talked of throughout Andalusia but the beautiful minstrel of the Alhambra. How could it be otherwise among a people so musical and gallant as the Andalusians, when the lute was magical in its powers, and the minstrel inspired by love!

While all Andalusia was thus music mad, a different mood prevailed at the court of Spain. Philip V., as is well known, was a miserable hypochondriac, and subject to all kinds of fancies. Sometimes he would keep to his bed for weeks together, groaning under imaginary complaints. At other times he would insist upon abdicating his throne, to the great annoyance of his royal spouse, who had a strong relish for the splendors of a court and the glories of a crown, and guided the sceptre of her imbecile lord with an expert and steady hand.

Nothing was found to be so efficacious in dispelling the royal megrims as the power of music; the queen took care, therefore, to have the best performers, both vocal and instrumental, at hand, and retained the famous Italian singer Farinelli about the court as a kind of royal physician.

At the moment we treat of, however, a freak had come over the mind of this sapient and illustrious Bourbon that surpassed all former vagaries. After a long spell of imaginary illness, which set all the strains of Farinelli and the consultations of a whole orchestra of court fiddlers at defiance, the monarch fairly, in idea, gave up the ghost, and considered himself absolutely dead.

This would have been harmless enough, and even convenient both to his queen and courtiers, had he been content to remain in the quietude befitting a dead man; but to their annoyance he insisted upon having the funeral ceremonies performed over him, and, to their inexpressible perplexity, began to grow impatient, and to revile bitterly at them for negligence and disrespect, in leaving him unburied. What was to be done? To disobey the king's positive commands was monstrous in the eyes of the obsequious courtiers of a punctilious court—but to obey him, and bury him alive, would be downright regicide!

  · In the midst of this fearful dilemma a rumor reached the court of the female minstrel who was turning the brains of all Andalusia. The queen despatched missions in all haste to summon her to St. Ildefonso, where the court at that time resided.

Within a few days, as the queen with her maids of honor was walking in those stately gardens, intended, with their avenues and terraces and fountains, to eclipse the glories of Versailles, the far-famed minstrel was conducted into her presence. The imperial Elizabetta gazed with surprise at the youthful and unpretending appearance of the little being that had set the world madding. She was in her picturesque Andalusian dress, her silver lute in hand, and stood with modest and downcast eyes, but with a simplicity and freshness of beauty that still bespoke her "the Rose of the Alhambra."

As usual she was accompanied by the ever-vigilant Fredegonda, who gave the whole history of her parentage and descent to the inquiring queen. If the stately Elizabetta had been interested by the appearance of Jacinta, she was still more pleased when she learnt that she was of a meritorious though impoverished line, and that her father had bravely fallen in the service of the crown. "If thy powers equal thy renown," said she, "and thou canst cast forth this evil spirit that possesses thy sovereign, thy fortunes shall henceforth be my care, and honors and wealth attend thee."

Impatient to make trial of her skill, she led the way at once to the apartment of the moody monarch.

Jacinta followed with downcast eyes through files of guards and crowds of courtiers. They arrived at length at a great chamber hung with black. The windows were closed to exclude the light of day; a number of yellow wax tapers in silver sconces diffused a lugubrious light, and dimly revealed the figures of mutes in mourning dresses, and courtiers who glided about with noiseless step and woebegone visage. In the midst of a funeral bed or bier, his hands folded on his breast, and the tip of his nose just visible, lay extended this would-be-buried monarch.

The queen entered the chamber in silence, and pointing to a footstool in an obscure corner, beckoned to Jacinta to sit down and commence.

At first she touched her lute with a faltering hand, but gathering confidence and animation as she proceeded, drew forth such soft aërial harmony, that all present could scarce believe it mortal. As to the monarch, who had already considered himself in the world of spirits, he set it down for some angelic melody or the music of the spheres. By degrees the theme was varied, and the voice of the minstrel accompanied the instrument. She poured forth one of the legendary ballads treating of the ancient glories of the Alhambra and the achievements of the Moors. Her whole soul entered into the theme, for with the recollections of the Alhambra was associated the story of her love. The funeral-chamber resounded with the animating strain. It entered into the gloomy heart of the monarch. He raised his head and gazed around: he sat up on his couch, his eye began to kindle—at length, leaping upon the floor, he called for sword and buckler.

The triumph of music, or rather of the enchanted lute, was complete; the demon of melancholy was cast forth; and, as it were, a dead man brought to life. The windows of the apartment were thrown open; the glorious effulgence of Spanish sunshine burst into the late lugubrious chamber; all eyes sought the lovely enchantress, but the lute had fallen from her hand, she had sunk upon the earth, and the next moment was clasped to the bosom of Ruyz de Alarcon.

The nuptials of the happy couple were celebrated soon afterwards with great splendor, and the Rose of the Alhambra became the ornament and delight of the court. "But hold—not so fast"—I hear the reader exclaim; "this is jumping to the end of a story at a furious rate! First let us know how Ruyz de Alarcon managed to account to Jacinta for his long neglect?" Nothing more easy; the venerable, time-honored excuse, the opposition to his wishes by a proud, pragmatical old father; besides, young people who really like one another soon come to an amicable understanding, and bury all past grievances when once they meet.

But how was the proud, pragmatical old father reconciled to the match?

Oh! as to that, his scruples were easily overcome by a word or two from the queen; especially as dignities and rewards were showered upon the blooming favorite of royalty. Besides, the lute of Jacinta, you know, possessed a magic power, and could control the most stubborn head and hardest breast.

And what came of the enchanted lute?

Oh, that is the most curious matter of all, and plainly proves the truth of the whole story. That lute remained for some time in the family, but was purloined and carried off, as was supposed, by the great singer Farinelli, in pure jealousy. At his death it passed into other hands in Italy, who were ignorant of its mystic powers, and melting down the silver, transferred the strings to an old Cremona fiddle. The strings still retain something of their magic virtues. A word in the reader's ear, but let it go no further: that fiddle is now bewitching the whole world,—it is the fiddle of Paganini!

From *The Alhambra*

THE GOVERNOR AND THE
NOTARY

The Veteran

AMONG the curious acquaintances I made in my rambles about
the fortress, was a brave and battered old colonel of Invalids, who
was nestled like a hawk in one of the Moorish towers. His history,
which he was fond of telling, was a tissue of those adventures, mishaps,
and vicissitudes that render the life of almost every Spaniard of note as
varied and whimsical as the pages of Gil Blas.

He was in America at twelve years of age, and reckoned among the
most signal and fortunate events of his life, his having seen General
Washington. Since then he had taken a part in all the wars of his
country; he could speak experimentally of most of the prisons and
dungeons of the Peninsula; had been lamed of one leg, crippled in his
hands, and so cut up and carbonadoed that he was a kind of walking
monument of the troubles of Spain, on which there was a scar for every
battle and broil, as every year of captivity was notched upon the tree of
Robinson Crusoe. The greatest misfortune of the brave old cavalier,
however, appeared to have been his having commanded at Malaga during a time of peril and confusion, and been made a general by the inhabitants, to protect them from the invasion of the French. This had en-
tailed upon him a number of just claims upon government, that I feared
would employ him until his dying day in writing and printing petitions
and memorials, to the great disquiet of his mind, exhaustion of his
purse, and penance of his friends; not one of whom could visit him
without having to listen to a mortal document of half an hour in
length, and to carry away half a dozen pamphlets in his pocket. This,
however, is the case throughout Spain; everywhere you meet with
some worthy wight brooding in a corner, and nursing up some pet
grievance and cherished wrong. Besides, a Spaniard who has a law-
suit, or a claim upon government, may be considered as furnished with
employment for the remainder of his life.

I have included an introductory chapter from *The Alhambra* as part of the tale
proper.—C.N.

I visited the veteran in his quarters in the upper part of the Torre del Vino, or Wine Tower. His room was small but snug, and commanded a beautiful view of the Vega. It was arranged with a soldier's precision. Three muskets and a brace of pistols, all bright and shining, were suspended against the wall, with a sabre and a cane hanging side by side, and above them two cocked hats, one for parade, and one for ordinary use. A small shelf, containing some half dozen books, formed his library, one of which, a little old mouldy volume of philosophical maxims, was his favorite reading. This he thumbed and pondered over day by day; applying every maxim to his own particular case, provided it had a little tinge of wholesome bitterness, and treated of the injustice of the world.

Yet he was social and kind-hearted, and provided he could be diverted from his wrongs and his philosophy, was an entertaining companion. I like these old weather-beaten sons of fortune, and enjoy their rough campaigning anecdotes. In the course of my visits to the one in question, I learnt some curious facts about an old military commander of the fortress, who seems to have resembled him in some respects, and to have had similar fortunes in the wars. These particulars have been augmented by inquiries among some of the old inhabitants of the place, particularly the father of Mateo Ximenes, of whose traditional stories the worthy I am about to introduce to the reader was a favorite hero.

IN former times there ruled, as governor of the Alhambra, a doughty old cavalier, who, from having lost one arm in the wars, was commonly known by the name of El Gobernador Manco, or "the one-armed governor." He in fact prided himself upon being an old soldier, wore his moustaches curled up to his eyes, a pair of campaigning boots, and a toledo as long as a spit, with his pocket-handkerchief in the basket-hilt.

He was, moreover, exceedingly proud and punctilious, and tenacious of all his privileges and dignities. Under his sway the immunities of the Alhambra, as a royal residence and domain, were rigidly exacted. No one was permitted to enter the fortress with fire-arms, or even with a sword or staff, unless he were of a certain rank; and every horseman was obliged to dismount at the gate, and lead his horse by the bridle. Now as the hill of the Alhambra rises from the very midst of the city of Granada, being, as it were, an excrescence of the capital, it must at all times be somewhat irksome to the captain-general, who commands the province, to have thus an *imperium in imperio,* a petty independent post in the very centre of his domains. It was rendered the more galling, in the present instance, from the irritable jealousy of the old governor, that took fire on the least question of authority and jurisdiction; and from the loose vagrant character of the people who had gradually nestled themselves within the fortress, as in a sanctuary, and thence carried on a system of roguery and depredation at the expense of the honest inhabitants of the city.

Thus there was a perpetual feud and heart-burning between the captain-general and the governor, the more virulent on the part of the latter, inasmuch as the smallest of two neighboring potentates is always the most captious about his dignity. The stately palace of the captain-general stood in the Plaza Nueva, immediately at the foot of the hill of the Alhambra; and here was always a bustle and parade of guards, and domestics, and city functionaries. A beetling bastion of the fortress over-looked the palace and public square in front of it; and on this bastion the old governor would occasionally strut backwards and forwards, with his toledo girded by his side, keeping a wary eye down upon his rival, like a hawk reconnoitring his quarry from his nest in a dry tree.

Whenever he descended into the city, it was in grand parade; on horseback, surrounded by his guards; or in his state coach, an ancient and unwieldy Spanish edifice of carved timber and gilt leather, drawn by eight mules, with running footmen, outriders, and lackeys; on which occasions he flattered himself he impressed every beholder with awe and admiration as vicegerent of the king; though the wits of Granada, particularly those who loitered about the palace of the captain-general, were apt to sneer at his petty parade, and, in allusion to the vagrant character of his subjects, to greet him with the appellation of "the king of the beggars." One of the most fruitful sources of dispute between these two doughty rivals was the right claimed by the governor to have all things passed free of duty through the city that were intended for the use of himself or his garrison. By degrees this privilege had given rise to extensive smuggling. A nest of *contrabandistas* took up their abode in the hovels of the fortress and the numerous caves in its vicinity, and drove a thriving business under the connivance of the soldiers of the garrison.

The vigilance of the captain-general was aroused. He consulted his legal adviser and factotum, a shrewd, meddlesome *escribano*, or notary, who rejoiced in an opportunity of perplexing the old potentate of the Alhambra, and involving him in a maze of legal subtleties. He advised the captain-general to insist upon the right of examining every convoy passing through the gates of his city, and penned a long letter for him in vindication of the right. Governor Manco was a straightforward cut-and-thrust old soldier, who hated an *escribano* worse than the devil, and this one in particular worse than all other *escribanos*.

"What!" said he, curling up his moustaches fiercely, "does the captain-general set his man of the pen to practise confusions upon me? I'll let him see an old soldier is not to be baffled by schoolcraft."

He seized his pen and scrawled a short letter in a crabbed hand, in which, without deigning to enter into argument, he insisted on the right of transit free of search, and denounced vengeance on any custom-house officer who should lay his unhallowed hand on any convoy protected by the flag of the Alhambra. While this question was agitated between the two pragmatical potentates, it so happened that a mule laden with supplies for the fortress arrived one day at the gate of Xenil, by which it was to traverse a suburb of the city on its way to the Alhambra. The convoy was headed by a testy old corporal, who had long served under the governor, and was a man after his own heart; as rusty and stanch as an old Toledo blade.

As they approached the gate of the city, the corporal placed the banner of the Alhambra on the pack-saddle of the mule, and drawing himself up to a perfect perpendicular, advanced with his head dressed to the front, but with the wary side-glance of a cur passing through hostile ground and ready for a snap and a snarl.

"Who goes there?" said the sentinel at the gate.

"Soldier of the Alhambra!" said the corporal, without turning his head.

"What have you in charge?"

"Provisions for the garrison."

"Proceed."

The corporal marched straight forward, followed by the convoy, but had not advanced many paces before a posse of custom-house officers rushed out of a small toll-house.

"Hallo there!" cried the leader. "Muleteer, halt, and open those packages."

The corporal wheeled round and drew himself up in battle array. "Respect the flag of the Alhambra," said he; "these things are for the governor."

"A *figo* for the governor and a *figo* for his flag. Muleteer, halt, I say."

"Stop the convoy at your peril!" cried the corporal, cocking his musket. "Muleteer, proceed."

The muleteer gave his beast a hearty thwack; the custom-house officer sprang forward and seized the halter; whereupon the corporal levelled his piece and shot him dead.

The street was immediately in an uproar.

The old corporal was seized, and after undergoing sundry kicks, and cuffs, and cudgellings, which are generally given impromptu by the mob in Spain as a foretaste of the after penalties of the law, he was loaded with irons and conducted to the city prison, while his comrades were permitted to proceed with the convoy, after it had been well rummaged, to the Alhambra.

The old governor was in a towering passion when he heard of this insult to his flag and capture of his corporal. For a time he stormed about the Moorish halls, and vapored about the bastions, and looked down fire and sword upon the palace of the captain-general. Having vented the first ebullition of his wrath, he despatched a message demanding the surrender of the corporal, as to him alone belonged the right of sitting in judgment on the offences of those under his command. The captain-general, aided by the pen of the delighted *escribano*, replied at great length, arguing that, as the offence had been committed within the walls of his city, and against one of his civil officers, it was clearly within his proper jurisdiction.

The governor rejoined by a repetition of his demand; the captain-general gave a surrejoinder of still greater length and legal acumen; the governor became hotter and more peremptory in his demands, and the captain-general cooler and more copious in his replies; until the old lion-hearted soldier absolutely roared with fury at being thus entangled in the meshes of legal controversy.

While the subtle *escribano* was thus amusing himself at the expense of the governor, he was conducting the trial of the corporal, who, mewed up in a narrow dungeon of the prison, had merely a small grated window at which to show his iron-bound visage and receive the consolations of his friends.

A mountain of written testimony was diligently heaped up, according to Spanish form, by the indefatigable *escribano*; the corporal was completely overwhelmed by it. He was convicted of murder, and sentenced to be hanged.

It was in vain the governor sent down remonstrance and menace from the Alhambra. The fatal day was at hand, and the corporal was put *in capilla*, that is to say, in the chapel of the prison, as is always done with culprits the day before execution, that they may meditate on their approaching end and repent them of their sins.

Seeing things drawing to extremity, the old governor determined to attend to the affair in person. For this purpose he ordered out his carriage of state, and, surrounded by his guards, rumbled down the avenue of the Alhambra into the city. Driving to the house of the *escribano*, he summoned him to the portal.

The eye of the old governor gleamed like a coal at beholding the smirking man of the law advancing with an air of exultation.

"What is this I hear," cried he, "that you are about to put to death one of my soldiers?"

"All according to law—all in strict form of justice," said the self-sufficient *escribano*, chuckling and rubbing his hands; "I can show your Excellency the written testimony in the case."

"Fetch it hither," said the governor. The *escribano* bustled into his office, delighted with having another opportunity of displaying his ingenuity at the expense of the hard-headed veteran. He returned with a satchel full of papers, and began to read a long deposition with professional volubility. By this time a crowd had collected, listening with outstretched necks and gaping mouths.

"Prithee, man, get into the carriage, out of this pestilent throng, that I may the better hear thee," said the governor.

· The *escribano* entered the carriage, when in a twinkling, the door was closed, the coachman smacked his whip,—mules, carriage, guards, and all dashed off at a thundering rate, leaving the crowd in gaping wonderment; nor did the governor pause until he had lodged his prey in one of the strongest dungeons of the Alhambra.

He then sent down a flag of truce in military style, proposing a cartel, or exchange of prisoners,—the corporal for the notary. The pride of the captain-general was piqued; he returned a contemptuous refusal, and forthwith caused a gallows, tall and strong, to be erected in the centre of the Plaza Nueva for the execution of the corporal.

"Oho! is that the game?" said Governor Manco. He gave orders, and immediately a gibbet was reared on the verge of the great beetling bastion that overlooked the Plaza. "Now," said he, in a message to the captain-general, "hang my soldier when you please; but at the same time that he is swung off in the square, look up to see your *escribano* dangling against the sky."

The captain-general was inflexible; troops were paraded in the square; the drums beat, the bell tolled. An immense multitude of amateurs gathered together to behold the execution. On the other hand, the governor paraded his garrison on the bastion, and tolled the funeral dirge of the notary from the Torre de la Campana, or Tower of the Bell.

The notary's wife pressed through the crowd, with a whole progeny of little embryo *escribanos* at her heels, and throwing herself at the feet of the captain-general, implored him not to sacrifice the life of her husband, and the welfare of herself and her numerous little ones, to a point of pride; "for you know the old governor too well," said she, "to doubt that he will put his threat into execution, if you hang the soldier."

The captain-general was overpowered by her tears and lamentations, and the clamors of her callow brood. The corporal was sent up to the Alhambra, under a guard, in his gallows garb, like a hooded friar, but with head erect and a face of iron. The *escribano* was demanded in exchange, according to the cartel. The once bustling and self-sufficient man of the law was drawn forth from his dungeon more dead than alive. All his flippancy and conceit had evaporated; his hair, it is said, had nearly turned gray with affright, and he had a down-cast, dogged look, as if he still felt the halter round his neck.

The old governor stuck his one arm akimbo, and for a moment surveyed him with an iron smile. "Henceforth, my friend," said he, "moderate your zeal in hurrying others to the gallows; be not too certain of your safety, even though you should have the law on your side; and above all, take care how you play off your schoolcraft another time upon an old soldier."

GOVERNOR MANCO AND THE SOLDIER

WHILE Governor Manco, or the "one-armed," kept up a show of military state in the Alhambra, he became nettled at the reproaches continually cast upon his fortress, of being a nestling-place of rogues and *contrabandistas*. On a sudden, the old potentate determined on reform, and setting vigorously to work, ejected whole nests of vagabonds out of the fortress and the gypsy caves with which the surrounding hills are honeycombed. He sent out soldiers, also, to patrol the avenues and footpaths, with orders to take up all suspicious persons.

One bright summer morning a patrol, consisting of the testy old corporal who had distinguished himself in the affair of the notary, a trumpeter, and two privates, was seated under the garden-wall of the Generalife, beside the road which leads down from the Mountain of the Sun, when they heard the tramp of a horse, and a male voice singing in rough though not unmusical tones an old Castilian campaigning-song.

Presently they beheld a sturdy, sunburnt fellow, clad in the ragged garb of a foot-soldier, leading a powerful Arabian horse caparisoned in the ancient Morisco fashion.

Astonished at the sight of a strange soldier descending, steed in hand, from that solitary mountain, the corporal stepped forth and challenged him.

"Who goes there?"

"A friend."

"Who and what are you?"

"A poor soldier just from the wars, with a cracked crown and empty purse for a reward."

By this time they were enabled to view him more narrowly. He had a black patch across his forehead, which, with a grizzled beard, added to a certain dare-devil cast of countenance, while a slight squint threw into the whole an occasional gleam of roguish good-humor.

Having answered the questions of the patrol, the soldier seemed to consider himself entitled to make others in return. "May I ask," said he, "what city is that which I see at the foot of the hill?"

"What city!" cried the trumpeter; "come, that's too bad. Here's a fellow lurking about the Mountain of the Sun, and demands the name of the great city of Granada!"

"Granada! *Madre di Dios!* can it be possible?"

"Perhaps not!" rejoined the trumpeter; "and perhaps you have no idea that yonder are the towers of the Alhambra."

"Son of a trumpet," replied the stranger, "do not trifle with me; if this be indeed the Alhambra, I have some strange matters to reveal to the governor."

"You will have an opportunity," said the corporal, "for we mean to take you before him." By this time the trumpeter had seized the bridle of the steed, the two privates had each secured an arm of the soldier, the corporal put himself in front, gave the word, "Forward—march!" and away they marched for the Alhambra.

The sight of a ragged foot-soldier and a fine Arabian horse, brought in captive by the patrol, attracted the attention of all the idlers of the fortress, and of those gossip groups that generally assemble about wells and fountains at early dawn. The wheel of the cistern paused in its rotations, and the slip-shod servant-maid stood gaping, with pitcher in hand, as the corporal passed by with his prize. A motley train gradually gathered in the rear of the escort.

Knowing nods and winks and conjectures passed from one to another. "It is a deserter," said one; "A *contrabandista*," said another; "A *bandolero*," said a third;—until it was affirmed that a captain of a desperate band of robbers had been captured by the prowess of the corporal and his patrol. "Well, well," said the old cronies, one to another, "captain or not, let him get out of the grasp of old Governor Manco if he can, though he is but one-handed."

Governor Manco was seated in one of the inner halls of the Alhambra, taking his morning's cup of chocolate in company with his confessor—a fat Franciscan friar, from the neighboring convent. A demure, dark-eyed damsel of Malaga, the daughter of his housekeeper, was attending upon him. The world hinted that the damsel, who, with all her demureness, was a sly buxom baggage, had found out a soft spot in the iron heart of the old governor, and held complete control over him. But let that pass—the domestic affairs of these mighty potentates of the earth should not be too narrowly scrutinized.

When word was brought that a suspicious stranger had been taken lurking about the fortress, and was actually in the lower court, in durance of the corporal, waiting the pleasure of his Excellency, the pride and stateliness of office swelled the bosom of the governor. Giving back his chocolate-cup into the hands of the demure damsel, he called for his basket-hilted sword, girded it to his side, twirled up his moustaches, took his seat in a large high-backed chair, assumed a bitter and forbidding aspect, and ordered the prisoner into his presence. The soldier was brought in, still closely pinioned by his captors, and guarded by the corporal. He maintained, however, a resolute, self-confident air, and returned the sharp, scrutinizing look of the governor with an easy squint, which by no means pleased the punctilious old potentate.

"Well, culprit," said the governor, after he had regarded him for a moment in silence, "what have you to say for yourself—who are you?"

"A soldier, just from the wars, who has brought away nothing but scars and bruises."

"A soldier—humph—a foot-soldier by your garb. I understand you have a fine Arabian horse. I presume you brought him too from the wars, besides your scars and bruises."

"May it please your Excellency, I have something strange to tell about that horse. Indeed I have one of the most wonderful things to relate. Something too that concerns the security of this fortress, indeed of all Granada. But it is a matter to be imparted only to your private ear, or in presence of such only as are in your confidence."

The governor considered for a moment, and then directed the corporal and his men to withdraw, but to post themselves outside of the door, and be ready at a call. "This holy friar," said he, "is my confessor, you may say anything in his presence;—and this damsel," nodding towards the handmaid, who had loitered with an air of great curiosity, "this damsel is of great secrecy and discretion, and to be trusted with anything."

The soldier gave a glance between a squint and a leer at the demure handmaid. "I am perfectly willing," said he, "that the damsel should remain."

When all the rest had withdrawn, the soldier commenced his story. He was a fluent, smooth-tongued varlet, and had a command of language above his apparent rank.

"May it please your Excellency," said he, "I am, as I before observed, a soldier, and have seen some hard service, but my term of enlistment being expired, I was discharged, not long since, from the army at Valladolid, and set out on foot for my native village in Andalusia. Yesterday evening the sun went down as I was traversing a great dry plain of Old Castile."

"Hold!" cried the governor, "what is this you say? Old Castile is some two or three hundred miles from this."

"Even so," replied the soldier, coolly, "I told your Excellency I had strange things to relate; but not more strange than true, as your Excellency will find, if you will deign me a patient hearing."

"Proceed, culprit," said the governor, twirling up his moustaches.

"As the sun went down," continued the soldier, "I cast my eyes about in search of quarters for the night, but as far as my sight could reach there were no signs of habitation. I saw that I should have to make my bed on the naked plain, with my knapsack for a pillow; but your Excellency is an old soldier, and knows that to one who has been in the wars, such a night's lodging is no great hardship."

The governor nodded assent, as he drew his pocket-handkerchief out of the basket-hilt to drive away a fly that buzzed about his nose.

"Well, to make a long story short," continued the soldier, "I trudged forward for several miles until I came to a bridge over a deep ravine, through which ran a little thread of water, almost dried up by the summer heat. At one end of the bridge was a Moorish tower, the upper end all in ruins, but a vault in the foundation quite entire. Here, thinks I, is a good place to make a halt; so I went down to the stream, and took a hearty drink, for the water was pure and sweet, and I was parched with thirst; then, opening my wallet, I took out an onion and a few crusts, which were all my provisions, and seating myself on a stone on the margin of the stream, began to make my supper,—intending afterwards to quarter myself for the night in the vault of the tower; and capital quarters they would have been for a campaigner just from the wars, as your Excellency, who is an old soldier, may suppose."

"I have put up gladly with worse in my time," said the governor, returning his pocket-handkerchief into the hilt of his sword.

"While I was quietly crunching my crust," pursued the soldier, "I heard something stir within the vault; I listened—it was the tramp of a horse. By and by a man came forth from a door in the foundation of the tower, close by the water's edge, leading a powerful horse by the bridle. I could not well make out what he was, by the starlight. It had a suspicious look to be lurking among the ruins of a tower, in that wild solitary place. He might be a mere wayfarer, like myself; he might be a *contrabandista*; he might be a *bandolero!* what of that? thank heaven and my poverty, I had nothing to lose; so I sat still and crunched my crust.

"He led his horse to the water, close by where I was sitting, so that I had a fair opportunity of reconnoitring him. To my surprise he was dressed in a Moorish garb, with a cuirass of steel, and a polished skullcap that I distinguished by the reflection of the stars upon it. His horse, too, was harnessed in the Morisco fashion, with great shovel stirrups. He led him, as I said, to the side of the stream, into which the animal plunged his head almost to the eyes, and drank until I thought he would have burst.

" 'Comrade,' said I, 'your steed drinks well; it's a good sign when a horse plunges his muzzle bravely into the water.'

" 'He may well drink,' said the stranger, speaking with a Moorish accent; 'it is a good year since he had his last draught.'

" 'By Santiago,' said I, 'that beats even the camels I have seen in Africa. But come, you seem to be something of a soldier, will you sit down and take part of a soldier's fare?' In fact, I felt the want of a companion in this lonely place, and was willing to put up with an infidel. Besides, as your Excellency well knows, a soldier is never very particular about the faith of his company, and soldiers of all countries are comrades on peaceable ground."

The governor again nodded assent.

"Well, as I was saying, I invited him to share my supper, such as it was, for I could not do less in common hospitality. 'I have no time to pause for meat or drink,' said he, 'I have a long journey to make before morning.'

" 'In what direction?' said I.

" 'Andalusia,' said he.

" 'Exactly my route,' said I; 'so, as you won't stop and eat with me, perhaps you will let me mount and ride with you. I see your horse is of a powerful frame; I'll warrant he'll carry double.'

" 'Agreed,' said the trooper; and it would not have been civil and soldierlike to refuse, especially as I had offered to share my supper with him. So up he mounted, and up I mounted behind him.

" 'Hold fast,' said he, 'my steed goes like the wind.'

" 'Never fear me,' said I, and so off we set.

"From a walk the horse soon passed to a trot, from a trot to a gallop, and from a gallop to a harum-scarum scamper. It seemed as if rocks, trees, houses, everything flew hurry-scurry behind us.

" 'What town is this?' said I.

" 'Segovia,' said he; and before the word was out of his mouth, the towers of Segovia were out of sight. We swept up the Guadarama Mountains, and down by the Escurial; and we skirted the walls of Madrid, and we scoured away across the plains of La Mancha. In this way we went up hill and down dale, by towers and cities, all buried in deep sleep, and across mountains, and plains, and rivers, just glimmering in the starlight.

"To make a long story short, and not to fatigue your Excellency, the trooper suddenly pulled up on the side of a mountain. 'Here we are,' said he, 'at the end of our journey.' I looked about, but could see no signs of habitation; nothing but the mouth of a cavern. While I looked I saw multitudes of people in Moorish dresses, some on horseback, some on foot, arriving as if borne by the wind from all points of the compass, and hurrying into the mouth of the cavern like bees into a hive. Before I could ask a question, the trooper struck his long Moorish spurs into the horse's flanks, and dashed in with the throng. We passed along a steep winding way, that descended into the very bowels of the mountain. As we pushed on, a light began to glimmer up, by little and little, like the first glimmerings of day, but what caused it I could not discern. It grew stronger and stronger, and enabled me to see everything around. I now noticed, as we passed along, great caverns, opening to the right and left, like halls in an arsenal. In some there were shields, and helmets, and cuirasses, and lances, and cimeters, hanging against the walls; in others there were great heaps of warlike munitions and camp-equipage lying upon the ground.

"It would have done your Excellency's heart good, being an old soldier, to have seen such grand provision for war. Then, in other caverns, there were long rows of horsemen armed to the teeth, with lances raised and banners unfurled, all ready for the field; but they all sat motionless in their saddles, like so many statues. In other halls were warriors sleeping on the ground beside their horses, and foot-soldiers in groups ready to fall into the ranks. All were in old-fashioned Moorish dresses and armor.

"Well, your Excellency, to cut a long story short, we at length entered an immense cavern, or I may say palace, of grotto-work, the walls of which seemed to be veined with gold and silver, and to sparkle with diamonds and sapphires and all kinds of precious stones. At the upper end sat a Moorish king on a golden throne, with his nobles on each side, and a guard of African blacks with drawn cimeters. All the crowd that continued to flock in, and amounted to thousands and thousands, passed one by one before his throne, each paying homage as he passed. Some of the multitude were dressed in magnificent robes, without stain or blemish, and sparkling with jewels; others in burnished and enamelled armor; while others were in mouldered and mildewed garments, and in armor all battered and dented and covered with rust.

"I had hitherto held my tongue, for your Excellency well knows it is not for a soldier to ask many questions when on duty, but I could keep silent no longer.

" 'Prithee, comrade,' said I, 'what is the meaning of all this?'

" 'This,' said the trooper, 'is a great and fearful mystery. Know,

O Christian, that you see before you the court and army of Boabdil the last king of Granada.'

"'What is this you tell me?' cried I. 'Boabdil and his court were exiled from the land hundreds of years agone, and all died in Africa.'

"'So it is recorded in your lying chronicles,' replied the Moor; 'but know that Boabdil and the warriors who made the last struggle for Granada were all shut up in the mountain by powerful enchantment. As for the king and army that marched forth from Granada at the time of the surrender, they were a mere phantom train of spirits and demons, permitted to assume those shapes to deceive the Christian sovereigns. And furthermore let me tell you, friend, that all Spain is a country under the power of enchantment. There is not a mountain cave, not a lonely watch-tower in the plains, nor ruined castle on the hills, but has some spellbound warriors sleeping from age to age within its vaults, until the sins are expiated for which Allah permitted the dominion to pass for a time out of the hands of the faithful. Once every year, on the eve of St. John, they are released from enchantment, from sunset to sunrise, and permitted to repair here to pay homage to their sovereign! and the crowds which you beheld swarming into the cavern are Moslem warriors from their haunts in all parts of Spain. For my own part, you saw the ruined tower of the bridge in Old Castile, where I have now wintered and summered for many hundred years, and where I must be back again by daybreak. As to the battalions of horse and foot which you beheld drawn up in array in the neighboring caverns, they are the spellbound warriors of Granada. It is written in the book of fate, that when the enchantment is broken, Boabdil will descend from the mountain at the head of this army, resume his throne in the Alhambra and his sway of Granada, and gathering together the enchanted warriors from all parts of Spain, will reconquer the Peninsula and restore it to Moslem rule.'

"'And when shall this happen?' said I.

"'Allah alone knows: we had hoped the day of deliverance was at hand; but there reigns at present a vigilant governor in the Alhambra, a stanch old soldier, well known as Governor Manco. While such a warrior holds command of the very outpost, and stands ready to check the first irruption from the mountain, I fear Boabdil and his soldiery must be content to rest upon their arms.'"

Here the governor raised himself somewhat perpendicularly, adjusted his sword, and twirled up his moustaches.

"To make a long story short, and not to fatigue your Excellency, the trooper, having giving me this account, dismounted from his steed.

"'Tarry here,' said he, 'and guard my steed while I go and bow the knee to Boabdil.' So saying, he strode away among the throng that pressed forward to the throne.

"'What's to be done?' thought I, when thus left to myself; 'shall I wait here until this infidel returns to whisk me off on his goblin steed, the Lord knows where; or shall I make the most of my time and beat a retreat from this hobgoblin community?' A soldier's mind is soon made up, as your Excellency well knows. As to the horse, he belonged to an avowed enemy of the faith and the realm, and was a fair prize according to the rules of war. So hoisting myself from the crupper into the saddle, I turned the reins, struck the Moorish stirrups into the sides of the steed, and put him to make the best of his way out of the passage by which he had entered. As we scoured by the halls where the Moslem horsemen sat in motionless battalions, I thought I heard the clang of armor and a hollow murmur of voices. I gave the steed another taste of the stirrups and doubled my speed. There was now a sound behind me like a rushing blast; I heard the clatter of a thousand hoofs; a countless throng overtook me. I was borne along in the press, and hurled forth from the mouth of the cavern, while thousands of shadowy forms were swept off in every direction by the four winds of heaven.

"In the whirl and confusion of the scene I was thrown senseless to the earth. When I came to myself, I was lying on the brow of a hill, with the Arabian steed standing beside me; for in falling, my arm had slipped within the bridle, which, I presume, prevented his whisking off to Old Castile.

"Your Excellency may easily judge of my surprise, on looking round, to behold hedges of aloes and Indian figs and other proofs of a southern climate, and to see a great city below me, with towers, and palaces, and a grand cathedral.

"I descended the hill cautiously, leading my steed, for I was afraid to mount him again, lest he should play me some slippery trick. As I descended I met with your patrol, who let me into the secret that it was Granada that lay before me, and that I was actually under the walls of the Alhambra, the fortress of the redoubted Governor Manco, the terror of all enchanted Moslems. When I heard this, I determined at once to seek your Excellency, to inform you of all that I had seen, and to warn you of the perils that surround and undermine you, that you may take measures in time to guard your fortress, and the kingdom itself, from this intestine army that lurks in the very bowels of the land."

"And prithee, friend, you who are a veteran campaigner, and have seen so much service," said the governor, "how would you advise me to proceed, in order to prevent this evil?"

"It is not for a humble private of the ranks," said the soldier, modestly, "to pretend to instruct a commander of your Excellency's sagacity, but it appears to me that your Excellency might cause all the caves and entrances into the mountains to be walled up with solid mason-work, so that Boabdil and his army might be completely corked up in their subterranean habitation. If the good father, too," added the soldier, reverently bowing to the friar, and devoutly crossing himself, "would consecrate the barricadoes with his blessing, and put up a few crosses and relics and images of saints, I think they might withstand all the power of infidel enchantments."

"They doubtless would be of great avail," said the friar.

The governor now placed his arm akimbo, with his hand resting on the hilt of his toledo, fixed his eye upon the soldier, and gently wagging his head from one side to the other,—

"So, friend," said he, "then you really suppose I am to be gulled with this cock-and-bull story about enchanted mountains and enchanted Moors? Hark ye, culprit!—not another word. An old soldier you may be, but you'll find you have an older soldier to deal with and one not easily outgeneralled. Ho! guards there! put this fellow in irons."

The demure handmaid would have put in a word in favor of the prisoner, but the governor silenced her with a look.

As they were pinioning the soldier, one of the guards felt something of bulk in his pocket, and drawing it forth, found a long leathern purse that appeared to be well filled. Holding it by one corner, he turned out the contents upon the table before the governor, and never did freebooter's bag make more gorgeous delivery. Out tumbled rings and jewels, and rosaries of pearls, and sparkling diamond crosses, and a profusion of ancient golden coin, some of which fell jingling to the floor, and rolled away to the uttermost parts of the chamber.

For a time the functions of justice were suspended; there was a universal scramble after the glittering fugitives. The governor alone, who was imbued with true Spanish pride, maintained his stately decorum, though his eye betrayed a little anxiety until the last coin and jewel was restored to the sack.

The friar was not so calm; his whole face glowed like a furnace, and his eyes twinkled and flashed at sight of the rosaries and crosses.

"Sacrilegious wretch that thou art!" exclaimed he; "what church or sanctuary hast thou been plundering of these sacred relics?"

"Neither one nor the other, holy father. If they be sacrilegious spoils, they must have been taken, in times long past, by the infidel trooper I have mentioned. I was just going to tell his Excellency when he interrupted me, that on taking possession of the trooper's horse, I unhooked a leathern sack which hung at the saddle-bow, and which I presume contained the plunder of his campaignings in the days of old, when the Moors overran the country."

"Mighty well; at present you will make up your mind to take up your quarters in a chamber of the Vermilion Tower, which, though not under a magic spell, will hold you as safe as any cave of your enchanted Moors."

"Your Excellency will do as you think proper," said the prisoner, coolly. "I shall be thankful to your Excellency for any accommodation in the fortress. A soldier who has been in the wars, as your Excellency well knows, is not particular about his lodgings. Provided I have a snug dungeon and regular rations, I shall manage to make myself comfortable. I would only entreat that while your Excellency is so careful about me, you would have an eye to your fortress, and think on the hint I dropped about stopping up the entrances to the mountain."

Here ended the scene. The prisoner was conducted to a strong dungeon in the Vermilion Tower, the Arabian steed was led to his Excellency's stable, and the trooper's sack was deposited in his Excellency's strong box. To the latter, it is true, the friar made some demur, questioning whether the sacred relics, which were evidently sacrilegious spoils, should not be placed in custody of the Church; but as the governor was peremptory on the subject, and was absolute lord in the Alhambra, the friar discreetly dropped the discussion, but determined to convey intelligence of the fact to the Church dignitaries in Granada.

To explain these prompt and rigid measures on the part of old Governor Manco, it is proper to observe, that about this time the Alpuxarra Mountains in the neighborhood of Granada were terribly infested by a gang of robbers, under the command of a daring chief named Manuel Borasco, who was accustomed to prowl about the country, and even to enter the city in various disguises, to gain intelligence of the departure of convoys of merchandise, or travellers with well-lined purses, whom they took care to waylay in distant and solitary passes of the road. These repeated and daring outrages had wakened the attention of government, and the commanders of the various posts had received instructions to be on the alert, and to take up all suspicious stragglers. Governor Manco was particularly zealous in consequence of the various stigmas that had been cast upon his fortress, and he now doubted not he had entrapped some formidable desperado of this gang.

In the meantime the story took wind, and became the talk, not merely of the fortress, but of the whole city of Granada. It was said that the noted robber Manuel Borasco, the terror of the Alpuxarras, had fallen into the clutches of old Governor Manco, and been cooped up by him in a dungeon of the Vermilion Tower; and every one who had been robbed by him flocked to recognize the marauder. The Vermilion Tower, as is well known, stands apart from the Alhambra on a sister hill, separated from the main fortress by the ravine down which passes the main avenue. There were no outer walls, but a sentinel patrolled before the tower. The window of the chamber in which the soldier was confined was strongly grated, and looked upon a small esplanade. Here the good folks of Granada repaired to gaze at him, as they would at a laughing hyena, grinning through the cage of a menagerie. Nobody, however, recognized him for Manuel Borasco, for that terrible robber was noted for a ferocious physiognomy, and had by no means the good-humored squint of the prisoner. Visitors came not merely from the city, but from all parts of the country; but nobody knew him, and there began to be doubts in the minds of the common people whether there might not be some truth in his story. That Boabdil and his army were shut up in the mountain, was an old tradition which many of the ancient inhabitants had heard from their fathers. Numbers went up to the Mountain of the Sun, or rather of St. Elena, in search of the cave mentioned by the soldier; and saw and peeped into the deep, dark pit, descending, no one knows how far, into the mountain, and which remains there to this day—the fabled entrance to the subterranean abode of Boabdil.

By degrees the soldier became popular with the common people. A freebooter of the mountains is by no means the opprobrious character in Spain that a robber is in any other country; on the contrary, he is a kind of chivalrous personage in the eyes of the lower classes. There is always a disposition, also, to cavil at the conduct of those in command; and many began to murmur at the high-handed measures of old Governor Manco, and to look upon the prisoner in the light of a martyr.

The soldier, moreover, was a merry, waggish fellow, that had a joke for every one who came near his window, and a soft speech for every female. He had procured an old guitar, also, and would sit by his window and sing ballads and love-ditties, to the delight of the women of the neighborhood, who would assemble on the esplanade in the evening and dance *boleros* to his music. Having trimmed off his rough beard, his sunburnt face found favor in the eyes of the fair, and the demure handmaid of the governor declared that his squint was perfectly irresistible. This kind-hearted damsel had from the first evinced a deep sympathy in his fortunes, and having in vain tried to mollify the governor, had set to work privately to mitigate the rigor of his dispensations. Every day she brought the prisoner some crumbs of comfort which had fallen from the governor's table, or been abstracted from his larder, together with, now and then, a consoling bottle of choice Val de Peñas, or rich Malaga.

While this petty treason was going on in the very centre of the old governor's citadel, a storm of open war was brewing up among his external foes. The circumstance of a bag of gold and jewels having been found upon the person of the supposed robber, had been reported, with many exaggerations, in Granada. A question of territorial jurisdiction was immediately started by the governor's inveterate rival, the captain-general. He insisted that the prisoner had been captured without the precincts of the Alhambra, and within the rules of his authority. He demanded his body, therefore, and the *spolia opima* taken with him. Due information having been carried likewise by the friar to the grand inquisitor of the crosses and rosaries, and other relics contained in the bag, he claimed the culprit as having been guilty of sacrilege, and insisted that his plunder was due to the Church, and his body to the next *auto-da-fe*. The feuds ran high. The governor was furious, and swore, rather than surrender his captive, he would hang him up within the Alhambra, as a spy caught within the purlieus of the fortress.

The captain-general threatened to send a body of soldiers to transfer the prisoner from the Vermilion Tower to the city. The grand inquisitor was equally bent upon despatching a number of the familiars of the Holy Office. Word was brought late at night to the governor of these machinations. "Let them come," said he; "they'll find me beforehand with them. He must rise bright and early who would take in an old soldier." He accordingly issued orders to have the prisoner removed, at daybreak, to the donjon keep within the walls of the Alhambra. "And d'ye hear, child," said he to his demure hand-maid, "tap at my door, and wake me before cock-crowing, that I may see to the matter myself."

The day dawned, the cock crowed, but nobody tapped at the door of the governor. The sun rose high above the mountain-tops, and glittered in at his casement, ere the governor was awakened from his morning dreams by his veteran corporal, who stood before him with terror stamped upon his iron visage.

"He's off! he's gone!" cried the corporal, gasping for breath.

"Who's off—who's gone?"

"The soldier—the robber—the devil, for aught I know. His dungeon is empty, but the door locked; no one knows how he has escaped out of it."

"Who saw him last?"

"Your handmaid; she brought him his supper."

"Let her be called instantly."

Here was new matter of confusion. The chamber of the demure damsel was likewise empty; her bed had not been slept in. She had doubtless gone off with the culprit, as she had appeared for some days past to have frequent conversations with him.

This was wounding the old governor in a tender part, but he had scarce time to wince at it, when new misfortunes broke upon his view. On going into his cabinet he found his strong box open, the leather purse of the trooper abstracted, and with it a couple of corpulent bags of doubloons.

But how, and which way, had the fugitives escaped? An old peasant, who lived in a cottage by the roadside leading up into the Sierra, declared that he had heard the tramp of a powerful steed, just before daybreak, passing up into the mountains. He had looked out at his casement, and could just distinguish a horseman, with a female seated before him.

"Search the stables!" cried Governor Manco. The stables were searched. All the horses were in their stalls, excepting the Arabian steed. In his place was a stout cudgel, tied to the manger, and on it a label bearing these words, "A Gift to Governor Manco, from an Old Soldier."

From *The Alhambra*

LEGEND OF THE TWO DISCREET STATUES

THERE lived once in a waste apartment of the Alhambra a merry little fellow, named Lope Sanchez, who worked in the gardens, and was as brisk and as blithe as a grasshopper, singing all day long. He was the life and soul of the fortress; when his work was over, he would sit on one of the stone benches of the esplanade, strum his guitar, and sing long ditties about the Cid, and Barnardo del Carpio, and Fernando del Pulgar, and other Spanish heroes, for the amusement of the old soldiers of the fortress; or would strike up a merrier tune, and set the girls dancing *boleros* and *fandangos*.

Like most little men, Lope Sanchez had a strapping buxom dame for a wife, who could almost have put him in her pocket; but he lacked the usual poor man's lot—instead of ten children he had but one. This was a little black-eyed girl about twelve years of age, named Sanchica, who was as merry as himself, and the delight of his heart. She played about him as he worked in the gardens, danced to his guitar as he sat in the shade, and ran as wild as a young fawn about the groves and alleys and ruined halls of the Alhambra.

It was now the eve of the blessed St. John, and the holiday-loving gossips of the Alhambra, men, women, and children, went up at night to the Mountain of the Sun, which rises above the Generalife, to keep their midsummer vigil on its level summit. It was a bright moon-light night, and all the mountains were gray and silvery, and the city, with its domes and spires, lay in shadows below, and the Vega was like a fairy land, with haunted streams gleaming among its dusky groves. On the highest part of the mountain they lit up a bonfire, according to an old custom of the country handed down from the

---

This tale, taken from *The Alhambra*, is supposed to be told by "a grave but, as I thought, somewhat sly old gentleman present, who, I believe, was the count's advocate or legal adviser." The count was Irving's neighbor in the Alhambra. The advocate assured his listeners, in Irving's words, that "two statues of nymphs in white marble, placed at the entrance of a vaulted passage . . . were connected with one of the great mysteries of the Alhambra; that there was a curious history concerning them, and, moreover, that they stood a living monument in marble of female secrecy and devotion."—C.N.

Moors. The inhabitants of the surrounding country were keeping a similar vigil, and bonfires, here and there in the Vega, and along the folds of the mountains, blazed up palely in the moonlight.

The evening was gayly passed in dancing to the guitar of Lope Sanchez, who was never so joyous as when on a holiday revel of the kind. While the dance was going on, the little Sanchica with some of her playmates sported among the ruins of an old Moorish fort that crowns the mountain, when, in gathering pebbles in the fosse, she found a small hand curiously carved of jet, the fingers closed, and the thumb firmly clasped upon them. Overjoyed with her good fortune, she ran to her mother with her prize. It immediately became a subject of sage speculation, and was eyed by some with superstitious distrust. "Throw it away," said one; "it's Moorish,—depend upon it, there's mischief and witchcraft in it." "By no means," said another; "you may sell it for something to the jewellers of the Zacatin." In the midst of this discussion an old tawny soldier drew near, who had served in Africa, and was as swarthy as a Moor. He examined the hand with a knowing look. "I have seen things of this kind," said he, "among the Moors of Barbary. It is a great virtue to guard against the evil eye, and all kinds of spells and enchantments. I give you joy, friend Lope, this bodes good luck to your child."

Upon hearing this, the wife of Lope Sanchez tied the little hand of jet to a ribbon, and hung it round the neck of her daughter.

The sight of this talisman called up all the favorite superstitions about the Moors. The dance was neglected, and they sat in groups on the ground, telling old legendary tales handed down from their ancestors. Some of their stories turned upon the wonders of the very mountain upon which they were seated, which is a famous hobgoblin region. One ancient crone gave a long account of the subterranean palace in the bowels of that mountain where Boabdil and all his Moslem court are said to remain enchanted. "Among yonder ruins," said she, pointing to some crumbling walls and mounds of earth on a distant part of the mountain, "there is a deep black pit that goes down, down into the very heart of the mountain. For all the money in Granada I would not look down into it. Once upon a time a poor man of the Alhambra, who tended goats upon this mountain, scrambled down into that pit after a kid that had fallen in. He came out again all wild and staring, and told such things of what he had seen that every one though his brain was turned. He raved for a day or two about the hobgoblin Moors that had pursued him in the cavern, and could hardly be persuaded to drive his goats up again to the mountain. He did so at last, but, poor man, he never came down again. The neighbors found his goats browsing about the Moorish ruins, and his hat and mantle lying near the mouth of the pit, but he was never more heard of."

The little Sanchica listened with breathless attention to his story. She was of a curious nature, and felt immediately a great hankering to peep into this dangerous pit. Stealing away from her companions, she sought the distant ruins, and, after groping for some time among them, came to a small hollow, or basin, near the brow of the mountain, where it swept steeply down into the valley of the Darro. In the centre of this basin yawned the mouth of the pit. Sanchica ventured to the verge, and peeped in. All was as black as pitch, and gave an idea of immeasurable depth. Her blood ran cold; she drew back, then peeped in again, then would have run away, then took another peep,— the very horror of the thing was delightful to her. At length she rolled a large stone, and pushed it over the brink. For some time it fell in silence; then struck some rocky projection with a violent crash; then rebounded from side to side, rumbling and tumbling, with a noise like thunder; then made a final splash into water, far below,—and all was again silent.

The silence, however, did not long continue. It seemed as if something had been awakened within this dreary abyss. A murmuring sound gradually rose out of the pit like the hum and buzz of a beehive. It grew louder and louder, there was the confusion of voices as of a distant multitude, together with the faint din of arms, clash of cymbals and clangor of trumpets, as if some army were marshalling for battle in the very bowels of the mountain.

The child drew off with silent awe, and hastened back to the place where she had left her parents and their companions. All were gone. The bonfire was expiring, and its last wreath of smoke curling up in the moonshine. The distant fires that had blazed along the mountains and in the Vega were all extinguished, and everything seemed to have sunk to repose. Sanchica called her parents and some of her companions by name, but received no reply. She ran down the side of the mountain, and by the gardens of the Generalife, until she arrived in the alley of trees leading to the Alhambra, when she seated herself on a bench of a woody recess, to recover breath. The bell from the watchtower of the Alhambra tolled midnight. There was a deep tranquillity as if all nature slept; excepting the low tinkling sound of an unseen stream that ran under the covert of the bushes. The breathing sweetness of the atmosphere was lulling her to sleep, when her eye was caught by something glittering at a distance, and to her surprise she beheld a long cavalcade of Moorish warriors pouring down the mountain side and along the leafy avenues. Some were armed with lances and shields; others, with cimeters and battle-axes, and with polished cuirasses that flashed in the moonbeams. Their horses pranced proudly and champed upon their bits, but their tramp caused no more sound than if they had been shod with felt, and the riders were all as pale as death. Among them rode a beautiful lady, with a crowned head and long golden locks entwined with pearls. The housings of her palfrey were of crimson velvet embroidered with gold, and swept the earth; but she rode all disconsolate, with eyes ever fixed upon the ground.

Then succeeded a train of courtiers magnificently arrayed in robes and turbans of divers colors, and amidst them, on a cream-colored charger, rode King Boabdil el Chico, in a royal mantle covered with jewels, and a crown sparkling with diamonds. The little Sanchica knew him by his yellow beard, and his resemblance to his portrait, which she had often seen in the picture-gallery of the Generalife. She gazed in wonder and admiration at this royal pageant, as it passed glistening among the trees; but though she knew these monarchs and courtiers and warriors, so pale and silent, were out of the common course of nature, and things of magic and enchantment, yet she looked on with a bold heart, such courage did she derive from the mystic talisman of the hand, which was suspended about her neck.

The cavalcade having passed by, she rose and followed. It continued on to the great Gate of Justice, which stood wide open; the old invalid sentinels on duty lay on the stone benches of the barbican, buried in profound and apparently charmed sleep, and the phantom pageant swept noiselessly by them with flaunting banner and triumphant state. Sanchica would have followed; but to her surprise she beheld an opening in the earth, within the barbican, leading down beneath the foundations of the tower. She entered for a little distance, and was encouraged to proceed by finding steps rudely hewn in the rock, and a vaulted passage here and there lit up by a silver lamp, which, while it gave light, diffused likewise a grateful fragrance. Venturing on, she came at last to a great hall, wrought out of the heart of the mountain, magnificently furnished in the Moorish style, and lighted up by silver and crystal lamps. Here, on an ottoman, sat an old man in Moorish dress, with a long white beard, nodding and dozing, with a staff in his hand, which seemed ever to be slipping from his grasp; while at a little distance sat a beautiful lady, in ancient Spanish dress, with a coronet all sparkling with diamonds, and her hair entwined with pearls, who was softly playing on a silver lyre. The little Sanchica now recollected a story she had heard among the

old people of the Alhambra, concerning a Gothic princess confined in
the centre of the mountains by an old Arabian magician, whom she
kept bound up in magic sleep by the power of music.

The lady paused with surprise at seeing a mortal in that enchanted
hall. "Is it the eve of the blessed St. John?" said she.

"It is," replied Sanchica.

"Then for one night the magic charm is suspended. Come hither,
child, and fear not. I am a Christian like thyself, though bound here
by enchantment. Touch my fetters with the talisman that hangs
about thy neck, and for this night I shall be free."

So saying, she opened her robes and displayed a broad golden band
round her waist, and a golden chain that fastened her to the ground.
The child hesitated not to apply the little hand of jet to the golden
band, and immediately the chain fell to the earth. At the sound the
old man woke and began to rub his eyes; but the lady ran her fingers
over the chords of the lyre, and again he fell into a slumber and began
to nod, and his staff to falter in his hand. "Now," said the lady,
"touch his staff with the talismanic hand of jet." The child did so, and
it· fell from his grasp, and he sank in a deep sleep on the ottoman.
The lady gently laid the silver lyre on the ottoman, leaning it against
the head of the sleeping magician; then touching the chords until
they vibrated in his ear,—"O potent spirit of harmony," said she, "continue thus to hold his senses in thraldom till the return of day. Now
follow me, my child," continued she, "and thou shalt behold the Alhambra as it was in the days of its glory, for thou hast a magic talisman
that reveals all enchantments." Sanchica followed the lady in silence.
They passed up through the entrance of the cavern into the barbican
of the Gate of Justice, and thence to the Plaza de los Algibes, or
esplanade within the fortress.

This was all filled with Moorish soldiery, horse and foot, marshalled
in squadrons, with banners displayed. There were royal guards also
at the portal, and rows of African blacks, with drawn cimeters. No
one spoke a word, and Sanchica passed on fearlessly after her conductor. Her astonishment increased on entering the royal palace, in
which she had been reared. The broad moonshine lit up all the halls
and courts and gardens almost as brightly as if it were day, but revealed a far different scene from that to which she was accustomed.
The walls of the apartments were no longer stained and rent by time.
Instead of cobwebs, they were now hung with rich silks of Damascus,
and the gildings and arabesque paintings were restored to their
original brilliancy and freshness. The halls, no longer naked and unfurnished, were set out with divans and ottomans of the rarest stuffs,

embroidered with pearls and studded with precious gems, and all the fountains in the courts and gardens were playing. The kitchens were again in full operation. Cooks were busy preparing shadowy dishes, and roasting and boiling the phantoms of pullets and partridges; servants were hurrying to and fro with silver dishes heaped up with dainties, and arranging a delicious banquet. The Court of Lions was thronged with guards, and courtiers, and *alfaquis*, as in the old times of the Moors; and at the upper end, in the saloon of judgment, sat Boabdil on his throne, surrounded by his court, and swaying a shadowy sceptre for the night. Notwithstanding all this throng and seeming bustle, not a voice nor a footstep was to be heard; nothing interrupted the midnight silence but the splashing of the fountains. The little Sanchica followed her conductress in mute amazement about the palace, until they came to a portal opening to the vaulted passages beneath the great tower of Comares. On each side of the portal sat the figure of a nymph, wrought out of alabaster. Their heads were turned aside, and their regards fixed upon the same spot within the vault. The enchanted lady paused, and beckoned the child to her. "Here," said she, "is a great secret, which I will reveal to thee in reward for thy faith and courage. These discreet statues watch over a treasure, hidden in old times by a Moorish king. Tell thy father to search the spot on which their eyes are fixed, and he will find what will make him richer than any man in Granada. Thy innocent hands alone, however, gifted as thou art also with the talisman, can remove the treasure. Bid thy father use it discreetly, and devote a part of it to the performance of daily masses for my deliverance from this unholy enchantment."

When the lady had spoken these words, she led the child onward to the little garden of Lindaraxa, which is hard by the vault of the statues. The moon trembled upon the waters of the solitary fountain in the centre of the garden, and shed a tender light upon the orange and citron trees. The beautiful lady plucked a branch of myrtle and wreathed it round the head of the child. "Let this be a memento," said she, "of what I have revealed to thee, and a testimonial of its truth. My hour is come; I must return to the enchanted hall. Follow me not, lest evil befall thee. Farewell. Remember what I have said, and have masses performed for my deliverance." So saying, the lady entered a dark passage leading beneath the Tower of Comares, and was no longer seen.

The faint crowing of a cock was now heard from the cottages below the Alhambra, in the valley of the Darro, and a pale streak of light began to appear above the eastern mountains. A slight wind arose, there was a sound like the rustling of dry leaves through the courts and corridors, and door after door shut to with a jarring sound.

Sanchica returned to the scenes she had so lately beheld thronged with the shadowy multitude, but Boabdil and his phantom court were gone. The moon shone into empty halls and galleries stripped of their transient splendor, stained and dilapidated by time, and hung with cobwebs. The bat flitted about in the uncertain light, and the frog croaked from the fish-pond.

Sanchica now made the best of her way to a remote staircase that led up to the humble apartment occupied by her family. The door, as usual, was open, for Lope Sanchez was too poor to need bolt or bar. She crept quietly to her pallet, and, putting the myrtle wreath beneath her pillow, soon fell asleep.

In the morning she related all that had befallen her to her father. Lope Sanchez, however, treated the whole as a mere dream, and laughed at the child for her credulity. He went forth to his customary labors in the garden, but had not been there long when his little daughter came running to him, almost breathless. "Father! father!" cried she, "behold the myrtle wreath which the Moorish lady bound round my head!"

Lope Sanchez gazed with astonishment, for the stalk of the myrtle was of pure gold, and every leaf was a sparkling emerald! Being not much accustomed to precious stones, he was ignorant of the real value of the wreath, but he saw enough to convince him that it was something more substantial than the stuff of which dreams are generally made, and that at any rate the child had dreamt to some purpose. His first care was to enjoin the most absolute secrecy upon his daughter. In this respect, however, he was secure, for she had discretion far beyond her years or sex. He then repaired to the vault, where stood the statues of the two alabaster nymphs. He remarked that their heads were turned from the portal, and that the regards of each were fixed upon the same point in the interior of the building. Lope Sanchez could not but admire this most discreet contrivance for guarding a secret. He drew a line from the eyes of the statues to the point of regard, made a private mark on the wall, and then retired.

All day, however, the mind of Lope Sanchez was distracted with a thousand cares. He could not help hovering within distant view of the two statues, and became nervous from the dread that the golden secret might be discovered. Every footstep that approached the place made him tremble. He would have given anything could he but have turned the heads of the statues, forgetting that they had looked precisely in the same direction for some hundreds of years, without any person being the wiser.

"A plague upon them," he would say to himself, "they'll betray all; did ever mortal hear of such a mode of guarding a secret?" Then on hearing any one advance, he would steal off, as though his very lurking near the place would awaken suspicion. Then he would return cautiously, and peep from a distance to see if everything was secure, but the sight of the statues would again call forth his indignation. "Ay, there they stand," would he say, "always looking, and looking, and looking, just where they should not. Confound them! they are just like all their sex; if they have not tongues to tattle with, they'll be sure to do it with their eyes."

At length, to his relief, the long anxious day drew to a close. The sound of footsteps was no longer heard in the echoing halls of the Alhambra; the last stranger passed the threshold, the great portal was barred and bolted, and the bat and the frog and the hooting owl gradually resumed their nightly vocations in the deserted palace.

Lope Sanchez waited, however, until the night was far advanced before he ventured with his little daughter to the hall of the two nymphs. He found them looking as knowingly and mysteriously as ever at the secret place of deposit. "By your leaves, gentle ladies," thought Lope Sanchez, as he passed between them, "I will relieve you from this charge that must have set so heavy in your minds for the last two or three centuries." He accordingly went to work at the part of the wall which he had marked, and in a little while laid open a concealed recess, in which stood two great jars of porcelain. He attempted to draw them forth, but they were immovable, until touched by the innocent hand of his little daughter. With her aid he dislodged them from their niche, and found, to his great joy, that they were filled with pieces of Moorish gold, mingled with jewels and precious stones. Before daylight he managed to convey them to his chamber, and left the two guardian statues with their eyes still fixed on the vacant wall.

Lope Sanchez had thus on a sudden become a rich man; but riches, as usual, brought a world of cares to which he had hitherto been a stranger. How was he to convey away his wealth with safety? How was he even to enter upon the enjoyment of it without awakening suspicion? Now, too, for the first time in his life the dread of robbers entered into his mind. He looked with terror at the insecurity of his habitation, and went to work to barricade the doors and windows; yet after all his precautions he could not sleep soundly. His usual gayety was at an end, he had no longer a joke or a song for his neighbors, and, in short, became the most miserable animal in the Alhambra. His old comrades remarked this alteration, pitied him heartily, and began to desert him; thinking he must be falling into want, and in danger of looking to them for assistance. Little did they suspect that his only calamity was riches.

The wife of Lope Sanchez shared his anxiety, but then she had ghostly comfort. We ought before this to have mentioned that Lope, being rather a light inconsiderate little man, his wife was accustomed, in all grave matters, to seek the counsel and ministry of her confessor Fray Simon, a sturdy, broad-shouldered, blue-bearded, bullet-headed friar of the neighboring convent of San Francisco, who was in fact the spiritual comforter of half the good wives of the neighborhood. He was, moreover, in great esteem among divers sisterhoods of nuns; who requited him for his ghostly services by frequent presents of those little dainties and knick-knacks manufactured in convents, such as delicate confections, sweet biscuits, and bottles of spiced cordials, found to be marvellous restoratives after fasts and vigils.

· Fray Simon thrived in the exercise of his functions. His oily skin glistened in the sunshine as he toiled up the hill of the Alhambra on a sultry day. Yet notwithstanding his sleek condition, the knotted rope round his waist showed the austerity of his self-discipline; the multitude doffed their caps to him as a mirror of piety, and even the dogs scented the odor of sanctity that exhaled from his garments, and howled from their kennels as he passed.

Such was Fray Simon, the spiritual counsellor of the comely wife of Lope Sanchez; and as the father confessor is the domestic confidant of women in humble life in Spain, he was soon acquainted, in great secrecy, with the story of the hidden treasure.

The friar opened his eyes and mouth, and crossed himself a dozen times at the news. After a moment's pause, "Daughter of my soul!" said he, "know that thy husband has committed a double sin—a sin against both state and church! The treasure he hath thus seized upon for himself, being found in the royal domains, belongs of course to the crown; but being infidel wealth, rescued as it were from the very fangs of Satan, should be devoted to the church. Still, however, the matter may be accommodated. Bring hither thy myrtle wreath."

When the good father beheld it, his eyes twinkled more than ever with admiration of the size and beauty of the emeralds. "This," said he, "being the first-fruits of this discovery, should be dedicated to pious purposes. I will hang it up as a votive offering before the image of San Francisco in our chapel, and will earnestly pray to him, this very night, that your husband be permitted to remain in quiet possession of your wealth."

The good dame was delighted to make her peace with heaven at so cheap a rate, and the friar, putting the wreath under his mantle, departed with saintly steps toward his convent.

When Lope Sanchez came home, his wife told him what had passed. He was excessively provoked, for he lacked his wife's devotion, and had for some time groaned in secret at the domestic visitations of the friar. "Woman," said he, "what hast thou done? thou hast put everything at hazard by thy tattling."

"What!" cried the good woman, "would you forbid my disburdening my conscience to my confessor?"

"No, wife! confess as many of your own sins as you please; but as to this money-digging, it is a sin of my own, and my conscience is very easy under the weight of it."

There was no use, however, in complaining; the secret was told, and, like water spilled on the sand, was not again to be gathered. Their only chance was that the friar would be discreet.

· The next day, while Lope Sanchez was abroad, there was an humble knocking at the door, and Fray Simon entered with meek and demure countenance.

"Daughter," said he, "I have earnestly prayed to San Francisco, and he has heard my prayer. In the dead of the night the saint appeared to me in a dream, but with a frowning aspect. 'Why,' said he, 'dost thou pray to me to dispense with this treasure of the Gentiles, when thou seest the poverty of my chapel? Go to the house of Lope Sanchez, crave in my name a portion of the Moorish gold, to furnish two candlesticks for the main altar, and let him possess the residue in peace."

When the good woman heard of this vision, she crossed herself with awe, and going to the secret place where Lope had hid the treasure, she filled the great leathern purse with pieces of Moorish gold, and gave it to the friar. The pious monk bestowed upon her, in return, benedictions enough, if paid by heaven, to enrich her race to the latest posterity; then slipping the purse in the sleeve of his habit, he folded his hands upon his breast, and departed with an air of humble thankfulness.

When Lope Sanchez heard of this second donation to the church, he had wellnigh lost his senses. "Unfortunate man," cried he, "what will become of me? I shall be robbed by piecemeal; I shall be ruined and brought to beggary!"

It was with the utmost difficulty that his wife could pacify him, by reminding him of the countless wealth that yet remained, and how considerate it was for San Francisco to rest contented with so small a portion.

Unluckily Fray Simon had a number of poor relations to be provided for, not to mention some half-dozen sturdy bullet-headed orphan children and destitute foundlings that he had taken under his care. He repeated his visits, therefore, from day to day, with solicitations on behalf of Saint Dominick, Saint Andrew, Saint James, until poor Lopez was driven to despair, and found that unless he got out of the reach of this holy friar he should have to make peace-offerings to every saint in the calendar. He determined, therefore, to pack up his remaining wealth, beat a secret retreat in the night, and make off to another part of the kingdom.

Full of his project he bought a stout mule for the purpose, and tethered it in a gloomy vault underneath the tower of the seven floors; the very place whence the Belludo, or goblin horse, is said to issue forth at midnight, and scour the streets of Granada, pursued by a pack of hellhounds. Lope Sanchez had little faith in the story, but availed himself of the dread occasioned by it, knowing that no one would be likely to pry into the subterranean stable of the phantom steed. He sent off his family in the course of the day, with orders to wait for him at a distant village of the Vega. As the night advanced he conveyed his treasure to the vault under the tower, and having loaded his mule, he led it forth and cautiously descended the dusky avenue.

Honest Lope had taken his measures with the utmost secrecy, imparting them to no one but the faithful wife of his bosom. By some miraculous revelation, however, they became known to Fray Simon. The zealous friar beheld these infidel treasures on the point of slipping forever out of his grasp, and determined to have one more dash at them for the benefit of the church and San Francisco. Accordingly, when the bells had rung for animas and all the Alhambra was quiet, he stole out of his convent, and descending through the Gate of Justice, concealed himself among the thickets of roses and laurels that border the great avenue. Here he remained, counting the quarters of hours as they were sounded on the bell of the watch-tower, and listening to the dreary hooting of owls, and the distant barking of dogs from the gypsy caverns.

At length he heard the tramp of hoofs, and, through the gloom of the overshading trees, imperfectly beheld a steed descending the avenue. The sturdy friar chuckled at the idea of the knowing turn he was about to serve honest Lope.

Tucking up the skirts of his habit, and wriggling like a cat watching a mouse, he waited until his prey was directly before him, when darting forth from his leafy covert, and putting one hand on the shoulder and the other on the crupper, he made a vault that would not have disgraced the most experienced master of equitation, and alighted well-forked astride the steed. "Ah ha!" said the sturdy friar, "we shall now see who best understands the game." He had scarce uttered the words when the mule began to kick, and rear, and plunge, and then set off full speed down the hill. The friar attempted to check him, but in vain. He bounded from rock to rock, and bush to bush; the friar's habit was torn to ribbons and fluttered in the wind, his shaven poll received many a hard knock from the branches of the trees, and many a scratch from the brambles. To add to his terror and distress, he found a pack of seven hounds in full cry at his heels, and perceived, too late, that he was actually mounted upon the terrible Belludo!

Away then they went, according to the ancient phrase, "pull devil, pull friar," down the great avenue, across the Plaza Nueva, along the Zacatin, around the Vivarrambla—never did huntsman and hound make a more furious run, or more infernal uproar. In vain did the friar invoke every saint in the calendar, and the holy Virgin into the bargain; every time he mentioned a name of the kind it was like a fresh application of the spur, and made the Belludo bound as high as a house. Through the remainder of the night was the unlucky Fray Simon carried hither and thither, and whither he would not, until every bone in his body ached, and he suffered a loss of leather too grievous to be mentioned. At length the crowing of a cock gave the signal of returning day. At the sound the goblin steed wheeled about, and galloped back for his tower. Again he scoured the Vivarrambla, the Zacatin, the Plaza Nueva, and the Avenue of Fountains, the seven dogs yelling and barking and leaping up, and snapping at the heels of the terrified friar. The first streak of day had just appeared as they reached the tower; here the goblin steed kicked up his heels, sent the friar a summerset through the air, plunged into the dark vault followed by the infernal pack, and a profound silence succeeded to the late deafening clamor.

Was ever so diabolical a trick played off upon a holy friar? A peasant going to his labors at early dawn found the unfortunate Fray Simon lying under a fig-tree at the foot of the tower, but so bruised and bedevilled that he could neither speak nor move. He was conveyed with all care and tenderness to his cell, and the story went that he had been waylaid and maltreated by robbers. A day or two elapsed before he recovered the use of his limbs; he consoled himself, in the meantime, with the thoughts that though the mule with the treasure had escaped him, he had previously had some rare pickings at the infidel spoils. His first care on being able to use his limbs was to search beneath his pallet, where he had secreted the myrtle wreath and the leathern pouches of gold extracted from the piety of Dame Sanchez. What was his dismay at finding the wreath, in effect, but a withered branch of myrtle, and the leathern pouches filled with sand and gravel!

Fray Simon, with all his chagrin, had the discretion to hold his tongue, for to betray the secret might draw on him the ridicule of the public and the punishment of his superior. It was not until many years afterwards, on his death-bed, that he revealed to his confessor his nocturnal ride on the Belludo.

Nothing was heard of Lope Sanchez for a long time after his disappearance from the Alhambra. His memory was always cherished as that of a merry companion, though it was feared, from the care and melancholy observed in his conduct shortly before his mysterious departure, that poverty and distress had driven him to some extremity. Some years afterwards one of his old companions, an invalid soldier, being at Malaga, was knocked down and nearly run over by a coach and six. The carriage stopped; an old gentleman, magnificently dressed, with a bag-wig and sword, stepped out to assist the poor invalid. What was the astonishment of the latter to behold in this grand cavalier his old friend Lope Sanchez, who was actually celebrating the marriage of his daughter Sanchica with one of the first grandees in the land.

The carriage contained the bridal party. There was Dame Sanchez, now grown as round as a barrel, and dressed out with feathers and jewels, and necklaces of pearls, and necklaces of diamonds, and rings on every finger, altogether a finery of apparel that had not been seen since the days of Queen Sheba. The little Sanchica had now grown to be a woman, and for grace and beauty might have been mistaken for a duchess, if not a princess outright. The bridegroom sat beside her— rather a withered, spindle-shanked little man, but this only proved him to be of the true blue blood; a legitimate Spanish grandee being rarely above three cubits in stature. The match had been of the mother's making.

Riches had not spoiled the heart of honest Lope. He kept his old comrade with him for several days; feasted him like a king, took him to plays and bull-fights, and at length sent him away rejoicing, with a big bag of money for himself, and another to be distributed among his ancient messmates of the Alhambra.

Lope always gave out that a rich brother had died in America and left him heir to a copper mine; but the shrewd gossips of the Alhambra insist that his wealth was all derived from his having discovered the secret guarded by the two marble nymphs of the Alhambra. It is remarked that these very discreet statues continue, even unto the present day, with their eyes fixed most significantly on the same part of the wall; which leads many to suppose there is still some hidden treasure remaining there well worthy the attention of the enterprising traveller. Though others, and particularly all female visitors, regard them with great complacency as lasting monuments of the fact that women can keep a secret.

From *The Alhambra*

SPANISH ROMANCE

IN the latter part of my sojourn in the Alhambra, I made frequent descents into the Jesuits' Library of the University; and relished more and more the old Spanish chronicles, which I found there bound in parchment. I delight in those quaint histories which treat of the times when the Moslems maintained a foothold in the Peninsula. With all their bigotry and occasional intolerance, they are full of noble acts and generous sentiments, and have a high, spicy, Oriental flavor, not to be found in other records of the times, which were merely European. In fact, Spain, even at the present day, is a country apart; severed in history, habits, manners, and modes of thinking, from all the rest of Europe. It is a romantic country; but its romance has none of the sentimentality of modern European romance; it is chiefly derived from the brilliant regions of the East, and from the high-minded school of Saracenic chivalry.

The Arab invasion and conquest brought a higher civilization, and a nobler style of thinking, into Gothic Spain. The Arabs were a quick-witted, sagacious, proud-spirited, and poetical people, and were imbued with Oriental science and literature. Wherever they established a seat of power, it became a rallying-place for the learned and ingenious; and they softened and refined the people whom they conquered. By degrees, occupancy seemed to give them an hereditary right to their foothold in the land; they ceased to be looked upon as invaders, and were regarded as rival neighbors. The Peninsula, broken up into a variety of states, both Christian and Moslem, became, for centuries, a great campaigning-ground, where the art of war seemed to be the principal business of man, and was carried to the highest pitch of romantic chivalry. The original ground of hostility, a difference of faith, gradually lost its rancor. Neighboring states, of opposite creeds, were occasionally linked together in alliances, offensive and defensive; so that the cross and crescent were to be seen side by side, fighting against some common enemy. In times of peace, too, the noble youth of either faith resorted to the same cities, Christian or Moslem, to school themselves in military science. Even in the temporary truces of sanguinary wars, the warriors who had recently striven together in the deadly conflicts of the field, laid aside their animosity, met at tournaments, jousts, and other military festivities, and exchanged the courtesies of gentle and generous spirits. Thus the opposite races became frequently mingled together in peaceful intercourse, or if any rivalry took place, it was in those high courtesies and nobler acts, which bespeak the accomplished cavalier. Warriors, of opposite creeds, became ambitious of transcending each other in magnanimity as well as valor. Indeed, the chivalric virtues were refined upon to a degree sometimes fastidious and constrained, but at other times inexpressibly noble and affecting. The annals of the times teem with illustrious instances of high-wrought courtesy, romantic generosity, lofty disinterestedness, and punctilious honor, that warm the very soul to read them. These have furnished themes for national plays and poems, or have been celebrated in those all pervading ballads, which are as the life-breath of the people, and thus have continued to exercise an influence on the national character, which centuries of vicissitude and decline have not been able to destroy; so that, with all their faults, and they are many, the Spaniards, even at the present day, are, on many points, the most high-minded and proud-spirited people of Europe. It is true, the romance of feeling derived from the sources I have mentioned, has, like all other romance, its affectations and extremes. It renders the Spaniard at times pompous and grandiloquent; prone to carry the *pundonor,* or point of honor, beyond the bounds of sober sense and sound morality; disposed, in the midst of poverty, to affect the *grande caballero,* and to look down with sovereign disdain upon "arts mechanical," and all the gainful pursuits of plebeian life; but this very inflation of spirit, while it fills his brain with vapors, lifts him above a thousand meannesses; and though it often keeps him in indigence, ever protects him from vulgarity.

In the present day, when popular literature is running into the low levels of life, and luxuriating on the vices and follies of mankind; and when the universal pursuit of gain is trampling down the early growth of poetic feeling, and wearing out the verdure of the soul, I question whether it would not be of service for the reader occasionally to turn to these records of prouder times and loftier modes of thinking; and to steep himself to the very lips in old Spanish romance.

With these preliminary suggestions, the fruit of a morning's reading and rumination in the old Jesuits' Library of the University, I will give him a legend in point, drawn forth from one of the venerable chronicles alluded to.

Legend of Don Munio Sancho de Hinojosa

IN the cloisters of the ancient Benedictine convent of San Domingo, at Silos, in Castile, are the mouldering yet magnificent monuments of the once powerful and chivalrous family of Hinojosa. Among these reclines the marble figure of a knight, in complete armor, with the hands pressed together, as if in prayer. On one side of his tomb is sculptured in relief a band of Christian cavaliers, capturing a cavalcade of male and female Moors; on the other side, the same cavaliers are represented kneeling before an altar. The tomb, like most of the neighboring monuments, is almost in ruins, and the sculpture is nearly unintelligible, excepting to the keen eye of the antiquary. The story connected with the sepulchre, however, is still preserved in the old Spanish chronicles, and is to the following purport.

In old times, several hundred years ago, there was a noble Castilian cavalier, named Don Munio Sancho de Hinojosa, lord of a border castle, which had stood the brunt of many a Moorish foray. He had seventy horsemen as his household troops, all of the ancient Castilian proof; stark warriors, hard riders, and men of iron; with these he scoured the Moorish lands, and made his name terrible throughout the borders. His castle-hall was covered with banners, cimeters, and Moslem helms, the trophies of his prowess. Don Munio was, moreover, a keen huntsman; and rejoiced in hounds of all kinds, steeds for the chase, and hawks for the towering sport of falconry. When not engaged in warfare his delight was to beat up the neighboring forests; and scarcely ever did he ride forth without hound and horn, a boar-spear in his hand, or hawk upon his fist, and an attendant train of huntsmen.

His wife, Doña Maria Palacin, was of a gentle and timid nature, little fitted to be the spouse of so hardy and adventurous a knight; and many a tear did the poor lady shed, when he sallied forth upon his daring enterprises, and many a prayer did she offer up for his safety.

As this doughty cavalier was one day hunting, he stationed himself in a thicket, on the borders of a green glade of the forest, and dispersed his followers to rouse the game, and drive it toward his stand. He had not been here long, when a cavalcade of Moors, of both sexes, came prankling over the forest-lawn. They were unarmed, and magnificently dressed in robes of tissue and embroidery, rich shawls of India, bracelets and anklets of gold, and jewels that sparkled in the sun.

At the head of this gay cavalcade rode a youthful cavalier, superior to the rest in dignity and loftiness of demeanor, and in splendor of attire; beside him was a damsel, whose veil, blown aside by the breeze, displayed a face of surpassing beauty, and eyes cast down in maiden modesty, yet beaming with tenderness and joy.

Don Munio thanked his stars for sending him such a prize, and exulted at the thought of bearing home to his wife the glittering spoils of these infidels. Putting his hunting-horn to his lips, he gave a blast that wrung through the forest. His huntsmen came running from all quarters, and the astonished Moors were surrounded and made captives.

The beautiful Moor wrung her hands in despair, and her female attendants uttered the most piercing cries. The young Moorish cavalier alone retained self-possession. He inquired the name of the Christian knight who commanded this troop of horsemen. When told that it was Don Munio Sancho de Hinojosa, his countenance lighted up. Approaching that cavalier, and kissing his hand, "Don Munio Sancho," said he, "I have heard of your fame as a true and valiant knight, terrible in arms, but schooled in the noble virtues of chivalry. Such do I trust to find you. In me you behold Abadil, son of a Moorish Alcalde. I am on the way to celebrate my nuptials with this lady; chance has thrown us in your power, but I confide in your magnanimity. Take all our treasure and jewels; demand what ransom you think proper for our persons, but suffer us not to be insulted nor dishonored."

When the good knight heard this appeal, and beheld the beauty of the youthful pair, his heart was touched with tenderness and courtesy. "God forbid," said he, "that I should disturb such happy nuptials. My prisoners in troth shall ye be, for fifteen days, and immured within my castle, where I claim, as conqueror, the right of celebrating your espousals."

So saying, he despatched one of his fleetest horsemen in advance, to notify Doña Maria Palacin of the coming of this bridal party; while he and his huntsmen escorted the cavalcade, not as captors, but as a guard of honor. As they drew near to the castle, the banners were hung out, and the trumpets sounded from the battlements; and on their nearer approach, the drawbridge was lowered, and Doña Maria came forth to meet them, attended by her ladies and knights, her pages and her minstrels. She took the young bride, Allifra, in her arms, kissed her with the tenderness of a sister, and conducted her into the castle. In the meantime, Don Munio sent forth missives in every direction, and had viands and dainties of all kinds collected from the country round; and the wedding of the Moorish lovers was celebrated with all possible state and festivity. For fifteen days the castle was given up to joy and revelry. There were tiltings and jousts at the ring, and bull-fights, and banquets, and dances to the sound of minstrelsy. When the fifteen days were at an end, he made the bride and bridegroom magnificent presents, and conducted them and their attendants safely beyond the borders. Such, in old times, were the courtesy and generosity of a Spanish cavalier.

Several years after this event, the king of Castile summoned his nobles to assist him in a campaign against the Moors. Don Munio Sancho was among the first to answer to the call, with seventy horsemen, all stanch and well-tried warriors. His wife, Doña Maria, hung about his neck. "Alas, my lord!" exclaimed she, "how often wilt thou tempt thy fate, and when will thy thirst for glory be appeased!"

"One battle more," replied Don Munio, "one battle more, for the honor of Castile, and I here make a vow that, when this is over, I will lay by my sword, and repair with my cavaliers in pilgrimage to the sepulchre of our Lord at Jerusalem." The cavaliers all joined with him in the vow, and Doña Maria felt in some degree soothed in spirit; still, she saw with a heavy heart the departure of her husband, and watched his banner with wistful eyes, until it disappeared among the trees of the forest.

·The king of Castile led his army to the plains of Salmanara, where they encountered the Moorish host, near to Ucles. The battle was long and bloody; the Christians repeatedly wavered and were as often rallied by the energy of their commanders. Don Munio was covered with wounds, but refused to leave the field. The Christians at length gave way, and the king was hardly pressed, and in danger of being captured.

Don Munio called upon his cavaliers to follow him to the rescue. "Now is the time," cried he, "to prove your loyalty. Fall to, like brave men! We fight for the true faith, and if we lose our lives here, we gain a better life hereafter."

Rushing with his men between the king and his pursuers, they checked the latter in their career, and gave time for their monarch to escape; but they fell victims to their loyalty. They all fought to the last gasp. Don Munio was singled out by a powerful Moorish knight, but having been wounded in the right arm, he fought to disadvantage, and was slain. The battle being over, the Moor paused to possess himself of the spoils of this redoubtable Christian warrior. When he unlaced the helmet, however, and beheld the countenance of Don Munio, he gave a great cry and smote his breast. "Woe is me!" cried he, "I have slain my benefactor! The flower of knightly virtue! the most magnanimous of cavaliers!"

While the battle had been raging on the plain of Salmanara, Doña Maria Palacin remained in her castle, a prey to the keenest anxiety. Her eyes were ever fixed on the road that led from the country of the Moors, and often she asked the watchman of the tower, "What seest thou?"

One evening, at the shadowy hour of twilight, the warden sounded his horn. "I see," cried he, "a numerous train winding up the valley. There are mingled Moors and Christians. The banner of my lord is in the advance. Joyful tidings!" exclaimed the old seneschal; "my lord returns in triumph, and brings captives!" Then the castle courts rang with shouts of joy; and the standard was displayed, and the trumpets were sounded, and the drawbridge was lowered, and Doña Maria went forth with her ladies, and her knights, and her pages, and her minstrels, to welcome her lord from the wars. But as the train drew nigh, she beheld a sumptuous bier, covered with black velvet, and on it lay a warrior, as if taking his repose: he lay in his armor, with his helmet on his head, and his sword in his hand, as one who had never been conquered, and around the bier were the escutcheons of the house of Hinojosa.

A number of Moorish cavaliers attended the bier, with emblems of mourning, and with dejected countenances; and their leader cast himself at the feet of Doña Maria, and hid his face in his hands. She beheld in him the gallant Abadil, whom she had once welcomed with his bride to her castle; but who now came with the body of her lord, whom he had unknowingly slain in battle!

The sepulchre erected in the cloisters of the convent of San Domingo was achieved at the expense of the Moor Abadil, as a feeble testimony of his grief for the death of the good knight Don Munio, and his reverence for his memory. The tender and faithful Doña Maria soon followed her lord to the tomb. On one of the stones of a small arch, beside his sepulchre, is the following simple inscription: *"Hic jacet Maria Palacin, uxor Munonis Sancij De Finojosa"*—Here lies Maria Palacin, wife of Munio Sancho de Hinojosa.

The legend of Don Munio Sancho does not conclude with his death. On the same day on which the battle took place on the plain of Salmanara, a chaplain of the Holy Temple at Jerusalem, while standing at the outer gate, beheld a train of Christian cavaliers advancing, as if in pilgrimage. The chaplain was a native of Spain, and as the pilgrims approached, he knew the foremost to be Don Munio Sancho de Hinojosa, with whom he had been well acquainted in former times. Hastening to the patriarch, he told him of the honorable rank of the pilgrims at the gate. The patriarch, therefore, went forth with a grand procession of priests and monks, and received the pilgrims with all due honor. There were seventy cavaliers beside their leader,—all stark and lofty warriors. They carried their helmets in their hands, and their faces were deadly pale. They greeted no one, nor looked either to the right or to the left, but entered the chapel, and kneeling before the sepulchre of our Saviour, performed their orisons in silence. When they had concluded, they rose as if to depart, and the patriarch and his attendants advanced to speak to them, but they were no more to be seen. Every one marvelled what could be the meaning of this prodigy. The patriarch carefully noted down the day, and sent to Castile to learn tidings of Don Munio Sancho de Hinojosa. He received for reply, that, on the very day specified, that worthy knight, with seventy of his followers, had been slain in battle. These, therefore, must have been the blessed spirits of those Christian warriors, come to fulfil their vow of pilgrimage to the Holy Sepulchre at Jerusalem. Such was Castilian faith in the olden time, which kept its word, even beyond the grave.

If any one should doubt of the miraculous apparition of these phantom knights, let him consult the "History of the Kings of Castile and Leon," by the learned and pious Fray Prudencio de Sandoval, Bishop of Pamplona, where he will find it recorded in the "History of King Don Alonzo VI.," on the hundred and second page. It is too precious a legend to be lightly abandoned to the doubter.

From *The Alhambra*

THE LEGEND OF THE
ENCHANTED SOLDIER

An Expedition in Quest of a Diploma

O NE of the most important occurrences in the domestic life of the Alhambra was the departure of Manuel, the nephew of Doña Antonia, for Malaga, to stand examination as a physician. I have already informed the reader that on his success in obtaining a degree depended in a great measure the union and future fortunes of himself and his cousin Dolores; at least so I was privately informed by Mateo Ximenes, and various circumstances concurred to corroborate his information. Their courtship, however, was carried on very quietly and discreetly, and I scarce think I should have discovered it, if I had not been put on the alert by the all-observant Mateo.

In the present instance, Dolores was less on the reserve, and had busied herself for several days in fitting out honest Manuel for his expedition. All his clothes had been arranged and packed in the neatest order, and above all she had worked a smart Andalusian travelling-jacket for him with her own hands. On the morning appointed for his departure, a stout mule on which he was to perform the journey was paraded at the portal of the Alhambra, and Tio Polo (Uncle Polo), an old invalid soldier, attended to caparison him. This veteran was one of the curiosities of the place. He had a leathern lantern visage, tanned in the tropics, a long Roman nose, and a black beetle eye. I had frequently observed him reading, apparently with intense interest, an old parchment-bound volume; sometimes he would be surrounded by a group of his brother invalids; some seated on the parapets, some lying on the grass listening with fixed attention, while he read slowly and deliberately out of his favorite work, sometimes pausing to explain or expound for the benefit of his less enlightened auditors.

I took occasion one day to inform myself of this ancient book, which appeared to be his *vade mecum,* and found it to be an odd volume of the works of Padre Benito Geronymo Feyjoo; and that one which treats about the magic of Spain, the mysterious caves of Salamanca and

Toledo, the purgatory of San Patricio (St. Patrick), and other mystic subjects of the kind. From that time I kept my eye upon the veteran.

On the present occasion I amused myself with watching him fit out the steed of Manuel with all the forecast of an old campaigner. First he took a considerable time in adjusting to the back of the mule a cumbrous saddle of antique fashion, high in front and behind, with Moorish stirrups like shovels; the whole looking like a relic of the old armory of the Alhambra; then a fleecy sheepskin was accommodated to the deep seat of the saddle; then a *maleta*, neatly packed by the hand of Dolores, was buckled behind; then a *manta* was thrown over it to serve either as cloak or couch; then the all-important *alforjas* carefully stocked with *provant*, were hung in front, together with the *bota*, or leathern bottle for either wine or water, and lastly the *trabucho*, which the old soldier slung behind, giving it his benediction. It was like the fitting out in old times of a Moorish cavalier for a foray or a joust in the Vivarrambla. A number of the *lazzaroni* of the fortress had gathered round, with some of the invalids, all looking on, all offering their aid, and all giving advice, to the great annoyance of Tio Polo.

When all was ready Manuel took leave of the household; Tio Polo held his stirrup while he mounted, adjusted the girths and saddle, and cheered him off in military style; then turning to Dolores, who stood admiring her cavalier as he trotted off, "Ah, Dolorocita," exclaimed he, with a nod and a wink, "*es muy guapo Manuelito in su Xaqueta,*" (Ah, Dolores, Manuel is mighty fine in his jacket). The little damsel blushed and laughed, and ran into the house.

Days elapsed without tidings from Manuel, though he had promised to write. The heart of Dolores began to misgive her. Had anything happened to him on the road? Had he failed in his examination? A circumstance occurred in her little household to add to her uneasiness and fill her mind with foreboding. It was almost equal to the escapado of her pigeon. Her tortoise-shell cat eloped at night and clambered to the tiled roof of the Alhambra. In the dead of the night there was a fearful caterwauling; some grimalkin was uncivil to her; then there was a scramble; then a clapper-clawing; then both parties rolled off the roof and tumbled from a great hight among the trees on the hillside. Nothing more was seen or heard of the fugitive, and poor Dolores considered it but a prelude to greater calamities.

At the end of ten days, however, Manuel returned in triumph, duly authorized to kill or cure; and all Dolores' cares were over. There was a general gathering in the evening of the humble friends and hangers-on of Dame Antonia to congratulate her and to pay their respects to *el Señor Medico*, who, peradventure, at some future day, might have all their lives in his hands. One of the most important of these guests was old Tio Polo; and I gladly seized the occasion to prosecute my acquaintance with him. "Oh Señor," cried Dolores, "you who are so eager to learn all the old histories of the Alhambra, Tio Polo knows more about them than any one else about the place. More than Mateo Ximenes and his whole family put together. *Vaya—Vaya*—Tio Polo, tell the Señor all those stories you told us one evening, about enchanted Moors, and the haunted bridge over the Darro, and the old stone pomegranates, that have been there since the days of King Chico."

It was some time before the old invalid could be brought into a narrative vein. He shook his head—they were all idle tales; not worthy of being told to a *cavallero* like myself. It was only by telling some stories of the kind myself I at last got him to open his budget. It was a whimsical *farrago*, partly made up of what he had heard in the Alhambra, partly of what he had read in Padre Feyjoo. I will endeavor to give the reader the substance of it, but I will not promise to give it in the very words of Tio Polo.

EVERYBODY has heard of the Cave of St. Cyprian at Salamanca, where in old times judicial astronomy, necromancy, chiromancy, and other dark and damnable arts were secretly taught by an ancient sacristan; or, as some will have it, by the Devil himself, in that disguise. The cave has long been shut up and the very site of it forgotten; though, according to tradition, the entrance was somewhere about where the stone cross stands in the small square of the seminary of Carvajal; and this tradition appears in some degree corroborated by the circumstances of the following story.

There was at one time a student of Salamanca, Don Vicente by name, of that merry but mendicant class, who set out on the road to learning without a penny in pouch for the journey, and who, during college vacations, beg from town to town and village to village to raise funds to enable them to pursue their studies through the ensuing term. He was now about to set forth on his wanderings; and being somewhat musical, slung on his back a guitar with which to amuse the villagers, and pay for a meal or a night's lodging.

As he passed by the stone cross in the seminary square, he pulled off his hat and made a short invocation to St. Cyprian, for good luck; when casting his eyes upon the earth, he perceived something glitter at the foot of the cross. On picking it up, it proved to be a seal-ring of mixed metal, in which gold and silver appeared to be blended. The seal bore as a device two triangles crossing each other, so as to form a star. This device is said to be a cabalistic sign, invented by King Solomon the Wise, and of mighty power in all cases of enchantment; but the honest student, being neither sage nor conjurer, knew nothing of the matter. He took the ring as a present from St. Cyprian in reward of his prayer; slipped it on his finger, made a bow to the cross, and strumming his guitar, set off merrily on his wandering.

The life of a mendicant student in Spain is not the most miserable in the world, especially if he has any talent at making himself agreeable. He rambles at large from village to village, and city to city, wherever curiosity or caprice may conduct him. The country curates, who, for the most part, have been mendicant students in their time, give him shelter for the night, and a comfortable meal, and often enrich him with several *quartos* or half-pence in the morning. As he presents himself from door to door in the streets of the cities, he meets with no harsh rebuff, no chilling contempt, for there is no disgrace attending his mendacity, many of the most learned men in Spain having commenced their career in this manner; but if, like the student in question, he is a good-looking varlet and a merry companion, and, above all, if he can play the guitar, he is sure of a hearty welcome among the peasants, and smiles and favors from their wives and daughters.

In this way, then, did our ragged and musical son of learning make his way over half the kingdom; with the fixed determination to visit the famous city of Granada before his return. Sometimes he was gathered for the night into the fold of some village pastor; sometimes he was sheltered under the humble but hospitable roof of the peasant. Seated at the cottage-door with his guitar, he delighted the simple folk with his ditties; or striking up a *fandango* or *bolero*, set the brown country lads and lasses dancing in the mellow twilight. In the morning he departed with kind words from host and hostess, and kind looks and, peradventure, a squeeze of the hand from the daughter.

At length he arrived at the great object of his musical vagabondizing, the far-famed city of Granada, and hailed with wonder and delight its Moorish towers, its lovely *vega*, and its snowy mountains glistening through a summer atmosphere. It is needless to say with what eager curiosity he entered its gates and wandered through its streets, and gazed upon its Oriental monuments. Every female face peering through a window or beaming from a balcony was to him a Zorayda or a Zelinda, nor could he meet a stately dame on the Alameda but he was ready to fancy her a Moorish princess, and to spread his student's robe beneath her feet.

His musical talent, his happy humor, his youth, and his good looks won him a universal welcome in spite of his ragged robes, and for several days he led a gay life in the old Moorish capital and its environs. One of his occasional haunts was the fountain of Avellanos, in the valley of Darro. It is one of the popular resorts of Granada, and has been so since the days of the Moors; and here the student had an opportunity of pursuing his studies of female beauty; a branch of study to which he was a little prone.

Here he would take his seat with his guitar, improvise love-ditties to admiring groups of *majos* and *majas*, or prompt with his music the ever-ready dance. He was thus engaged one evening when he beheld a padre of the church advancing, at whose approach every one touched the hat. He was evidently a man of consequence; he certainly was a mirror of good if not of holy living; robust and rosy-faced, and breathing at every pore with the warmth of the weather and the exercise of the walk. As he passed along he would every now and then draw a *maravedi* out of his pocket and bestow it on a beggar with an air of signal beneficence. "Ah, the blessed father!" would be the cry; "long life to him, and may he soon be a bishop!"

To aid his steps in ascending the hill he leaned gently now and then on the arm of a handmaid, evidently the pet-lamb of this kindest of pastors. Ah, such a damsel! Andalus from head to foot; from the rose in her hair, to the fairy shoe and lacework stocking; Andalus in every movement; in every undulation of the body:—ripe, melting Andalus!— But then so modest!—so shy!—ever, with downcast eyes, listening to the words of the padre; or, if by chance she let flash a side glance, it was suddenly checked and her eyes once more cast to the ground.

The good padre looked benignantly on the company about the fountain, and took his seat with some emphasis on a stone bench, while the handmaid hastened to bring him a glass of sparkling water. He sipped it deliberately and with a relish, tempering it with one of those spongy pieces of frosted eggs and sugar so dear to Spanish epicures, and on returning the glass to the hand of the damsel pinched her cheek with infinite loving-kindness.

"Ah, the good pastor!" whispered the student to himself; "what a happiness would it be to be gathered into his fold with such a pet-lamb for a companion!"

But no such good fare was likely to befall him. In vain he essayed those powers of pleasing which he had found so irresistible with country curates and country lasses. Never had he touched his guitar with such skill; never had he poured forth more soul-moving ditties, but he had no longer a country curate or country lass to deal with. The worthy priest evidently did not relish music, and the modest damsel never raised her eyes from the ground. They remained but a short time at the fountain; the good padre hastened their return to Granada. The damsel gave the student one shy glance in retiring; but it plucked the heart out of his bosom!

He inquired about them after they had gone. Padre Tomás was one of the saints of Granada, a model of regularity; punctual in his hour of rising; his hour of taking a *paseo* for an appetite; his hours of eating; his hour of taking his *siesta;* his hour of playing his game of *tresillo,* of an evening, with some of the dames of the cathedral circle; his hour of supping, and his hour of retiring to rest, to gather fresh strength for another day's round of similar duties. He had an easy sleek mule for his riding; a matronly housekeeper skilled in preparing tid-bits for his table; and the pet-lamb, to smooth his pillow at night and bring him his chocolate in the morning.

Adieu now to the gay, thoughtless life of the student; the side-glance of a bright eye had been the undoing of him. Day and night he could not get the image of this most modest damsel out of his mind. He sought the mansion of the padre. Alas! it was above the class of houses accessible to a strolling student like himself. The worthy padre had no sympathy with him; he had never been *estudiante sopista,* obliged to sing for his supper. He blockaded the house by day, catching a glance of the damsel now and then as she appeared at a casement; but these glances only fed his flame without encouraging his hope. He serenaded her balcony at night, and at one time was flattered by the appearance of something white at a window. Alas, it was only the night cap of the padre.

Never was lover more devoted; never damsel more shy; the poor student was reduced to despair. At length arrived the eve of St. John, when the lower classes of Granada swarm into the country, dance away the afternoon, and pass midsummer's night on the banks of the Darro and the Xenil. Happy are they who on this eventful night can wash their faces in those waters just as the cathedral bell tells midnight, for at that precise moment they have a beautifying power. The student, having nothing to do, suffered himself to be carried away by the holiday-seeking throng until he found himself in the narrow valley of the Darro, below the lofty hill and ruddy towers of the Alhambra. The dry bed of the river; the rocks which border it; the terraced gardens which overhang it, were alive with variegated groups, dancing under the vines and fig-trees to the sound of the guitar and castanets.

The student remained for some time in doleful dumps, leaning against one of the huge misshapen stone pomegranates which adorn the ends of the little bridge over the Darro. He cast a wistful glance upon the merry scene, where every cavalier had his dame; or, to speak more appropriately, every Jack his Jill; sighed at his own solitary state, a victim to the black eye of the most unapproachable of damsels, and repined at his ragged garb, which seemed to shut the gate of hope against him.

By degrees his attention was attracted to a neighbor equally solitary with himself. This was a tall soldier, of a stern aspect and grizzled beard, who seemed posted as a sentry at the opposite pomegranate. His face was bronzed by time; he was arrayed in ancient Spanish armor, with buckler and lance, and stood immovable as a statue. What surprised the student was, that though thus strangely equipped, he was totally unnoticed by the passing throng, albeit that many almost brushed against him.

"This is a city of old time peculiarities," thought the student, "and doubtless this is one of them with which the inhabitants are too familiar to be surprised." His own curiosity, however, was awakened, and being of a social disposition, he accosted the soldier.

"A rare old suit of armor that which you wear, comrade. May I ask what corps you belong to?"

·The soldier gasped out a reply from a pair of jaws which seemed to have rusted on their hinges.

"The royal guard of Ferdinand and Isabella."

"Santa Maria! Why, it is three centuries since that corps was in service."

"And for three centuries have I been mounting guard. Now I trust my tour of duty draws to a close. Dost thou desire fortune?"

The student held up his tattered cloak in reply.

"I understand thee. If thou hast faith and courage, follow me, and thy fortune is made."

"Softly, comrade, to follow thee would require small courage in one who has nothing to lose but life and an old guitar, neither of much value; but my faith is of a different matter, and not to be put in temptation. If it be any criminal act by which I am to mend my fortune, think not my ragged coat will make me undertake it."

The soldier turned on him a look of high displeasure. "My sword," said he, "has never been drawn but in the cause of the faith and the throne. I am a Cristiano viejo; trust in me and fear no evil."

The student followed him wondering. He observed that no one heeded their conversation, and that the soldier made his way through the various groups of idlers unnoticed, as if invisible.

Crossing the bridge, the soldier led the way by a narrow and steep path past a Moorish mill and aqueduct, and up the ravine which separates the domains of the Generalife from those of the Alhambra. The last ray of the sun shone upon the red battlements of the latter, which beetled far above; and the convent bells were proclaiming the festival of the ensuing day. The ravine was overshadowed by fig-trees, vines, and myrtles, and the outer towers and walls of the fortress. It was dark and lonely, and the twilight-loving bats began to flit about. At length the soldier halted at a remote and ruined tower, apparently intended to guard a Moorish aqueduct. He struck the foundation with the but-end of his spear. A rumbling sound was heard, and the solid stones yawned apart, leaving an opening as wide as a door.

"Enter in the name of the Holy Trinity," said the soldier, "and fear nothing." The student's heart quaked, but he made the sign of the cross, muttered his *Ave Maria*, and followed his mysterious guide into a deep vault cut out of the solid rock under the tower, and covered with Arabic inscriptions. The soldier pointed to a stone seat hewn along one side of the vault. "Behold," said he, "my couch for three hundred years." The bewildered student tried to force a joke. "By the blessed St. Anthony," said he, "but you must have slept soundly, considering the hardness of your couch."

· "On the contrary, sleep has been a stranger to these eyes, incessant watchfulness has been my doom. Listen to my lot. I was one of the royal guards of Ferdinand and Isabella; but was taken prisoner by the Moors in one of their sorties, and confined a captive in this tower. When preparations were made to surrender the fortress to the Christian sovereigns, I was prevailed upon by an Alfaqui, a Moorish priest, to aid him in secreting some of the treasures of Boabdil in this vault. I was justly punished for my fault. The Alfaqui was an African necromancer, and by his infernal arts, cast a spell upon me—to guard his treasures. Something must have happened to him, for he never returned, and here have I remained ever since, buried alive. Years and years have rolled away; earthquakes have shaken this hill; I have heard stone by stone of the tower above tumbling to the ground, in the natural operation of time; but the spellbound walls of this vault set both time and earthquakes at defiance.

"Once every hundred years, on the festival of St. John, the enchantment ceases to have thorough sway; I am permitted to go forth and post myself upon the bridge of the Darro, where you met me, waiting until some one shall arrive who may have power to break this magic spell. I have hitherto mounted guard there in vain. I walk as in a cloud, concealed from mortal sight. You are the first to accost me for now three hundred years. I behold the reason. I see on your finger the seal-ring of Solomon the Wise, which is proof against all enchantment.

With you it remains to deliver me from this awful dungeon, or to leave me to keep guard here for another hundred years."

The student listened to this tale in mute wonderment. He had heard many tales of treasures shut up under strong enchantment in the vaults of the Alhambra, but had treated them as fables. He now felt the value of the seal-ring, which had, in a manner, been given to him by St. Cyprian. Still, though armed by so potent a talisman, it was an awful thing to find himself *tête-à-tête* in such a place with an enchanted soldier, who, according to the laws of nature, ought to have been quietly in his grave for nearly three centuries.

A personage of this kind, however, was quite out of the ordinary run, and not to be trifled with, and he assured him he might rely upon his friendship and good-will to do everything in his power for his deliverance.

"I trust to a motive more powerful than friendship," said the soldier.

He pointed to a ponderous iron coffer, secured by locks inscribed with Arabic characters. "That coffer," said he, "contains countless treasure in gold and jewels and precious stones. Break the magic spell by which I am enthralled, and one half of this treasure shall be thine."

"But how am I to do it?"

"The aid of a Christian priest and a Christian maid is necessary. The priest to exorcise the powers of darkness; the damsel to touch this chest with the seal of Solomon. This must be done at night. But have a care. This is solemn work, and not to be effected by the carnal-minded. The priest must be a *Cristiano viejo*, a model of sanctity; and must mortify the flesh, before he comes here, by a rigorous fast of four-and-twenty hours: and as to the maiden, she must be above reproach, and proof against temptation. Linger not in finding such aid. In three days my furlough is at an end; if not delivered before midnight of the third, I shall have to mount guard for another century."

"Fear not," said the student, "I have in my eye the very priest and damsel you describe; but how am I to regain admission to this tower?"

"The seal of Solomon will open the way for thee."

The student issued forth from the tower much more gayly than he had entered. The wall closed behind him, and remained solid as before.

The next morning he repaired boldly to the mansion of the priest, no longer a poor strolling student, thrumming his way with a guitar; but an ambassador from the shadowy world, with enchanted treasures to bestow. No particulars are told of his negotiation, excepting that the zeal of the worthy priest was easily kindled at the idea of rescuing an old soldier of the faith and a strong-box of King Chico from the very clutches of Satan; and then what alms might be dispensed, what churches built, and how many poor relatives enriched with the Moorish treasure!

As to the immaculate handmaid, she was ready to lend her hand, which was all that was required, to the pious work; and if a shy glance now and then might be believed, the ambassador began to find favor in her modest eyes.

The greatest difficulty, however, was the fast to which the good padre had to subject himself. Twice he attempted it, and twice the flesh was too strong for the spirit. It was only on the third day that he was enabled to withstand the temptations of the cupboard; but it was still a question whether he would hold out until the spell was broken.

At a late hour of the night the party groped their way up the ravine by the light of a lantern, and bearing a basket with provisions for exorcising the demon of hunger so soon as the other demons should be laid in the Red Sea.

The seal of Solomon opened their way into the tower. They found the soldier seated on the enchanted strong-box, awaiting their arrival. The exorcism was performed in due style. The damsel advanced and touched the locks of the coffer with the seal of Solomon. The lid flew open; and such treasures of gold and jewels and precious stones as flashed upon the eye!

"Here's cut and come again!" cried the student, exultingly, as he proceeded to cram his pockets.

"Fairly and softly," exclaimed the soldier. "Let us get the coffer out entire, and then divide."

They accordingly went to work with might and main; but it was a difficult task; the chest was enormously heavy, and had been imbedded there for centuries. While they were thus employed the good dominie drew on one side and made a vigorous onslaught on the basket, by way of exorcising the demon of hunger which was raging in his entrails. In a little while a fat capon was devoured, and washed down by a deep potation of Val de peñas; and, by way of grace after meat, he gave a kind-hearted kiss to the pet-lamb who waited on him. It was quietly done in a corner, but the tell-tale walls babbled it forth as if in triumph. Never was chaste salute more awful in its effects. At the sound the soldier gave a great cry of despair; the coffer, which was half raised, fell back in its place and was locked once more. Priest, student, and damsel found themselves outside of the tower, the wall of which closed with a thundering jar. Alas! the good padre had broken his fast too soon!

When recovered from his surprise, the student would have re-entered the tower, but learnt to his dismay that the damsel, in her fright, had let fall the seal of Solomon; it remained within the vault.

In a word, the cathedral bell tolled midnight; the spell was renewed; the soldier was doomed to mount guard for another hundred years, and there he and the treasure remain to this day—and all because the kind-hearted padre kissed his handmaid. "Ah, father! father!" said the student, shaking his head ruefully, as they returned down the ravine, "I fear there was less of the saint than the sinner in that kiss!"

Thus ends the legend as far as it has been authenticated. There is a tradition, however, that the student had brought off treasure enough in his pocket to set him up in the world; that he prospered in his affairs, that the worthy padre gave him the pet-lamb in marriage, by way of amends for the blunder in the vault; that the immaculate damsel proved a pattern for wives as she had been for handmaids, and bore her husband a numerous progeny; that the first was a wonder; it was born seven months after her marriage, and though a seven-months' boy, was the sturdiest of the flock. The rest were all born in the ordinary course of time.

The story of the enchanted soldier remains one of the popular traditions of Granada, though told in a variety of ways; the common people affirm that he still mounts guard on midsummer eve, beside the gigantic stone pomegranate on the bridge of the Darro; but remains invisible excepting to such lucky mortal as may possess the seal of Solomon.

NOTES TO THE ENCHANTED SOLDIER.

Among the ancient superstitions of Spain, were those of the existence of profound caverns in which the magic arts were taught, either by the Devil in person, or some sage devoted to his service. One of the most famous of these caves was at Salamanca. Don Francisco de Torreblanca makes mention of it in the first book of his work on magic, C. 2, No. 4. The Devil was said to play the part of oracle there; giving replies to those who repaired thither to propound fateful questions, as in the celebrated cave of Trophonius. Don Francisco, though he records this story, does not put faith in it; he gives it however as certain, that a sacristan, named Clement Potosi, taught secretly the magic arts in that cave. Padre Feyjoo, who inquired into the matter, reports it as a vulgar belief, that the Devil himself taught those arts there; admitting only seven disciples at a time, one of whom, to be determined by lot, was to be devoted to him body and soul forever. Among one of these sets of students was a young man, son of the Marquis de Villena, on whom, after having accomplished his studies, the lot fell. He succeeded, however, in cheating the Devil, leaving him his shadow instead of his body.

Don Juan de Dios, Professor of Humanities in the university, in the early part of the last century, gives the following version of the story, extracted, as he says, from an ancient manuscript. It will be perceived he has marred the supernatural part of the tale, and ejected the Devil from it altogether.

As to the fable of the cave of San Cyprian, says he, all that we have been able to verify is, that where the stone cross stands, in the small square or place called by the name of the Seminary of Carvajal, there was the parochial church of San Cyprian. A descent of twenty steps led down to a subterranean sacristy, spacious and vaulted like a cave. Here a sacristan once taught magic, judicial astrology, geomancy, hydromancy, pyromancy, acromancy, chiromancy, necromancy, etc.

The extract goes on to state that seven students engaged at a time with the sacristan, at a fixed stipend. Lots were cast among them which one of their number should pay for the whole, with the understanding that he on whom the lot fell, if he did not pay promptly, should be detained in a chamber of the sacristy until the funds were forthcoming. This became thenceforth the usual practice.

On one occasion the lot fell on Henry de Villena, son of the marquis of the same name. He having perceived that there had been trick and shuffling in the casting of the lot, and suspecting the sacristan to be cognizant thereof, refused to pay. He was forthwith left in limbo. It so happened, that in a dark corner of the sacristy was a huge jar or earthen reservoir for water, which was cracked and empty. In this the youth contrived to conceal himself. The sacristan returned at night with a servant, bringing lights and a supper. Unlocking the door, they found no one in the vault, and a book of magic lying open on the table. They retreated in dismay, leaving the door open, by which Villena made his escape. The story went about that through magic he had made himself invisible. The reader has now both versions of the story, and may make his choice. I will only observe that the sages of the Alhambra incline to the diabolical one.

This Henry de Villena flourished in the time of Juan II., King of Castile, of whom he was uncle. He became famous for his knowledge of the natural sciences; and hence in that ignorant age was stigmatized as a necromancer. Fernan Perez de Guzman, in his account of distinguished men, gives him credit for great learning, but says he devoted himself to the arts of divination, the interpretation of dreams, of signs, and portents.

At the death of Villena, his library fell into the hands of the king, who was warned that it contained books treating of magic, and not proper to be read. King Juan ordered that they should be transported in carts to the residence of a reverend prelate to be examined. The prelate was less learned than devout. Some of the books treated of mathematics, others of astronomy, with figures and diagrams, and planetary signs; others of chemistry or alchemy, with foreign and mystic words. All these were necromancy in the eyes of the pious prelate, and the books were consigned to the flames, like the library of Don Quixote.

THE SEAL OF SOLOMON.—The device consists of two equilateral triangles, interlaced so as to form a star, and surrounded by a circle. According to Arab tradition, when the Most High gave Solomon the choice of blessings, and he chose wisdom, there came from heaven a ring, on which this device was engraven. This mystic talisman was the arcanum of his wisdom, felicity, and grandeur; by this he governed and prospered. In consequence of a temporary lapse from virtue he lost the ring in the sea, and was at once reduced to the level of ordinary men. By penitence and prayer he made his peace with the Deity, was permitted to find his ring again in the belly of a fish, and thus recovered his celestial gifts. That he might not utterly lose them again, he communicated to others the secret of the marvellous ring.

This symbolical seal we are told was sacrilegiously used by the Mohammedan infidels; and before them by the Arabian idolaters, and before them by the Hebrews, for "diabolical enterprises and abominable superstitions." Those who wish to be more thoroughly informed on the subject, will do well to consult the learned Father Athanasius Kirker's treatise on the *Cabala Sarracenica*.

A word more to the curious reader. There are many persons in these sceptical times who affect to deride everything connected with the occult sciences, or black art; who have no faith in the efficacy of conjurations, incantations, or divinations; and who stoutly contend that such things never had existence. To such determined unbelievers the testimony of past ages is as nothing; they require the evidence of their own senses, and deny that such arts and practices have prevailed in days of yore, simply because they meet with no instance of them in the present day. They cannot perceive that, as the world became versed in the natural sciences, the supernatural became superfluous and fell into disuse; and that the hardy inventions of art superseded the mysteries of magic. Still, say the enlightened few, those mystic powers exist, though in a latent state, and untasked by the ingenuity of men. A talisman is still a talisman, possessing all its indwelling and awful properties; though it may have lain dormant for ages at the bottom of the sea, or in the dusty cabinet of the antiquary.

The signet of Solomon the Wise, for instance, is well known to have held potent control over genii, demons, and enchantments; now who will positively assert that the same mystic signet, wherever it may exist, does not at the present moment possess the same marvellous virtues which distinguished it in the olden time? Let those who doubt repair to Salamanca, delve into the cave of San Cyprian, explore its hidden secrets, and decide. As to those who will not be at the pains of such investigation, let them substitute faith for incredulity, and receive with honest credence the foregoing legend.

From *The Alhambra*

WOLFERT'S ROOST

Chronicle I

ABOUT five-and-twenty miles from the ancient and renowned city of Manhattan, formerly called New Amsterdam, and vulgarly called New York, on the eastern bank of that expansion of the Hudson known among Dutch mariners of yore as the Tappan Zee, being in fact the great Mediterranean Sea of the New Netherlands, stands a little, old-fashioned stone mansion, all made up of gable ends, and as full of angles and corners as an old cocked hat. It is said, in fact, to have been modelled after the cocked hat of Peter the Headstrong, as the Escurial was modelled after the gridiron of the blessed St. Lawrence. Though but of small dimensions, yet, like many small people, it is of mighty spirit, and values itself greatly on its antiquity, being one of the oldest edifices, for its size, in the whole country. It claims to be an ancient seat of empire,—I may rather say an empire in itself,—and, like all empires, great and small, has had its grand historical epochs. In speaking of this doughty and valorous little pile, I shall call it by its usual appellation of "The Roost"; though that is a name given to it in modern days, since it became the abode of the white man.

Its origin, in truth, dates far back in that remote region commonly called the fabulous age, in which vulgar fact becomes mystified and tinted up with delectable fiction. The eastern shore of the Tappan Sea was inhabited in those days by an unsophisticated race, existing in all the simplicity of nature; that is to say, they lived by hunting and fishing, recreated themselves occasionally with a little tomahawking and scalping. Each stream that flows down from the hills into the Hudson had its petty sachem, who ruled over a hand's-breadth of forest on either side, and had his seat of government at its mouth. The chieftain who ruled the Roost was not merely a great warrior, but a medicine-man, or prophet, or conjurer, for they all mean the same thing in Indian parlance. Of his fighting propensities evidences still remain, in various arrowheads of flint, and stone battle-axes, occasionally digged up about the Roost; of his wizard powers we have a token in a spring which wells up at the foot of the bank, on the very margin of the river, which, it is said, was gifted by him with rejuvenating powers, something like the renowned Fountain of Youth in the Floridas, so anxiously but vainly sought after by the veteran Ponce de Leon. This story, however, is stoutly contradicted by an old Dutch matter-of-fact tradition, which declares that the spring in question was smuggled over from Holland in a churn, by Femmetie Van Blarcom, wife of Goosen Garret Van Blarcom, one of the first settlers, and that she took it up by night, unknown to her husband, from beside their farm-house near Rotterdam; being sure she should find no water equal to it in the new country;—and she was right.

The wizard sachem had a great passion for discussing territorial questions, and settling boundary lines; in other words, he had the spirit of annexation. This kept him in continual feud with the neighboring sachems, each of whom stood up stoutly for his hand-breadth of territory; so that there is not a petty stream nor rugged hill in the neighborhood that has not been the subject of long talks and hard battles. The sachem, however, as has been observed, was a medicine-man as well as warrior, and vindicated his claims by arts as well as arms; so that, by dint of a little hard fighting here, and hocuspocus (or diplomacy) there, he managed to extend his boundary line from field to field, and stream to stream, until it brought him into collision with the powerful sachem of Sing-Sing.* Many were the sharp conflicts between these rival chieftains for the sovereignty of a winding valley, a favorite hunting-ground watered by a beautiful stream called the Pocantico. Many were the ambuscades, surprisals, and deadly onslaughts that took place among its fastnesses, of which it grieves me much that I cannot pursue the details, for the gratification of those gentle but bloody-minded readers, of both sexes, who delight in the romance of the tomahawk and scalping-knife. Suffice it to say, that the wizard chieftain was at length victorious, though the victory is attributed, in Indian tradition, to a great medicine, or charm, by which he laid the sachem of Sing-Sing and his warriors asleep among the rocks and recesses of the valley, where they remain asleep to the present day, with their bows and war-clubs beside them. This was the origin of that potent and drowsy spell, which still prevails over the valley of Pocantico, and which has gained it the well-merited appellation of Sleepy Hollow. Often, in secluded and quiet parts of that valley, where the stream is overhung by dark woods and

---

* A corruption of the old Indian name, O-sin-sing. Some have rendered it, O-sin-song, or, O-sing-song, in token of its being a great market town, where anything might be had for a mere song. Its present melodious alternation to Sing-Song is said to have been made in compliment to a Yankee singing-master, who taught the inhabitants the art of singing through their nose.

rocks, the ploughman, on some calm and sunny day, as he shouts to his oxen, is surprised to hear faint shouts from the hill-sides in reply; being, it is said, the spellbound warriors, who half start from their rocky couches and grasp their weapons, but sink to sleep again.

The conquest of the Pocantico was the last triumph of the wizard sachem. Notwithstanding all his medicines and charms, he fell in battle, in attempting to extend his boundary line to the east, so as to take in the little wild valley of the Sprain; and his grave is still shown, near the banks of the pastoral stream. He left, however, a great empire to his successors, extending along the Tappan Sea, from Yonkers quite to Sleepy Hollow, and known in all records and maps by the Indian name of Wicquaes-Keck.

The wizard sachem was succeeded by a line of chiefs of whom nothing remarkable remains on record. One of them was the very individual on whom master Hendrick Hudson and his mate Robert Juet made that sage experiment gravely recorded by the latter in the narrative of the discovery.

"Our master and his mate determined to try some of the cheefe men of the country, whether they had any treacherie in them. So they took them down into the cabin, and gave them so much wine and aqua vitæ, that they were all quite merrie; one of them had his wife with him, which sate so modestly as any of our country women would do in a strange place. In the end, one of them was drunke; and that was strange to them, for they could not tell how to take it."*

How far master Hendrick Hudson and his worthy mate carried their experiment with the sachem's wife, is not recorded; neither does the curious Robert Juet make any mention of the after consequences of this grand moral test; tradition, however, affirms that the sachem, on landing, gave his modest spouse a hearty rib-roasting, according to the connubial discipline of the aboriginals; it farther affirms that he remained a hard drinker to the day of his death, trading away all his lands, acre by acre, for aqua vitæ; by which means the Roost and all its domains, from Yonkers to Sleepy Hollow, came in the regular course of trade, and by right of purchase, into the possession of the Dutchmen.

The worthy government of the New Netherlands was not suffered to enjoy this grand acquisition unmolested. In the year of 1654, the losel Yankees of Connecticut, those swapping, bargaining, squatting, enemies of the Manhattoes, made a daring inroad into this neighborhood, and founded a colony called Westchester, or, as the ancient Dutch records term it, Vest Dorp, in the right of one Thomas Pell, who

---

* See Juet's *Journal*, Purchas' *Pilgrams*.

pretended to have purchased the whole surrounding country of the Indians, and stood ready to argue their claims before any tribunal of Christendom.

This happened during the chivalrous reign of Peter Stuyvesant, and roused the ire of that gunpowder old hero. Without waiting to discuss claims and titles, he pounced at once upon the nest of nefarious squatters, carried off twenty-five of them in chains to the Manhattoes; nor did he stay his hand, nor give rest to his wooden leg, until he had driven the rest of the Yankees back into Connecticut, or obliged them to acknowledge allegiance to their High Mightinesses. In revenge, however, they introduced the plague of witchcraft into the province. This doleful malady broke out at Vest Dorp, and would have spread throughout the country had not the Dutch farmers nailed horse-shoes to the doors of their houses and barns, sure protections against witchcraft, many of which remain to the present day.

The seat of empire of the wizard sachem now came into the possession of Wolfert Acker, one of the privy councillors of Peter Stuyvesant. He was a worthy, but ill-starred man, whose aim through life had been to live in peace and quiet. For this he had emigrated from Holland, driven abroad by family feuds and wrangling neighbors. He had warred for quiet through the fidgety reign of William the Testy, and the fighting reign of Peter the Headstrong, sharing in every brawl and rib-roasting, in his eagerness to keep the peace and promote public tranquillity. It was his doom, in fact, to meet a head-wind at every turn, and be kept in a constant fume and fret by the perverseness of mankind. Had he served on a modern jury, he would have been sure to have eleven unreasonable men opposed to him.

At the time when the province of the New Netherlands was wrested from the domination of their High Mightinesses by the combined forces of Old and New England, Wolfert retired in high dudgeon to this fastness in the wilderness, with the bitter determination to bury himself from the world, and live here for the rest of his days in peace and quiet. In token of that fixed purpose, he inscribed over his door (his teeth clinched at the time) his favorite Dutch motto, "Lust in Rust" (pleasure in quiet.) The mansion was thence called Wolfert's Rust (Wolfert's Rest), but by the uneducated, who did not understand Dutch, Wolfert's Roost; probably from its quaint cockloft look, and from its having a weathercock perched on every gable.

Wolfert's luck followed him into retirement. He had shut himself up from the world, but he had brought with him a wife, and it soon passed into a proverb throughout the neighborhood that the cock of the Roost was the most henpecked bird in the country. His house too was reputed to be harassed by Yankee witchcraft. When the weather was quiet everywhere else, the wind, it was said, would howl and whistle about the gables; witches and warlocks would whirl about upon the weathercocks, and scream down the chimneys; nay, it was even hinted that Wolfert's wife was in league with the enemy, and used to ride on a broomstick to a witches' Sabbath in Sleepy Hollow. This, however, was all mere scandal, founded perhaps on her occasionally flourishing a broomstick in the course of a curtain lecture, or raising a storm within doors, as termagant wives are apt to do, and against which sorcery horse-shoes are of no avail.

Wolfert Acker died and was buried, but found no quiet even in the grave; for if popular gossip be true, his ghost has occasionally been seen walking by moonlight among the old gray moss-grown trees of his apple orchard.

Chronicle II

THE next period at which we find this venerable and eventful pile rising into importance, was during the dark and troublous time of the revolutionary war. It was the keep or stronghold of Jacob Van Tassel, a valiant Dutchman of the old stock of Van Tassels, who abound in Westchester County. The name, as originally written, was Van Texel, being derived from the Texel in Holland, which gave birth to that heroic line.

The Roost stood in the very heart of what at that time was called the debatable ground, lying between the British and American lines. The British held possession of the city and island of New York; while the Americans drew up towards the Highlands, holding their head-quarters at Peekskill. The intervening country from Croton River to Spiting Devil Creek was the debatable ground in question, liable to be harried by friend and foe, like the Scottish borders of yore.

It is a rugged region, full of fastnesses. A line of rocky hills extends through it like a backbone sending out ribs on either side; but these rude hills are for the most part richly wooded, and enclose little fresh pastoral valleys watered by the Neperan, the Pocantico,* and other

---

* The Neperan, vulgarly called the Saw-Mill River, winds for many miles through a lovely valley, shrouded by groves, and dotted by Dutch farm-houses, and empties itself into the Hudson at the ancient Dorp of Yonkers. The Pocantico, rising among woody hills, winds in many a wizard maze through the sequestered haunts of Sleepy Hollow. We owe it to the indefatigable researches

beautiful streams, along which the Indians built their wigwams in the olden time.

In the fastnesses of these hills, and along these valleys, existed, in the time of which I am treating, and indeed exist to the present day, a race of hard-headed, hard-handed, stout-hearted yeomen, descendants of the primitive Nederlanders. Men obstinately attached to the soil, and neither to be fought nor bought out of their paternal acres. Most of them were strong Whigs, throughout the war; some, however, were Tories, or adherents to the old kingly rule, who considered the revolution a mere rebellion, soon to be put down by his majesty's forces. A number of these took refuge within the British lines, joined the military bands of refugees, and became pioneers or leaders to foraging parties sent out from New York to Scour the country and sweep off supplies for the British Army.

In a little while the debatable ground became infested by roving bands, claiming from either side, and all pretending to redress wrongs and punish political offences; but all prone in the exercise of their high functions—to sack hen-roosts, drive off cattle, and lay farm-houses under contribution; such was the origin of two great orders of border chivalry, the Skinners and the Cow Boys, famous in revolutionary story; the former fought, or rather marauded, under the American, the latter, under the British banner. In the zeal of service, both were apt to make blunders, and confound the property of friend and foe. Neither of them in the heat and hurry of a foray had time to ascertain the politics of a horse or cow, which they were driving off into captivity; nor, when they wrung the neck of a rooster, did they trouble their heads whether he crowed for Congress or King George.

To check these enormities, a confederacy was formed among the yeomanry who had suffered from these maraudings. It was composed for the most part of farmers' sons, bold, hard-riding lads, well armed, and well mounted, and undertook to clear the country round of Skinner and Cow Boy, and all other border vermin; as the Holy Brotherhood in old times cleared Spain of the banditti which infested her highways.

Wolfert's Roost was one of the rallying places of this confederacy, and Jacob Van Tassel one of its members. He was eminently fitted for the service; stout of frame, bold of heart, and like his predecessor, the

---

of MR. KNICKERBOCKER, that those beautiful streams are rescued from modern commonplace, and reinvested with their ancient Indian names. The correctness of the venerable historian may be ascertained by reference to the records of the original Indian grants to the Herr Frederick Philipsen, preserved in the county clerk's office at White Plains.

warrior sachem of yore, delighting in daring enterprises. He had an Indian's sagacity in discovering when the enemy was on the maraud, and in hearing the distant tramp of cattle. It seemed as if he had a scout on every hill, and an ear as quick as that of Fine Ear in the fairy tale.

The foraging parties of tories and refugees had now to be secret and sudden in their forays into Westchester County; to make a hasty maraud among the farms, sweep the cattle into a drove, and hurry down to the lines along the river road, or the valley of the Neperan. Before they were half-way down, Jacob Van Tassel, with the holy brotherhood of Tarrytown, Petticoat Lane, and Sleepy Hollow, would be clattering at their heels. And now there would be a general scamper for King's Bridge, the pass over Spiting Devil Creek, into the British lines. Sometimes the moss-tropers would be overtaken, and eased of part of their booty. Sometimes the whole cavalgada would urge its headlong course across the bridge with thundering tramp and dusty whirlwind. At such times their pursuers would rein up their steeds, survey that perilous pass with wary eye, and, wheeling about, indemnify themselves by foraging the refugee region of Morrisania.

· While the debatable land was liable to be thus harried, the great Tappan Sea, along which it extends, was likewise domineered over by the foe. British ships of war were anchored here and there in the wide expanses of the river, mere floating castles to hold it in subjection. Stout galleys armed with eighteen pounders, and navigated with sails and oars, cruised about like hawks, while row-boats made descents upon the land, and foraged the country along shore.

It was a sore grievance to the yeomanry along the Tappan Sea to behold that little Mediterranean ploughed by hostile prows, and the noble river of which they were so proud reduced to a state of thraldom. Councils of war were held by captains of market-boats and other river-craft, to devise ways and means of dislodging the enemy. Here and there on a point of land extending into the Tappan Sea, a mud work would be thrown up, and an old field-piece mounted, with which a knot of rustic artillerymen would fire away for a long summer's day at some frigate dozing at anchor far out of reach; and reliques of such works may still be seen overgrown with weeds and brambles, with peradventure the half-buried fragment of a cannon which may have burst.

Jacob Van Tassel was a prominent man in these belligerent operations; but he was prone, moreover, to carry on a petty warfare of his own for his individual recreation and refreshment. On a row of hooks above the fireplace of the Roost, reposed his great piece of ordnance, —a duck, or rather goose-gun, of unparalleled longitude, with which it was said he could kill a wild-goose half way across the Tappan Sea. Indeed, there are as many wonders told of this renowned gun, as of the enchanted weapons of classic story. When the belligerent feeling was strong upon Jacob, he would take down his gun, sally forth alone, and prowl along shore, dodging behind rocks and trees, watching for hours together any ship or galley at anchor or becalmed, as a valorous mouser will watch a rat-hole. So sure as a boat approached the shore, bang went the great goose-gun, sending on board a shower of slugs and buckshot; and away scuttled Jacob Van Tassel through some woody ravine. As the Roost stood in a lonely situation, and might be attacked, he guarded against surprise by making loop-holes in the stone walls, through which to fire upon an assailant. His wife was stout-hearted as himself, and could load as fast as he could fire; and his sister, Nochie Van Wurmer, a redoubtable widow, was a match, as he said, for the stoutest man in the country. Thus garrisoned, his little castle was fitted to stand a siege, and Jacob was the man to defend it to the last charge of powder.

In the process of time the Roost became one of the secret stations, or lurking-places, of the Water Guard. This was an aquatic corps in the pay of government, organized to range the waters of the Hudson, and keep watch upon the movements of the enemy. It was composed of nautical men of the river, and hardy youngsters of the adjacent country, expert at pulling an oar or handling a musket. They were provided with whale-boats, long and sharp, shaped like canoes, and formed to lie lightly on the water, and be rowed with great rapidity. In these they would lurk out of sight by day, in nooks and bays, and behind points of land, keeping a sharp look-out upon the British ships, and giving intelligence to head-quarters of any extraordinary movement. At night they rowed about in pairs, pulling quietly along with muffled oars, under shadow of the land, or gliding like spectres about frigates and guard-ships to cut off any boat that might be sent to shore. In this way they were a source of constant uneasiness and alarm to the enemy.

The Roost, as has been observed, was one of their lurking-places; having a cove in front where their whale-boats could be drawn up out of sight, and Jacob Van Tassel being a vigilant ally, ready to take a part in any "scout or scrummage" by land or water. At this little warrior nest the hard-riding lads from the hills would hold consultations with the chivalry of the river, and here were concerted divers of those daring enterprises which resounded from Spiting Devil Creek even unto Anthony's Nose. Here was concocted the midnight invasion of New York Island, and the conflagration of Delancy's Tory mansion, which makes such a blaze in revolutionary history. Nay, more, if the Traditions of the Roost may be credited, here was meditated, by Jacob Van Tassel and his compeers, a nocturnal foray into New York itself, to surprise and carry off the British commanders, Howe and Clinton, and put a triumphant close to the war.

There is no knowing whether this notable scheme might not have been carried into effect, had not one of Jacob Van Tassel's egregious exploits along shore with his goose-gun, with which he thought himself a match for anything, brought vengeance on his house.

It so happened, that in the course of one of his solitary prowls he descried a British transport aground; the stern swung toward shore within point-blank shot. The temptation was too great to be resisted. Bang! went the great goose-gun, from the covert of the trees, shivering the cabin-windows and driving all hands forward. Bang! bang! the shots were repeated. The reports brought other of Jacob's fellow bush-fighters to the spot. Before the transport could bring a gun to bear, or land a boat to take revenge, she was soundly peppered, and the coast evacuated.

This was the last of Jacob's triumphs. He fared like some heroic spider that has unwittingly ensnared a hornet to the utter ruin of his web. It was not long after the above exploit that he fell into the hands of the enemy in the course of one of his forays, and was carried away prisoner to New York. The Roost itself, as a pestilent rebel nest, was marked out for signal punishment. The cock of the Roost being captive, there was none to garrison it but his stout-hearted spouse, his redoubtable sister, Nochie Van Wurmer, and Dinah, a strapping negro wench. An armed vessel came to anchor in front; a boat full of men pulled to shore. The garrison flew to arms; that is to say, to mops, broomsticks, shovels, tongs, and all kinds of domestic weapons,—for unluckily the great piece of ordnance, the goose-gun, was absent with its owner. Above all, a vigorous defence was made with that most potent of female weapons, the tongue. Never did invaded hen-roost make a more vociferous outcry. It was all in vain. The house was sacked and plundered, fire was set to each corner, and in a few moments its blaze shed a baleful light far over the Tappan Sea. The invaders then pounced upon the blooming Laney Van Tassel, the beauty of the Roost, and endeavored to bear her off to the boat. But here was the real tug of war. The mother, the aunt, and the strapping negro wench, all flew to the rescue. The struggle continued down to the very water's edge, when a voice from the armed vessel at anchor ordered the spoilers to desist; they relinquished their prize, jumped into their boats, and pulled off, and the heroine of the Roost escaped with a mere rumpling of her feathers.

As to the stout Jacob himself, he was detained a prisoner in New York for the greater part of the war; in the meantime the Roost remained a melancholy ruin, its stone walls and brick chimneys alone sanding, the resorts of bats and owls. Superstitious notions prevailed about it. None of the country people would venture alone at night down the rambling lane which led to it, overhung with trees, and crossed here and there by a wild wandering brook. The story went that one of the victims of Jacob Van Tassel's great goose-gun had been buried there in unconsecrated ground.

Even the Tappan Sea in front was said to be haunted. Often in the still twilight of a summer evening, when the sea would be as glass, and the opposite hills would throw their purple shadows half across it, a low sound would be heard as of the steady, vigorous pull of oars, though not a boat was to be descried. Some might have supposed that a boat was rowed along unseen under the deep shadows of the opposite shores; but the ancient traditionists of the neighborhood knew better. Some said it was one of the whale-boats of the old Water Guard, sunk by the British ships during the war, but now permitted to haunt its old cruising grounds; but the prevalent opinion connected it with the awful fate of Rambout Van Dam of graceless memory. He was a roistering Dutchman of Spiting Devil, who in times long past had navigated his boat alone one Saturday the whole length of the Tappan Sea, to attend a quilting frolic at Kakiat, on the western shore. Here he had danced and drunk until midnight, when he entered his boat to return home. He was warned that he was on the verge of Sunday morning; but he pulled off nevertheless, swearing he would not land until he reached Spiting Devil, if it took him a month of Sundays. He was never seen afterwards; but may be heard plying his oars, as above mentioned,—being the Flying Dutchman of the Tappan Sea, doomed to ply between Kakiat and Spiting Devil until the day of judgment.

Chronicle III

THE revolutionary war was over. The debatable ground had once more become a quiet agricultural region; the border chivalry had turned their swords into plough-shares, and their spears into pruning-hooks, and hung up their guns, only to be taken down occasionally in a campaign against wild pigeons on the hills, or wild ducks upon the Hudson. Jacob Van Tassel, whilome carried captive to New York, a flagitious rebel, had come forth from captivity a "hero of seventy-six." In a little while he sought the scenes of his former triumphs and mishaps, rebuilt the Roost, restored his goose-gun to the hooks over the fireplace, and reared once more on high the glittering weathercocks.

Years and years passed over the time-honored little mansion. The honeysuckle and the sweetbrier crept up its walls; the wren and the Phœbe-bird built under the eaves; it gradually became almost hidden among trees, through which it looked forth, as with half-shut eyes, upon the Tappan Sea. The Indian spring, famous in the days of the wizard sachem, still welled up at the bottom of the green bank; and the wild brook, wild as ever, came babbling down the ravine, and threw itself into the little cove where of yore the Water Guard harbored their whale-boats.

Such was the state of the Roost many years since, at the time when Diedrich Knickerbocker came into this neighborhood, in the course of his researches among the Dutch families for materials for his immortal history. The exterior of the eventful little pile seemed to him full of promise. The crow-step gables were of the primitive architecture of the province. The weathercocks which surmounted them had crowed in the glorious days of the New Netherlands. The one above the porch had actually glittered of yore on the great Vander Heyden palace at Albany.

The interior of the mansion fulfilled its external promise. Here were records of old times; documents of the Dutch dynasty, rescued from the profane hands of the English by Wolfert Acker, when he retreated from New Amsterdam. Here he had treasured them up like buried gold, and here they had been miraculously preserved by St. Nicholas, at the time of the conflagration of the Roost.

Here then did old Diedrich Knickerbocker take up his abode for a time, and set to work with antiquarian zeal to decipher these precious documents, which, like the lost books of Livy, had baffled the research of former historians; and it is the facts drawn from these sources which give his work the preference, in point of accuracy, over every other history.

It was during his sojourn in this eventful neighborhood that the historian is supposed to have picked up many of those legends, which have since been given by him to the world, or found among his papers. Such was the legend connected with the old Dutch Church of Sleepy Hollow. The Church itself was a monument of by-gone days. It had been built in the early time of the province. A tablet over the portal bore the names of its founders,—Frederick Filipson, a mighty man of yore, patroon of Yonkers, and his wife Katrina Van Courtland, of the Van Courtlands of Croton; a powerful family connection,—with one foot resting on Spiting Devil Creek, and the other on the Croton River.

Two weathercocks, with the initials of these illustrious personages, graced each end of the Church, one perched over the belfry, the other over the chancel. As usual with ecclesiastical weathercocks, each pointed a different way; and there was a perpetual contradiction between them on all points of windy doctrine; emblematic, alas! of the Christian propensity to schism and controversy.

In the burying-ground adjacent to the Church, reposed the earliest fathers of a wide rural neighborhood. Here families were garnered together, side by side, in long platoons, in this last gathering place of kindred. With pious hand would Diedrich Knickerbocker turn down the weeds and brambles which had overgrown the tombstones, to decipher inscriptions in Dutch and English, of the names and virtues of succeeding generations of Van Tassels, Van Warts, and other historical worthies, with their portraitures faithfully carved, all bearing the family likeness to cherubs.

The congregation in those days was of a truly rural character. City fashions had not as yet stole up to Sleepy Hollow. Dutch sun-bonnets and honest homespun still prevailed. Everything was in primitive style, even to the bucket of water and tin cup near the door in summer, to assuage the thirst caused by the heat of the weather or the drought of the sermon.

The pulpit, with its widespreading sounding-board, and the communion-table, curiously carved, had each come from Holland in the olden time, before the arts had sufficiently advanced in the colony for such achievements. Around these on Sundays would be gathered the elders of the church, gray-headed men, who led the psalmody, and in whom it would be difficult to recognize the hard-riding lads of yore, who scoured the debatable land in the time of the revolution.

The drowsy influence of Sleepy Hollow was apt to breathe into this sacred edifice; and now and then an elder might be seen with his handkerchief over his face to keep off the flies, and apparently listening to the dominie; but really sunk into a summer slumber, lulled by the sultry notes of the locust from the neighboring trees.

And now a word or two about Sleepy Hollow, which many have rashly deemed a fanciful creation, like the Lubberland of mariners. It was probably the mystic and dreamy sound of the name which first tempted the historian of the Manhattoes into its spellbound mazes. As he entered, all nature seemed for the moment to awake from its slumbers and break forth in gratulations. The quail whistled a welcome from the cornfield; the loquacious cat-bird flew from bush to bush with restless wing proclaiming his approach, or perked inquisitively into his face as if to get a knowledge of his physiognomy. The woodpecker tapped a tattoo on the hollow apple-tree, and then peered round the trunk, as if asking how he relished the salutation; while the squirrel scampered along the fence, whisking his tail over his head by way of a huzza.

Here reigned the golden mean extolled by poets, in which no gold was to be found and very little silver. The inhabitants were of the primitive stock, and had intermarried and bred in and in, from the earliest time of the province, never swarming far from the parent hive, but dividing and sub-dividing their parental acres as they swarmed.

Here were small farms, each having its little portion of meadow and cornfield; its orchard of gnarled and sprawling apple-trees; its garden, in which the rose, the marigold, and hollyhock, grew sociably with the cabbage, the pea, and the pumpkin; each had its low-eaved mansion redundant with white-headed children; with an old hat nailed against the wall for the housekeeping wren; the coop on the grass-plot, where the motherly hen clucked round with her vagrant brood: each had its stone well, with a moss-covered bucket suspended to the long balancing-pole, according to antediluvian hydraulics; while within doors resounded the eternal hum of the spinning wheel.

Many were the great historical facts which the worthy Diedrich collected in these lowly mansions, and patiently would he sit by the old Dutch housewives with a child on his knee, or a purring grimalkin on his lap, listening to endless ghost stories spun forth to the humming accompaniment of the wheel.

The delighted historian pursued his explorations far into the foldings where the Pocantico winds its wizard stream among the mazes of its old Indian haunts; sometimes running darkly in pieces of woodland beneath balancing sprays of beech and chestnut; sometimes sparkling between grassy borders in fresh, green intervales; here and there receiving the tributes of silver rills which came whimpering down the hill-sides from their parent springs.

In a remote part of the Hollow, where the Pocantico forced its way down rugged rocks, stood Carl's mill, the haunted house of the neighborhood. It was indeed a goblin-looking pile: shattered and time-worn, dismal with clanking wheels and rushing streams, and all kinds of uncouth noises. A horse-shoe nailed to the door to keep off witches, seemed to have lost its power; for as Diedrich approached, an old negro thrust his head all dabbled with flour out of a hole above the water-wheel, and grinned and rolled his eyes, and appeared to be the very hobgoblin of the place. Yet this proved to be the great historic genius of the Hollow, abounding in that valuable information never to be acquired from books. Diedrich Knickerbocker soon discovered his merit. They had long talks together seated on a broken millstone, heedless of the water and the clatter of the mill; and to his conference with that African sage many attribute the surprising, though true story, of Ichabod Crane and the Headless Horseman of Sleepy Hollow. We refrain, however, from giving farther researches of the historian of the Manhattoes during his sojourn at the Roost, but may return to them in future pages.

Reader! the Roost still exists. Time, which changes all things, is slow in its operations on a Dutchman's dwelling. The stout Jacob Van Tassel, it is true, sleeps with his fathers; and his great goose-gun with him: yet his stronghold still bears the impress of its Dutch origin. Odd rumors have gathered about it, as they are apt to do about old mansions, like moss and weather-stains. The shade of Wolfert Acker still walks his unquiet rounds at night in the orchard; and a white figure has now and then been seen seated at a window and gazing at the moon, from a room in which a young lady is said to have died of love and green apples.

Mementos of the sojourn of Diedrich Knickerbocker are still cherished at the Roost. His elbow-chair and antique writing-desk maintain their place in the room he occupied, and his old cocked-hat still hangs on a peg against the wall.

From *Wolfert's Roost*

THE CREOLE VILLAGE

A Sketch From a Steamboat
[First published in 1837]

IN travelling about our motley country, I am often reminded of
Ariosto's account of the moon, in which the good paladin Astolpho
found everything garnered up that had been lost on earth. So I am
apt to imagine that many things lost in the Old World are treasured
up in the New; having been handed down from generation to generation, since the early days of the colonies. A European antiquary, therefore, curious in his researches after the ancient and almost obliterated
customs and usages of his country, would do well to put himself upon
the track of some early band of emigrants, follow them across the
Atlantic, and rummage among their descendants on our shores.

In the phraseology of New England might be found many an old
English provincial phrase long since obsolete in the parent country,
with some quaint relics of the Roundheads; while Virginia cherishes
peculiarities characteristic of the days of Elizabeth and Sir Walter
Raleigh.

In the same way, the sturdy yeomanry of New Jersey and Pennsylvania keep up many usages fading away in ancient Germany; while
many an honest, broad bottomed custom, nearly extinct in venerable
Holland, may be found flourishing in pristine vigor and luxuriance in
Dutch villages, on the banks of the Mohawk and the Hudson.

In no part of our country, however, are the customs and peculiarities
imported from the Old World by the earlier settlers kept up with
more fidelity than in the little, poverty-stricken villages of Spanish and
French origin, which border the rivers of ancient Louisiana. Their
population is generally made up of the descendants of those nations,
married and interwoven together, and occasionally crossed with a slight
dash of the Indian. The French character, however, floats on top, as,
from its buoyant qualities, it is sure to do, whenever it forms a particle,
however small, of an intermixture.

In these serene and dilapidated villages, art and nature stand still,
and the world forgets to turn round. The revolutions that distract

other parts of this mutable planet, reach not here, or pass over without leaving any trace. The fortunate inhabitants have none of that public spirit which extends its cares beyond its horizon, and imports trouble and perplexity from all quarters in newspapers. In fact, newspapers are almost unknown in these villages; and, as French is the current language, the inhabitants have little community of opinion with their republican neighbors. They retain, therefore, their old habits of passive obedience to the decrees of government, as though they still lived under the absolute sway of colonial commandants, instead of being part and parcel of the sovereign people, and having a voice in public legislation.

A few aged men, who have grown gray on their hereditary acres, and are of the good old colonial stock, exert a patriarchal sway in all matters of public and private import; their opinions are considered oracular, and their word is law.

The inhabitants, moreover, have none of that eagerness for gain, and rage for improvement, which keep our people continually on the move, and our country towns incessantly in a state of transition. There the magic phrases, "town lots," "water privileges," "railroads," and other comprehensive and soul-stirring words from the speculator's vocabulary, are never heard. The residents dwell in the houses built by their forefathers, without thinking of enlarging or modernizing them, or pulling them down and turning them into granite stores. The trees under which they have been born, and have played in infancy, flourish undisturbed; though, by cutting them down, they might open new streets, and put money in their pockets. In a word, the almighty dollar, that great object of universal devotion throughout our land, seems to have no genuine devotees in these peculiar villages; and unless some of its missionaries penetrate there, and erect banking-houses and other pious shrines, there is no knowing how long the inhabitants may remain in their present state of contented poverty.

In descending one of our great western rivers in a steamboat, I met with two worthies from one of these villages, who had been on a distant excursion, the longest they had ever made, as they seldom ventured far from home. One was the great man, or Grand Seigneur of the village; not that he enjoyed any legal privileges or power there, everything of the kind having been done away when the province was ceded by France to the United States. His sway over his neighbors was merely one of custom and convention, out of deference to his family. Besides, he was worth full fifty thousand dollars, an amount almost equal, in the imaginations of the villagers, to the treasures of King Solomon.

This very substantial old gentleman, though of the fourth or fifth generation in this country, retained the true Gallic feature and deportment, and reminded me of one of those provincial potentates that are to be met with in the remote parts of France. He was of a large frame, a ginger-bread complexion, strong features, eyes that stood out like glass knobs, and a prominent nose, which he frequently regaled from a gold snuff-box, and occasionally blew with a colored handkerchief, until it sounded like a trumpet.

He was attended by an old negro, as black as ebony, with a huge mouth, in a continual grin; evidently a privileged and favorite servant, who had grown up and grown old with him. He was dressed in creole style, with white jacket and trousers, a stiff shirt-collar, that threatened to cut off his ears, a bright Madras handkerchief tied round his head, and large gold ear-rings. He was the politest negro I met with in a western tour, and that is saying a great deal, for, excepting the Indians, the negroes are the most gentlemanlike personages to be met with in those parts. It is true they differ from the Indians in being a little extra polite and complimentary. He was also one of the merriest; and here, too, the negroes, however we may deplore their unhappy condition, have the advantage of their masters. The whites are, in general, too free and prosperous to be merry. The cares of maintaining their rights and liberties, adding to their wealth, and making presidents engross all their thoughts and dry up all the moisture of their souls. If you hear a broad, hearty, devil-may-care laugh, be assured it is a negro's.

Besides this African domestic, the seigneur of the village had another no less cherished and privileged attendant. This was a huge dog, of the mastiff breed, with a deep, hanging mouth, and a look of surly gravity. He walked about the cabin with the air of a dog perfectly at home, and who had paid for his passage. At dinner-time he took his seat beside his master, giving him a glance now and then out of a corner of his eye, which bespoke perfect confidence that he would not be forgotten. Nor was he. Every now and then a huge morsel would be thrown to him, peradventure the half-picked leg of a fowl, which he would receive with a snap like the springing of a steel trap,—one gulp, and all was down; and a glance of the eye told his master that he was ready for another consignment.

The other village worthy, travelling in company with the seigneur, was of a totally different stamp. Small, thin, and weazen-faced, as Frenchmen are apt to be represented in caricature, with a bright, squirrel-like eye, and a gold ring in his ear. His dress was flimsy, and sat loosely on his frame, and he had altogether the look of one with but little coin in his pocket. Yet, though one of the poorest, I was assured he was one of the merriest and most popular personages in his native village.

Compère Martin, as he was commonly called, was the factotum of the place—sportsman, schoolmaster, and land-surveyor. He could sing, dance, and above all, play on the fiddle, an invaluable accomplishment in an old French creole village, for the inhabitants have a hereditary love for balls and *fêtes*. If they work but little, they dance a great deal; and a fiddle is the joy of their heart.

What had sent Compère Martin travelling with the Grand Seigneur I could not learn. He evidently looked up to him with great deference, and was assiduous in rendering him petty attentions; from which I concluded that he lived at home upon the crumbs which fell from his table. He was gayest when out of his sight, and had his song and his joke when forward among the deck passengers; but, altogether, Compère Martin was out of his element on board of a steamboat. He was quite another being, I am told, when at home in his own village.

Like his opulent fellow-traveller, he too had his canine follower and retainer,—and one suited to his different fortunes,—one of the civilest, most unoffending little dogs in the world. Unlike the lordly mastiff, he seemed to think he had no right on board of the steamboat; if you did but look hard at him, he would throw himself upon his back, and lift up his legs, as if imploring mercy. At table he took his seat a little distance from his master; not with the bluff, confident air of the mastiff, but quietly and diffidently; his head on one side, with one ear dubiously slouched, the other hopefully cocked up; his under-teeth projecting beyond his black nose, and his eye wistfully following each morsel that went into his master's mouth.

If Compère Martin now and then should venture to abstract a morsel from his plate, to give to his humble companion, it was edifying to see with what diffidence the exemplary little animal would take hold of it, with the very tip of his teeth, as if he would almost rather not, or was fearful of taking too great a liberty. And then with what decorum would he eat it! How many efforts would he make in swallowing it, as if it stuck in his throat; with what daintiness would he lick his lips; and then with what an air of thankfulness would he resume his seat, with his teeth once more projecting beyond his nose, and an eye of humble expectation fixed upon his master.

It was late in the afternoon when the steamboat stopped at the village which was the residence of these worthies. It stood on the high bank of the river, and bore traces of having been a frontier trading-post. There were the remains of stockades that once protected it from the Indians, and the houses were in the ancient Spanish and French colonial taste, the place having been successively under the domination of both those nations prior to the cession of Louisiana to the United States.

The arrival of the seigneur of fifty thousand dollars, and his humble companion, Compère Martin, had evidently been looked forward to as an event in the village. Numbers of men, women, and children, white, yellow, and black, were collected on the river bank; most of them clad in old-fashioned French garments, and their heads decorated with colored handkerchiefs, or white nightcaps. The moment the steamboat came within sight and hearing, there was a waving of handkerchiefs, and a screaming and bawling of salutations and felicitations, that baffle all description.

The old gentleman of fifty thousand dollars was received by a train of relatives, and friends, and children, and grandchildren, whom he kissed on each cheek, and who formed a procession in his rear, with a legion of domestics, of all ages, following him to a large, old-fashioned French house, that domineered over the village.

His black *valet de chambre*, in white jacket and trousers, and gold ear-rings, was met on the shore by a boon, though rustic companion, a tall negro fellow, with a long good-humored face, and the profile of a horse, which stood out from beneath a narrow-rimmed straw hat, stuck on the back of his head. The explosions of laughter of these two varlets on meeting and exchanging compliments, were enough to electrify the country round.

The most hearty reception, however, was that given to Compère Martin. Everybody, young and old, hailed him before he got to land. Everybody had a joke for Compère Martin, and Compère Martin had a joke for everybody. Even his little dog appeared to partake of his popularity, and to be caressed by every hand. Indeed, he was quite a different animal the moment he touched the land. Here he was at home; here he was of consequence. He barked, he leaped, he frisked about his old friends, and then would skim round the place in a wide circle, as if mad.

I traced Compère Martin and his little dog to their home. It was an old ruinous Spanish house, of large dimensions, with verandas overshadowed by ancient elms. The house had probably been the residence, in old times, of the Spanish commandant. In one wing of this crazy, but aristocratical abode, was nestled the family of my fellow-traveller; for poor devils are apt to be magnificently clad and lodged, in the cast-off clothes and abandoned palaces of the great and wealthy.

The arrival of Compère Martin was welcomed by a legion of women, children, and mongrel curs; and, as poverty and gayety generally go hand-in-hand among the French and their descendants, the crazy mansion soon resounded with loud gossip and light-hearted laughter.

As the steamboat paused a short time at the village, I took occasion to stroll about the place. Most of the houses were in the French taste, with casements and rickety verandas, but most of them in flimsy and ruinous condition. All the wagons, ploughs, and other utensils about the place were of ancient and inconvenient Gallic construction, such as had been brought from France in the primitive days of the colony. The very looks of the people reminded me of the villages of France.

From one of the houses came the hum of a spinning-wheel, accompanied by a scrap of an old French *chanson*, which I have heard many a time among the peasantry of Languedoc, doubtless a traditional song, brought over by the first French emigrants, and handed down from generation to generation.

Half a dozen young lasses emerged from the adjacent dwellings, reminding me, by their light step and gay costume, of scenes in ancient France, where taste in dress comes natural to every class of females. The trim bodice and colored petticoat, and little apron, with its pockets to receive the hands when in an attitude for conversation; the colored kerchief wound tastefully round the head, with a coquettish knot perking above one ear; and the neat slipper and tight-drawn stocking, with its braid of narrow ribbon embracing the ankle where it peeps from its mysterious curtain. It is from this ambush that Cupid sends his most inciting arrows.

While I was musing upon the recollections thus accidentally summoned up, I heard the sound of a fiddle from the mansion of Compère Martin, the signal, no doubt, for a joyous gathering. I was disposed to turn my steps thither, and witness the festivities of one of the very few villages I had met with in my wide tour that was yet poor enough to be merry; but the bell of the steamboat summoned me to re-embark.

As we swept away from the shore, I cast back a wistful eye upon the moss-grown roofs and ancient elms of the village, and prayed that the inhabitants might long retain their happy ignorance, their absence of all enterprise and improvement, their respect for the fiddle, and their contempt for the almighty dollar.* I fear, however, my prayer is

---

* This phrase, used for the first time in this sketch, has since passed into current circulation, and by some has been questioned as savoring of irreverence. The author, therefore, owes it to his orthodoxy to declare that no irreverence was intended even to the dollar itself; which he is aware is daily becoming more and more an object of worship.—w.i.

doomed to be of no avail. In a little while the steamboat whirled me to an American town, just springing into bustling and prosperous existence.

The surrounding forest had been laid out in town lots; frames of wooden buildings were rising from among stumps and burnt trees. The place already boasted a court-house, a jail, and two banks, all built of pine boards, on the model of Grecian temples. There were rival hotels, rival churches, and rival newspapers; together with the usual number of judges and generals and governors; not to speak of doctors by the dozen, and lawyers by the score.

The place, I was told, was in an astonishing career of improvement, with a canal and two railroads in embryo. Lots doubled in price every week; everybody was speculating in land; everybody was rich; and everybody was growing richer. The community, however, was torn to pieces by new doctrines in religion and in political economy; there were camp-meetings, and agrarian meetings; and an election was at hand, which, it was expected, would throw the whole country into a paroxysm.

Alas! with such an enterprising neighbor, what is to become of the poor little creole village!

From *Wolfert's Roost*

MOUNTJOY;

or, Some Passages Out of the Life of a Castle-builder

I WAS born among romantic scenery, in one of the wildest parts of the Hudson, which at that time was not so thickly settled as at present. My father was descended from one of the old Huguenot families, that came over to this country on the revocation of the Edict of Nantz. He lived in a style of easy, rural independence, on a patrimonial estate that had been for two or three generations in the family. He was an indolent, good-natured man, took the world as it went, and had a kind of laughing philosophy, that parried all rubs and mishaps, and served him in the place of wisdom. This was the part of his character least to my taste; for I was of an enthusiastic, excitable temperament, prone to kindle up with new schemes and projects, and he was apt to dash my sallying enthusiasm by some unlucky joke; so that whenever I was in a glow with any sudden excitement, I stood in mortal dread of his good humor.

Yet he indulged me in every vagary, for I was an only son, and of course a personage of importance in the household. I had two sisters older than myself, and one younger. The former were educated at New York, under the eye of a maiden aunt; the latter remained at home, and was my cherished playmate, the companion of my thoughts. We were two imaginative little beings, of quick susceptibility, and prone to see wonders and mysteries in everything around us. Scarce had we learned to read, when our mother made us holiday presents of all the nursery literature of the day, which at that time consisted of little books covered with gilt paper, adorned with "cuts," and filled wih tales of fairies, giants, and enchanters. What draughts of delightful fiction did we then inhale! My sister Sophy was of a soft and tender nature. She would weep over the woes of the Children in the Wood, or quake at the dark romance of Blue-Beard, and the terrible mysteries of the blue chamber. But I was all for enterprise and adventure. I burned to emulate the deeds of that heroic prince who delivered the white cat from her enchantment; or he of no less royal blood and doughty emprise, who broke the charmed slumber of the Beauty in the Wood!

The house in which we lived was just the kind of place to foster such propensities. It was a venerable mansion, half villa, half farmhouse. The oldest part was of stone, with loopholes for musketry, having served as a family fortress in the time of the Indians. To this there had been made various additions, some of brick, some of wood, according to the exigencies of the moment; so that it was full of nooks and crooks, and chambers of all sorts and sizes. It was buried among willows, elms, and cherry-trees, and surrounded with roses and hollyhocks, with honeysuckle and sweetbrier clambering about every window. A brood of hereditary pigeons sunned themselves upon the roof; hereditary swallows and martins built about the eaves and chimneys; and hereditary bees hummed about the flower-beds.

Under the influence of our story-books every object around us now assumed a new character, and a charmed interest. The wild flowers were no longer the mere ornaments of the fields, or the resorts of the toilful bee; they were the lurking-places of fairies. We would watch the humming-bird, as it hovered around the trumpet-creeper at our porch, and the butterfly as it flitted up into the blue air, above the sunny tree-tops, and fancy them some of the tiny beings from fairy land. I would call to mind all that I had read of Robin Goodfellow, and his power of transformation. Oh, how I envied him that power! How I longed to be able to compress my form into utter littleness, to ride the bold dragon-fly, swinging on the tall bearded grass, follow the ant into his subterraneous habitation, or dive into the cavernous depths of the honeysuckle!

While I was yet a mere child, I was sent to a daily school, about two miles distant. The schoolhouse was on the edge of a wood, close by a brook overhung with birches, alders, and dwarf-willows. We of the school who lived at some distance came with our dinners put up in little baskets. In the intervals of school hours, we would gather round a spring, under a tuft of hazel-bushes, and have a kind of picnic; interchanging the rustic dainties with which our provident mothers had fitted us out. Then, when our joyous repast was over, and my companions were disposed for play, I would draw forth one of my cherished story-books, stretch myself on the greensward, and soon lose myself in its bewitching contents.

I became an oracle among my schoolmates, on account of my superior erudition, and soon imparted to them the contagion of my infected fancy. Often in the evening, after school hours, we would sit on the trunk of some fallen tree in the woods, and vie with each other in telling extravagant stories, until the whip-poor-will began his nightly moaning, and the fire-flies sparkled in the gloom. Then came the perilous journey homeward. What delight we would take in getting up wanton panics, in some dusky part of the wood; scampering like frightened deer, pausing to take breath, renewing the panic, and scampering off again, wild with fictitious terror!

Our greatest trial was to pass a dark, lonely pool, covered with pond-lilies, peopled with bull-frogs and water-snakes, and haunted by two white cranes. Oh! the terrors of that pond! How our little hearts would beat, as we approached it; what fearful glances we would throw around! And if by chance a plash of a wild duck, or the guttural twang of a bull-frog, struck our ears as we stole quietly by—away we sped, nor paused until completely out of the woods. Then, when I reached home, what a world of adventures and imaginary terrors would I have to relate to my sister Sophy!

As I advanced in years, this turn of mind increased upon me, and became more confirmed. I abandoned myself to the impulses of a romantic imagination, which controlled my studies, and gave a bias to all my habits. My father observed me continually with a book in my hand, and satisfied himself that I was a profound student; but what were my studies? Works of fiction, tales of chivalry, voyages of discovery, travels in the East; everything, in short, that partook of adventure and romance. I well remember with what zest I entered upon that part of my studies which treated of the heathen mythology, and particularly of the sylvan deities. Then indeed my school-books became dear to me. The neighborhood was well calculated to foster the reveries of a mind like mine. It abounded with solitary retreats, wild streams, solemn forests, and silent valleys. I would ramble about for a whole day, with a volume of Ovid's *Metamorphoses* in my pocket, and work myself into a kind of self-delusion, so as to identify the surrounding scenes with those of which I had just been reading. I would loiter about a brook that glided through the shadowy depths of the forest, picturing it to myself the haunt of Naiades. I would steal round some bushy copse that opened upon a glade, as if I expected to come suddenly upon Diana and her nymphs; or to behold Pan and his satyrs bounding, with whoop and halloo, through the woodland. I would throw myself, during the panting heats of a summer noon, under the shade of some widespreading tree, and muse and dream away the hours, in a state of mental intoxication. I drank in the very light of day, as nectar, and my soul seemed to bathe with ecstasy in the deep blue of a summer sky.

In these wanderings nothing occurred to jar my feelings, or bring me back to the realities of life. There is a repose in our mighty forests that gives full scope to the imagination. Now and then I would hear the distant sound of the wood-cutter's axe, or the crash of some tree which he had laid low; but these noises, echoing along the quiet landscape, could easily be wrought by fancy into harmony with its illusions. In general, however, the woody recesses of the neighborhood were peculiarly wild and unfrequented. I could ramble for a whole day, without coming upon any traces of cultivation. The partridge of the wood scarcely seemed to shun my path, and the squirrel, from his nut-tree, would gaze at me for an instant, with sparkling eye, as if wondering at the unwonted intrusion.

I cannot help dwelling on this delicious period of my life; when as yet I had known no sorrow, nor experienced any worldly care. I have since studied much, both of books and men, and of course have grown too wise to be so easily pleased; yet with all my wisdom, I must confess I look back with a secret feeling of regret to the days of happy ignorance, before I had begun to be a philosopher.

It must be evident that I was in a hopeful training, for one who was to descend into the arena of life, and wrestle with the world. The tutor, also, who superintended my studies, in the more advanced stage of my education, was just fitted to complete the *fata morgana* which was forming in my mind. His name was Glencoe. He was a pale, melancholy-looking man, about forty years of age; a native of Scotland, liberally educated, and who had devoted himself to the instruction of youth, from taste rather than necessity; for, as he said, he loved the human heart, and delighted to study it in its earlier impulses. My two elder sisters, having returned home from a city boarding-school, were likewise placed under his care, to direct their reading in history and belles-lettres.

We all soon became attached to Glencoe. It is true we were at first somewhat prepossessed against him. His meagre, pallid countenance, his broad pronunciation, his inattention to the little forms of society, and an awkward and embarrassed manner, on first acquaintance, were much against him; but we soon discovered that under this unpromising exterior existed the kindest urbanity, the warmest sympathies, the most enthusiastic benevolence. His mind was ingenious and acute. His reading had been various, but more abstruse than profound; his memory was stored, on all subjects, with facts, theories, and quotations, and crowded with crude materials for thinking. These, in a moment of excitement, would be, as it were, melted down and poured forth in the lava of a heated imagination. At such moments, the change in the whole man was wonderful. His meagre form would acquire a dignity and grace; his long, pale visage would flash with a hectic glow; his eyes would beam with intense speculation; and there would be pathetic tones and deep modulations in his voice, that delighted the ear, and spoke movingly to the heart.

But what most endeared him to us, was the kindness and sympathy with which he entered into all our interests and wishes. Instead of curbing and checking our young imaginations with the reins of sober reason, he was a little too apt to catch the impulse, and be hurried away with us. He could not withstand the excitement of any sally of feeling or fancy, and was prone to lend heightening tints to the illusive coloring of youthful anticipation.

Under his guidance my sisters and myself soon entered upon a more extended range of studies; but while they wandered, with delighted minds, through the wide field of history and belles-lettres, a nobler walk was opened to my superior intellect.

The mind of Glencoe presented a singular mixture of philosophy and poetry. He was fond of metaphysics, and prone to indulge in abstract speculations, though his metaphysics were somewhat fine-spun and fanciful, and his speculations were apt to partake of what my father most irreverently termed "humbug." For my part, I delighted in them, and the more especially because they set my father to sleep, and completely confounded my sisters. I entered, with my accustomed eagerness, into this new branch of study. Metaphysics were now my passion. My sisters attempted to accompany me, but they soon faltered, and gave out before they had got half way through Smith's Theory of Moral Sentiments. I, however, went on, exulting in my strength. Glencoe supplied me with books, and I devoured them with appetite, if not digestion. We walked and talked together under the trees before the house, or sat apart, like Milton's angels, and held high converse upon the themes beyond the grasp of the ordinary intellects. Glencoe possessed a kind of philosophic chivalry, in imitation of the old peripatetic sages, and was continually dreaming of romantic enterprises in morals, and splendid systems for the improvement of society. He had a fanciful mode of illustrating abstract subjects, peculiarly to my taste; clothing them with the language of poetry, and throwing round them almost the magic hues of fiction. "How charming," thought I, "is divine philosophy";

> "Not harsh and crabbed, as dull fools suppose,
> But musical as is Apollo's lute;
> And a perpetual feast of nectar'd sweets,
> Where no crude surfeit reigns."

I felt a wonderful self-complacency at being on such excellent terms with a man whom I considered on a parallel with the sages of antiquity, and looked down with a sentiment of pity on the feebler intellects of my sisters, who could comprehend nothing of metaphysics. It is true, when I attempted to study them by myself I was apt to get in a fog; but when Glencoe came to my aid, everything was soon as clear to me as day. My ear drank in the beauty of his words; my imagination was dazzled with the splendor of his illustrations. It caught up the sparkling sands of poetry that glittered through his speculations, and mistook them for the golden ore of wisdom. Struck with the facility with which I seemed to imbibe and relish the most abstract doctrines, I conceived a still higher opinion of my mental powers, and was convinced that I also was a philosopher.

I was now verging toward man's estate, and though my education had been extremely irregular,—following the caprices of my humor, which I mistook for the impulses of my genius,—yet I was regarded with wonder and delight by my mother and sisters, who considered me almost as wise and infallible as I considered myself. This high opinion of me was strengthened by a declamatory habit, which made me an oracle and orator at the domestic board. The time was now at hand, however, that was to put my philosophy to the test.

We had passed through a long winter, and the spring at length opened upon us, with unusual sweetness. The soft serenity of the weather, the beauty of the surrounding country, the joyous notes of the birds, the balmy breath of flower and blossom, all combined to fill my bosom with indistinct sensations and nameless wishes. Amid the soft seductions of the season I lapsed into a state of utter indolence, both of body and mind. Philosophy had lost its charms for me. Metaphysics—faugh! I tried to study; took down volume after volume, ran my eye vacantly over a few pages, and threw them by with distaste. I loitered about the house, with my hands in my pockets, and an air of complete vacancy. Something was necessary to make me happy; but what was that something? I sauntered to the apartments of my sisters, hoping their conversation might amuse me. They had walked out, and the room was vacant. On the table lay a volume which they had been reading. It was a novel. I had never read a novel, having conceived a contempt for works of the kind, from hearing them universally condemned. It is true, I had remarked they were universally read; but I considered them beneath the attention of a philosopher, and never would venture to read them, less I should lessen my mental superiority in the eyes of my sisters. Nay, I had taken up a work of the kind, now and then, when I knew my sisters were observing me, looked into it for a moment, and then laid it down, with a slight supercilious smile. On the present occasion, out of mere listlessness, I took up the volume, and turned over a few of the first pages. I thought I heard some one coming, and laid it down. I was mistaken; no one was near, and what I had read, tempted my curiosity to read a little farther. I leaned against a window-frame, and in a few minutes was completely lost in the story. How long I stood there reading I know not, but I believe for nearly two hours. Suddenly I heard my sisters on the stairs, when I thrust the book into my bosom, and the two other volumes, which lay near, into my pockets, and hurried out of the house to my beloved woods. Here I remained all day beneath the trees, bewildered, bewitched; devouring the contents of these delicious volumes; and only returned to the house when it was too dark to peruse their pages.

This novel finished, I replaced it in my sisters' apartment, and looked for others. Their stock was ample, for they had brought home all that were current in the city; but my appetite demanded an immense supply. All this course of reading was carried on clandestinely, for I was a little ashamed of it, and fearful that my wisdom might be called in question; but this very privacy gave it additional zest. It was "bread eaten in secret"; it had the charm of a private amour.

But think what must have been the effect of such a course of reading on a youth of my temperament and turn of mind; indulged, too, amidst romantic scenery, and in the romantic season of the year. It seemed as if I had entered upon a new scene of existence. A train of combustible feelings were lighted up in me, and my soul was all tenderness and passion. Never was youth more completely love-sick, though as yet it was a mere general sentiment, and wanted a definite object. Unfortunately, our neighborhood was particularly deficient in female society, and I languished in vain for some divinity, to whom I might offer up this most uneasy burden of affections. I was at one time seriously enamoured of a lady whom I saw occasionally in my rides reading at the window of a country-seat, and actually serenaded her with my flute; when, to my confusion, I discovered that she was old enough to be my mother. It was a sad damper to my romance; especially as my father heard of it, and made it the subject of one of those household jokes, which he was apt to serve up at every meal-time.

I soon recovered from this check, however, but it was only to relapse into a state of amorous excitement. I passed whole days in the fields, and along the brooks; for there is something in the tender passion that makes us alive to the beauties of Nature. A soft sunshine morning infused a sort of rapture into my breast; I flung open my arms, like the Grecian youth in Ovid, as if I would take in and embrace the balmy atmosphere.* The song of the birds melted me to tenderness. I would lie by the side of some rivulet for hours, and form garlands of the flowers on its banks, and muse on ideal beauties, and sigh from the crowd of undefined emotions that swelled my bosom.

In this state of amorous delirium, I was strolling one morning along a beautiful wild brook which I had discovered in a glen. There was one place where a small waterfall, leaping from among rocks into a natural basin, made a scene such as a poet might have chosen as the haunt of some shy Naiad. It was here I usually retired to banquet on my novels. In visiting the place this morning, I traced distinctly, on the margin of the basin, which was of fine clear sand, the prints of a female foot, of the most slender and delicate proportions. This was sufficient for an imagination like mine. Robinson Crusoe himself, when he discovered the print of a savage foot on the beach of his lonely island, could not have been more suddenly assailed with thick-coming fancies.

I endeavored to track the steps, but they only passed for a few paces along the fine sand, and then were lost among the herbage. I remained gazing in reverie upon this passing trace of loveliness. It evidently was not made by any of my sisters, for they knew nothing of this haunt; besides, the foot was smaller than theirs; it was remarkable for its beautiful delicacy.

My eye accidentally caught two or three half withered wild-flowers, lying on the ground. The unknown nymph had doubtless dropped them from her bosom! Here was a new document of taste and sentiment. I treasured them up as invaluable relics. The place, too, where I found them, was remarkably picturesque, and the most beautiful part of the brook. It was overhung with a fine elm, entwined with grapevines. She who could select such a spot, who could delight in wild brooks, and wild flowers, and silent solitudes, must have fancy, and feeling, and tenderness; and, with all these qualities, she must be beautiful!

But who could be this Unknown, that had thus passed by, as in a morning dream, leaving merely flowers and fairy footsteps to tell of her loveliness! There was a mystery in it that bewildered me. It was so vague and disembodied, like those "airy tongues that syllable men's names" in solitude. Every attempt to solve the mystery was vain. I could hear of no being in the neighborhood to whom this trace could be ascribed. I haunted the spot, and became more and more enamoured. Never, surely, was passion more pure and spiritual, and never lover in more dubious situation. My case could only be compared with that of

---

* Ovid's *Metamorphoses*, Book vii.

the amorous prince, in the fairy tale of *Cinderella*; but he had a glass slipper on which to lavish his tenderness. I, alas! was in love with a footstep!

The imagination is alternately a cheat and a dupe; nay, more, it is the most subtle of cheats, for it cheats itself, and becomes the dupe of its own delusions. It conjures up "airy nothings," gives to them a "local habitation and a name," and then bows to their control as implicitly as if they were realities. Such was now my case. The good Numa could not more thoroughly have persuaded himself that the nymph Egeria hovered about her sacred fountain, and communed with him in spirit, than I had deceived myself into a kind of visionary intercourse with the airy phantom fabricated in my brain. I constructed a rustic seat at the foot of the tree where I had discovered the footsteps. I made a kind of bower there, where I used to pass my mornings, reading poetry and romances. I carved hearts and darts on the tree, and hung it with garlands. My heart was full to overflowing, and wanted some faithful bosom into which it might relieve itself. What is a lover without a confidante? I thought at once of my sister Sophy, my early playmate, the sister of my affections. She was so reasonable, too, and of such correct feelings, always listening to my words as oracular sayings, and admiring my scraps of poetry, as the very inspirations of the Muse. From such a devoted, such a rational being, what secrets could I have?

I accordingly took her, one morning, to my favorite retreat. She looked around, with delighted surprise, upon the rustic seat, the bower, the tree carved with emblems of the tender passion. She turned her eyes upon me to inquire the meaning.

"O Sophy," exclaimed I, clasping both her hands in mine, and looking earnestly in her face, "I am in love!"

She started with surprise.

"Sit down," said I, "and I will tell you all."

She seated herself upon the rustic bench, and I went into a full history of the footstep, with all the associations of idea that had been conjured up by my imagination.

Sophy was enchanted; it was like a fairy tale: she had read of such mysterious visitations in books, and the loves thus conceived were always for beings of superior order, and were always happy. She caught the illusion, in all its force; her cheek glowed; her eye brightened.

"I dare say she's pretty," said Sophy.

"Pretty!" echoed I, "she is beautiful!" I went through all the reasoning by which I had logically proved the fact to my own satisfaction. I dwelt upon the evidences of her taste, her sensibility to the beauties of Nature; her soft meditative habit, that delighted in solitude; "Oh," said I, clasping my hands, "to have such a companion to wander through these scenes; to sit with her by this murmuring stream; to wreathe garlands round her brow; to hear the music of her voice mingling with the whisperings of these groves——"

"Delightful! delightful!" cried Sophy; "what a sweet creature she must be! She is just the friend I want. How I shall dote upon her! Oh, my dear brother! you must not keep her all to yourself. You must let *me* have some share of her!"

I caught her to my bosom: "You shall—you shall!" cried I, "my dear Sophy; we will all live for each other!"

The conversation with Sophy heightened the illusions of mind; and the manner in which she had treated my day-dream, identified it with facts and persons, and gave it still more the stamp of reality. I walked about as one in a trance, heedless of the world around, and lapped in an elysium of the fancy.

In this mood I met, one morning, with Glencoe. He accosted me with his usual smile, and was proceeding with some general observations, but paused and fixed on me an inquiring eye.

"What is the matter with you?" said he; "you seem agitated; has anything in particular happened?"

"Nothing," said I, hesitating; "at least nothing worth communicating to you."

"Nay, my dear young friend," said he, "whatever is of sufficient importance to agitate you, is worthy of being communicated to me."

"Well—but my thoughts are running on what you would think a frivolous subject."

"No subject is frivolous that has the power to awaken strong feelings."

"What think you," said I, hesitating, "what think you of love?"

Glencoe almost started at the question. "Do you call that a frivolous subject?" replied he. "Believe me, there is none fraught with such deep, such vital interest. If you talk, indeed, of the capricious inclination awakened by the mere charm of perishable beauty, I grant it to be idle in the extreme; but that love which springs from the concordant sympathies of virtuous hearts; that love which is awakened by the perception of moral excellence, and fed by meditation on intellectual as well as personal beauty; that is a passion which refines and enobles the human heart. Oh, where is there a sight more nearly approaching to the intercourse of angels, than that of two young beings, free from the sins and follies of the world, mingling pure thoughts, and looks, and feelings, and becoming as it were soul of one soul, and heart of

one heart! How exquisite the silent converse that they hold; the soft
devotion of the eye, that needs no words to make it eloquent! Yes, my
friend, if there be anything in this weary world worthy of heaven, it
is the pure bliss of such a mutual affection!"

The words of my worthy tutor overcame all farther reserve. "Mr.
Glencoe," cried I, blushing still deeper, "I am in love!"

"And is that what you were ashamed to tell me? Oh, never seek to
conceal from your friend so important a secret. If your passion be unworthy, it is for the steady hand of friendship to pluck it forth: if
honorable, none but an enemy would seek to stifle it. On nothing does
the character and happiness so much depend, as on the first affection
of the heart. Were you caught by some fleeting or superficial charm—
a bright eye, a blooming cheek, a soft voice, or a voluptuous form—I
would warn you to beware; I would tell you that beauty is but a
passing gleam of the morning, a perishable flower; that accident may
becloud and blight it, and that at best it must soon pass away. But
were you in love with such a one as I could describe; young in years,
but still younger in feelings; lovely in person, but as a type of the
mind's beauty; soft in voice, in token of gentleness of spirit; blooming
in countenance, like the rosy tints of morning kindling with the
promise of a genial day; an eye beaming with the benignity of a happy
heart; a cheerful temper, alive to all kind impulses, and frankly diffusing its own felicity; a self-poised mind, that needs not lean on others
for support; an elegant taste, that can embellish solitude, and furnish
out its own enjoyments—"

"My dear sir," cried I, for I could contain myself no longer, "you
have described the very person!"

"Why then, my dear young friend," said he, affectionately pressing
my hand, "in God's name, love on!"

For the remainder of the day I was in some such state of dreamy
beatitude as a Turk is said to enjoy when under the influence of
opium. It must be already manifest how prone I was to bewilder myself with picturings of the fancy, so as to confound them with existing
realities. In the present instance, Sophy and Glencoe had contributed
to promote the transient delusion. Sophy, dear girl, had as usual joined
with me in my castle-building, and indulged in the same train of imaginings, while Glencoe, duped by my enthusiasm, firmly believed that I
spoke of a being I had seen and known. By their sympathy with my
feelings, they in a manner became associated with the Unknown in my
mind, and thus linked her with the circle of my intimacy.

In the evening our family party was assembled in the hall, to enjoy
the refreshing breeze. Sophy was playing some favorite Scotch airs on

the piano, while Glencoe, seated apart, with his forehead resting on his hand, was buried in one of those pensive reveries, that made him so interesting to me.

"What a fortunate being I am!" thought I, "blessed with such a sister and such a friend! I have only to find out this amiable Unknown, to wed her, and be happy! What a paradise will be my home, graced with a partner of such exquisite refinement! It will be a perfect fairy bower, buried among sweets and roses. Sophy shall live with us, and be the companion of all our enjoyments. Glencoe, too, shall no more be the solitary being that he now appears. He shall have a home with us. He shall have his study, where, when he pleases, he may shut himself up from the world, and bury himself in his own reflections. His retreat shall be held sacred; no one shall intrude there; no one but myself, who will visit him now and then, in his seclusion, where we will devise grand schemes together for the improvement of mankind. How delightfully our days will pass, in a round of rational pleasures and elegant enjoyments! Sometimes we will have music; sometimes we will read; sometimes we will wander through the flower-garden, when I will smile with complacency on every flower my wife has planted; while in the long winter evenings, the ladies will sit at their work and listen, with hushed attention, to Glencoe and myself, as we discuss the abstruse doctrines of metaphysics."

From this delectable reverie I was startled by my father's slapping me on the shoulder: "What possesses the lad?" cried he; "here have I been speaking to you half a dozen times, without receiving an answer."

"Pardon me, sir," replied I; "I was so completely lost in thought, that I did not hear you."

"Lost in thought! And pray what were you thinking of? Some of your philosophy, I suppose."

"Upon my word," said my sister Charlotte, with an arch laugh, "I suspect Harry's in love again."

"And if I were in love, Charlotte," said I, somewhat nettled, and recollecting Glencoe's enthusiastic eulogy of the passion, "if I were in love, is that a matter of jest and laughter? Is the tenderest and most fervid affection that can animate the human breast to be made a matter of cold-hearted ridicule?"

My sister colored. "Certainly not, brother! nor did I mean to make it so, nor to say anything that should wound your feelings. Had I really suspected that you had formed some genuine attachment, it would have been sacred in my eyes; but—but," said she, smiling, as if at some whimsical recollection, "I thought that you—you might be indulging in another little freak of the imagination."

"I'll wager any money," cried my father, "he has fallen in love again with some old lady at a window!"

"Oh, no!" cried my dear sister Sophy, with the most gracious warmth; "she is young and beautiful."

"From what I understand," said Glencoe, rousing himself, "she must be lovely in mind as in person."

I found my friends were getting me into a fine scrape. I began to perspire at every pore, and felt my ears tingle.

"Well, but," cried my father, "who is she?—what is she? Let us hear something about her."

This was no time to explain so delicate a matter. I caught up my hat and vanished out of the house.

The moment I was in the open air, and alone, my heart upbraided me. Was this respectful treatment to my father—to such a father too—who had always regarded me as the pride of his age—the staff of his hopes? It is true, he was apt sometimes, to laugh at my enthusiastic flights, and did not treat my philosophy with due respect; but when had he ever thwarted a wish of my heart? Was I then to act with reserve toward him, in a matter which might affect the whole current of my future life? "I have done wrong," thought I; "but it is not too late to remedy it. I will hasten back, and open my whole heart to my father!"

I returned accordingly, and was just on the point of entering the house, with my heart full of filial piety, and a contrite speech upon my lips, when I heard a burst of obstreperous laughter from my father, and a loud titter from my two elder sisters.

"A footstep?" shouted he, as soon as he could recover himself; "in love with a footstep! why, this beats the old lady at the window!" And then there was another appalling burst of laughter. Had it been a clap of thunder, it could hardly have astounded me more completely. Sophy, in the simplicity of her heart, had told all, and had set my father's risible propensities in full action.

Never was poor mortal so thoroughly crest-fallen as myself. The whole delusion was at an end. I drew off silently from the house, shrinking smaller and smaller at every fresh peal of laughter; and, wandering about until the family had retired, stole quietly to my bed. Scarce any sleep, however, visited my eyes that night. I lay overwhelmed with mortification, and meditating how I might meet the family in the morning. The idea of ridicule was always intolerable to me: but to endure it on a subject by which my feelings had been so much excited, seemed worse than death. I almost determined, at one time, to get up, saddle my horse, and ride off, I knew not whither.

At length I came to a resolution. Before going down to breakfast I sent for Sophy, and employed her as an ambassador to treat formally in the matter. I insisted that the subject should be buried in oblivion; otherwise I would not show my face at table. It was readily agreed to; for not one of the family would have given me pain for the world. They faithfully kept their promise. Not a word was said of the matter; but there were wry faces, and suppressed titters, that went to my soul; and whenever my father looked me in the face, it was with such a tragic-comical leer—such an attempt to pull down a serious brow upon a whimsical mouth—that I had a thousand times rather he had laughed outright.

For a day or two after the mortifying occurrence mentioned, I kept as much as possible out of the way of the family, and wandered about the fields and woods by myself. I was sadly out of tune: my feelings were all jarred and unstrung. The birds sang from every grove, but I took no pleasure in their melody; and the flowers of the field bloomed unheeded around me. To be crossed in love is bad enough; but then one can fly to poetry for relief, and turn one's woes to account in soul-subduing stanzas. But to have one's whole passion, object and all, annihilated, dispelled, proved to be such stuff as dreams are made of, or, worse than all, to be turned into a proverb and a jest—what consolation is there in such a case?

I avoided the fatal brook where I had seen the footstep. My favorite resort was now the banks of the Hudson, where I sat upon the rocks and mused upon the current that dimpled by, or the waves that laved the shore; or watched the bright mutations of the clouds, and the shifting lights and shadows of the distant mountain. By degrees a returning serenity stole over my feelings; and a sigh now and then, gentle and easy, and unattended by pain, showed that my heart was recovering its susceptibility.

As I was sitting in this musing mood, my eye became gradually fixed upon an object that was borne along by the tide. It proved to be a little pinnace, beautifully modelled, and gayly painted and decorated. It was an unusual sight in this neighborhood, which was rather lonely; indeed it was rare to see any pleasure barks in this part of the river. As it drew nearer, I perceived that there was no one on board: it had apparently drifted from its anchorage. There was not a breath of air; the little bark came floating along on the glassy stream, wheeling about with the eddies. At length it ran aground, almost at the foot of the rock on which I was seated. I descended to the margin of the river, and drawing the bark to shore, admired its light and elegant proportions, and taste with which it was fitted up. The benches were covered with cushions, and its long streamer was of silk. On one of the cushions lay a lady's glove, of delicate size and shape, with beautifully tapered fingers. I instantly seized it and thrust it in my bosom: it seemed a match for the fairy footstep that had so fascinated me.

In a moment all the romance of my bosom was again in a glow. Here was one of the very incidents of fairy tale; a bark sent by some invisible power, some good genius, or benevolent fairy, to waft me to some delectable adventure. I recollected something of an enchanted bark, drawn by white swans, that conveyed a knight down the current of the Rhine, on some enterprise connected with love and beauty. The glove, too, showed that there was a lady fair concerned in the present adventure. It might be a gauntlet of defiance, to dare me to the enterprise.

In the spirit of romance, and the whim of the moment, I sprang on board, hoisted the light sail, and pushed from shore. As if breathed by some presiding power, a light breeze at that moment sprang up, swelled out the sail, and dallied with the silken streamer. For a time I glided along under steep umbrageous banks, or across deep sequestered bays; and then stood out over a wide expansion of the river, toward a high rocky promontory. It was a lovely evening: the sun was setting in a congregation of clouds that threw the whole heavens in a glow, and were reflected in the river. I delighted myself with all kinds of fantastic fancies, as to what enchanted island or mystic bower, or necromantic palace, I was to be conveyed by the fairy bark.

In the revel of my fancy, I had not noticed that the gorgeous congregation of clouds which had so much delighted me, was, in fact, a gathering thunder-gust. I perceived the truth too late. The clouds came hurrying on, darkening as they advanced. The whole face of Nature was suddenly changed, and assumed that baleful and livid tint predictive of a storm. I tried to gain the shore; but, before I could reach it, a blast of wind struck the water, and lashed it at once into foam. The next moment it overtook the boat. Alas! I was nothing of a sailor; and my protecting fairy forsook me in the moment of peril. I endeavored to lower the sail, but in so doing I had to quit the helm; the bark was overturned in an instant, and I was thrown into the water. I endeavored to cling to the wreck, but missed my hold: being a poor swimmer, I soon found myself sinking, but grasped a light oar that was floating by me. It was not sufficient for my support: I again sank beneath the surface; there was a rushing and bubbling sound in my ears, and all sense forsook me.

How long I remained insensible, I know not. I had a confused notion of being moved and tossed about, and of hearing strange beings and strange voices around me; but all was like a hideous dream. When I at length recovered full consciousness and perception, I found myself in bed, in a spacious chamber, furnished with more taste than I had been accustomed to. The bright rays of a morning sun were intercepted by curtains of a delicate rose color, that gave a soft, voluptuous tinge to every object. Not far from my bed, on a classic tripod, was a basket of beautiful exotic flowers, breathing the sweetest fragrance.

"Where am I? How came I here?"

I tasked my mind to catch at some previous event, from which I might trace up the thread of existence to the present moment. By degrees I called to mind the fairy pinnace, my daring embarkation, my adventurous voyage, and my disastrous shipwreck. Beyond that all was chaos. How came I here? What unknown region had I landed upon? The people that inhabited it must be gentle and amiable, and of elegant tastes, for they loved downy beds, fragrant flowers, and rose-colored curtains.

While I lay thus musing, the tones of a harp reached my ear. Presently they were accompanied by a female voice. It came from the room below; but in the profound stillness of my chamber not a modulation was lost. My sisters were all considered good musicians, and sang very tolerably; but I had never heard a voice like this. There was no attempt at difficult execution, or striking effect; but there were exquisite inflexions, and tender turns, which art could not reach. Nothing but feeling and sentiment could produce them. It was soul breathed forth in sound. I was always alive to the influence of music; indeed I was susceptible of voluptuous influences of every kind,—sounds, colors, shapes, and fragrant odors. I was the very slave of sensation.

I lay mute and breathless, and drank in every note of this siren strain. It thrilled through my whole frame, and filled my soul with melody and love. I pictured to myself, with curious logic, the form of the unseen musician. Such melodious sounds and exquisite inflexions could only be produced by organs of the most delicate flexibility. Such organs do not belong to coarse, vulgar forms; they are the harmonious results of fair proportions and admirable symmetry. A being so organized must be lovely.

Again my busy imagination was at work. I called to mind the Arabian story of a prince, borne away during sleep by a good genius, to the distant abode of a princess of ravishing beauty. I do not pretend to say that I believed in having experienced a similar transportation; but it was my inveterate habit to cheat myself with fancies of the kind, and to give the tinge of illusion to surrounding realities.

The witching sound had ceased, but its vibrations still played round

my heart, and filled it with a tumult of soft emotions. At this moment
a self-upbraiding pang shot through my bosom. "Ah, recreant!" a voice
seemed to exclaim, "is this the stability of thine affections? What! hast
thou so soon forgotten the nymph of the fountain? Has one song,
idly piped in thine ear, been sufficient to charm away the cherished
tenderness of a whole summer?"

The wise may smile; but I am in a confiding mood, and must confess
my weakness. I felt a degree of compunction at this sudden infidelity,
yet I could not resist the power of present fascination. My peace of
mind was destroyed by conflicting claims. The nymph of the fountain
came over my memory, with all the associations of fairy footsteps, shady
groves, soft echoes, and wild streamlets; but this new passion was produced by a strain of soul-subduing melody, still lingering in my ear,
aided by a downy bed, fragrant flowers, and rose-colored curtains.
"Unhappy youth!" sighed I to myself, "distracted by such rival passions,
and the empire of thy heart thus violently contested by the sound of a
voice and the print of a footstep!"

I had not remained long in this mood, when I heard the door of the
room gently opened. I turned my head to see what inhabitant of this
enchanted palace should appear; whether page in green, hideous
dwarf, or haggard fairy. It was my own man Scipio. He advanced with
cautious step, and was delighted, as he said, to find me so much myself
again. My first questions were as to where I was, and how I came there?
Scipio told me a long story of his having been fishing in a canoe, at the
time of my hare-brained cruise; of his noticing the gathering squall,
and my impending danger; of his hastening to join me, but arriving just
in time to snatch me from a watery grave; of the great difficulty in restoring me to animation; and of my being subsequently conveyed, in a
state of insensibility, to this mansion.

"But where am I?" was the reiterated demand.

"In the house of Mr. Somerville."

"Somerville—Somerville!" I recollected to have heard that a gentleman
of that name had recently taken up his residence at some distance from
my father's abode, on the opposite side of the Hudson. He was commonly known by the name of "French Somerville," from having passed
part of his early life in France, and from his exhibiting traces of French
taste in his mode of living and the arrangements of his house. In fact,
it was in his pleasure-boat, which had got adrift, that I had made my
fanciful and disastrous cruise. All this was simple, straightforward matter of fact, and threatened to demolish all the cobweb romance I had
been spinning, when fortunately I again heard the tinkling of a harp.
I raised myself in bed, and listened.

"Scipio," said I, with some little hesitation, "I heard some one singing just now. Who was it?"

"Oh, that was Miss Julia."

"Julia! Julia! Delightful! what a name! And, Scipio—is she—is she pretty?"

Scipio grinned from ear to ear. "Except Miss Sophy, she was the most beautiful young lady he had ever seen."

I should observe, that my sister Sophia was considered by all the servants a paragon of perfection.

Scipio now offered to remove the basket of flowers; he was afraid their odor might be too powerful; but Miss Julia had given them that morning to be placed in my room.

These flowers, then, had been gathered by the fairy fingers of my unseen beauty: that sweet breath, which had filled my ear with melody, had passed over them. I made Scipio hand them to me, culled several of the most delicate, and laid them on my bosom.

Mr. Somerville paid me a visit not long afterward. He was an interesting study for me, for he was the father of my unseen beauty, and probably resembled her. I scanned him closely. He was a tall and elegant man, with an open, affable manner, and an erect and graceful carriage. His eyes were bluish-gray, and, though not dark, yet at times were sparkling and expressive. His hair was dressed and powdered, and being lightly combed up from his forehead, added to the loftiness of his aspect. He was fluent in discourse, but his conversation had the quiet tone of polished society, without any of those bold flights of thought, and picturings of fancy, which I so much admired.

My imagination was a little puzzled at first, to make out of this assemblage of personal and mental qualities, a picture that should harmonize with my previous idea of the fair unseen. By dint, however, of selecting what it liked, and rejecting what it did not like, and giving a touch here and a touch there, it soon finished out a satisfactory portrait.

"Julia must be tall," thought I, "and of exquisite grace and dignity. She is not quite so courtly as her father, for she has been brought up in the retirement of the country. Neither is she of such vivacious deportment; for the tones of her voice are soft and plaintive, and she loves pathetic music. She is rather pensive—yet not too pensive; just what is called interesting. Her eyes are like her father's, except that they are of a purer blue, and more tender and languishing. She has light hair—not exactly flaxen, for I do not like flaxen hair, but between that and auburn. In a word, she is a tall, elegant, imposing, languishing, blue-eyed, romantic looking beauty." And having thus finished her picture, I felt ten times more in love with her than ever.

I felt so much recovered, that I would at once have left my room, but Mr. Somerville objected to it. He had sent early word to my family of my safety; and my father arrived in the course of the morning. He was shocked at learning the risk I had run, but rejoiced to find me so much restored, and was warm in his thanks to Mr. Somerville for his kindness. The other only required, in return, that I might remain two or three days as his guest, to give time for my recovery, and for our forming a closer acquaintance, a request which my father readily granted. Scipio accordingly accompanied my father home, and returned with a supply of clothes, and with affectionate letters from my mother and sisters.

The next morning, aided by Scipio, I made my toilet with rather more care than usual, and descended the stairs with some trepidation, eager to see the original of the portrait which had been so completely pictured in my imagination.

On entering the parlor, I found it deserted. Like the rest of the house, it was furnished in a foreign style. The curtains were of French silk, there were Grecian couches, marble tables, pier-glasses, and chandeliers. What chiefly attracted my eye, were documents of female taste that I saw around me,—a piano with an ample stock of Italian music; a book of poetry lying on the sofa; a vase of fresh flowers on a table, and a portfolio open with a skilful and half finished sketch of them. In the window was a Canary bird, in a gilt cage; and near by, the harp that had been in Julia's arms. Happy harp! But where was the being that reigned in this little empire of delicacies?—that breathed poetry and song, and dwelt among birds and flowers, and rose-colored curtains?

Suddenly I heard the hall-door fly open, the quick pattering of light steps, a wild, capricious strain of music, and the shrill barking of a dog. A light frolic nymph of fifteen came tripping into the room, playing on a flageolet, with a little spaniel ramping after her. Her gypsy hat had fallen back upon her shoulders; a profusion of glossy brown hair was blown in rich ringlets about her face, which beamed through them with the brightness of smiles and dimples.

At sight of me she stopped short, in the most beautiful confusion, stammered out a word or two about looking for her father, glided out of the door, and I heard her bounding up the staircase, like a frightened fawn, with the little dog barking after her.

When Miss Somerville returned to the parlor, she was quite a different being. She entered, stealing along by her mother's side, with noiseless step and sweet timidity; her hair was prettily adjusted, and a soft blush mantled on her damask cheek. Mr. Somerville accompanied the ladies, and introduced me regularly to them. There were many kind inquiries, and much sympathy expressed on the subject of my nautical accident, and some remarks upon the wild scenery of the neighborhood, with which the ladies seemed perfectly acquainted.

"You must know," said Mr. Somerville, "that we are great navigators, and delight in exploring every nook and corner of the river. My daughter, too, is a great hunter of the picturesque, and transfers every rock and glen to her portfolio. By the way, my dear, show Mr. Mountjoy that pretty scene you have lately sketched." Julia complied, blushing, and drew from her portfolio a colored sketch. I almost started at the sight. It was my favorite brook. A sudden thought darted across my mind. I glanced down my eye, and beheld the divinest little foot in the world. Oh, blissful conviction! The struggle of my affections was at an end. The voice and the footstep were no longer at variance. Julia Somerville was the nymph of the fountain!

What conversation passed during breakfast I do not recollect, and hardly was conscious of at the time, for my thoughts were in complete confusion. I wished to gaze on Miss Somerville, but did not dare. Once, indeed, I ventured a glance. She was at that moment darting a similar one from under a covert of ringlets. Our eyes seemed shocked by the rencontre, and fell; hers through the natural modesty of her sex, mine through a bashfulness produced by the previous workings of my imagination. That glance, however, went like a sunbeam to my heart.

A convenient mirror favored my diffidence, and gave me the reflection of Miss Somerville's form. It is true it only presented the back of her head, but she had the merit of an ancient statue; contemplate her from any point of view, she was beautiful. And yet she was totally different from everything I had before conceived of beauty. She was not the serene, meditative maid that I had pictured the nymph of the fountain; nor the tall, soft, languishing, blue-eyed, dignified being that I had fancied the minstrel of the harp. There was nothing of dignity about her; she was girlish in her appearance, and scarcely of the middle size; but then there was the tenderness of budding youth; the sweetness of the half-blown rose, when not a tint or perfume has been withered or exhaled; there were smiles and dimples, and all the soft witcheries of ever varying expression. I wondered that I could ever have admired any other style of beauty.

After breakfast Mr. Somerville departed to attend to the concerns of his estate, and gave me in charge of the ladies. Mrs. Somerville also was called away by household cares, and I was left alone with Julia! Here then was the situation which of all others I had most coveted. I was in the presence of the lovely being that had so long been the desire of my heart. We were alone; propitious opportunity for a lover! Did I seize upon it? Did I break out in one of my accustomed rhapsodies? No such thing! Never was being more awkwardly embarrassed.

"What can be the cause of this?" thought I. "Surely I cannot stand in awe of this young girl. I am of course her superior in intellect, and am never embarrassed in company with my tutor, notwithstanding all his wisdom."

It was passing strange. I felt that if she were an old woman, I should be quite at my ease; if she were even an ugly woman, I should make out very well; it was her beauty that overpowered me. How little do lovely women know what awful beings they are, in the eyes of inexperienced youth! Young men brought up in the fashionable circles of our cities will smile at all this. Accustomed to mingle incessantly in female society, and to have the romance of the heart deadened by a thousand frivolous flirtations, women are nothing but women in their eyes; but to a susceptible youth like myself, brought up in the country, they are perfect divinities.

Miss Somerville was at first a little embarrassed herself; but, somehow or other, women have a natural adroitness in recovering their self-possession; they are more alert in their minds and graceful in their manners. Besides, I was but an ordinary personage in Miss Somerville's eyes; she was not under the influence of such a singular course of imaginings as had surrounded her, in my eyes, with the illusions of romance. Perhaps, too, she saw the confusion in the opposite camp, and gained courage from the discovery. At any rate, she was the first to take the field.

Her conversation, however, was only on commonplace topics, and in an easy, well-bred style. I endeavored to respond in the same manner; but I was strangely incompetent to the task. My ideas were frozen up; even words seemed to fail me. I was excessively vexed at myself, for I wished to be uncommonly elegant. I tried two or three times to turn a pretty thought, or to utter a fine sentiment; but it would come forth so trite, so forced, so mawkish, that I was ashamed of it. My very voice sounded discordantly, though I sought to modulate it into the softest tones. "The truth is," thought I to myself, "I cannot bring my mind down to the small talk necessary for young girls; it is too masculine and robust for the mincing measure of parlor gossip. I am a philosopher; and that accounts for it."

The entrance of Mrs. Somerville at length gave me relief. I at once breathed freely, and felt a vast deal of confidence come over me. "This is strange," thought I, "that the appearance of another woman should revive my courage; that I should be a better match for two women than one. However, since it is so, I will take advantage of the circumstance, and let this young lady see that I am not so great a simpleton as she probably thinks me."

I accordingly took up the book of poetry which lay upon the sofa. It was Milton's *Paradise Lost*. Nothing could have been more fortunate; it afforded a fine scope for my favorite vein of grandiloquence. I went largely into a discussion of its merits, or rather an enthusiastic eulogy of them. My observations were addressed to Mrs. Somerville, for I found I could talk to her with more ease than to her daughter. She appeared perfectly alive to the beauties of the poet, and disposed to meet me in the discussion; but it was not my object to hear her talk; it was to talk myself. I anticipated all she had to say, overpowered her with the copiousness of my ideas, and supported and illustrated them by long citations from the author.

While thus holding forth, I cast a side-glance to see how Miss Somerville was affected. She had some embroidery stretched on a frame before her, but had paused in her labor, and was looking down, as if lost in mute attention. I felt a glow of self-satisfaction; but I recollected, at the same time, with a kind of pique, the advantage she had enjoyed over me in our *tête-à-tête*. I determined to push my triumph, and accordingly kept on with redoubled ardor, until I had fairly exhausted my subject, or rather my thoughts.

I had scarce come to a full stop, when Miss Somerville raised her eyes from the work on which they had been fixed, and turning to her mother, observed: "I have been considering, mamma, whether to work these flowers plain, or in colors."

Had an ice-bolt been shot to my heart, it could not have chilled me more effectually. "What a fool," thought I, "have I been making myself,—squandering away fine thoughts and fine language upon a light mind and an ignorant ear! This girl knows nothing of poetry. She has no soul, I fear, for its beauties. Can any one have real sensibility of heart, and not be alive to poetry! However, she is young; this part of her education has been neglected; there is time enough to remedy it. I will be her preceptor. I will kindle in her mind the sacred flame, and lead her through the fairy land of song. But, after all, it is rather unfortunate that I should have fallen in love with a woman who knows nothing of poetry."

I passed a day not altogether satisfactory. I was a little disappointed that Miss Somerville did not show more poetical feeling. "I am afraid, after all," said I to myself, "she is light and girlish, and more fitted to pluck wild flowers, play on the flageolet, and romp with little dogs, than to converse with a man of my turn."

I believe however, to tell the truth, I was more out of humor with myself. I thought I had made the worst first appearance that ever hero made, either in novel or fairy tale. I was out of all patience when I called to mind my awkward attempts at ease and elegance, in the *tête-à-tête*. And then my intolerable long lecture about poetry, to catch the applause of a heedless auditor! But there I was not to blame. I had certainly been eloquent; it was her fault that the eloquence was wasted. To meditate upon the embroidery of a flower, when I was expatiating on the beauties of Milton! She might at least have admired the poetry, if she did not relish the manner in which it was delivered; though that was not despicable, for I had recited passages in my best style, which my mother and sisters had always considered equal to a play. "Oh, it is evident," thought I, "Miss Somerville has very little soul!"

Such were my fancies and cogitations during the day, the greater part of which was spent in my chamber; for I was still languid. My evening was passed in the drawing-room, where I overlooked Miss Somerville's portfolio of sketches. They were executed with great taste, and showed a nice observation of the peculiarities of Nature. They were all her own, and free from those cunning tints and touches of the drawing-master, by which young ladies' drawings, like their heads, are dressed up for company. There was no garish and vulgar trick of colors, either; all was executed with singular truth and simplicity.

"And yet," thought I, "this little being, who has so pure an eye to take in, as in a limpid brook, all the graceful forms and magic tints of Nature, has no soul for poetry!"

Mr. Somerville, toward the latter part of the evening, observing my eye to wander occasionally to the harp, interpreted and met my wishes with his accustomed civility.

"Julia, my dear," said he, "Mr. Mountjoy would like to hear a little music from your harp; let us hear, too, the sound of your voice."

Julia immediately complied, without any of that hesitation and difficulty by which young ladies are apt to make the company pay dear for bad music. She sang a sprightly strain, in a brilliant style, that came thrilling playfully over the ear; and the bright eye and dimpling smile showed that her little heart danced with the song. Her pet Canary bird, who hung close by, was wakened by the music, and burst forth into an emulating strain. Julia smiled with a pretty air of defiance, and played louder.

After some time the music changed, and ran into a plaintive strain, in a minor key. Then it was that all the former witchery of her voice came over me; then it was that she seemed to sing from the heart and to the heart. Her fingers moved about the chords as if they scarcely touched them. Her whole manner and appearance changed; her eyes beamed with the softest expression; her countenance, her frame,—all seemed subdued into tenderness. She rose from the harp, leaving it still vibrating with sweet sounds, and moved toward her father to bid him good-night.

His eyes had been fixed on her intently during her performance. As she came before him, he parted her shining ringlets with both his hands, and looked down with the fondness of a father on her innocent face. The music seemed still lingering in its lineaments, and the action of her father brought a moist gleam in her eye. He kissed her fair forehead, after the French mode of parental caressing: "Good-night, and God bless you," said he, "my good little girl!"

Julia tripped away with a tear in her eye, a dimple in her cheek, and a light heart in her bosom. I thought it the prettiest picture of paternal and filial affection I had ever seen.

When I retired to bed a new train of thoughts crowded into my brain. "After all," said I to myself, "it is clear this girl has a soul, though she was not moved by my eloquence. She has all the outward signs and evidences of poetic feeling. She paints well, and has an eye for Nature. She is a fine musician, and enters into the very soul of song. What a pity that she knows nothing of poetry! But we will see what is to be done. I am irretrievably in love with her; what then am I to do? Come down to the level of her mind, or endeavor to raise her to some kind of intellectual equality with myself? That is the most generous course. She will look up to me as a benefactor. I shall become associated in her mind with the lofty thoughts and harmonious graces of poetry. She is apparently docile; besides the difference of our ages will give me an ascendency over her. She cannot be above sixteen years of age, and I am full turned of twenty." So, having built this most delectable of air-castles, I fell asleep.

The next morning I was quite a different being. I no longer felt fearful of stealing a glance at Julia; on the contrary, I contemplated her steadily, with the benignant eye of a benefactor. Shortly after breakfast I found myself alone with her, as I had on the preceding morning; but I felt nothing of the awkwardness of our previous tête-à-tête. I was elevated by the consciousness of my intellectual superiority, and should almost have felt a sentiment of pity for the ignorance of the lovely little being, if I had not felt also the assurance that I should be able to dispel it. "But it is time," thought I, "to open school."

Julia was occupied in arranging some music on her piano. I looked over two or three songs; they were Moore's Irish Melodies.

"These are pretty things," said I, flirting the leaves over lightly, and giving a slight shrug, by way of qualifying the opinion.

"Oh, I love them of all things!" said Julia, "they're so touching!"

"Then you like them for the poetry?" said I, with an encouraging smile.

"Oh, yes; she thought them charmingly written."

Now was my time. "Poetry," said I, assuming a didactic attitude and air,—"poetry is one of the most pleasing studies to occupy a youthful mind. It renders us susceptible of the gentle impulses of humanity, and cherishes a delicate perception of all that is virtuous and elevated in morals, and graceful and beautiful in physics. It—"

I was going on in a style that would have graced a professor of rhetoric, when I saw a light smile playing about Miss Somerville's mouth, and that she began to turn over the leaves of a music book. I recollected her inattention to my discourse of the preceding morning. "There is no fixing her light mind," thought I, "by abstract theory; we will proceed practically." As it happened, the identical volume of Milton's *Paradise Lost* was lying at hand.

"Let me recommend to you, my young friend," said I, in one of those tones of persuasive admonition, which I had so often loved in Glencoe, —"let me recommend to you this admirable poem: you will find in it sources of intellectual enjoyment far superior to those songs which have delighted you." Julia looked at the book, and then at me, with a whimsically dubious air. "Milton's *Paradise Lost?*" said she; "oh, I know the greater part of that by heart."

I had not expected to find my pupil so far advanced; however, the *Paradise Lost* is a kind of school-book, and its finest passages are given to young ladies as tasks.

"I find," said I to myself, "I must not treat her as so complete a novice; her inattention, yesterday, could not have proceeded from absolute ignorance, but merely from a want of poetic feeling. I'll try her again."

I now determined to dazzle her with my own erudition, and launched into a harangue that would have done honor to an institute. Pope, Spenser, Chaucer, and the old dramatic writers were all dipped into, with the excursive flight of a swallow. I did not confine myself to English poets, but gave a glance at the French and Italian schools: I passed over Ariosto in full wing, but paused on Tasso's *Jerusalem Delivered.* I dwelt on the character of Clorinda: "There's a character," said I, "that you will find well worthy a woman's study. It shows to what exalted heights of heroism the sex can rise; how gloriously they may share even in the stern concerns of men."

"For my part," said Julia, gently taking advantage of a pause,—"for my part, I prefer the character of Sophronia."

I was thunderstruck. She then had read Tasso! This girl that I had been treating as an ignoramus in poetry! She proceeded, with a slight glow of the cheek, summoned up perhaps by a casual glow of feeling:—

"I do not admire those masculine heroines," said she, "who aim at the bold qualities of the opposite sex. Now Sophronia only exhibits the real qualities of a woman, wrought up to their highest excitement. She is modest, gentle, and retiring, as it becomes a woman to be; but she has all the strength of affection proper to a woman. She cannot fight for her people, as Clorinda does, but she can offer herself up, and die, to serve them. You may admire Clorinda, but you surely would be more apt to love Sophronia; at least," added she, suddenly appearing to recollect herself, and blushing at having launched into such a discussion,—"at least, that is what papa observed, when we read the poem together."

"Indeed," said I, dryly, for I felt disconcerted and nettled at being unexpectedly lectured by my pupil,—"indeed, I do not exactly recollect the passage."

"Oh," said Julia, "I can repeat it to you"; and she immediately gave it in Italian.

Heavens and earth!—here was a situation! I knew no more of Italian than I did of the language of Psalmanazar. What a dilemma for a would-be-wise man to be placed in! I saw Julia waited for my opinion.

"In fact," said I, hesitating, "I—I do not exactly understand Italian."

"Oh," said Julia, with the utmost *naïveté*, "I have no doubt it is very beautiful in the translation."

I was glad to break up school and get back to my chamber, full of the mortification which a wise man in love experiences on finding his mistress wiser than himself. "Translation! translation!" muttered I to myself, as I jerked the door shut behind me. "I am surprised my father has never had me instructed in the modern languages. They are all-important. What is the use of Latin and Greek? No one speaks them; but here, the moment I make my appearance in the world, a little girl slaps Italian in my face. However, thank Heaven, a language is easily learned. The moment I return home, I'll set about studying Italian; and to prevent future surprise, I will study Spanish and German at the same time; and if any young lady attempts to quote Italian upon me again, I'll bury her under a heap of High Dutch poetry!"

I felt now like some mighty chieftain, who has carried the war into a weak country, with full confidence of success, and been repulsed and obliged to draw off his forces from before some inconsiderable fortress.

"However," thought I, "I have as yet brought only my light artillery into action; we shall see what is to be done with my heavy ordnance. Julia is evidently well versed in poetry; but it is natural she should be so; it is allied to painting and music, and is congenial to the light graces of the female character. We will try her on graver themes."

I felt all my pride awakened; it even for a time swelled higher than my love. I was determined completely to establish my mental superiority, and subdue the intellect of this little being: it would then be time to sway the sceptre of gentle empire, and win the affections of her heart.

Accordingly, at dinner I again took the field *en potence*. I now addressed myself to Mr. Somerville, for I was about to enter upon topics in which a young girl like her could not be well versed. I led, or rather forced, the conversation into a vein of historical erudition, discussing several of the most prominent facts of ancient history and accompanying them with sound, indisputable apothegms.

Mr. Somerville listened to me with the air of a man receiving information. I was encouraged, and went on gloriously from theme to theme of school declamation. I sat with Marius on the ruins of Carthage; I defended the bridge with Horatius Cocles; thrust my hand into the flame with Martius Scævola, and plunged with Curtius into the yawning gulf; I fought side by side with Leonidas, at the straits of Thermopylæ; and was going full drive into the battle of Platæa, when my memory, which is the worst in the world, failed me, just as I wanted the name of the Lacedæmonian commander.

"Julia, my dear," said Mr. Somerville, "perhaps you may recollect the name of which Mr. Mountjoy is in quest?"

Julia colored slightly: "I believe," said she, in a low voice,— "I believe it was Pausanias."

This unexpected sally, instead of reinforcing me, threw my whole scheme of battle into confusion, and the Athenians remained unmolested in the field.

I am half inclined, since, to think Mr. Somerville meant this as a sly hit at my schoolboy pedantry; but he was too well-bred not to seek to relieve me from my mortification. "Oh!" said he, "Julia is our family book of reference for names, dates, and distances, and has an excellent memory for history and geography."

I now became desperate; as a last resource, I turned to metaphysics. "If she is a philosopher in petticoats," thought I, "it is all over with me."

Here, however, I had the field to myself. I gave chapter and verse of my tutor's lectures, heightened by all his poetical illustrations; I even went farther than he had ever ventured, and plunged into such depths of metaphysics, that I was in danger of sticking in the mire at the bottom. Fortunately, I had auditors who apparently could not detect my flounderings. Neither Mr. Somerville nor his daughter offered the least interruption.

When the ladies had retired, Mr. Somerville sat some time with me; and as I was no longer anxious to astonish, I permitted myself to listen, and found that he was really agreeable. He was quite communicative, and from his conversation I was enabled to form a juster idea of his daughter's character, and the mode in which she had been brought up. Mr. Somerville had mingled much with the world, and with what is termed fashionable society. He had experienced its cold elegancies, and gay insincerities; its dissipation of the spirits, and squanderings of the heart. Like many men of the world, though he had wandered too far from Nature ever to return to it, yet he had the good taste and good feeling to look back fondly to its simple delights, and to determine that his child, if possible, should never leave them. He had superintended her education with scrupulous care, storing her mind with the graces of polite literature, and with such knowledge as would enable it to furnish its own amusement and occupation, and giving her all the accomplishments that sweeten and enliven the circle of domestic life. He had been particularly sedulous to exclude fashionable affectations; all false sentiment, false sensibility, and false romance. "Whatever advantages she may possess," said he, "she is quite unconscious of them. She is a capricious little being, in everything but her affections; she is, however, free from art; simple, ingenuous, innocent, amiable, and, I thank God! happy."

Such was the eulogy of a fond father, delivered with a tenderness that touched me. I could not help making a casual inquiry whether, among the graces of polite literature, he had included a slight tincture of metaphysics. He smiled, and told me he had not.

On the whole, when, as usual, that night I summed up the day's observations on my pillow, I was not altogether dissatisfied. "Miss Somerville," said I, "loves poetry, and I like her the better for it. She has the advantage of me in Italian: agreed; what is it to know a variety of languages, but merely to have a variety of sounds to express the same idea? Original thought is the ore of the mind; language is but the accidental stamp and coinage, by which it is put into circulation. If I can furnish an original idea, what care I how many languages she can translate it into? She may be able, also, to quote names, and dates, and latitudes, better than I; but that is a mere effort of the memory. I admit she is more accurate in history and geography than I; but then she knows nothing of metaphysics."

I had now sufficiently recovered to return home; yet I could not think of leaving Mr. Somerville's without having a little farther conversation with him on the subject of his daughter's education.

"This Mr. Somerville," thought I, "is a very accomplished, elegant man; he has seen a good deal of the world, and, upon the whole, has profited by what he has seen. He is not without information, and, as far as he thinks, appears to think correctly; but after all, he is rather superficial, and does not think profoundly. He seems to take no delight in those metaphysical abstractions that are the proper aliment of masculine minds." I called to mind various occasions in which I had indulged largely in metaphysical discussions, but could recollect no instance where I had been able to draw him out. He had listened, it is true, with attention, and smiled as if in acquiescence, but had always appeared to avoid reply. Besides, I had made several sad blunders in the glow of eloquent declamation; but he had never interrupted me, to notice and correct them, as he would have done had he been versed in the theme.

"Now it is really a great city," resumed I, "that he should have the entire management of Miss Somerville's education. What a vast advantage it would be, if she could be put for a little time under the superintendence of Glencoe. He would throw some deeper shades of thought into her mind, which at present is all sunshine; not but that Mr. Somerville has done very well, as far as he has gone; but then he has merely prepared the soil for the strong plants of useful knowledge. She is well versed in the leading facts of history, and the general course of belles-lettres," said I; "a little more philosophy would do wonders."

I accordingly took occasion to ask Mr. Somerville for a few moments' conversation in his study, the morning I was to depart. When we were alone, I opened the matter fully to him. I commenced with the warmest eulogium of Glencoe's powers of mind, and vast acquirements, and ascribed to him all my proficiency in the higher branches of knowledge. I begged, therefore, to recommend him as a friend calculated to direct the studies of Miss Somerville; to lead her mind, by degrees, to the contemplation of abstract principles, and to produce habits of philosophical analysis; "which," added I, gently smiling, "are not often cultivated by young ladies." I ventured to hint, in addition, that he would find Mr. Glencoe a most valuable and interesting acquaintance for himself; one who would stimulate and evolve the powers of his mind; and who might open to him tracts of inquiry and speculation to which perhaps he had hitherto been a stranger.

Mr. Somerville listened with grave attention. When I had finished, he thanked me in the politest manner for the interest I took in the welfare of his daughter and himself. He observed that, as regarded himself, he was afraid he was too old to benefit by the instructions of Mr. Glencoe, and that as to his daughter, he was afraid her mind was but little fitted for the study of metaphysics. "I do not wish," continued he, "to strain her intellects with subjects they cannot grasp, but to make her familiarly acquainted with those that are within the limits of her capacity. I do not pretend to prescribe the boundaries of female genius, and am far from indulging the vulgar opinion that women are unfitted by Nature for the highest intellectual pursuits. I speak only with reference to my daughter's taste and talents. She will never make a learned woman; nor in truth do I desire it; for such is the jealousy of our sex, as to mental as well as physical ascendency, that a learned woman is not always the happiest. I do not wish my daughter to excite envy, nor to battle with the prejudices of the world; but to glide peaceably through life, on the good-will and kind opinion of her friends. She has ample employment for her little head in the course I have marked out for her; and is busy at present with some branches of natural history, calculated to awaken her perceptions to the beauties and wonders of Nature, and to the inexhaustible volume of wisdom constantly spread open before her eyes. I consider that woman most likely to make an agreeable companion, who can draw topics of pleasing remark from every natural object; and most likely to be cheerful and contented, who is continually sensible of the order, the harmony, and the invariable beneficence that reign throughout the beautiful world we inhabit.

"But," added he, smiling, "I am betraying myself into a lecture, instead of merely giving a reply to your kind offer. Permit me to take the liberty, in return, of inquiring a little about your own pursuits. You speak of having finished your education; but of course you have a line of private study and mental occupation marked out; for you must know the importance, both in point of interest and happiness, of keeping the mind employed. May I ask what system you observe in your intellectual exercises?"

"Oh, as to system," I observed, "I could never bring myself into anything of the kind. I thought it best to let my genius take its own course, as it always acted the most vigorously when stimulated by inclination."

Mr. Somerville shook his head. "This same genius," said he, "is a wild quality, that runs away with our most promising young men. It has become so much the fashion, too, to give it the reins, that it is now thought an animal of too noble and generous a nature to be brought to the harness. But it is all a mistake. Nature never designed these high endowments to run riot through society, and throw the whole system into confusion. No, my dear sir; genius, unless it acts upon system, is very apt to be a useless quality to society; sometimes an injurious, and certainly a very uncomfortable one, to its possessor. I have had many opportunities of seeing the progress through life of young men who were accounted geniuses, and have found it too often end in early exhaustion and bitter disappointment; and have as often noticed that these effects might be traced to a total want of system. There were no habits of business, of steady purpose, and regular application superinduced upon the mind; everything was left to chance and impulse, and native luxuriance, and everything of course ran to waste and wild entanglement. Excuse me if I am tedious on this point, for I feel solicitous to impress it upon you, being an error extremely prevalent in our country, and one into which too many of our youth have fallen. I am happy, however, to observe the zeal which still appears to actuate you for the acquisition of knowledge, and augur every good from the elevated bent of your ambition. May I ask what has been your course of study for the last six months?"

Never was question more unluckily timed. For the last six months I had been absolutely buried in novels and romances.

·Mr. Somerville perceived that the question was embarrassing, and with his invariable good breeding, immediately resumed the conversation, without waiting for a reply. He took care, however, to turn it in such a way as to draw from me an account of the whole manner in which I had been educated, and the various currents of reading into which my mind had run. He then went on to discuss briefly, but impressively, the different branches of knowledge most important to a young man in my situation; and to my surprise I found him a complete master of those studies on which I had supposed him ignorant, and on which I had been descanting confidently.

He complimented me, however, very graciously, upon the progress I had made, but advised me for the present to turn my attention to the physical rather than the moral sciences. "These studies," said he, "store a man's mind with valuable facts, and at the same time repress self-confidence, by letting him know how boundless are the realms of knowledge, and how little we can possibly know. Whereas metaphysical studies, though of an ingenious order of intellectual employment, are apt to bewilder some minds with vague speculations. They never know how far they have advanced, or what may be the correctness of their favorite theory. They render many of our young men verbose and declamatory, and prone to mistake the aberrations of their fancy for the inspirations of divine philosophy."

I could not but interrupt him, to assent to the truth of these remarks, and to say that it had been my lot, in the course of my limited experience, to encounter young men of the kind, who had overwhelmed me by their verbosity.

Mr. Somerville smiled. "I trust," said he kindly, "that you will guard against these errors. Avoid the eagerness with which a young man is apt to hurry into conversation, and to utter the crude and ill-digested notions which he has picked up in his recent studies. Be assured that extensive and accurate knowledge is the slow acquisition of a studious lifetime; that a young man, however pregnant his wit and prompt his talent, can have mastered but the rudiments of learning, and, in a manner attained the implements of study. Whatever may have been your past assiduity, you must be sensible that as yet you have but reached the threshold of true knowledge; but at the same time, you have the advantage that you are still very young, and have ample time to learn."

Here our conference ended. I walked out of the study, a very different being from what I was on entering it. I had gone in with the air of a professor about to deliver a lecture; I came out like a student, who had failed in his examination, and been degraded in his class.

· "Very young," and "on the threshold of knowledge!" This was extremely flattering to one who had considered himself an accomplished scholar and profound philosopher!

"It is singular," thought I; "there seems to have been a spell upon my faculties ever since I have been in this house. I certainly have not been able to do myself justice. Whenever I have undertaken to advise, I have had the tables turned upon me. It must be that I am strange and diffident among people I am not accustomed to. I wish they could hear me talk at home!"

"After all," added I, on farther reflection,—"after all, there is a great deal of force in what Mr. Somerville has said. Somehow or other, these men of the world do now and then hit upon remarks that would do credit to a philosopher. Some of his general observations came so home, that I almost thought they were meant for myself. His advice about adopting a system of study, is very judicious. I will immediately put it in practice. My mind shall operate henceforward with the regularity of clock-work."

How far I succeeded in adopting this plan, how I fared in the farther pursuit of knowledge, and how I succeeded in my suit to Julia Somerville, may afford matter for a farther communication to the public, if this simple record of my early life is fortunate enough to excite any curiosity.

From *Wolfert's Roost*

THE WIDOW'S ORDEAL;

or, a Judicial Trial by Combat

THE world is daily growing older and wiser. Its institutions vary with its years, and mark its growing wisdom; and none more so than its modes of investigating truth, and ascertaining guilt or innocence. In its nonage, when man was yet a fallible being, and doubted the accuracy of his own intellect, appeals were made to Heaven in dark and doubtful cases of atrocious accusation.

The accused was required to plunge his hand in boiling oil, or to walk across red-hot plough-shares, or to maintain his innocence in armed fight and listed field, in person or by champion. If he passed these ordeals unscathed, he stood acquitted, and the result was regarded as a verdict from on high.

It is somewhat remarkable that, in the gallant age of chivalry, the gentler sex should have been most frequently the subjects of these rude trials and perilous ordeals; and that, too, when assailed in their most delicate and vulnerable part,—their honor.

In the present very old and enlightened age of the world, when the human intellect is perfectly competent to the management of its own concerns, and needs no special interposition of Heaven in its affairs, the trial by jury has superseded these superhuman ordeals; and the unanimity of twelve discordant minds is necessary to constitute a verdict. Such a unanimity would, at first sight, appear also to require a miracle from Heaven; but it is produced by a simple device of human ingenuity. The twelve jurors are locked up in their box, there to fast until abstinence shall have so clarified their intellects that the whole jarring panel can discern the truth, and concur in a unanimous decision. One point is certain, that truth is one and is immutable; until the jurors all agree, they cannot all be right.

It is not our intention, however, to discuss this great judicial point, or to question the avowed superiority of the mode of investigating truth adopted in this antiquated and very sagacious era. It is our object merely to exhibit to the curious reader one of the most memorable cases of judicial combat we find in the annals of Spain. It occurred at the bright commencement of the reign, and in the youthful, and, as yet, glorious days of Roderick the Goth; who subsequently tarnished his fame at home by his misdeeds, and, finally lost his kingdom and his life on the banks of the Guadalete, in that disastrous battle which gave up Spain a conquest to the Moors. The following is the story:

There was once upon a time a certain Duke of Lorraine, who was acknowledged throughout his domains to be one of the wisest princes that ever lived. In fact there was no one measure adopted by him that did not astonish his privy councillors and gentlemen in attendance; and he said such witty things, and made such sensible speeches, that the jaws of his high chamberlain were well-nigh dislocated from laughing with delight at one, and gaping with wonder at the other.

This very witty and exceedingly wise potentate lived for half a century in single blessedness; at length his courtiers began to think it a great pity so wise and wealthy a prince should not have a child after his own likeness, to inherit his talents and domains; so they urged him most respectfully to marry, for the good of his estate and the welfare of his subjects.

He turned their advice over in his mind some four or five years, and then sent forth emissaries to summon to his court all the beautiful maidens in the land, who were ambitious of sharing a ducal crown. The court was soon crowded with beauties of all styles and complexions, from among whom he chose one in the earliest budding of her charms, and acknowledged by all the gentlemen to be unparalleled for grace and loveliness. The courtiers extolled the duke to the skies for making such a choice, and considered it another proof of his great wisdom. "The duke," said they, "is waxing a little too old; the damsel, on the other hand, is a little too young; if one is lacking in years, the other has a superabundance; thus a want on one side is balanced by an excess on the other, and the result is a well-assorted marriage."

The duke, as is often the case with wise men who marry rather late, and take damsels rather youthful to their bosoms, became dotingly fond of his wife, and very properly indulged her in all things. He was, consequently, cried up by his subjects in general, and by the ladies in particular, as a pattern for husbands; and, in the end, from the wonderful docility with which he submitted to be reined and checked, acquired the amiable and enviable appellation of Duke Philibert the wife-ridden.

There was only one thing that disturbed the conjugal felicity of this paragon of husbands: though a considerable time elapsed after his marriage, there was still no prospect of an heir. The good duke left no means untried to propitiate Heaven. He made vows and pilgrimages, he fasted and he prayed, but all to no purpose. The courtiers were all astonished at the circumstance. They could not account for it. While the meanest peasant in the country had sturdy brats by dozens, without putting up a prayer, the duke wore himself to skin and bone with penances and fastings, yet seemed farther off from his object than ever.

At length the worthy prince fell dangerously ill, and felt his end approaching. He looked sorrowfully and dubiously upon his young and tender spouse, who hung over him with tears and sobbings. "Alas!" said he, "tears are soon dried from youthful eyes, and sorrow lies lightly on a youthful heart. In a little while thou wilt forget in the arms of another husband him who has loved thee so tenderly."

"Never! never!" cried the duchess. "Never will I cleave to another! Alas, that my lord should think me capable of such inconstancy!"

The worthy and wife-ridden duke was soothed by her assurances; for he could not brook the thought of giving her up even after he should be dead. Still he wished to have some pledge of her enduring constancy.

"Far be it from me, my dearest wife," said he, "to control thee through a long life. A year and a day of strict fidelity will appease my troubled spirit. Promise to remain faithful to my memory for a year and a day, and I will die in peace."

The duchess made a solemn vow to that effect, but the uxorious feelings of the duke were not yet satisfied. "Safe bind, safe find," thought he; so he made a will, bequeathing to her all his domains, on condition of her remaining true to him for a year and a day after his decease; but, should it appear that, within that time, she had in anywise lapsed from her fidelity, the inheritance should go to his nephew, the lord of a neighboring territory.

Having made his will, the good duke died and was buried. Scarcely was he in his tomb, when his nephew came to take possession, thinking, as his uncle had died without issue, the domains would be devised to him of course. He was in a furious passion when the will was produced, and the young widow declared inheritor of the dukedom. As he was a violent, high-handed man, and one of the sturdiest knights in the land, fears were entertained that he might attempt to seize on the territories by force. He had, however, two bachelor uncles for bosom counsellors,—swaggering, rakehelly old cavaliers, who, having led loose and riotous lives, prided themselves upon knowing the world, and being deeply experienced in human nature. "Prithee, man, be of good cheer," said they; "the duchess is a young and buxom widow. She has just buried our brother, who, God rest his soul! was somewhat too much given to praying and fasting, and kept his pretty wife always tied to his girdle. She is now like a bird from a cage. Think you she will keep her vow? Pooh, pooh—impossible! Take our words for it—we know mankind, and, above all, womankind. She cannot hold out for such a length of time; it is not in womanhood,—it is not in widowhood; we know it, and that's enough. Keep a sharp lookout upon the widow, therefore, and within the twelvemonth you will catch her tripping, and then the dukedom is your own."

The nephew was pleased with this counsel, and immediately placed spies round the duchess, and bribed several of her servants to keep watch upon her, so that she could not take a single step, even from one apartment of her palace to another, without being observed. Never was young and beautiful widow exposed to so terrible an ordeal.

The duchess was aware of the watch thus kept upon her. Though confident of her own rectitude, she knew that it is not enough for a woman to be virtuous,—she must be above the reach of slander. For the whole term of her probation, therefore, she proclaimed a strict non-intercourse with the other sex. She had females for cabinet ministers and chamberlains, through whom she transacted all her public and private concerns; and it is said that never were the affairs of the dukedom so adroitly administered.

All males were rigorously excluded from the palace; she never went out of its precincts, and whenever she moved about its courts and gardens, she surrounded herself with a bodyguard of young maids of honor, commanded by dames renowned for discretion. She slept in a bed without curtains, placed in the centre of a room illuminated by innumerable wax tapers. Four ancient spinsters, virtuous as Virginia, perfect dragons of watchfulness, who only slept during the daytime, kept vigils throughout the night, seated in the four corners of the room on stools without backs or arms, and with seats cut in checkers of the hardest wood, to keep them from dozing.

Thus wisely and wearily did the young duchess conduct herself for twelve long months, and slander almost bit her tongue off in despair, at finding no room even for a surmise. Never was ordeal more burdensome, or more enduringly sustained.

The year passed away. The last, odd day arrived, and a long, long day it was. It was the twenty-first of June, the longest day in the year. It seemed as if it would never come to an end. A thousand times did the duchess and her ladies watch the sun from the windows of the palace, as he slowly climbed the vault of heaven, and seemed still more slowly to roll down. They could not help expressing their wonder, now and then, why the duke should have tagged this supernumerary day to the end of the year, as if three hundred and sixty-five days were not sufficient to try and task the fidelity of any woman. It is the last grain that turns the scale—the last drop that overflows the goblet—and the last moment of delay that exhausts the patience. By the time the sun sank below the horizon, the duchess was in a fidget that passed all bounds, and, though several hours were yet to pass before the day regularly expired, she could not have remained those hours in durance to gain a royal crown, much less a ducal coronet. So she gave orders, and her palfrey, magnificently caparisoned, was brought into the court-yard of the castle, with palfreys for all her ladies in attendance. In this way she sallied forth, just as the sun had gone down. It was a mission of piety,—a pilgrim cavalcade to a convent at the foot of a neighboring mountain,—to return thanks to the blessed Virgin, for having sustained her through this fearful ordeal.

The orisons performed, the duchess and her ladies returned, ambling gently along the border of a forest. It was about the mellow hour of twilight when night and day are mingled, and all objects are indistinct. Suddenly some monstrous animal sprang from out a thicket, with fearful howlings. The female body-guard was thrown into confusion, and fled different ways. It was some time before they recovered from their panic, and gathered once more together; but the duchess was not to be found. The greatest anxiety was felt for her safety. The hazy mist of twilight had prevented their distinguishing perfectly the animal which had affrighted them. Some thought it a wolf, others a bear, others a wild man of the woods. For upwards of an hour did they beleaguer the forest, without daring to venture in, and were on the point of giving up the duchess as torn to pieces and devoured, when, to their great joy, they beheld her advancing in the gloom, supported by a stately cavalier.

He was a stranger knight, whom nobody knew. It was impossible to distinguish his countenance in the dark; but all the ladies agreed that he was of noble presence and captivating address. He had rescued the duchess from the very fangs of the monster, which, he assured the ladies, was neither a wolf, nor a bear, nor yet a wild man of the woods, but a veritable fiery dragon, a species of monster peculiarly hostile to beautiful females in the days of chivalry, and which all the efforts of knight-errantry had not been able to extirpate.

The ladies crossed themselves when they heard of the danger from which they had escaped, and could not enough admire the gallantry of the cavalier. The duchess would fain have prevailed on her deliverer to accompany her to her court; but he had no time to spare, being a knight-errant who had many adventures on hand, and many distressed damsels and afflicted widows to rescue and relieve in various parts of the country. Taking a respectful leave, therefore, he pursued his wayfaring, and the duchess and her train returned to the palace. Throughout the whole way, the ladies were unwearied in chanting the praises of the stranger knight; nay, many of them would willingly have incurred the danger of the dragon to have enjoyed the happy deliverance of the duchess. As to the latter, she rode pensively along, but said nothing.

No sooner was the adventure of the wood made public than a whirlwind was raised about the ears of the beautiful duchess. The blustering nephew of the deceased duke went about, armed to the teeth, with a swaggering uncle at each shoulder, ready to back him, and swore the duchess had forfeited her domain. It was in vain that she called all the saints, and angels, and her ladies in attendance into the bargain, to witness that she had passed a year and a day of immaculate fidelity. One fatal hour remained to be accounted for; and into the space of one little hour sins enough may be conjured up by evil tongues to blast the fame of a whole life of virtue.

The two graceless uncles, who had seen the world, were ever ready to bolster the matter through, and as they were brawny, broad-shouldered warriors, and veterans in brawl as well as debauch, they had great sway with the multitude. If any one pretended to assert the innocence of the duchess, they interrupted him with a loud ha! ha! of derision. "A pretty story, truly," would they cry, "about a wolf and a dragon, and a young widow rescued in the dark by a sturdy varlet, who dares not show his face in the daylight. You may tell that to those who do not know human nature; for our parts, we know the sex, and that's enough."

If, however, the other repeated his assertion, they would suddenly knit their brows, swell, look big, and put their hands upon their swords. As few people like to fight in a cause that does not touch their own interests, the nephew and the uncles were suffered to have their way, and swagger uncontradicted.

The matter was at length referred to a tribunal composed of all the dignitaries of the dukedom, and many and repeated consultations were held. The character of the duchess throughout the year was as bright and spotless as the moon in a cloudless night; one fatal hour of darkness alone intervened to eclipse its brightness. Finding human sagacity incapable of dispelling the mystery, it was determined to leave the question to Heaven; or in other words, to decide it by the ordeal of the sword,—a sage tribunal in the age of chivalry. The nephew and two bully uncles were to maintain their accusation in listed combat, and six months were allowed to the duchess to provide herself with three champions, to meet them in the field. Should she fail in this, or should her champions be vanquished, her honor would be considered as attainted, her fidelity as forfeit, and her dukedom would go to the nephew as a matter of right.

With this determination the duchess was fain to comply. Proclamations were accordingly made, and heralds sent to various parts; but day after day, week after week, and month after month elapsed, without any champion appearing to assert her loyalty throughout that darksome hour. The fair widow was reduced to despair, when tidings reached her of grand tournaments to be held at Toledo, in celebration of the nuptials of Don Roderick, the last of the Gothic kings, with the Morisco princess Exilona. As a last resort, the duchess repaired to the Spanish court, to implore the gallantry of its assembled chivalry.

The ancient city of Toledo was a scene of gorgeous revelry on the event of the royal nuptials. The youthful king, brave, ardent, and magnificent, and his lovely bride, beaming with all the radiant beauty of the East, were hailed with shouts and acclamations whenever they appeared. Their nobles vied with each other in the luxury of their attire, their prancing steeds, and splendid retinues; and the haughty dames of the court appeared in a blaze of jewels.

In the midst of all this pageantry, the beautiful but afflicted Duchess of Lorraine made her approach to the throne. She was dressed in black, and closely veiled; four duennas of the most staid and severe aspect, and six beautiful demoiselles, formed her female attendants. She was guarded by several very ancient, withered, and gray-headed cavaliers; and her train was borne by one of the most deformed and diminutive dwarfs in existence.

Advancing to the foot of the throne, she knelt down, and, throwing up her veil, revealed a countenance so beautiful that half the courtiers present were ready to renounce wives and mistresses, and devote themselves to her service; but when she made known that she came in quest of champions to defend her fame, every cavalier pressed forward to offer his arm and sword, without inquiring into the merits of the case; for it seemed clear that so beautious a lady could have done nothing but what was right; and that, at any rate, she ought to be championed in following the bent of her humors, whether right or wrong.

Encouraged by such gallant zeal, the duchess suffered herself to be raised from the ground, and related the whole story of her distress. When she concluded, the king remained for some time silent, charmed by the music of her voice. At length, "As I hope for salvation, most beautiful duchess," said he, "were I not a sovereign king, and bound in duty to my kingdom, I myself would put lance in rest to vindicate your cause; as it is, I here give full permission to my knights, and promise lists and a fair field, and that the contest shall take place before the walls of Toledo, in presence of my assembled court."

As soon as the pleasure of the king was known, there was a strife among the cavaliers present for the honor of the contest. It was decided by lot, and the successful candidates were objects of great envy, for everyone was ambitious of finding favor in the eyes of the beautiful widow.

Missives were sent summoning the nephew and his two uncles to Toledo, to maintain their accusation, and a day was appointed for the combat. When the day arrived all Toledo was in commotion at an early hour. The lists had been prepared in the usual place, just without the walls, at the foot of the rugged rocks on which the city is built, and on that beautiful meadow along the Tagus, known by the name of the King's Garden. The populace had already assembled, each one eager to secure a favorable place; the balconies were filled with the ladies of the court, clad in their richest attire, and bands of youthful knights, splendidly armed and decorated with their ladies' devices, were managing their superbly caparisoned steeds about the field. The king at length came forth in state, accompanied by the queen Exilona. They took their seats in a raised balcony, under a canopy of rich damask; and, at sight of them, the people rent the air with acclamations.

The nephew and his uncles now rode into the field, armed *cap-a-pie*, and followed by a train of cavaliers of their own roystering cast, great swearers and carousers, arrant swashbucklers, with clanking armor and jingling spurs. When the people of Toledo beheld the vaunting and discourteous appearance of these knights, they were more anxious than ever for the success of the gentle duchess; but, at the same time, the sturdy and stalwart frames of these warriors showed that whoever won the victory from them must do it at the cost of many a bitter blow.

As the nephew and his riotous crew rode in at one side of the field, the fair widow appeared at the other, with her suite of gray-headed courtiers, her ancient duennas and dainty demoiselles, and the little dwarf toiling along under the weight of her train. Every one made way for her as she passed, and blessed her beautiful face, and prayed for success to her cause. She took her seat in a lower balcony, not far from the sovereigns; and her pale face, set off by her mourning weeds, was as the moon, shining forth from among the clouds of night.

The trumpets sounded for the combat. The warriors were just entering the lists, when a stranger knight, armed in panoply, and followed by two pages and an esquire, came galloping into the field, and, riding up to the royal balcony, claimed the combat as a matter of right.

"In me," cried he, "behold the cavalier who had the happiness to rescue the beautiful duchess from the peril of the forest, and the misfortune to bring on her this grievous calumny. It was but recently, in the course of my errantry, that tidings of her wrongs have reached my ears, and I have urged hither at all speed, to stand forth in her vindication."

No sooner did the duchess hear the accents of the knight than she recognized his voice, and joined her prayers with his that he might enter the lists. The difficulty was to determine which of the three champions already appointed should yield his place, each insisting on the honor of the combat. The stranger knight would have settled the point, by taking the whole contest upon himself; but this the other knights would not permit. It was at length determined, as before, by lot, and the cavalier who lost the chance retired murmuring and disconsolate.

The trumpets again sounded—the lists were opened. The arrogant nephew and his two drawcansir uncles appeared so completely cased in steel, that they and their steeds were like moving masses of iron. When they understood the stranger knight to be the same that had rescued the duchess from her peril, they greeted him with the most boisterous derision.

"O ho! sir Knight of the Dragon," said they, "you who pretend to champion fair widows in the dark, come on, and vindicate your deeds of darkness in the open day."

The only reply of the cavalier was to put lance in rest, and brace himself for the encounter. Needless is it to relate the particulars of a battle, which was like so many hundred combats that have been said and sung in prose and verse. Who is there but must have foreseen the event of a contest where Heaven had to decide on the guilt or innocence of the most beautiful and immaculate of widows?

The sagacious reader, deeply read in this kind of judicial combats, can imagine the encounter of the graceless nephew and the stranger knight. He sees their concussion, man to man, and horse to horse, in mid career, and sir Graceless hurled to the ground and slain. He will not wonder that the assailants of the brawny uncles were less successful in their rude encounter; but he will picture to himself the stout stranger spurring to their rescue, in the very critical moment; he will see him transfixing one with his lance, and cleaving the other to the chine with a back stroke of his sword, thus leaving the trio of accusers dead upon the field, and establishing the immaculate fidelity of the duchess, and her title to the dukedom, beyond the shadow of a doubt.

The air rang with acclamations; nothing was heard but praises of the beauty and virtue of the duchess, and of the prowess of the stranger knight; but the public joy was still more increased when the champion raised his visor, and revealed the countenance of one of the bravest cavaliers of Spain, renowned for his gallantry in the service of the sex, and who had been round the world in quest of similar adventures.

That worthy knight, however, was severely wounded, and remained for a long time ill of his wounds. The lovely duchess, grateful for having twice owed her protection to his arm, attended him daily during his illness, and finally rewarded his gallantry with her hand.

The king would fain have had the knight establish his title to such high advancement by farther deeds of arms; but his courtiers declared that he already merited the lady, by thus vindicating her fame and fortune in a deadly combat to *outrance*; and the lady herself hinted that she was perfectly satisfied of his prowess in arms, from the proofs she had received of his achievement in the forest.

· Their nuptials were celebrated with great magnificence. The present husband of the duchess did not pray and fast like his predecessor, Philibert the wife-ridden; yet he found greater favor in the eyes of Heaven, for their union was blessed with a numerous progeny: the daughters chaste and beauteous as their mother; the sons stout and valiant as their sire, and renowned like him, for relieving disconsolate damsels and desolate widows.

From *Wolfert's Roost*

THE GRAND PRIOR OF MINORCA

A Veritable Ghost Story

"Keep my wits, heaven! They say spirits appear
To melancholy minds, and the graves open!"
FLETCHER

The Knight of Malta

IN the course of a tour in Sicily, in the days of my juvenility, I passed some little time at the ancient city of Catania, at the foot of Mount Ætna. Here I became acquainted with the Chevalier L——, an old Knight of Malta. It was not many years after the time that Napoleon had dislodged the knights from their island, and he still wore the insignia of his order. He was not, however, one of those reliques of that once chivalrous body, who have been described as "a few wornout old men, creeping about certain parts of Europe, with the Maltese cross on their breasts"; on the contrary, though advanced in life, his form was still lithe and vigorous. He had a pale, thin, intellectual visage, with a high forehead, and a bright, visionary eye. He seemed to take a fancy to me, as I certainly did to him, and we soon became intimate. I visited him occasionally at his apartments, in the wing of an old palace, looking toward Mount Ætna. He was an antiquary, a virtuoso, and a connoisseur. His rooms were decorated with mutilated statues, dug up from Grecian and Roman ruins; old vases, lachrymals, and sepulchral lamps. He had astronomical and chemical instruments, and black-letter books, in various languages. I found that he had dipped a little in chimerical studies, and had a hankering after astrology and alchemy. He affected to believe in dreams and visions, and delighted in the fanciful Rosicrucian doctrines. I cannot persuade myself, however, that he really

---

I have removed the quotation marks which in the original version serve only to clutter Don Luis's account of his torments of conscience.—C.N.

believed in all these; I rather think he loved to let his imagination carry him away into the boundless fairy-land which they unfolded.

In company with the chevalier, I made several excursions on horseback about the environs of Catania, and the picturesque skirts of Mount Ætna. One of these led through a village which had sprung up on the very track of an ancient eruption, the houses being built of lava. At one time we passed, for some distance, along a narrow lane, between two high dead convent-walls. It was a cut-throat-looking place, in a country where assassinations are frequent; and just about midway through it we observed blood upon the pavement and the walls, as if a murder had actually been committed there.

The chevalier spurred on his horse, until he had extricated himself completely from this suspicious neighborhood. He then observed that it reminded him of a similar blind alley in Malta, infamous on account of the many assassinations that had taken place there; concerning one of which he related a long and tragical story, that lasted until we reached Catania. It involved various circumstances of a wild and supernatural character, but which he assured me were handed down in tradition, and generally credited by the old inhabitants of Malta.

As I like to pick up strange stories, and as I was particularly struck with several parts of this, I made a minute of it, on my return to my lodgings. The memorandum was lost, with several of my travelling papers, and the story had faded from my mind, when recently, on perusing a French memoir, I came suddenly upon it, dressed up, it is true, in a very different manner, but agreeing in the leading facts, and given upon the word of that famous adventurer, the Count Cagliostro.

I have amused myself, during a snowy day in the country, by rendering it roughly into English, for the entertainment of a youthful circle round the Christmas fire. It was well received by my auditors, who, however, are rather easily pleased. One proof of its merits is, that it sent some of the youngest of them quaking to their beds, and gave them very fearful dreams. Hoping that it may have the same effect upon the ghost-hunting reader, I subjoin it. I would observe, that wherever I have modified the French version of the story, it has been in conformity to some recollection of the narrative of my friend, the Knight of Malta.

ABOUT the middle of the last century, while the Knights of Saint John of Jerusalem still maintained something of their ancient state and sway in the island of Malta, a tragical event took place there, which is the groundwork of the following narrative.

It may be as well to premise, that, at the time we are treating of, the

Order of Saint John of Jerusalem, grown excessively wealthy, had degenerated from its originally devout and warlike character. Instead of being a hardy body of "monk-knights," sworn soldiers of the Cross, fighting the Paynim in the Holy Land, or scouring the Mediterranean, and scourging the Barbary coasts with their galleys, or feeding the poor, and attending upon the sick at their hospitals, they led a life of luxury and libertinism, and were to be found in the most voluptuous courts of Europe. The order, in fact, had become a mode of providing for the needy branches of the Catholic aristocracy of Europe. "A commandery," we are told, was a splendid provision for a younger brother; and men of rank, however dissolute, provided they belonged to the highest aristocracy, became Knights of Malta, just as they did bishops, or colonels of regiments, or court chamberlains. After a brief residence at Malta, the knights passed the rest of their time in their own countries, or only made a visit now and then to the island. While there, having but little military duty to perform, they beguiled their idleness by paying attention to the fair.

There was one circle of society, however, into which they could not obtain currency. This was composed of a few families of the old Maltese nobility, natives of the island. These families, not being permitted to enroll any of their members in the order, affected to hold no intercourse with its chevaliers; admitting none into their exclusive coteries but the Grand Master, whom they acknowledged as their sovereign, and the members of the chapter which composed his council.

To indemnify themselves for this exclusion, the chevaliers carried their gallantries into the next class of society, composed of those who held civil, administrative, and judicial situations. The ladies of this class were called *honorate*, or honorables, to distinguish them from the inferior orders; and among them were many of superior grace, beauty, and fascination.

Even in this more hospitable class, the chevaliers were not all equally favored. Those of Germany had the decided preference, owing to their fair and fresh complexions, and the kindliness of their manners; next to these, came the Spanish cavaliers, on account of their profound and courteous devotion, and most discreet secrecy. Singular as it may seem, the chevaliers of France fared the worst. The Maltese ladies dreaded their volatility, and their proneness to boast of their amours, and shunned all entanglement with them. They were forced, therefore, to content themselves with conquests among females of the lower orders. They revenged themselves, after the gay French manner, by making the "honorate" the objects of all kinds of jests and mystifications; by prying into their tender affairs with the more favored chevaliers, and making them the theme of song and epigram.

About this time a French vessel arirved at Malta, bringing out a distinguished personage of the Order of Saint John of Jerusalem, the Commander de Foulquerre, who came to solicit the post of commander-in-chief of the galleys. He was descended from an old and warrior line of French nobility, his ancestors having long been seneschals of Poitou, and claiming descent from the first Counts of Angouleme.

The arrival of the commander caused a little uneasiness among the peaceably inclined, for he bore the character, in the island, of being fiery, arrogant, and quarrelsome. He had already been three times at Malta, and on each visit had signalized himself by some rash and deadly affray. As he was now thirty-five years of age, however, it was hoped that time might have taken off the fiery edge of his spirit, and that he might prove more quiet and sedate than formerly. The commander set up an establishment befitting his rank and pretensions; for he arrogated to himself an importance greater even than that of the Grand Master. His house immediately became the rallying-place of all the young French chevaliers. They informed him of all the slights they had experienced or imagined, and indulged their petulant and satirical vein at the expense of the *honorate* and their admirers. The chevaliers of other nations soon found the topics and tone of conversation at the commander's irksome and offensive, and gradually ceased to visit there. The commander remained at the head of a national *clique*, who looked up to him as their model. If he was not as boisterous and quarrelsome as formerly, he had become haughty and overbearing. He was fond of talking over his past affairs of punctilio and bloody duel. When walking the streets, he was generally attended by a ruffling train of young French chevaliers, who caught his own air of assumption and bravado. These he would conduct to the scenes of his deadly encounters, point out the very spot where each fatal lunge had been given, and dwell vaingloriously on every particular.

Under his tuition the young French chevaliers began to add bluster and arrogance to their former petulance and levity; they fired up on the most trivial occasions, particularly with those who had been most successful with the fair; and would put on the most intolerable drawcansir airs. The other chevaliers conducted themselves with all possible forbearance and reserve; but they saw it would be impossible to keep on long, in this manner, without coming to an open rupture.

Among the Spanish cavaliers was one named Don Luis de Lima Vasconcellos. He was distantly related to the Grand Master; and had been enrolled at an early age among his pages, but had been rapidly promoted by him, until, at the age of twenty-six, he had been given the richest Spanish commandery in the order. He had, moreover, been fortunate with the fair, with one of whom, the most beautiful *honorata* of Malta, he had long maintained the most tender correspondence.

The character, rank, and connections of Don Luis put him on a par with the imperious Commander de Foulquerre, and pointed him out as a leader and champion to his countrymen. The Spanish cavaliers repaired to him, therefore, in a body; represented all the grievances they had sustained and the evils they apprehended, and urged him to use his influence with the commander and his adherents to put a stop to the growing abuses.

Don Luis was gratified by this mark of confidence and esteem on the part of his countrymen, and promised to have an interview with the Commander de Foulquerre on the subject. He resolved to conduct himself with the utmost caution and delicacy on the occasion; to represent to the commander the evil consequences which might result from the inconsiderate conduct of the young French chevaliers, and to entreat him to exert the great influence he so deservedly possessed over them, to restrain their excesses. Don Luis was aware, however, of the peril that attended any interview of the kind with this imperious and fractious man, and apprehended, however it might commence, that it would terminate in a duel. Still it was an affair of honor, in which Castilian dignity was concerned; beside, he had a lurking disgust at the overbearing manners of De Foulquerre, and perhaps had been somewhat offended by certain intrusive attentions which he had presumed to pay to the beautiful *honorata*.

It was now Holy Week; a time too sacred for worldly feuds and passions, especially in a community under the dominion of a religious order: it was agreed, therefore, that the dangerous interview in question should not take place until after the Easter holidays. It is probable, from subsequent circumstances, that the Commander de Foulquerre had some information of this arrangement among the Spanish cavaliers, and was determined to be beforehand, and to mortify the pride of their champion, who was thus preparing to read him a lecture. He chose Good Friday for his purpose. On this sacred day it is customary, in Catholic countries, to make a tour of all the churches, offering up prayers in each. In every Catholic church, as is well known, there is a vessel of holy water near the door. In this, every one, on entering, dips his fingers, and makes therewith the sign of the cross on his forehead and breast. An office of gallantry, among the young Spaniards, is to stand near the door, dip their hands in the holy vessel, and extend them courteously and respectfully to any lady of their acquaintance who may enter; who thus receives the sacred water at second hand, on the tips of her fingers, and proceeds to cross herself with all due decorum. The Spaniards, who are the most jealous of lovers, are impatient when this piece of devotional gallantry is proffered to the object of their affections by any other hand: on Good Friday, therefore, when a lady makes a tour of the churches, it is the usage among them for the inamorato to follow her from church to church, so as to present her the holy water at the door of each; thus testifying his own devotion, and at the same time preventing the officious services of a rival.

On the day in question Don Luis followed the beautiful *honorata*, to whom, as has already been observed, he had long been devoted. At the very first church she visited, the Commander de Foulquerre was stationed at the portal, with several of the young French chevaliers about him. Before Don Luis could offer her the holy water, he was anticipated by the commander, who thrust himself between them, and, while he performed the gallant office to the lady, rudely turned his back upon her admirer, and trod upon his feet. The insult was enjoyed by the young Frenchmen who were present: it was too deep and grave to be forgiven by Spanish pride; and at once put an end to all Don Luis's plans of caution and forbearance. He repressed his passion for the moment, however, and waited until all the parties left the church: then, accosting the commander with an air of coolness and unconcern, he inquired after his health, and asked to what church he proposed making his second visit. "To the Magisterial Church of St. John." Don Luis offered to conduct him thither by the shortest route. His offer was accepted, apparently without suspicion, and they proceeded together. After walking some distance, they entered a long, narrow lane, without door or window opening upon it, called the "Strada Stretta," or narrow street. It was a street in which duels were tacitly permitted, or connived at, in Malta, and were suffered to pass as accidental encounters. Everywhere else they were prohibited. This restriction had been instituted to diminish the number of duels formerly so frequent in Malta. As a further precaution to render these encounters less fatal, it was an offence, punishable with death, for any one to enter this street armed with either poniard or pistol. It was a lonely, dismal street, just wide enough for two men to stand upon their guard and cross their swords; few persons ever traversed it, unless with some sinister design; and on any preconcerted *duello*, the seconds posted themselves at each end, to stop all passengers and prevent interruption.

In the present instance, the parties had scarce entered the street, when Don Luis drew his sword, and called upon the commander to defend himself.

De Foulquerre was evidently taken by surprise: he drew back, and attempted to expostulate; but Don Luis persisted in defying him to the combat.

After a second or two, he likewise drew his sword, but immediately lowered the point.

"Good Friday!" ejaculated he, shaking his head: "one word with you; it is full six years since I have been in a confessional: I am shocked at the state of my conscience; but within three days—that is to say, on Monday next—"

Don Luis would listen to nothing. Though naturally of a peaceable disposition, he had been stung to fury; and people of that character, when once incensed, are deaf to reason. He compelled the commander to put himself on his guard. The latter, though a man accustomed to brawl and battle, was singularly dismayed. Terror was visible in all his features. He placed himself with his back to the wall, and the weapons were crossed. The contest was brief and fatal. At the very first thrust the sword of Don Luis passed through the body of his antagonist. The commander staggered to the wall, and leaned against it.

"On Good Friday!" ejaculated he again, with a failing voice and despairing accents. "Heaven pardon you!" added he; "take my sword to Têtefoulques, and have a hundred masses performed in the chapel of the castle, for the repose of my soul!" With these words he expired.

The fury of Don Luis was at an end. He stood aghast, gazing at the bleeding body of the commander. He called to mind the prayer of the deceased for three days' respite, to make his peace with Heaven; he had refused it; had sent him to the grave, with all his sins upon his head! His conscience smote him to the core; he gathered up the sword of the commander, which he had been enjoined to take to Têtefoulques, and hurried from the fatal Strada Stretta.

The duel, of course, made a great noise in Malta, but had no injurious effect on the worldly fortunes of Don Luis. He made a full declaration of the whole matter, before the proper authorities; the chapter of the order considered it one of those casual encounters of the Strada Stretta, which were mourned over, but tolerated; the public, by whom the late commander had been generally detested, declared that he deserved his fate. It was but three days after the event that Don Luis was advanced to one of the highest dignities of the order, being invested by the Grand Master with the Priorship of the kingdom of Minorca.

From that time forward, however, the whole character and conduct of Don Luis underwent a change. He became a prey to a dark melancholy, which nothing could assuage. The most austere piety, the severest penances, had no effect in allaying the horror which preyed upon his mind. He was absent for a long time from Malta, having gone, it was said, on remote pilgrimages: when he returned, he was more haggard than ever. There seemed something mysterious and inexplicable in this disorder of his mind. The following is the revelation, made by himself, of the horrible visions or chimeras by which he was haunted:—

When I had made my declaration before the chapter, said he, my provocations were publicly known,—I had made my peace with man; but it was not so with God, nor with my confessor, nor with my own conscience. My act was doubly criminal, from the day on which it was committed, and from my refusal to a delay of three days, for the victim of my resentment to receive the sacraments. His despairing ejaculation, "Good Friday! Good Friday!" continually rang in my ears. "Why did I not grant the respite!" cried I to myself; "was it not enough to kill the body, but must I seek to kill the soul!"

On the night following Friday I started suddenly from my sleep. An unaccountable horror was upon me; I looked wildly around. It seemed as if I were not in my apartment, nor in my bed, but in the fatal Strada Stretta, lying on the pavement. I again saw the commander leaning against the wall; I again heard his dying words, "Take my sword to Têtefoulques, and have a hundred masses performed in the chapel of the castle, for the repose of my soul!"

On the following night I caused one of my servants to sleep in the same room with me. I saw and heard nothing, either on that night or any of the nights following, until the next Friday, when I had again the same vision, with this difference, that my valet seemed to be lying some distance from me on the pavement of the Strada Stretta. The vision continued to be repeated on every Friday night, the commander always appearing in the same manner, and uttering the same words: "Take my sword to Têtefoulques, and have a hundred masses performed in the chapel of the castle, for the repose of my soul!"

On questioning my servant on the subject, he stated that on these occasions he dreamed that he was lying in a very narrow street, but he neither saw nor heard anything of the commander.

I knew nothing of this Têtefoulques, whither the defunct was so urgent I should carry his sword. I made inquiries, therefore, concerning it, among the French chevaliers. They informed me that it was an old castle, situated about four leagues from Poitiers, in the midst of a forest. It had been built in old times, several centuries since, by Foulques Taillefer (or Fulke Hack-iron), a redoubtable hard-fighting Count of Angouleme, who gave it to an illegitimate son, afterwards created

Grand Seneschal of Poitou, which son became the progenitor of the Foulquerres of Têtefoulques, hereditary seneschals of Poitou. They further informed me, that strange stories were told of this old castle, in the surrounding country, and that it contained many curious reliques. Among these were the arms of Foulques Taillefer, together with those of the warriors he had slain; and that it was an immemorial usage with the Foulquerres to have the weapons deposited there which they had wielded either in war or single combat. This, then, was the reason of the dying injunction of the commander respecting his sword. I carried this weapon with me wherever I went; but still I neglected to comply with his request.

The vision still continued to harass me with undiminished horror. I repaired to Rome, where I confessed myself to the Grand Cardinal penitentiary, and informed him of the terrors with which I was haunted. He promised me absolution, after I should have performed certain acts of penance, the principal of which was to execute the dying request of the commander, by carrying his sword to Têtefoulques, and having the hundred masses performed in the chapel of the castle for the repose of his soul.

I set out for France as speedily as possible, and made no delay in my journey. On arriving at Poitiers, I found that the tidings of the death of the commander had reached there, but had caused no more affliction than among the people of Malta. Leaving my equipage in the town, I put on the garb of a pilgrim, and taking a guide, set out on foot for Têtefoulques. Indeed the roads in this part of the country were impracticable for carriages.

I found the castle of Têtefoulques a grand but gloomy and dilapidated pile. All the gates were closed, and there reigned over the whole place an air of almost savage loneliness and desertion. I had understood that its only inhabitants were the concierge, or warder, and a kind of hermit who had charge of the chapel. After ringing for some time at the gate, I at length succeeded in bringing forth the warder, who bowed with reverence to my pilgrim's garb. I begged him to conduct me to the chapel, that being the end of my pilgrimage. We found the hermit there, chanting the funeral service; a dismal sound to one who came to perform a penance for the death of a member of the family. When he had ceased to chant, I informed him that I came to accomplish an obligation of conscience, and that I wished him to perform a hundred masses for the repose of the soul of the commander. He replied that, not being in orders, he was not authorized to perform mass, but that he would willingly undertake to see that my debt of conscience was discharged. I laid my offering on the altar, and would have placed the sword of the commander there likewise. "Hold!" said the hermit, with a melancholy shake of the head, "this is no place for so deadly a weapon, that has so often been bathed in Christian blood. Take it to the armory; you will find there trophies enough of like character. It is a place into which I never enter."

The warder here took up the theme abandoned by the peaceful man of God. He assured me that I would see in the armory the swords of all the warrior race of Foulquerres, together with those of the enemies over whom they had triumphed. This, he observed, had been a usage kept up since the time of Mellusine, and of her husband, Geoffrey à la Grand-dent, or Geoffrey with the Great-tooth.

I followed the gossiping warder to the armory. It was a great dusky hall, hung round with Gothic-looking portraits of a stark line of warriors, each with his weapon, and the weapons of those he had slain in battle, hung beside his picture. The most conspicuous portrait was that of Foulques Taillefer (Fulke Hack-iron), Count of Angouleme, and founder of the castle. He was represented at full length, armed cap-a-pie, and grasping a huge buckler, on which were emblazoned three lions passant. The figure was so striking, that it seemed ready to start from the canvas; and I observed beneath this picture a trophy composed of many weapons, proofs of the numerous triumphs of this hard-fighting old cavalier. Besides the weapons connected with the portraits, there were swords of all shapes, sizes, and centuries, hung round the hall, with piles of armor placed, as it were, in effigy.

On each side of an immense chimney were suspended the portraits of the first seneschal of Poitou (the illegitimate son of Foulques Taillefer) and his wife, Isabella de Lusignan, the progenitors of the grim race of Foulquerres that frowned around. They had the look of being perfect likenesses; and as I gazed on them, I fancied I could trace in their antiquated features some family resemblance to their unfortunate descendant whom I had slain! This was a dismal neighborhood, yet the armory was the only part of the castle that had a habitable air; so I asked the warder whether he could not make a fire, and give me something for supper there, and prepare me a bed in one corner.

"A fire and a supper you shall have, and that cheerfully, most worthy pilgrim," said he; "but as to a bed, I advise you to come and sleep in my chamber."

"Why so?" inquired I; "why shall I not sleep in this hall?"

"I have my reasons; I will make a bed for you close to mine."

I made no objections, for I recollected that it was Friday, and I dreaded the return of my vision. He brought in billets of wood, kindled a fire in the great overhanging chimney, and then went forth to prepare my supper. I drew a heavy chair before the fire, and seating myself in it, gazed musingly round upon the portraits of the Foulquerres and the antiquated armor and weapons, the mementos of many a bloody deed. As the day declined, the smoky draperies of the hall gradually became confounded with the dark ground of the paintings, and the lurid gleams from the chimney only enabled me to see visages staring at me from the gathering darkness. All this was dismal in the extreme, and somewhat appalling; perhaps it was that state of my conscience that rendered me peculiarly sensitive and prone to fearful imaginings.

At length the warder brought in my supper. It consisted of a dish of trout and some crawfish taken in the fosse of the castle. He procured also a bottle of wine, which he informed me was wine of Poitou. I requested him to invite the hermit to join me in my repast, but the holy man sent back word that he allowed himself nothing but roots and herbs, cooked with water. I took my meal, therefore, alone, but prolonged it as much as possible, and sought to cheer my drooping spirits by the wine of Poitou, which I found very tolerable.

When supper was over I prepared for my evening devotions. I have always been very punctual in reciting my breviary; it is the prescribed and bounden duty of all cavaliers of the religious orders; and I can answer for it, is faithfully performed by those of Spain. I accordingly drew forth from my pocket a small missal and a rosary, and told the warder he need only designate to me the way to his chamber, where I could come and rejoin him when I had finished my prayers.

He accordingly pointed out a winding staircase opening from the hall. "You will descend this staircase," said he, "until you come to the fourth landing-place, where you enter a vaulted passage, terminated by an arcade, with a statue of the blessed Jeanne of France; you cannot help finding my room, the door of which I will leave open; it is the sixth door from the landing-place. I advise you not to remain in this hall after midnight. Before that hour you will hear the hermit ring the bell, in going the rounds of the corridors. Do not linger here after that signal."

The warder retired, and I commenced my devotions, I continued at them earnestly, pausing from time to time to put wood upon the fire. I did not dare to look much around me, for I felt myself becoming a prey to fearful fancies. The pictures appeared to become animated. If I regarded one attentively, for any length of time, it seemed to move the eyes and lips. Above all, the portraits of the Grand Seneschal and his lady, which hung on each side of the great chimney, the progenitors of the Foulquerres of Têtefoulques, regarded me, I thought, with angry and baleful eyes; I even fancied they exchanged significant glances with each other. Just then a terrible blast of wind shook all the casements, and, rushing through the hall, made a fearful rattling and clashing among the armor. To my startled fancy, it seemed something supernatural.

At length I heard the bell of the hermit, and hastened to quit the hall. Taking a solitary light, which stood on the supper-table, I descended the winding staircase, but before I had reached the vaulted passage leading to the statue of the blessed Jeanne of France, a blast of wind extinguished my taper. I hastily remounted the stairs, to light it again at the chimney; but judge of my feelings, when, on arriving at the entrance to the armory, I beheld the Seneschal and his lady, who had descended from their frames, and seated themselves on each side of the fireplace!

"Madam, my love," said the Seneschal, with great formality and in anticipated phrase, "what think you of the presumption of this Castilian, who comes to harbor himself and make wassail in this our castle, after having slain our descendant, the commander, and that without granting him time for confession?"

"Truly, my lord," answered the female spectre, with no less stateliness of manner, and with great asperity of tone—"truly, my lord, I opine that this Castilian did a grievous wrong in this encounter, and he should never be suffered to depart hence, without your throwing him the gauntlet." I paused to hear no more, but rushed again down stairs to seek the chamber of the warder. It was impossible to find it in the darkness and in the perturbation of my mind. After an hour and a half of fruitless search, and mortal horror and anxieties, I endeavored to persuade myself that the day was about to break, and listened impatiently for the crowing of the cock; for I thought if I could hear his cheerful note, I should be reassured; catching, in the disordered state of my nerves, at the popular notion that ghosts never appear after the first crowing of the cock.

At length I rallied myself, and endeavored to shake off the vague terrors which haunted me. I tried to persuade myself that the two figures which I had seemed to see and hear, had existed only in my troubled imagination. I still had the end of a candle in my hand, and determined to make another effort to relight it and find my way to bed, for I was ready to sink with fatigue. I accordingly sprang up the staircase, three steps at a time, stopped at the door of the armory, and peeped cautiously in. The two Gothic figures were no longer in the chimney-corners, but I neglected to notice whether they had reascended to their frames. I entered and made desperately for the fireplace, but scarce had I advanced three strides, when Messire Foulques Taillefer stood before me, in the centre of the hall, armed cap-a-pie, and standing in guard, with the point of his sword silently presented to me. I would have re-treated to the staircase, but the door of it was occupied by the phantom figure of an esquire, who rudely flung a gauntlet in my face. Driven to fury, I snatched down a sword from the wall: by chance it was that of the commander, which I had placed there. I rushed upon my fantastic adversary, and seemed to pierce him through and through; but at the same time I felt as if something pierced my heart, burning like a red-hot iron. My blood inundated the hall, and I fell senseless.

When I recovered consciousness, it was broad day, and I found my-self in a small chamber, attended by the warder and the hermit. The former told me that on the previous night he had awakened long after the midnight hour, and perceiving that I had not come to his chamber, he had furnished himself with a vase of holy water, and set out to seek me. He found me stretched senseless on the pavement of the armory, and bore me to his room. I spoke of my wound, and the quantity of blood that I had lost. He shook his head, and knew nothing about it; and to my surprise, on examination, I found myself perfectly sound and unharmed. The wound and blood, therefore, had been all delusion. Neither the warder nor the hermit put any questions to me, but ad-vised me to leave the castle as soon as possible. I lost no time in comply-ing with their counsel, and felt my heart relieved from an oppressive weight, as I left the gloomy and fate-bound battlements of Têtefoulques behind me.

I arrived at Bayonne, on my way to Spain, on the following Friday. At midnight I was startled from my sleep, as I had formerly been; but it was no longer by the vision of the dying commander. It was old Foulques Taillefer who stood before me, armed cap-a-pie, and present-ing the point of his sword. I made the sign of the cross, and the spec-tre vanished, but I received the same red-hot thrust in the heart which I had felt in the armory, and I seemed to be bathed in blood. I would have called out, or have risen from my bed and gone in quest of suc-cor, but I could neither speak nor stir. This agony endured until the crowing of the cock, when I fell asleep again; but the next day I was ill, and in a most pitiable state. I have continued to be harrassed by the same vision every Friday night; no acts of penitence and devotion have been able to relieve me from it; and it is only a lingering hope in divine mercy that sustains me, and enables me to support so lamentable a visitation.

The Grand Prior of Minorca wasted gradually away under this con-stant remorse of conscience and this horrible incubus. He died some

716 THE COMPLETE TALES OF WASHINGTON IRVING

time after having revealed the preceding particulars of his case, evidently the victim of a diseased imagination.

The above relation has been rendered, in many parts literally, from the French memoir, in which it is given as a true story: if so, it is one of those instances in which truth is more romantic than fiction.

From *Wolfert's Roost*

A CONTENTED MAN

IN the garden of the Tuileries there is a sunny corner under the wall of a terrace which fronts the south. Along the wall is a range of benches commanding a view of the walks and avenues of the garden. This genial nook is a place of great resort in the latter part of autumn, and in fine days in winter, as it seems to retain the flavor of departed summer. On a calm, bright morning, it is quite alive with nursery-maids and their playful little charges. Hither also resort a number of ancient ladies and gentlemen, who with laudable thrift in small pleasures and small expenses, for which the French are to be noted, come here to enjoy the sunshine and save firewood. Here may often be seen some cavalier of the old school, when the sunbeams have warmed his blood into something like a glow, fluttering about like a frost-bitten moth thawed before the fire, putting forth a feeble show of gallantry among the antiquated dames, and now and then eyeing the buxom nursery-maids with what might almost be mistaken for an air of libertinism.

Among the habitual frequenters of this place I had often remarked an old gentleman whose dress was decidedly anti-revolutional. He wore the three-cornered cocked hat of the *ancien régime*; his hair was frizzed over each ear into *ailes de pigeon*, a style strongly savoring of Bourbonism; and a queue stuck out behind, the loyalty of which was not to be disputed. His dress, though ancient, had an air of decayed gentility, and I observed that he took his snuff out of an elegant though old-fashioned gold box. He appeared to be the most popular man on the walk. He had a compliment for every old lady, he kissed every child, and he patted every little dog on the head; for children and little dogs are very important members of society in France. I must observe, however, that he seldom kissed a child without, at the same time, pinching the nursery-maid's cheek; a Frenchman of the old school never forgets his *devoirs* to the sex.

I had taken a liking to this old gentleman. There was an habitual expression of benevolence in his face, which I have very frequently remarked in these relics of the politer days of France. The constant interchange of those thousand little courtesies which imperceptibly sweeten life, has a happy effect upon the features, and spreads a mellow evening charm over the wrinkles of old age.

Where there is a favorable predisposition, one soon forms a kind of tacit intimacy by often meeting on the same walks. Once or twice I accommodated him with a bench, after which we touched hats on passing each other; at length we got so far as to take a pinch of snuff together out of his box, which is equivalent to eating salt together in the East; from that time our acquaintance was established.

I now became his frequent companion in his morning promenades, and derived much amusement from his good-humored remarks on men and manners. One morning, as we were strolling through an alley of the Tuileries, with the autumnal breeze whirling the yellow leaves about our path, my companion fell into a peculiarly communicative vein, and gave me several particulars of his history. He had once been wealthy, and possessed of a fine estate in the country and a noble hotel in Paris; but the revolution, which effected so many disastrous changes, stripped him of everything. He was secretly denounced by his own steward during a sanguinary period of the revolution, and a number of the bloodhounds of the Convention were sent to arrest him. He received private intelligence of their approach in time to effect his escape. He landed in England without money or friends, but considered himself singularly fortunate in having his head upon his shoulders, several of his neighbors having been guillotined as a punishment for being rich.

When he reached London he had but a louis in his pocket, and no prospect of getting another. He ate a solitary dinner on beefsteak, and was almost poisoned by port wine, which from its color he had mistaken for claret. The dingy look of the chop-house, and of the little mahogany-colored box in which he ate his dinner, contrasted sadly with the gay saloons of Paris. Everything looked gloomy and disheartening. Poverty stared him in the face; he turned over the few shillings he had of change; he did not know what was to become of him; and—went to the theatre!

He took his seat in the pit, listened attentively to a tragedy of which he did not understand a word, and which seemed made up of fighting, and stabbing, and scene-shifting, and began to feel his spirits sinking within him; when, casting his eyes into the orchestra, what was his surprise to recognize an old friend and neighbor in the very act of extorting music from a huge violincello.

As soon as the evening's performance was over he tapped his friend on the shoulder; they kissed each other on each cheek, and the musician took him home, and shared his lodgings with him. He had learned music as an accomplishment; by his friend's advice he now turned to it as a means of support. He procured a violin, offered himself for the orchestra, was received, and again considered himself one of the most fortunate men upon earth.

Here, therefore, he lived for many years during the ascendency of the terrible Napoleon. He found several emigrants living like himself by the exercise of their talents. They associated together, talked of France and of old times, and endeavored to keep up a semblance of Parisian life in the centre of London.

They dined at a miserable cheap French *restaurateur* in the neighborhood of Leicester Square, where they were served with a caricature of French cookery. They took their promenade in St James's Park, and endeavored to fancy it the Tuileries; in short, they made shift to accommodate themselves to everything but an English Sunday. Indeed, the old gentleman seemed to have nothing to say against the English, whom he affirmed to be *braves gens;* and he mingled so much among them, that at the end of twenty years he could speak their language almost well enough to be understood.

The downfall of Napoleon was another epoch in his life. He had considered himself a fortunate man to make his escape penniless out of France, and he considered himself fortunate to be able to return penniless into it. It is true that he found his Parisian hotel had passed through several hands during the vicissitudes of the times, so as to be beyond the reach of recovery; but then he had been noticed benignantly by government, and had a pension of several hundred francs, upon which, with careful management, he lived independently, and, as far as I could judge, happily.

As his once splendid hotel was now occupied as a *hôtel garni,* he hired a small chamber in the attic; it was but, as he said, changing his bedroom up two pair of stairs,—he was still in his own house. His room was decorated with pictures of several beauties of former times, with whom he professed to have been on favorable terms; among them was a favorite opera-dancer, who had been the admiration of Paris at the breaking out of the revolution. She had been a *protégée* of my friend, and one of the few of his youthful favorites who had survived the lapse of time and its various vicissitudes. They had renewed their acquaintance, and she now and then visited him; but the beautiful Psyche, once the fashion of the day and the idol of the *parterre,* was now a shrivelled, little old woman, warped in the back, and with a hooked nose.

The old gentleman was a devout attendant upon levees; he was most zealous in his loyalty, and could not speak of the royal family without a burst of enthusiasm, for he still felt towards them as his companions in exile. As to his poverty he made light of it, and indeed had a good-humored way of consoling himself for every cross and privation. If he had lost his château in the country, he had half a dozen royal palaces, as it were, at his command. He had Versailles and St. Cloud for his country resorts, and the shady alleys of the Tuileries and the Luxembourg for his town recreation. Thus all his promenades and relaxations were magnificent, yet cost nothing. When I walk through these fine gardens, said he, I have only to fancy myself the owner of them, and they are mine. All these gay crowds are my visitors, and I defy the grand seignior himself to display a greater variety of beauty. Nay, what is better, I have not the trouble of entertaining them. My estate is a perfect *Sans Souci*, where every one does as he pleases, and no one troubles the owner. All Paris is my theatre, and presents me with a continual spectacle. I have a table spread for me in every street, and thousands of waiters ready to fly at my bidding. When my servants have waited upon me I pay them, discharge them, and there's an end; I have no fears of their wronging or pilfering me when my back is turned. Upon the whole, said the old gentleman, with a smile of infinite good-humor, when I think upon the various risks I have run, and the manner in which I have escaped them, when I recollect all that I have suffered, and consider all that I at present enjoy, I cannot but look upon myself as a man of singular good fortune.

Such was the brief history of this practical philosopher, and it is a picture of many a Frenchman ruined by the revolution. The French appear to have a greater facility than most men in accommodating themselves to the reverses of life, and of extracting honey out of the bitter things of this world. The first shock of calamity is apt to overwhelm them; but when it is once past, their natural buoyancy of feeling soon brings them to the surface. This may be called the result of levity of character, but it answers the end of reconciling us to misfortune, and if it be not true philosophy, it is something almost as efficacious. Ever since I have heard the story of my little Frenchman, I have treasured it up in my heart; and I thank my stars I have at length found, what I had long considered as not to be found on earth—a contented man.

P. S.—There is no calculating on human happiness. Since writing the foregoing, the law of indemnity, has been passed, and my friend restored to a great part of his fortune. I was absent from Paris at the time, but on my return hastened to congratulate him. I found him magnificently lodged on the first floor of his hotel. I was ushered, by a servant in livery, through splendid saloons, to a cabinet richly furnished, where I found my little Frenchman reclining on a couch. He received me with his usual cordiality; but I saw the gayety and benevolence of his countenance had fled; he had an eye full of care and anxiety.

I congratulated him on his good fortune. "Good fortune?" echoed he; "bah! I have been plundered of a princely fortune, and they give me a pittance as an indemnity."

Alas! I found my late poor and contented friend one of the richest and most miserable men in Paris. Instead of rejoicing in the ample competency restored to him, he is daily repining at the superfluity withheld. He no longer wanders in happy idleness about Paris, but is a repining attendant in the antechambers of ministers. His loyalty has evaporated with his gayety; he screws his mouth when the Bourbons are mentioned, and even shrugs his shoulders when he hears the praises of the king. In a word, he is one of the many philosophers undone by the law of indemnity; and his case is desperate, for I doubt whether even another reverse of fortune, which should restore him to poverty, could make him again a happy man.

From *Wolfert's Roost*

GUESTS FROM GIBBET ISLAND

A Legend of Communipaw

FOUND AMONG THE KNICKERBOCKER PAPERS AT WOLFERT'S ROOST

WHOEVER has visited the ancient and renowned village of Communipaw may have noticed an old stone building, of most ruinous and sinister appearance. The doors and window-shutters are ready to drop from their hinges; old clothes are stuffed in the broken panes of glass, while legions of half-starved dogs prowl about the premises, and rush out and bark at every passer-by, for your beggarly house in a village is most apt to swarm with profligate and ill-conditioned dogs. What adds to the sinister appearance of this mansion is a tall frame in front, not a little resembling a gallows, and which looks as if waiting to accommodate some of the inhabitants with a well-merited airing. It is not a gallows, however, but an ancient sign-post; for this dwelling in the golden days of Communipaw was one of the most orderly and peaceful of village taverns, where public affairs were talked and smoked over. In fact, it was in this very building that Oloffe the Dreamer and his companions concerted that great voyage of discovery and colonization in which they explored Buttermilk Channel, were nearly shipwrecked in the strait of Hell Gate, and finally landed on the island of Manhattan, and founded the great city of New Amsterdam.

Even after the province had been cruelly wrested from the sway of their High Mightinesses by the combined forces of the British and the Yankees, this tavern continued its ancient loyalty. It is true, the head of the Prince of Orange disappeared from the sign, a strange bird being painted over it, with the explanatory legend of "DIE WILDE GANS," or, The Wild Goose; but this all the world knew to be a sly riddle of the landlord, the worthy Teunis Van Gieson, a knowing man, in a small way, who laid his finger beside his nose and winked, when any one studied the signification of his sign, and observed that his goose was hatching, but would join the flock whenever they flew over the water; an enigma which was the perpetual recreation and delight of the loyal but fat-headed burghers of Communipaw.

Under the sway of this patriotic, though discreet and quiet publican, the tavern continued to flourish in primeval tranquillity, and was the resort of true-hearted Nederlanders, from all parts of Pavonia; who met here quietly and secretly, to smoke and drink the downfall of Briton and Yankee, and success to Admiral Van Tromp.

The only drawback on the comfort of the establishment was a nephew of mine host, a sister's son, Yan Yost Vanderscamp by name, and a real scamp by nature. This unlucky whipster showed an early propensity to mischief, which he gratified in a small way by playing tricks upon the frequenters of the Wild Goose,—putting gunpowder in their pipes, or squibs in their pockets, and astonishing them with an explosion, while they sat nodding around the fireplace in the bar-room; and if perchance a worthy burgher from some distant part of Pavonia lingered until dark over his potation, it was odds but young Vanderscamp would slip a brier under his horse's tail, as he mounted, and send him clattering along the road, in neck or nothing style, to the infinite astonishment and discomfiture of the rider.

It may be wondered at, that mine host of the Wild Goose did not turn such a graceless varlet out of doors; but Teunis Van Gieson was an easy-tempered man, and, having no child of his own, looked upon his nephew with almost parental indulgence. His patience and good-nature were doomed to be tried by another inmate of his mansion. This was a cross-grained curmudgeon of a negro, named Pluto, who was a kind of enigma in Communipaw. Where he came from, nobody knew. He was found one morning, after a storm, cast like a sea-monster on the strand, in front of the Wild Goose, and lay there, more dead than alive. The neighbors gathered round, and speculated on his production of the deep; whether it were fish or flesh, or a compound of both, commonly yclept a merman. The kind-hearted Teunis Van Gieson, seeing that he wore the human form, took him into his house, and warmed him into life. By degrees, he showed signs of intelligence, and even uttered sounds very much like language, but which no one in Communipaw could understand. Some thought him a negro just from Guinea, who had either fallen overboard, or escaped from a slave-ship. Nothing, however, could ever draw from him any account of his origin. When questioned on the subject, he merely pointed to Gibbet Island, a small rocky islet which lies in the open bay, just opposite Communipaw, as if that were his native place, though everybody knew it had never been inhabited.

In the process of time, he acquired something of the Dutch language; that is to say, he learnt all its vocabulary of oaths and maledictions, with just words sufficient to string them together. *"Donder en blicksem!"* (thunder and lightning) was the gentlest of his ejaculations. For years he kept about the Wild Goose, more like one of those familiar spirits, or household goblins, we read of, than like a human being. He acknowledged allegiance to no one, but performed various domestic offices, when it suited his humor; waiting occasionally on the guests, grooming the horses, cutting wood, drawing water; and all this without being ordered. Lay any command on him, and the stubborn sea-urchin was sure to rebel. He was never so much at home, however, as when on the water, plying about in skiff or canoe, entirely alone, fishing, crabbing, or grabbing for oysters, and would bring home quantities for the larder of the Wild Goose, which he would throw down at the kitchen-door, with a growl. No wind nor weather deterred him from launching forth on his favorite element; indeed, the wilder the weather, the more he seemed to enjoy it. If a storm was brewing, he was sure to put off from shore; and would be seen far out in the bay, his light skiff dancing like a feather on the waves, when sea and sky were in a turmoil, and the stoutest ships were fain to lower their sails. Sometimes on such occasions he would be absent for days together. How he weathered the tempest, and how and where he subsisted, no one could divine, nor did any one venture to ask, for all had an almost superstitious awe of him. Some of the Communipaw oystermen declared they had more than once world around him; could navigate from the Hook to Spiting Devil waves, and after a while come up again, in quite a different part of the bay; whence they concluded that he could live under water like that notable species of wild-duck commonly called the hell-diver. All began to consider him in the light of a foul-weather bird, like the Mother Carey's chicken, or stormy petrel; and whenever they saw him putting far out in his skiff, in cloudy weather, made up their minds for a storm.

The only being for whom he seemed to have any liking was Yan Yost Vanderscamp, and him he liked for his very wickedness. He in a manner took the boy under his tutelage, prompted him to all kinds of mischief, aided him in every wild harum-scarum freak, until the lad became the complete scapegrace of the village, a pest to his uncle and to every one else. Nor were his pranks confined to the land; he soon learned to accompany old Pluto on the water. Together these worthies would cruise about the broad bay, and all the neighboring straits and rivers; poking around in skiffs and canoes; robbing the set nets of the fishermen; landing on remote coasts, and laying waste orchards and watermelon patches; in short, carrying on a complete system of piracy, on a small scale. Piloted by Pluto, the youthful Vanderscamp soon became acquainted with all the bays, rivers, creeks, and inlets of the watery seen him suddenly disappear, canoe and all, as if plunged beneath the on the darkest night, and learned to set even the terrors of Hell Gate at defiance.

At length negro and boy suddenly disappeared, and days and weeks elapsed, but without tidings of them. Some said they must have run away and gone to sea; others jocosely hinted that old Pluto, being no other than his namesake in disguise, had spirited away the boy to the nether regions. All, however agreed in one thing, that the village was well rid of them.

In the process of time, the good Teunis Van Gieson slept with his fathers, and the tavern remained shut up, waiting for a claimant, for the next heir was Yan Yost Vanderscamp, and he had not been heard of for years. At length, one day, a boat was seen pulling for shore, from a long, black, rakish-looking schooner, that lay at anchor in the bay. The boat's crew seemed worthy of the craft from which they debarked. Never had such a set of noisy, roistering, swaggering varlets landed in peaceful Communipaw. They were outlandish in garb and demeanor, and were headed by a rough, burly, bully ruffian, with fiery whiskers, a copper nose, a scar across his face, and a great Flaunderish beaver slouched on one side of his head, in whom, to their dismay, the quiet inhabitants were made to recognize their early pest, Yan Yost Vanderscamp. The rear of this hopeful gang was brought up by old Pluto, who had lost an eye, grown grizzly-headed, and looked more like a devil than ever. Vanderscamp renewed his acquaintance with the old burghers, much against their will, and in a manner not at all to their taste. He slapped them familiarly on the back, gave them an iron grip of the hand, and was hail-fellow well met. According to his own account, he had been all the world over, had made money by bags full, had ships in every sea, and now meant to turn the Wild Goose into a country-seat, where he and his comrades, all rich merchants from foreign parts, might enjoy themselves in the interval of their voyages.

Sure enough, in a little while there was a complete metamorphose of the Wild Goose. From being a quiet, peaceful Dutch public-house, it became a most riotous, uproarious private dwelling; a complete rendezvous for boisterous men of the seas, who came here to have what they called a "blow-out" on dry land, and might be seen at all hours, lounging about the door, or lolling out of the windows, swearing among themselves and cracking rough jokes on every passer-by. The house was fitted up, too, in so strange a manner: hammocks slung to the walls, instead of bedsteads; odd kinds of furniture, of foreign fashion; bamboo couches, Spanish chairs; pistols, cutlasses, and blunderbusses, suspended on every peg; silver crucifixes on the mantelpieces, silver candle-sticks and porringers on the tables, contrasting oddly with the pewter and Delf ware of the original establishment. And then the strange amusements of these sea-monsters! Pitching Spanish dollars, instead of quoits; firing blunderbusses out of the window; shooting at a mark, or at any unhappy dog, or cat, or pig, or barn-door fowl, that might happen to come within reach.

The only being who seemed to relish their rough waggery was old Pluto; and yet he led but a dog's life of it, for they practised all kinds of manual jokes upon him, kicked him about like a foot-ball, shook him by his grizzly mop of wool, and never spoke to him without coupling a curse by way of adjective, to his name, and consigning him to the infernal regions. The old fellow, however, seemed to like them the better the more they cursed him, though his utmost expression of pleasure never amounted to more than the growl of a petted bear, when his ears are rubbed.

Old Pluto was the ministering spirit at the orgies of the Wild Goose; and such orgies as took place there! Such drinking, singing, whooping, swearing; with an occasional interlude of quarrelling and fighting. The noisier grew the revel, the more old Pluto plied the potations, until the guests would become frantic in their merriment, smashing everything to pieces, and throwing the house out of the windows. Sometimes, after a drinking bout, they sallied forth and scoured the village, to the dismay of the worthy burghers, who gathered their women within doors, and would have shut up the house. Vanderscamp, however, was not to be rebuffed. He insisted on renewing acquaintance with his old neighbors, and on introducing his friends, the merchants, to their families; swore he was on the lookout for a wife, and meant, before he stopped, to find husbands for all their daughters. So, will-ye, nill-ye, sociable he was; swaggered about their best parlors, with his hat on one side of his head; sat on the good-wife's nicely waxed mahogany table, kicking his heels against the carved and polished leg; kissed and tousled the young *vrows*; and, if they frowned and pouted, gave them a gold rosary, or a sparkling cross, to put them in good-humor again.

Sometimes nothing would satisfy him, but he must have some of his old neighbors to dinner at the Wild Goose. There was no refusing him, for he had the complete upper hand of the community, and the peaceful burghers all stood in awe of him. But what a time would the quiet, worthy men have, among these rake-hells, who would delight to astound them with the most extravagant gunpowder tales, embroidered with all kinds of foreign oaths, clink the can with them, pledge them in deep potations, bawl drinking-songs in their ears, and occasionally fire pistols over their heads, or under the table, and then laugh in their faces, and ask them how they liked the smell of gunpowder.

Thus was the little village of Communipaw for a time like the unfortunate wight possessed with devils; until Vanderscamp and his brother merchants would sail on another trading voyage, when the Wild Goose would be shut up and everything relapse into quiet, only to be disturbed by his next visitation.

The mystery of all these proceedings gradually dawned upon the tardy intellects of Communipaw. These were the times of the notorious Captain Kidd, when the American harbors were the resorts of piratical adventurers of all kinds, who, under pretext of mercantile voyages, scoured the West Indies, made plundering descents upon the Spanish Main, visited even the remote Indian Seas, and then came to dispose of their booty, have their revels, and fit out new expeditions in the English colonies.

Vanderscamp had served in this hopeful school, and, having risen to importance among the buccaneers, had pitched upon his native village and early home, as a quiet, out-of-the-way, unsuspected place, where he and his comrades, while anchored at New York, might have their feasts, and concert their plans, without molestation.

At length the attention of the British government was called to these piratical enterprises, that were becoming so frequent and outrageous. Vigorous measures were taken to check and punish them. Several of the most noted free-booters were caught and executed, and three of Vanderscamp's chosen comrades, the most riotous swash-bucklers of the Wild Goose, were hanged in chains on Gibbet Island, in full sight of their favorite resort. As to Vanderscamp himself, he and his man Pluto again disappeared, and it was hoped by the people of Communipaw that he had fallen in some foreign brawl, or been swung on some foreign gallows.

For a time, therefore, the tranquillity of the village was restored; the worthy Dutchmen once more smoked their pipes in peace, eying with peculiar complacency their old pests and terrors, the pirates, dangling and drying in the sun, on Gibbet Island.

This perfect calm was doomed at length to be ruffled. The fiery persecution of the pirates gradually subsided. Justice was satisfied with the examples that had been made, and there was no more talk of Kidd, and the other heroes of like kidney. On a calm summer evening, a boat, somewhat heavily laden, was seen pulling into Communipaw. What was the surprise and disquiet of the inhabitants to see Yan Yost Vanderscamp seated at the helm, and his man Pluto tugging at the oar! Vanderscamp, however, was apparently an altered man. He brought

home with him a wife, who seemed to be a shrew, and to have the upper hand of him. He no longer was the swaggering, bully ruffian, but affected the regular merchant, and talked of retiring from business, and settling down quietly, to pass the rest of his days in his native place.

The Wild Goose mansion was again opened, but with diminished splendor, and no riot. It is true, Vanderscamp had frequent nautical visitors, and the sound of revelry was ocasionally overheard in his house; but everything seemed to be done under the rose, and old Pluto was the only servant that officiated at these orgies. The visitors, indeed, were by no means of thc turbulent stamp of their predecessors; but quiet mysterious traders; full of nods, and winks, and hieroglyphic signs, with whom, to use their cant phrase, "everything was smug." Their ships came to anchor at night, in the lower bay; and, on a private signal, Vanderscamp would launch his boat, and, accompanied solely by his man Pluto, would make them mysterious visits. Sometimes boats pulled in at night, in front of the Wild Goose, and various articles of merchandise were landed in the dark, and spirited away, nobody knew whither. One of the more curious of the inhabitants kept watch, and caught a glimpse of the feature of some of these night visitors, by the casual glance of a lantern, and declared that he recognized more than one of the freebooting frequenters of the Wild Goose, in former times; whence he concluded that Vanderscamp was at his old game, and that this mysterious merchandise was nothing more nor less than piratical plunder. The more charitable opinion, however, was, that Vanderscamp and his comrades, having been driven from their old line of business by the "oppressions of government," had resorted to smuggling to make both ends meet.

Be that as it may, I come now to the extraordinary fact which is the butt-end of this story. It happened, late one night, that Yan Yost Vanderscamp was returning across the broad bay, in his light skiff, rowed by his man Pluto. He had been carousing on board of a vessel, newly arrived, and was somewhat obfuscated in intellect, by the liquor he had imbibed. It was a still, sultry night; a heavy mass of lurid clouds was rising in the west, with the low muttering of distant thunder. Vanderscamp called on Pluto to pull lustily, that they might get home before the gathering storm. The old negro made no reply, but shaped his course so as to skirt the rocky shores of Gibbet Island. A faint creaking overhead caused Vanderscamp to cast up his eyes, when, to his horror, he beheld the bodies of his three pot companions and brothers in iniquity dangling in the moonlight, their rags fluttering, and their chains creaking, as they were slowly swung backward and forward by the rising breeze.

"What do you mean, you blockhead!" cried Vanderscamp, "by pulling so close to the island?"

"I thought you'd be glad to see your old friends once more," growled the negro; "you were never afraid of a living man, what do you fear from the dead?"

"Who's afraid?" hiccoughed Vanderscamp, partly heated by liquor, partly nettled by the jeer of the negro; "who's afraid? Hang me, but I would be glad to see them once more, alive or dead, at the Wild Goose. Come, my lads in the wind!" continued he, taking a draught and flourishing the bottle above his head, "here's fair weather to you in the other world; and if you should be walking the rounds to-night, odds fish! but I'll be happy if you will drop in to supper."

A dismal creaking was the only reply. The wind blew loud and shrill, and as it whistled round the gallows, and among the bones, sounded as if they were laughing and gibbering in the air. Old Pluto chuckled to himself, and now pulled for home. The storm burst over the voyagers, while they were yet far from shore. The rain fell in torrents, the thunder crashed and pealed, and the lightning kept up an incessant blaze. It was stark midnight before they landed at Communipaw.

Dripping and shivering, Vanderscamp crawled homeward. He was completely sobered by the storm, the water soaked from without having diluted and cooled the liquor within. Arrived at the Wild Goose, he knocked timidly and dubiously at the door; for he dreaded the reception he was to experience from his wife. He had reason to do so. She met him at the threshold, in a precious ill-humor.

"Is this a time," said she, "to keep people out of their beds, and to bring home company, to turn the house upside down?"

"Company?" said Vanderscamp, meekly; "I have brought no company with me, wife?"

"No, indeed! they have got here before you, but by your invitation; and blessed-looking company they are, truly!"

Vanderscamp's knees smote together. "For the love of heaven, where are they, wife?"

"Where?—why in the blue room, up-stairs, making themselves as much at home as if the house were their own."

Vanderscamp made a desperate effort, scrambled up to the room, and threw open the door. Sure enough, there at a table, on which burned a light as blue as brimstone, sat the three guests from Gibbet Island, with halters round their necks, and bobbing their cups together, as if they were hob-or-nobbing, and trolling the old Dutch freebooter's glee, since translated into English:

> "For three merry lads be we,
> And three merry lads be we;
> I on the land, and thou on the sand,
> And Jack on the gallows-tree."

Vanderscamp saw and heard no more. Starting back with horror, he missed his footing on the landing-place, and fell from the top of the stairs to the bottom. He was taken up speechless, either from the fall or the fright, and was buried in the yard of the little Dutch church at Bergen, on the following Sunday.

From that day forward the fate of the Wild Goose was sealed. It was pronounced a *haunted house*, and avoided accordingly. No one inhabited it but Vanderscamp's shrew of a widow and old Pluto, and they were considered but little better than its hobgoblin visitors. Pluto grew more and more haggard and morose, and looked more like an imp of darkness than a human being. He spoke to no one, but went about muttering to himself; or, as some hinted, talking with the devil, who, though unseen, was ever at his elbow. Now and then he was seen pulling about the bay alone in his skiff, in dark weather, or at the approach of nightfall; nobody could tell why, unless, on an errand to invite more guests from the gallows. Indeed, it was affirmed that the Wild Goose still continued to be a house of entertainment for such guests, and that on stormy nights the blue chamber was occasionally illuminated, and sounds of diabolical merriment were overheard, mingling with the howling of the tempest. Some treated these as idle stories, until on one such night, it was about the time of the equinox, there was a horrible uproar in the Wild Goose, that could not be mistaken. It was not so much the sound of revelry, however, as strife, with two or three piercing shrieks, that pervaded every part of the village. Nevertheless, no one thought of hastening to the spot. On the contrary, the honest burghers of Communipaw drew their nightcaps over their ears, and buried their heads under the bedclothes, at the thoughts of Vanderscamp and his gallows companions.

The next morning some of the bolder and more curious undertook to reconnoitre. All was quiet and lifeless at the Wild Goose. The door yawned wide open, and had evidently been open all night, for the storm had beaten into the house. Gathering more courage from the silence and apparent desertion, they gradually ventured over the threshold. The house had indeed the air of having been possessed by devils. Everything was topsy-turvy; trunks had been broken open, and chests of drawers and corner cupboards turned inside out, as in a time of general sack and pillage; but the most woeful sight was the widow of Yan Yost Vanderscamp, extended a corpse on the floor of the blue chamber, with the marks of a deadly gripe on the windpipe.

All now was conjecture and dismay at Communipaw; and the disappearance of old Pluto, who was nowhere to be found, gave rise to all kinds of wild surmises. Some suggested that the negro had betrayed the house to some of Vanderscamp's buccaneering associates, and that they had decamped together with the booty; others surmised that the negro was nothing more nor less than a devil incarnate, who had now accomplished his ends, and made off with his dues.

Events, however, vindicated the negro from this last implication. His skiff was picked up, drifting about the bay, bottom upward, as if wrecked in a tempest; and his body was found, shortly afterward, by some Communipaw fishermen, stranded among the rocks of Gibbet Island, near the foot of the pirates gallows. The fishermen shook their heads and observed that old Pluto had ventured once too often to invite guests from Gibbet Island.

From *Wolfert's Roost*

THE EARLY EXPERIENCES OF
RALPH RINGWOOD

*Noted Down from His Conversations: by Geoffrey Crayon, Gent**

I AM a Kentuckian by residence and choice, but a Virginian by
birth. The cause of my first leaving the "Ancient Dominion," and
emigrating to Kentucky, was a jackass! You stare, but have a little patience, and I'll soon show you how it came to pass. My father, who
was of one of the old Virginian families, resided in Richmond. He was
a widower, and his domestic affairs were managed by a housekeeper
of the old school, such as used to administer the concerns of opulent
Virginian households. She was a dignitary that almost rivalled my
father in importance, and seemed to think everything belonged to her;
in fact, she was so considerate in her economy, and so careful of expense, as sometimes to vex my father, who would swear she was dis-
gracing him by her meanness. She always appeared with that ancient
insignia of housekeeping trust and authority, a great bunch of keys
jingling at her girdle. She superintended the arrangements of the table at every meal, and saw that the dishes were all placed according to
her primitive notions of symmetry. In the evening she took her stand
and served out tea with a mingled respectfulness and pride of station
truly exemplary. Her great ambition was to have everything in order,

---

* Ralph Ringwood, though a fictitious name, is a real personage,—the late Governor [William P.] Duval of Florida. I have given some anecdotes of his early and
eccentric career, in, as nearly as I can recollect, the very words in which he related
them. They certainly afford strong temptations to the embellishments of fiction;
but I thought them so strikingly characteristic of the individual and of the scenes
and society into which his peculiar humors carried him, that I preferred giving
them in their original simplicity.—w.i.

We can take with a large grain of salt Irving's disclaimer of fictionalizing here.
He would have had to have had a phonographic memory to support his assertion that
he has produced the very words in which Duval related his experiences. I have
removed the awkward quotation marks from the original version. They were not
always characteristic of his method.—c.n.

and that the establishment under her sway should be cited as a model of good housekeeping. If anything went wrong, poor old Barbara would take it to heart, and sit in her room and cry, until a few chapters in the Bible would quiet her spirits, and make all calm again. The Bible, in fact, was her constant resort in time of trouble. She opened it indiscriminately, and whether she chanced among the Lamentations of Jeremiah, the Canticles of Solomon, or the rough enumeration of the tribes in Deuteronomy, a chapter was a chapter, and operated like balm to her soul. Such was our good old housekeeper Barbara; who was destined, unwittingly, to have a most important effect upon my destiny.

It came to pass, during the days of my juvenility, while I was yet what is termed "an unlucky boy," that a gentleman of our neighborhood, a great advocate for experiments and improvements of all kinds took it into his head that it would be an immense public advantage to introduce a breed of mules, and accordingly imported three jacks to stock the neighborhood. This in a part of the country where the people cared for nothing but blood horses! Why, sir, they would have considered their mares disgraced, and their whole stud dishonored, by such a misalliance. The whole matter was a town-talk, and a town scandal. The worthy amalgamator of quadrupeds found himself in a dismal scrape; so he backed out in time, abjured the whole doctrine of amalgamation, and turned his jacks loose to shift for themselves upon the town common. There they used to run about and lead an idle, good-for-nothing, holiday life, the happiest animals in the country.

It so happened that my way to school lay across the common. The first time that I saw one of these animals, it set up a braying and frightened me confoundedly. However, I soon got over my fright, and seeing that it had something of a horse look, my Virginian love for anything of the equestrian species predominated, and I determined to back it. I accordingly applied at a grocer's shop, procured a cord that had been round a loaf of sugar, and made a kind of halter; then, summoning some of my school-fellows, we drove master Jack about the common until we hemmed him in in an angle of a "worm-fence." After some difficulty we fixed the halter round his muzzle, and I mounted. Up flew his heels, away I went over his head, and off he scampered. However, I was on my legs in a twinkling, gave chase, caught him, and remounted. By dint of repeated tumbles I soon learned to stick to his back, so that he could no more cast me than he could his own skin. From that time, master Jack and his companions had a scampering life of it, for we all rode them between school-hours, and on holiday afternoons; and you may be sure school-boys' nags are never permitted to suffer the grass to grow under their feet. They soon became so knowing, that they took to their heels at sight of a schoolboy; and we were generally much longer in chasing than we were in riding them.

Sunday approached, on which I projected an equestrian excursion on one of these long-eared steeds. As I knew the jacks would be in great demand on Sunday morning, I secured one over night, and conducted him home, to be ready for an early outset. But where was I to quarter him for the night? I could not put him in the stable; our old black groom George was as absolute in that domain as Barbara was within doors, and would have thought his stable, his horses, and himself disgraced by the introduction of a jackass. I recollected the smoke-house,—an outbuilding appended to all Virginian establishments, for the smoking of hams and other kinds of meat. So I got the key, put master Jack in, locked the door, returned the key to its place, and went to bed, intending to release my prisoner at an early hour, before any of the family were awake. I was so tired, however, by the exertions I had made in catching the donkey, that I fell into a sound sleep, and the morning broke without my waking.

·Not so with dame Barbara, the housekeeper. As usual, to use her own phrase, "she was up before the crow put his shoes on," and bustled about to get things in order for breakfast. Her first resort was to the smoke-house. Scarce had she opened the door, when master Jack, tired of his confinement, and glad to be released from darkness, gave a loud bray, and rushed forth. Down dropped old Barbara; the animal trampled over her, and made off for the common. Poor Barbara! She had never before seen a donkey; and having read in the Bible that the Devil went about like a roaring lion, seeking whom he might devour, she took it for granted that this was Beelzebub himself. The kitchen was soon in a hubbub; the servants hurried to the spot. There lay old Barbara in fits; as fast as she got out of one, the thoughts of the Devil came over her, and she fell into another, for the good soul was devoutly superstitious.

As ill luck would have it, among those attracted by the noise, was a little, cursed, fidgety, crabbed uncle of mine; one of those uneasy spirits that cannot rest quietly in their beds in the morning, but must be up early, to bother the household. He was only a kind of half-uncle, after all, for he had married my father's sister; yet he assumed great authority on the strength of this left-handed relationship, and was a universal intermeddler and family pest. This prying little busybody soon ferreted out the truth of the story, and discovered, by hook and by crook, that I was at the bottom of the affair, and had locked up the donkey in the smoke-house. He stopped to inquire no farther, for he was one of those testy curmudgeons with whom unlucky boys are always in the wrong. Leaving old Barbara to wrestle in imagination with the Devil, he made for my bedchamber, where I still lay wrapped in rosy slumbers, little dreaming of the mischief I had done, and the storm about to break over me.

In an instant I was awakened by a shower of thwacks, and started up in wild amazement. I demanded the meaning of this attack, but received no other reply than that I had murdered the housekeeper; while my uncle continued whacking away during my confusion. I seized a poker, and put myself on the defensive. I was a stout boy for my years, while my uncle was a little wiffet of a man; one that in Kentucky we would not call even an "individual"; nothing more than a "remote circumstance." I soon, therefore, brought him to a parley, and learned the whole extent of the charge brought against me. I confessed to the donkey and the smoke-house, but pleaded not guilty of the murder of the housekeeper. I soon found out that old Barbara was still alive. She continued under the doctor's hands, however, for several days; and whenever she had an ill turn, my uncle would seek to give me another flogging. I appealed to my father, but got no redress. I was considered an "unlucky boy," prone to all kinds of mischief; so that prepossessions were against me, in all cases of appeal.

I felt stung to the soul at all this. I had been beaten, degraded, and treated with slighting when I complained. I lost my usual good spirits and good-humor; and, being out of temper with everybody, fancied everybody out of temper with me. A certain wild, roving spirit of freedom, which I believe is as inherent in me as it is in the partridge, was brought into sudden activity by the checks and restraints I suffered. "I'll go from home," thought I, "and shift for myself." Perhaps this notion was quickened by the rage for emigrating to Kentucky which was at that time prevalent in Virginia. I had heard such stories of the romantic beauties of the country, of the abundance of game of all kinds, and of the glorious independent life of the hunters who ranged its noble forests, and lived by the rifle, that I was as much agog to get there as boys who live in seaports are to launch themselves among the wonders and adventures of the ocean.

After a time, old Barbara got better in mind and body, and matters were explained to her; and she became gradually convinced that it was not the Devil she had encountered. When she heard how harshly I had been treated on her account, the good old soul was extremely grieved, and spoke warmly to my father in my behalf. He had himself remarked the change in my behavior, and thought punishment might have been carried too far. He sought, therefore, to have some conversation with me and to soothe my feelings; but it was too late. I frankly told him the course of mortification that I had experienced, and the fixed determination I had made to go from home.

"And where do you mean to go?"

"To Kentucky."

"To Kentucky! Why, you know nobody there."

"No matter; I can soon make acquaintances."

"And what will you do when you get there?"

"Hunt!"

My father gave a long, low whistle, and looked in my face with a serio-comic expression. I was not far in my teens, and to talk of setting off alone for Kentucky, to turn hunter, seemed doubtless the idle prattle of a boy. He was little aware of the dogged resolution of my character; and his smile of incredulity but fixed me more obstinately in my purpose. I assured him I was·serious in what I said, and would certainly set off for Kentucky in the spring.

Month after month passed away. My father now and then adverted slightly to what had passed between us; doubtless for the purpose of sounding me. I always expressed the same grave and fixed determination. By degrees he spoke to me more directly on the subject, endeavoring earnestly but kindly to dissuade me. My only reply was, "I had made up my mind."

Accordingly, as soon as the spring had fairly opened, I sought him one day in his study, and informed him I was about to set out for Kentucky, and had come to take my leave. He made no objection, for he had exhausted persuasion and remonstrance, and doubtless thought it best to give way to my humor, trusting that a little rough experience would soon bring me home again. I asked money for my journey. He went to a chest, took out a long green silk purse, well filled, and laid it on the table. I now asked for a horse and servant.

"A horse!" said my father, sneeringly, "why, you would not go a mile without racing him, and breaking your neck; and as to a servant, you cannot take care of yourself, much less of him."

"How am I to travel, then?"

"Why, I suppose you are man enough to travel on foot."

He spoke jestingly, little thinking I would take him at his word; but I was thoroughly piqued in respect to my enterprise; so I pocketed the purse, went to my room, tied up three or four shirts in a pocket-hand-kerchief, put a dirk in my bosom, girt a couple of pistols round my waist, and felt like a knight-errant armed *cap-a-pie,* and ready to rove the world in quest of adventures.

My sister (I had but one) hung round me and wept, and entreated me to stay. I felt my heart swell in my throat; but I gulped it back to its place, and straightened myself up: I would not suffer myself to cry. I at length disengaged myself from her, and got to the door.

"When will you come back?" cried she.

"Never, by heavens!" cried I, "until I come back a member of Congress from Kentucky. I am determined to show that I am not the tail-end of the family."

Such was my first outset from home. You may suppose what a greenhorn I was, and how little I knew of the world I was launching into.

I do not recollect any incident of importance, until I reached the borders of Pennsylvania. I had stopped at an inn to get some refreshment; as I was eating in a back room, I overheard two men in the bar-room conjecture who and what I could be. One determined, at length, that I was a runaway apprentice, and ought to be stopped, to which the other assented. When I had finished my meal, and paid for it, I went out at the back door, lest I should be stopped by my supervisors. Scorning, however, to steal off like a culprit, I walked round to the front of the house. One of the men advanced to the front door. He wore his hat on one side, and had a consequential air that nettled me.

"Where are you going, youngster?" demanded he.

"That's none of your business!" replied I, rather pertly.

"Yes, but it is though! You have run away from home, and must give an account of yourself."

He advanced to seize me, when I drew forth a pistol. "If you advance another step, I'll shoot you!"

He sprang back as if he had trodden upon a rattle-snake, and his hat fell off in the movement.

"Let him alone!" cried his companion; "he's a foolish mad-headed boy, and don't know what he's about. He'll shoot you, you may rely on it."

He did not need any caution in the matter; he was afraid even to pick up his hat; so I pushed forward on my way without molestation. This incident, however, had its effect upon me. I became fearful of sleeping in any house at night, lest I should be stopped. I took my meals in the houses, in the course of the day, but would turn aside at night into some wood or ravine, make a fire and sleep before it. This I considered was true hunter's style, and I wished to inure myself to it.

At length I arrived at Brownsville, leg-weary and wayworn, and in a shabby plight, as you may suppose, having been "camping out" for some nights past. I applied at some of the inferior inns, but could gain no admission. I was regarded for a moment with a dubious eye, and then informed they did not receive foot-passengers. At last I went boldly to the principal inn. The landlord appeared as unwilling as the rest to receive a vagrant boy beneath his roof; but his wife interfered in the midst of his excuses, and, half elbowing him aside,—

"Where are you going, my lad?" said she.

"To Kentucky."

"What are you going there for?"

"To hunt."

She looked earnestly at me for a moment or two. "Have you a mother living?" said she at length.

"No, madam; she has been dead for some time."

"I thought so!" cried she, warmly. "I knew if you had a mother living, you would not be here." From that moment the good woman treated me with a mother's kindness.

I remained several days beneath her roof, recovering from the fatigue of my journey. While here, I purchased a rifle, and practised daily at a mark, to prepare myself for a hunter's life. When sufficiently recruited in strength I took leave of my kind host and hostess, and resumed my journey.

. At Wheeling I embarked in a flat-bottomed family boat, technically called a broad-horn, a prime river conveyance in those days. In this ark for two weeks I floated down the Ohio. The river was as yet in all its wild beauty. Its loftiest trees had not been thinned out. The forest overhung the water's edge, and was occasionally skirted by immense canebrakes. Wild animals of all kinds abounded. We heard them rushing through the thickets and plashing in the water. Deer and bears would frequently swim across the river; others would come down to the bank, and gaze at the boat as it passed. I was incessantly on the alert with my rifle; but, somehow or other, the game was never within shot. Sometimes I got a chance to land and try my skill on shore. I shot squirrels, and small birds, and even wild turkeys; but though I caught glimpses of deer bounding away through the woods, I never could get a fair shot at them.

In this way we glided in our broad-horn past Cincinnati, the "Queen of the West," as she is now called, then a mere group of log-cabins; and the site of the bustling city of Louisville, then designated by a solitary house. As I said before, the Ohio was as yet a wild river; all was forest, forest, forest! Near the confluence of Green River with the Ohio I landed, bade adieu to the broad-horn, and struck for the interior of Kentucky. I had no precise plan; my only idea was to make for one of the wildest parts of the country. I had relatives in Lexington and other settled places, to whom I thought it probable my father would write concerning me; so, as I was full of manhood and independence, and resolutely bent on making my way in the world without assistance or control, I resolved to keep clear of them all.

In the course of my first day's trudge I shot a wild turkey, and slung it on my back for provisions. The forest was open and clear from underwood. I saw deer in abundance, but always running, running. It seemed to me as if these animals never stood still.

At length I came to where a gang of half-starved wolves were feasting on the carcass of a deer which they had run down, and snarling and snapping, and fighting like so many dogs. They were all so ravenous and intent upon their prey that they did not notice me, and I had time to make my observations. One, larger and fiercer than the rest, seemed to claim the larger share, and to keep the others in awe. If any one came too near him while eating, he would fly off, seize and shake him, and then return to his repast. "This," thought I, "must be the captain; if I can kill him, I shall defeat the whole army." I accordingly took aim, fired, and down dropped the old fellow. He might be only shamming dead; so I loaded and put a second ball through him. He never budged; all the rest ran off, and my victory was complete.

.It would not be easy to describe my triumphant feelings on this great achievement. I marched on with renovated spirit, regarding myself as absolute lord of the forest. As night drew near, I prepared for camping. My first care was to collect dry wood, and make a roaring fire to cook and sleep by, and to frighten off wolves, and bears, and panthers. I then began to pluck my turkey for supper. I had camped out several times in the early part of my expedition; but that was in comparatively more settled and civilized regions, where there were no wild animals of consequence in the forest. This was my first camping out in the real wilderness, and I was soon made sensible of the loneliness and wildness of my situation.

In a little while a concert of wolves commenced; there might have been a dozen or two, but it seemed to me as if there were thousands. I never heard such howling and whining. Having prepared my turkey, I divided it into two parts, thrust two sticks into one of the halves, and planted them on end before the fire,—the hunter's mode of roasting. The smell of roast meat quickened the appetites of the wolves, and their concert became truly infernal. They seemed to be all around me, but I could only now and then get a glimpse of one of them, as he came within the glare of the light.

I did not much care for the wolves, who I knew to be a cowardly race, but I had heard terrible stories of panthers, and began to fear their stealthy prowlings in the surrounding darkness. I was thirsty, and heard a brook bubbling and tinkling along at no great distance, but absolutely dared not go there, lest some panther might lie in wait and spring upon me. By-and-by a deer whistled. I had never heard one before, and thought it must be a panther. I now felt uneasy lest he might climb the trees, crawl along the branches overhead, and plump down upon me; so I kept my eyes fixed on the branches, until my head ached. I more than once thought I saw fiery eyes glaring down from among the leaves. At length I thought of my supper, and turned to see if my half turkey was cooked. In crowding so near the fire, I had pressed the meat into the flames, and it was consumed. I had nothing to do but roast the other half, and take better care of it. On that half I made my supper, without salt or bread. I was still so possessed with the dread of panthers, that I could not close my eyes all night, but lay watching the trees until daybreak, when all my fears were dispelled with the darkness; and as I saw the morning sun sparkling down through the branches of the trees, I smiled to think how I suffered myself to be dismayed by sounds and shadows; but I was a young woodsman, and a stranger in Kentucky.

Having breakfasted on the remainder of my turkey and slaked my thirst at the bubbling stream, without farther dread of panthers, I resumed my wayfaring with buoyant feelings. I again saw deer, but, as usual, running, running! I tried in vain to get a shot at them, and began to fear I never should. I was gazing with vexation after a herd in full scamper, when I was startled by a human voice. Turning round I saw a man at a short distance from me in a hunting-dress.

"What are you after, my lad?" cried he.

"Those deer," replied I, pettishly; "but it seems as if they never stand still."

Upon that he burst out laughing. "Where are you from?" said he.

"From Richmond."

"What! In old Virginny?"

"The same."

"And how on earth did you get here?"

"I landed at Green River from a broad-horn."

"And where are your companions?"

"I have none."

"What!—all alone?"

"Yes."

"Where are you going?"

"Anywhere."

"And what have you come here for?"

"To hunt."

"Well," said he, laughingly, "you'll make a real hunter; there's no mistaking that! Have you killed anything?"

"Nothing but a turkey; I can't get within shot of a deer; they are always running."

"Oh, I'll tell you the secret of that. You're always pushing forward, and starting the deer at a distance, and gazing at those that are scampering; but you must step as slow and silent and cautious as a cat, and keep your eyes close round you, and lurk from tree to tree, if you wish to get a chance at deer. But come, go home with me. My name is Bill Smithers; I live not far off; stay with me a little while, and I'll teach you how to hunt."

I gladly accepted the invitation of honest Bill Smithers. We soon reached his habitation, a mere log-hut, with a square hole for a window, and a chimney made of sticks and clay. Here he lived, with a wife and child. He had "girdled" the trees for an acre or two around, preparatory to clearing a space for corn and potatoes. In the meantime he maintained his family entirely by his rifle, and I soon found him to be a first-rate huntsman. Under his tutelage I received my first effective lessons in "woodcraft."

The more I knew of a hunter's life, the more I relished it. The country, too, which had been the promised land of my boyhood, did not, like most promised lands, disappoint me. No wilderness could be more beautiful than this part of Kentucky in those times. The forests were open and spacious, with noble trees, some of which looked as if they had stood for centuries. There were beautiful prairies, too, diversified with groves and clumps of trees, which looked like vast parks, and in which you could see the deer running, at a great distance. In the proper season, these prairies would be covered in many places with wild strawberries, where your horse's hoofs would be dyed to the fetlock. I thought there could not be another place in the world equal to Kentucky;—and I think so still.

After I had passed ten or twelve days with Bill Smithers, I thought it time to shift my quarters, for his house was scarce large enough for his own family, and I had no idea of being an encumbrance to any one. I accordingly made up my bundle, shouldered my rifle, took a friendly leave of Smithers and his wife, and set out in quest of a Nimrod of the wilderness, one John Miller, who lived alone, nearly forty miles off, and who I hoped would be well pleased to have a hunting companion.

I soon found out that one of the most important items in woodcraft, in a new country, was the skill to find one's way in the wilderness. There were no regular roads in the forests, but they were cut up and perplexed by paths leading in all directions. Some of these were made by the cattle of the settlers, and were called "stock-tracks," but others had been made by the immense droves of buffaloes which roamed about the country from the flood until recent times. These were called buffalo-tracks, and traversed Kentucky from end to end, like highways. Traces of them may still be seen in uncultivated parts, or deeply worn in the rocks where they crossed the mountains. I was a young woodsman, and sorely puzzled to distinguish one kind of track from the other, or to make out my course through this tangled labyrinth. While thus perplexed, I heard a distant roaring and rushing sound; a gloom stole over the forest. On looking up, when I could catch a stray glimpse of the sky, I beheld the clouds rolled up like balls, the lower part as black as ink. There was now and then an explosion, like a burst of cannonry afar off, and the crash of a falling tree. I had heard of hurricanes in the woods, and surmised that one was at hand. It soon came crashing its way, the forest writhing, and twisting, and groaning before it. The hurricane did not extend far on either side, but in a manner ploughed a furrow through the woodland, snapping off or uprooting trees that had stood for centuries, and filling the air with whirling branches. I was directly in its course, and took my stand behind an immense poplar, six feet in diameter. It bore for a time the full fury of the blast, but at length began to yield. Seeing it falling, I scrambled nimbly round the trunk like a squirrel. Down it went, bearing down another tree with it. I crept under the trunk as a shelter, and was protected from other trees which fell around me, but was sore all over, from the twigs and branches driven against me by the blast.

This was the only incident of consequence that occurred on my way to John Miller's, where I arrived on the following day, and was received by the veteran with the rough kindness of a backwoodsman. He was a gray-haired man, hardy and weather-beaten, with a blue wart, like a great bead, over one eye, whence he was nick-named by the hunters, "Blue-bead Miller." He had been in these parts from the earliest settlements, and had signalized himself in the hard conflicts with the Indians, which gained Kentucky the appellation of "the Bloody Ground." In one of these fights he had an arm broken; in another he had narrowly escaped, when hotly pursued, by jumping from a precipice thirty feet high into a river.

Miller willingly received me into his house as an inmate, and seemed pleased with the idea of making a hunter of me. His dwelling was a small log-house, with a loft or garret of boards, so that there was ample room for both of us. Under his instruction, I soon made a tolerable proficiency in hunting. My first exploit of any consequence was killing a bear. I was hunting in company with two brothers, when we came upon the track of Bruin, in a wood where there was an undergrowth of canes and grape-vines. He was scrambling up a tree, when I shot him through the breast; he fell to the ground, and lay motionless. The brothers sent in their dog, who seized the bear by the throat. Bruin raised one arm, and gave the dog a hug that crushed his ribs. One yell, and all was over. I don't know which was first dead, the dog or the bear. The two brothers sat down and cried like children over their unfortunate dog. Yet they were mere rough huntsmen, almost as wild and untamable as Indians; but they were fine fellows.

By degrees I became known, and somewhat of a favorite among the hunters of the neighborhood; that is to say, men who lived within a circle of thirty or forty miles, and came occasionally to see John Miller, who was a patriarch among them. They lived widely apart, in log-huts and wigwams, almost with the simplicity of Indians, and wellnigh as destitute of the comforts and inventions of civilized life. They seldom saw each other; weeks, and even months would elapse, without their visiting. When they did meet, it was very much after the manner of Indians; loitering about all day, without having much to say, but becoming communicative as evening advanced, and sitting up half the night before the fire, telling hunting-stories, and terrible tales of the fights of the Bloody Ground.

Sometimes several would join in a distant hunting expedition, or rather campaign. Expeditions of this kind lasted from November until April, during which we laid up our stock of summer provisions. We shifted our hunting-camps from place to place, according as we found the game. They were generally pitched near a run of water, and close by a canebrake, to screen us from the wind. One side of our lodge was open towards the fire. Our horses were hoppled and turned loose in the canebrakes, with bells round their necks. One of the party stayed at home to watch the camp, prepare the meals, and keep off the wolves; the others hunted. When a hunter killed a deer at a distance from the camp, he would open it and take out the entrails; then climbing a sapling, he would bend it down, tie the deer to the top, and let it spring up again, so as to suspend the carcass out of reach of the wolves. At night he would return to the camp, and give an account of his luck. The next morning early he would get a horse out of the cane-brake and bring home his game. That day he would stay at home to cut up the carcass, while the others hunted.

Our days were thus spent in silent and lonely occupations. It was only at night that we would gather together before the fire, and be sociable. I was a novice, and used to listen with open eyes and ears to the strange and wild stories told by the old hunters, and believed everything I heard. Some of their stories bordered upon the supernatural. They believed that their rifles might be spellbound, so as not to be

THE COMPLETE TALES OF WASHINGTON IRVING

able to kill a buffalo, even at arm's length. This superstition they had derived from the Indians, who often think the white hunters have laid a spell upon their rifles. Miller partook of this superstition, and used to tell of his rifle's having a spell upon it; but it often seemed to me to be a shuffling way of accounting for a bad shot. If a hunter grossly missed his aim, he would ask, "Who shot last with his rifle?"—and hint that he must have charmed it. The sure mode to disenchant the gun was to shoot a silver bullet out of it.

By the opening of spring we would generally have quantities of bear's meat and venison salted, dried, and smoked, and numerous packs of skins. We would then make the best of our way home from our distant hunting-grounds, transporting our spoils, sometimes in canoes along the rivers, sometimes on horseback over land, and our return would often be celebrated by feasting and dancing, in true backwoods style. I have given you some idea of our hunting; let me now give you a sketch of our frolicking.

It was on our return from a winter's hunting in the neighborhood of Green River, when we received notice that there was to be a grand frolic at Bob Mosely's to greet the hunters. This Bob Mosely was a prime fellow throughout the country. He was an indifferent hunter, it is true, and rather lazy, to boot; but then he could play the fiddle, and that was enough to make him of consequence. There was no other man within a hundred miles that could play the fiddle, so there was no having a regular frolic without Bob Mosely. The hunters, therefore, were always ready to give him a share of their game in exchange for his music, and Bob was always ready to get up a carousal whenever there was a party returning from a hunting expedition. The present frolic was to take place at Bob Mosely's own house, which was on the Pigeon-Roost Fork of the Muddy, which is a branch of Rough Creek, which is a branch of Green River.

Everybody was agog for the revel at Bob Mosely's; and as all the fashion of the neighborhood was to be there, I thought I must brush up for the occasion. My leathern hunting-dress which was the only one I had, was somewhat the worse for wear, it is true, and considerably japanned with blood and grease; but I was up to hunting expedients. Getting into a periogue, I paddled off to a part of the Green River where there was sand and clay, that might serve for soap; then, taking off my dress, I scrubbed and scoured it, until I thought it looked very well. I then put it on the end of a stick, and hung it out of the periogue to dry, while I stretched myself very comfortably on the green bank of the river. Unluckily a flaw struck the periogue, and tipped over the stick; down went my dress to the bottom of the river, and I never saw it more. Here was I, left almost in a state of nature. I managed to make a kind of Robinson Crusoe garb of undressed skins, with the hair on, which enabled me to get home with decency; but my dream of gayety and fashion was at an end; for how could I think of figuring in high life at the Pigeon Roost, equipped like a mere Orson?

Old Miller, who really began to take some pride in me, was confounded when he understood that I did not intend to go to Bob Mosely's; but when I told him my misfortune, and that I had no dress, "By the powers," cried he, "but you *shall* go, and you shall be the best dressed and the best mounted lad there!"

He immediately set to work to cut out and make up a hunting-shirt, of dressed deer-skin, gayly fringed at the shoulders, and leggins of the same, fringed from hip to heel. He then made me a rakish raccoon-cap, with a flaunting tail to it, mounted me on his best horse; and I may say, without vanity, that I was one of the smartest fellows that figured on that occasion at the Pigeon-Roost Fork of the Muddy.

It was no small occasion, either, let me tell you. Bob Mosely's house was a tolerably large bark shanty, with a clapboard roof; and there were assembled all the young hunters and pretty girls of the country for many a mile round. The young men were in their best hunting-dresses, but not one could compare with mine; and my raccoon-cap, with its flowing tail, was the admiration of everybody. The girls were mostly in doe-skin dresses; for there was no spinning and weaving as yet in the woods, nor any need of it. I never saw girls that seemed to me better dressed, and I was somewhat of a judge, having seen fashions at Richmond. We had a hearty dinner, and a merry one; for there was Jemmy Kiel, famous for raccoon-hunting, and Bob Tarleton, and Wesley Pigman, and Joe Taylor, and several other prime fellows for a frolic, that made all ring again, and laughed that you might have heard them a mile.

After dinner we began dancing, and were hard at it when, about three o'clock in the afternoon, there was a new arrival—the two daughters of old Simon Schultz; two young ladies that affected fashion and late hours. Their arrival had nearly put an end to all our merriment. I must go a little round about in my story to explain to you how that happened.

As old Schultz, the father, was one day looking in the canebrakes for his cattle, he came upon the track of horses. He knew they were none of his, and that none of his neighbors had horses about that place. They must be stray horses, or must belong to some traveller who had lost his way, as the track led nowhere. He accordingly followed it up, until he came to an unlucky peddler, with two or three pack-horses, who had been bewildered among the cattle-tracks, and had wandered for two or three days among woods and canebrakes, until he was almost famished.

Old Schultz brought him to his house, fed him on venison, bear's meat, and hominy, and at the end of a week put him in prime condition. The peddler could not sufficiently express his thankfulness, and when about to depart, inquired what he had to pay. Old Schultz stepped back with surprise. "Stranger," said he, "you have been welcome under my roof. I've given you nothing but wild meat and hominy, because I had no better, but have been glad of your company. You are welcome to stay as long as you please; but, by Zounds! if any one offers to pay Simon Schultz for food, he affronts him!" So saying, he walked out in a huff.

The peddler admired the hospitality of his host, but could not reconcile it to his conscience to go away without making some recompense. There were honest Simon's two daughters, two strapping, red-haired girls. He opened his packs and displayed riches before them of which they had no conception; for in those days there were no country stores in those parts, with their artificial finery and trinketry; and this was the first peddler that had wandered into that part of the wilderness. The girls were for a time completely dazzled, and knew not what to choose; but what caught their eyes most were two looking-glasses, about the size of a dollar, set in gilt tin. They had never seen the like before, having used no other mirror than a pail of water. The peddler presented them these jewels without the least hesitation; nay, he gallantly hung them round their necks by red ribbons, almost as fine as the glasses themselves. This done, he took his departure, leaving them as much astonished as two princesses in a fairy-tale, that have received a magic gift from an enchanter.

It was with these looking-glasses hung round their necks as lockets, by red ribbons that old Schultz's daughters made their appearance at three o'clock in the afternoon, at the frolic at Bob Mosely's, on the Pigeon-Roost Fork of the Muddy.

By the powers, but it was an event! Such a thing had never before been seen in Kentucky. Bob Tarleton, a strapping fellow, with a head like a chestnut-burr, and a look like a boar in an apple-orchard, stepped up, caught hold of the looking-glass of one of the girls, and gazing at it for a moment, cried out, "Joe Taylor, come here! come here! I'll be darn'd if Patty Schultz ain't got a locket that you can see your face in, as clear as in a spring of water!"

In a twinkling all the young hunters gathered round old Schultz's daughters. I, who knew what looking-glasses were, did not budge. Some of the girls who sat near me were excessively mortified at finding themselves thus deserted. I heard Peggy Pugh say to Sally Pigman, "Goodness knows it's well Schultz's daughters is got them things round their necks, for it's the first time the young men crowded round them!"

I saw immediately the danger of the case. We were a small community, and could not afford to be split up by feuds. So I stepped up to the girls, and whispered to them: "Polly," said I, "those lockets are powerful fine, and become you amazingly, but you don't consider that the country is not advanced enough in these parts for such things. You and I understand these matters, but these people don't. Fine things like these may do very well in the old settlements, but they won't answer at the Pigeon-Roost Fork of the Muddy. You had better lay them aside for the present, or we shall have no peace."

Polly and her sister luckily saw their error; they took off the lockets, laid them aside, and harmony was restored; otherwise, I verily believe there would have been an end of our community. Indeed, notwithstanding the great sacrifice they made on this occasion, I do not think old Schultz's daughters were ever much liked afterwards among the young women.

This was the first time that looking-glasses were ever seen in the Green River part of Kentucky.

I had now lived some time with old Miller, and had become a tolerably expert hunter. Game, however, began to grow scarce. The buffalo had gathered together, as if by universal understanding, and had crossed the Mississippi, never to return. Strangers kept pouring into the country, clearing away the forests, and building in all directions. The hunters began to grow restive. Jemmy Kiel, the same of whom I have already spoken for his skill in raccoon catching came to me one day. "I can't stand this any longer," said he, "we're getting too thick here. Simon Schultz crowds me so that I have no comfort of my life."

"Why, how you talk!" said I; "Simon Schultz lives twelve miles off."

"No matter; his cattle run with mine, and I've no idea of living where another man's cattle can run with mine. That's too close neighborhood; I want elbow room. This country, too, is growing too poor to live in; there's no game; so two or three of us have made up our minds to follow the buffalo to the Missouri, and we should like to have you of the party." Other hunters of my acquaintance talked in the same manner. This set me thinking; but the more I thought, the more I was perplexed. I had no one to advise with; old Miller and his associates knew of but one mode of life, and I had no experience in any other but I had a wider scope of thought. When out hunting alone, I used to for-

get the sport, and sit for hours together on the trunk of a tree, with
rifle in hand, buried in thought, and debating with myself: "Shall I
go with Jemmy Kiel and his company, or shall I remain here? If I remain here, there will soon be nothing left to hunt. But am I to be a
hunter all my life? Have not I something more in me than to be
carrying a rifle on my shoulder, day after day, and dodging about
after bears, and deer, and other brute beasts?" My vanity told me I had;
and I called to mind my boyish boast to my sister, that I would never
return home until I returned a member of Congress from Kentucky;
but was this the way to fit myself for such a station?

Various plans passed through my mind, but they were abandoned
almost as soon as formed. At length I determined on becoming a lawyer.
True it is, I knew almost nothing. I had left school before I had learnt
beyond the "Rule of Three." "Never mind," said I to myself, resolutely,
"I am a terrible fellow for hanging on to anything when I've once
made up my mind; and if a man has but ordinary capacity, and will set
to work with heart and soul, and stick to it, he can do almost anything." With this maxim, which has been pretty much my main stay
throughout life, I fortified myself in my determination to attempt the
law. But how was I to set about it? I must quit this forest life, and go
to one or other of the towns, where I might be able to study and to attend the courts. This, too, required funds. I examined into the state
of my finances. The purse given me by my father had remained un-
touched, in the bottom of an old chest up in the loft, for money was
scarcely needed in these parts. I had bargained away the skins acquired in hunting, for a horse and various other matters, on which, in
case of need, I could raise funds. I therefore thought I could make shift
to maintain myself until I was fitted for the bar.

I informed my worthy host and patron, old Miller, of my plan. He
shook his head at my turning my back upon the woods when I was in a
fair way of making a first-rate hunter; but he made no effort to dissuade me. I accordingly set off in September, on horseback, intending
to visit Lexington, Frankfort, and other of the principal towns, in
search of a favorable place to prosecute my studies. My choice was made
sooner than I expected. I had put up one night at Bardstown, and
found, on inquiry, that I could get comfortable board and accommodation in a private family for a dollar and a half a week. I liked the place,
and resolved to look no farther. So the next morning I prepared to
turn my face homeward, and take my final leave of forest life.

I had taken my breakfast, and was waiting for my horse, when, in
pacing up and down the piazza, I saw a young girl seated near a window, evidently a visitor. She was very pretty, with auburn hair and

blue eyes, and was dressed in white. I had seen nothing of the kind since I had left Richmond, and at that time I was too much of a boy to be much struck by female charms. She was so delicate and dainty-looking, so different from the hale, buxom, brown girls of the woods; and then her white dress!—it was perfectly dazzling! Never was poor youth more taken by surprise and suddenly bewitched. My heart yearned to know her; but how was I to accost her? I had grown wild in the woods, and had none of the habitudes of polite life. Had she been like Peggy Pugh, or Sally Pigman, or any other of my leathern-dressed belles of the Pigeon Roost, I should have approached her without dread; nay, had she been as fair as Schultz's daughters, with their looking-glass lockets, I should not have hesitated; but that white dress and those auburn ringlets, and blue eyes, and delicate looks quite daunted while they fascinated me. I don't know what put it into my head, but I thought, all at once, that I would kiss her! It would take a long acquaintance to arrive at such a boon, but I might seize upon it by sheer robbery. Nobody knew me here. I would just step in, snatch a kiss, mount my horse, and ride off. She would not be the worse for it; and that kiss—oh! I should die if I did not get it!

I gave no time for the thought to cool, but entered the house, and stepped lightly into the room. She was seated with her back to the door, looking out at the window, and did not hear my approach. I tapped her chair, and as she turned and looked up, I snatched as sweet a kiss as ever was stolen, and vanished in a twinkling. The next moment I was on horseback, galloping homeward, my very ears tingling at what I had done.

On my return home, I sold my horse and turned everything to cash, and found, with the remains of the paternal purse, that I had nearly four hundred dollars,—a little capital which I resolved to manage with the strictest economy.

It was hard parting with old Miller, who had been like a father to me; it cost me, too, something of a struggle to give up the free, independent, wild-wood life I had hitherto led; but I had marked out my course, and have never been one to flinch or turn back.

I footed it sturdily to Bardstown, took possession of the quarters for which I had bargained, shut myself up, and set to work with might and main to study. But what a task I had before me! I had everything to learn; not merely law, but all the elementary branches of knowledge. I read and read for sixteen hours out of the four-and-twenty, but the more I read the more I became aware of my own ignorance, and shed bitter tears over my deficiency. It seemed as if the wilderness of knowledge expanded and grew more perplexed as I advanced. Every height gained only revealed a wider region to be traversed, and nearly filled me with despair. I grew moody, silent, and unsocial, but studied on doggedly and incessantly. The only person with whom I held any conversation, was the worthy man in whose house I was quartered. He was honest and well-meaning, but perfectly ignorant, and I believe would have liked me much better if I had not been so much addicted to reading. He considered all books filled with lies and impositions, and seldom could look into one without finding something to rouse his spleen. Nothing put him into a greater passion than the assertion that the world turned on its own axis every four-and-twenty hours. He swore it was an outrage upon common sense. "Why, if it did," said he, "there would not be a drop of water in the well by morning, and all the milk and cream in the dairy would be turned topsy-turvy!" And then to talk of the earth going round the sun! "How do they know it? I've seen the sun rise every morning and set every evening for more than thirty years. They must not talk to *me* about the earth's going round the sun!"

At another time he was in a perfect fret at being told the distance between the sun and moon. "How can any one tell the distance?" cried he. "Who surveyed it? who carried the chain? By Jupiter! they only talk this way before me to annoy me. But then there's some people of sense who give in to this cursed humbug! There's Judge Broadnax, now, one of the best lawyers we have; isn't it surprising he should believe in such stuff? Why, sir, the other day I heard him talk of the distance from a star he called Mars to the sun! He must have got it out of one or other of those confounded books he's so fond of reading; a book some impudent fellow has written, who knew nobody could swear the distance was more or less."

For my own part, feeling my own deficiency in scientific lore, I never ventured to unsettle his conviction that the sun made his daily circuit round the earth; and for aught I said to the contrary, he lived and died in that belief.

I had been about a year at Bardstown, living thus studiously and reclusely, when, as I was one day walking the street, I met two young girls, in one of whom I immediately recalled the little beauty whom I had kissed so impudently. She blushed up to the eyes, and so did I; but we both passed on without further sign of recognition. This second glimpse of her, however, caused an odd fluttering about my heart. I could not get her out of my thoughts for days. She quite interfered with my studies. I tried to think of her as a mere child, but it would not do; she had improved in beauty, and was tending toward womanhood: and then I myself was but little better than a stripling.

However, I did not attempt to seek after her, or even to find out who she was, but returned doggedly to my books. By degrees she faded from my thoughts, or if she did cross them occasionally, it was only to increase my despondency, for I feared that, with all my exertions, I should never be able to fit myself for the bar, or enable myself to support a wife.

One cold stormy evening I was seated, in dumpish mood, in the bar-room of the inn, looking into the fire and turning over uncomfortable thoughts, when I was accosted by someone who had entered the room without my perceiving it. I looked up, and saw before me a tall, and, as I thought, pompous-looking man, arrayed in smallclothes and kneebuckles, with powdered head, and shoes nicely blacked and polished; a style of dress unparalleled in those days in that rough country. I took a pique against him from the very portliness of his appearance and stateliness of his manner, and bristled up as he accosted me. He demanded if my name was not Ringwood.

I was startled, for I supposed myself perfectly *incog.*; but I answered in the affirmative.

. "Your family, I believe, lives in Richmond."

My gorge began to rise. "Yes, sir," replied I, sulkily, "my family does live in Richmond."

"And what, may I ask, has brought you into this part of the country?"

"Zounds, sir!" cried I, starting on my feet, "what business is it of yours? How dare you to question me in this manner?"

The entrance of some persons prevented a reply; but I walked up and down the bar-room, fuming with conscious independence and insulted dignity, while the pompous-looking personage, who had thus trespassed upon my spleen, retired without proffering another word.

The next day, while seated in my room, someone tapped at the door, and, on being bid to enter, the stranger in the powdered head, smallclothes, and shining shoes and buckles, walked in with ceremonious courtesy.

My boyish pride was again in arms, but he subdued me. He was formal, but kind and friendly. He knew my family and understood my situation, and the dogged struggle I was making. A little conversation, when my jealous pride was once put to rest, drew everything from me. He was a lawyer of experience and of extensive practice, and offered at once to take me with him and direct my studies. The offer was too advantageous and gratifying not to be immediately accepted. From that time I began to look up. I was put into a proper track, and was enabled to study to a proper purpose. I made acquaintance, too, with some of the young men of the place who were in the same pursuit, and was encouraged at finding that I could "hold my own" in argument with them. We instituted a debating-club, in which I soon became prominent and popular. Men of talents, engaged in other pursuits, joined it, and this diversified our subjects and put me on various tracks of inquiry. Ladies, too, attended some of our discussions, and this gave them a polite tone and had an influence on the manners of the debaters. My legal patron also may have had a favorable effect in correcting any roughness contracted in my hunter's life. He was calculated to bend me in an opposite direction, for he was of the old school; quoted "Chesterfield" on all occasions, and talked of Sir Charles Grandison, who was his *beau ideal*. It was Sir Charles Grandison, however, Kentuckyized.

I had always been fond of female society. My experience, however, had hitherto been among the rough daughters of the backwoodsmen, and I felt an awe of young ladies in "store clothes," delicately brought up. Two or three of the married ladies of Bardstown, who had heard me at the debating-club, determined that I was a genius, and undertook to bring me out. I believe I really improved under their hands, became quiet where I had been shy or sulky, and easy where I had been impudent.

I called to take tea one evening with one of these ladies, when, to my surprise, and somewhat to my confusion, I found with her the identical blue-eyed little beauty, whom I had so audaciously kissed. I was formally introduced to her, but neither of us betrayed any sign of previous acquaintance, except by blushing to the eyes. While tea was getting ready, the lady of the house went out of the room to give some directions, and left us alone.

Heavens and earth, what a situation! I would have given all the pittance I was worth, to have been in the deepest dell of the forest. I felt the necessity of saying something in excuse of my former rudeness, but I could not conjure up an idea, nor utter a word. Every moment matters were growing worse. I felt at one time tempted to do as I had done when I robbed her of the kiss,—bolt from the room, and take to flight; but I was chained to the spot, for I really longed to gain her good-will.

At length I plucked up courage, on seeing that she was equally confused with myself, and walking desperately up to her, I exclaimed:

"I have been trying to muster up something to say to you, but I cannot. I feel that I am in a horrible scrape. Do have pity on me, and help me out of it!"

A smile dimpled about her mouth, and played among the blushes of her cheek. She looked up with a shy but arch glance of the eye, that expressed a volume of comic recollection; we both broke into a laugh, and from that moment all went on well.

A few evenings afterward I met her at a dance, and prosecuted the acquaintance. I soon became deeply attached to her, paid my court regularly, and before I was nineteen years of age had engaged myself to marry her. I spoke to her mother, a widow lady, to ask her consent. She seemed to demur; upon which, with my customary haste, I told her there would be no use in opposing the match, for if her daughter chose to have me, I would take her, in defiance of her family, and the whole world.

She laughed, and told me I need not give myself any uneasiness; there would be no unreasonable opposition. She knew my family, and all about me. The only obstacle was, that I had no means of supporting a wife, and she had nothing to give with her daughter.

No matter; at that moment everything was bright before me. I was in one of my sanguine moods. I feared nothing, doubted nothing. So it was agreed that I should prosecute my studies, obtain a license, and as soon as I should be fairly launched in business, we would be married.

I now prosecuted my studies with redoubled ardor, and was up to my ears in law, when I received a letter from my father, who had heard of me and my whereabouts. He applauded the course I had taken, but advised me to lay a foundation of general knowledge, and offered to defray my expenses if I would go to college. I felt the want of a general education, and was staggered with this offer. It militated somewhat against the self-dependent course I had so proudly, or rather conceitedly, marked out for myself, but it would enable me to enter more advantageously upon my legal career. I talked over the matter with the lovely girl to whom I was engaged. She sided in opinion with my father, and talked so disinterestedly, yet tenderly, that if possible, I loved her more than ever. I reluctantly, therefore, agreed to go to college for a couple of years, though it must necessarily postpone our union.

Scarcely had I formed this resolution, when her mother was taken ill, and died, leaving her without a protector. This again altered all my plans. I felt as if I could protect her. I gave up all idea of collegiate studies; persuaded myself that by dint of industry and application I might overcome the deficiencies of education, and resolved to take out a license as soon as possible.

That very autumn I was admitted to the bar, and within a month afterward was married. We were a young couple,—she not much above sixteen, I not quite twenty,—and both almost without a dollar in the world. The establishment which we set up was suited to our circumstances: a log-house, with two small rooms; a bed, a table, a half-dozen chairs, a half-dozen knives and forks, a half-dozen spoons; everything by half-dozens; a little Delft ware; everything in a small way: we were so poor, but then so happy!

We had not been married many days when court was held at a country town, about twenty-five miles distant. It was necessary for me to go there, and put myself in the way of business; but how was I to go? I had expended all my means on our establishment; and then, it was hard parting with my wife so soon after marriage. However, go I must. Money must be made, or we should soon have the wolf at the door. I accordingly borrowed a horse, and borrowed a little cash, and rode off from my door, leaving my wife standing at it, and waving her hand after me. Her last look, so sweet and beaming, went to my heart. I felt as if I could go through fire and water for her.

I arrived at the county town on a cool October evening. The inn was crowded, for the court was to commence on the following day. I knew no one, and wondered how I, a stranger and a mere youngster, was to make my way in such a crowd, and to get business. The public room was thronged with the idlers of the country, who gather together on such occasions. There was some drinking going forward, with much noise, and a little altercation. Just as I entered the room, I saw a rough bully of a fellow, who was partly intoxicated, strike an old man. He came swaggering by me, and elbowed me as he passed. I immediately knocked him down, and kicked him into the street. I needed no better introduction. In a moment I had a dozen rough shakes of the hand and invitations to drink, and found myself quite a personage in this rough assembly.

The next morning the court opened. I took my seat among the lawyers, but felt as a mere spectator, not having a suit in progress or prospect, not having any idea where business was to come from. In the course of the morning, a man was put at the bar charged with passing counterfeit money, and was asked if he was ready for trial. He answered in the negative. He had been confined in a place where there were no lawyers, and had not had an opportunity of consulting any. He was told to choose counsel from the lawyers present, and to be ready for trial on the following day. He looked round the court, and selected me. I was thunderstruck. I could not tell why he should make such a choice. I, a beardless youngster, unpractised at the bar, perfectly unknown. I felt diffident, yet delighted, and could have hugged the rascal.

Before leaving the court, he gave me one hundred dollars in a bag, as a retaining fee. I could scarcely believe my senses; it seemed like a dream. The heaviness of the fee spoke but lightly in favor of his innocence, but that was no affair of mine. I was to be advocate, not judge, nor jury. I followed him to jail, and learned from him all the particulars of his case: thence I went to the clerk's office, and took minutes of the indictment. I then examined the law on the subject, and prepared my brief in my room. All this occupied me until midnight, when I went to bed, and tried to sleep. It was all in vain. Never in my life was I more wide awake. A host of thoughts and fancies kept rushing through my mind; the shower of gold that had so unexpectedly fallen into my lap; the idea of my poor little wife at home, that I was to astonish with my good fortune! But then the awful responsibility I had undertaken!—to speak for the first time in a strange court; the expectations the culprit had evidently formed of my talents; all these, and a crowd of similar notions, kept whirling through my mind. I tossed about all night, fearing the morning would find me exhausted and incompetent; in a word, the day dawned on me, a miserable fellow!

I got up feverish and nervous. I walked out before breakfast, striving to collect my thoughts, and tranquillize my feelings. It was a bright morning; the air was pure and frosty. I bathed my forehead and my hands in a beautiful running stream; but I could not allay the fever heat that raged within. I returned to breakfast, but could not eat. A single cup of coffee formed my repast. It was time to go to court, and I went there with a throbbing heart. I believe if it had not been for the thoughts of my little wife, in her lonely log-house, I should have given back to the man his hundred dollars, and relinquished the cause. I took my seat, looking, I am convinced, more like a culprit than the rogue I was to defend.

When the time came for me to speak, my heart died within me. I rose embarrassed and dismayed, and stammered in opening my cause. I went on from bad to worse, and felt as if I was going down hill. Just then the public prosecutor, a man of talents, but somewhat rough in his practice, made a sarcastic remark on something I had said. It was like an electric spark, and ran tingling through every vein in my body. In an instant my diffidence was gone. My whole spirit was in arms. I answered with promptness and bitterness, for I felt the cruelty of such an attack upon a novice in my situation. The public prosecutor made a kind of apology; this, from a man of his redoubted powers, was a vast concession. I renewed my argument with a fearless glow; carried the case through triumphantly, and the man was acquitted.

This was the making of me. Everybody was curious to know who this new lawyer was, that had thus suddenly risen among them, and bearded the attorney-general at the very outset. The story of my *début* at the inn, on the preceding evening, when I had knocked down a bully, and kicked him out of doors, for striking an old man, was circulated, with favorable exaggerations. Even my very beardless chin and juvenile countenance were in my favor, for the people gave me far more credit than I really deserved. The chance business which occurs in our country courts came thronging upon me. I was repeatedly employed in other causes; and by Saturday night, when the court closed, and I had paid my bill at the inn, I found myself with a hundred and fifty dollars in silver, three hundred dollars in notes, and a horse that I afterwards sold for two hundred dollars more.

Never did miser gloat on his money with more delight. I locked the door of my room, piled the money in a heap upon the table, walked round it, sat with my elbows on the table and my chin upon my hands, and gazed upon it. Was I thinking of the money? No! I was thinking of my little wife at home. Another sleepless night ensued; but what a night of golden fancies and splendid air-castles! As soon as morning dawned, I was up, mounted the borrowed horse with which I had come to court, and led the other, which I had received as a fee. All the way I was delighting myself with the thoughts of the surprise I had in store for my little wife; for both of us had expected nothing but that I should spend all the money I had borrowed, and should return in debt.

Our meeting was joyous, as you may suppose; but I played the part of the Indian hunter, who, when he returns from the chase, never for a time speaks of his success. She had prepared a snug little rustic meal for me, and while it was getting ready, I seated myself at an old-fashioned desk in one corner, and began to count over my money and put it away. She came to me before I had finished and asked who I had collected the money for.

"For myself, to be sure," replied I, with affected coolness; "I made it at court."

She looked me for a moment in the face, incredulously. I tried to keep my countenance, and to play Indian, but it would not do. My muscles began to twitch; my feelings all at once gave way. I caught her in my arms; laughed, cried, and danced about the room, like a crazy man. From that time forward, we never wanted for money.

I had not been long in successful practice, when I was surprised one day by a visit from my woodland patron, old Miller. The tidings of my prosperity had reached him in the wilderness, and he had walked one hundred and fifty miles on foot to see me. By that time I had improved my domestic establishment and had all things comfortable about me. He looked around him with a wondering eye, at what he considered luxuries and superfluities; but supposed they were all right, in my altered circumstances. He said he did not know, upon the whole, but that I acted for the best. It is true, if game had continued plenty, it would have been a folly for me to quit a hunter's life; but hunting was pretty nigh done up in Kentucky. The buffalo had gone to Missouri; the elk were nearly gone also; deer, too, were growing scarce; they might last out his time, as he was growing old, but they were not worth setting up life upon. He had once lived on the borders of Virginia. Game grew scarce there; he followed it up across Kentucky, and now it was again giving him the slip; but he was too old to follow it farther.

He remained with us three days. My wife did everything in her power to make him comfortable; but at the end of that time he said he must be off again to the woods. He was tired of the village, and of having so many people about him. He accordingly returned to the wilderness, and to hunting life. But I fear he did not make a good end of it; for I understand that a few years before his death he married Sukey Thomas, who lived at the White Oak Run.

From *Wolfert's Roost*

THE COUNT VAN HORN

DURING the minority of Louis XV., while the Duke of Orleans was Regent of France, a young Flemish nobleman, the Count Antoine Joseph Van Horn, made his sudden appearance in Paris, and by his character, conduct, and the subsequent disasters in which he became involved, created a great sensation in the high circles of the proud aristocracy. He was about twenty-two years of age, tall, finely formed, with a pale, romantic countenance, and eyes of remarkable brilliancy and wildness.

He was one of the most ancient and highly esteemed families of European nobility, being of the line of the Princes of Horn and Overique, sovereign Counts of Hautekerke, and hereditary Grand Veneurs of the empire.

The family took its name from the little town and seigneurie of Horn, in Brabant; and was known as early as the eleventh century among the little dynasties of the Netherlands, and since that time, by a long line of illustrious generations. At the peace of Utrecht, when the Netherlands passed under subjection to Austria, the house of Van Horn came under the domination of the Emperor. At the time we treat of, two of the branches of this ancient house were extinct; the third and only surviving branch was represented by the reigning prince, Maximilian Emanuel Van Horn, twenty-four years of age, who resided in honorable and courtly style on his hereditary domains at Baussigny, in the Netherlands, and his brother, the Count Antoine Joseph, who is the subject of this memoir.

The ancient house of Van Horn, by the intermarriage of its various branches with the noble families of the Continent, had become widely connected and interwoven with the high aristocracy of Europe. The Count Antoine, therefore, could claim relationship to many of the proudest names in Paris. In fact, he was grandson, by the mother's side, of the Prince de Ligne, and even might boast of affinity to the Regent (the Duke of Orleans) himself. There were circumstances, however, connected with his sudden appearance in Paris, and his previous story, that placed him in what is termed "a false position"; a word of baleful significance in the fashionable vocabulary of France.

The young Count had been captain in the service of Austria, but had been cashiered for irregular conduct, and for disrespect to Prince Louis of Baden, commander-in-chief. To check him in his wild career, and bring him to sober reflection, his brother the Prince caused him to be arrested, and sent to the old castle of Van Wert, in the domains of Horn. This was the same castle in which, in former times, John Van Horn, Stadtholder of Gueldres, had imprisoned his father; a circumstance which has furnished Rembrandt with the subject of an admirable painting. The governor of the castle was one Van Wert, grandson of the famous John Van Wert, the hero of many a popular song and legend. It was the intention of the Prince that his brother should be held in honorable durance, for his object was to sober and improve, not to punish and afflict him. Van Wert, however, was a stern, harsh man, of violent passions. He treated the youth in a manner that prisoners and offenders were treated in the strongholds of the robber counts of Germany in old times; confined him in a dungeon, and inflicted on him such hardships and indignities, that the irritable temperament of the young count was roused to continual fury, which ended in insanity. For six months was the unfortunate youth kept in this horrible state, without his brother the Prince being informed of his melancholy condition, or of the cruel treatment to which he was subjected. At length, one day, in a paroxysm of frenzy, the Count knocked down two of his jailers with a beetle, escaped from the castle of Van Wert, and eluded all pursuit; and after roving about in a state of distraction, made his way to Baussigny, and appeared like a spectre before his brother.

The Prince was shocked at his wretched, emaciated appearance, and his lamentable state of mental alienation. He received him with the most compassionate tenderness, lodged him in his own room, appointed three servants to attend and watch over him day and night, and endeavored, by the most soothing and affectionate assiduity, to atone for the past act of rigor, with which he reproached himself. When he learned, however, the manner in which his unfortunate brother had been treated in confinement, and the course of brutalities that had led to his mental malady, he was aroused to indignation. His first step was to cashier Van Wert from his command. That violent man set the Prince at defiance, and attempted to maintain himself in his government and his castle, by instigating the peasants, for several leagues round, to revolt. His insurrection might have been formidable against the power of a petty prince; but he was put under the ban of the empire, and seized as a state prisoner. The memory of his grandfather, the oft-sung John Van Wert, alone saved him from a gibbet; but he was imprisoned in the strong tower of Hornop-Zee. There he remained until he was eighty-two years of age, savage, violent, and unconquered to the last; for we are told that he never ceased fighting and thumping as long as he could close a fist or wield a cudgel.

In the meantime, a course of kind and gentle treatment and wholesome regimen, and, above all, the tender and affectionate assiduity of his brother the Prince, produced the most salutary effects upon Count Antoine. He gradually recovered his reason; but a degree of violence seemed always lurking at the bottom of his character, and he required to be treated with the greatest caution and mildness, for the least contradiction exasperated him.

In this state of mental convalescence he began to find the supervision and restraints of brotherly affection insupportable; so he left the Netherlands furtively, and repaired to Paris, whither, in fact, it is said he was called by motives of interest, to make arrangements concerning a valuable estate which he inherited from his relative the Princess d'Epinay.

On his arrival in Paris, he called upon the Marquis of Créqui, and other of the high nobility with whom he was connected. He was received with great courtesy; but, as he brought no letters from his elder brother, the Prince, and as various circumstances of his previous history had transpired, they did not receive him into their families, nor introduce him to their ladies. Still they fêted him in bachelor style, gave him gay and elegant suppers at their separate apartments, and took him to their boxes at the theatres. He was often noticed, too, at the doors of the most fashionable churches, taking his stand among the young men of fashion; and at such times his tall, elegant figure, his pale but handsome countenance, and his flashing eyes, distinguished him from among the crowd, and the ladies declared that it was almost impossible to support his ardent gaze.

The Count did not afflict himself much at his limited circulation in the fastidious circles of the high aristocracy. He relished society of a wilder and less ceremonious cast; and meeting with loose companions to his taste, soon ran into all the excesses of the capital, in that most licentious period. It is said that, in the course of his wild career, he had an intrigue with a lady of quality, a favorite of the Regent, that he was surprised by that prince in one of his interviews, that sharp words passed between them, and that the jealousy and vengeance thus awakened ended only with his life.

About this time, the famous Mississippi scheme of [John] Law was at its height, or rather it began to threaten that disastrous catastrophe which convulsed the whole financial world. Every effort was making to keep the bubble inflated. The vagrant population of France was swept off from the streets at night, and conveyed to Havre de Grace, to be shipped to the projected colonies; even laboring people and mechanics were thus crimped and spirited away. As Count Antoine was in the habit of sallying forth at night, in disguise, in pursuit of his pleasures, he came near being carried off by a gang of crimps; it seemed, in fact, as if they had been lying in wait for him, as he had experienced very rough treatment at their hands. Complaint was made of his case by his relation, the Marquis de Créqui, who took much interest in the youth; but the Marquis received mysterious intimations not to interfere in the matter, but to advise the Count to quit Paris immediately: "If he lingers he is lost!" This has been cited as a proof that vengeance was dogging at the heels of the unfortunate youth, and only watching for an opportunity to destroy him.

Such opportunity occurred but too soon. Among the loose companions with whom the Count had become intimate, were two who lodged in the same hotel with him. One was a youth only twenty years of age, who passed himself off as the Chevalier d'Étampes, but whose real name was Lestang, the prodigal son of a Flemish banker. The other, named Laurent de Mille, a Piedmontese, was a cashiered captain, and at the time an esquire in the service of the dissolute Princess de Carignan, who kept gambling-tables in her palace. It is probable that gambling propensities had brought these young men together, and that their losses had driven them to desperate measures; certain it is, that all Paris was suddenly astounded by a murder which they were said to have committed. What made the crime more startling, was, that it seemed connected with the great Mississippi scheme, at that time the fruitful source of all kinds of panics and agitations. A Jew, a stock-broker, who dealt largely in shares of the bank of Law, founded on the Mississippi scheme, was the victim. The story of his death is variously related. The darkest account states, that the Jew was decoyed by these young men into an obscure tavern, under pretext of negotiating with him for bank shares, to the amount of one hundred thousand crowns, which he had with him in his pocket-book. Lestang kept watch upon the stairs. The Count and De Mille entered with the Jew into a chamber. In a little while there were heard cries and struggles from within. A waiter passing by the room, looked in, and seeing the Jew weltering in his blood, shut the door again, double-locked it, and alarmed the house. Lestang rushed down stairs, made his way to the hotel, secured his most portable effects, and fled the country. The Count and De Mille endeavored to escape by the window, but were both taken, and conducted to prison.

A circumstance which occurs in this part of the Count's story, seems to point him out as a fated man. His mother, and his brother, the Prince Van Horn, had received intelligence some time before, at Baussigny, of the dissolute life the Count was leading at Paris, and of his losses at play. They despatched a gentleman of the Prince's household to Paris, to pay the debts of the Count, and persuade him to return to Flanders; or, if he should refuse, to obtain an order from the Regent for him to quit the capital. Unfortunately the gentleman did not arrive at Paris until the day after the murder.

The news of the Count's arrest and imprisonment, on a charge of murder, caused a violent sensation among the high aristocracy. All those connected with him, who had treated him hitherto with indifference, found their dignity deeply involved in the question of his guilt or innocence. A general convocation was held at the hotel of the Marquis de Créqui, of all the relatives and allies of the house of Horn. It was an assemblage of the most proud and aristocratic personages of Paris. Inquiries were made into the circumstances of the affair. It was ascertained beyond a doubt, that the Jew was dead, and that he had been killed by several stabs of a poniard. In escaping by the window, it was said that the Count had fallen, and been immediately taken; but that De Mille had fled through the streets, pursued by the populace, and had been arrested at some distance from the scene of the murder; that the Count had declared himself innocent of the death of the Jew, and that he had risked his own life in endeavoring to protect him; but that De Mille, on being brought back to the tavern, confessed to a plot to murder the broker, and rob him of his pocket-book, and inculpated the Count in the crime.

Another version of the story was, that the Count Van Horn had deposited with the broker bank shares to the amount of eighty-eight thousand livres; that he had sought him in this tavern, which was one of his resorts, and had demanded the shares; that the Jew had denied the deposit; that a quarrel had ensued, in the course of which the Jew struck the Count in the face; that the latter, transported with rage, had snatched up a knife from a table and wounded the Jew in the shoulder; and that thereupon De Mille, who was present, and who had likewise been defrauded by the broker, fell on him, and despatched him with blows of a poniard, and seized upon his pocket-book; that he had offered to divide the contents of the latter with the Count, *pro rata*, of what the usurer had defrauded them; that the latter had refused the proposition with disdain; and that, at a noise of persons approaching, both had attempted to escape from the premises, but had been taken.

Regard the story in any way they might, appearances were terribly against the Count, and the noble assemblage was in great consternation.

What was to be done to ward off so foul a disgrace and to save their illustrious escutcheons from this murderous stain of blood? Their first attempt was to prevent the affair from going to trial, and their relative from being dragged before a criminal tribunal, on so horrible and degrading a charge. They applied therefore, to the Regent, to intervene his power, to treat the Count as having acted under an access of his mental malady, and to shut him up in a madhouse. The Regent was deaf to their solicitations. He replied, coldly, that if the Count was a madman, one could not get rid too quickly of madmen who were furious in their insanity. The crime was too public and atrocious to be hushed up, or slurred over; justice must take its course.

Seeing there was no avoiding the humiliating scene of a public trial, the noble relatives of the Count endeavored to predispose the minds of the magistrates before whom he was to be arraigned. They accordingly made urgent and eloquent representations of the high descent, and noble and powerful connections of the Count; set forth the circumstances of his early history, his mental malady, the nervous irritability to which he was subject, and his extreme sensitiveness to insult or contradiction. By these means they sought to prepare the judges to interpret every thing in favor of the Count; and, even if it should prove that he had inflicted the mortal blow on the usurer, to attribute it to access of insanity provoked by insult.

To give full effect to these representations, the noble conclave determined to bring upon the judges the dazzling rays of the whole assembled aristocracy. Accordingly, on the day that the trial took place, the relations of the Count, to the number of fifty-seven persons, of both sexes and of the highest rank, repaired in a body to the Palace of Justice, and took their stations in a long corridor which led to the court-room. Here, as the judges entered, they had to pass in review this array of lofty and noble personages, who saluted them mournfully and significantly as they passed. Any one conversant with the stately pride and jealous dignity of the French noblesse of that day, may imagine the extreme state of sensitiveness that produced this self-abasement. It was confidently presumed, however, by the noble suppliants, that having once brought themselves to this measure, their influence over the tribunal would be irresistible. There was one lady present, however, Madame de Beauffremont, who was affected with the Scottish gift of second sight, and related such dismal and sinister apparitions as passing before her eyes, that many of her female companions were filled with doleful presentiments.

Unfortunately for the Count, there was another interest at work, more powerful even than the high aristocracy. The infamous but all-potent Abbé Dubois, the grand favorite and bosom counsellor of the Regent, was deeply interested in the scheme of Law and the prosperity of his bank, and of course in the security of the stock-brokers. Indeed, the Regent himself is said to have dipped deep in the Mississippi scheme. Dubois and Law, therefore, exerted their influence to the utmost to have the tragic affair pushed to the extremity of the law, and the murderer of the broker punished in the most signal and appalling manner. Certain it is, the trial was neither long nor intricate. The Count and his fellow-prisoner were equally inculpated in the crime, and both were condemned to a death the most horrible and ignominious—to be broken alive on the wheel!

As soon as the sentence of the court was made public, all the nobility, in any degree related to the house of Van Horn, went into mourning. Another grand aristocratical assemblage was held, and a petition to the Regent, on behalf of the Count, was drawn out and left with the Marquis de Créqui for signature. This petition set forth the previous insanity of the Count, and showed that it was an hereditary malady in his family. It stated various circumstances in mitigation of his offence, and implored that his sentence might be commuted to perpetual imprisonment.

Upward of fifty names of the highest nobility, beginning with the Prince de Ligne, and including cardinals, archbishops, dukes, marquises, etc., together with ladies of equal rank, were signed to this petition. By one of the caprices of human pride and vanity, it became an object of ambition to get enrolled among the illustrious suppliants; a kind of testimonial of noble blood, to prove relationship to a murderer! The Marquis de Créqui was absolutely besieged by applicants to sign, and had to refer their claims to this singular honor to the Prince de Ligne, the grandfather of the Count. Many who were excluded were highly incensed, and numerous feuds took place. Nay, the affronts thus given to the morbid pride of some aristocratical families, passed from generation to generation; for, fifty years afterward, the Duchess of Mazarin complained of a slight which her father had received from the Marquis de Créqui, which proved to be something connected with the signature of this petition.

This important document being completed, the illustrious body of petitioners, male and female, on Saturday evening, the eve of Palm Sunday, repaired to the Palais Royal, the residence of the Regent, and were ushered with great ceremony, but profound silence, into his hall of council. They had appointed four of their number as deputies to present the petition, viz.: the Cardinal de Rohan, the Duke de Havré, the Prince de Ligne, and the Marquis de Créqui. After a little while, the deputies were summoned to the cabinet of the Regent. They entered, leaving the assembled petitioners in a state of the greatest anxiety. As time slowly wore away, and the evening advanced, the gloom of the company increased. Several of the ladies prayed devoutly; the good Princess of Armagnac told her beads.

The petition was received by the Regent with a most unpropitious aspect. "In asking the pardon of the criminal," said he, "you display more zeal for the house of Van Horn than for the service of the King." The noble deputies enforced the petition by every argument in their power. They supplicated the Regent to consider that the infamous punishment in question would reach not merely the person of the condemned, not merely the house of Van Horn, but also the genealogies of princely and illustrious families, in whose armorial bearings might be found quarterings of this dishonored name.

"Gentlemen," replied the Regent, "it appears to me the disgrace consists in the crime, rather than in the punishment."

The Prince de Ligne spoke with warmth: "I have in my genealogical standard," said he, "four escutcheons of Van Horn, and of course have four ancestors of that house. I must have them erased and effaced, and there would be so many blank spaces, like holes, in my heraldic ensigns. There is not a sovereign family which would not suffer through the rigor of your Royal Highness; nay, all the world knows that in the thirty-two quarterings of Madame, your mother, there is an escutcheon of Van Horn."

"Very well," replied the Regent, "I will share the disgrace with you, gentlemen."

Seeing that a pardon could not be obtained, the Cardinal de Rohan and the Marquis de Créqui left the cabinet; but the Prince de Ligne and the Duke de Havré remained behind. The honor of their houses, more than the life of the unhappy Count, was the great object of their solicitude. They now endeavored to obtain a minor grace. They represented that in the Netherlands and in Germany there was an important difference in the public mind as to the mode of inflicting the punishment of death upon persons of quality. That decapitation had no influence on the fortunes of the family of the executed, but that the punishment of the wheel was such an infamy, that the uncles, aunts, brothers, and sisters of the criminal, and his whole family, for three succeeding generations, were excluded from all noble chapters, princely abbeys, sovereign bishoprics, and even Teutonic commanderies of the Order of Malta. They showed how this would operate immediately upon the fortunes of a sister of the Count, who was on the point of being received as a canoness into one of the noble chapters.

While this scene was going on in the cabinet of the Regent, the illustrious assemblage of petitioners remained in the hall of council, in the most gloomy state of suspense. The re-entrance from the cabinet of the Cardinal de Rohan and the Marquis de Créqui, with pale downcast countenances, had struck a chill into every heart. Still they lingered until near midnight, to learn the result of the after application. At length the cabinet conference was at an end. The Regent came forth and saluted the high personages of the assemblage in a courtly manner. One old lady of quality, Madame de Guyon, whom he had known in his infancy, he kissed on the cheek, calling her his "good aunt." He made a most ceremonious salutation to the stately Marchioness de Créqui, telling her he was charmed to see her at the Palais Royal, "a compliment very ill-timed," said the Marchioness, "considering the circumstance which brought me there." He then conducted the ladies to the door of the second saloon, and there dismissed them, with the most ceremonious politeness.

The application of the Prince de Ligne and the Duke de Havré, for a change of the mode of punishment, had, after much difficulty, been successful. The Regent had promised solemnly to send a letter of commutation to the attorney-general, on Holy Monday, the 25th of March, at 5 o'clock in the morning. According to the same promise, a scaffold would be arranged in the cloister of the Conciergerie, or prison, where the Count would be beheaded on the same morning, immediately after having received absolution. This mitigation of the form of punishment gave but little consolation to the great body of petitioners, who had been anxious for the pardon of the youth: it was looked upon as all-important, however, by the Prince de Ligne, who, as has been before observed, was exquisitely alive to the dignity of his family.

The Bishop of Bayeux and the Marquis de Créqui visited the unfortunate youth in prison. He had just received the communion in the chapel of the Conciergerie, and was kneeling before the altar, listening to a mass for the dead, which was performed at his request. He protested his innocence of any intention to murder the Jew, but did not deign to allude to the accusation of robbery. He made the Bishop and the Marquis promise to see his brother the Prince, and inform him of this his dying asseveration.

Two other of his relations, the Prince Rebecq-Montmorency and the Marshal Van Isenghien, visited him secretly, and offered him poison, as the means of evading the disgrace of a public execution. On his refusing to take it, they left him with high indignation. "Miserable man!" said they, "you are fit only to perish by the hand of the executioner!"

The Marquis de Créqui sought the executioner of Paris, to bespeak an easy and decent death for the unfortunate youth. "Do not make him suffer," said he; "uncover no part of him but the neck, and have his body placed in a coffin before you deliver it to his family." The executioner promised all that was requested, but declined a *rouleau* of a hundred louis-d'ors which the Marquis would have put into his hand. "I am paid by the King for fulfilling my office," said he; and added, that he had already refused a like sum offered by another relation of the Marquis.

The Marquis de Créqui returned home in a state of deep affliction. There he found a letter from the Duke de St. Simon, the familiar friend of the Regent, repeating the promise of that Prince, that the punishment of the wheel should be commuted to decapitation.

"Imagine," says the Marchioness de Créqui, who in her memoirs gives a detailed account of this affair, "imagine what we experienced, and what was our astonishment, our grief, and indignation, when, on Tuesday the 26th of March, an hour after midday, word was brought us that the Count Van Horn had been exposed on the wheel in the Place de Grève, since half-past six in the morning, on the same scaffold with the Piedmontese, De Mille, and that he had been tortured previous to execution!"

One more scene of aristocratic pride closed this tragic story. The Marquis de Créqui, on receiving this astounding news, immediately arrayed himself in the uniform of a general officer, with his cordon of nobility on the coat. He ordered six valets to attend him in grand livery, and two of his carriages, each with six horses, to be brought forth. In this sumptuous state he set off for the Place de Grève, where he had been preceded by the Princes de Ligne, de Rohan, de Croüy, and the Duke de Havré.

The Count Van Horn was already dead, and it was believed that the executioner had had the charity to give him the *coup de grâce*, or "death-blow," at eight o'clock in the morning. At five o'clock in the evening, when the Judge Commissary left his post at the Hotel de Ville, these noblemen, with their own hands, aided to detach the mutilated remains of their relation; the Marquis de Créqui placed them in one of his carriages, and bore them off to his hotel, to receive the last sad obsequies.

The conduct of the Regent in this affair excited general indignation. His needless severity was attributed by some to vindictive jealousy; by others to the persevering machinations of Law and the Abbé Dubois. The house of Van Horn, and the high nobility of Flanders and Germany, considered themselves flagrantly outraged; many schemes of vengeance were talked of, and a hatred engendered against the Regent that followed him through life, and was wreaked with bitterness upon his memory after his death.

The following letter is said to have been written to the Regent by the Prince Van Horn, to whom the former had adjudged the confiscated effects of the Count:—

"I do not complain, sir, of the death of my brother, but I complain that your Royal Highness has violated in his person the rights of the kingdom, the nobility, and the nation. I thank you for the confiscation of his effects; but I should think myself as much disgraced as he, should I accept any favor at your hands. *I hope that God and the King may render to you as strict justice as you have rendered to my unfortunate brother.*"

From *Wolfert's Roost*

DON JUAN
A SPECTRAL RESEARCH

"I have heard of spirits walking with aërial bodies, and have been
wondered at by others; but I must only wonder at myself, for, if they
be not mad, I 'me come to my own buriall."

SHIRLEY'S "WITTY FAIRIE ONE"

EVERYBODY has heard of the fate of Don Juan, the famous
libertine of Seville, who, for his sins against the fair sex and other
minor peccadilloes, was hurried away to the infernal regions. His story
has been illustrated in play, in pantomime, and farce, on every stage in
Christendom, until at length it has been rendered the theme of the
opera of operas, and embalmed to endless duration in the glorious music
of Mozart. I well recollect the effect of this story upon my feelings in
my boyish days, though represented in grotesque pantomime; the awe
with which I contemplated the monumental statue on horseback of
the murdered commander, gleaming by pale moonlight in the convent
cemetery; how my heart quaked as he bowed his marble head, and accepted the impious invitation of Don Juan; how each footfall of the
statue smote upon my heart, as I heard it approach, step by step, through
the echoing corridor, and beheld it enter, and advance, a moving
figure of stone, to the supper-table! But then the convivial scene in the
charnel-house, where Don Juan returned the visit of the statue, was
offered a banquet of skulls and bones, and on refusing to partake, was
hurled into a yawning gulf under a tremendous shower of fire! These
were accumulated horrors enough to shake the nerves of the most
pantomime-loving school-boy. Many have supposed the story of Don
Juan a mere fable. I myself thought so once; but "seeing is believing." I
have since beheld the very scene where it took place, and now to indulge any doubt on the subject, would be preposterous.

I was one night perambulating the streets of Seville, in company with
a Spanish friend, a curious investigator of the popular traditions and
other good-for-nothing lore of the city, and who was kind enough to
imagine he had met, in me, with a congenial spirit. In the course of our
rambles, we were passing by a heavy dark gateway, opening into the

courtyard of a convent, when he laid his hand upon my arm: "Stop!" said he; "this is the convent of San Francisco; there is a story connected with it, which I am sure must be known to you. You cannot but have heard of Don Juan and the marble statue."

"Undoubtedly," replied I; "it has been familiar to me from childhood."

"Well, then, it was in the cemetery of this convent that the events took place."

"Why, you do not mean to say that the story is founded on fact?"

"Undoubtedly it is. The circumstances of the case are said to have occurred during the reign of Alfonso XI. Don Juan was of the noble family of Tenorio, one of the most illustrious houses of Andalusia. His father, Don Diégo Tenorio was a favorite of the King, and his family ranked among the *veintecuatros*, or magistrates, of the city. Presuming on his high descent and powerful connections, Don Juan set no bounds to his excesses; no female, high or low, was sacred from his pursuit; and he soon became the scandal of Seville. One of his most daring outrages was, to penetrate by night into the palace of Don Gonzalo de Ulloa, Commander of the Order of Calatrava, and attempt to carry off his daughter. The household was alarmed; a scuffle in the dark took place; Don Juan escaped, but the unfortunate commander was found weltering in his blood, and expired without being able to name his murderer. Suspicions attached to Don Juan; he did not stop to meet the investigations of justice and the vengeance of the powerful family of Ulloa, but fled from Seville, and took refuge with his uncle, Don Pedro Tenorio, at that time ambassador at the court of Naples. Here he remained until the agitation occasioned by the murder of Don Gonzalo had time to subside; and the scandal which the affair might cause to both the families of Ulloa and Tenorio had induced them to hush it up. Don Juan, however, continued his libertine career at Naples, until at length his excesses forfeited the protection of his uncle the ambassador, and obliged him again to flee. He had made his way back to Seville, trusting that his past misdeeds were forgotten, or rather trusting to his daredevil spirit and the power of his family, to carry him through all difficulties.

"It was shortly after his return, and while in the height of his arrogance, that on visiting this very convent of Francisco, he beheld on a monument the equestrian statue of the murdered commander, who had been buried within the walls of this sacred edifice, where the family of Ulloa had a chapel. It was on this occasion that Don Juan, in a moment of impious levity, invited the statue to the banquet, the awful catastrophe of which has given such celebrity to his story."

"And pray how much of this story," said I, "is believed in Seville?" "The whole of it by the populace, with whom it has been a favorite tradition since time immemorial, and who crowd to the theatres to see it represented in dramas written long since by Tyrso de Molina, and another of our popular writers. Many in our higher ranks also, accustomed from childhood to this story, would feel somewhat indignant at hearing it treated with contempt. An attempt has been made to explain the whole, by asserting that, to put an end to the extravagances of Don Juan, and to pacify the family of Ulloa, without exposing the delinquent to the degrading penalties of justice, he was decoyed into this convent under false pretext, and either plunged into a perpetual dungeon, or privately hurried out of existence; while the story of the statue was circulated by the monks, to account for his sudden disappearance. The populace, however, are not to be cajoled out a ghost-story by any of these plausible explanations; and the marble statue still strides the stage, and Don Juan is still plunged into the infernal regions, as an awful warning to all rake-helly youngsters, in like case offending."

· While my companion was relating these anecdotes, we had traversed the exterior courtyard of the convent, and made our way into a great interior court, partly surrounded by cloisters and dormitories, partly by chapels, and having a large fountain in the centre. The pile had evidently once been extensive and magnificent; but it was for the greater part in ruins. By the light of the stars, and of twinkling lamps placed here and there in the chapels and corridors, I could see that many of the columns and arches were broken; the walls were rent and riven; while burnt beams and rafters showed the destructive effects of fire. The whole place had a desolate air; the night breeze rustled through grass and weeds flaunting out of the crevices of the walls, or from the shattered columns; the bat flitted about the vaulted passages, and the owl hooted from the ruined belfry. Never was any scene more completely fitted for a ghost-story.

While I was indulging in picturings of the fancy, proper to such a place, the deep chant of the monks from the convent church came swelling upon the ear. "It is the vesper service," said my companion; "follow me."

Leading the way across the court of the cloisters, and through one or two ruined passages, he reached the portal of the church, and pushing open a wicket, cut in the folding-doors, we found ourselves in the deep arched vestibule of the sacred edifice. To our left was the choir, forming one end of the church, and having a low vaulted ceiling, which gave it the look of a cavern. About this were ranged the monks, seated on stools, and chanting from immense books placed on music-stands, and having the notes scored in such gigantic characters as to be legible from every part of the choir. A few lights on these music-stands dimly illumined the choir, gleamed on the shaven heads of the monks, and threw their shadows on the walls. They were gross, blue-bearded, bullet-headed men, with bass voices, of deep metallic tone, that reverberated out of the cavernous choir.

To our right extended the great body of the church. It was spacious and lofty; some of the side chapels had gilded grates, and were decorated with images and paintings, representing the sufferings of our Saviour. Aloft was a great painting by Murillo, but too much in the dark to be distinguished. The gloom of the whole church was but faintly relieved by the reflected light from the choir, and the glimmering here and there of a votive lamp before the shrine of the saint.

As my eye roamed about the shadowy pile, it was struck with the dimly seen figure of a man on horseback, near a distant altar. I touched my companion, and pointed to it: "The spectre statue!" said I.

"No," replied he; "it is the statue of the blessed St. Iago; the statue of the commander was in the cemetery of the convent, and was destroyed at the time of the conflagration. But," added he, "as I see you take a proper interest in these kind of stories, come with me to the other end of the church, where our whisperings will not disturb these holy fathers at their devotions, and I will tell you another story that has been current for some generations in our city, by which you will find that Don Juan is not the only libertine that has been the object of supernatural castigation in Seville."

I accordingly followed him with noiseless tread to the farther part of the church, where we took our seats on the steps of an altar opposite to the suspicious-looking figure on horseback, and there, in a low, mysterious voice, he related to me the following narrative:

"There was once in Seville a gay young fellow, Don Manuel de Manara by name, who, having come to a great estate by the death of his father, gave the reins to his passions, and plunged into all kinds of dissipation. Like Don Juan, whom he seemed to have taken for a model, he became famous for his enterprises among the fair sex, and was the cause of doors being barred and windows grated with more than usual strictness. All in vain. No balcony was too high for him to scale; no bolt nor bar was proof against his efforts; and his very name was a word of terror to all the jealous husbands and cautious fathers of Seville. His exploits extended to country as well as city; and in the village dependent on his castle scarce a rural beauty was safe from his arts and enterprises.